NAÏVE HOPE

SETTING THE RECORD STRAIGHT

One Woman's Tale of Domestic Violence, a Tyrant 'Christian' Husband and Surviving Church Control

When Ruin, Terrorism and Death Threats Are Not Enough

The Festering Legacy One Cruel Soul Creates

Marni Chronicles Her Journey from Despair to Wisdom

By Siri Eschel

Based on a True Story

COPYRIGHT and LEGAL NOTICE

This Book is Copyright © 2016 and Beyond: Siri Eschel (the 'Author'). All rights reserved worldwide.

Reproduction or translation of any part of this work beyond that permitted by section 107 or 108 of the 1976 United States Copyright Act without permission of the copyright owner is unlawful. Requests for permission or further information should be addressed to the Author. No part of this Book whether eBook or hardcopy may be translated or reproduced or transmitted in any form or by any means, electronic or mechanical, including photocopying, recording, or by an information storage and retrieval system without the express permission of the Author.

First Printing, **August 2016**

Published by Healing Knowhow Publishing,
2/36 Wallarah Rd, Gorokan, 2263, Australia

National Library of Australia Cataloguing-in-Publication entry:
Creator: Eschel, Siri, Author

Title: Naive hope : setting the record straight : one woman's tale
of domestic violence, a tyrant 'christian'
husband and surviving church control. When
ruin, terrorism and death threats are not
enough, the festering legacy one cruel
soul creates / by Siri Eschel.

ISBN: 9780992392475 (paperback)

Subjects: Abused wives--Fiction.
Wife abuse--Fiction.
Abusive men--Religious life--Fiction.

Dewey Number: A823.4

Foreword

Acknowledgements and Dedication

Thank you to my friend Leonie. Without your help I could not have put this all together.

To all the Soul's whose hearts have yearned for love, light and truth in the hope that the change you make is in yourself.

Naïve Hope:

A story of moving beyond Blind Faith

'Hope is a tease, designed to prevent us from accepting reality' Downton Abbey

'And the truth will set you free...'

PROLOGUE

IDENTITY CRISIS; TO LIE OR TO DIE?

1980

The day had started off pleasantly enough; birds twittering, new plants freshly cosseted and tended, surrounding areas weeded. The really tall grass had been hand-cut with Jim's machete, and fresh cut grass smells filled our garden. All seemed at peace, without a hint of what was to come. The garden smells of harmony and the air is rich with Spring promise. It is not until I go into the bedroom to change out of my earth smeared clothing that the atmosphere begins to change.

Jim follows me. There is no longer that sense of camaraderie we had shared as we worked together. His mouth is now set in a grim line and I can only guess at what thoughts he has conjured up to be grim about. His blue eyes have taken on a darker grey hue.

Jim now closes the door behind him as he enters the bedroom. He is currently still facing me with one hand behind his back. There are still bits of grass sticking to his shirt, and patches of sweat under his armpits through the exertions of the day. I assume he is also in the bedroom to change his clothing. I smile and carry on.

As I busy myself changing my clothes, Jim now reaches behind himself and turns the door lock. I hear its click and I know what he has done. The air in the bedroom seems to have grown murkier, with an almost tangible sinister quality. It is that old familiar feeling, seeping and creeping through the room again, like cigarette smoke that seems to invade and soak into everything around it.

That is when I become alert to his mood. Now I dare to begin to question things, waiting for his next step as I start to feel butterflies and discomfort – what is he going to do to me now? Apart from his face and growing demeanour, there is nothing I dare say to question him about closing the door, and a part of me knows that I have to let this play itself out, as usual, whatever it is. Past experience has shown me that when that door locks behind us he is not about to give me a gold bracelet, nor woo me with tender love ... oh, no!

As quickly as I have looked up I now look away so that I am not challenged with a 'What are *you* looking at?' from him.

Jim is now firmly placed in between me and the bedroom door.

'I want to show you something,' he states by way of explanation to his actions. Or actually as a form of cover, something that succeeds in jolting me with total surprise when I see what he actually reveals. There is nothing as yet in his voice to prepare me for what he has to 'show'.

Now he brings his arm around to the front of him – in his hand is the machete he had used on cutting down the tall grass earlier. I gulp. This could be innocent, but in this atmosphere, it does not look good. I pray he really is just going to show me something connected with this knife. *Keep calm, Marni. Don't get too excited just yet.*

Dare I question the locked door, to divert his attention? *Just exactly what is the problem, what have I supposed to have done this time?* Is it just that the machete is not sharp enough? Did it get damaged and he is going to blame me? But then why the locked door? This makes no sense.

My, how the mind races when it feels under threat.

Yet I do feel under threat. If our conversation has not yet conveyed that, then Jim's demeanour certainly is doing a sterling job of it. There is a further shift in the air, a glimmer of danger...

He lifts the knife up to near my face. I naturally move away from it, but he keeps it firmly and clearly in my view, held upright, the sharp end facing me. There is a glint in his eye, a dark and dangerous fixed stare... His face has changed again to *that face* of his – the one that is not only looking for trouble, but has already found it.

This machete is a really long large curved knife. It is used for cutting through lots of thick grass easily, even for splitting coconuts. It is not a pleasant thing to be right next to with uncovered skin. And even though it is now clean, it is still not a pretty or comforting sight.

'So what have you got to tell me, Marni?' he growls. He moves the knife infinitesimally, as if to highlight the importance of answering his question.

This is not about the garden, this is not about the work we have just been doing. This is about something else entirely different. This has come from left field. Again. For I have no idea what he is referring to. All I know is that now I am getting scared. *Now* I am excited - I begin to tremble inside.

'What about?' I ask, trying to keep my voice steady.

'Don't come that with me' he grunts, inching his body closer toward me. 'You know what about. I can see it in your face'.

'?' I blinked in answer.

Yes, that's not a misprint – that '?' means that I was stumped. It was an unspoken 'What the...?' moment. An incoherent moment in time. Again, I repeat, I had absolutely *no idea* what he was talking about. Nor what he was thinking – which is a danger for me, as I now didn't have a chance to sort this out amicably in order to set his mind at rest.

I check inwardly to see what my face is doing and what it has been doing. And it is clear that I do not see what it is that he thinks he sees. My scared barometer is rising. I am now in a seriously tricky situation, for this knife thing is totally new to me. Before it has only been his fists, and they are powerful enough as it is. But bringing a knife into the picture is a whole new ball game.

'What's going on at work? Who is it that you fancy?' he intimates, as he moves the knife forward enough to touch my neck with the tip of the machete.

The feeling of cold powerful steel against a vulnerable point fires my imagination – and this is precisely what he has intended to do. He wants me scared. And I am. *Bloody scared!* My imagination is already picturing blood... Dare I move my head back more? No, he will only follow the movement. Just stand your ground, you have done nothing to be ashamed of, Marni.

Foreword

'There's no-one at work' I say. '*Nothing's* going on at work' I blurt out. And there isn't. I have always had to tell him everything about work. This is fact. My face registers my emotions and it is again like living in a glass house – what I feel, you can see. But there is *no-one* at work. Or maybe I don't even know it myself? And as usual, I begin to doubt myself. Bad move, Marni. Because even this thought is now caught on his mind camera and will register in my face, won't it?

And the truth is this; I am *not* after anyone at work, I do *not 'fancy'* anyone at work. I am possibly fascinated by a couple of people there, not having been around others like them before, but the thoughts of 'fancying' or flirting are furthest from my mind. I am even labelled *'The Ice Lady'* at work because I refuse to share the smutty office jokes, because I refuse to flirt, to get caught up in the intrigues, to join in at the same level with them, even though I admit that I am learning to thaw out my self-righteous attitude to others and to be a bit more accepting of other ways of living and being. But as to *carrying on* with anyone, I daren't even let any thoughts of that enter my mind – my husband would kill me – well, right now that looks like it's possibly going to be true whether I did or not. It would be more than stupid of me to consider doing *anything* like that with a husband such as this.

Jim holds the machete closer down to my throat, getting closer to the jugular vein. Despite my statement, he continues to question me as if he has some sort of proof. But it is all in his head, this idea that I am carrying on with someone.

'I *know* there's someone else' he states threateningly. 'Who is it?'

The man is nuts. He's *insane*! What is in possession of his mind? This is an insane moment! Nothing is making sense... Vivid pictures race through my mind... I am now terrified. *Oh God, Oh God, Oh God, Jesus help me* pleeease...

Jim's cold eyes watch me, like a snake sizing up its prey looking for where to strike its venom next...

The inner quivering has spread to my limbs, and now I am visibly shaking so badly that my knees are giving way and I have slowly, carefully sat on the edge of the bed, his hand and the knife following my slow move downward very closely. Tears well up in my eyes at the injustice and accusations, at these lies and at my own fears.

I *know* that what he is saying is not true. I don't know where he gets it from. *God* knows it. I keep doubting myself, checking my past thoughts, scouring my mind for any possible forgotten misdemeanour, any ignored slip - while he continues to keep on questioning me, over and over and over.

'Who is it?' 'I will find out.' 'What's his name?' The machete stays close to my neck. He won't believe me when I tell him the truth, and I am beginning to think that at any minute he might crack up and slice me up.

This man has already punched me, broken my ribs, threatened me, insulted me, interrogated me, stripped me of money, falsely accused me and kept me on egg shells for such a long time – and now he was resorting to weapons... My worst fears begin to yammer at me. For one never knew what it was that was going to trigger him next.

Neither did he, and this was the power he exerted over others. The dance he tangoed for his own kicks. And also what makes this dark side of him so dangerous. A victim to his own feelings or inclinations, apparently without any compassion or impulse control.

I am now beginning to think that I might not see this night through. My continuing to tell him 'The Truth' was just not working, and this time it wasn't just a hit or a punch, or about him throwing me around – it was a knife! A bloody big sharp dangerous *knife*!

My stomach begins a painful churning, fear fires through my body. Blood rushes to my head, drains from my limbs, I cannot think straight, and I fear in case I am blushing. Ridiculous really, as I was probably as white as a ghost. *He will think I am guilty if I blush* I stupidly think to myself, but I cannot stop that. I am fighting to regain control of my own limbs as I feel this weakness flow through them.

Foreword

I search my conscience again – even *I* now doubted myself, he was so sure of this. No! I have *not* been unfaithful to him in *any* way. I repeat this with conviction. But still he refuses to hear it.

The knife only wanders centimetres away through this bizarre conversation, but continues to return to that cold presence against my flesh. Far too close for any sense of fleeting relief.

I am now genuinely terrified and my thoughts have followed on to make its own conclusions for I am seeing my own death; I am beginning to wonder what will happen to the boys if he kills me... Yet how can I make this man believe me when I tell him the truth? Jim's eyes are so intent, so dark, so full of anger and hate that I don't know how long before something inevitably happens, the 'wrong' thing is unavoidably said. And with that the 'snap' occurs like I have seen before when he has lunged at me - with his fist ready and already reaching at me as I am frozen in my surprise so that there is no time to react in any way other than to take the hit. He is not seeing 'me', he is seeing something or someone else. He does not want to hear me. He does not want to know the truth. What else can I do? What alternative is there? I wildly cast about in my mind – what else is there but The Truth? I have *always* told him the truth. *Yes, but does he believe you? Is that what he wants to hear? No?* Then *what* does he want to hear? *Why, a lie of course!*

To Lie or Not To Lie. That Is The Question!

And so the interrogation proceeds... I have no idea where this will lead... I have tried everything else, I will try *this*...

Into my mind pops 'reverse psychology' – and so I take a gamble – I do the only thing that I could think of to do in the situation now – I tell him what he *wants* to hear.

> *Maybe if I give him what he wants,* which is to hear that he is right after all and that I actually *have* been fancying someone, then just maybe he will settle down somewhat and not hurt me. Just maybe. Arguing with him is getting him angrier. *Go the other way, Marni!* I have to try. He

sure has his mind made up that I have been unfaithful. He doesn't want to hear that I hadn't. Let's just agree. *Make up a story, Marni – quick – pick on anyone at work, the first male name that comes into your head.*

Jim again clearly and determinedly said he *knows* that I was fancying someone; I take a chance. I agree. 'Yes, you're right.'

The look of satisfaction on his face belies any fact that he doesn't want his accusation to be a truth. He is getting something out of this! But what?

Now Jim says that he *knows* that I work with this someone; I have no option but to follow up this lie, so I agree. 'Yes, there is someone that I fancy at work.' My course is now set; the knife is being lowered from my face. His threatening posture is being replaced with some form of twisted pleasure.

He now says that he knows that I had kissed him; I agree. 'Yes, I didn't mean to, but it just happened.' Amazingly, Jim is getting calmer rather than angrier...

He asks for a name – so I give him a name. He asks me when it happened; so I make something up.

And he is accepting this. No, he is *loving* this! I am so conflicted. Yes, I am safe. For the moment. But!!! I have *given in* – I have given this man what he wants. Part of me feels out of danger, but it seems to be a numb safety, like somehow part of me feels resigned. Another part of me is drowning in something else...

I realise that I will now say anything, *try* anything, to get out of the situation, believe me. How would it be for my kids to get up in the morning, and find me in pieces all over the house, blood everywhere? How will they cope with him when he is prison for murder? Attempting to make sense of it all, I realise that I had to do whatever it took to diffuse the situation. By this time, I am now begging, and asking him for forgiveness. I now see myself as being separate from my thoughts, I am looking at the physical me, and I am watching things as they happen. I think they call this disassociation. I see myself because I am outside of myself, looking at the situation, seeing me begging him, seeing him lording it over me with that malicious gleam in his eye and the machete still dangerously close to my throat.

I seem to have lost all sense of self, all sense of my own standards. I am no longer me. I watch myself as if in a fog. And seeing as it is expected, I say that I am sorry for it, and 'it won't happen again'.

I find that I am now pledging myself over and over to him – that I am sorry and will only be faithful to him – and somehow this seems to be helping alleviate some of the drama. I can't remember everything after that to make it end, what was said that gave him permission to put the machete away, how it was that he calmed down – I suspect it was partly the act of his demand to prove it to him by having sex as he wanted; Good old sex as proof of my 'allegiance'! Or more correctly, giving him sexual gratification– I cannot call it 'making love' because I cannot call any of his actions or motives a 'love' of *any* kind.

There is now a disconnect within me. I have broken my own barriers – have wounded myself in some way. I feel that he has won somehow, and that I have lost. And I have. Self-respect.

But what I do clearly remember is this; I take away with me a firm resolve somewhere deep within me – I *swear* to myself that *if I survived* the night, if I got out of that situation and lived to tell the tale, if I made it out of the bedroom alive, *that I would find a way to leave him, to escape!* That I would *never,* **ever** *tell a lie to save myself from him again* – the emotional, moral and spiritual cost was too much for me. I could not and *would* not live with myself if I could only survive by lying about who I was. It simply was not worth it. **I would rather be dead!**

This was to be the first of the two most significant occasions, the first of the two extreme events initiated by Jim that thrust me face to face with my own mortality, my own boundaries, my own honour.

The incidents were mounting and accumulating, the scales getting heavier, the balance was shifting, and this huge wedge of bastardly and dastardly misery and disgust caused through him had somehow lodged a hold in my consciousness - and was now beyond any more of my forgiveness or acceptance.

Foreword

How did I come to be in such a situation as this? If I was married to a man who claimed to 'love God' and who claimed to be a 'Born-Again Christian', then how on earth could he act in such a way? And how was it I had allowed things to get to this point?

In order to understand this, I need to understand who I am, who he is. What sort of a person allows another to terrorize them like this? How much more could I, would I take?

Some of the answer lies in my own beginnings... in the childhood preparation for ongoing violence and terrorism...

RATIONALE

August 2016

This work is based on a true story. The resources are from the heroine's – if we dare call her that - own hand-written and typewritten memoirs and notes, diaries and documents as well as extensive personal interviews. She wishes to remain anonymous at this stage, and thus prefers the work to be labelled as Fiction. However... Some of the names have been changed to protect the innocent, some of the names have not been changed, also to protect as well as to inform the innocent. And to provide veracity to events that may be recognised by any 'victims' who may identify themself in this journal.

Very few of us have been gifted with our own personal life manual. One that might provide us with fool-proof guidance to the many mysteries, events and encounters we call life. Life just simply (or not so simply) seems to happen, no matter what it is we plan for.

This may well be despite the fact that we may think or believe that we have really smart, and clearly workable, plans... as many so-called 'failures' can attest to. The assumption then is that there are no guarantees in life, and good and supposedly bad things can happen to any one of us. Even good folk. And it is the true tone of the person that dictates how they respond to it, how they handle it.

It takes time to write a book, and even though this work was finally completed and edited in 2016, it would be remiss if the original introduction notes by our heroine were not included at this point. And here they are.

It is August 2014

I was brought up not to complain. I was not allowed to say how I felt or to expect attention to my discomforts. To hear the words 'always complaining' about others and the associated contempt with that statement, and then to have it applied to yourself as a small child is almost as unpleasant as saying nothing and putting up with one's worry or distress. Becoming an adult, one would think that having a voice would be a natural part of life.

Foreword

Involvement with a church professing the 'love of God' would surely bring the comfort it advertised, and a kindly ear to share one's burdens and anxiety with. Getting married to a 'Born-Again' Christian would happily bring a partner who would care for you as devotedly as you cared for him.

Not so.

There has been no Champion for me, no defender of my rights, no recourse when I was damaged and abused.

My own anger at the injustices heaped on me has caused me to examine myself. And the reasons for writing this book. Did I want revenge? Did I seek punishment on the church and its agent, my husband, who had been given total unreserved control over me?

No.

What I want is validation. What I want is for my voice to be heard. What I want is accountability. What I want is for the truth to be told. The truth about the man who systematically set about destroying my life, my reputation, my home, my happiness, my family and who *still* holds family court and credence in what was once my own family. Where is the justice? Where is the Champion?

Would his sons ever challenge him or his behaviours when they finally learn of the truth? Will they ever dare to confront him about his unspeakable behaviours? Would they finally defy 'keeping the peace' in order to question the labels he had tarred and feathered me with all those years ago, and still continues to do so with his silent complicity and complacency? How can there be peace when any one family member is in pain? (And each member of the family is in pain, one way or another.) How can there be healing unless that which is still causing wounding has not been first examined and dealt with?

Only when one who is no longer under the thumb and out of the shadow of the legacy of control and bullying can one speak up and challenge. And challenge I do.

This book is my voice. This book is my challenge. This book is my justice.

Foreword

Hello. My name is Marni, and I am still sitting here typing everything that I can remember. This is my own personal story of how I survived abuse. Some thought has been given to the 'why' of things, though this has not always successfully been answered in every instance of the events described, but thus it is in life. However along the way, I have found answers to some of my questions and I trust that others may perhaps find various insights scattered through these pages.

This is the story of someone who simply wanted to do and be the best she could. This aspiration followed me throughout my life, and my biggest challenge was to become wiser to the darkness of others without it contaminating my own heart.

My story begins where most stories really begin, my birth, which was right at the end of war-time in England. The tale escalates with my conversion to a religious cult, though the other members would certainly not call it that, going to great lengths to disown that label. And indeed, this group still appears to have some credence in many cities. But cult it became to me.

From this climactic event, things occurred that governed not only my life, but affected the lives of my as-yet unborn children as well. No event happens in isolation, and there is often a background that can lead up to it. It is for this reason as well as for greater clarity and understanding of the events that I also give the reader the fertile soil of my family foundations, and consequently the backdrop as to how some of the ensuing events were allowed to grow and flourish. For that which led to my conversion and my early marriage is essential in setting the stage for the abuse that followed. Responses do not happen in seclusion. They may well happen, though, according to a preconceived or patterned way of thinking, being or doing. Generally.

This account may be a bit of a strange tale in places indeed, yet everything that is conveyed here is true and happened the way I relate. Even as I review and go back over my life in the editing and rereading of events, I could be forgiven for not believing it happened the way it did – that is, if I hadn't actually lived through it all. And that is the difference – I did actually live through all of this. And somehow I can still smile!

Foreword

I was only seventeen when I got married – yes, rather naïve and just a wee bit young, hey? I knew little of the world, really, and mistakenly trusted and counted on others older and wiser for their guidance. Bring into this mix the out-of-touch attitudes of a church that is more interested in making a name for itself and increasing the number of conversions and its members rather than in the actual happiness of all the individuals of its flock. And with that added extra ingredient of putting the unpalatable behind one instead of dealing with it (and dealing with it at root level,) we have the ingredients that can create an interesting recipe, full of disastrous equations.

It has taken me many months to come to this place, in fact years, and now I am clearer as to how I begin my tale. For before my life in the church, there was another 'me' that needs to be considered. It was a very different world back in the forties and fifties. Many young people today have no idea of the skills one had to learn, or the things that were required then for us just to get by, as there is such emphasis via technical media today on being Special and of having to immortalise one's existence in some way through fame, celebrity, 'selfies' and social media in order to validate oneself.

I sometimes kept diaries which proved helpful later in recalling the dates of events. Fortunately, over the last few years I have also developed the habit of taking note and documenting buried memories and their associated feelings as they surfaced whilst examining events. As these recollections and instances were being documented, I found that other memories, concealed memories, memories that had been deeply buried and repressed, began emerging in more graphic detail – and it became clear that these were essential to acknowledge and deal with.

In the recalling of these events, many of the flashbacks were accompanied with strong emotion – the same ones that I felt at the time that they originally happened. These sometimes became very overwhelming for me – it was as if I was living through them all over again. I realised I had not always been able to resolve these before. I couldn't always afford to experience them fully back then – for who would be there to take care of me whilst I navigated through them? Or for my children when they were part of this story. Who could I count on within my family or social circle to be there just for me? There was no-one. I had to be strong just to get through. I didn't always know that this was about 'getting through'. I think I thought that this was my life and simply addressed each problem that emerged as best I could, digging as far back as my heart, soul, mind and emotions were able or prepared to reveal and to release at the time. And I realised later that old conditioning and a tendency to only see the best, or to only think on the best, had a part in this.

Under peculiar circumstances I lived a Christian life, and yet still experienced cruelty and abuse. I was not only terrorised, but I was also slandered and declaimed for no longer yielding to such ignorant brutality. My children were taken from me, I lost my home, my health, and sometimes even my will to live.

How does an intelligent young woman get trapped into such a relationship like this? A supposedly blessed association that was destined to become such a sadistic one? And just what kept her there? Why did she not simply leave? With such a strong faith in God, how come things turned out the way they did?

It took many years to answer these questions for myself, and to eventually reclaim those parts of me that had died. A lot of fear had to be overcome to finally face the monster who had deliberately tried to destroy me. His lies and denials have had their day. Here I share it all with you. For this story is my way of setting the record straight. I bore the shame of the events at the time alone. Now I am exposing it for what it is and was, and handing the shame back to its initiator and its author. I now correct the Falsehoods that have been made about me and that I had not been given audience to redress.

This is my attempt to set the record straight. And to make clear the events that led to my awakening.

This is my voice.

IN THE BEGINNING

*~ Humble Benchill ~ No Voice ~ School ~ Celebration ~ Scary Sounds
~ Mixed Bag ~ Grammar School ~ Bobby Dazzler ~ Anaemic
~ Working Class ~ Don't Break Her Spirit ~ Ways and Means
~ Latch-Key Kids ~ What About Me... ~ Home Dead End
~ Nightmares ~ Nightlights And Chrissie ~ To Be or Not to Be
~ Seeking Freedom ~ Greek God ~ Anniversary Crossroad
~ Faith and Hope ~ Fate Butts In ~ The Church*

HUMBLE BENCHILL

My story begins in Benchill, a humble suburb of Wythenshawe, Manchester. It was a new estate at the time that our small family first moved there in 1949, and we found that we were positioned on the outskirts of the developing township of Wythenshawe, yet still within easy reach of rich and luscious farmlands. There was growing opportunity for work and we were positioned within easy walking distance to the nearest bus-stop that travelled regularly into Manchester Town as it was called in those days. Manchester boasted a thriving city which was graced with the once famous flowering Piccadilly Gardens even though it was in the industrial mid-north of England. These gardens were often visited as a special treat by the local Mancunians, and it rated highly next to a visit to the Zoo as 'the place to go', no matter one's age. Various local tea rooms and major shops sustained the attraction, and many considered a 'day in town' as a special treat.

At the time of our move there I was aged four. I have memories of watching the van with our few meagre belongings being unloaded into the empty and bare house. My parents were unknowingly destined to live in this rented council house until they were both hospitalised sixty years of tenancy later in 2008. At that time of moving in, it was considered to be the latest brand new housing estate in Manchester. This part of Wythenshawe was located not too far from the Ringway Airport which over time became one of the major airports in the North of England.

The brand new residential estate was comprised of houses designed as almost-semi-detached residences in that they were built in groups of two red bricked houses attached in mirrored design together with their front doors practically right next door to each other, though separated externally by a mutual fence or row of hedges front and rear. These two houses were then attached to another similar pair, which were separated on the ground floor only by ten foot high tunnels right through to the back of the houses, and was named locally as a guinnel – pronounced gi-nul. This gave ease of access to the back garden area, mainly composed of resistant clay which took much labour, time, phosphate and energy to make vegetable productive. Equipped with an inside toilet and coal-hole (a small room for storing the coal and coke used for burning and heating), the house was an improvement to some degree on what my mother had been used to in the early days of wedded bliss. For immediately after she was married she had moved away from my stern and stoic grandparents whom she had been living with in Wigan, to try to manage by herself in Liverpool. Dad was still in the army and it was a few more years before she could persuade him to leave that behind and support her practically in raising a family.

Liverpool had taken a bit of a pounding by bombs during the Second World War but I believe that Manchester had fared a bit better. Because our new home was set in an avenue, which faced another similar mirror avenue, this gave some of the residential Council housing a mite of variety and some seclusion. This was one of the reasons why mum had chosen this location as it was ideal for children who actively played outside in those days, and it provided some safety from the increasing growth in the number of hazards, such as buses, cars and motorbikes on the nearby roads and more main thoroughfares.

The avenue boasted a huge oak tree, and quickly became the local children's friend and gathering place. For many years, around fifty actually, it stood sentinel on one side of the avenue, shady in summer, bare and quiet in winter, and perfect for climbing all year round. It eventually boasted steel pegs for the slow climber, and later progressed to wearing a huge rubber tyre on one of its thick and sturdy limbs, which served as the local swing for many. And ugly as it may have seemed to some, it was a welcoming and promising sight to the growing number of children as the estate gradually became green with fresh plantings and a community of sorts was established.

There was a local primary school already within easy walking distance, with the promise of secondary schools being tabled for future building. A short walk to the local Haverley School required a minimum amount of care crossing the road near the bus route, and a friendly kind of teacher helped the attending children to partly enjoy the process of Growen'-Up and Lurnin'.

The school was a mixture of children from various backgrounds. I had heard talk from time to time on the 'classes', Britain apparently having a variety of these particular ways of defining various stratas and lifestyles of status and position. To put it simply, the rich, the titled and those of independent means were usually included in the 'upper class' section, then there was the 'middle class' which was the moderately wealthy and the upper professionals. Underneath these (or considered as so by these other classes) were the 'working class' which included traders and tradesman. And in some quarters, these were also considered as 'lower class'. I suspect that this class system may have variations in differing districts but that is a sketch of the fundamentals.

Based on family and neighbourhood talk, I had somehow always assumed we were middle class. Mum had even once termed us as 'upper middle class', which must have been when she was a factory charge-hand with staff under her and she could begin to see her way money wise through her increased wages. And I think this front of 'middle class' was what dad attempted to present to the world. One day, after hearing other children talking about the concept and its labels and disputing what I had heard from my parents, I had become confused about it all, and so I asked my parents what 'class' we really were. They initially fobbed me off with claiming we were 'middle class'. But my friends had mentioned that we were not that, but said that we were actually poor. I was still confused. Mum mumbled things like 'white collar', 'blue collar' and 'middle class'. But this still didn't quite feel right, so I questioned for further definition; mum came up with us being 'blue-collar' class, which seemed to include factory workers, which she was at the time. She might have been in munitions during the war, and war-time had seen a total mixture of all times of class of both rich and poor women all pulling together for the 'cause', but we were no longer at war, and dad was now working on building sites. As a foreman, he was 'blue collar', which both my parents considered was a kind of middle class. Later I came to realise this wasn't quite the truth of it. For we were mostly just plain 'working class'.

And in reality, despite my dad's aspirations and with his lousy luck at the behind-the-shops-gambling and both my parent's attempts to woo and socially impress neighbours and friends, we were really pretty poor. Like most in the neighbourhood. Leastways that was the end result.

When I had asked about whether we were poor or not, mum pointed out some neighbours who lived round the corner as actually being 'poor' because they had six children and had holes in almost everything they wore. Even though we were not quite that bad, we weren't that far from them sometimes.. There was only some marginal differences. In retrospect I realized that we actually were poor, as most people were right after the war, but my parents were somewhat more ambitious (it would appear) than some of our immediate neighbours.

We were pretty short of hugs growing up. In the days of such deprivation, a lot of people had the attitude that if they gave too much, it would be 'spoiling the child'. The Baby Boomers were to emerge around the time that rationing stopped, but for some years after the war, there was still a sense of deficiency and scarcity which drove some to stockpile as soon as they could afford to. In my own family, hugs were few and far between, as were 'treats'. Cadbury chocolate was our main form of special treat, along with ice cream, which was far rarer. When dad was in a good mood, or guilty for some misdemeanour that had cause friction in the family, he would buy a block of chocolate and break it into squares. These he would hand round on a plate for us to take one at a time until he thought we had had enough, or the entire block was gone. Depending on how he felt. There has long been an association of this chocolate with love for me, though I hesitate to buy it now because of its current Halal connections. The many phrases on child care and child rearing that were bandied around in our house in those days included such pearls, or rather 'nuts', of teaching as

Naïve Hope

the following: Children should be seen and not heard; Spare the rod and spoil the child; They have to learn they can't have it all their own way; Do as I do, not as I say; What's yours is mine, and what's mine is my own; You must learn to share with others. And for me in particular and on many an occasion; we are (or I am) only doing this for your own good; you are the oldest, so you should know better. Ha!

If only they had realised that emotional pain as well as physical pain can be dispelled by enough hugs! But there was a shortage in our lives, and probably had always been in their own lives... Pain left unacknowledged and untreated can dog one for years; alcohol can deaden the pain, tobacco can temporarily lift it, shopping can attempt to replace it, sex can distract from it, but until that *pain of unlovedness* is dealt with, it will simply re-occur or continue to cause pain.

Trauma for some can cause deep bruising of the psyche and heart and can filter down deep into the body to settle in the very bones - and even marrow - in the body.

No Voice

One of the most impactful memories and experiences of my life, apart from the uncomfortable early days in Wigan with the grandparents was my Tonsillectomy.

This (horrifying) experience was Ice Cream coated. Or so they convinced me. When I was about four years of age, I was diagnosed with Tonsillitis. This is a condition of severe inflammation at the back of the throat where one can hardly swallow without acute pain. My tonsils would swell up, and I would find it difficult in breathing. After a series of successive coughs and colds, my tonsils flared seriously and painfully. This all took place in the days when doctors were God, and one NEVER disobeyed them. Otherwise, the alternative was death, for the doctor was ALWAYS right! If you ignored what he said, and did not follow to the letter what he instructed, then you would surely DIE. Talk about the fear of God! The doctor informed mum and dad that the only option to my swollen tonsils was a Tonsillectomy, which would remove the offending anatomy and stop the pain. No understanding that the tonsils had a function. They were simply 'of no use' and now needed to be removed so that they would stop getting swollen. Medical opinion and knowledge at that time did not take into account that as everybody had tonsils, why would the body deliberately create bits that had absolutely no function just for the sheer heck of it? In a climate where the norm is to remove what offends, this they duly did.

However, getting me into hospital was another proposition. As soon as mum told me what was to happen, that I would need to go to hospital and would go to sleep whilst they took out what was hurting me, I went into panic and tears. In some way, I knew what would happen to me and simply didn't want to experience it. It would mean leaving my own home, being without my mother, being forced and made to 'sleep' and having my body cut. Reassurances from the doctor and mum failed miserably. Almost. Until they tempted me with ice cream!

The deal was that I could have as much Ice Cream to eat as my little heart could want, or my little stomach could fit in. Now, you must understand something first. We are talking Ice Cream here. We are talking about a very special treat and highly prized in those days. We are talking about something that was a rarity in the days shortly after the war. The days of yore when Ice Cream was fresh, creamy, natural, yummy and something quite different from today's Ice Creams. To have Ice Cream then was a marvellous experience that lasted for hours, if not days, after.

For some strange reason I definitely did NOT want to go into hospital – I was fair afraid of the idea. But they had obviously paid attention to my response and interest in ice cream. I eventually succumbed to their cajoling, and allowed myself to be carted off, clinging to mum, to hospital. The separation from mum was a sight to behold. A grip of all my might and tears and fears would have given the impression that this was a fight to the death for me... Looking back, though, it is understandable that it seemed that my world was falling apart, melodramatic as this sounds. Children truly need comfort, safety and stability. And *pretending* about something doesn't help them to deal with the realities of life in the long run. And they were pretending all right.

Naïve Hope

When I woke up from the operation, I was in a hospital cot with high sides so that I couldn't climb over. Feeling so very sickly and woozy it was a while before I could gather myself together. My memory of it now is so very clear. I am in a cot, a kind of small bed, with wooden rails around it to prevent me getting out onto the hospital floor. I am feeling sick and seedy from the anaesthetic. I want my mummy and she is not there. And my throat is hurting so bad. I thought they were going to make it better, take away the pain. Why, oh why, is it hurting me so much, so bad. It is hot, and sore, and throbbing, and I want my mummy, and I am all alone. I can't swallow, it hurts so much. I can't talk, cause that hurts, too. I want to get out of the cot, but I cannot, I want to cry for my mummy, and I try to speak, but I cannot, I can only croak.

When the nurse saw me looking round a bit wildly, she brought my mum from the waiting room into the ward and allowed mum to give me some comfort, though I wasn't allowed to leave this horrible cot. My throat hurt like hell, it was the worst pain I had experienced in my short life. Feeling like the inside of the back of my throat and my swallowing area was shredded into tiny pieces, I could hardly swallow, and if I did accidentally swallow, I doubled over in pain and clutched at my throat.

Mum had been promising me the ice cream, and sure enough the ice cream came around for the children in my ward. The tears are spilling down my face, and I am so unhappy, and a nurse comes up and asks me if I want some Ice Cream. She says that the ice cream will make my throat feel better and soothe it and cool it down for me so that it hurts less. So I manage to stop my sobbing for a little, and I look up with tears to listen to her. And so she gets me some ice cream.

But it *doesn't* make my throat better. Even just one sip of this when swallowed causes me acute agony. I cannot swallow it. I cannot swallow, or call out, or speak, or cry properly. So I cannot have my ice cream. I couldn't believe it! Hadn't they promised me that it would help to soothe my throat? Wasn't this the reason I had allowed myself to be brought here? Why did it hurt so much? What had happened? I couldn't speak, and I couldn't swallow.

Little children are whizzing by me in little pedal-push cars. They are all eating their ice cream. Nobody else is in pain like me, they are all moving about, and eating happily. Eventually my mother is allowed to visit me. I still cannot speak. I still cannot swallow. I am still crying wet tears down my cheeks. And my mum wants to take me home. I am so sad and unhappy, I want to go home. I want my mummy.

And then, all too short, far too soon, the nurses tell mum that visiting time was over and she has to leave. Oh My God! I am devastated. Tears streaming down my face, choking back on the inevitable swallows and back-mucous, I was in total torture and misery. Each swallow was a nightmare, each attempt to cry was a torture. I clung and clung and clung to mum's hand, but stronger fingers than mine extricated me from her and shooed her out of the door. The nurse ushers her out, away from me, out of my sight. I remember she did not want to leave me, seeing the distress on my face, and hearing my chokes, and seeing how I couldn't swallow or cry out or speak. But she obeys, and goes. Sobs from deep within shook me. Nobody paid any attention. What could they do? Well, maybe a couple of hugs might have helped... But they were all far too busy! And I am left, all alone with my tears, trying to internally swallow down my pain, my frustration, my betrayal, my loneliness, my powerlessness, my voicelessness. Nobody cares. And nobody did. I was just 'that tiresome little tyke who can't stop crying'.

For a couple of days I could not eat or swallow without severe pain, my condition was so painful and the doctors could not release me until I was better, and so they had to wait until I could eat again. I withdrew into my own little world of total isolation and misery. I felt I was being punished and couldn't work it out. But most of all, I felt totally *betrayed*. Their promises were broken, their words were just lies. By the time I was ready to go home, I hadn't been able to down *any* ice cream, and I felt cheated and deceived. They had tricked me. They didn't care about me. But I *needed* mum and dad, didn't I? I have no alternative other than to push the hurt out of my mind and let the memory and pain sink into my being so that I can carry on with life; after all, I am now out of hospital and home and able to start taking fluids.

Naïve Hope

After a sensitive period of recover, I can at last tentatively swallow again.

The impact on my psyche was devastating and affected me for most of my life. Those of you who have read any child development books will understand the stories and beliefs that my heart and emotions created as a result of this experience. A sample of the potent beliefs developed as a consequence, and continually played out in my life are as follows:

1. Nobody cares
2. They promise, but they don't deliver
3. They lie to me, I do what they want, but they cheat
4. I am not important enough
5. I cannot have what I want

Meanwhile, a little child has to find a way to move on.

Life goes on.

The operation certainly alleviated the coughs, colds and sore throats. However, removing the tonsils does *not* stop problems, for from that point on, every cold now became bronchitis. The tonsils had acted as a defence to stop germs reaching my lungs... but I didn't know this until I was an adult, and I dare say, not many in the medical profession realised this then, either. Ah well. Sometimes progress is a good thing. Though a more advanced solution would be to find out the *cause* of these coughs and colds, and to deal with these causes instead of simply dealing with the symptoms... And in time, this is what I did; and along the way I discovered that supporting the immune system rather than pill-popping, which was then the new norm with doctors, made a great difference to my ability to fight off infections like this.

During my childhood, as for many children, a series of illnesses hit me, and apparently I nearly died from this bombardment. Though we didn't know it at the time, Glandular Fever, which was just one of the onslaughts I experienced early on, can still affect one later on in life.

With the existing prevailing restrictions on good protein or even simply sufficient food to eat, many people experienced nutritional deprivation. By the age of eleven I was wearing a dental plate to replace the resultant loss of adult teeth.

Growing up with such difficulties required the development of good old British stoicism – though in some this was often experienced as hardness of heart and a lock-down of feelings. The war had many costs, numerous ramifications. Many had had to overcome the loss of the brightest and fairest, and indeed the fondest, whether it be a parent, a lover, friend or child. Trauma was repressed and those warriors who survived the fighting or destruction by bombardment were well served if they got a stint away at a seaside nursing home. Generally there was a bit more understanding then for the weary wounded and their timely acknowledgement of 'shell-shock' would be equivalent to our current label of Post Traumatic Stress Syndrome or PTSD. Though back then there was at least an attempt to rectify some of the damage done. Not so in more recent times, as returning troops are left to fend for themselves, and, sadly, are often unable to do so.

One of our local doctors, a Dr Fowler (yes, I still remember his name), was obviously an astute man and would have been blind not to notice the various inflictions on mum that were presented as consistently clumsy attempts to manoeuvre through dangerous doorways. Or down steps. Such were the 'reasons' for her bruises and marks. Not given to drink, not that I noticed anyway, for there were never many alcoholic bottles in evidence at home, should she be believed mum may well have appeared to the world at large to be a surprisingly clumsy woman; yet one who somehow managed to work very capably and efficiently with machinery in the local factory, and to maintain a very light and accurate step at the dancehall she occasionally visited with dad. When things were going well.

These physical solo altercations with wood or masonry (*self-inflicted?*) were a bit of a contradiction, possibly? And there were the odd occasions calling for essential Health Service home visits for after hours 'accidents'.

Naïve Hope

Having to see dad's particular handy-work on mum's face, and my later experiences of having to help and even nurse her as she suffered spontaneous abortions from being kicked down the stairs were all filed away as 'beyond my control' whilst I, like mum, simply got on with life.

As regards alcohol that I ever saw in the house, there wasn't much really. In the top shelf in the pantry we had the odd bottle of sherry that mum would occasionally use for cooking or baking, though I never actually saw her drink it unless she tasted it when she was cooking with it. Nor dad. I only ever saw them drink alcohol properly at Christmas really. For at those festive times there would always be a bottle of Cherry Brandy, a bottle of Sweet Sherry, and in later years, mum and dad would also have on hand a bottle of a milky drink called Malibu, I think, that tastes of coconuts, and another creamy one called Bailey's Irish Cream.

With me being born just exactly nine months after they were married everyone breathing an audible sigh at my birth event, I later heard. The next family arrival at two years of age was by my brother, Ian. By this time, we had accumulated some furniture. This was followed by a sister four years later when I was aged six. Joan was the fair-haired child in the family. Mum's Christian name was Ann and Dad's first name was John, so they joined their names together to get Jo-an, Joan. And they were so excited about having her, not like when Ian was due.

Yet despite butter-wouldn't-melt-in-the-mouth looks, Joan turned out to be a real trouble maker, a renegade, a liar and the most sneaky and selfish person I ever came to know. Joan showed very quickly what type of soul she was as she proved to be a really spoilt brat. At the time, I was 'responsible' for her and was put to work in baby-sitting or 'minding' her at every opportunity. I would be held accountable for everything that she did wrong, every cry she made, every hurt she suffered and I often got punished for these. She was also the favoured one, the lucky one, the one who dad always picked up the moment he came home. She was always getting Ian and myself into trouble, and always getting out of any blame. She wouldn't do as she was told, and I would get the blame. She would deliberately cause problems and pretend it had nothing to do with her.

I have no idea how she managed to get away with what she got away with, but she did. I think we all resented her on some level; mum, Ian and myself. The theory that I later developed is that a man is not really ready for children until he is in his thirties, usually around thirty-three years of age onwards. Dad was thirty-three when Joan arrived, and the sun shone out of her backside. In his eyes she could do no wrong. And we all felt his love pouring into her, and it felt like there was none left over for any of us. Yet we all took great care of her, though it's possible that some of our 'respect' for her was based on just what she could do to cause trouble for us.

Of course, this could all have simply been dad's final acceptance of his responsibilities, or yet another case of applying his love back into the family between bouts of taking it elsewhere... Whatever the reason, Joan ruled. What she wanted was what she got. Even to demanding, on Christmas Day, that I share my meager Christmas presents with her, though she wouldn't share with me.

In later life this little viper really showed who she was as she betrayed the whole family with lies and theft. She still holds a position as a Minister, or rather 'Pastor' though I know she scored that dubious title in a very suspect way; through marrying the son of a Pastor and through nepotism and entitlement being bestowed this title by his dad. She is still connected with ministries in one of the Throngs of God associations in Manchester, and I daresay she is still cheating elderly folks as she did my parents towards the end of their lives. But that is another story.

School

It was a chaotic family, a disorganized life, a fraught home and a fearful confusing existence. With parents who were just too engrossed in their own dramas and conflicts. They wanted to send me to a local school a few miles away, which had come on the recommendation of neighbours; mostly Catholic. The kids already attending there told me that I would be initiated with the (undignified) welcome rite should I attend it. This means having one's head thrust down the toilet and flushed. I knew that these kids meant it, and that they indeed wished me harm and my life

Naïve Hope

would there would be more of the same. The first day Mum took me to the school despite my protestations and begging, I managed to grab hold of the railings and to grip on for dear life. I howled, I screamed, I wept. Mum relented. This was the only time in my life that I resisted my parent's wishes. So I ended up being sent to another primary, but this was even closer and felt safer.

Though still feeling generally misunderstood and fearful at school, I discovered and adored one teacher who actually seemed to see 'me' and to speak directly to me. For I guess by this time I was accustomed to being fobbed off and ignored, and I generally felt invisible and unimportant to most people. She was my English teacher, and teased out of me the confidence to exercise my intelligence and ability for the English language. A portly woman, with a mature tidy and open face, well past marriageable age, she was what was termed back in those days as a 'spinster'. Always with a neat bun at the nape of her neck, and often wearing those woolen twin sets of matching jumper and cardigan worn together with mid calf length plain woolen skirts, Miss Hunter was my savior and the highlight of my school days. It was as though the soul of this woman saw *my* soul. This seemed to let me know that she somehow knew that I existed. For an impressionable and sensitive six year old, having her for the first couple of years of school life gave me some sort of hope. I aspired to do all things well for her, and found that I could. Because she believed in me.

Bless her wherever she is right now.

Being the eldest didn't give me any special rights or privileges. Rather it gave me responsibilities far too early in life. And the price of not meeting one's responsibilities was direct punishment. In those days. It was to be many years later that I learned not to automatically duck when someone raised their arm near me.

Being told to 'Shut Up!' was a common thing, and this was usually followed by a short sharp and sometimes stinging clip around the ears or on the back of the head. We certainly learned to beware on occasion, but I often got into trouble when I could not stop myself from demanding fairness in life, whether defending a wrongly accused sibling, arguing over an unjustified broken promise or jumping to mum's aid when she had been erroneously made wrong by dad.

Happy events were few and far between. There wasn't really much to celebrate, though children can be resilient and attempt to be happy with whatever they find to hand.

Celebration

And we had certainly learned to make the most of little. One such occasion occurred that embraced the whole of the country. I still vaguely recall the Coronation of Queen Elisabeth in 1953. And all of the grandness, the pomp and ceremony, the magic, the colour, the flag-wavings, the celebrations. Oh my! I was all of eight years old.

Being in Manchester, and not in the grand city of London, did nothing to dampen this opportunity to forget about the harsh realities of life. Every single person seemed to embrace it. There were major preparations made in schools, halls, streets and homes. Shops elbowed in on the occasion, providing cups and saucers, mugs, books, cards, tea-towels, special photographs or wall pictures, ribbons, flags, teapots ... anything that could hold an imprint of the British flag and a picture of the Princess Elizabeth and the Crown of England. Pictures of the Royal Coaches, the Palace, Westminster Hall, indeed *anything* that had any connection to the forthcoming Coronation was fair game for making a penny... But this blatant marketing didn't seem to detract from the occasion and everyone bought *something*, no matter how small the memento. It was wonderful and amazing and at eight years old it was absolutely fascinating for me. Many of us dreamed of being a little princess or of having even just *one* of their lovely dresses. Most every family I knew bought flags to wave, and at least one or two items marking this special occasion, the favourites being a Coronation mug, plate or a wall plaque.

I remember that the following Christmas I was thrilled to receive a jigsaw puzzle of the queen in a lovely blue dress wearing one of her amazing tiaras. The dress so dazzled me, for it was totally covered with sequins. My eyes had never been filled with such richness and beauty before. For as long as it lasted, I treasured that jigsaw...

Naïve Hope

These dreams and fantasies helped to get me through some of the more mundane aspects of life. Such as trying to eat burnt potatoes – yes, I know – how can you burn boiling potatoes? But mum did. It was a regular occurrence. She would put the pot on the stove on a high gas flame and then forget it. She was good at that. The water would boil dry and burn the bottoms of the potatoes black. We lost several pots that couldn't be rescued over the years. And interestingly I remember that on one occasion dad said nothing, and sat there eating the burnt potatoes, even slathering them in butter whilst expecting us all to do the same. I wasn't old enough to guess the real story behind that event!

SCARY SOUNDS

But there were other things that caused friction in our house, and I often felt an element of fear there.

I remember quite clearly listening intently whilst lying in my bed at night for sounds of distress from mum. Many was the night I would hear her cry out 'Oooh, John, please don't do that – it hurts' – I didn't know what they were doing, I only know that I felt mum was in pain, and fearful. Which made me feel in pain and fearful. It seemed that I would lie in bed ready to jump out of it at any moment and daring to risk braving dad's wrath with the excuse of 'I can't sleep' in order to stop *any* thing that I heard was causing mum pain. Listening so intently, I would hear the blood rushing and pulsing through my ears. Needless to say, I developed excellent night hearing once I had learned to distinguish the sounds. Of course I didn't always fully understand what was happening and thank goodness for that for I was far too young to know then of the things that can happen between couples. But in some way it put me on some kind of long-term alert, and I would sometimes have nightmares and even wet the bed. For which I paid in shame or smacks. I did grow out of it, though. Both Ian and myself suffered from this, and I was later to learn that bladder function is affected by fear. So, no surprises there then, though we were quite ignorant of this at the time.

However, being so sensitive, I think I was more prone to the dark moods of others and I do remember having a puzzling experience one day. I must have been around **nine years of age**, and one day when I ran out to play I found that I was rather confused upon discovering that I had lost whatever spring I had previously had in my step – it seemed like running and moving in life from that point on now just felt 'heavy' and joyless. In fact it was to be many years later that I was to rediscover the meaning and indeed the experience of joy.

Mixed Bag

Though we were quite deprived in many ways that I was totally unaware of back then, we didn't want for pets – somehow there was always a cat or kitten around, or a dog, or a bird – usually engineered by mum. This is possibly where we got some love from, unconditional or otherwise.

And sometimes there was more than one pet. I don't know how mum managed this, for dad was definitely the Master of our house. However, it happened. And over the years we went through the usual suspects of pets during school years: guinea pigs, a hamster, budgerigars, dove (mum's personal choice, this one), chickens, worms, white mice, and one year my brother even got a grass snake. And somehow amongst the family dysfunctions, rows, fights and disharmony we could sometimes still rescue time and dredge up some fun in school holidays.

Memories I can dig up include rounds of monopoly, playing cards, charades, 'hang-man', battleships, and the usual skipping, tree climbing, planting of plants, growing carrot-tops, drawing and colouring-in, jigsaws, knitting, sewing, and even one year watching chicklets hatch from fertilized chicken eggs care of the old 'back-to-back' coal oven in our kitchen. This was an oven connected to the coal fire that fronted into the lounge room, and was also meant to double as a (temperamental) solution in lieu of a heater for our hot water. Bath times could be very cold affairs, with very little hot bath water to go around. And marked with wet discomfort as we often had to use the same soggy towel as the previous bather.

Sleeping was not necessarily a place of comfort or safety either. I was always cold. The blankets were sparse, few in number and ineffective.

Naïve Hope

Often in winter and on many an occasion my feet froze, even though I called out that I was so cold I was actually shivering and couldn't stop from feeling the cold. My hot water bottle had absolutely no effect on the cold damp cheap sheets and blanket, for there weren't enough blankets to fix the problem. We often had our overcoats thrown over the bed to try and keep some heat in. Even dad's army greatcoat of wool was totally ineffectual. And so very heavy that it cut off circulation and hurt my ankles and toes even more. I marvel now at the array of heating that is almost mandatory in English homes. And so it should be.

Life could be so dispiriting that I would threaten to leave home - to run away like I had heard somewhere in a movie. I was determined not to live under the same roof as people who were so insensitive, who were so rowdy and argumentative, so selfish, so hurtful and over-riding that at that point I would have walked to the moon and back if I was able.

I think I was about ten years old when it was the third time I had gotten to this point of declaring that I would leave and not come back that my parents shifted tack on this one. And smartly so. Instead of threatening me with punishments or confining me to my room as before, they now helped me pack my school satchel with a jumper and spare socks, and even gave me a bottle of water and a sandwich to go, waving goodbye to me at the front door! Initially I was relieved for I was in the full throes of righteous indignation, and just couldn't wait to get out of that house! But twenty minutes into my journey, walking away from home and dad in particular, my initial rage spent, I had no idea where I was to go or to end up, nor what would happen to me when and if I got to wherever this place was that I was supposed to be going to.

Who did I know besides family that could help me or take me in? Where could I sleep that night, for it was already late afternoon? What would I do for food and money after eating this sandwich? Yes, you guessed it. You get the picture. Wearily trudging back home defeated, I dejectedly knocked at the front door to be let back in again. Resigned to the family crap with none of my own resources and far too young and tender to be out in the world, I again submitted and subjected myself to the chaotic laws and rules of the incomprehensible minds and hearts of my parents and family.

Life went on. Inexorably.

GRAMMAR SCHOOL

I somehow passed the Eleven-Plus Primary School Leaving Exam and fortunately good marks meant that secondary school for me was the new local grammar school. This felt like such a privilege to be part of its first year beginnings. Blessed with brand new furnishings and surroundings, it was lovely to have new seats and desks. However, time also brought with it a mixture of experiences that sometimes left me feeling like an outsider whose parents couldn't always afford extras. But I got through, and still have very fond memories and respect in particular for the headmaster, Dr Gilpin, as well as some of the teachers including Mr. Fisher the French and Music teacher, Miss Ilse and the Math's teacher, Mr. Hutchinson. I didn't really excel in all the Math's subjects but was quite interested and did relatively well all things considered. These teachers in particular were very fair, and though from time to time I had detentions, usually for not finishing homework in time, they were always respectful and I couldn't help but admire them and their fair dealings. Maybe they could see below the surface?

Mum and dad had little time to support us in our schooling, and for me in particular, there was no time to attend any events I was involved in at school unless they were summoned to it. Or rather, mum was. Dad was always too busy, or working or some such other whatever. At age twelve, I took part in a school play held at Poundswick Grammar, the *only* school play I was ever in actually, and this went unseen by both my parents. Disheartening as it was, I had come to expect nothing less. Too many children, too much to do, not important enough etc.

However, the next time our family doctor, the friendly and understanding Dr Fowler visited us, he exclaimed on my part in the play and how I had everybody laughing even though I only had a few lines. 'Really brought it alive' he said. 'One of the few bright spots in it all' and he beamed at me, eyes twinkling with delight and encouragement. Did he too see me? I wonder.

Naïve Hope

How I had wished that dad would have been there.

Let me say at this point that when dad did pay us any attention, he was the sun to my winter. He was my hero, and I only ever wanted his admiration and encouragement. The tiny dribs and drabs he gave to me prevented me from hating him totally, though I still think a girl's heart can continue to seek a different kind of love and acceptance from her father than from her mother. In later years, he became a kindly loving grandparent, but back then... he was a tyrant and a bully with very little tolerance and generally very demanding. He would bark and yell like a drill sergeant, and his attempts at our compliance did more to freeze and scare us than to elicit correct action.

To be honest and to be fair though, these horrors were sometimes interspersed with moments of consideration, but not enough to sustain the hearts that were needing his love, attention and care. Nor to sway the overall balance from fear to safety and nurture.

There needs to be some form of balance, but one where the goodwill, the tenderness, the fulfillment of a guardian's trust far outweighs any oversights or mistakes made on his part. He is entrusted with the hearts of his daughters, and it is his duty, responsibility and privilege to treat this with the utmost respect and care. If he can. And this is the rub. For many men had no such role models...

The essential role of a loving father cannot be more emphasized, especially for a daughter. Where else is she going to learn about the important men she allows into her life and her heart? Where else can she discover safety and be assured that she deserves respect and valuing. A father sets down her initial 'love-equation' for a partner, and if this is faulty or destructive it can take many years, many tears, and even many scars before she may be able – if at all – to rewrite her own love-equation for her most intimate of relationships.

I realize that dad was an angry man. Many were during and after the war.

I wasn't allowed to be angry as a little girl. There was more than enough anger to go around between my parents and when things were actually peaceful, there would still somehow be something going on or some sort of fight or stand-off with 'the neighbours'. I think and guess I probably held onto and stored my anger as hurt and pain. I had both seen and felt that anger was very scary and hurt others, and I didn't want to do that. And anyway I usually got punished if I dared come close to showing any. So hurt was a safer emotion to deal with for me. And for my parents. In fact, in later life I got to feel this hidden anger erupt at things totally unrelated, and had to work out ways to clear it from my system. Feelings just don't vanish because they are ignored, particularly those associated with pain, anger or sadness – they bury into the body, emerging either when it's safe or when it is triggered again...

BOBBY DAZZLER

However it still didn't stop me from registering what was wrong and unfair. One day I was really challenged with all of this, and came face to face with a life-defining situation that could have changed the destiny for the whole of the family. If only.....

Mum and dad were at it like hammer and tongues again in the lounge-room, when dad suddenly slapped her so hard she fell on the floor. He was red and bulging in the face, so angry and so scary, leaning over her and shouting at her. I hated violence and I always got upset whenever I saw anger of this kind. My courage and desire to defend mum got the better of me. My reaction was immediate. And extreme.

'Don't you hit her!' I yelled. 'Stop that right now', I literally screamed out at him. I didn't want him to hurt her anymore and I would do all I could to stop it. My righteous indignation was well and truly riled. My face was burning and my hands became fists clenched by my side. Nothing in the world could make this outrage right in my eyes...

Dad turned his rage onto me. With flashing eyes he advanced toward me. 'Stop hitting mum', dared I, for I was now screaming, frantic with panic and rage, and also now, fear.

'Or what?', he sneered.

'Or we'll call the police!' I bluffed.

Naïve Hope

'Shut up and stay out of this', dad yelled over me as I tried to cover mum's prostrate body with mine.

My little brother Ian was watching wide-eyed, having also naturally been summoned by all that was going on. He started to cry and dad shouted at him to shut up. I was crying and sobbing myself by this time, trying to control my voice and my shaking hands.

'And you shut up too' he yelled again at me.

Ian and I looked at each other, wondering who dad was going to attack next, who would be first for the next thwack, the next thump of a punch. Even though Ian had pushed his hands into his mouth to try and stop his tears and moans, he couldn't stop his sobs from breaking through.

Mum struggled to find her voice, now, the initial shock at being slapped to the floor (and by this champion boxer) giving way to concern at the escalation of the situation. She now also had to protect her children, for they were getting involved in this. Finding her breathe, she attempted to pacify both my brother and myself and she was trying to scramble her way up from off the floor. 'Kids, you stay out of this. It's alright', she croaked. But it was too late, and now it was our turn...

Emotions were far too high and dad had been challenged. Dad got really rough with us both then, and as mum struggled to find her legs and her voice, and I tried to cover her modesty by pulling her skirt back over her knees, dad slapped Ian hard across the head, then pushed him out the lounge-room door telling him to get to his bedroom and he'd deal with him later. Ian's attempts at not crying must have triggered this attack at that point. One down, two to go, he must have thought for then he promptly turned back to attack mum again. It was obviously all her fault, all of this trouble. Right?

I shouted then I screamed at him not to hit her again, both daring and begging him to stop. 'Don't hit her, dad, please don't hit her' I howled, amid tears, fear and frustration. Who was going to stop this man, who was going to help us out of all this?

Our voices were raised so high I figured all of the neighbours would hear us and do something. Surely someone would come and stop this row, this thing that felt like it might end in murder...

But the next thing that I knew was that I got a stinging slap across the face which knocked me onto the couch and out of his way. Then dad turned back to hit mum and he punched her down to the floor again, this time hitting her in the stomach. This tall handsome charming man had again become a wild uncontrollable animal, a tyrant and bully, beating a helpless woman. But this time I had dared to challenge him and to interfere with what he was doing.

I had had enough. I took action. I was not going to stand by and let him do whatever he wanted. I could not hit him back, I stood no chance. I did not dare to hit him with any object that could be used as a weapon, he would still overpower me. I could not stop him; I had to get someone who *could* stop him. My face red, streaked with tears, indignant at what this man was doing, even though he was my dad, I ran to the lounge door which led to the front door and the stairway to our bedrooms. As I grabbed it open, I saw Ian just outside the door, too scared to go to his room and await what would surely come to him after dad had dealt with mum. I grabbed his hand saying 'Come on Ian, we are going to get the Police' and I threw the front door open. I made sure that my dad could hear us, and shouted my intentions out to him.

'We're going for the police, and they will lock you away for this, dad. Just you see', I threatened, running as fast as my feet would allow whilst dragging Ian behind me. My timing was good, dad could not reach us in time to stop us due to his position on the other side of the room. But he heard my shouts as Ian and I took off at a fast run.

'I am going for the Police, they will stop you. Mum, we're going to get the Police on to dad. We'll be back as soon as we can with the Police'. I no longer cared who heard me, this man *had* to be stopped. Blow what the neighbours think, if they can't help, then the police will!

I ran out of the avenue, leaving the front door open, heading in the direction of the Police Station and dragging Ian after me.

Naïve Hope

Dad didn't catch us. He didn't follow us. We didn't hear the sound of his motor bike chasing after us though we were expecting to, and we just ran and ran and ran. Crazy thoughts and fears assaulted my senses, whilst I tried to quieten Ian and drag him along at the same time.

Is dad coming after us? Will we get to the police station in time? Will he be there waiting to stop us? Was mum dead? Had he killed her? Would we be in time to stop him? What would we find when we came back with the police?

Pausing for breath along the way, we kept checking to see if he was in pursuit and were ready to hide in the nearest garden, guinnel or pathway if we saw him coming. Our goal was to let the Police know what this man had been doing. And to stop him. For Good!

Ian was coughing and almost choking with crying and running, and I was still red-faced and wet-eyed as we came to within twenty meters of the Police Station. There was a public bench facing the station. We paused to wipe our eyes and to catch our breath and adjust our clothing as I had pulled Ian's shirt out with my dragging. Whilst running I had been trying to think through what we were going to say when we finally got to the station.

Stopping at the bench when we finally arrived there gave us both an opportunity to gather our thoughts and our breath whilst making ourselves presentable, and for me to better review our plan. Going to the police was an unprecedented step.

Then it hit me. 'What are we actually going to *say* to them? What words am I going to use to explain?' I said to Ian... He looked blankly at me. It was obvious to him. But I had had time to think. And I only had limited thinking and solutions given all that I knew of life and of our situation at this point in time.

I talked it out aloud to Ian, telling him my thoughts and fears on this, as we worked out how we would ask for help and what we would say in words. We knew what dad had done but how do you tell a Policeman that your dad is hitting, no *beating*, your mum like this? Then I paused considering the ramifications. The consequences of what telling the police would achieve.

Wrong!

Not a good thing to do, making yourself responsible for the outcome of others, but that is what I did. Ian and I took this moment to get our story straight so that we would make sense and get things in the right order. We tried to assess things and consider what would happen when we went inside that station door – there would be no going back because this was a serious thing, and once you did it, you couldn't un-did it. Ian was set – yet I still hesitated...

Okay, now we need to go into the Police Station and ask them to come home with us and to stop dad beating up mum. And us. 'Cause he will probably give us both the belt when we get home. [The 'belt' meant that he would use that thick Army issue belt of his on us complete with its heavy buckle as he had done before. It leaves terrible welts and can cut into the skin.] *And then what will happen? Well, they will come back with us and stop dad. And then what. Well, they will take him to the Police Station, and put him in jail. And then what... Well they will lock him up in jail, won't they? Then mum will be safe. And... and what else... and dad won't be able to go to work anymore. But mum also won't have a husband any more. And we won't have a dad anymore. And we will starve because we won't have enough money to live on anymore. And then mum will blame us and we will all die. And I will be to blame for telling the police. And I will be blamed for dragging you here with me, Ian. It will be all **my** fault if dad is put in jail.*

Don't expect adult reasoning from a child, especially one who has been slapped stupid around the head and terrified in such a way! And just wants everyone to be happy.

Ian argued, begged me not to stop but to go right inside and tell them and stop dad. But I just couldn't! It wasn't that I didn't have the guts. It was that I was terrified about creating an even *worse* situation. No child should be faced with such a gut-wrenching life decision as this! No child should be forced to argue about getting help for their family. We didn't know what would really happen, how could we? We were children! And in those days, dad would probably have just gotten a caution and a warning, but nothing would have been done about it – because not much was done about

Naïve Hope

men hitting women back then. Nor in some places even now. But then, in Manchester, in Benchill, those were the times.

We weren't to know that, for we only knew what we had heard and what we saw on the telly or in comics or read in books. And we had always respected and avoided the Police and knew that they had powers to put bad people away for a very long time!

We reluctantly headed back for 'home'...

It must have taken us over half an hour to drag our feet back home to face the music and to cover what had initially been a ten minute run. Unsure as to what we would find, we first carefully looked through all of the windows before going through the guinnel and round to the back of the house. Everything was quiet. All the doors were closed. There were no broken windows or broken furniture outside the house.

Was mum still alive? Had we been gone too long? Should we have brought the police after all? We were now very disappointed with ourselves that we hadn't resolved the problem and bought the police but also scared about what would await us. We breathed a sigh of relief when we confirmed that his motorbike was missing from the guinnel. Dad was out. Within a few moments we realized that we needn't have feared further right then as dad was *definitely* not in, and mum was recovering from her beating.

Inside the house, we gathered round mum as she lay on the couch, ministering as best we could, putting the kettle on to make her a cup of tea, tidying up the mess that dad's rampage had caused, picking up the broken glass and broken crockery that had been part of his explosion, bringing her wet flannels and clean towels, aspirins and plasters for her cuts. We swept and cleared and tidied and wiped.

It was a subdued house for the rest of the afternoon and evening and we didn't see dad that night. He must have gone to some friend's house. We got no punishment later, either, from dad for this venture to the Police station. It was actually a couple of days before he came back home again. Maybe dad was too embarrassed or ashamed for his behaviour, I have no idea.

Mum meanwhile just slumped, or she walked around like someone sleep-walking. Ian and I were concerned about dad going missing, but we could do nothing about it, and we almost blamed ourselves that it was because *we* had gone for the Police. Now I had another concern; I worried and worried what would happen if he *didn't* come back 'home' and so we both tried to support mum and not cause her any further stress. We tip-toed around the place, being as well behaved as possible.

Joan was totally oblivious to what had been happening and didn't make things any easier, being as demanding as ever. But at least mum was alive, and dad was not in jail, and he did finally come home.

Things quietened down for a little while until the next eruption, but dad didn't do quite as much damage in front of us again. Instead, it tended to happen after we had gone to bed and were assumed to be asleep. And storming off on his motorbike now became a more familiar event.

If only....

Family was a real conundrum to me. In a time when families had to stick together to survive, we did just that, kind of. 'Family is important', 'Be loyal to your family', 'Stand by your family' – familiar phrases back then. I saw 'family' as the other members who needed help and taking care of, and it took a long time for me to work out that I, too, was a family member, and I *too* deserved the very same considerations. A very long time!

In truth, real family is really about who has got your back, who is there to be counted on and relied upon. Not just about who is *related* to you!

ANAEMIC

As a young girl around twelve and at the end of my first year at Poundswick Grammar School, I was diagnosed as Anaemic and also as being underweight.

The shortage of good food over the years, together with the following post-war period of rationing and the struggles of mum

Naïve Hope

and dad to make ends meet had really told on my health. In all, I was pretty undernourished as a child and in my teen years, and I had lost several important and prominent adult teeth by the age of eleven. The lack of proper dental support had sealed the fate of these teeth, for when acute pain had hit, and even when the caries and decay was so totally obvious that it indicated immediate attention, my parents would instead resort to stuffing the black holes with tobacco, or even cloves. Though this was intended to ease pain, it often did very little, and even painkillers did little to assuage the sharp and shooting nerve pains for me. The pain was horrific and unnecessarily prolonged; until my parents were finally forced to have these teeth removed for me. Cleaning the teeth might have been a regular part of our regime, but real care and concern seemed to fly over my parents heads. Indeed my two front adult teeth had fallen to the Grim Reaper this way. Eating apples was impossible, and some foods I just couldn't enjoy. Not to mention the embarrassment!

Fortunately, the school nurse had brought attention to my plight and dental treatment was arranged, which included creating a dental plate for some of the missing teeth. Thank god for that. And this meant that I dare smile again without being laughed and jeered at… It was common to hear 'All I want for Christmas is my two front teeth'… Though it was a truth for me at the time. I can laugh about all this now, and indeed had to learn to laugh at the time, though with my mouth closed… It was a happy day when I could open my mouth and see teeth!

I do remember being told that some of this delay of treatment was because of the cost, and I also know of the post-war struggles for nutrition and proper welfare, yet I also remember that dad was not averse to a horsey and greyhound betting habit.

My local doctor, the friendly Dr Fowler, declared that I was undernourished and severely anaemic and badly in need of health care and support and ordered on a script that I be sent away to a convalescent home in the North of Wales. Called 'The Margaret Beaven Memorial Convalescent Home', the home was located in Heswall, a Welsh sea-side suburb practically opposite England. It was a lovely big house set up as a recovery home for deprived and undernourished children. This lovely place had been specifically set up to help children recover from illness. I was duly packed off by train and met at the platform. The whole experience made quite an impact on me, for though I was somewhat like a fish out of water in such strange surroundings, I also relished and revelled in the clean and regular crisp fresh bed sheets and plentifully fresh and nourishing food, sun, sea, play, care and attention.

The staff were exemplary and though I often felt lonely being away from home for this the first time in my life, I did not feel totally unsupported there.

Here I was fed well, experienced weekly clean, crisp bed sheets for the first time ever, was encouraged to eat to my heart's content, and got to just 'play'. Yes, we had a few chores to do, and regular Sunday service to attend, but it was all over quickly and became an interesting exercise in so many ways. I could add here that I wrote practically every day to my parents, and when I ran out of money for stamps and envelopes, I had to ask for more money, which usually arrived in the form of a two-shillings-and-sixpence-postal-order. The other girls were getting postal orders of five shillings to a whole pound a week, but I knew my parents were poor, and didn't want to be a burden on them, so I always struggled with having to ask them for money, and only did so when I was quite desperate.

There was a local little gift shop where the girls would go, accompanied by one of the nurses, and buy little mementos, or books to colour in or read, magazines or comics, handkerchiefs, or knicky-knacks, as well as the inevitable sweets or lollies.

We wore a kind of uniform – a loose tunic type of dress in similar ginghams, so there was no differentiation from me and a couple of others previously labelled underprivileged. And for Sunday services, we were dressed in blouses, ties, skirts, blazers, and even shoes and socks, all to match. We noticed that there were a group of boys attending church services too, all dressed in a similar kind of uniform, though a different colour scheme, and with trousers, of course.

It was originally intended that I only stay for a period of three weeks, 'to build her up'. But after an accident with a huge wooden bench, when it was my turn to sweep up, I had to stay a further

Naïve Hope

three weeks to recover from the loss of my big toe nails and to settle me down again. Though I must confess, I felt even guiltier about being away from home, and even more home-sick the longer I stayed. I didn't realise that this was really good for me, and just couldn't wait to get back home. All the same, I also suspect that I felt embarrassed by my lack of funds, and also about the damage to my toes. I did indeed make a couple of friends whilst there, but they too had to leave after three weeks, so I sometimes felt quite lonely that those I had developed connections with had moved on. Our short friendships gave me some happy memories though, especially when we got down to the sand at the beach, and also played on the swings there. A couple of the nurses were absolutely fantastic, but the only name I can remember is Nurse Rathbone. They observed while we played, and nothing seemed to be too much trouble to them.

One of the girls that I really liked and felt good around was called Norma Forster, and we wrote for a short time, but I think that our individual family demands plus the lack of family finances in my case eventually came in to play. We lost touch.

She had long, fine blonde hair, and was a skinny as I was when I first arrived at the Home. But I managed to put on some weight. Probably due to my being inactive for several weeks when lying in bed, and also learning (through loneliness, sheer boredom and home-sickness) how to develop a taste for whole jugs of the creamiest custard which was served up regularly at our meal times. Best I ever tasted!

Here at this home, I really 'fattened-up' with good hearty roasts, fresh sea air, clean sheets (Oh, my!), regular baths, developing a taste for lots and lots of creamy custard, and even sporting a bit of a tan.

Apparently the local doctor was well satisfied with the results when we next visited him, and mum was quite proud of me fitting my school uniform better. Though Dr Fowler didn't know all of the details of things between mum and dad, he was our family doctor, attending to all of us. So he would have probably developed his own impressions and opinions regarding our family as well as its impact on me personally. I think he had a soft spot for me, and I know I always felt comfortable around him.

Our house had originally been on farm land. We still lived within easy walking distance of fields and orchards – in the beginning. This has all now changed, and indeed altered very quickly in the following twenty-five years. There was once an old mill and millpond that has since long disappeared, and the old dark and ancient corner house near Crossacres that we thought was haunted is no more. The playing fields that resided right next to them are now a collection of shops and pavements with the fancy name 'Civic Centre'. The hill we used to toboggan down on HollyHedge Road in winter using pieces of board has long since vanished. The sloping slide has been land-filled and a block of flats now fills the space between the shops and St Luke's Church. Many of the fields of my memories, my romantic escape spaces and places have long since been eaten up by suburban residential housing and shopping centres and the nearest local fields are now many miles and many minutes drive away from that spot. Such is 'progress'.

Working Class

Mum did as much as she could mending, sewing and knitting clothes, and these skills she also passed on to me through necessity. I learned how to darn socks, a valuable skill back then, as well as how to turn a hem and shorten trousers. Mum certainly wasn't professional, but despite this lack, through self taught home renovation skills and through recycling and redesigning jumble sale charity purchases we managed to stay reasonably clothed and mended. Polishing the front door knocker with Brasso, using Cardinal Red Step polish for the front door step, sweeping, mopping, helping put sheets through the washing machine wringer, preparing food, making beds according to dad's Army 'apple-pie' tucking in method; these were a few of our regular chores.

Growing up, one accepts many things. A child often has no more skills at comparison than a pet kitten, no further ability to question than a goldfish. It is not until later, when there has been experience at life, when one is aware that there are other ways,

Naïve Hope

other stories, that one begins to navigate and often to label events that take place in their life. And it is often later again, that one revisits those labels, those memories, and begins to re-sort and to reshuffle them in an attempt to make a more current assessment of them - in order to answer further questions to life and the self.

Dad was often a complete mystery to me, as was mum, though in different ways. I only ever yearned for his love and favour. And spent many years both loving and hating him, usually for what I saw him do to mum as I was growing up ...

Dad had been very respected and successful in the army, becoming an officer and a trainer with medals and awards as the champion of his regiment in boxing and also in diving – this was evidenced by the silver cups and trophies that I and my two-years-younger brother Ian had to polish every couple of weeks. Dad was a handsome man, and a striking physical specimen. A Commando trainer, mainly stationed overseas during and after the war in India or Egypt, he had been very well regarded. Fit, healthy, active charming, he was sometimes mistaken for Errol Flynn, whilst mum resembled a cross between the popular Greer Garson and Ingrid Bergman.

Within a few years of the war ending, dad had been called home to help mum manage with her firstborn – me. But becoming a civilian again, and working on 'civvy street' (as they called it when one was out of the armed forces and seeking employment as a civilian looking for 'normal' work) was a big change, and so again, life did not smile kindly on dad. Now, having been used to his orders being obeyed without question, dad found his world included disgruntled and mean bosses cutting corners and doing shoddy work now ruling over him. Not a happy chappie!

Oh, he could work hard, he was extremely smart and capable, and had a fine physique, and was respected by any men he had under him, often gaining promotions as he was a natural leader.

However, he was used to leading and to being accountable. Now he had to learn to hold his tongue about things that he felt were wrong, for the men or for the job. This meant he had to be schtumm about things *most* of the time, which he could not always do, and when it became obvious to *him* that his current boss was a fool, then if he couldn't use his fists he would certainly use his words!

And next thing you know he would have to 'sign-up' for employment again and begin to look for another job. So home life was always somewhat chaotic, and often loud and noisy. And upsetting.

Don't Break Her Spirit

It was also this very thing of dad being used to having his orders obeyed that almost broke me totally. I remember on one occasion, I must have been about eight years old, and I hadn't 'performed' to his satisfaction. That is, I had somehow not prevented my siblings from doing something that they shouldn't have done. I had been, after all, left in command of my brother and sister, delegated to do so by dad, whilst he was busying himself with some other obviously more important task. Which was taking apart yet again, some component of his motorbike... with screws and bolts and tools laid out on the table. And because Ian and Joan had touched something that they shouldn't have, that I couldn't stop them from doing anyway, and because they wouldn't always listen to me, the blame stopped with me. If I had held them down to stop them, even that would incur his wrath if they protested. But I hadn't done that, I was just too busy and occupied with keeping *two* children out of trouble. I didn't yet have eyes in the back of my head for this task. So I failed in preventing their little grabby grubby touchy feely fingers from playing with something that dad had put down whilst he attended to another component of his current task.

Dad lost it!

He now goes into his sergeant major routine, yelling at me as though I am one of his troops. He advances, and fearfully I keep stepping backward until I feel a wall behind me and I can shrink no further from him. He is now towering over me. I have no voice to be heard over his. Except for my sobs, his forcefulness silences me. As if in a film, numb with his explosiveness, frozen in time, I withdrew from my own body and I see myself cowering in the corner by the window, attempting to avoid his venom and rage. He

Naïve Hope

is red in the face, the veins popping out on his neck, and I actually thought he was going to punch me. I could feel the energy of his volatile and fiery breath on my face, blowing back the fringe from my forehead. I cannot recount the words he used now, I was in too much shock, and indeed, part of me had stepped outside of myself, the pain of his unreasonable force being too much to bear. It was probably something along the lines of 'I told you not to let anybody touch these. You have let me down, not doing what I ask. I ask you to do a simple job, to look after your brother and sister, and ...lazy and... stupid and... disobedient and... blah blah blah'.

More than anything, I remember the pain in my throat, and the choking and sobbing coming from the pit of my stomach. I was gasping for breath. I just wanted to pour myself into the ground like a puddle and disappear under the house. Fortunately, mum came home from the shops, and seeing what was going on, she intervened. She had left dad in charge of us whilst she went shopping. But we were not entertaining enough, valuable enough, at this point in time, to be any competition to keep him from tinkering with his beloved motor bike. Yet he was taking it all out on me. Mum didn't challenge him about that, but she could see what was happening, and obviously identified.

'John', she yelled – she had to yell, and to yell loud to be heard over his tirade – 'John, *stop* that, there is no need for that. Can't you see that you will break her spirit yelling like that?'

She somehow could see what he was doing, treating me like a disobedient willful army cadet who knew better and who needed humiliation and face-ranting to knock sense into him, instead of the little child that I was. She had to shout several times at him before he heard her, even tugging at his arm to pull him away from his pinning me down in the corner, but I remember those words, for a part of my mind had recognized and knew that this *was* what he was doing to me. She was able to pull him away when he finally came to his senses, and she continued to attempt to calm him down. But mum also saw that I was shaking and white, and so she pulled me to her and cuddled some comfort into me. Again she reminded him that I was just a child, not one of his soldiers or trainees, and that he couldn't treat a child like that. But something in me *had* been broken, though I didn't know it at the time. Sure, years later, I remembered this incident and thought that mum had rescued me just in time and that my spirit was fine. But further reviewing and experiences showed to me that he *had* damaged me that day. The forceful message that my heart, subconscious and neurology had received so strongly from him now included this: *my very survival and safety depends on a man's (dad's) capacity to love or to hurt me...*

He broke something in me that day, and there was no attempt to fix it. And this 'breaking' did not serve me in my life. This damage had left me wide open to further abuse, and I didn't yet know it. A boundary of 'self' and my identity had been destroyed. This was a *monumental* failure as a parent. I was never lacking in courage, but the helplessness against violence, and the threat of it, at the hands of an important, loved and trusted one had been implanted into my very nervous system. And had part-blinded my own Soul.

Even though he could be such a brute, dad was also a frustrated poet and writer. He had some artistic tendencies, and he used to boast of an ancestor well known for these talents. But words didn't pay the rent... or the groceries...

Money was always such a loaded issue in our house. Later I came to realize that dad did some gambling, as well as drinking and dancing. Quite the spiff as it turned out. And an excellent dancer. I remember a huge argument because he had gotten himself a new suit, and mum had been struggling trying to clothe us. The words and the shoes that got thrown at him that day... even as he stormed out of the house and into the avenue to get on his motorbike and escape... Mum was lucky she didn't get a fat lip for her feisty abuse, but I think it was because he knew that he was in the wrong all things considered. They fought like cats and dogs when they got started sometimes. However, he got his way after all, and the suit stayed.

Because I never saw him actually drunk, for many years I had no idea of this side of things at all. I was to later learn that he had become accustomed to good quality things when in the army and found it extremely hard to adapt to marriage and fatherhood. Especially the expenses of children. He wasn't in the army anymore though.

Naïve Hope

And when the family multiplied to four girls and one boy, all living in a two bedroom council house, the pressure was really on!

It is probably obvious by now that it was not the best childhood growing up.

Living in denied poverty, and having difficulty with connecting with the better-off children I often felt isolated. Mum and dad in actuality had little emotional time for us, or indeed any time of value. And when I eventually discovered and considered their history and their own deprivations I could see some of the reason for their behaviours. But as a child, this was not explained, nor would it have been fully understood if it had been.

Discipline was definitely the old fashioned kind – children were to be seen and not heard, not allowed to throw tantrums nor express anger, had slaps on the legs or head for simple infringements and sent to bed early without supper (or dinner as it is called in Australia) if they refused to eat what was set before them. We even had it reheated – and sometimes not – the following morning for breakfast on occasion. Yukk! Generally many children learned to clean their plates totally and developed an alertness for trouble and a physical kind of armoring in their nervous system and physiology.

WAYS AND MEANS

As children, we each had very little pocket money. In an attempt to have some regular spends - as it was called back then, I remember that around age thirteen I got some work doing a newspaper round. For finally mum and dad had bought me a bike for my birthday. This was a *huge* gift, and besides giving me some freedom also meant that I could earn some pocket money. This now also relieved them of any further need to continue to supply any further spends, paltry though it had been. I didn't care, for I now had wheels. And the first flush of earning a few shillings compensated for getting up in the dark and cold to deliver the early morning papers. There was more of a struggle delivering the evening papers, as I was now at grammar school I also had more homework, yet I still had to fit in home chores and my paper round with my school work.

I suffered intermittently from anemia through early childhood and into my teens. This issue continued in later years as I remained susceptible for some time to the occasional adult bout of low blood iron.

Living with such an uncaring and very chaotic family further added to my nervous and sensitive nature. The continual exposure to family fights, arguments and tensions together with the ever-present load of numerous family chores and premature responsibilities I was not as energetic as I would liked to have been. I wasn't allowed out unless I had done my chores. Or until dad felt like letting me leave the house - whichever it was on the day.

With the abundance of fights and the many restrictions on freedom, unless and until all duties and jobs were done there was little real free time. Consequently I had limited energy to sustain the paper round I wanted in order to provide me with some pocket money - but I continued my efforts, the heart being the master that kept me going. I tried for two paper rounds. The first newsagent eventually sacked me for not turning up to deliver, having given me some grace for the late start on my very first delivery. The fact was that my not-so-darling brother Ian sometimes 'borrowed' my bike or rather took it without asking me, but he never repaired any punctures to the tyres. So when it came time for me to start the round and to pick up the newspapers, I would often discover that he had left it without repairing any puncture that he had caused. He didn't tell me, just left it lying in the back garden with two flat tyres as though this was his right.

No matter my pleas, Ian simply ignored my requests to stop doing this or to fix it himself, but no amount of complaining to mum or dad changed things. He would just use the bike and dump it so often that it seemed to become a habit. Finding out that there was yet another puncture just as you are going on your round made fulfilling any paper run impossible. Unable to repair punctures after school in time to get to the shop for my paper-round, or to even replace the necessary puncture kits bought with *my* pocket money, meant that I couldn't and didn't turn up. This called the death-knell to my money-making and independence aspirations on any newspaper round. Both newsagents had attempted to cover my round last minute, but in the end, each had let me go. A small part of me seemed to close up with these seeming injustices, but I had to resign myself to the situation, though I couldn't understand why Ian didn't want to do the right thing and fix up what he had destroyed. Even though there was only two years age difference between us, he seemed to have a totally different attitude to respecting other people's things than I did. Or maybe it was a passive-aggressive way of getting to me...

However, over time I moved on.

Ian and I had a love-hate relationship. I would stand up for him if he was threatened, or feel for him if he was unjustly punished, and even attempt to comfort him when he was in pain. But we also fought like cat and dog. Literally, physical fights. He would blow up and get extremely emotional if I got the better of him in anything, or if I refused to let him have his own way.

He would get so worked up that he would throw himself on the ground, whether or not I had laid a finger on him, just because he couldn't catch me or hit me. He would howl and yowl and hold his breath until he turned blue in the face, finally exhausting himself and then physically his body would become kind of loose, all of his rage and energy expended. I could not believe it the first time I saw it! I was really worried about him, though I was also scared in case he was doing a false 'feint' and intended to jump up and chase me again as soon as I got close to him.

Yes, he had tried this trick of dropping crying and yowling to the floor. Then of launching himself at me to catch me when I got close enough. But this time, his face went blue. I thought he had fainted, and he kind of had. Running for mum who was in the back garden hanging out washing, she came upstairs and put him to bed. We both got told off for what had happened to him. But I hadn't touched him and he had been chasing me because I had disagreed with him. Because I refused to bow to his will, he had created this rageful state that had caused his blackout.

It was a ridiculous state of affairs. But things didn't improve, and I learned that I had to remove myself from him, for his rages were getting scarier. It could get so bad that I would have to run away from him and lock myself in the bedroom I shared with my sisters. This lasted for as long as the bedroom door lock held out. One awful day, it yielded to his attacks, and we fell to on each other with fists and hair pulling and whatever kids do when in such a state. After throwing of things and exhausting ourselves and the accompanying tears by both parties, we had to stop. And review the mess we had made as reality set in. And try to fix it up before our parents saw it.

We both felt, I think, that Mum and dad were never really any good at clear justice, and often took sides, even avoiding the main issues and focusing mainly on the damage done and not the 'why' of the fight. Ignoring the real causes of the problems which had prompted these fights, we all just continued to roll along repeating the same patterns.

Until one day dad decided that he would teach Ian to 'box'.

Somehow because dad was the champion boxer of his regiment and had trained Commandos, he now set-to to teach Ian how to defend himself. In hindsight, this is quite unbelievable. For it was clearly stated at the time that not only was this for defending himself from other boys who would pick a fight with him, but also to defend himself against me. Before this, if Ian had lost his temper and hit me, I had either hit him back or run. Now there would be an imbalance, and so it was even doubly important that I get behind that bedroom door, and find ways to keep the door shut.

There was a huge old wooden army trunk that dad had brought back with him from the war. Mum used it to store our meager bedding and clothing in and it was in the 'girls' bedroom. Ian slept in a tiny room that was over the stairwell, and it was called the 'boxroom' because of its shape. Just big enough to get a single bed in, and to use the tiny shelfing space that was positioned over the stairwell for his books or clothes, Ian as the only male child had this as his own room, whereas I had to share the second bedroom with my other sister, Joan, and later with Tina, when she arrived when I was age twelve. This heavy box was now used to prop against the bedroom door. With me sitting on it and pushing it against the door, Ian could not gain entry. As long as the windows were also shut – for it was not past him to scale the drainpipe to 'get-back' at me – I was safe. And I would have to sit and wait until mum or dad returned home.

Naïve Hope

I learned not to be tempted out when Ian put on one of his blue fits, as mum said it was only because he had worked himself up so much, and that when he lost consciousness, he would begin to breath normally again. If it was genuine, then he would recover naturally, and if it was not genuine, then he couldn't fool me or catch me to hurt me.

Latch-Key Kids

It wasn't all fighting between us, though, as some events created a sort of alliance. Along the way, both Ian and myself discovered the joys of being 'latch-key' kids.

With both dad, and mum of necessity, at work, we would often arrive home from school to an empty house. We enjoyed (if one may stretch the use of the word here) periods of finding the door key hanging behind the letterbox mouth placed at and in the front door. This gave us immediate access to protection from the weather and furnished us some comfort from being outside. On other occasions such as if there had been reports of a local burglary, we were allowed to possess our own key which was attached to a string around our neck. Or rather mine, as I was the oldest. Then there were long spells when we weren't allowed into the house. I trace it back to those times when we came home so hungry that we had attacked a loaf of bread and made ourselves what were called 'butties' – commonly known as sandwiches. However, our hunger often dictated the width of these supposed snacks, and we would venture into 'doorstop' land – really thick slices of bread and butter. These were in the days when there was really only butter, before margarine was so brain-washing-ly advertised. And butter was very costly. And we could really lay the butter on, especially when there was no jam or any other topping to be had. So 'doorstops' it was. Until they took the key off us again.

We were hungry kids – what did they expect? Well, it is obvious that they didn't expect us to eat so much and it was no wonder that I had so many nutrition and nourishment problems. For this was all we could get – when we could get it. For the rest, we just went hungry.

Ian and I did, that is. For Joan was a totally different matter. Dad still doted on her.

Our sister Joan only had to ask to get her special little treats, over and above any special considerations on her choices of meals. Oh, and I forgot to say, I had to collect her from school at some stage when she wasn't being looked after at the child care centre. She got chubbier and we got leaner.

I was so glad when walking to and from my Grammar School took so much time that I could no longer collect the little brat, though I never ever thought of her *then* as this, just as someone who somehow magically managed to cause trouble and yet get out of trouble – continually. Other arrangements were made for Joan.

Being a latch-key kid meant that Ian and I were also prey to the older school boys whose parents were late home working, too. They made up their own gangs, and you didn't cross them on purpose if you could help it. Fortunately, Ian and myself managed to avoid most of the gang troubles, though at Bonfire season the fight for burning and bonfire matter – commonly known as 'bongy-wood' – caused many minor rumbles. Guy Fawkes night was mostly worth it, though, and some kind neighbours always seemed to find a way of giving me and Ian some sticky toffee apples on sticks or some treacle toffee. And dad would never let neighbours think that we couldn't afford fireworks, so we always had something to fire off.

There were also hard times when we weren't allowed in the house after school until either mum or dad was home, and we spent some very cold times sitting in a windy guinnel without a chair or cushion, or even a dry square of pavement to stand on. Waiting for some food, warmth and a parent to come home was a real trial then. One couldn't even put their satchel on the ground because of rain, and if it snowed or hailed, we could no longer feel our feet or hands. Many were the colds and chest complaints that we suffered through this sort of arrangement. Mind you, being in those houses without any sort of heating was a trial anyway. Winter required that there was a fire to warm our feet only after dad came home from work and I eventually excelled at clearing out the ashes and preparing the perfect fire ready for the lit match.

Naïve Hope

Considering how difficult those times were, and how little we were actually really looked after in the way we should have been, and how prone we were to the predatory ways of others, I am quite proud that I avoided any real trouble and kept out of the way of most of the boys, especially the rebels. I was brain-washed about 'saving yourself' for marriage, kept on an honour system not to 'mess around with boys' (which, bugger it, I honoured) and I was very helpful and compliant, all things considered.

At ages fifteen and sixteen, I found a part-time job and was working for a supermarket in Altrincham, two buses away, on Friday nights and all day Saturdays. This gave me some pocket money, and I would willingly give half to the family budget. The rest would have to cover me for spends, the pictures, any 'treats' I might like, clothing items beyond school uniform, and after school activities etc. Mum began to visit the store, and eventually she developed a pattern of coming into the shop to whatever stall I was working on. I would serve her with as much as she could cram into her shopping bag, only charging her approximately 2/6p (two shillings and sixpence). It was mainly always food or knitting wool that she bought. She was just so grateful for this extra addition to her shopping budget that I didn't know how to stop. I look back and consider myself so lucky that I wasn't caught, charged or arrested for this.

The things I did to help my parents! But I guess I would have done anything to help, and I often did.

Part of the small amount I could keep for myself from my meager pay helped to cover items of clothing that were purchased from the Jumble Sales I attended, and I quickly learned how to adapt and cut down many clothes to fit. At school I got the name-tag Make-Do-And-Mend-Marni. Not flattering, but honest and accurate.

Eventually Joan was displaced as youngest by the next sister Tina, who was born six years after her. Tina was born premature and also had Yellow Jaundice. Mum had several complications with her birth, and it was with relief that Tina survived and made it home to join us. But this didn't deter our Joan, for she simply took to making further trouble to get the attention she wanted.

Whilst I am on the subject of being honest... Here I have to confess to something else that I did that I am not that proud of. And this something I did all by myself – no coercion or feeling sorry for someone else – purely self motivated... It wasn't till later that I came to understand the reasons that lay behind why I did what I did and to learn to be more understanding toward myself. I was lucky that things turned out the way they did for they could have been much worse and pushed me in a totally alien direction ...

WHAT ABOUT ME...

When young girls mature and begin to develop, their world seems to expand, to take on different dimensions. There is an inner world that begins to assemble itself. Image is impressed on them, even if only for the fact that they are developing breasts and are therefore looked at differently. Like any teenager, my interaction in the world was shifting, and I could feel the pressures that lifted my mind from more than school, more than chores, more than reading. I was also quickly and consciously becoming more aware of what other girls had and what I didn't. And I guess a whole lot of incidents and emotions culminated in this event; emotionally unavailable parents, deprivation of proper protection and nurturing and unclear family standards at attempts to keep us all honest versus the reality of poverty, hypocrisy and family materialistic neediness and lack.

Let me beg some understanding from you as I lay my heart out here, for this was to become a memorable lesson for me...

One day during school holidays I went into town with my friend Chrissie, who was also a bit of a misfit herself. We had gone there to occupy ourselves and because we had each earned enough pocket money to pay for the bus fare. A grand adventure in those days for us. The lovely big store windows with their beautiful new clothes would fire any girls dream, and whenever we had been in the city with parents previously, we would be rushed past these windows as neither of our parents had the time nor the money (nor the inclination) to ever consider buying such lovely (or 'too-expensive') items. Obviously garments fit only for the posh or those with money to spare.

Naïve Hope

Today we were free from such constraints. We began to drink in these lovely clothes in Manchester city centre; at Littlewoods, Marks and Spencer's then in the windows of C & A Modes. And then we began to dare to daydream. Neither of us had much money, but we could dream couldn't we?

There we were, kind of window shopping when each of us saw different garments in the C & A Modes flash and sumptuous windows that we both fell in love with.

The thing that took my heart was a beautiful blue brushed mohair skirt. Its deep rich color hypnotized me. Chrissie saw a skirt that excited her and we were both inspired to actually dare to try our dream finds on. Slim line and tailored, my skirt was fully lined – *fully lined* - and when I put it on, I did *not* want to take it off. The feel of the silk lining against my skin was amazing; I had never felt anything like that before. Nor had anything else fitted so perfectly. I had never worn anything like it – it was what *real* people wore!

I could not afford it. Totally out of my price range.

But I was fed up with hand-me-downs, cut-me-downs, blow-me-downs and cheapies. This skirt felt so classy, so warm and luxurious! It was *beautiful*!

And I *wanted* it!

So in the dressing rooms Chrissie and I looked at each other in our new finds... for she too had found a skirt that she really, really wanted, and also couldn't afford. Chrissie was just as deprived as I was, having lost her father many years before when he had been expelled from the family home due to his drinking. We knew we couldn't afford them, so we reluctantly took them off again. There we were, in the changing rooms, both holding these skirts that we couldn't possibly afford, but that we had fallen in love with... and we were having to put them back on the clothes rack again. We looked at each other again, and something seemed to click for us both...and there and then on the spot we rebelliously decided that we would do whatever it took to have them and to keep them. I think we *needed* them as much as wanted them... We were both so smitten that we hatched a devious little plan.

Feverishly, we worked out that we could keep these skirts *under* the clothing we originally had on, and just walk out *wearing* the skirts! We figured that they would only search our bags if they suspected us, and so wouldn't find the skirts. We swore to each other to admit to nothing. *Nothing!*

So, to cut to the chase, we walked out of the store and into the street, so relieved that we were now going to be on our way home – with our beautiful skirts.

That is until we both felt a tap on our shoulders, and turned to find a store walker addressing us both to 'Please open your bags as we believe that you have some unpaid for items in your shopping.'

Oh My God!

We were escorted back into the store, not realizing that we did not have to submit to do so. When nothing was found in our bags, we were still detained and questioned further. We were actually each put into separate rooms, and the door locked whilst we were individually questioned! Not a nice feeling. I was so determined, so in love with this beautiful work of art that I was somehow set against my habitual honesty and I was resolute not to say anything; I really *really* wanted to keep that skirt. Somehow it was a symbol to me that I *could have* lovely things, just like the other girls at school. But Chrissie crumbled first under the pressure when questioned and gave in very quickly, confessing to our wearing the items and as to how we had hidden them.

So then we had to undress *and* give them up *and* go to the police station *and* sit in a cell 'to think about things whilst we contact your parents'.

And await our parents. Shamefacedly. And embarrassingly.

We had to appear in juvenile court within a short time, but the discomfort at home didn't help and was little talked about, though the unspoken language of judgment and shame and disappointment with me and in me was like a tangible fog in the house. And I was forbidden to speak to or play with Chrissie…

Fortunately for us the judge for juvenile offenders was a wise man and saw something other than the obvious. Somehow he saw past two errant teenagers and glimpsed the basically good girls that we

Naïve Hope

really were and had been; we got off with a caution and small fine as well as a suspended probation. I think that the judge grasped that we were both deprived, parentally and materially and realized that more serious punishments could push one or both of us in the wrong direction. It was a disorienting experience, and I never ever did anything like that again. However, it didn't stop me from still feeling deprived.

After a good Talking To from my parents, with them now realizing that this was not my normal behavior, they became (temporarily at least) a bit more aware to paying a little more attention to me for a while. I served the due home punishment for causing such embarrassment and concern. But within a very short time things pretty much went back to how they had always been.

I had felt naked. Naked, humiliated and destitute. That small moment of warmth and that sweet smell of luxury and possession had been so fleeting – and so costly.

Though the experience helped to prevent me from ever doing something like that again, I felt I had lost something; that something as precious as that skirt was always going to be just out of my reach. Even though I was lucky to avoid more serious consequences, my needs were still not really addressed or properly looked at. And the family financial situation didn't change; dad didn't stop his gambling, didn't really pay any more attention, nor stop his intermittent womanizing – and he continued to squander money!

For all her faults, whilst I was growing up and even despite this episode, in her own way mum tried to love us all, but was generally pretty caught up in her own stuff. In retrospect, it was at around eight years of age that I had somehow been made into a kind of stand-in or pseudo-mum. I was expected to feel responsible to do a better job than any normal eight year old was assumed to manage, and criticized and punished if I didn't do things to a certain standard. I understand the role that the first-born often has to play in family dynamics – now – but this was a huge responsibility and was well above and beyond what any normal eight year old should be required to handle. Looking after my siblings was only part of it, taking over some of the food preparation duties for when mum got home from work, having to watch the time of an evening to make sure dinner was ready on time, cleaning up and dish-washing after, and at weekends a whole list of things were required to be done before I was free to do any of the things that I wanted to do. I worked hard to be allowed to go to the picture-house or play outside and along with all this I somehow felt it my job to look after mum when she was down, and in fact the whole family. I guess that someone had to, and mum often struggled to see past herself, though when I remember how it was between her and dad this is not so surprising.

With my tendency to over-conscientiousness and of others feelings and attitudes towards me, I did not yet understand how sensitive I was, nor that I would often 'pick up' on these feelings - especially when dad would come home in a mood, or mum came home from work as a kind of zombie. I just knew when to tread carefully as if on egg-shells... and got quite good at 'reading' his moods and taking appropriate action in order to avoid bad moods escalating.

It was a difficult final school year as I was still expected to help in family emergencies such as when one of my siblings was ill and had to be kept off school. I had often been called upon to stay at home to help 'the family'. There had also been those other intermittent demands on me to help mum when dad had had a go at her, as well as support mum through her final pregnancy; all of which forced me to take off time from study.

Considering these disadvantages and that I was a smart and intelligent kid I could have done much better with a settled home life given the opportunity. And even possibly, with some belief and encouragement in my ability and worth, done magnificently.

Oh what a blessing when one has good parents, ones that really want for their children to be happy and well and to find their passion in life, their confidence in themselves, and a partner to bring them joy.

Home Dead End

By now dad had had a couple of affairs which were hushed up. One day he disappeared for a whole week or more. I thought he had left

Naïve Hope

us all for good when I came home from work and found mum in hysterics.

'Your father has left us,' she ranted, wild-eyed. 'He has gone off with his bit of fluff, his fancy lady,' she continued, whilst I looked on in shock. Waving the bank book around she shouted 'He has emptied the family bank account and spent it on his *fancy-woman* and there is *nothing* left. What are we to do? How will we manage?' She was almost beside herself.

Some of this had been money from my wages I was later to discover. But it was clear that dad had indeed gone and probably wasn't coming back.

I remember feeling such utmost panic and despair at the realization that my own father had left us all. And later I was to understand that this was linked to the pain of abandonment. I was still too young to fully understand the whole situation, all I knew was what I saw my mother going through, and the severe and deep emotions that coursed through me as I went through the various tidal waves of feelings as each realization of what mum was describing hit home to me. Dad had left us. And for another woman, which to me meant another family! And he had taken all the bank money with him. How could he do this? *Why* would he do this? How would we cope now? Why did he leave? What did we do wrong? There had been fights before, rants and cursing, slammed doors, the roar of the motorbike, the silence after the whirlwind as things sank in. Then the heightened activity of renewed focus on the debris left behind as the destruction and aftermath was cleaned, sorted, tidied up or thrown in the bin. But nothing quite like this. This felt more final. Dad had never emptied the family bank account before...

My mind was in a whirlwind – I could not make sense of it.

Mum was in hysterics, anger mixed with screams of pain, curses mixed with moans of loss... She flew round the house and flung anything dad had not taken with him into a battered bag. She was going to take it round there 'right now' and show this 'tart' what she thought of her for taking her man away.

'Stuck-up little Miss Perfect,' I heard her mutter as she slammed things around. 'Let's see how *she* manages with four children, a house and a job to manage.'

Eventually she remembered that we were all in shock along with her, and she started to calm down and to comfort the little ones. I could only support her and help her tidy up, help to prepare some form of supper, help to pet and hug the littlies. All the time I was wondering if we would ever see dad again... Mum was so wrapped up in her own pain, her own envy and enmity of this other woman, her own abandonment that there was no space to reassure me.

Mum withdrew into her own inner world, functioning only for essential things, coming home from work with barely a word to any of us, doing only the basics, and we all continued to tread on egg shells, not wishing to add to any problems.

I don't know whether she actually went round there with dad's stuff or not, but I do know that within a couple of weeks or so, dad had come home again. No apology, no explanation, no given reason. That elephant in the room was totally avoided.

It was icy for a while at home. Still don't know the story, and as they are both dead now I never will. Later on, things did eventually pick up for a while, and dad must have made it up to mum in some way that satisfied her to some degree. I don't know how they did it, but they managed to reconcile and I do remember that at some time later after that, I saw them dancing a waltz in the lounge room again, enjoying each other as they used to. They knew how to be romantic with each other, but Boy! Did they know how to row!

However and as was to be expected things didn't last this way for long, and the usual interactions of arguing, rowing, fighting then making up in a romantic and memorable way was now giving way to a more consistent and different flavour at home.

Mum was becoming more and more like a zombie, hardly speaking when she wasn't working, mostly resentful, bitter or kind of quiet and listless like she had been bombed, and it showed in the cooking she attempted. Me – well I was trying to manage as best I could, supervising the kids when around, but trying to be out whenever possible between chores, and attending to my own domestic

Naïve Hope

requirements, though often still daring to act as the referee in their fights (sometimes at the cost of a well-aimed blow at me).

I wonder now if mum was taking anything... Some sort of over-the-counter powder? Possibly.

Nightmares

The mind is always seeking a solution, a way out...

There is only so much that a person can tolerate before something collapses or changes.

There was this reality in my life, of hardship, worry, disappointment, lack of recognition. Yet a part of me seemed to want to dream of better things. Hope would be extinguished, and then Hope would try to flare again at the slightest encouragement. A roller coaster sometimes, though the down times of despair were more frequent, and the dark periods were growing longer and merging into each other more.

Emotional dysfunction and mismanagement was the way of our family, though there were no words for this, no frame of reference, no understanding or measuring gage, no intelligence or awareness – merely reaction, venting, recycling and misdirecting. Old issues were brought in and mixed with current ones, a kind of 'kitchen-sink'-ing of grievances; problems were never really solved with thought out solutions to prevent further recurrences; policing or monitoring of behaviours and consequences were all skewed and applied to the children (including me) alone; no real emotional recognition or leadership was available; truth and fairness often got thrashed over the head with entitlement; favouritism was the Ace card.

I was desperate to be free of all of this despair, this isolation, this invisibility, this doomed game.

It was during my final year at school and whilst I was working part-time that I had had enough. I was just sixteen years old, and saw no hope for myself. In fact, looking back, I am surprised that I managed to pull myself together enough to finish school...

Well, I almost didn't...

I had little joy in my life, did not feel supported or nurtured and no-one seemed to be aware of what I needed. That's how it felt. And the reality was that my parents were heading for a split. Mum had met some man in a park when we were there one day whilst dad was 'playing up' yet again. She later confided to me that even though she and this man had only held hands and hadn't yet so much as kissed, she felt that he was such a gentleman and that they had felt such a connection that she was thinking of leaving dad and of taking us all with her to join him as he had invited her to. She had been seriously thinking about it for a week or so before she shared this information with me.

'How do you feel about that?' she asked me. 'Do you think I should leave your father for someone who wants to take care of us all?'

I didn't really know how to answer. As she talked about him, I did actually remember this man she was speaking of, and at the time he seemed a very pleasant and kind man in my eyes, too. So it seemed to me. And dad wasn't really present to us, and there were always fights and so on... all this went on in my mind. But did I really want to leave all I knew to move in with this 'kind man'? I couldn't answer because I didn't really know what it would entail. But I did say 'Whatever you think is the best thing to do, then that's ok with me.' I would rather be with mum than with dad, after all.

Of *course* I couldn't make a decision for her... She eventually realised this was too much of an ask of me. This was a big step mum was considering. But the way dad was at the time, I got why this was such a temptation. However mum had morals, and even though dad was out most nights, apparently she wasn't going the same way.

As it turned out, mum rethought her vows and it all fell through and mum once again seemed to go into her own little world. Even though we stayed and it would appear that she had sacrificed this possible chance at happiness, nothing improved at home. It all seemed doomed and pointless.

For many years, since as far back as I could remember, I had been continually having two repetitive dreams.

The first one was about walking on my way to the local shops (we usually walked, as there was no bus route there). I am on Panfield Road and heading toward the Church which is at the bottom of the hill, in order to turn left towards HollyHedge Shops. Suddenly, there is a huge fire moving towards me. I turn and start to walk, but the fire still follows, growing larger. Then I run, but the fire moves closer and closer to me. No matter how fast or hard I run, the fire is always hot on my heels. I can do nothing to escape it. I usually awoke with my heart racing just as I feared it would engulf me. I never understood this dream until much later in my life.

The other dream I often had was about me standing at the top of the stairs at home – then I would somehow start to slowly fall, somehow turning in mid-air so that as I landed, I would end up on my back, looking back up to the top of the stairs, and feeling as I was falling and landing a strange semi-painful sensation in my nervous system, followed by a kind of painful numbness in my body, and then feel totally unable to move. Often in my dream, dad would be standing at the top of the stairs, looking down at me as I fall.

I later understood these dreams as representational of my situation. It was to be many, many years later when I finally ceased to have them but not until after I was divorced.

Nightlights and Chrissie

A couple of things helped keep me sane and not totally despairing of life.

As a young girl, there would be nights of overwhelm from all the drama and hopelessness, times when I would be lying in bed, hating my life, and wanting oblivion; and then I would hear the drone of engines. Not motor vehicle or truck engines, but the steady increasing and imagination-inspiring sound of the drone of aeroplanes making their majestic way silhouetted across the night sky, with their myriad of promising lights, moving toward some exotic destination or to a heart filled homecoming. I would get out of bed as quickly and quietly as I could, and gaze and gaze, watching and waiting for a glimpse of these travelling lights, in hope of transport 'away from all this'. I would dream of trips away to foreign places I had heard about, of travel in planes, of going somewhere far, far away. And wondering about the people who were in those planes. And one day hoping one would be me. These night lights helped to remind me that there was more to life than 'just this'.

My friend Chrissie lived in the same avenue. Not a 'pretty' girl, she was big boned, strong and quite masculine-looking for a girl. She too had trouble keeping 'in' with the other girls. So we both teamed up. Our favourite game was 'Cowboys & Indians', with me being the cowgirl and she being the Indian. When she had a band around her forehead, and had put in a feather from one of our chickens, she indeed did look very much like an Indian. A solid Capricorn, we became friends out of necessity, but this friendship sustained us through many unhappy experiences. We would take off on school holidays, to walk many miles away into the country. Living not too far from the Manchester Airport, which was then called Ringway Airport, we would take some homemade sandwiches, a bottle of water, and an apple, put them in our schoolbags, and hoisting them onto our backs, we would walk and talk for miles. I remember us 'raiding' a farm one time, digging madly into the field whilst the workers were at the other end of the field using a mechanical hoe and digger, raking up the potatoes. We filled our bags full of spuds, and, hearing them raise the alarm, we struggled off with bags full, knowing that they wouldn't be able to catch us in time. But did we bolt! Mum was thrilled with what we brought home. Fresh out of the ground, they tasted so yummy. As mum was always struggling for provisions, this was a godsend to her.

Chrissie was very herbal smart for a young kid. Once I fell into a patch of weeds and I got badly stung with stinging nettles, so much so that my whole leg started to swell. Chrissie got out the little metal billycan she had carried with her, and boiled some stinging nettles & dandelion leaves in the water and forced me to drink the 'brew'. It tasted pretty yucky to my sweet tooth, but I persevered. She also put some on to the actual swellings. Eventually the welts would ease, and I would start to feel better, and able to make it home again. She seemed to know all sorts of sundry interesting titbits. When we played at her house, her grandma, a very old-fashioned lady, would chase me away from the house. At Chrissie's

Naïve Hope

insistence, I would hide round a corner of the house and she would sneak out with a tin can with string attached and then run back inside. We would talk down the tin cans to each other, just like a telephone; the sound vibrations running along the string. She was a kind of life saver in my childhood, and I wish her well still wherever she is now.

We were friends for many years, gradually starting to drift apart when we both attended different secondary schools. We often caught up in school holidays if she didn't go away with her mother, brother and grandma. Many years later we reconnected with each other again.

TO BE OR NOT TO BE

Despite the occasional respite and the odd moment of sanity from our family hamster wheel of family drama, histrionics and neglect, living lacked purpose. I felt thwarted.

Life felt futile. There seemed to be little peace or meaning to life. Hope had not only turned its face away, it had totally disappeared.

This was when I decided to end it all. I had had enough. It was pointless and I was numb. I embarked on a serious attempt to commit suicide.

My parents were always careful with tablets and pills of any kind, and kept all of the family pills and medicines up on the top shelf, wrapped in severe threats. Dad had a healthy respect of drugs and often refused to use even pre-packaged foods, including tomato sauce, if the ingredients weren't labelled. I was very aware that certain pills were dangerous. This could be my answer!

I made plans. I bought pills, pills that I understood to be dangerous and lethal from the chemist. I chose the night. My mind was set. I was going to find my escape!

This particular night, armed with a bottle of water and whole bottle of these pills, I downed the lot, one by one, in anticipation of sweet relief. As I was falling asleep, sinking into a weird space, I remember saying an old prayer to myself *'If I die before I wake, I pray the Lord my soul to take. If I die whilst I sleep, I pray the Lord my soul to keep.'*

More than anything, I wanted peace and rest. Or total oblivion. Anything but this...

Darkness descends.

From somewhere on the edge of my consciousness I became aware of a light. Then I gradually became aware of a ringing in my ears. I couldn't move. Then the ringing in my ears became an aggressive painful sound, worse than a real alarm clock ringing *inside* my ears. It felt like it was trying to break the sound barrier. The light was getting stronger, and it wasn't as blurred as it was before.

Where are the Angels? My eyes hurt! My ears hurt! Oh rats! I am **still** *in my bedroom. I am still* **alive***.*

Oh, my head! Why is the room spinning? Why do I feel like I have cotton-wool in my brain?

Can I move my arms? No. Try again... Oh, now I can just about move myself. Do I still have the use of my hands or are these real lead weights on them? No. They are just feeling heavy. Everything feels heavy. I feel like I think it would be to have been hit by a truck!

Then I realise that the alarm actually *is* ringing! I attempt to get up to turn it off. And I struggle to sit upright. I can't. I can barely move! It takes several attempts to find my hands and my legs and work out where my face is to touch it. Time slows down again. Ages and hours later, it is still ringing in my head, this sound. I have barely moved. I am starting to 'wake' up...

My bid to end it all is a miserable failure, and I am forced to face the world. Again. Eventually I manage to work my limbs and fingers and I turn it off, but there is still ringing in my ears. It is a muffled sound, like I am underwater and it is constant. I wonder what happened and I recall my botched attempt. I can't even win when I want to escape it all, can I? I find myself having to force my hands and fingers and feet to work again to get me to my Saturday job in Altrincham. Dressing was a slow disconnected trial of perseverance. Getting on and off the buses to work was almost a hit and miss experiment. My mind was not my own, my body felt like it was four feet off the ground, and my head felt like it was stretched at least ten to fifteen feet above me. I had trouble placing

Naïve Hope

one foot in front of the other. I was expecting to fall over or simply 'slide' at any moment... and for most of that day I was 'out-of-it' – I was indeed lucky to make it home, where I skipped dinner and crept to bed as soon as I could, head still filled with cotton-wool and ears still filled with muffled underwater ringing.

And you know, no-one noticed!

Mum and dad so wound up in themselves, they failed to see anything wrong. Years later when I thought about this, I could not comprehend that. At the time, I was so filled with shock at still being alive, and so full of despair at life, and so on-automatic, that I simply just tried to keep moving and get myself safely to work. I was still alive – couldn't seem to avoid *that* and anyway, what would I say? I was too shocked, disappointed and ashamed at my own perceived failure.

I couldn't even win at death, never mind life!

Why did I even *consider* such an action, as to not just *want* to be dead, but to actively *try* to be dead? There were many reasons, but I think a major contributing factor was that I had absolutely no control over my life or its direction. No Hope. No real nurturing. Life seemed to lack any meaning other than work, rows, fights. And more work, rows, fights.

As a young child and as far back as I can remember I have asked the following questions of myself and probably annoyed my parents with these same wonderings too; Why are we here? Who am I? What is this all about?

I wasn't any closer to the answer before or after this experience. I still wished I was dead, but I didn't know how to accomplish it successfully and in a quick and reasonably pain-free way.

Yet.

And even though I was still physically alive, another part of me somewhere inside had certainly died.

Yet Life went on.

My last year of school was a difficult time, but things were about to change – again...

I look back at all of these times and I see my life like a cork bobbing around on a sea of life and crises – I confess that I had little idea *then* (and for quite some time) that I could plan my life the way I wanted. In all honesty, whatever I had wanted or planned for simply hadn't happened or been *allowed* to happen anyway, so my view and acceptance back then was justifiably predictable. Looking at what I learned from my parents, this fatalism was also understandable. Hadn't they been through two huge wars, and experienced the Great Depression? My young head did not yet have any comprehension of this, and incoming information on life was limited to that which was gleaned from those around me, by example and by word. Warnings from the older generation were plentiful. Books that I read appeared to be filled with honour, duty, romance and justice, though stories of strong or successful women and freedom for women were still limited; and my need and dependence for home nurture was probably a part of the equation of such chain-ings that kept me asleep in these circumstances.

And if I am totally truthful, did I really *know* what I wanted? When years later I asked this question of myself and of others who were my clients, the response is usually to start to list what I *don't* want... what we *don't* want... Men appear to be simpler and more direct in this, for they seem to know more clearly what it is that they want – at the time, anyway – and don't seem to have the same issue in whether or not they can *have* what they want. Generally. Sure, they may change their mind and want something else later, but they don't necessarily see the same obstacles most women do. The mental wiring is different. Or the opportunities...

This iteration of what one *doesn't* want, though, can often be vital to discovering what one *does* want... This step of turning *around* the negative to a positive statement on the item in question is not always pursued; and therein lay some of my powerlessness as a female. It was easier (and habitual) to see or to identify what didn't suit, what I really didn't like, and then to learn to put up with it.

Dealing with what turns up, the making of adjustments, is often more readily seen as the solution as opposed to creating what *one really wants*. Women are great at adaptation, and just as it can be a huge plus, it can also become a prison when one gets used to

Naïve Hope

responding to life continually in this way. Though I am speaking of the culture for women at this particular time in my life.

Things are changing now and women are taking control of their lives and goals at early ages, however back then, choices were limited.

So in a climate of fate, in circumstances of dictation, momentous and life changing opportunities may occur. And some may be recognised. Or availed of.

Or not...

Seeking Freedom

I struggled to complete my studies, trying to lose myself in the distractions offered me by a few acquaintances at school, then by bouncing back to focus on my school subjects. The final year was a mixture of dread, despair, angst and the smell of career promise for other students that felt so uncertain to me.

Shortly after leaving school my examination results had come through. I had done tests on six subjects and passed on four, coming away with two G.C.E.'s 'O' Level (English General Certificate of Education which was equivalent to Matriculation in Australia) and two U.L.C.I.'s (Union of Lancashire & Cheshire Institute equivalent to the Australian School Leaving certification). It was to be many years later that I did Tertiary education and other Certifications, obtaining Diplomas and several professional qualifications.

Considering the amount of time that I had been forced to take off from school for various domestic reasons – though I must confess to the occasional indefinable inner dissatisfaction and tetchiness that made me want to wag school on a couple of occasions – I had not done too badly. Achieving two school leaving and general matriculation certificates at least qualified me for more than a life of working at Woolworths, and indicated that I certainly did have some intelligence. English Language, Literature, Art and Math's were my tickets to work beyond being a check-out chick for the rest of my life!

In that final school year, besides doing final school exams, I had also been entered for a scholarship by the Headmaster. Within another couple of weeks I was amazed to receive a formal letter addressed to myself personally in an official looking envelope. Mum and dad handed it to me after I came home one night from working at Woolworths. Like some other local teens, I had increased my weekend hours to also work during the weekdays during school holidays. This had been helping to occupy my time until results and direction became clear. I had nothing better to do, after all.

Not only that, mum and dad never took us away on holidays anyway, so it's hard to miss what you never had – said someone, who had absolutely *no* idea of what they were talking about, hey? Anyway...

Imagine my surprise when I read that I was being offered a hairdressing apprenticeship with full training at the Domestic and Trades College in Manchester. I had to read it several times to understand what it was saying and what it all meant.

And what it was offering me.

Hope!

Someone valued me and wanted to help me improve my life. *Someone* was handing me a ticket to freedom, a ticket to self-exploration, to a career and a position. Hairdressing!

Is this what I wanted...? Well, it might possibly mean more financial struggle for me, but future earning prospects were high and what a *great* opportunity to do something I had always enjoyed playing around with... And good wages down the track. The art of 'back-combing' hair to tease volume into it for my girlfriends (and myself) to create bee-hives or the bouffant look was such fun, and I was developing an interest and an eye for fashion. Wasn't I able to wear reasonably fashionable items through my make-do-and-mend skills? Mum had cut all our hair at home to save on hairdressing fees, and so I thought I could take that over too as well as get to see how to do some of the amazing things that were done with hair. Hadn't I also taken to sometimes cutting my own hair (like film star Kim Novak) and also coloring and even

Naïve Hope

home-perming it myself? Now I could work with hair and beauty, and become professional at it. Even though I only remember going to a hairdressers for a cut *once* in my life, this didn't persuade me from this path. For when faced with this offer, I realized that I really enjoyed and appreciated beauty, fashion and doing hair (not that I could yet much afford it); for Art had been my best subject, and I was excellent at it.

And after all of the dramas of career counseling with the school careers advisor (and certain key others) regarding my still undecided career direction this seemed like a heaven sent opportunity.

As I had excelled in art I had initially wanted to be an artist. This was what I had started leaning towards in my heart, but when it had come to actually looking at vocations and 'career paths' both my mum and art teacher had decided against me following up on this and went to great pains to talk me out of it. The reasons that they gave me were vague and based on something about commercial artists not being allowed to do their own stuff, but always having to work for someone else. Isn't that a usual condition of employment anyway? So this I found confusing. Though I argued the point, any point, I couldn't get either of my parents nor Mr. Wilson, the art teacher, to change their mind.

When asked what it was that I 'wanted' to do again (though it was becoming more a case of what I was being 'allowed' to do), I considered my next choice carefully and decided that I would love to train as an air hostess. I had loved watching all those planes from my bedroom window with a yearning to fly with them. And on frequent walking trips to Ringway Airport with Chrissie, as well as the rare trip-treat with dad on his motorbike, we would stand at the end of the runway flightpath and feel the planes as they passed overhead - this had obviously contributed to my fascination as well as a future travel bug. Part of my childhood survival support system had been through this daydreaming and bedtime escapism from my bedroom window imagining flight and freedom. I loved hearing the drone of the airplanes and to watch them as they passed by, wishing and hoping that *'One day, I will be on a plane and visit exotic places, and get far away from all this'*, which just may have influenced me to some degree, hey?

But, again, I was discouraged from this career option, the job being disdainfully described as 'only a glorified waitress's job'! Despite the hard training that the air hostess did and the then current strict requirements, it didn't come close to being entertained by my parents as an acceptable or permitted option for me.

So when I received this amazing news that I had *won* the scholarship I was just so over the moon. I waved the letter happily in front of mum and dad, I was so thrilled with the results. I could dare to dream again! Elation burst into my chest and mind.

I welcomed the spark of Hope into my heart...

And I was so excited at winning *something*! At being recognized as having some degree of worthiness and ability. For that's what it felt like just then. At getting a chance at doing something that I enjoyed! Even if I couldn't follow my beloved art, I could create art with hair!

Floating down from my euphoria, I turned my attention back to mum and dad, and how pleased they would be with this scholarship... What a saving with it all being paid for!

I had little noticed their silence whilst I had been reading and absorbing my letter. My thoughts had raced to take in what this apprenticeship had meant, and the details of what was being covered by the scholarship included in the letter. I think I must have read some of it out loud as well, but I was too involved in this significant event to notice straight away.

Funny thing, but when I finally handed it over for mum and dad to read, at first they seemed to be very quiet and somewhat disconcerted. At first I thought they just hadn't heard me right... Or that they had misunderstood just exactly what this news was offering me...

Being the eldest, I knew that they had had high hopes for me, and I had performed as best as I could; even with the lack of proper support and other disadvantages that had been placed before me. Loss of time had made it difficult but I *had* applied myself.

So I guess I naively and secretly kind of hoped and expected them to be proud and supportive of me, and I also proudly figured that there would be good pay down the track for me and the family.

Naïve Hope

After all, I was brought up with the idea that if you do the right thing, you get rewarded. Right? Well look what happened for Cinderella!

Hmm. So this continuing discomfort was not quite the reaction I was hoping for, or expecting, or had given any thought to. They then sat me down. They next told me that I had done well, but they couldn't afford to let me go. 'Oh, that's easy!' I thought. They hadn't read the letter properly – I had won a *Scholarship* – there *was* no cost! I explained that *they* didn't have to pay, I had *won* this, and *all* expenses and even bus fares would be paid.

'It won't cost you anything! And I can keep my weekend job to help out,' I joyfully exclaimed.

But it fell on deaf ears. Did they not understand? Neither mum nor dad could look me full in the face. They just kept insisting that I could *not* attend the Domestic & Trades College scholarship because *they* couldn't afford it. I still didn't understand what they were saying. It was a Scholarship – it was free!

Come on, help me here... My Hope is starting to tremble... Dad just sat on the couch, letting mum do most of the explaining.

'No, you don't understand, Marni. We can't *afford* for you *not* to be working and helping the family out. We can't afford to have you do any training. You *have* to get a job, and *soon*, so we can all manage.'

'But..., but...' I said, beginning to realize where this was leading.

'It's your duty to help your family...' they both said straight-faced as they dispassionately insisted.

The family needed my wages. *Now*. They could not afford to have me *not* working full-time. All arguments were exhausted, all appeals denied, all pleas disowned.

I was in shock. Stunned. Wordless now. Hope drifted out of the room and far away... The upshot of this, when it finally sank into my frazzled and confused brain was that even though I had this opportunity, I had *no* option but to pass it up as this was what was expected, demanded and required of me, and that I go out to work full-time to contribute to the family coffers. Or as it actually turned out later, to dad's pockets.

'So what do I do about the letter?' I asked, still confused as to how this could happen. 'Write them and let them know you can't follow up on it', was the short shrift solution I received back. And with a heavy heart I sealed shut the door to that life.

Accordingly it was that again, later and still stunned, I had to work once more down the list of suitable work positions and opportunities for school leaver's jobs and going alphabetically the rulers of my life tied in my Math's results to Accounting of some form.

Thus it was sorted. And a part of me died. I was again resigned to my fate, and there was to be no escape.

And here's a thing – many years later I was sharing this story with a good friend who couldn't seem to understand that I accepted all this. The question they asked me was simple – to them -: 'Why didn't you just leave home and get a place of your own and do the training?' You know, it had never occurred to me, had never entered my head to do so – in those days that sort of 'selfishness' wasn't conceivable, let alone considered as an option. It was unheard of in my community. Family stuck together. Family helped each other. Though it took me many years to realize that *I* often got forgotten for the sake of *family*, which seemed to include everyone else's needs but mine. I was family wasn't I? But I didn't think of this at the time, and so being a good girl, family duty won out. The world has certainly changed.

Consequently and inevitably a job was located for me as a trainee cost clerk with Ferranti's Rocket Missile Base located near Peel Hall; application letters were sent, interviews attended and employment confirmed. I had fulfilled my obligations and earned my right to live as the dutiful daughter. Again I felt I had no control over my life or choices, and indeed this was my experience. But at least I was now viewed as a responsible employable person and not lumped in with those who were still struggling to either identify or to find work. I could not afford to dwell on this thwarting. To view it another way, I didn't have to go on the dole or be tossed onto the heap of the unemployable.

Naïve Hope

So off I set to do the best I could.

I swallowed my hurt and staved off my grief with a forced attitude of proving myself a good employee. Ready to meet the challenges as best I could. Willing to learn. And learn I did.

There were hardships in store still to come. As there were no direct buses (unless you took a series of two or three that did roundabout routes) I had to walk most days to the site, except for my training day in the city, as the allowance of two pounds from my monthly wages of six pounds was not sufficient to support my costs. For this meager amount had to cover the costs of my own lunches, nylon stockings for work, shoe repairs, my own clothing or even regular bus fares. The walk was about five miles, most of it over flat fields, in the middle of winter, without any shelter. And without as yet, a decent winter coat.

My six monthly pay rise for being such a good trainee cost apprentice went up to eight pounds per month, from which my allowance was increased to the princely sum of two pounds and *ten* shillings per month. In those days, it was twenty shillings to the pound. On dad's instructions my wages packet still had to be handed directly to mum and she was to give me my 'allowance' from that.

I was to learn many, many years later from mum that whatever she had received from me in wages dad had reduced the housekeeping to her by that same exact amount. So mum was no better off from my working. I had basically been funding dad and not the family. And unbeknown to me, that money that dad had gained through my pay actually went on socializing, drinks for his dancing buddies, gambling and his motorbike!

After almost a year of battling colds through the cold winter walks to work, I searched the papers and found another better paid job in Manchester in the city. This was too far to walk and now I had to be allowed to catch the bus to Shude Hill, as it was then, - working at a shoe retail shop, where I was continually going up and down stairs to bring the right shoe sizes down for the customer to try on. If we did not have the desired sizes on display or they were not in the showroom upstairs I had to locate them and this was hard work with those stairs. But at least the walking and climbing was generally indoors and offered some weather protection.

I was now working full time for six days per week and getting home a bit later. For this hard effort, I was rewarded with the sum of five whole pounds per week wages.

From my wages packet I was handed back one whole pound per week for myself, and boy did I earn it. Though this gave me enough money to cover my costs, it didn't exactly put me into a position of wealth.

The echo of this enforced learning that impacted on me in later life was that I didn't deserve much, that I had to work hard for what I got, and that if I did the right thing by others then I would hopefully be eventually looked after – providing the needs of others were met first. What a dream, hey? Yes, I know, that silly Cinderella dream again. Took me a while to wake-up from that one!

And to add insult to injury, my nasty, self-absorbed, inconsiderate and virulent sister, Joan, later made a scathing and hurtful comment to me about these work choices. Around forty years later on one of my regular visits to family, she 'kindly shared' that mum had been 'quite disappointed with your Grammar School education, for she (mum) didn't benefit much from it, and you didn't really do the best you could with it.' This said with that sarcastic semi-smile on her face, the one that seems to say 'There, so take that!' I was floored that mum could even *think* that, much less *say* it! And how *wrong*...

Maybe some part of me knew that I was simply being used to prop up family expenditure, but it was certainly not known to me on a conscious level. After all, that is not the right thing to do, is it? If you are being asked to pay your way at home, or rather, if you are being handed out your '*spends*' from your own pay packet, and have no idea where the money is going, but you are told that it is to help 'the family', then one would expect that the money being taken from you is actually going to 'family'.

And not to *dad*!

Duped unwittingly, and not aware! And it also begs the question – 'Just what would you do if you *had* been aware, Marni?' To be honest, I have absolutely no idea... How appalling, but I was so stuck in 'doing the right thing', fear of not obeying, and so totally wound up in family issues, that I could not see my own life and my own crises or direction clearly. When it comes to experiencing trauma in family and in childhood, it is not surprising that there seemed to be so few choices for me, or so few independent thoughts in my head. I had absolutely no idea of how I functioned, or of the interplay in relationships that had created or maintained these dysfunctional attitudes and sabotages that had kept me 'in my place'. Then.

Did this serve as a momentous climax or even just as an interesting prelude and a ripe opportunity for anything, anything, that would free me from such oppression? Not necessarily. Not then. I didn't consider leaving home for one mini-second. It never entered my head. I was the eldest, and it was *my* duty and up to *me* to help out with the family. End of!

It is not surprising therefore that when I met my future husband (Jim) and in the circumstances that I met him, that I thought that things would be different; I believed the promises made by God, I thought He, and Jim, would love me, protect me and look after me. For after all, this was a Preacher Man, 'man of God' wasn't he? Instead I ended up jumping out of the frying pan and into the fire, losing all autonomy over my finances yet again. But I am getting ahead of myself. Even before my school Scholarship offer and let-down, I had been fighting my battles with Hope.

But my own war was still far from over...

Meanwhile, some sort of pattern develops as I trudge to work and walk my butt off to get people's correct shoes. I am gaining in independence of some sort. Not yet cognisant as to my true situation, having my own regular money and knowing that I was conscientious at what I was doing was equipping me to further my social life and to unconsciously seek solutions to my own personal unhappiness within the confines of my current situation.

Greek God

On some level I think I must have accepted all of this, the family and work situation, as my fate.

But one has secret labyrinths in the mind.

The mind is always seeking a solution, a way out...

After my attempt at ending it all, things fell into a numbed out kind of existence.

After a while I got to hear from other teens how they had fun, and this was the time of Elvis Presley, Tommy Steel and the advent of after school teen 'night-school'. The saving grace was one of the local schools club which put on rock and roll or 'jive' (which was emerging) nights weekly. All very innocent stuff, you could get a cup of tea or coffee if you could afford it included in the admission cost of a shilling.

But the young school girls were learning by observing – clothes, makeup, hairstyles, dance steps – and participating. Sure there were a few rough kids, but generally it was a great place to practice dance steps and 'groom' for pre-adulthood. I *loved* it. The boys were mostly quite shy, but those that were brave enough to dare to engage on the dance floor became very good at the dance steps. The school gym was converted into the 'social dance club' a couple of nights a week after the local teens worked off their exuberance, and some of these guys often stayed to play pool, or to watch or join in with dance efforts.

I began to live for these nights, and even though I could only afford to buy my clothes from jumble sales and have to alter or redesign them, I was starting to develop my own style and confidence. And occasionally through my part-time job I would buy new material and make the odd brand new outfit.

I was beginning to have a reason to live again. Though chained to the grindstone, the dancing gave me something that hadn't yet been taken away from me...

Graduating from the 'Rackhouse' School dance to the Locarno Ballroom in Sale, near Altrincham where the older kids and working teens danced on Saturday nights was exciting. It was a

Naïve Hope

whole new grown up world. This place had a disco ball! I was fascinated! I would still visit the local school club occasionally, but at weekends there was this whole new world waiting for me. There was some alcohol on the premises, but it was all so very tame back then, with only the occasional beer being consumed. I never saw anyone drunk, and didn't drink myself, so it wasn't a problem. [I didn't have a problem with alcohol, I still don't. I don't drink much, as my dad, for all his faults, taught me respect of alcohol, and it was he who gave me my first drinking lesson of 'sip and respect' *and* he backed it up by his never being drunk that I ever saw or knew of.] So it was all very innocent.

And this was where I first met my Greek God.

Actually it was on the bus ride to the Locarno.

This was when I first saw him, and later danced with him – and when we did, something 'went off' in my insides.

Tall, dark and handsome will forever be my thoughts on him, and 'Greek God' will always be my watchword for Bob Hopkins. He was wearing the tight pants of the day, called 'drainpipes', though they weren't skin tight like some guys. Black leather jacket, neat pressed white shirt, a thin black tie, pointed 'winkle-picker' black shoes, and coiffed hair in a forehead flounce. He was tall and well proportioned, with an attractive face possessing high crafted cheek bones. A neat and sexy moustache complemented his strong sharp eyebrows, perfectly placed over brooding dark brown laughing eyes and attractive Grecian nose. And what a smile!

We both did double takes when we first laid eyes on each other on the bus. He flirted with me a little bit but behaved as a gentleman. Me and my school chum and dance friend, Susan Entwistle, didn't suspect he was going to the same place as us until he was getting off at the same bus stop. He waved goodbye to me and indicated he was meeting a friend. We didn't say where we were going, nor did he. But things had been set in motion. To my surprise we bumped into each other at the Locarno. Things just naturally developed from there, and he was calling on me very soon, dating me, and became my first real boyfriend. I was still naïve, but I dared to think that maybe life could actually be getting better, even though my parents were still in this terrible emotional dead place.

Meanwhile, I had a boyfriend. And he was taking me out to places. And on his motorbike! Great! Maybe things are looking up for me. He really liked me, was gorgeous and could afford treats.

Wow! Maybe life had some treats in store after all...

Mum and dad gave him the once over, and dad ensured that Bob knew he was a past boxer. Not that I think this bothered Bob. They talked motorbikes the moment they met. I was fortunate in that Bob had presented himself in a really good light when he had approached mum and dad for our first date. The fact that he was only a little older than myself, and that he was taking me dancing, a pastime close to their own hearts, and that he promised to bring me home early, and *always did so*, was a help. And maybe they realized that I was going to have a boyfriend anyway. Sooner or later.

With Bob in my life, things were changing for me in subtle ways. He took me out places, he kept his word and he kept his promises. He took me for rides on his motorbike. He introduced me to his sister and his mother. He was proud of me. All of this brought me confidence. I was beginning to gain some sense of personal style over my looks, noting trends, and even sensing what was coming up. Between finding good jumble sale suit buys that I could transform to fit me and the current styles, I was now also able to save and buy the odd measure of material and sew my own outfits.

I was beginning to look pretty attractive and I was learning the art of makeup. Having adjusted to living on a mini-budget, I was beginning to explore and also enjoying being appreciated. And because I was getting a little older and could always be trusted to come home at the appointed hour, usually around ten o'clock, with the odd special occasion of eleven o'clock, and I was still pitching in with the housework, I was allowed these new privileges.

I enjoyed this space for a while. At home things were pretty much as they were before but this outlet and attention helped me to further endure erratic home life...

Naïve Hope

ANNIVERSARY CROSSROAD

We progress to 1961. It was in this year that mum and dad went through an extraordinary experience, one which affected and changed our whole family and dictated my life for the next twenty years and more.

There we all were, just another day in our Marjetson household. Coming home to strife and dysfunction, unhappy people coupled together in pure survival mode, slipping away from each other but with no other ideas or options as to how to change things, bound or locked by life, responsibilities and children. Three wage earners with me working for very little, and having most of it taken off me by my parents. Yet things weren't really improving materially as much as they could.

On several occasions I had heard mum mumble something about leaving him, I knew she couldn't and wouldn't for she had also told me this, too. Even so, it was feeling to me like my parents were close to splitting up. Every time they got together in the same room, it would either be ice or fireworks. I dreaded being home.

Then their wedding anniversary loomed. They usually liked to celebrate things, even though there would often be disagreements.

We no longer went to church much, not since that one morning at service when I was about nine years old. Mum had always encouraged us to go to church on Sundays and where possible, Ian and I would attend Sunday School. That is until the day I wanted change from God. Then they kicked me out. Let me explain...

I only had sixpence for spends for the whole week (which was much less pocket-money than my neighbourhood friends) and I knew we had to put *something* on the offering plate when it was passed round – this was supposedly for the poor, though I later thought that it was rather more for church upkeep and wages with the poor being a 'poor second' (pardon the pun).

As I had only been given my sixpence coin pocket money late on the Saturday, there had been no chance to buy anything yet and with it now being Sunday, there was nowhere open to get any change for the sixpenny piece before church. So I thought about it and decided on a fair plan; and set it in action. It was simply this –

when the plate came around, I would put my sixpence down first and then pick up a thrupenny bit in exchange.

This was easier than messing around with pennies, so threepence it was going to be. Easy. No fuss. And so it came to pass...

When it came time for the collection bowl on the Sunday at church, I did put in my sixpence and I did take out a three pence piece. A natural exchange after all; God got a whole three pence which was a more than generous half of my pocket money spends, and I still had some money to last me through the week. However, the picking up was observed by the steward handling the bowl - but not the putting down.

Well! This was *so* frowned upon, and I was in big trouble. We were all waylaid after the service and I was put through the third degree. No amount of explanation would convince them other than I had stolen from the church offering.

No, I didn't steal, not at all.

Mum saw what had happened and actually understood and agreed with me; she defended me as she knew I wasn't a liar, knew that I had been given sixpence and that now I only had thrupence (or threepence); she saw the logic in my action, and she basically stood up for me and told them. But the church was adamant that what goes into the bowl *stays* in the bowl. How dare I? 'Just not done!' And so on. So mum told them politely where to put their offering plate. I was after all, an innocent child simply wanting some spends, and even though I had little myself, I had given *half* of what I had to the church. So in a snoot, and also with some embarrassment, we stopped attending the Methodist Church. And what a miserable and droopy experience it always had been. Mournful would be a good word to describe it. Since that time, mum and church had had a strained relationship.

Originally mum had been Church of England, and before this episode we were basically Protestant as opposed to Catholic - and had leaned toward the local Methodist church. This was the answer given when asked the inevitable question on the subject. But despite all of this, and despite devout Catholics living in the avenue alongside other denominations of churchgoers, this was not the reason mum and dad stayed together. Even though they did not know what real peace was, they were co-dependent on each other for far too many things, and in particular I later realized, they needed each other to argue with and fight with. And to make-up with.

Their arguments were always so dramatic, but on the occasions they were in sync, nothing gave us kids more pleasure and awe than to watch them waltz together in the living room, or to see dad literally swoop mum up in his arms. We always delighted in these moments when love appeared to be in the building.

Maybe these moments of pure elation were addictive...? For this dance of hell, fighting, drama and love – well it *was* like an addiction. That was probably what it was, addiction and now a pattern of behavior.

And as I told you, the year before mum had seriously been thinking about leaving dad after meeting this man by accident in the park, and because of this incredible connection they had felt. But her dilemma and the reason she had not followed through was because of how it would affect everyone, I think. And I guess underneath it all, it really challenged her about how much she really loved dad, and whether she would want to live without him. They were so joined and entwined despite their fighting.

So this particular wedding anniversary the June of 1961, and after my 16th birthday, dad went out in a snit on his motorbike. Mum went and stood at the garden entry, gazing after him with a blank look on her face as he exited the avenue.

For some reason dad doubled back home.

'Anne, I'm thinking of going to Gawsworth Hall, to see my ancestors burial grounds. It's a lovely ride in the country, and I wondered if you would like to come, seeing as it's a special day and all. And you haven't been out for a while... It's up to you.'

This invitation was offered as he propped himself on his motorbike at the garden gate. Still a handsome looking man, still very much in his prime, with his charm and charisma, he must have looked very attractive to mum as he waited for her response.

Surprised mum with this sudden return I thought mum was going to shoot out further verbal vitriol as she had most of the week, but she suddenly deflated, and said half-heartedly 'Well it's been a while since I've been to the countryside on the motorbike, so if Marni will take care of things here, then I guess I will come.' Not given much to gracefulness, is mum, hey? But at least they weren't arguing. I agreed, feeling that this was an important step somehow.

So off they went. And we kids were a little surprised that she hadn't raise any more arguments or nasty comments.

We were even more surprised when they later came back.

They had totally changed!

You would be forgiven for thinking that they had either won the Pools lottery or were blind drunk! They were singing at the tops of their voices and as alive as I had ever seen them before.

Their faces alight, the story unfolded about how they had been in the ancestral church graveyard (of all places) when a man standing under a tree approached them and preached to them. And the short version of what transpired is that this became their conversion testimony of how they confessed their sins to God and took Jesus into their hearts, right there, kneeling on the gravestones. For several weeks we kids observed them to see if this 'thing' would go away, but they seemed so happy and had started going to this church several days a week, coming back singing and laughing.

If you know anything about the type of 'faith' they had become involved in, you will know that most of the 'Born-Again' types of religions are very fervent, zealous and emotional. Years later, after my own experiences, I realized that in these services, with their clapping and jigging in the aisles, they were being given permission to experience their emotions, free from guilt and judgment, and that they were happy because of their new belief that they were 'going to heaven'.

They had become Pentecostal Born-Again Christians.

A reason to rejoice, if that's what you believe in – and if life is pretty ordinary otherwise! 'Jesus Saves' was the preacher's and church message, and they had been 'saved'. Saved from the consequences of their 'sins', saved from hell damnation, saved to serve God.

Suffice it to say, they got change at a time in their life just when they craved it. This conversion fulfilled a real need for them both. Something had had to change from the way things had been going. However, the underlying fundamental flaws in family and relating skills or even simply in self-responsibility, self-development or understanding were never really addressed in the church. Nor could they be. The emphasis was on how lost they were without God, and without the beliefs of this group of believers...

To put it bluntly, over time this all became a prop and a crutch for their lives. The Charismatic aspect of the church and its preachings only served to keep them in a different type of fear and dependency than before. Everything was met with a Bible quote, every disagreement, argument or contrary opinion solved by one. However, I jump ahead.

I am not going to go much into religions, faiths or cults here, even though I have done some study on the subject: except to say that the Pentecostals claimed unique right-ness - or righteousness, if you prefer - because of their highlighting of and focus on the Baptism of the Holy Spirit on the Day of Pentecost. This automatically elevated them (in their eyes) to a more comprehensive standing, and also indicated that all other factions, religions, faiths and beliefs weren't quite up to the mark.

Mum and dad were still in this same space for many weeks. No fights, no rows, no slammed doors, insults etc... Peace actually reigned for a time. Within weeks, my brother and sisters were going to church and were supposedly converted. Rather, being as young as they were, I think they were rather impressed or enlisted into it. How can a child make an educated decision on such a thing, really?

Then, and as a matter of course, and I guess because neither Bob nor myself were showing any real interest in all of this religious fervor and activity my boyfriend and I were more and more pressured into attending one of the meetings.

I still didn't feel drawn to join in with what mum and dad were doing. But the evangelization process had been well honed. The conversion pressure process was well proven. We were targeted and we were being 'prayed for'... And anyone who has studied prayer or the power of intention or focused energy can understand what could happen. Back then I knew none of this, however.

Bob and I graciously gave in to attend a meeting, as we were told it was just an information night. And I guess I was a little curious as to what it was all about. But it turned out to be a special 'appeal' night, a conversion meeting – what I later discovered that meant is that there is the 'preaching of the word' (the 'word' being specific carefully chosen quotes from the Bible) then a direct (and repeated) appeal to take Jesus into your heart after admitting that you were 'a sinner' and needed 'saving'; 'Jesus Saves!'

Yes, I felt the guilt and fear of what awaited me if I did not pay attention to 'the state of my soul', but I also felt the love of Christ and thought I saw an image of what living a godly life would be like…

Very confronting stuff, yet for a heart that seeks for a higher sense of things, for solutions to problems, for genuine peace, it was a no-brainer that I would seriously consider the options at this specific cross-road I was being warned that I was standing at…

In my heart I told myself that 'Well, I've seen what it's done for mum and dad. So I will give this a go, and if it doesn't work for me, then I will stop.'

Despite my own proviso, I fully opened my heart to The Lord, and accepted Him as my Saviour, and my Lord. I made a total commitment and a sincere dedication.

Yes, in a way I had been trapped into this step, for there was no way I would have sought this out, but don't get me wrong – I entered fully into this commitment, and there followed many spiritual experiences, and the sense of a very close and personal connection with the Lord Jesus Christ as I opened my heart fully to Him and the idea of Him. We believed in the baptism of the Holy Spirit (all scriptural, as I said) and life seemed 'alive' again. And I certainly felt it.

Naïve Hope

Within weeks of my conversion I was baptized in water, as was Bob, and not long after had an experience of Baptism by the Holy Spirit. This was a physical experience as well as a spiritual one, and not long after I was able to 'Speak in Tongues' and interpret such things in church. Each experience it seemed my spiritual devotion drew me closer to God, and I felt that I couldn't help myself. There was no doubt I had been touched by God, or more realistically, *I had allowed myself to open myself spiritually and to act on it*. But the church was more than this. It was a particular way of *interpreting* the Word of God, and a way of *holding* together a congregation in order that this congregation continue to support itself and its ministers. It was just another group, really. Yes, you could have spiritual events, spiritual experiences if you had a true heart, but I later realised that you could have these anyway with or without a church.

But I was a trusting soul. It was another twenty years before I was able to see how one-sided this path of Hope was and that it really hadn't delivered what it had promised.

FAITH AND HOPE

Being a sincere type of person, I don't like to 'give my word' for something or make a promise and then not to deliver on it. I know what that hurt feels like, having been let-down so often growing up, and not wishing to put someone else through that same pain. So having made the decision to follow the Lord, no matter how manipulated or pressured I had been to do so, I gave myself wholeheartedly to it, and started studying the Bible in earnest. Love for Jesus filled my heart and opened me fully to God and the Lord – or what I *thought* was God...

But I had also found a new friend. I had met Jesus, and somewhere in the preachings, I had heard that he was also our brother as well as our Saviour. This meant that I now had a new father, as in Father God, and a new brother. And I was also hearing that I could count on them! Considering my lack of male support growing up, and my lack of loving fathering, the image of a God that cared and that was loving and who kept His word gave me something that I never had before – a sense of being able to count on someone who wouldn't let me down. This connection with the Divine was something that my soul craved. And so in turn, neither would I then let Him down, neither God nor His son Jesus. I could think of him at any time and pray to him and they would always hear me. Praise The Lord! And so 'Praise the Lord', 'Hallelujah', 'God is good', began to infiltrate into my daily conversations.

Bob was pretty good about things really. Even though he had made the same sort of decision, he was not so full-on with it as I was, and was content to come to church and the meetings with me. We attended a Billy Graham evening when the evangelist was storming Britain, and Bob was ok with it all. But he still wanted to take me out to the cinemas and dancing. And I was thrilled when he took me to my first ever music concert! I think he was far more grounded than me, and he appeared to have had a more settled home life than me.

However, the dark clouds of guilt, control, judgment and fear began to hover over me, when night after night, meeting after meeting, I was continually told that 'the devil' was after my soul, and that dancing, drinking, music, make-up, magazines, even the newspapers, were full of the devil's work and words, and that he was lying in wait to stop me from 'loving God'. There was not anything left untouched that had any fun in it other than worshipping and praying to God – and in particular his son Jesus. It was evangelism gone mad...

But this was the beginning of the '60s – the start of 'free love', hippies and 'flower-power'. The energy of the times was prompting people to pursue love, freedom or peace in a variety of ways. Against the backdrop of this energy and the questing of the masses, my own personal shift and change was taking place. However, ingrained restraints were also coming into play...

I was sixteen. I was limited in affairs of 'the world'. I was accustomed to crises, and of having to do it tough. I had no real sense of identity yet and a still undeveloped sense of independence, and had such a sensitive inner soul that this dedication to God all made a kind of sense to me. I was now attending nearly all of the meetings at the church as well as Bible Study. Lofty thoughts of helping others less fortunate than myself were replacing thoughts

Naïve Hope

of pleasure and play. Veiled guilt for I knew not what made its presence felt as appeals were continually charged at the church flock in exhortation to 'good works' and of 'being worthy' of the Lord. This sensitive soul was impressed, had to be impressed, by it all – not in a flighty sensational way, but in a devout and seriously considered way.

My life had been if nothing else to this point, serious.

In true Pentecostal style, at a prayer meeting I had a kind of energy exchange with the 'laying on of hands', where the Pastor prays a blessing and places his hand on your forehead – which covers the place between the brow and can reach up to the crown of the head. This was part of the baptism of the Holy Spirit, as at Pentecost, which is where this particular religious branch, or cult, got its name. This *laying on of hands* can allow the Holy Spirit, the Shekinah Glory, to flow through the being, and possibly endow one with the ability to *speak in tongues* and to see visions. And because my heart and spirit was truly open and seeking God, I certainly felt the impact, and found that words and sounds were struggling to be released from my mouth. A kind of praising of God but in a language that I had no idea of consciously. I got lost in God, then. This, to me, was a heightened spiritual experience. Some short time later, I would see pictures and images in meetings when others were 'speaking in tongues'. The Pastor told me that I had the ability to 'interpret' the 'tongues' of others, and I felt blessed.

Within months of my conversion, I studied for and became one of the Sunday School teachers at the Church. Top marks. All seriousness and salvation and 'Hallelujah's'. I was having what I considered to be real spiritual experiences and could re-visit those feelings and places again when I prayed. And the church was such a happy place, with its freedom of demonstrating exuberance and its habit of jigging in the aisles.

But this step to working for the church was still a few months away... Meanwhile, I am still enjoying my relationship with Bob, and the outings we were having together. Though this was not to last as the Christian judgmental rot began to set in.

And I did not see what was behind it.

Life was now taking on more and more of the church practices and recommendations; tithing, worship, meetings, witnessing, works of charity, prayer, Bible-reading. And a hidden dose of self-righteousness and condemnation.

Worldly-Fun was frowned upon; Bob knew how to have fun, and so my relationship with Bob began to face its challenges. Bob was becoming very serious about *us*, and whilst I enjoyed this worshipping attention, I was being torn in two directions.

We were out walking to the local shops one day, too close to use his motorbike. Holding my hand as we walked along, he was discussing his potential opportunities at work and his future plans. I was only partly listening as I didn't really understand the structure of his engineering position, but my ears pricked up when I heard him mention marriage. Marriage? I tuned in, because the word jarred me somehow. Bob was saying that in a few months' time we would become engaged, then plan on getting married and having children. Apparently he could afford a ring by that time, having paid off his bike, and then we could plan for our future together. But my mind had heard the words 'marriage and children'... I found myself looking at him, nodding my head, but my mind and heart had split. Gone! Upped and raced down the road, running as fast as they could from any mention of being in the position of prisoner of the kitchen and bedroom. For that is what it felt like. Yet at the time there were no words to describe what I was feeling, for something was so scared within me, that I was unable to recognize what was happening, let alone speak it. For I was not yet ready to even *consider* the possibility of having a child, let alone bringing one up after what I had seen my mother go through; the abortions, the pain, the life sentence of dependency on a man and the lack of true safety with him. Yet if I was married, I would be expected to have children, wouldn't I? And with that a good many fears that I had absorbed subconsciously from my mother's life and my childhood began their whispering rat-tat-tatting at me. A part of me began to pull away from Bob without me knowing it; our relationship was about to come undone.

On the spiritual and church front, yet another battle was being fought. How can you enjoy a night out with your boyfriend when you are considered as being out in 'the devils playground', when

Naïve Hope

you are no longer one of 'the flock' but are now acting as part of 'the world'? (These apparently are the only two options.) And I was being taught that I was to 'Be *in* the world, but not *of* the world'. Bob tried to make sense of these apparent limitations placed by the church by 'talking sense' into me. But I was confused and torn by what I was hearing from the pulpit of disloyalty to God, together with the accompanying threats of hell-fire and with what Bob had to offer me, which was also scary though I hadn't yet consciously recognized this.

When continual hammerings of guilt, shame, service, sacrifice, doing good and saving others is the only thing that you get to hear from church and from home, and you have no other comparisons to check it against, and you live in a house where this is the only acceptable way of life, and you cannot afford to even contemplate any other way of life because ... well, because ... well frankly because you don't *know* any other way, and it doesn't even *occur* to you to leave home and make choices and decisions for yourself. Why that's, well, that's simply *selfish*! And we all know that that's *evil*.

'Worldly' things were usually attributed as ploys of the Devil. This makes for a very narrow experience of life, when doing spiritual things such as praying, worship, study, giving, or serving were perceived as 'right, acceptable, godly' and the *only* way to be acceptable to God. And because I was part programmed to serve in the family, there was little argument that I could conceive of to foster or even contemplate.

I wonder if I had been mentally and emotionally stronger, would I have given so much weight to these doomsayers, would I have seen through the propaganda and their view on things, would I have been ready to interpret the Bible in a more healthy and realistic way? Who can say...?

This tendency to be somewhat spiritual to begin with, to be the responsible eldest daughter, to want to find a higher cause now seems in hindsight to have been perfect fertile ground for the fear and sacrifice hallmarking the preachings and perceptions of pastor and sheeple-flock - which also rather unfortunately fitted in nicely with my own inner and as yet unrecognized aspirations along those lines. This tendency sometimes got played out in my sentimentality, my love of things romantic, and belief in happy endings, in true spiritual and heart love, old-fashioned qualities of honour, devotion and respect, and the dream of being rescued by the gallant Prince or *gentleman*. Progressive, realistic and courageous in many other ways, I was very naïve and innocent in matters of the heart and of the world. Cinderella was still firmly entrenched as an echo of my own heart, I felt so like her.

Fairy stories and children's tales are often the stuff of childhood, but when one clings to fairytale endings without having a wise guide to point the way through the roses and briars of reality and falsehood (the correct role of a good parent actually), then one can find oneself becoming unable to read life's signposts – and even become somewhat blind...

To manage my life, books had carried me in pain free escape to the lands of happy endings where my mind and heart were momentarily safe and where I dared to feel a kind of happiness, however fleeting. These were what had sometimes carried me through the waves of riotous and frightening family life. Some tales were also not just romantic and promised rewards for good behavior. The story of *The Ugly Duckling* was part of a series of books and also was a familiar song from Danny Kaye. This was reinforced in the family by dad, who I later learned had always felt 'left-out' and 'not fitting in' with family and peers during his own childhood.

I remember my father telling me a similar story of the ugly little chicken, and of how this little orphaned bird was so out of place with everyone else. This felt so like me. And the story goes that this ugly little bird found life hard as it tried to find an acceptable place with its 'brothers and sister'. These other little chicklets and chickens were part of the family of the mother hen that had found this little ugly-bird and had adopted it even though it looked somewhat different; it had a large bill not really built for pecking for seeds and insects off the rough ground, it had funny big feet with skin between that made scratching at the earth difficult. And it could never understand why the other chickens avoided the rain and the pond, yet it felt right at home in it. The others laughed and called it names when it grew its long neck and teased it when it had to bend it so much to fit into the chicken hutch coup to sleep at night. But one day when it was looking at how different its reflection in the pond was from the other birds that it shared with, it also saw reflected up in the sky a group of migrating birds flying overhead on their way to better pastures. They too saw the 'ugly bird' down below and so they called out to it to join them. Then the bird realized that *it* was one of *these* other graceful and beautiful white birds and not part of this flock after all, and it took off and flew up to join them. It had found its own kind. It realized that it was really a *swan*, and not a chicken, nor a duck. What had been perceived as ugly and cumbersome was actually very graceful and powerful. Part of me so resonated with this story, that I not only felt but also thought that I knew in some way that it was true.

Maybe Christians were part of 'my flock'? This need to identify can be very strong, so strong that it can override other considerations. And the changes in my family had been undeniable.

I thought that I would somehow become more graceful and be able to serve God in some way. Little did I know how this would transpire in my life. Meanwhile, I was still learning what God wanted from me, according to what I was being taught through Bible study and from sermons.

Whilst I was enjoying my time with this new boyfriend, my search for meaning was being channeled through these new experiences and new understandings. So my emotional needs, my relational needs, and my spiritual needs were now being met in diverse ways.

However, there was some inner conflict that was growing, another path that I was unknowingly being channeled along by fate.

Things were again about to change...

Fate Butts In

One pleasant Sunday afternoon, Bob took me out for a motorbike ride to the city. On the way I remembered an invitation to us both from a church member, Mary Strawthorne, to attend an Open Air Meeting in Platt Fields in Manchester. Out of curiosity, I suggested we drop in to take a quick look at what this was about. An Open Air Meeting is where a group of people, in this case Born-Again

Christians or 'Believers', gather in the outdoors. And sing a couple of hymns. And as it turned out, to preach 'The Word' from the Bible, appealing to the public to hand their lives over to God and in particular, the Lord Jesus Christ. It was also expected that several of the group give public testimony to their own personal story as to how they were converted, or 'Came to The Lord' as it was often referred to. The scriptural focus tended to be on the New Testament, rather than the Old Testament; most Christians know that the Old Testament was generally perceived as a kind of Part A and the fulfillment of the prophecies of its foretold Saviour as the New Testament Part B. Usually after the Open Air Meeting, the group also 'Witness': that is that they hand out tracts or religious pamphlets and they speak up or 'bear Witness' to their Conversion one on one to anyone interested. This is strongly recommended as essential by our church as a sign you are a true Christian. It also gained a lot of respect in this same group. There would be much 'Amen'-ing, 'Praise the Lord'-ing and 'Hallelujah'-ing as those not directly speaking gave support to those that were. Bibles were prominent, later to be joined with musical instruments, and the atmosphere was one of sincere and serious God business...

On this fateful day, we arrived in time to see some of the gathering stand up and give the story of their experience with the Lord Jesus. All making life-changing claims, they seemed very proud to do so. Then a young man whose face seemed aglow with fervor and zeal proclaimed his experience loudly. He gave his own personal conversion testimony; saying his name was Jim and he spoke of how he used to drink and smoke before he was 'saved' and of how his life had drastically changed since he opened his heart to the Lord. He had 'seen the light'. Indeed, his face seemed to hold some light. Here was this short yet very fit and enthusiastic young man, dressed in an old fashioned check jacket (the first I had seen in a very long time), standing cockily with his Bible under his arms, chest out and shoulders back, holding his ground and speaking very convincingly, loudly and forthrightly of his love for Jesus and that 'Jesus Saves'. I was mightily impressed.

Mary and Stuart were also attending the meeting, looking on with beatific smiles on their faces. I was enthralled with Jim's testimony, and listened to the end. Then there was an appeal to

Naïve Hope

people who wanted to accept Jesus into their lives to attend the church or to simply speak with any one of the members present. As soon as Jim had finished his speech, Mary brought him over to introduce Bob and myself to him. As it later turned out, Bob's grip was *super*-firm when he shook hands with Jim. Possibly a bit too firm for the situation...?

Now, my man Bob was three years older than me, and he was over six feet tall, whilst I was only five foot seven inches. We looked the perfect couple, and *seemed* the perfect couple, yet I was *comparing* him to this unusual and short old-fashioned man...

What was I thinking of to even *do* a comparison on Bob and Jim? What was in my head that I should even *want* to compare this plain Jim with my yummy man?

Bob was a honey, with his motorbike kit on over his lithe fit body; black leather motorbike pants and bomber jacket. Underneath he wore a smart shirt and tie with a modern pullover. He was considerate, progressive, kind, exciting. I still to this day ever refer to him as my 'Greek God', my 'tall, dark and handsome'. With his black hair in a modern cut, penetrating dark eyes and a hint of a moustache, he was an extremely attractive man, had a promising future, and importantly, he swore he loved me to bits. And he showed it!

Ok, so what if not long into our relationship he had spoken to me about getting engaged and in the same conversation about then getting married and of having kids. And what if, at this premature mention of having children together, I felt like I had wanted to run away. At the time I didn't realize that this reaction was related to having seen what had happened with mum and dad, and the spontaneous abortions I had witnessed due to dad's abuses. And I did not as yet realize or recognize that I was shy and frightened at the thought of having children, and fearful of being imprisoned like mum had been. Nor that this was why I felt this discomfort, just that 'I don't want to talk about it just now because ... because... well because...' (I sometimes couldn't really find words nor clarity on my own thoughts and so I would come usually up with a change of subject). Actually, I was *terrified*, but also in denial and not yet emotional smart or savvy enough to recognize this reaction in me, nor of my motivation of what later happened after this revelation by him.

But I digress. Why *am* I wanting to know more about this short and stocky preacher when I have this *lovely* man?

This 'model-preacher' Jim had a short-back-and-sides-cut with a centre parting; a *centre parting*! I didn't know *anyone* who still had that! So totally old fashioned in those days, and not what I usually looked for in a rescuing prince or a hero. Jim must have been almost five foot eight inches if that. Almost an inch taller than me. He was so *short*! I later discovered that he was four years older than me, and from an Irish background. He had a real air of what I thought was confidence about him and somehow looked like he had stepped out of some old-fashioned magazine or paper. Someone I would *never* normally entertain as a boyfriend nor even be attracted to! But what grabbed me, and grab me it did, was the fact of him speaking so loudly and proudly about his faith. I remember thinking to myself 'Now there's a man who *loves God*, who would not harm me, but would protect me, just like he's doing now for his beliefs'.

Hah! Oops, sorry, couldn't help myself. Back to the story...

Bob and Jim thought differently. Or so it seemed to me. Even though Jim was nowhere near as intelligent as Bob, he seemed to have different values and seemed genuine in his expressed desire to help others to 'know' The Lord! And this desire for positive change was more in line with where my own head and heart lay.

It didn't bother me when later I found that Jim had had trouble doing his school-leaving exam. That is why he ended up in the Navy doing menial tasks until he proved himself good with peeling potatoes and scrubbing floors and had worked his way up to assisting with cooking, then assistant cook.

A clear demonstration of his intelligence and ability – or rather, limit of it - and one which went totally over my head! But then I always tended to just accept people as they were...

I was to learn many years later that Jim was also a champion boxer on his ship, and had been taught boxing at school, winning medals and awards. *This* was what gave him his confidence!

Naïve Hope

But it also gave him a direct similarity to an aspect of my father's character... Some subconscious equation here...?

Bob was an intelligent man, already owned a motorbike and had good taste. He was well set for a successful career in engineering and he had so many other things going for him. But I wasn't as influenced as my mother was, or many other women I had heard talking about partners, when it came to being beguiled by money, position or salary, especially not now that I was a Christian and satisfying that sensitive and spiritual side of myself.

I didn't know it then, but soon Bob was about to become toast, and I was about to be roast for a good many years. For when I let Jim begin to fill the role of a 'hero' in my head, I had actually fallen into a false idea; I accepted this false advertising and charm, based on my needs, not based on facts, but on yearnings and perceptions. And hidden in there, my own inherited 'love-equation'...

Don't get me wrong, this Jim was a very sincere, very charming young man that I saw, *on the surface,* but underneath it also later transpired that he was also a very wounded and tormented young man that the church later did very little to help apart from preaching at and sustaining the need for and reliance upon a Jesus, a Saviour. I was still a wide-eyed young Christian convert and wasn't yet old enough or experienced enough in life to be able to recognise any of this.

However, within the dynamics that were taking place, little did I realize just how out of touch I was with who I *really* was, how marred I had been by my childhood, how affected by my lack of nurturing, how little I knew of myself and of what I really required to be happy. So much illusion I had accepted and I sought. Just when does maturity kick in and allow one to see a situation for what it really is? When does one learn to ask oneself the vital questions rather than making excuses or assuming that all will be as one would wish it to be?

I was as wounded as him, in a way, though in an entirely different way... For I was prepared to believe what I saw, prepared to give the benefit of the doubt, prepared to accept and to hope for the good in everyone...

But not everyone is like this.

This picture of a young and virile 'Man of God' (that is what I thought at the time, yessiree) standing up against the world (yes, more church-influence) challenged my own status quo - again.

Not only that, but with the challenge of the church culture of having fun outside of the church frowned upon, and my just beginning to have fun in my young life, things were colliding. Alongside that, I hadn't as yet faced my own unrecognized fears of marriage and children and all of that responsibility. And these new and glorified 'higher' goals of bringing others to a 'better way' and 'life eternal' were creating a form of crisis within me.

Amongst all of this, I think I kind of got lost. Not that I had yet found myself. But I had 'found Jesus', and the experiences that this afforded me seemed to be very real. I now loved Jesus with all my heart, and had dedicated myself to him and his service. My mind saw and set a future in serving the Lord, in making what I saw as positive changes in the world. In helping others get to heaven rather than go to hell. Or so I thought. I thought I was loving God, but I had fallen for a Cause, an idea, an ideal.

My, how our ego can fool us...

At the time that all of this was taking place, the church was beginning its international campaign of Divine Healing. A film was being made by Granada Television which was then televised throughout England, Russia, Europe, and I am not too sure where else. This was part of the push for 'Revival Meetings' by the Throngs of God who were behind our Pentecostal Church. Pastors Parratt and Williams were the two Divine Healing Evangelists, and their normal Sunday night Healing Services had also been included as part of the TV broadcast. They then took their ministry on the road for several weeks, working across Europe and visiting churches in any countries that were interested or who invited them, before they came home weary and triumphant. As for efficacy of their work, well my own mother claimed to have been healed from a variety of diseases, and had been due for operations that were now no longer necessary. Mum had fallen pregnant again after this healing of a septic pelvis, fibroids and other allied problems, and this was to be the last child (thank god!) for mum and dad.

Naïve Hope

Hence the naming of my youngest sibling as Faith for she was born after these healings and without any further problems. But I must confess that I also met a few who claimed that they had not received a long lasting healing. It had obviously worked for some, but not all. But the failures were blamed either upon their faith (or lack of it) or that God wasn't ready to heal them just yet... yes, I know, very obvious neat side-stepping, hey?

In all, there was a lot of excitement at the church, and this was enough to engage Bob's interest, and also fulfilled my increasing curiosity, thirst and need to know more of this new 'faith' that I had adopted. Things had been going along fine for a while, but the pressure not to partake in the things of the world was continual. I had no answer to this yet. Something was to precipitate another crisis...

Fate seems ever interwoven with events that took place around this whole thing. For I can't say it was only one thing that forced events, merely that in retrospect it seemed totally out of my hands. Not that I didn't contribute to the outcome...

An important note on Fate: *Jim went to the same church as Bob and I.*

Yes, he wasn't just a member of the Throngs of God group of churches dotted around Manchester. He was a member of *my* church, *our* church. There he was, at *our* church, involved in all sorts of church things, being so kind to the elderly and seeming to be so gentle and understanding... I didn't even know that. Hadn't seen him when Bob and I had been there. So whilst I was looking the other way, my hidden little mind was now glutton-ing itself and busy making sneaky comparisons...

Adding up two and two doesn't always yield four...

Or in this case, one and two...

This was now another shadow struggling over my status quo.

Something had to break. And break it did. What happened next was a deal-breaker and it ended my relationship with Bob. The scene is still etched clearly on my mind. Wondering about it all again now, it clearly demonstrates how little I knew of myself and of how I functioned at the time.

Not long after the Open Air meeting and our subsequent bumping into Jim at church, Bob and I are sitting in my kitchen, baby-sitting whilst mum and dad are out at one of the church meetings. We are reasonably cosy, and chatting about things in general. He is talking about another concert he was thinking of taking me to, and I am doing a bit of humming and harr-ing over it, dealing with my inner conflict of the guilt over *daring* to enjoy myself whilst others suffer... ridiculous in hindsight, but that was me back then... Wanting yet not recognizing how starved of enjoyment I had been, yet willing to give what little came into my life up to the four winds simply because others did not have what I had... This was the theme, though the reality was that I also had very little compared to what many others had. Did I see this, entertain this? No, I wasn't able to, or I was just too willing – or prone – to accept guilt and to want to help and fix those I thought needed it. Did I think I was better than them? Not that I was or am aware of. Did I think that by helping others, I would be helped? Possibly. Martyr –complex? Cinderella? Probably.

Anyway, feeling somewhat uncomfortable with my inability to truly define the inner conflicts within about what I would like versus what the church would like versus what I thought I should be doing versus what I was actually doing versus where I was heading etc etc and etc, I suddenly blurt something out to Bob.

'Bob, what would you do if Jim asked me out?'

Where did that come from, I thought to myself – he certainly hasn't asked me out, he hasn't even flirted with me. But before I had a chance for further reflection on this, Bob had jumped up and caught me by the hair on the back of my head. Pulling my head back to look at him, his dark eyes flashing into mine, he growls 'What! *When* was this? And just *what* did you say to him?'

Intense! Scary!

I was so surprised. Shocked even. Swallowing quickly, I exclaimed 'No, he hasn't asked me. I was just wondering. Nothing's happened between us.'

Naïve Hope

I was back pedaling, wondering what the hell had caused me to utter such a thing out loud. Bob was the picture of pure ferocious jealousy. I was scared. And shaken.

He gradually loosened his hold, but it wasn't over yet. The top of his well-defined cheekbones now had red blotches, but his eyes were still flashing. I was interrogated further until Bob was satisfied that neither Jim nor I had gone behind his back or done something untoward. Which was fair enough. However...

This incident sealed not only his fate, but mine. For now my ruminations were out in the open, and I had to face them consciously. Had I wanted to see just how much Bob felt for me, find out just how much he cared? Did I want him to step up to some mark that I perceived Jim was at in his spirituality that Bob hadn't yet attained? Was I trying to engender some sort of rivalry? Was I testing Bob? Was my inner conflict forcing some sort of crisis in my relationship?

Whatever was fully behind all of this, what *had* happened was that a dark side of Bob had revealed itself, just as my own unexpected revelation now disclosed my *own* lack of satisfaction with myself and with my perceived function or direction in life. That Bob was capable of jealousy might be great when you wanted to know someone had strong feelings for you, but really scary when they got in a lather about it and loomed darkly over you. In retrospect and in truth, I guess after glimpsing Bob's jealousy, I somehow felt Jim was a softer option in the long run. This view of his sinister jealousy flung me right back into dark memories of violent fights between mum and dad, something I swore that I wanted never to be a part of again. I wanted a happy marriage, a safe marriage, for this was what my soul craved.

Deep in my heart I had vowed that I would never ever let my children go through what I had gone through, that my children would never see what I had seen. I intended never to marry a man who was violent like my father. I had grown up with fear, and I didn't want to be married in fear. And I had felt a moment of fear with Bob.

Frankly Bob didn't think there was much romance to be had in church, anyway. He was fighting a losing battle with my ridiculous martyring programming. As for me, I wasn't really aware of what was happening with me internally either, for in retrospect there was such inner confusion with my ideals, new beliefs, the search for identity and meaning, as well as some real fear of repeating the disaster of my parent's marriage. And I was being seduced by the glamour and glory of missions and causes.

With my ill-thought out and badly timed question about Jim, it's possible that somehow Fate had flipped a coin into the air, and with Bob's response that coin toss had come down tails...

It was over, cracked, done, though the façade still held for a few days as the fall-out filtered through.

I really was now too scared to continue the relationship. Not that I had quite grasped this fully yet, for I was still ruminating over my own faux pas as well as considering this emerging reluctance to see Bob again. I did not have Jim waiting in the wings, in fact I had *no* idea if he had even noticed my existence apart from his politeness and the necessary congregation involvements.

Within days my resistance took hold, and I found excuses not to be available for dates with Bob, until I eventually got the courage to tell him I just couldn't see him anymore. I had had to work out for myself what the reasons were for this difficulty in continuing. Though there had been absolutely nothing happening between Jim and myself, and 'nothing' had continued to happen; it was not about making a swap of partners. One of the real reasons for me now was my fear of Bob and of his possible temper and anger. To make things simpler for him to accept though, I stuck to my guns about my discomfort with the church decrees on worldly enjoyment as the main reason for ending it. And this was the truth, in a truth. For without this, I probably wouldn't have tried Bob's sense of loyalty.

Had I stayed with Bob, this may well have been an entirely different story. However, with that spectre of violence in my history and childhood, and that instant and momentary combustion in him, I think that it is possible that it would have been too much a part of our relationship somewhere. I didn't want to risk it.

Naïve Hope

THE CHURCH

Our Pastor, Pastor Parratt, introduced me to the Youth Group shortly after I was no longer dating Bob. The group met regularly, and helped out with Sunday School classes as well as coming up with ideas and support of and for the youth in the church, and ideas to help the old and infirm.

The Throngs of God Church itself was a stone building with some stain glass windows still in place. Double entry doors at the front, proper wooden congregation benches to sit on, raised platform – in all a lovely church.

Attending this type of Church was in itself a very interesting experience. So very different to the Methodist, Protestant and Church of England Churches that I had attended in my youth. Intent on pomp and ritual, gravity and austerity, they were clearly about duty and God as an unapproachable Being.

But in the Saviour Full Gospel Church, there was singing and whoops of celebration off the congregation. To an onlooker, it may initially seem almost irreverent. Until one was invited to join in and express one's joy and worship of the Lord. Looking back, I think it was some kind of emotional 'fix'. The 'Laugh' workshops of today probably produce the same result, I think. For the sad, lonely, down at luck, and those having a hard time, it was an alternative to being at home alone on a Sunday.

GOD IS LOVE. JESUS SAVES.

These were the most common slogans, sorry, 'messages' on the Church billboard. The common theme was evangelical; 'For God so loved the world that he gave his only begotten Son that whosoever believeth in Him shall not perish but have eternal life'. Neat! God loves you, He sacrificed and died for your sins. Then comes the follower, the hook; 'He that denies me before men, him will I deny before my father which is in heaven' (Matthew). Interpreted as; 'If you don't go round 'confessing' (witnessing) that God died for you, then you will not receive eternal life: You are going to Hell! Heathens now included the 'un-saved; *anyone* who didn't believe in exactly the same way!

The message looks like Love, but feels like a threat. A great marketing concept, built on fear, punishment and reward. There are so many arguments that I have with this concept now, but back then, it all made perfect sense to me. Because IT FIT!

Home life was still confusing, though. It was an emotional morass. Mum and dad were still fighting, although there had been a cessation of enemy engagement for a while after their initial conversion. They were, however, a lot quicker to make up as threats of Hell-Fire became part of the fabric of life. And the Pastor's gifts of the right words at the right time sweet-talked them back from the edge of calamity and seemed to help them sort out to some satisfactory degree (for them) whatever current ripples and rages threatened to again irreversibly upturn the family boat.

I was still the stalwart baby sitter and home assistant. Helping to get the children ready for church and Sunday School on time was now added to my duties and became for me a regular challenge. And when we arrived for the meetings at Throngs of God Church even though the conduct of the people was so very different, I eventually learned to warm to the emotiveness, the feel-good of raised arms, the belting out in voice and verse. Watching some of the coloured people in church doing their little jigs and dances in the aisle at first bemused me, though I eventually gave myself permission to just go with the flow with the occasional foray into the aisle alongside them and their apparent joyousness. I might not be able to jive on the dance floor, but I could jig in the aisle. At least there was some freedom in the singing if there was little in the lesson from the Pastor or one of his 'invited guests' from the wooden eagle-decorated pulpit. Hell-Fire and Salvation were the favourite key preaching subjects. Many 'Amen's and 'Praise the Lord's rang out during sermons and sessions.

When the Pastor noted our family attending together regularly he approached me about being a Youth Group leader. He took me aside and told me that he wanted me to do a Sunday School Teacher course and the Youth Leader's course as he said he could see that I was a very intelligent young woman. He could obviously pick how willing I was to serve God, too. And I guess he could see that the current youth needed some intelligence and spark to encourage them. Little did I realize that he was grooming me not just for the youth leadership, but also as a 'helpmeet' for some other young Christian man. That's how the Bible refers to the wives or women in the Bible who are good and support their men. Hints were continually thrown around about following the Lord and His ways and not the world's or the Devil's ways. Little choice was offered other than to accept their interpretations if you were still 'young in the Lord' and learning about God and His ways. I was also being encouraged by the Pastor in a way I wasn't encouraged by my own father. And I so wanted to be loved and to love. I listened. And I accepted the sugar-coated offer, though in reality, I didn't question and simply obeyed. Duh!

1961 moved into 1962 and I am now totally aligned to the church.

Thinking that I have a bit more autonomy there, at the least I had a bit more peer identity in the Youth Group. That is my reading the sense of 'belonging' that was engendered and the revival of some sort of meaning in my life. I had more freedom from home if what I did was considered by my parents as connected with church activities. Sure there were lots of younger children, but there were a few people my own age. Malcolm was a Jamaican, and was a bit older than me by a few years. It I remember correctly he would have been around twenty. A very handsome young man. Bright eyes, white teeth, friendly smile, easy and soft vocal tone, very fit body though he had a very slight limp, and was always respectful. Ken was stringy and skinny, wore glasses and was a bit nerdy in today's terminology. Around age nineteen I didn't find him appealing in more than a Christian way. Marion was around twenty-two. Helpful though quiet and intense, she was solidly built and favoured wearing kilts and blazers a lot. She had a bit of a turn in her eye and she could be even more serious than I was. For without realizing it I was a very solemn young woman indeed. I took life very seriously indeed, and became more so in Christianity, it being such a life and death issue for one's very soul! It took me twenty years to learn to really laugh and to laugh truly, from the heart and from the belly. But back then, my laugh was a bit shrill, and rather self-conscious.

Jim was also part of the Youth Group. The Pastor would call the older youth to 'progress' meetings whilst engineering reasons for Jim and I to talk together about lessons and ideas for the youth.

Because we would all meet regularly to talk and encourage each other, there became a natural gravitation. After Youth meetings you might find the three of us, Malcolm, Jim and myself, caught up in some Bible topic or adding further details to some possible endeavour or idea. So if I was looking for a similar mind, a friend I could talk to about what interested me then, someone who also seemed to share my sincere desires, it would appear that this seemingly thoughtful and very charming young Irish man would be the closest to it. My love of dancing was now being curtailed and channeled elsewhere. The travel to and from work in the city for six days of the week, together with its intense and tiring physical activity was forcing me to rethink my job. Again. Now that I was so involved with the church, and there were sometimes Saturday church meetings and open-air meetings, I found a job closer to home. This was as an apprentice copy reader at the William Morris Printing Press in Sharston. I excelled at this position, with my love of English coming to the fore again, and the two lovely ancient men that I worked with were gentility and kindness itself, and both had adorable senses of humour. They tolerated my forays into Christianity and managed to curtail my attempts at their conversion without offending me.

Despite the religious changes, there was still not much room for anything else at home other than mum and dad and their disasters and dramas, though these were new dramas now. Together with my own confused teenage hormones of self identity, a longing for romantic love and an emerging subconscious desire to be other than someone else's family slave, it was inevitable I find solace elsewhere. Not least of which was the Pastor's own ideas and suggestions that often brought us in on similar endeavours. Was this part of his plan? (Certainly it was, I say in hindsight. For without me, Jim would have fallen off the Christian wagon very quickly.) Something is definitely building. Though I couldn't yet put my finger just on what was being anticipated... In all 1962 had been a hugely eventful year, with change all around. And still more to come.

1962 THE SCENE IS SET
Marriage and Early Married Life

~ Strange Romance ~ Two Day Countdown ~ The Big Day!
~ Why Jim? ~ Married Life ~ Don't Look ~ Shoulder Shoves
~ Christian Wife ~ Sheila

STRANGE ROMANCE

The very first book that I really read for myself was a Christmas present; *Black Beauty* by Anna Sewell. My imagination was taken a hold of, and I was so enthralled and involved by this story that it gave me cause to forever love and enjoy reading. I was earlier introduced to the story of Cinderella by my parents. And when the Walt Disney classic cartoon production came out, I was totally hooked. In some ways, my life mirrored the poor hard-working and kindly Cinderella, so I nursed a hope that if I was kind and helpful and did what was expected of me, then I too could and would be rewarded in the same way. I will not insult your intelligence on how unlikely this is for most young women today. Sure it's *possible*, but not necessarily *probable*.

But I really did buy it. And what a great way to keep young women in a certain mindset...

It was all about needing someone else to rescue the damsel – true romantic stuff – and would that it was true in some ways. But in so many ways it does not create a realistic expectation or a true picture of real life. Without putting down the dream that there *is* someone for everyone, I wasn't warned of the compromise in my own autonomy or identity I would be making by expecting 'My Prince' to come along to rescue me. This I learned later. I guess in some way, I needed rescuing, for I was pretty much plugged into family, duty, responsibility, service. And I had no concept of rescuing myself. Yet!

Meanwhile, life happens.

Belonging to the church influenced so many areas of my life, and further tempered my attitudes and expectations. The martyr image

I was continually being presented with fed into and further reinforced my own predisposition and survival mode of ensuring others were okay first and further infused other things in life for me. Whereas I had begun enjoying my handsome man, this was offset by guilt or discomfort at enjoying life (or myself) in some way and I think had negated these beginnings of joyful exploration of who I was, and that habitual other side of me again stepped forward to be counted; The Helper. It would also appear that there was still some conflict with being rescued, and now Helper and Cinderella were attempting to live together in the same person, though my rescuer was now the Lord Jesus Christ and the call of service to work for Him. Talk about confusion!

And in my efforts to follow the Lord with such a serious conscience, things were still changing within me. My own search and need to be loved genuinely influenced my decisions. God is Love, so if I love and serve Him, then He will love me and things will naturally sort themselves out. Yes? Trust… That's what I am called to do, isn't it? Belief. Faith. Without any physical evidence, the challenge is to believe anyway. Blind obedience really. Place your trust and hope in the Lord, for He cares for you. With this desire to do good, to follow the Lord genuinely – and completely - I am looking for ways to do so. I do not see the down side, for I am in for the long haul.

The Pastor asks me to help Jim with his Youth Leader assignments, which I do without thinking about. So now when Jim and I both qualify it is almost inevitable that we gravitate together even more as we both function as joint Youth Leaders at Pastor Parratt's personal, persistent and persuasive instigations. We find ourselves visiting the inmates at Strangeways Prison in Manchester together, to bring them words of hope and comfort. And it begins to feel like a purposeful partnership. We seem to be pushed together by circumstances continually, and all connected with work for the Lord.

But I am getting ahead of myself and this was well before we had made any moves toward each other at all. It was mainly what Jim represented that I thought I wanted – the beginning of the belief that men might not be violent, jealous, threatening, selfish or cruel in their relationships or indeed in the world. That some men

Naïve Hope

actually followed love. And a higher cause. And were kind. And had substance... Strange dream indeed!

Anyway, shortly after my seventeenth birthday we had stayed back and talked one night after a Youth meeting.

Neither of us seemed to know what was happening between us. There was a really strange and electrified atmosphere, though it wasn't necessarily charged with lust or romance. But something was going on. It was like something *inevitable* was happening – like magnets being forced or drawn together. We talked about church and beliefs; I was fascinated with his story; we had the same goals – to change the world; we both wanted to be missionaries ....

And somehow that night, we became an item. In fact what actually happened at the end of all our talking, at the end of the turning over of all these ideas, Jim took my hand, looked at me and said 'By Faith, we'll get engaged, and if it's God's Will, we'll get married'. Then he gave me my first kiss. Or should I say, my first peck.

Yup! That's exactly how it happened!

And it all felt so inevitable!

No fireworks, just projected admiration at a man who claimed to be - and whom I then saw - as Standing Up For God and declaring to everyone his change through his conversion. Basically, I had turned everything Over To God, and had fallen into Service again. And along with this I now gave myself permission to Fall In Love with this idea of 'Love'. After all, it was In God's Hands, wasn't it? And this at the ripe old age of seventeen!

By this time I had missed my last bus home, and in those days we had no phone. I could be in serious trouble as I always usually had to be home by 11pm. But my parents knew that I was at church and their faith in me was strong – and they had instructed me well. Part of me wasn't one bit concerned, anyway. Surely they knew they could trust me. (How predictable and well-trained I was, hey? Such a 'good girl'!) So the next thing to do was to find somewhere acceptable to sleep for the night. And so that is how I found myself being ridden to Jim's home on the cross-bar of Jim's bicycle. Not as quick as a motorbike, but I thought that I was safe, and things just felt so ... well ... *'fate'd*....

The bike felt like a Rolls Royce to me... Spring was in the air in Manchester! And I had caught a good dose of it. Maybe Jim had too. We were both so happy about it, even though it had been such a strange and unusual start to our relationship. The lack of initial romantic attraction showed that God was in this, didn't it? (So I thought!) And so now I was in heaven! And right now I am so in love. Or rather I am soo in love with the idea of love! I was glowing! I was going to be with a man who loved God! And who would treat me right. All part of God's Grand Plan. We would do great things together. And I was safe!

My rapture was so great, that even Audrey Hepburn in *A Nun's Story* could not possibly have felt the same dedication to a worthier cause than I did to mine. My religious fervor now encompassed this act of devotion and service to God through marriage. We are on a mission, and it is all part of God's plan.

There is a shift in gear as I come back to reality when we arrive at Jim's home. I am greeted with a shopfront with a dirty window that has an old curtain or sheet hung up directly behind it. We pass boxes and 'things' that have been parked in this area. This was all very strange to me but I put aside my mental chatter about how bizarre it all is, for I am still on a wave of glory, and I focus on my need for shelter, for a place to be safe tonight. I trustingly follow on through after Jim, as he heads toward a closed door. Going through to the back of this shop front, we enter the 'lounge' room of his mum's and dad's home. It was in far worse state than my own home, but who am I to judge?

In this back space, this little tiny area packed with shabby furniture that you have to pick your way around and where a fireplace stands nursing a fading glow is obviously where it all happened, where life was lived with his family. It was small, and crammed up, but clean. An old faded couch and an arm chair near an almost cold fireplace, which Jim got blazing into flames quickly, offers me some comfort and warmth. With a pot of hot strong tea in my hands and a woolly blanket over my knees, I began to feel more settled for the night. It was way past midnight, and I was not used to being out this late, but I manage to find enough padding and cushions to gain some sleep-sitting-up-comfort and tried to get some shut-eye. Jim took himself off upstairs to bed. And I dozed.

Naïve Hope

Early in the morning, I heard creaking, coughing and sighing as his parents moved about and came downstairs into the little side scullery-kitchen off this small room. His mum shuffles through from the stairs and into the kitchen, turning to glance at me as she realizes that I was there. A double-take, then...

Well, the *look* she gave me when she saw me sitting there!

'Who're you?' she challenges in a broad Irish accent and wearing a mighty frown. I introduced myself, explaining that I had missed the last bus and her son had been kind enough to let me stay there for the night. She disappears into the kitchen with a 'harrumph' and the same frown, and when Jim comes downstairs a few minutes later there are raised voices in there. The words 'hussy', 'tart', 'lies', 'bad' were some of the words I heard said. I sit there holding my breath in case I am kicked out onto the street as a result of these exchanges. Eventually Jim emerges from the kitchen with a smile bringing some thick hot toast and a mug of strong tea for me. By this time I was desperate to use the toilet, and had to go through the scullery and past his mum and her frown to get there. And by this time I was also beginning to think that the frown was permanent.

But when she found out the true facts and later got to know me, she was a totally different person toward me. And sure enough I eventually got to see her smile, and to earn respect from her. That is, when she was sober. In all honesty, at these temperate times she had a good and simple heart.

Meantime I had to get the early bus back home and explain my lack of presence to my own parents. And this unreal story of our engagement.

Oh boy!

My face glowed as I told mum and dad of the events of the previous evening... I was in love. Well I was in love *with* love! Actually, with the *idea* of love! *Though I didn't realize that then.* It was enough for me that I was engaged to a man of God and I had a future that was in line with my inner calling. Though there were some restrained congratulations, and a few praising the Lords, there was also a bit of a stunned atmosphere as my parents began to come to terms with a couple of things. I would be getting married and leaving home; no more of Marni's wages. I was marrying a Christian; mum was jealous. I would be moving closer to Jim's parents; no more free baby-sitting for them. Also no more fight refereeing. No more a few things. But how could they argue with what the Pastor was encouraging and what God was allowing? Debate on the subject was silenced, there was no parental counseling and they accepted what they saw as inevitable, even though Jim and I hardly knew each other...

In all, Jim and I had only actually known each other for just a few months, though in a way it felt like years.

Like every other young girl growing up at that time, I automatically assumed that at some stage I would get married and have my own family. That was also what the glossy magazines that were circulating were full of, and a natural part of a young girl's inner world. It was the practice, and it was expected. Though I had absolutely no idea as to how this would come about. I knew at least that there would be an engagement first.

And in my heart I believed in romance. I certainly wanted love; I wanted to be loved and to give love. In those days a popular song was called 'Love and Marriage' and the lyrics went like this: 'Love and marriage go together like a horse and carriage ... you can't have one without the other.' But I hadn't obsessed about it, even though I would sometimes imagine myself being rescued at some stage by a good looking man who would be devoted to me and care for me. And I for him. Usually after a difficult day or a huge family row!

I had still to learn that romance and marriage and being rescued were not necessarily as I thought they were. Nor a natural progression in life. And right now I was being challenged as my previous understanding and expectations of all the normal rituals of going steady, courting, delighting in dating, having fun and being adored were turned upside down as I struggled to serve God in this new situation.

Reflecting on this very unusual form of proposal, and on what later eventuated as my wedding, I compare myself with the young girls and women of today who appear to obsess over it all. Serious and purposeful Planning seems to begin from during secondary school.

Naïve Hope

Dreaming about 'the dress' seems to occupy so much mind and time. So many women have planned the day before working out the sort of man they want to marry. They dream and design their wedding dress and some even their engagement and wedding rings. I am amazed that there is so much focus on the actual event, yet so little on *what* being married is really about and on *who* they will marry. I can't remember obsessing over the ceremony like this, though I do remember in school writing my name as Mrs. Saunders over and over when I had a crush on a boy in my class who never even noticed me...

I had seen getting married as somewhere in the distant future and not of immediate consequence, and anyway, I had been too caught up in events happening around me and in the church and in what my parents would say or do. Interestingly, though, as it turned out, both the type of wedding I had and the kind of man I married were both very ordinary - if not outright disasters - so I truly cannot claim to be an authority on this really, can I?

In due course, we were engaged for only four months, having gotten engaged in the April, just days after my seventeenth birthday. The ring came a couple of weeks after Jim's proposal, when he took me shopping to the local pawn shops for something affordable. Apparently, he wasn't well off. But I knew that already, didn't I? After all, I had taken note of mum's conversations with other wives – and that she had married for love and not for money. Not that I realized that this repeated phrase had taken root in my subconscious. I thought this *was* love.

Where did I hear the phrase, 'Align yourself with a God-fearing man and (you can) change the world'? No idea. But this seemed to be an overriding theme. Did it matter that Jim wasn't as gushing himself, as abandoned as myself, in expression of our future mission? Did he say anything to cause any doubt about his commitment to this proposal? No.

So just what did dating young Christians do that was acceptable without doing the things of the world? Reading the Bible and praying together was a top priority, and doing charitable things like visiting and ministering to others together. This had a very different flavor than any other dating that I had done before. Yet I somehow simply accepted it. We were all expected to tithe (and we did) which meant that a tenth of our earnings went to the church, so there wasn't much to spend on treats and entertainment anyway. And weren't we supposed to put aside the 'pleasures of the flesh' anyway? I had chosen a road less travelled. And my hope in the future was placed in the hands of the Lord. Yes, 'Jesus Saves'...

The wedding would take place at some reasonably suitable time in the future. But within a month we were setting the date for the August. This was because we were advised or rather ultimated by the Pastor to get married quickly; or be refused the breaking of the bread (Holy Communion) at church. Why was this?

Well, what happened was that during our engagement I slept with Jim - before marriage. There was no lust or real romance involved, no seduction, no teasing or leading on; after all, the closest to romance I ever got from him was him buying me a cup of coffee after us both visiting the prisoners in Strangeways Prison one day – for Christians didn't have fun. Or do Dinners Out. Or go dancing or to the movies.

So how did it happen?

One day, or rather one night, Jim had attended a Prayer Meeting with my parents and a couple of other Christians at my home in Wythenshawe. For some reason it went on longer than usual, and so he missed his bus home. We made up a make-shift bed for the night in front of the fireplace downstairs. After saying 'Goodnight' I trotted upstairs after mum and dad. However, late cups of tea brought on a call of nature... Now the toilet is downstairs, and one has to pass through the living room to get to it.

So coming downstairs I had to walk past Jim as he lay in front of the low burning fire. It flickered on his face and he smiled at me. I whisperingly explained that I had to go out the back, and was sorry for disturbing him. He was fine with that, but having trouble falling asleep. When I came back from the toilet out the back I went to open the hall door to go back upstairs to bed. I turned to see him pick up his Bible to read it again by the firelight. So I thought I would give him a kiss goodnight.

Naïve Hope

I could not resist kneeling down to do so, and as I did so, he moved over to allow me to share some part of his bedding. There was no thought in my head of anything other than to make him feel comfortable and to share my admiration with him. Then Jim gently pulls me down to lie alongside him and kisses me more deeply. Still being somewhat naïve in this type of worldly matter (or possible consequences), yet it feeling so perfectly natural in light of the life of service we were contemplating together, it was just an organic development and consequence that I lay down beside him for a hug, and from that it was then such a natural step to progress to give myself to him that night. I didn't seduce him, but neither did he force me. It simply felt natural and inevitable. No fireworks, not a great experience, just an act of love and compliance. And I had no idea as yet of the pleasure that a woman could experience, not for a few more years...

I had somehow felt that our relationship was sealed and that this was the natural way of things. And so we had made love. For that is what it was. Not sex, just love. Lovemaking to me was a spiritual and a heart experience. Later I came to realize that for some sex is purely an earthy need, for some even a dirty deed, but I could not approach it like that. I did not contemplate any sense of shame as this act together had simply unfolded. I already had begun to see my life as entwined with his. Bigger picture visions had taken over. I had imagined us as missionaries together, and this seemed to be the way the Lord had planned it. It seemed natural to acknowledge what we had before God. I take my leave and go back to bed, acknowledging God's Hand in my life.

We were engaged. We were betrothed. This was my duty and path, and if it wasn't God's Will He would *surely* let us know. And we had all recently been reading the writings of Solomon in the Bible, on how he treasured and cherished his Beloved. Moving stuff!

In the morning Jim returns home and all appears as normal, with me convinced that something like that wouldn't have happened if God wasn't in this with us.

But the next thing I know is that at the next church service the Pastor calls us both over and asks us to stay behind after the congregation starts to move off for home. I had no idea what this was about and so was not prepared for what was to happen next. Apparently, without saying a word about it to me, Jim had been to see the Pastor in order to 'confess' to him about our 'carnality'.

Not a word to me about this, just Jim taking it upon himself to go to the Pastor and tell him what had happened. To me it hadn't felt wrong. But apparently it *was* wrong. Even though we were engaged – see – 'I have this ring to prove it!'

'No! Not good enough. You must cease, or get married immediately, or I will have to insist you no longer receive the bread and wine at church. And if you disobey you will be out, excommunicated. You will not be welcome in this church again.' Thus spake and decreed Pastor Parratt, our minister. This was very black and white to him, and was definitely 'not allowed'.

A word aside here; this man was so ignorant of correct counsel for young couples. Not only that, he was not even aware of the goings on amongst his own family. For your information and possible interest, the Pastor's own son later had an affair and subsequently left his wife for another church-going woman (who was in fact my sister Joan, then calling herself Joanne). She seduced the Pastor's son thus engineering his divorce. Meanwhile Jim's Best Man, who was the Pastor's own son-in-law, was later found guilty of sexual predatory actions causing the failure of his own marriage and his eviction from the church. But not before he had corrupted several young minds. All this came out later, though I find it all so very Ironic now. However, at this time Jim's total acceptance of the Pastor's decree was the over-rider – and though I felt it unrealistic, I gave in to the church's teachings and the inevitable 'moral' demands. And the Bible statements quoted state clearly that there was to be no sex before marriage. I thought God lived in my heart and showed me the way, but obviously not so...

Well.

The pressure and guilt within and from Jim set things in stone. Even though I was ok with not sleeping with Jim again, I could not one hundred percent guarantee that this would not ever happen, and as I had already now committed myself to Jim I felt that this *must* be the *right* thing to do. After all, the Pastor was very clear that in order to stay in God's Grace we had to follow his instructions. I did not want to undertake the bread and wine during the communion service if it was considered a sin or a lie, nor did I want ex-communication, but in my heart of hearts I truly could not understand what all the fuss was about. A part of me heard that one shouldn't sleep with someone before marriage and I could see the point. Indeed I had been brought up this way by my parents, always encouraged to hold on to my Virtue until after marriage. But the connection had felt so natural. However, who was I to argue? What did I really know of these things? And as Youth Leaders it is up to us to set good examples to others and refrain and resist 'sin and temptation' by getting married, and as soon as possible.

Did I have any preconceptions as to the kind of man I would eventually marry? Well, it was too far off in the distant future and all I had considered so far was that I wanted someone who wouldn't beat me like mum got beaten. And that he would be faithful. I guess I *hoped* he would be handsome, romantic, love dancing, be kind. Apart from these vague and random thoughts, the answer really would be 'No'. Did I have any guidelines as to the appropriate choice of partner, ideas as to the best potential qualities for success in marriage? NO. Not a clue! Never been discussed! No talks, support, suggestions, advice. I guess mainly because of the *cult*-ivating (yes, that hyphen is deliberate) by the church of my parents and myself, my conscience listened to what was required of me and then unquestioningly handed over.

A date had to be sourced to accomplish the shift from 'sin' to acceptable sex between committed partners in marriage.

The only date that we could see as a possible was in the August, as we had already booked and paid a deposit for the Youth Convention in Scotland alongside the rest of the church Youth. Strained finances meant that we could not afford anything else for another year or so. Could we last out that long working in such close proximity with each other? Neither of us was sure that we could. So this would have to be it, this trip would have to double as our honeymoon. Purely an exercise in expediency and expenditure this was the only way we could mark the nuptials presently.

So, still reeling in confusion from the shame attached to an act of love and giving, and the Pastor's insistent pressure, *and* Jim's ongoing guilt, the plans were now laid which naturally involved my parents.

After all, we had only been together for a short time, and here we were - engaged in the April and planning our wedding in the August. Almost but not quite a Shotgun Wedding; though without the Shot. For I certainly wasn't pregnant. And we hadn't slept together since that embarrassing confession.

Now another interesting dynamic began to emerge. When mum knew of the looming and hurried date of the wedding, she became somewhat testy with me. I think she began to see that I was escaping the prison she saw herself in, and she became caught up in jealousy that I had a *Christian* man from the very *start* of my marriage, whereas she had been through the storms of violence and infidelity with dad, a 'worldly' man, from the very beginning of *her* marriage. This attitude slowly reared its head through her snide remarks.

In effect, I really didn't get the real support that I needed from her, nor from dad. For I was not really offered any other choices to the Pastor's dictates, nor later, even when violence reared its head in my own marriage. One would have thought there would have been some education or advice from either one or the other of my parents on what to look for in the choice of a marriage partner. That I would have been wised-up in some way. The only things I heard when growing up were echoed by a popular song at the time: 'Love and marriage go together like a horse and carriage, you can't have one without the other' and also as I mentioned mum often said to me that it's better to 'Marry for love and not for money'. Oh, I remember another one: 'Can't live with them, can't live without them'. Charming, hey?

But one also has to remember the times in which we were living; some had been impacted long-term by the lacks and deprivations experienced during the Great Depression and World War Two. This had brought a change in how people courted and in decisions regarding marriage that were to last for many years. Many people had been wounded with the brutality and deprivations of wartime,

Naïve Hope

many good and upstanding young men had gone to fight for their country and their families and they did not return. Often common sense had taken a back seat in the face of a chance at some sort of romantic happiness. Leastways this is an excuse I give my parents for their abysmal lack in proper parental guidance with ideas as to what to look for to make a good marriage. If they had have been on the case, they might have seen things I hadn't, and helped to point me in the right direction or ask the right questions. But that didn't happen – and in truth I don't really know if they would have known what to say anyway.

And so things were arranged, and on a shoe-string budget, we used the planned upcoming Youth Convention Week away as our honeymoon. Not an ideal way to plan one's wedding, but my life was already so different to so many of my old school chums and friends there was no way that I could gauge it differently. I went along with it all. I thought I was Doing The Right Thing. And had no one really to talk to about all of this, no other ideas or comparisons to measure it against, nor any real counsel from mum and dad. And after all, I was being called to a life of sacrifice, wasn't I? Whether it was in darkest Africa or here in England, my life was dedicated to doing God's Will. And if I really was going to be a missionary alongside Jim, as we had talked about with the Pastor, then it wasn't about the trimmings, was it?

Looking back, I seemed to be living a strange kind of life, but then my life had felt strange for many, many years. Not at all as I had ever imagined it, whenever I had dared to imagine it. There was little romance, and our times together were mainly spent in Bible study, prayer or some sort of church activity. I hadn't really 'traveled' apart from school day excursions and my time at the convalescent home. As the dutiful daughter, I had towed the line with my family obligations, and knew very little of how a *happy* marriage was conducted.

Most of my previous personal expectations on life had proved fruitless, so I simply lived it as it happened. For wasn't I placing myself in God's hands, and wasn't I promised that He cared for me? Maybe this was the answer to life, the answer for *my* life, to what it was all about; to follow the exhortations in the Bible, to follow Him and do the Right Thing, to seek that which is holy and good and to seek the best and do it. Right now I am taking this huge step and thinking that I am doing it because that is what God wants. And for me at that time, that seemed to be the way...

'Delight thyself also in the Lord and He shall give thee the desires of thine heart.'

I didn't fully know the desires of my own heart yet, even though I probably thought that I did, but having a man that I could share life with, my faith in God with and help others with was a pretty good start... I didn't know what would happen next, what would happen after the honeymoon, except to trust and serve God as best I could. After all, God had sacrificed for us. It was now expected that we sacrifice for Him. 'Not my will, but Thy Will be done.'

On a practical level, Jim had secured a flat above a shop just two doors away from his mum and dad. It was a corner position on a bus route, and as he said, 'Mum and dad can keep an eye on you,' though exactly what that meant at that time, I wasn't really sure. So I settled to the thought that they could or would assist me if I needed any help. I could not as yet imagine what sort of help I would need but I bowed to his more mature years. It was obvious that in some ways things would change when I got married. I had absolutely no idea and no preparation for how it would really be. And didn't think to ask anyone... Well, I guess most people don't really know either, do they?

However, the next phase on the course of my life is now set. The wheels are turning. This is the start of a new adventure. I step forward again in faith, and I engage Hope to see me through.

Two Day Countdown

Time moves us forward inevitably and speedily to our August marriage rendezvous. And as some can vouch, the closer it gets to the inevitable, the more inevitably a person is revealed...

What I was totally unaware of was this man's capacity for anger. And also, if I am totally honest here, my own martyring tendency - again.

I had learned to read my dad's anger, and knew when to watch for thumps and blows, which generally I did, though I had been caught

Naïve Hope

out a few times when my sense of injustice caused me to dare to bravely confront him on behalf of mum or a sibling. But with their religious conversion, I had hoped we could be done with all of the violence that we had previously experienced as children. Things had shifted, certainly. But old habits die hard and they began to re-emerge in a different version. Arguments were now around the Bible, and who was being obedient or forgiving or loving or some such... There was less violence, but it hadn't disappeared from the family's communication vocabulary just yet. However and interestingly, the words 'Hypocrite' and 'Sin' together with the odd Bible quote now joined the usual verbal slander and array of vocal slings at certain choice moments.

Meanwhile, plans have been laid for the wedding, arrangements made, notices published and all the other things needful for our marriage had somehow been conjured up out of thin air. Fragile, bare-boned, on a budget, but at least the absolute essentials had been organised. The same pawnbroker had a secondhand wedding ring at a price we could just afford, and a further promise was made by Jim to renew my tiny engagement ring when it was financially possible. Dress, check. Ring, check. Church, check. And so the essential short list went.

Except that there was still so little that we knew about each other. He was from a totally different background to me, and I was so very naïve that I didn't consider any of this. I thought God's Love would solve all our problems!

What was life with this man going to be like? We had only just starting to talk about things other than the necessities required in our getting married. And day shortly before our set date, I was introduced to a blaze of Jim's latent anger and his potential for unreasonableness. For the first time I had a warning of what life was really going to be like. Just two days before we are due to exchange our vows at the altar.. Despite this I also didn't yet realize just how impelled I felt to go through with this, and just how set-up on some level that this marriage was...

This is what happened - We are walking to the bus stop one rainy night after church, and the rain had momentarily stopped. The glow of zeal that had been present during the church service had disappeared from his face, the enthusiasm I had mistaken as the 'light of God' was now replaced by ill-humour, scowls and contrariness.

He had his Bible tucked under his arm as usual - his Bible was his pride and joy – a big deal and fuss was made at our church in those days about the sort of Bible you had, and the chosen version spoke volumes about what you did and didn't believe and respect. It was like comparing cars, a kind of competition, though some would probably deny that. Much was made about interpretations, and so Jim's chosen Bible was a large King James Version which was highly recommended by the Pastor as *the* one being closest to the truth of interpretation. It had gold leaf along the edges, and was bound in leather. He had saved up to buy this treasure, and he would tuck it under his arm to show what he believed in. Like a badge or a uniform – Soldier of Christ type of thing. He rarely went anywhere without it unless he was going to work.

Jim totally lost his cool. Discussing the imminent arrangements we were talking about what would happen after we got married, and Jim was waxing strong about where I would work. I was surprised to learn that immediately after I returned back from the 'honeymoon' I would now be expected to give up my current job in Sharston in order to work near him. In fact Jim wanted me to work in the *same place* as him. He was actually telling me *where* I could work, and what sort of job I had to look for. This was totally unexpected to me and I was so surprised and amazed that I *dared* to question him about it.

That was when he tossed a hissy-fit, and he actually *threw* his Bible on the road with a violent slam, and simply stormed off, leaving it there!

Wow! I was stunned.

Well his Bible, his pride and joy was on the path, in the rain and dirt, having flung-fallen open at a page. He had stormed off, and would not respond to my calls to him to come back. He had yelled something like 'Then the wedding is off'.

I was sad, but I also calmly thought that that was that. I didn't feel huge loss, just some sadness and acceptance. I now wonder if I

Naïve Hope

wasn't a bit relieved, but cannot truly remember feeling that, just feeling a bit numb and resigned. Probably still stunned that he had turned on me like this and showed such *anger,* such volatility.

Little did I know that this was a message to me, though I couldn't see it then. A warning and a sample of what was to come, a peep through the chink in the curtains that surrounded this man. A sign-post to say 'Falling Rocks Ahead, Drive Slow' kind of warning. I had no concept of life's sign-posts as yet, unfortunately...

But I couldn't just leave his Bible sitting there in the rain. Could I?

Well, actually I could, and really I should have. It was his action, and therefore his responsibility. But like an idiot, though I thought I was being respectful, I picked it up and wiped it off. And I needed to get it back to him, because I couldn't leave it there in the rain. Could I? And I didn't want to take it home with me. There was only one solution to not taking it with me... I walked round to his mum's house and knocked on the door. I just wanted to hand it in to her for him for when he got home. And go.

But she wouldn't take it off me, and she told me to come inside. I didn't want to, but she refused to take the Bible off me and kept insisting that I come in out of the rain. I had resigned myself to the wedding not going ahead by this time, and I simply wanted to go home. But she suddenly disappears and I wonder what on earth to do next; do I leave the Bible on the floor here and simply leave? I am not given to rudeness, so I am considering how I can drop this off and exit quickly. The next thing I know Jim comes out and takes the Bible off me and starts to apologise profusely to me. In retrospect, I think maybe his mum had asked him what had happened, and he had told her something, and so she had made him apologise.

Somewhere inside I felt a bit numb toward him, and I still didn't realize that I had just had a huge signal, a mega warning regarding the volatility of this guy, though his mum just kept saying 'wedding nerves'. And when I got back home and relayed the story to mum she said the same thing. Despite my experience with dad, and some ability to read him to some degree, Jim was a different fish, and kept a lot hidden; I didn't yet know how to read his signals, so I had missed what this incident was really telling me.

You know, I am so glad that I am revisiting these events and detailing these things because now I can see them all in a different light. I can understand more clearly as to what was going on when I got married. How events kind of stacked up to create what was created.

In some way I had complied, obeyed, submitted. I had passed (or failed, depending on how you look at it) the test of picking up after him – if this was indeed a test to see just how far he could go, or even, of how far I would go. Unfortunately, this was to become a template for our lives together. Though with arrangements made, social expectations, family reputation and subtle religious pressure highlighting the forthcoming nuptials, (*and* there being no apparent or acknowledged reason why his behavior should affect the proceedings,) I allowed my attention to be diverted again to all that was in motion, and all of the effort from others that had been involved to get to this point. After all, hadn't mum made herself a new outfit for the occasion, hadn't she made my sisters Tina and Joan bridesmaid dresses, hadn't I been given some decent shop-bought outfits for my 'honeymoon' passed on by my chief bridesmaid, Mary? Don't get me wrong, I was sooo grateful, for considering our financial situation, this was the best we could do. The subtle messages I got from those around me was all about the effort and sacrifice that people were making on my behalf so that this day was possible for me. I couldn't just spurn or discount that because of a *little hiccup*, could I?

The overriding sense was to just get on with it. Somehow, I managed to get myself together, and bury this blemish on the start to our new life together. Any moments of inner question or doubt were met with a hope and trust that this was a one-off and that it was only a case of jitters or nerves.

And after all, wasn't God In Charge?

> *Trust and Obey*
> *For there's no other way*
> *To be happy in Jesus*
> *Than to Trust and Obey*
> Revival Hymn

Naïve Hope

What I do not yet realize is that this has been destined. My sense of inevitability is being played out. Short of being run over by a bus, this marriage will go ahead. When there is unfinished business on any level, events can conspire to allow for them to be replayed in order to be finished.

THE BIG DAY!

The Big Day. *No going back now.* And so it was.

Let me be clear here that the engagement ring, wedding ring and wedding dress were all second-hand. Interesting portend or not? Hmm.

As organized, the wedding took place at our usual family place of worship, Throngs of God Church in Old Trafford. And Pastor Parratt performed the rites.

And the friends that had assisted in – or rather paved the way for - Jim's conversion, Mary and Stuart, were naturally involved. Naturally; because they were significant in Jim's joining the church and helpful in some of the wedding support. Mary was my bridesmaid, and I was wearing her Wedding Dress which she had graciously given me as we were both the same slim fit. Someone else bought flowers for the church. Someone else used their Kodak camera and took some pictures to mark the occasion. I was up late the night before putting ringlets into my sisters' hair, and up early the following day to take them out and dress them. I was the only one available to do it, and had to rush to get dressed myself.

There was no taking it easy, no relaxing breakfast for me, none of me being the centre of attention and being pampered as is the standard of today. No help for me. But I was only seventeen and so very naïve. In a way, I didn't expect help anyway, for I didn't really know what happened for others getting married. This was the first wedding I had been a part of.

Getting married on a shoestring, it appears that we had somehow managed all of the essentials. And mum had been busy preparing for what was to follow in way of celebration - a grand At-Home Reception consisting of a few home-made sandwiches and cakes for the select wedding party of Jim's mum & his siblings and our family. And that was it! No bridal showers, no hen's night, no reveling or dreaming. Just sheer practicality. One step up from mum's Registry Office wedding.

The wedding vows were the time-old ones, there was no other option given, and when I had enquired about it I was told that this was the Pentecostal position and it was promptly backed up with biblical quotes.

At the altar, Jim and I duly spoke the ancient verses:

> *I, ___, take thee, ___, to be my wedded husband/wife, to have and to hold, from this day forward, for better, for worse, for richer, for poorer, in sickness and in health, to love, honour and* cherish/ obey, *till death do us part, forsaking all others and cleaving only unto thee, according to God's holy ordinance; and thereto I pledge thee my troth*

Note the interesting difference in our promises:

> *The Bride: to Love, Honour and* Obey
>
> *The Groom: to Love, Honour and* Cherish

Little was I to know that many years later I would greatly regret these words, committing me as they did to this doomed relationship. For many years, I had no other thought than to be completely faithful to that which I had promised. I meant my vows and took them seriously.

I think we both did at the time. I was by now well accustomed to doing my duty. Though the interpretation of my wedding vows into real life situations just might have been a bit unclear.

After the ceremony, Kodak Brownie pictures were taken, with several interesting ones showing Jim holding my free arm, the one not holding my flowers, being gripped between both his hands. I do remember I hardly moved from the steps of the church because of his hold on me. But at the time, I just accepted it. This was all new to me after all. The Pastor came up and beamingly placed both of his hands on each of our shoulders, saying how pleased he was and how blessed we were. At the time, I thought so too, being caught up in the emotion of the day and the meaning and intent of

Naïve Hope

my commitment. After all, hadn't he said from the pulpit on our wedding day that he saw great things ahead for us both?

It was an interesting drive up to the Youth Convention immediately after the ceremony and after I had taken a quick bite of sandwich. Jim and I travelled with the Youth Group as arranged, taking a ribbing from them on our being just married. But I was still in a bit of a daze and still adjusting to all that had happened. It had been a hectic day from the very start, and I hadn't had a chance to catch my breath yet.

The bus was an open affair, seats set on either side of the aisle in sets of two so that it was four across. Jim and I had chosen front seats, being the stars so to speak of the day. And I also needed to be near the front so I could see where we were going as I sometimes got travel sick. This was going to be a long drive, so best not take any chances. I got up momentarily from my seat because a friend had called me to a couple of seats behind. However, when I got back to my seat next to Jim, I could no longer sit next to him.

This was because one girl, who was around nineteen years old and should have known better, had now begun to make a general nuisance of herself. Her name was Lillian, and she kept sitting on Jim's lap, throwing her arms around his neck and taking up the whole two seats in this way. Jim didn't seem to have any problem with any of this and even appeared to be in control generally; he totally allowed this, joking about it, and I couldn't understand why he did.

I asked her not to, and if she wouldn't mind moving, but *I* was the one who was told off by Jim for not being *kind* to her! I wasn't being a prima donna, I wasn't trying to take any kudos, nor was I demanding any so-called rights. But I later realized why I was so upset with this. After all, this was my *wedding day*, for crying out loud!

And another portend on what I had to contend with later, though I successfully swallowed this incident down under the Christian heading 'be kind...' and 'do unto others...'; For I did not as yet see the double standards set by some men, little recognizing misogyny when I came across it.

However, this incident was glossed over by Jim, and we embarked on our married life. The wedding night was nothing special, though I did view it through starry eyes, still. We had much to learn about sex and love-making, and I approached it as an act of loving service. For hadn't I scored an upright and God-fearing Christian man?

There were often good days early on, but as I think back there was still a bit of a shadow over things, though I tended to always be doing my best to make things work, make things right, make things better. It sometimes felt like something else was missing, but I wasn't sure what. Bible reading and praying gave me temporary space and peace and I would often think that it was something that I was failing to do or to be, so I applied myself to being or doing better. Jim was trying too in his own way. But it began to become clear to me that he was just as testy as dad could be. Were all men like this? Probably.

Though if you ask me that same question now you would get a quite different answer.

Why Jim?

Why did I end up getting married to this guy? How come this had happened? Someone who would never have been on my partner or romance radar? I think by now you are getting a sense of some of the components that became part of the mosaic in this union.

Time has given me further insights into it all. And it wasn't just about me, for there were other factors besides my own inner misunderstood or immature floundering. So just what else propelled me into this romance-less and dutiful liaison? Apart from being guilt-ed or manoeuvred into it by the Pastor, you mean? Which you possibly may have gathered from what you have read so far. Good question!

Well I have explained how we kind of ended up working with the youth together. But I have some further reflections to add.

Apart from the fact that when Jim asked me, if you can call it asking, the whole proposition of marriage had been dependent on

God's Will-ingness – yes, I know, don't say it, letting someone else decide is irresponsible.

At the time it had been more of a statement from Jim than a request or even any sort of question.

'If it is God's Will we will get married.'

God seemed so real to me, and following God's Will so important... there seemed no question in my mind that if it wasn't God's will, then it would *not* go ahead anyway. My belief in God was so real that some part of me figured that God would stop it if it wasn't meant to be. The engineering by the Pastor to bring us together wasn't at all apparent to me at that time. Not till much much later. My own conscious overriding thought seemed to be the huge difference between Jim and other boys I had known who had felt to me like they were trying to get into my pants and sweet talk me. The picture that Jim presented was all about helping others, talking about God, standing up for the right and the good. This appealed to the altruistic side of me and was such a relief for me to not to have to fight overt sexual attention. Programming to protect my 'virtue' had begun early, not that my parents had necessarily adhered to the same practice, but rather that they had discouraged me from any promiscuity...

I think I also subconsciously sensed the little-boy-lost in Jim, and felt his need and that I could help him. Little did I realize how damaged he was and that this was to be a challenge way beyond me.

A choice of partner is often based not just on present situations, choices and standards alone. It can sometimes be based on things that we are totally unaware of. Such as what we experienced growing up. How our parents were together, with each other. Psychological and emotional dynamics and experiences seen and lived through. There are so many things that drive us in our decisions. That is until we change – often consciously - what can only be described as our programming and patterning.

Right now, and not starting at any particular place, I am taking a moment here to examine my understandings of life back then, and of what may have contributed to my getting married at that time and with that particular man. It was such a mixture of things. Jim had a presence, a charisma of sorts which was obvious when I first saw him in the park. He had a great deal of Irish charm, a very great deal. Most Irish, it seems, have been blessed (or cursed) with a kiss of the Blarney... He could be very attentive and appear very understanding when he wanted to, needed to or chose to. So much so, that later people could not entertain that he might be anything other than who he presented himself to be. This aspect became apparent the first time I sought help after he had first started abusing me. They couldn't conceive that he could be like that. Just like I initially couldn't see it.

But underneath this charm and apparent calm, he was prey to very deep emotions and erratic feelings. His zeal for the church had entranced me and seemed to match my own commitment to a higher cause. (This spiritual stuff could get quite heady for me at times.) His emotional neediness was matched by my own needing to be needed, and in some way, I somehow took on the role not only of fiancé then wife, but also of nurturer and mother. To him!

I guess I was used to this role, and so it was an unrecognized yet natural progression. I must confess that I was not aware of how married life was supposed to play out. I knew my parents had a volatile relationship - though in some ways they were making attempts to change that - and I guess I might have idealistically maintained a focus on those times when they were romantic together and were in happier minds. I thought in some way that this was what was possible. This was the picture that I often presented myself with in the silences after the rows... And I thought that as I had married someone who was interested in being the best he could be that he would be a good man. A kind of kaleidoscope of all of dad's good bits, and the Pastor's good bits without dad's crap or anger and violence etc. After all I had chosen a totally different man than my mother had, hadn't I?

Well, *hadn't I?*

I think my vision of our future together was a picture of peace, caring, respect, joint mission and understanding, and a willingness to discover God's plans for us together. In my mind I thought this was real love as opposed to romantic love, that I would be taken

Naïve Hope

Naïve Hope

care of, and that what I had to give would be honoured, used correctly, and would be effective. I somehow assumed that this was the way it would be for me, despite what I had seen to the contrary growing up. Like most young people, I guess I thought I could do it better than my parents, avoid the same mistakes... I also thought our joining together might be a bit *Different* as we had come together through The Lord or rather through circumstances that *could* be read as having the Lord's Hand upon them. Not very realistic, but then I *was* only seventeen. And naïve and gullible, giving others the benefit of the doubt, just as I would wish them to give the same to me.

As I write this, it is through hindsight that I can now add further understandings on how such a pair of mismatched people could be coupled like this. Sure the church had a lot to do with it, the Pastor in particular. So did my own immaturity and inexperience, for I was really far too young to realize fully what I was doing, and hadn't had a lot of experience with boys, even though I had had a couple of boyfriends. This was in the days when seeing a boy was a matter of holding hands, an exchange of addresses first, and of boys coming to the house to ask permission to take you out, then of writing letters to make arrangements for a Date; and so prospective friends were safely vetted to some degree. Not only that, but this was in the day when dating whilst still at school tended to be less permissive than they seem to be in current times. Dating was a much more transparent affair than it is today, leastways this was *my* experience.

So what other components contributed to a situation like this one; an unusual proposal that might possibly and probably not have occurred like this in today's western world? Where a deal was struck even before the first kiss had been exchanged? Well back then my parents had come through a major war as well as a major Depression. These experiences had coloured entire generations. Traditional methods of courtship were changing. War alters things, for Death can become a reality. During war, there is no guarantee of time, or of life. Dad had been billeted in Eritrea in the Middle East training commandos during the Second World War, so he got to see others leave and not come back. Mum had been working on munitions, and had lived through some of the bombings in Liverpool. This had changed how many met a potential partner, and when you did meet a likely someone, you grasped at the chance of love – you celebrated *life*. If you waited, you missed out. Many conventions were forsaken. There was little time for 'courting', for checking of compatibilities, for the meeting of prospective future parents, for being aware of and pursuing future prospects – if you loved someone, if you felt that chemistry, then you went for it – a *Get Love Where You Can* mentality still tended to prevail. Consequently, there was probably a general pervasive lack of inability for accurate discernment in making the best or most appropriate choices when it came to choosing partners, or in making a wise decision regarding love. Particularly amongst the ordinary people. Spouses that had made disastrous matches generally simply stayed married because that was what was done back then.

As regards the criteria for my own choice of partner, I didn't receive much instruction on what made a Good Match. Well actually, not any. Further - because of the family's religious conversion experience - there was a general additional blindness in operation that limited true clarity; after all, wasn't this the Jimmy that preached in the parks and gardens? Then he must be alright for he has given everything up for God and loves God. This proves that he has a pure heart then, doesn't it? Well, actually no, it *doesn't*. But I wasn't to know that back then.

So let's get to the bottom of this – if we can...

And in all honesty there was more to this than just what was going on in my everyday 3D lives, for in esoteric terms I later discovered there were other lessons for me still to learn and that this man and I had been together before. But then that is another story for another book. Right now is the time to set the records straight as to events in *this* life with the most accurate and honest account that I can give.

Getting back to *why* on Earth I married *Jim*... Such a bog-standard Irish ijeet as it turns out.

Being honest here, too, another reason now comes to mind, and this is probably the first time I have considered this idea.

Naïve Hope

*This might well have simply been a chance to **do what** I **wanted**, mightn't it?*

Getting married was a reason to leave home, wasn't it? This was something that my parents *couldn't* argue about! They had stopped other things from happening in my life, but this time I just may have God on my side, hey? For another thing lurking in the back of my mind was that they had already once before prevented my chance to date a thoroughly respectable guy before Bob had come along. When I was sixteen they had stopped me from dating Eric Cavanagh. He was aged twenty-one, five years my senior at the time. We had met whilst dancing, and he paid proper respect to the conventions of the day, coming round to my house on his motorbike to personally ask my dad for his permission to take me out on a date. Eric was six feet tall, dark, solid, respectful. He was a look alike for an American hunk of a guy that used to be in a TV serial, Clint Walker. He and dad got on great and they talked motorbikes for a bit, as dad was a great motorbike fan and owned a couple himself at the time. Dad could now assess him and he actually said that he was ok. But then mum interfered, holding fast to the age difference and making a real fuss. Because I was only sixteen, she thought that he was too old for me and somehow persuaded dad to agree. And even though Eric had solemnly promised that he would 'take great care of' me, seemed very respectful, had promised to honour me, and to bring me back at whatever time they dictated, they still refused to let me see him ever again. This broke my heart at the time, for I could not understand their reasoning. It seemed to me that any chance of fun in my life was taken away by them. But those are the intense and sometimes unreasonable feelings of a sixteen year old. I did eventually recover from the disappointment. As I had learned to do. Though not from the memory!

This had seemed like just another nail in the coffin of their control over me and my life. For as is now clearly shown by history they had also exercised their power over my chance of taking up the scholarship, they had kept most of my wages, and with this boyfriend deprivation they had again showed that they had management over most of my life choices.

But they couldn't argue with the Pastor, and they couldn't argue about me marrying a 'man of God' now could they? And they were still so wound up and bound up in their own dramas that they wouldn't miss me anyway. I think I was so tired and fed up of having to always be looking after someone else.

I had been the eldest of five children, all living in a two bedroom house. Looking after kids and working for the family coffers was a fact of my life and was always going to be my lot if I stayed home. And I wanted to save the world, didn't I? I daresay somewhere in my mind were dreams of making a difference in some other part of the world. And if I joined with Jim who loves the Lord the same as me, well, we could make a difference, couldn't we? I would then be following *God's Will* wouldn't I? Convicting and enticing heady stuff!

And just WHO refuses GOD?

I add to this another aspect. One where I had allowed myself to fall in love; I had actually allowed myself to *'Fall'* in love, which denotes a descending, a dropping, a kind of collapse into something. Thinking that there was a safe space at the bottom of this descent, I had permitted myself to dream of those things that I so wanted and I didn't yet have into the situation. But that is not all, for in my desire to be this goody-two-shoes and to see love all around me, I sought something else within the man; I thought that I saw the possibility of the purity or love of God. The bit I actually fell in love with was with the *God within a man*, the bit I *thought* I saw. Or rather, hoped that I saw. Stupidly, I didn't even recognise the Goddess within myself. I was *still* allowing myself to be under the wrong influences, and I didn't even know my own mind. And I agreed to *Fall* in love with his God within, but a God that was external to myself. As Julia Roberts in *Pretty Woman* says; 'Big Mistake. Huge!'

My altruistic nature got a good dose of Hope whilst my subconscious was working overtime, with dreams of escape for a higher cause, of missions rescuing lost souls, and of finally being taken care of by someone who would care for me as Christ loved and cared for his church; and I would be free of having to baby-sit, problem-solve, sacrifice, tolerate the still horrible family fights, cook meals for everyone, and I would be an independent and married woman with her own rights. I had served my family since the age of eight years of age with everything I had. Now it was my time, to love and be loved. To be cared for. To be respected. Yeah, sister, right on sister – I don't think! For that's certainly not how it all turned out.

Goodness me, what a dream... What an illusion... What a *Hope*...

Wow, I had never seen all of this so consciously back then... not in the entirety that I now view it. Yet on other levels, these were all parts of the equation that caused me to take the path I did as there was not just the one thing that dictated the outcome. I think that all of these things contributed in some way or other whether or not they acted alone or combined as a major force in any decision making process.

In these latter ruminations, I also now realize that even though I had left home, I hadn't left my duties behind, for years later I found myself looking after Jim emotionally (and domestically) as if he was a child. The start, I think, indeed the beginning of my being caught in this web, had been set-up from the day we started teaching the Sunday School kids together. I must have picked up on a subconscious level that he needed looking after. I think that the Pastor had seen that Jim's intentions and his ability were probably miles apart; for making it my role to keep Jim satisfied and on the straight and narrow was where the Pastor had been nudging me. Jim certainly needed to be loved, though that wasn't my initial *conscious* reaction to him. All the same, after we got married, I definitely unwittingly defaulted into Mother Role again. This surely was an unconscious habit of mine and when one doesn't recognize a pattern, one is often (and usually) unable to prevent it from happening again.

Time and distance always furnishes further clarity.

Thinking back to ancient times, to the history of patient and persistent mothers, for some reason I later mused on this – *Just why did women put up with the things that they did...?*

Is it that women are the ones better equipped to put up with the atrocious, messy and noisy behaviors, wants and needs of demanding infants and children? When others not directly related could or would want to hand it right back over or walk away. Or even desire to throw the difficult or deafening infant out. And don't tell me that no mother would never, ever, not even for a split second, want to get rid of her child; for my own experience of being absolutely *driven* by a demanding and upset infant when one is sleep-deprived, exhausted from feeding, ignored and unsupported by her partner and still healing from the birth trauma will bear out that dreadful milli-second of desire to be free and unfrazzled.

Fortunately, our pro-life hormones are generally in full swing, though it can be a difficult trial for those suffering from post-partum issues or who have had a difficult and physically exhausting pregnancy. Some women might later wonder what on earth prevented them from walking out on all of this. Is it because the love of a mother and the role of a mother can be so very powerful, overcoming many adverse issues and situations?

Or is it because of an essential and necessary blind spot in womanhood that guarantees the perpetuation of the species? Women see the *potential* in their children, despite their ugliness, scryking, messiness, smelliness, mistakes and handicaps. But many mothers later have to learn that potential is not necessarily possibility nor even probability. And we can make the mistake of transferring this expectation or excuse onto our partner and instead of acting like an equal, we can fall into the *Improving and Mothering* pattern. I have seen it happen and I fear and **know** that I did this myself.

I later developed a pet theory on this patience of women to stand by their partner and to trust that the potential they could see would eventually eventuate; it is what I call the *'faulty* Mother-Gene'. Just like a mother may initially tend to think or want to believe that her child is different or special or will somehow change the world, this can be transferred to the partner. If he is indeed gifted, this can become an unshakable success partnership, though there is no guarantee that all of her needs will be met; *Behind every good man is a good woman.* Though I dare to add here that 'Behind every good woman is a good woman' as there are not many women that I know of that have been unquestioningly and competently supported by her husband or male partner.

Getting back to this *'faulty* Mother-Gene'; which in my opinion can affect hormones that keep one patiently expecting the revelation and reality of the *potential* of a being, *whether or not* that being is capable of actually realizing or materializing it in their life time, or within their own capabilities or even their own chosen endeavours.

These things, I think, contributed to background scenery in my journeying at this point and time. The clarity gained further down my path of how the church and the Pastor had been at work behind the veil and that I had been 'recruited' by the Pastor to keep Jim in the church was an illuminating and liberating realisation. Willing fodder, I had been dedicated, genuine and capable, and I had wanted to serve and please God. Who else would have put up with him otherwise? Don't answer that one – I just had a horrible picture of some other poor woman ending up with him... but still, I didn't deserve what was eventually dished out by him.

Well these are some possible reasons of how I ended up with this man. It certainly wasn't a romantic and sweeping love affair. I guess I could just as well close my eyes and stick a pin in any or each of these possible reasons I have listed, and it would have contributed in some way or another.

Married Life

Our first week of married life was under the smirking, judgmental eyes of the youth, the convention staff and the Pastors running the centre schedules. Not much opportunity for romance, but then I was managing to create my own sense of rightness and romance in my own reality, convinced as I was that this was God's Will and His Doing. This carried me through, and even though there weren't fireworks, there was closeness and there was gratitude and there was that sense that we were both facing the same adventure together. A rare and very brief time of companionship and comfort. He led, and I followed.

Jim made arrangements for us to move into the vacant flat practically next door to his parents right in the heart of Hulme, near Moss Side in Manchester. We were to live our first year or so at number 80 Preston Street. The flat was accessed by a long flight of stairs, leading to an open space over the shop below; it had bare unpolished floorboards throughout, no cupboards or storage space, and was very noisy at night as it overlooked a busy intersection. Pretty bare place really. Well, it had previously been used for storage. And this was where we went directly Jim and I got back to Manchester from the Convention Centre.

There was already an old kitchen table in the flat, and our bed and bedding had been bought through hire purchase – in those days we didn't have credit cards – along with the dining table and two plain armchairs, which were delivered whilst we were away. Finances initially were very tight as I had left my copy reader position in Wythenshawe. Travel wasn't viable, but Jim had already insisted anyway that I get work closer to home and to him – isn't this what we had argued over two days before the wedding? Yes, it was. But he was the boss, eh. I had coped with being on my own shoestring budget, so it was just another step to learn how to manage more expense, but with two wages to get by. Familiar with household chores I was surprised when Jim was adamant that I learn how to scrub the bare floors *his* way. Making me get down on my hands and knees, he showed me how I must use the scrubbing brush. Mopping was insufficient apparently, even though I had scrubbed the front door step and mopped the kitchen at home for several years. Part of his training on board ship when he was in the Merchant Navy, yes, but I had no choice but to comply, after all, it was my new domestic job description to become a good Wife. I was also shown how to chop vegetables. His way. So I learned to do it his way.

I learned to stack my groceries on the kitchen table, leaning them on the edge pushed up and closest to the wall. It was a sparse bare life there and I will leave it at that. Our wedding presents were the absolute basics for any couple to manage; two plates, two cups, two knives, two forks, two spoons, potato peeler, sharp knife, two pots, two tea towels and two towels, two wooden spoons, a dish mop, a floor mop and bucket, scrubbing brush and a sweeping brush. Bemused that this was all that we got, nevertheless, I was extremely grateful, for how else could I have managed the housework and basics?

Fortunately I had had plenty of experience with a sewing machine and knitting needles, and whenever possible used mums sewing machine until I owned my own again. This helped solve the problem of soft furnishings to a degree, though we, or rather I, had to save to buy the materials for this. But I had always had a good eye for a bargain.

I remember when mum and dad had first moved to Manchester with very little furniture. There were some wooden packing boxes that we used until we could afford a proper couch. They often joked that when we had visitors they would say to them 'Welcome. Just draw up a floor-board and sit by the fire'. And now mum and dad reminded me that I was at the beginning of my marriage and that we had a chance to work together to build a home like they had done. So that is how I came to see it. Each new little acquisition, no matter how small, would be another step toward my dream of a home filled with love and beauty and dedicated to the Lord.

I do eventually get over this God-thing and religious over-focus. But right then this is how I saw it all.

Whatever floating or vague ideas I may have had about how it would be to be married, it slowly became apparent that there was not much place for real consideration for *my* wishes. I am allowed to say things but that doesn't mean they are heard or acted on. This is not quite the partnership and teamwork that had been touted as the making of a successful marriage from the pulpit... Rather it was looking like the Boss and the skivvy...

Jim worked on an upper level in an office of Remington Rand, and his job was to visit and service typewriters and copying machines and printers, which were just emerging as part of the evolving office equipment.

It is now clear that getting a similar job as a copy reader, a costing clerk or even to continue to work in an office again is dependent entirely on what is available in the same Paper Mills building where Jim was employed. Housing all manner of paper works still, this huge stark and imposing building also had given over floor-space to various smaller endeavours. A number of other companies occupied several floor levels and the Paper Works itself was now confined to the ground floor and basement, intent on the refinement of paper, rather than the manufacturing of it.

I just didn't get the reason why Jim was insisting on this. Hadn't this come up just before our wedding? Hadn't he seen that I didn't agree with him then? Doesn't he realize I am capable of better prospects than working in a factory? Again I dare to question him on this, recognizing that my earning capacity was increasing as I had been gathering experience and as I proved my skills and intelligence. This of course would eventually earn us better money than me working in a factory... or so I thought.

'But why can't I get a job elsewhere? Why does it *have* to be in the same place as you? What if they don't have any vacancies for the sort of work that I do?' I asked Jim, still not quite understanding what this was about.

'Well, then, you take whatever they can give you.'

'But what if they don't have anything suitable, anything that I can actually do?' I was still struggling with the concept.

'Then you take *anything*, even if it's a cleaner's job. My mum is a cleaner, and if it is good enough for her, then it's good enough for you,' he insists.

'But if I can earn more than a cleaner...' Here he interrupted me; 'Look, this way it's easier for me to *Keep An Eye On You*. This is only *For Your Own Good*. This is only for your own *Protection*.'

'What protection? Why do I need protection – from what? What can happen to me? I can take buses and...' Again, he interrupted me, now becoming more and more obviously agitated with my questioning of him on this.

'You could get attacked. You could get raped. You could get mugged. You're working in the same place so that I can go to work with you and come home with you. And that's that!'

What?!

I didn't know of anyone who had been attacked, let alone raped, and it just wasn't part of my reality. The only time I had come even *close* to anything that resembled being overpowered was by a kind of boyfriend (though he was toast after this) was when he pushed me threateningly into some bushes... and I had responded with my own threats to scream, as well as indignation and anger at his

Naïve Hope

daring to even think about it – which had covered my own fear very well. My body had tensed ready to react which I am sure he felt, for I had been prepared to fight this, whatever the cost or damage, in order to protect myself and preserve my integrity. So this *protection* thing seemed a bit weird to me. Hadn't I been working and travelling quite well by myself for some time now? Why would something happen now?

The difference was this; I was married and I *belonged* to Jim now...! Initially I had supposed it was protection from Unbelievers, but on reflection, he was *controlling* his assets (me) yet he chose to see it as *protecting*.

His decree is quite clear and firm; I give this stance up and I take whatever is available for me, accept work from whoever is willing to employ me. Despite my capabilities. In view of my marital status, I am not given any option of course. It was now quite naturally expected that I obey my husband's wishes, as the church beliefs and creeds gave him power *over* me.

And I had *promised* to obey him as part of my wedding vows. Yes, that is what I had promised... and that is what I inevitably did. Slowly, in increments, my autonomy is being eroded, and this is just the beginning, even though I do not recognise it yet. I am only seventeen, still learning about life and myself.

Making sense of my Christian and my married life now became a habitual linking together of biblical quotes, freely brought out and aired when there was even just one word of similarity to any given situation. Things go wrong; 'God knows best'. Things go *terribly* wrong; 'Who can know the mind of God?', 'Cast your burdens upon the Lord for He careth for You', 'Trust in the Lord and He shall deliver thee', 'The heart of man is corrupt', 'Do good that thy days may be long', 'Delight thyself also in the Lord and He shall give thee the desires of thine heart', 'He shall defeat thine enemies...' etc.

Considering that our lives literally revolved around church, and that this Full Gospel Church conducted meetings every Monday, Wednesday and Friday nights (Bible Study or Prayer Meetings), as well as Saturday night, and twice on Sunday (morning and late afternoon services, as well as the Youth Meeting on a Tuesday night), one could live their whole life at church... And this continual influence gave one little chance to reflect on other ways, other thoughts, other perceptions, other things. Of course, one then-popular-flavour-of-the-month-quote bandied around was about 'keeping busy for God' and avoiding being in 'the devil's playground' which was, of course, 'the World'. 'You are *in* the world, not *of* the world' gained a lot of validity with the advent of rock and roll, the Beatles, and other temptations away from serving-the-Lord...

Caught up in the events and in the dream of promised love and security that I thought marriage would bring, I had really had little opportunity or encouragement to reflect on such a momentous decision, such a life-changing act, such a change in my potential status as becoming a wife. The details of the wedding, together with its mystery and confused expectations had been my prime focus. Though Jim had promised to love, honour and to *cherish* me, interestingly this was always conveniently left out of any discussions together, the focus being on my own role as an obedient wife; and you know, it took me years to realise that he had been so derelict in this. This is what can happen when one is operating in Survival Mode. Or trying to continually be a Good Person.

Really, as a young Christian girl, dedicated to doing what is right, and to serving the Lord, and who now had her husband as The Head over her, and coupling all of that along with a pretty familiar dysfunction in my own family's dynamics and relationships, I was pretty much on track; I was following the path and habits set down before me. Now was not the time for me to challenge these issues. And anyway, right now I wouldn't have been able to see the mismatches and inequalities; too many Bible quotes stood between me and logic, too much 'duty' existed between me and self-worth. I was too busy with high ideas of 'Work out your own salvation in fear and trembling' (yep, that's another direct biblical quote) and was pretty used, anyway, to not having control over my own life, and so it was so easy to allow all of this to happen.

The childhood preparation for the choices I was making is an easy explanation, though what I also find interesting is that I didn't rebel in any way. Actually, let me rephrase that, or rather correct it

Naïve Hope

– for I *did* rebel, I *did* make attempts to seek justice. At the risk of sounding like a victim, it was the continual quashing down of these attempts that predisposed me to accepting what I was not able to change... For many things I learned growing up I wasn't aware of until much later in life, not yet recognising them as what had been drummed into me growing up. The unravelling of many of these things was an enlightening experience that I would have wished had occurred earlier in my history. Nevertheless, from the age of three onwards I was taught that 'You can't have everything you want. You get what you're given.' Another one was 'You have to learn that dreams don't buy food!' along with 'You have to share.' And the old perennial; 'Money doesn't grow on trees, you know'. Very limited thinking in those days, but that was the reality for most people emerging from the deprivations from war. But that 'You get what you're given' was a real humdinger for me, as, once it was absorbed into my subconscious, kept me from reaching out without aid, permission, support or gifting of someone else. 'Go for your dreams' and 'You can be whatever you want to be, have anything you want' simply was not part of the thinking of my family, my social group, my church and I daresay a good percentage of the population at that time.

But this was *my* life, and *I* allowed these decisions to be *my* decisions. Ultimately *I* am responsible. Though to be truly congruous and responsible for something does usually require a certain amount of authority in the same area. However...

They say it takes two people to get married, and nobody had held a gun to my head. Well not a real gun.

Not then anyway.

So I apply for a job at Jim's instruction, working my way through applications to all of the places in the same mills where Jim is employed and I eventually find a job in a huge paper manufacturing company. This employment was a sheer waste of my skills from Ferranti's etc but it paid. The position was working with and handling huge labelling and gumming paper machines in one of the Paper Mills there. Dangerous work if you didn't pay attention, but I avoided injury and kept all my fingers. I did witness a couple of nasty incidents, but managed to avoid anything untoward for myself in the short time that I was there.

In my head, I was working towards our future, and toward whatever God had planned for us in our working together for Him. In fact and reality, I had become my husband's 'possession' – for a 'wife' according to the Bible was a 'helpmeet' or helpmate – and there to help her husband, and it would appear, existing for no other reason than to do so. Continuing to be blinded by Doing The Right Thing and of being Counted Worthy, this all connected in with my previous experience of the initial most-important-man in my life – my father. What I didn't really see at the time, though I felt it, was that I had given up any claim to doing what I wanted to do, I had been stripped of my own autonomy and my rights to independent thinking. I was reduced to flicking large sheets of paper into a huge printing machine which could also take a hand with it if care was lacking, and my freedom of movement outside work had been totally constricted and restricted. We would travel to work together, and he would accompany me home. I would be monitored at any potentially free time. Anyone who has studied psychopaths and sociopaths, narcissists and the mentally aberrated will recognise the gradual removal of independent thought, action, social, emotional, financial and mental freedoms as various control mechanisms devised to bring another under their dominion.

I am learning my place. I dutifully work at the mill. Jim and I attend prayer meetings together, still working with the Youth Group, though there is now some variation in our duties, and various occasions where he alone attends to just the young males in the group.

Jim however, is allowed whatever freedom he desires. He was free to travel to London for weekends or days away to do update courses connected with new machine models, and he would meet up and mix with people on the training courses. During these times, I was of necessity entrusted to keep myself safe, though on one early occasion, his mother actually came to meet me to accompany me home. Not much help really, as she was quite drunk anyway, and accordingly a pain and not a protection as such. Meanwhile, Jim fell into the habit of bringing back smiling photographs of girls he had met away. No photos of guys, just girls. Of course they were

Naïve Hope

supposedly Christian girls, part of the 'brethren' he encountered, but were they *all* Christian doing the same course at the same time? And only females? Confusingly, I wasn't sure if he met them only at the course, or if they went to the local church or both. And one didn't overly question Jim. For peace and expediency I think, I believed everything he told me about these trips away, which had been happening during our engagement and after we married. Including his visits to the local Gospel Churches which he explained occupied his spare time whilst away. This, though, was not without some sort of jealous and mistrustful niggle at this attractive Virginia Lennox-Grey and her striking girl friend, Linda. Time later revealed that this sense that I felt at the time, of there being something more between him and one of these girls, may well have been a true intuition; instructed by the church to always give the benefit of the doubt, and not liking the discomfort that suspicion brought, I accepted what he said dismissing my distrust.

I trusted, and foolishly.

My own intelligence and naivety proved to be a two-edged sword as one often inhibited the other. There was never any conscious recognition of how much I was missing by getting married so early. I can honestly say that it wasn't until in much later years, long after the dust had settled that I ever even contemplated this concept. My thoughts of idealism overshadowed reason, and commitment to a Higher Cause took precedence to what should have been loyalty to my own heart and soul.

If I trusted Jim, it was to become clear that he didn't trust me.

Don't Look

Within two months of being married, I had received my first 'side-thump' off him.

Travelling home late one afternoon after an Open Air meeting at Alexander Park, Jim and I are sitting side by side together, with me against the window. This was so that no one would touch me 'by mistake' as they grazed past. It was always at Jim's insistence that I sat next to the window. Sure, it could be seen as a protection against being accidentally banged by someone's bag or parcel but I don't think that that was always necessarily the case. The bus wasn't full at this point, but soon we found ourselves sitting in front of a young man. Not that I had actually noticed him until Jim drew my attention to him as I shall relate here.

The double seat was on the upper deck section of the large double-decker red Manchester bus, and at this point we are going past a row of shops with displays still clearly visible in the windows. I didn't usually get much chance to go window shopping or to look at clothes. It was just not done in those days – I was a Christian married woman and that meant domestic and church responsibilities as well as a requirement to lead a spotless life – which meant that I was expected to set an example of thrift and humility.

But, I am also still only seventeen years old...

Looking out of the bus window I saw a dress in a shop-window as we passed by and it really caught my eye. It was a simple black shift, a classic yet modest design, and something that I just might possibly be allowed to wear. Knowing that we probably couldn't afford anything like that anyway, and wondering if I could make something similar, I got lost in looking. Permitting myself a moment to dream about it, I naturally paid as much attention as the window scope would let me. I wanted to take in as much of the dress visually as I could, because I didn't know if I would ever see it again. Sitting next to the window which is on my left side, I peered out and let my eyes and head follow the dress whilst I drank in the details, which occasioned a bit of a neck crane as the shop passed me by and out of sight. A perfectly normal thing to do, I would have thought.

NO. Not so!

I am suddenly jolted in my seat as I feel a hurtful and very sharp dig in my ribs, and I turn around on impulse to see what on earth has caused it. It is Jim.

Jim had punched me as sharply as he could at that angle to get my attention, but in a way that could not be witnessed by others. This is my first 'side-thump', my first sign of potential violence. He is glaring at me. I had no idea why, and so leant toward him to ask him what was the matter, but instead of an explanation I got more of the same as he growled through gritted teeth at a level only I could hear over the bus engine noise these words; 'Turn around! The guy sitting behind you will think you are looking at HIM!'

What?

'But I am only, ...' was as far as he would let me speak. His glare instructed me that he was not only *not pleased*, but that it would be *dangerous* for me to speak any more about this whilst on the bus, and in public! I shut up. Not difficult to do.

I was gobsmacked. Metaphorically speaking. Though the effect also felt physical. He was obviously very upset with me, and I didn't know why. What did I do to warrant this? I immediately turned my head back to look straight ahead, taking in what had happened. Replaying the tape of my actions and his responses. I was trying to understand it, though I was not getting very far. But he had made his point. I came to realise that the point was: '*Only look where I say you can.*' According to Jim.

From that point on I was terrified of looking where I wasn't supposed to. And on arriving home, I received a glaring righteous lecture on *Not Attracting Attention*. All this because I part turned in my seat. And I don't think the guy behind us, whoever he was, had the least idea, nor the least care, as regards me looking out of a bus window!

Cheesh, only seventeen hey? This man was twenty-one years old. Yet here we were, and in different ways and for different reasons, both accepting his ridiculous decisions. For I think that he thought that because he was older he was therefore wiser and more mature. Which of course, by all accounts, would be the normal logic and assumption at the time. To a degree this was correct, for he had experienced more in life than I had to date. But common assumption isn't necessarily an accurate assumption.

And we were married! And probably would have a family together? Well, to be honest, I didn't even think that far ahead at that time. Thinking wasn't required of me, nor really allowed for me. But we were certainly joined for life... I realise now that he had awakened a fear in me, and I was to become more fearful as time went on.

Things like this I couldn't understand, but I could understand being ruled, as my own father had been a tartar and dictator. So I guess that I had to accept my fate, try to adjust, do the right thing, and get on with it. What other option was there?

But I obviously didn't forget. This is not about not forgiving, for I had to learn to forgive, and forgive, and then forgive some more. But when pain is associated with something, it is not so easy to forget, for we are wired to learn by pleasure and to learn by pain.

I didn't realise that I had been and was being cultivated by the church, and now by this man, for his own ends. That is an interesting word: *cultivated*. It usually indicates a nurturing in preparation for harvesting and in part this is true. I now see another meaning in it. Let me explain.

At church and as Youth Leaders we were eventually trained to argue down any other faith, religion or set of beliefs with the Bible. We knew what each religion's points of differences were and the biblical quotations and related interpretations to oint out and demonstrate that the Pentecostal way was the 'correct' and only way, and I became really good at recognising and applying the appropriate relevant scriptures. We were also taught that our church, the Pentecostals, part of the Throngs of God guys, us Good Guys, were definitely NOT a religion. They were very clear on this. No, no, No; *We* are *not* a religion. *We* don't belong with the rest of them. Ours is a FAITH, a way of life, a following of the Lord with the Pentecostal Baptism of the Holy Spirit, which *no* other faith or religion has. We are special. We speak in Tongues so we have direct access to God and the Holy Spirit. Ours is *not* a *religion*. *Ours* is a *Faith*! Big Difference!

Well, let me tell you, I have since discovered that *it is* a religion. And not only that, it is a CULT. Brainwashing to serve and to do things that are not in your best interests even when supposedly in the name of God, is definitely *not* built on God's Love. Separation and being the only ones that will end up in 'Heaven' is the hallmark of any cult. I was absolutely cultivated; *Cult*-ivated. And harvested by the Pastor to help Jim to be a Christian. I did not recognise the sacrifice I was undertaking. I was not being called to be a missionary to the masses, or the underprivileged, I was being used to be a missionary support to this man Jim. And I had no idea!

Brainwashing is like having the thoughts you were familiar with being replaced by others, usually with a promise, a reward or a threat; whatever it takes to make you change your mind. When you have an open mind, one that is ready to accept or believe, or do what is perceived or presented as 'the right thing', you have less resistance. When you have a pre-disposition to believing the best of others, you don't have much chance at weighing things or examining these new 'truths' that are being presented to you. When you give your word and promise to follow as I did, then you have very little chance indeed. You are learning; open to learn, willing to learn, ready to learn. Your boundaries are replaced, reset, your mindset adjusted, your walls fall down. Reprogramming takes place. Women may lose their autonomy to a larger degree basically because of the impact and presence of control and shame merely for being female that is being hammered at them. And if your sex has to wear the guilt of Eve over and over, you can more easily fall to the belief that women are lesser than men, and then you are in deep shit. For it takes a lot to climb out of all this.

This side-thump is a precursor, a warning of more to come if I continue to goad the beast; a quick hit out with a fist in temper rather than a directed and targeted punch to the face or the stomach. If I had known then what I know now, I like to think that maybe I could have stopped this somehow, or move out until he learned to treat me better. But I didn't know better myself, so how could I teach him that? It is a sad truth that the nervous system and neurology can become wired to a particular way through constant abuse, and the fear of those fists, and the remembrance of my father's treatment of us mostly overrides and blots out any other alternatives. Reclaiming your brain, autonomy, self-worth and identity can take some time. But it's worth it! For me at this time, that concept was still a way off in my future. Right now I am still in the grip of control mechanisms that are *not* under my control.

Within a few months of our marriage, Jim's quick temper starts to emerge more clearly. Was I as argumentative as he makes me out to be? Or is it simply that he couldn't handle anyone else's opinion or ideas that differed from his? From my perspective, I am as eager as any young bride to make a happy home life, and have unwittingly subconsciously learnt from my mother what my *place* was in it and it is being reinforced by Jim. But a repeat of my parent's marriage style was not what I had signed up for, for surely I am in a different situation to mum; for Jim and I are on the same Christian team – this man is a Born-Again Christian after all, and he truly loves God and the Lord Jesus.

So he kept saying, and I had no real cause to doubt him at that time, being verbally pummelled continually mentally and emotionally by the church on the sinful nature of man (and woman) and our inherent need for a Saviour. My 'sins' were sometimes simply the fact of being a woman, for it is taught that women started original sin in the garden (so the pass-the-parcel-of-inadequate-male-self-responsibility goes) and women are therefore historically responsible for so many problems for men.

Such tempting Jezebels, we women were, no matter what we wear.

And as for vanity, women require strict instructions to wear hats in church in order not to distract others with their flamboyant or elaborate hairstyles... We are all often compared either to Mary mother of Jesus or Mary the harlot, with doses of comparisons to Martha, Ruth, Delilah, Salome and any other female that had earned infamous or otherwise notation in the scriptures. Depending on what your perceived offence was. All are archetypes of submissive serving women, or, if a woman dared to stand up for herself, then she was damned, dangerous or sent by the Devil and therefore not to be copied.

Men were generally spared such direct and clearly opposite comparisons to the same degree, although Doubting Thomas was a favourite male label applied to both genders to encourage more blind faith.

What kept women in the church? Good question, difficult answer. Personally, my own experiences later revealed that if you have been made to feel controlled or less-than, or are wearing guilt, self-doubt or fear, then it is easy to be persuaded that you *need* a Saviour, that you are not good enough without one, and that the consequences of not having one are so dire that it threatens your very Soul. Some women get caught up in it because they have a need to help others, seeing their own needs as less important. Include that the enthusiasm and bliss that everyone got through singing in the churches typically abandoned and ecstatic way as well as the encouragement to dance in the aisles, and the opportunity to unburden yourself publicly (or privately) for any wrong-doing – and without a drop of alcohol needing to be taken – *and* to receive God's forgiveness all tended to result in a feeling of well-being that helped negate any surfacing fear of hell's fire. Church could give one a real side benefit of a 'hit' of hormone-high! Could it be addictive? Of course. And especially to those Souls who tended toward more addiction capacity than others. Easy to swap one addiction, say alcohol or smoking, for fanaticism and zeal for God.

Church usually made me feel better, and that was mainly because I thought that I needed it, and it was the only place I was allowed any form of self expression and social connection. All other forms were not only shunned, they were judged detrimental and dangerous. This does tend to keep one's blinkers on. Learning that a face aglow with zeal doesn't automatically mean that they are in God's Light was a lesson for me to learn later!

Shoulder Shoves

Married life is all so new to me. Learning how to conduct myself is still a major focus. Adjusting to work at the paper mill without any resentment I unthinkingly saw as just another Christian challenge. I daresay that Jim was having to do some of his own adjusting as well.

One particular day Jim comes home from work and seems to already be in a foul mood. I have no idea what has happened to cause this, and I am sure it is not me. Nor the meal that I am preparing, which nevertheless gives Jim cause to complain. I am a bit harassed, but doing my best. This is not good enough, though. It is not being done to Jim's specifications, and he is getting madder by the minute. Leastways that is the excuse for his rising temper.

As I turn away from the stove top, Jim is in my face. 'Don't look at me like that' he growls. 'Who do you think you are?'

I have no real answer for this because I don't know what this is about. But I rearrange my face to what I think is a less offensive face, trying to be willing to hear what his problem is. He doesn't sound like a man I want to cross right now. He lifts his hand.

Jim is right handed, and as he is facing me, when he shoves me it is with this right hand. Or rather, when he shoves my shoulder. This pushes me towards the sink. Takes little effort, but this is not enough, for he shoves me again, more sharply this time.

'Let this be a warning to you', he sneers, turning away. I am relieved, scared and bothered. I have done nothing wrong that I am aware of, but it is obvious that something is going on. Dare I ask him? Or will I just get more of the same?

My decision is finally this; *'Best stay out of his way when he is like this.'* So I quietly go about the chores, and he does eventually get over it, though I never do find out what it was. 'For better, for worse' is in my ears. Ah well, could be worse. At least he hadn't punched me like dad did. He loves God, after all, and he will be his usual self again soon. So I thought!

CHRISTIAN WIFE

No matter how I try to excel in my wifely duties at home I still score hefty and inescapable bouts of accusations of having pride (even for something as domestically mundane as when I succeed in finally getting something rusty or filthy into a sparkling state again), of not keeping my own counsel (when daring to speak up or have an opinion contrary to the management of the establishment; Jim), or of anything that was not of how a Christian wife was supposed to be. Or rather of how Jim demands that I be, according to what is being fed to him by the current church interpretations, the Pastors, the fakeness and falsities of church members with their carefully manufactured temperate and blameless masks and facades, and a multitude of insincere policies fabricated with the flimsiest of scriptural thread, that were designed to keep the flock (and women in particular) in conformity. There was the odd genuine soul who simply wished for peace and love and light to reign, but I now believe that they were few and far between.

Insincere – In-Sin-sear... seared by sin... Sorry, got carried away with the word and just saw this glimmer of hidden meaning.

Jim is now 'master' over me, according to the Bible. Hard when you have a spontaneous and extrovert streak, despite my serious-mindedness. The Pastor and my parents had also in their own ways given him permission to treat me as such by standing by and doing nothing .

Maybe if my own father had given me more self belief, more encouragement, more support and attention, been a better father and role model really, then I would have found it easier to recognise the degree of abuse that was happening, instead of accepting on some level that this was a part of married life. But even so, would it have compensated for the rupture within my own psyche caused by his determination to break my will as a child? That damage was to go unknown, unseen, unrecognised by me for many more years to come. So instead, *I* compensate...

As a Youth Leader and prospective spouse, I had already begun paying close attention to Proverbs 31 which describes the perfect wife. A woman whose price is above rubies. And whose sacrifices are what keeps her family not only functioning, but prospering. Now my life was a crash-course in attempting such lofty examples and in obeying and doing what Jim thought I should be doing, whilst also learning about humility. This was how it seemed and subsequently what I thought at the time. In my heart and in our conversation together, Jim and I had great admiration for the evangelists of the day, thinking that they were bringing light into the world. I knew that this would take some sacrifice, and often saw my tribulations as preparation for this. But that was not really what I was being called to do, was it? The wives of the evangelists were their support, and I was learning about all that. Over time I realised that we were never really going to go down that missionary road, no matter the talk on it. Jim simply didn't have it in him. And I was now bound to him.

Maybe there was an inner conflict with his inability to be what he talked. I chose not to see him as the weak man that he was, but as a more romanticised distraught soul willing to follow God to the ends of the earth, and simply having trouble in doing so. And seeing that he needed my help. God love me, what a silly girl. And how many other women have been fooled by that thought; if I love him enough, give him enough, he will change. And in line with this mission, I was quickly waking up to the reality of life with this man, and having to redefine my thoughts about my purpose. I did not as yet fully understand my real role in this relationship, seeing only my support and help-meet role.

My first black eye and swollen mouth was deliberate. I had not cooked the food the way he wanted, and heavens-to-Betsy it was late being put on the table. No, he didn't hit me because of that but because I dared to speak back to him about it. A man doesn't want his woman daring to question him or challenge him when he has had a bad day, does he? He doesn't want to know what problems she has had with feeding the baby, or trying to get the place clean. Easier to find fault with what is in front of him than to dig that deep. Consequently, all manner of faults were found, things that he thought I had done wrong at other times were thrown at me, and this also justifies his physical attack.

The real problem I suspect in hindsight was probably something going on at work that he couldn't handle, and he had to blame *someone* for his feeling shitty about things. Andpossibly his dark shadow side has been hassling him with all manner of temptations and thoughts that his own personal shame forbids him from owning up to. So naturally he found fault with me, and I copped it.

This fault finding slowly started to become a pattern. If I didn't call in to see his parents when they had told him to tell me to do so, this too would do it. A possible lapse in memory (even if that was truly what it really was) held no excuse, instead I was perceived as being offensive and rude to his mum and dad. 'But I forgot.' 'No you didn't, you did it on *purpose*.'

When someone hits you and it's unjustified, one feels a sense of outrage. In any event *of course* it's totally unjustified - at *any time* - unless you are in the boxing ring. However, when this outrage is expressed, and you are not in control of the situation but the perpetrator is, and you dare to challenge, then it's likely you risk *further* unjustified hits. And so it was. I knew that I was not to blame for his bad mood, but I didn't yet have the words for it. I knew that he had no right to hit me like he did, but he had the upper hand, literally, and he had the experience of fighting this way. And he had the power and the force, and he didn't hesitate to use it *against* me.

And this is something many people don't always realise, not unless they have been subjected to it. When someone is much stronger and more powerful than you are, and they are allowed to get away with their bad behaviour, and fear is part of the equation, then it is no matter who or what is right or wrong. The maxim '*Might is Right*' holds sway. And when one is sworn to loyalty and has made sincere oaths to honour and obey, there is little recourse from that path.

At the time, I felt and knew that what was happening was wrong, and that we had to get some sort of help. Was this what God wanted for my life? Really?

So I ran home to mum and dad at the first onset of 'Black-eye'-itis. My first instinct had been to escape from him, and I somehow think in my own heart that my parents would offer me shelter. And the fact that his abuse has now been exposed will make him realise that this was now unacceptable behaviour. Hadn't I married him to avoid this very thing? Hadn't I chosen him because he had promised that he had given his heart to God and would follow Him? Hadn't he claimed that he was different man now that he was a Christian?

Mum and dad will help me. They will point out to him that God is love, and not violence. They have stopped their physical abuse and fighting now so they can get him to stop this. So I thought.

So I arrive at their doorstep in tears, sporting my injury. Telling them what he has done, I sought their help and support. Did I get it? What counsel did they give me? Not much. Well, they both looked at each other when I showed them what Jim had done to me. There was a kind of shocked silence in the air. Then they found their tongues and asked me how it happened, and I explain what had taken place. I am not only surprised, I am flattened that all it seemed that they could do was to make excuses for him and generally appeared powerless to intervene. They had no answer, no solution to the problem. He is my husband now, after all. What? And this is OK?

Did my dad take him on one side and say to him 'Now, lad, this is *my* daughter, and it's *your* job to look after her, not hit her. If you lay another finger on her again, you will have *me* to deal with. Right?' The answer to that is 'No'. Did he do anything to fight for me, to protect me? Again, 'No'. Did he tell Jim that he was supposed to be *following* Christ's example of peace and turning the other cheek? If you guessed another 'No' then you already realise the situation and have obviously been paying attention. This father of mine, this supposed Christian father didn't do a *thing* to help me. He was bigger than Jim and probably stronger. But he did nothing, *nothing* to help me. Thank you, dad.

I cannot tell you how I felt over this. I go to my parents for help, for support, for love, and I get *nothing*. What I did get was this; mum's jealousy and resentment that I had had the opportunity to marry a Christian man when she had no such chance. This *still* comes through. Though I must confess that there was a moment when she showed some sadness that I too had copped such a deal in marriage. But her comment that stung me then and every time thereafter that I thought of it was this remarkable peace of non-wisdom: *'You've made your bed, now lie in it.'* No solutions, just that!

What amazing support, mum. Thank you very much.

Afterwards Jim was sorry of course. He seemed appalled at what he had done, and looked truly repentant and full of remorse. Particularly when he was faced with the *very* evident marks and bruises and actually *saw* what he had done. Of course the whole fucking *world* was going to see those marks and bruises now. *Now* he couldn't hide from what he had done, could he? So maybe it was a good idea that I had shown this to my parents. Now maybe he will show some contrition. If he still wants acceptance in the church.

Jim's shame is thrown back at him with my exposure before mum and dad. And it seems that he is genuinely affected by his own behaviour, for he now tries to make it up with apologies, flowers, and chocolates. He was now attentive, charming, helpful and considerate. He suddenly plays the man I first mistook him for in the beginning, the man I thought that I would marry. He displays loving and caring, and this helps to wipe the pain and hurt away. I sincerely thought he meant it, and that he had seen the error of his ways. And that he wouldn't want to embarrass himself in front of my parents like that again.

Humility, for a short time, was his garment. *Till the next time.* We lurch along to the next event in our union together.

SHEILA

Meanwhile, there is a ray of light. For some hope is rekindled with the appearance in my life of Sheila.

I had few friends, indeed I had none really since getting pregnant. Sure, the folk at church were by and large quite friendly. Some of them were a bit snobbish, some gossipy, some extremely judgmental, some just glad to have others around, some boring, some needy, some plain stupid like most communities or groups of people. Some were very cliquey, and some very magnanimous. No one really bad, that is no-one obviously so at that time that I was aware of, though little I knew of things that were hidden from the congregation. Though that is another story.

But no-one really who was a close friend. No one bothered to come visit me and see how I was coping with things.

After I got married, as events would have it, I did make one very good friend, and her name was Sheila Williams.

Sheila is engaged to Jim's brother, John, who was also still living at home with his parents. But Johnny likes to drink occasionally and have certain nights out with the boys. Sheila is around the same age as me, shorter than I am, and with blue eyes and blonde naturally wavy hair. Her sense of humour is outrageous, but she is also smart. It turns out that through Jim she attended the church and made a commitment to the Lord. This qualifies her, in Jim's eyes, as suitable companion material on the nights that she is waiting for John to come home from work or when he is out with the boys. After all, she is just a couple of doors away waiting for Johnny.

Sheila has also had a conversion experience, but unlike me, she is not as obsessive as I was, and she had more supportive parents who had their feet on the ground. Sheila was a very grounded and practical person.

Consequently she wasn't easily bull-dozed and she was totally capable of making her own decisions. The fact that she still came to the same church from time to time made her continue to be palatable to Jim, together with his brother connection. When American preachers such as Billy Graham, Oral Roberts or T L Osborn did the Revival rounds in Manchester, she also came along with us. Bless her.

Sheila was my 'light relief' and she would occasionally sneak in magazines for me to look at, as they weren't allowed in the house. And keep me up with some of the current popular music. Though it wasn't strictly allowed – that is it wouldn't have been if Jim had been present - she often hums the latest pop songs to me. And in later years when she called round and Jim was out, she would dare switch the radio on and find the best music, and we would have a little jig in the kitchen. Until we would heard Jim's key in the door and she would quickly turn it off again. This way, I couldn't be accused of turning on 'the devils music'. I remember that one of her favourites was 'Good Vibrations' by the Beach Boys.

We click. And I find that most Saturday nights, she keeps me company whilst Jim is at church and Johnny is with his mates at the local pub. Sheila doesn't drink and she finds his mates a bit too much to handle, so this works out so well for both of us. Though I often talk about God to her, through her groundedness and sensibleness, we manoeuvre our way through to other subjects, finding similarities that help to further cement our friendship. Sheila becomes a part of my life, and I dearly love her for what she brings to it.

I find that I can be myself with her, and always feel better for her visits. It never occurs to me to tell her about Jim's abuse. Probably because I hope that it is behind us for my focus is on the future.

Naïve Hope

We have a shared love of comedy. Morecombe and Wise, an English comedy duo, had a TV program that I had watched pre-Christianity and these we both take great delight in retelling excerpts to each other over and over. Amazingly gentle funny men. Sheila and I often joke about being like them, she is alluded to as 'the-one-with-the-short-fat-hairy-legs', and I am supposedly 'the-tall-good-looking-one-with-the-glasses'. Or we simply called each other 'Sunshine". There were times when we imitated them with their signature gentle slap/ tapping on both sides of the face, just like Eric Morecombe did. I don't know how I would have fared without Sheila being there and her unquestioning support and acceptance. And humour.

She was extremely smart to break it off with Jim's brother, for the apples didn't fall far from the tree. Even after she and Johnny split up due to his drunkenness and poor social habits, she still visited. Suffice it to say that eventually Sheila had enough of Johnny's drinking and so she ended the relationship, giving him his engagement ring back. Johnny continued drinking and eventually he killed himself by default. This was about five or six years later. Falling asleep whilst smoking in bed one night, drunk, he started a fire that finished both him and his apartment. Though a shock to the family, none of them really learned from this for within a few short years, another brother, Danny, died from Sclerosis of the Liver through alcohol.

Even after Sheila got married to a lovely non-Born-Again man called Peter, she kept our friendship going. It was always an easy relationship, no matter the changes in our lives. She doesn't preach at me, doesn't judge me but simply accepts me. Such a relief and a blessing!

1963

~ Firstborn ~ Pride Leads to Hell ~ The Birth ~ Sin and Saviours
~ Seal of Baptism ~ Preacher Jim ~ Moran, James Moran

FIRSTBORN

Nothing seems to last for long and inside a short period of time there is another shift in my life. Within a matter of months of marriage, and still just seventeen years old, I find that I have fallen pregnant. Surprise!

When Bob had talked of marriage and children, I had wanted to run. I hadn't even considered children with Jim. I hadn't considered *anything*, as I had quite literally 'handed my life over to the Lord'. I had *totally* placed my life in God's hands. (Though in actual fact, I had placed it in Jim's hands, which I could not see at the time.) When one relinquishes self-responsibility, one also surrenders self-autonomy. So, the hierarchy in my life was: God first as Lord over all, then Jim as the master over the woman, then the woman's devotion and sacrifice to her husband and others in service. Where was Marni in all this? God knows, for I certainly didn't – except that she was busy doing what she was told.

In some peculiar way, the news of pregnancy felt inevitable. Again, it felt predestined. I was surprised too, sure, though it is generally the usual consequence of sex, yes? Too late to run, yet not as strange as when Bob had mentioned having children. But Jim and I had never talked of having children. Only about God. Initially.

More importantly, it also felt like something that I could not avoid. Similar to the sense around my engagement, there was a sense of predestination... Both in being pregnant to Jim and in this inevitable result of our marriage. Who was this little soul that was coming into the world to join us?

There was a strange sense of familiarity about all of this. Like I had done this before. And with Jim. This sense of the unavoidable was again present, hidden with a whispering 'Ah-hah' moment

Naïve Hope

somewhere inside. Inescapable and inexorable, we were now all three of us along for the ride...together.

On a conscious level, visions of missionary work as a couple with a child were now being tempered with the simple married couple future I had fantasised about, and my current situation had not totally dismissed such aspirations to be like other well-known missionaries. These Glamour Christians were being promoted in the church just as the pop stars were being promoted in the world. T.L Osborn, Oral Roberts, and other prominent missionaries were pictured with their good wives and offspring, all bright and shiny faced, beaming their goodness out to the world, smiling in the face of the devil, intent on the battle to convert the heathen and the condemned. Ok, Lord, if this is what you are calling me to, then so be it.

Our first Christmas together as a married couple was in the flat near his parents. Buses came vibrating round the corner, and we were slap bang on that noisy busy intersection. Being used to walking some distance to the bus-stop in Benchill, I was still adjusting to the much closer noise and associated activity together with the bump and thrum and reverberations as buses changed gears and either slowed down or sped up to take in or drop off passengers directly outside Jim's parents house. We didn't have much to call our own that first year, but we were both still in the early stages of it all. Sometimes there was love in the air. Then there would arise the contamination of discomfort or angst of some sort or another.

Jim was literally my boss. What he says goes.

I still worked full-time until I was about six months pregnant. The time is fast approaching when I am considered as being too large and too cumbersome to risk sitting on those high stools or fit behind the safety bar at work. Manoeuvring the high stool operators seat is just too dangerous. I had to give up work. Of course, this created problems with our finances, as we were still paying off our furniture on credit. Ultimately, these were repossessed, much to my shame and embarrassment. We got to keep the bed however, as they couldn't on-sell that. But what a wakeup call. This pushed us to look for cheaper accommodation, maybe a small room instead of a full one bedroom flat? But right then we still had a bed and we were both learning about financial management.

The church was closer for me from the flat than from Wythenshawe, but now I am pregnant and really starting to show and it becomes increasingly difficult to go to work and take care of domestic duties as well as attend the *many* church meetings.

Bible Study and Prayer Meeting nights were also held at private homes as well as Church. Sunday morning Service was Holy Communion (or Breaking of Bread as Throngs of God people termed it) and both Saturday and Sunday Nights at church were a combination of Prayer Meeting, Revival Service and Preaching. Alongside this the Youth Groups met on Monday nights and Saturday nights. Sunday School took place Sunday afternoons. We were pretty much committed to getting to as many meetings as we could. It was expected of us as Youth Leaders and therefore as examples for God that we attend as often as possible, to avoid getting distracted by the world at large and the Devil behind the glamour in the world. Etcetera. There was also a monetary collection every single meeting, as well as the tithing that was the main income of the church – that is a pledged tenth of one's income. Yup, could be a good gig. Built into church expectation, there was a biblical precedent and a promised future reward for all this, though the reward certainly took a long time coming to us.

Now that I am waddling and find that sitting for long is uncomfortable, I do not attend as many meetings. I also find it hard going to walk to church, though none of this stops Jim and he is still as committed to as many meetings as before.

My pregnancy would have been a most miserable affair without her presence and character. Encouraging me in my discomfort, for I grew extremely large really quickly, I share baby patterns and recipes with her, and dare a few gossipy tidbits of news items.

She also now encourages me with the idea of Jim attending ante-natal classes, as this is her own thinking and preference on the subject of pregnancy. Sheila obviously has been thinking about when the same thing happens to her. My life of dealing with crisis after crisis has left me little time to plan for success, and my preoccupation with letting God take care of things if I do what He wants is not serving me in familiarizing myself with the ways of the world. Not that I am aware of this just yet. Thank god that she is in my life. Such a blessing.

Giving up work means that I am now totally dependent on Jim financially for a while. This places extra pressure on him, and he is not home as often as he could be, whilst my life is more and more insulated and inhibited, with no money to spend during the day, and only his parents for any sort of company. My own mother and father are too busy with the church or it is' too far away' for them to travel to visit me also. Meanwhile, I am preparing myself for the birth, and so grateful for Sheila's occasional visits, and that I have someone who I can laugh with.

Knitting baby clothes occupies some time, but can be boring or tiring. I am often left alone at home now, spending many lonely evenings waiting for Jim to get back not having any real friends. Church *acquaintances* aplenty, but no-one I can really talk to.

I cannot open my heart to his parents, now can I? There is no way that I can share any fears that I have, particularly in view of his parents not being 'Born-Again'. It would be like letting the 'side' down to share any problems or concerns, especially as we were telling people that God would take care of them. This tended to diminish one's ability to share one's problems, so short of a disaster or an accident any communications are based around mundane things. I still feel very confused when it comes to sex. I wondered what all the fuss was about, but I remain somewhat sheltered from the full experience until well after I give birth. It was mainly missionary position and all over quickly, and I often felt frustrated or had a kind of 'That's' It?' feeling afterwards without knowing why. And the word 'orgasm' had never touched my virgin ears.

It was to be quite a while and several years later after I read a sex education book (off Jim!) that I actually had a 'G' spot. Mind you, I think I would have found it extremely embarrassing to have spoken to someone about such things, not unless they would dare to share similar issues with me. And that wasn't about to happen soon. So I tuck it away as another mystery of life.

I turn eighteen in the April and our firstborn is due to be born in the July. It will be eleven months after our wedding that my confinement is scheduled, just a month before our first wedding anniversary. So anyone who had been doing the nine month countdown finally had to admit that it wasn't a shotgun wedding! Hah!

Pride leads to Hell

Well anyway, we move on. A further lesson, or memory if you prefer, I would like to share with you is the day I was Taken Down A Peg.

Currently, I am now in the habit, and have been so for many years, of reviewing my life around Christmas and New Year, to see what I have accomplished, to see what I have survived. To see where I want to go next. Back then, when I was married, I used to try to do something similar at birthdays. Though there was less focus on Where To Next, as family life pretty much sorted all that for me and the reigning needs governed the day so to speak. It was more a sense of acknowledging that I was a year older, and wondering what had changed for me in that year.

Anyway, because I am a Christian, I am discouraged from wearing make-up, or tizz my hair, or dress in any way that is sexy or showy - the emphasis is always on being modest at all times. I *never* showed any cleavage at church, out shopping, or even home life for the most part of my life. Something I much regret later, as the bloom of my youth began to fade and those haunting words 'if you've got it, flaunt it' taunted me with recrimination over my too-inhibited mode of dress. Not that I wish that I had been given to exhibition or to parade inappropriately. That is not me. It's more the sense of a lack of appreciation over how well I actually was put together. Too many women berate their bodies, always willing to find something 'wrong' about their face, their hair, their butt, their tum, their legs etc. Too little acknowledgement of their best points. Despite the focus on modesty and sobriety and even though the church women aren't fashionistas, there is some competition at church – it shows in the choice of hats, shoes and discreet make-up and perfume. You couldn't attend church as a woman back then

Naïve Hope

without wearing a hat, or at the very least, a headscarf. This was because of certain statements made in the Bible about women's head covering in church. Yet, you were still expected to wear your best to church, and pay attention to this so as to Honour the Lord.

That last year as a teenager at school, and before getting engaged I still wore a smidgin' of discreet make-up. When I went out dancing with my friends, I wore full makeup, even though my skin didn't really need foundation. Now I sometimes get away with a touch of a natural coloured lipstick, but little else, though I do make efforts with my hair and headscarves.

So we come to the day I was *Taken Down a Peg*. It is shortly after my eighteenth birthday, and I am six months pregnant. Such a lot has changed since I got married. I am not necessarily looking my best radiant self at this stage, and am still settling into married life. I am in need of a happy moment, feeling lonely as I do, and as large as I do. Sheila is busy with her other things just now but she still pops down when she can. Meanwhile, I decide to see if I can remember what I look like, as the girl in the mirror doesn't look so very happy to me right now. I am also feeling a bit sentimental, approaching the last few months of pregnancy, and thinking of what having a baby entails.

I get out the few photos I have from home, the home I shared with mum and dad and I settle down on a kitchen chair. I am looking through the few photos I have of myself as a child, and my school photos, and doing a bit of a dreamy thing about 'I wonder how my old school friends are doing and where they are now'. Not that I had many real friends, but I had developed some friendly acquaintances with some school chums which had been over-stretched when I became a Christian and I was expected to hassle them into church. So having gone through the pictures I am looking at my last school photograph, a single portrait of myself, not the group photograph, for I didn't know where that had gone to; only this one has survived.

I remember I had done my own hair for the photos. I had coloured it all by myself. Though it had turned out more of a reddish colour than the true gold-blonde it was supposed to be. But that didn't matter. I had help with perming it from one of mum's next door neighbour friends, Lily – I didn't have the money to get it done professionally – and it had all turned out really well. In fact I was rather proud of my efforts to improve myself. You see, my hair is so very fine, and back then, it was like silk. Clips, plaits, waves, ringlets, ribbons, even hair-teasing just didn't stay in – everything just slipped off back to soft, shiny and flat. Not a lot I could do with it, until I discovered that perming it gave it some grip and it could hold a style. Big bouffant hair was becoming the fashion and I couldn't make it like that without a perm.

So there I am, looking at this photo of myself pre-Christian, pre-marriage and pre-children, and seeing myself as at least pretty and well-presented back then, and realising that this was in fact the best and most flattering photo of myself that I possessed. It was a moment of happiness that I had managed to have such a picture of myself before all of the responsibilities of a young family. Something I could show to my children when they grew up, something that showed them who their mum had been. I am lost in thought with my photos and even though I hear Jim coming back from church, I don't hear him open the kitchen door.

Meanwhile, Jim has come into the room and is quietly watching me. Asking me what I am doing, I happily share with him the photo, saying that I thought it was the best photo of myself that I had. I hand it to him so he can see it, and he takes it off me and looks at it. He studies it for a moment or two and I await his comment.

I am not prepared for what happens next. There is now a feeling of disapproval that touches me. I reach up to take it back from him, but he holds onto it. With a glint in his eye and a sneer on his face he snatches the photo away from the scope of my hand.

'Pride goeth before a fall' he disparages me, and taking the photo he goes to the toilet. Standing over the toilet bowl with the door wide open where I can clearly see him, and before I can stop him, he deliberately and maliciously tears the photo into little pieces and holding them in sight, he releases them into the bowl. Then he triumphantly flushes all the pieces away – all before I realise what he is doing or can move to stop him.

Naïve Hope

As the toilet flushed this last precious personal memory of pre-marriage away, I am too stunned to do anything except ask 'Why did you do that? That was the only one I had!'

'Because you are too proud. And Pride goes before a fall', he sneeringly announces. Turning on his heels he walks out of the room. As far as he is concerned that is that. End of story. He actually leaves the room and leaves me there with part of my self-identity in tatters. I am astonished, bewildered, shocked. Am I too proud? I do not know. It doesn't feel like I am, for all I feel is pain. Pain and hurt. And confusion. My self-esteem is in tatters.

And another part of me dies that day.

And do you know, to this day, I *do not* think that he didn't realise what he was doing. He *realised* all right. I recognise now that he was keeping me 'in my place'. How mean and childish, how *cruel*, ripping my image and self-image apart like that. Why did he do such a thing? Why did he have to hurt me like that? God knows. What on earth was he afraid of? Another question I ask myself years later is what pay-off did he get from being so cruel and self righteous?

Can you imagine my surprise when, also years later, I came across his collection of - intact - boxing award photographs. And certificates. Him, Jim, sitting there proudly, grinning over his prizes and cups?

Proud? Nah! Not Jim! Mr Perfect – Not!

Just a real control bully freak *hypocrite*. And still using his bullying power for the 'Glory of God'? Huh! 'Nuff said!

This nasty destruction took some recovering. It did hit, after all, at the image of who I was. Its message became 'You are nobody, you are unmemorable'. Turning back to prayer to ease my pain, I had no alternative other than to accept this action of his. I was certainly humbled. After all, he was the head over me, wasn't he? But it did not stop me from remembering this act. Things are getting to be more than I can bear. Again. But I see no way out, no end to this. Yet.

Time moves on and the lack of outdoor space and too many stairs forces us to rethink our living situation. Looking for something cheaper, the Pastor informs us of a ground-floor apartment near him. It is owned by his own brothers and there might be room for expansion into the other let rooms later as two elderly sisters rented these. Near him was very accurate, just a few houses away!

This is not my obvious choice, you understand, though I bow to Jim's insistence. It is a nice enough large old house with high ceilings, and has several storeys that include a cellar, located in a much nicer part of town. In actual fact it's just a few short miles from Jim's parents via a short bus ride, but those miles show huge changes in both English terrain and in culture. Easier to get to church from there, too. Very few stairs, *and* we have a back yard for Joseph and any further children! Closeness to the Pastor wasn't necessarily on my list of prerequisites, though Jim thinks it important.

In all it could have been much worse. Well... in all honesty, what with its mismatched and peeling wallpaper, shipped paint, patchy lino and general air of make-do about it, not that much worse. With my eye for aesthetics, I just had to accept and adapt to this bog-standard rental and do the best I could.

So soon we have moved on and moved away from Jim's parents and we are living five doors down from the Pastor and his family in Upper Chorlton Road, Chorlton-cum-Hardy. While we live here Jim seems to initially be behaving himself, but this wasn't for long, as inevitably Jim again has a jealous conniption.

I am accused of infidelity. Again. Whether something has been seen by him as a flirtation or exaggerated in his own mind to something so much more, I am not guilty.

Whatever it is he thinks he sees, it is not my experience. And my intent is not the one he claims it is. His jealousy and bad thoughts live in his head, not in mine. And to prove it, I get a black eye and a sore jaw. Undeserved? Yes, definitely! I had done nothing wrong and I *know* that I have done nothing wrong - I need to get help on this. Do I go to mum and dad again? Nah! No point, really, unless I want my face rubbed in it. So I make my way to Mary and Stuart's, those stalwarts of the Christian Church, and my – our - friends. They won't stand for this nonsense; they do not 'do' violence... And Jim has a healthy almost worshipful respect for them. Their response is to speak with Jim, or rather Stuart speaks with him whilst Mary consoles me. The result? Jim is chastised and I am mollified. And things are sweet and peaceful for a while... I think and believe that the problem is solved, and that after this Jim will be more mindful.

For some reason I still don't tell Sheila about Jim's abuse and violence. I think I saw it as somehow betraying him back then. How ridiculous!

The Birth

Jim somehow agrees to attend antenatal classes with me as I call on his promise to attend the birth process; we embark on the Lamaze method of preparation for a natural birth. A brave thing for him to do, but then, he owes me doesn't he? I didn't get myself pregnant all by myself, and not only that, the swing for men to support their wives in labour is taking hold in current thinking and in maternity circles and appears to be fully acceptable and indeed encouraged by our church and even by the Pastor, so he has been given permission from other significant quarters.

The forecast birth date arrives and on the due day our first child is born naturally after a normal labour, though without any drugs. We have a little boy. He arrives shortly after lunch. Because it is my request, and totally encouraged by the pre-natal staff, Jim stays with me to attend and support me during the birth. And he really did try his best to be there for me. Ok, so he was pressured into it, for I had held as firm as I dared about it, but there was also a part of him that was willing to try the new, and I have to acknowledge that. In the maternity ward delivery room, I called on all I had been taught during the pre-natal classes, drawing on the Lamaze breathing and pain techniques which I had been practising, but still found it to be an extremely exhausting and very painful experience. The staff kept insisting that I was going to be ages as this was a first-time birth, and consequently they had no painkilling drugs or gas on hand when I was actually ready to deliver. Throughout all of this, Jim and I both held fast to the *belief* that the baby would be born by lunch-time. Why? Because the due date was today, and lunch was half-way through the day. We believed that God would make it so. Gosh, but belief can be strong sometimes, can't it?

The staff didn't have the same point of view, and even though my waters had broken very early in the morning, they fully expected me to be longer seeing as this was a first birth. Dilations were initially slow, so this was understandable. Without painkillers, and with Jim trying to rub my back, it felt like a very painful ordeal. And I was not relishing a long labour, if this was the pain level I had to bear.

But then, around lunchtime, things began to happen quickly. The overwhelming sensation and imperative given me by my own body to just *p-u-s-h* took me by surprise, and the challenge for me was to hold back that push sensation until I was actually on the right table in the right room... not easy! Even the delivery doctor was taken unawares and in his excitement he tore through his rubber gloves a couple of times until he eventually managed to get on a pair that held. Too late for painkilling support of any kind, it is suddenly panic and pain and pushing and... then abruptly it is all over, and peace seems to reign momentarily.

For from the moment I looked into the face of my son, and felt him in my arms, the pain was behind me and I was just enthralled with this little being that I felt so connected to. There followed moments when I was sure he could really see me, and I really felt that he could recognise me like I did him. To me, it felt like I already knew him, and when I looked into his eyes, I could feel that recognition, that connection, and would become almost teary with it. And of course, we did know each other. The familiarity was real.

He was a healthy little boy, and I relished this new soul who had joined us and whom we named Joseph Stephen.

We had not known the sex of baby before birth, not in those days, so we had played with names for boys and girls. The tradition in Jim's family had been that the firstborn boy was always called James Henly. This had happened for many generations. However, I challenged that tradition. On purely practical grounds, I could not see the sense in having three heads turn when you called a name, and the immediacy of getting the required 'Jim's' attention being lost in having to explain exactly which Jim you were calling

Naïve Hope

to... It was already a problem when Jim and his father would both turn round to see who I was speaking to, let alone confuse a child too. I stuck by my guns with this one, and after enough explanations, they – Jim and his father, Jim – eventually gave way. I had won that round, but not that war. In order to achieve this concession, I had to forfeit the right to name my first son myself, and Jim took over this lordly duty, combing the Bible for the name he thought best. Eventually Joseph the dreamer and dream interpreter and Stephen the martyr won out. In retrospect, what burdens to put upon a child! But my own biblical blindness also won out and I conceded – at least he would escape being called Jim! However, I did claim the right to name our next child if and when there was one.

It was to be many years later that I learned that Jim actually nursed an idea that I found to be quite upsetting and quite perverse – it seems that he doubted my explanation of this naming and he conveniently thought that I wouldn't call our first born son James Henly because he wasn't actually Jim's son! If I had known this at the time, I think I would have left him there and then for his ever daring to doubt my loyalty, fidelity, honesty and devotion! But then was *not* the time for such revelations. I knew none of this. Such is our life together, and more is afoot...

In those days, directly after birth, it was the normal practise that new mums stayed in hospital for a week or two to recover, and often had help from family, particularly the new mum's own mother, for the first few weeks until new mum got the hang of things. So the plan was that after the delivery and first few days in hospital that we all stay at my parents in Benchill for a couple of weeks more. Mum and dad had offered up their bedroom, and were quite happy to sleep on the new bed-cum-couch in the living room downstairs. This would give Jim and myself and the new baby the privacy we needed. It was July and also the school holidays, and fortunately most of my siblings were away either at school camp or staying over with friends.

This aid and time for acclimatisation would have been idyllic in setting me up as a new mum and in my feeling supported. Would have been. Further cracks now showed in our relationship and Jim now reveals another side I had no idea of, exposing more of who he *really* was, though I still was far too naïve and not yet equipped to recognise it.

So...We are still staying at mum and dad's and I am pretty engrossed in re-learning and re-membering about baby nursing and breast feeding, and coping with the challenges and demands both physically, emotionally and mentally, even though I had done so much mothering myself alongside mum. There is still such a lot to focus on when it is your own child and you have sole responsibility, so I am busy learning as much as I can on changing nappies, bathing, feeding, etc etc. Maybe it was all too much for Jim. Prior to the birth, he had taken to sleeping tablets occasionally, as he sometimes found trouble sleeping, and would often stay up late to read the Bible.

It was about a week into this early post-natal adjusting period at mum's that Jim just upped and left. He simply disappeared. Not a word spoken. Took off. I had no idea of what was running through his mind, but I soon found out way. Talk about dramatic! The first indication took me by surprise.

I was in the middle of attending to Joseph's nappy and getting ready to breast-feed him when I heard the front door slam, yet no one had come in the house. Something didn't feel right. Had someone come in loudly or did someone leave angrily? I sorted baby's nappy out quickly, then as soon as it was convenient I went up to the bedroom to find Jim and to see if it was him and how he was. I found instead a note on the bed telling me that he had taken the whole bottle of his sleeping tablets and that he was getting on the bus and going where I couldn't find him or stop him from ending his life. I was shocked. Amazed. Stunned. And I panicked. What *was* going on?

My breasts were full to bursting with milk, but I had to find Jim. I gave baby Joseph to mum, even though he was crying, and shouted to dad what had happened. Grabbing breast pads and tissues and still dripping milk, I ran out of the house to go to the bus stop to stop Jim getting on the bus, but he was nowhere to be seen. Dad had been alerted by all of the ruckus and came in from the garden shed to see what the commotion was about and he saw Jim's note. Dad grabbed his coat and he then went in search of Jim, finding me at the bus stop. He took over the chase, sending me back home to nurse the baby and saying he would contact the police to help as he caught the next bus after Jim,.

Dad followed through. I was worried and upset and confused. Many hours later I was informed that Jim had been found and that he was in hospital after having his stomach pumped out. He had collapsed on the bus. Of course! Find an audience so you will be taken care of, 'cause this is not about a serious suicide bid, but to get attention and to feel important in some way! This may sound a bit callous, but I am looking at this from the viewpoint of what I know of him today. However, at that time we were all totally confused as to what had happened and why.

The reason he did such a thing, or should I say the reason he *gave* for doing such a thing that he gave me later beggars belief; it was (he says) because my *mum* had said to him 'Do you *want* a cup of tea?' *instead* of 'Would you *like* a cup of tea'. Not a word to anyone about it all, he had gone to the bedroom and sulked and sulked and made this big thing about it all. And thrown a hissy fit, but in a passive-aggressive way. And also in a punishing, selfish, vindictive way. He was making it all about him. He just couldn't cope because he wasn't getting the attention he demanded.

Communication – what a difficult thing it can be at times! But along with that one also needs honesty! I look back now and think to myself 'Nuts! He was Nuts!' and wonder why I didn't think that at the time. I just automatically went into 'Rescuer' mode. Again. Duh!

Mind you, when a woman is having (and when she has just had) a baby, her brain becomes a bit 'mushy' due to all the hormones coursing through her in such large quantities – which are necessary to equip her for the mammoth task of nurturing life and birthing it, and then nursing it. It is surprising that many people seem to have the attitude that you just have a baby and nothing much changes except a temporary 'bump', then a 'bit of extra fat after' and within a couple of weeks you magically 'snap' back into how things were *exactly* before it all began. No, no, no! This is *not* what happens. Though this initial concept a woman may have has been known to change when she *actually* embarks upon and experiences such a process.

Mind you, it's a bit disconcerting for men too, when a new bub comes along. But I guess that I expected Jim to have more understanding and to be able to support me through the intensely challenging experience that having a baby can be. It certainly does require a mature man to handle it, and at twenty-two years of age, some males have not necessarily gained that much maturity yet, though this admittedly depends on his capability, understanding and upbringing.

Jim survives this suicide attempt, naturally, having ensured that he is found whilst surrounded by others. Within a day or so of his release from hospital, we return back to our flat with some awkwardness. The role of being mother to Joseph is now fully upon me, but I needs must temper it with being 'mum' to Jim as well. An increased attempt at watching my 'p's and q's' is emphasised in order for us to retain any form of equilibrium. Though I suspect that was too ambitious a state to aim for...

Normal sexual relations begin again - for impatient Jim –after the usual six weeks post natal period, whether I am ready or not. The reason for this wait for indulgence is questioned over and over by him until he hears it from a medical professional himself.

Meanwhile, in Wythenshawe, things have also moved on. My brother Ian has had a huge fight and left home, though I had no idea where he went to. And so it falls to Joan to bear the brunt of dad's ill will. She is no longer the 'shining-one', no longer the favoured one. For her habit of lying on the bed reading magazines or comics is not conducive to her fulfilling the role that I had vacated. Now Joan is expected to not only 'do her bit' but to pull up slack for what I used to do, and what had been defaulted to Ian to do after I had married. With both Ian and myself out of the picture and off the hook, Joan was now 'It'. No surprise to tell that she not only failed abysmally, she became highly resentful, seeking a way of getting back at this injustice now served upon her. Later, Joan, who had changed her name at the time to Joanna, (a habit of first name tweaking she developed over the years – Joan, Joanne, Joanna, back to Joanne, back to Joanna) was to write later in her church newsletter about the time she had planned to knife dad to death. Yes, a Christian herself at the time, so she claims, yet she crept into mum and dad's bedroom with a knife intent on stabbing him through the heart. The fact that the intensified sound of her own heart beats and the fear of dad waking as he turned over in his sleep was the only thing that prevented her from doing so is beside the point. I never, in all my years of abuse at his hands, dreamt of doing such a thing.

Not long after this episode, at age thirteen, Joan ran away from home to the Pastor's house. Begging sanctuary, she persuaded the Pastor, over time, to adopt her, spinning and embellishing on her home stories. Though she was too old for legal adoption she was completely integrated into the family and had a name change, formally becoming a Parratt, and further ingratiating herself with the family in such a way that she learned to play the piano through them and she became the church pianist, always on the platform at meetings. Over time, she also came between the Pastor's son and his wife. He divorced and Joan conveniently stepped into the breach, completing her coup by shortly being made a minister by good old dad-in-law. But that is another story.

SIN AND SAVIOURS

Meanwhile, the dye now cast in our little family of three, we endeavour to make a little home for ourselves with what we have; Jim working hard and Witnessing hard and me allocated to home duties and taking care of domestic issues and to a degree, I am content. Being a mother is satisfying, and I enjoy watching Joseph grow and develop. Now that the birth is over it is easier for me to focus on my lot, and on how I can improve it, and I enjoy the moments I can share with my son. And momentarily, Jim is again pleasant and charming. When things are going right, and Jim is attentive, then life is great and somehow gives life some meaning.

However, I never can quite understand how he can change his moods so quickly. For change again they do, and on these occasions I examine myself regularly to see where I am to blame or what I have done to cause the shift. Or not done. Conscientious and a mite scared, I try to anticipate his needs ahead of time, as I endeavored to do with my dad.

Like most women after childbirth, within a few months I am also attempting to regain my figure to some degree, not necessarily for fashions sake, but because I knew that one didn't necessarily have to 'go-to-seed' after birth.

And more practically, because I just couldn't *afford* new clothes. I wear my maternity smocks still until I could eventually fit into my pre-pregnancy dresses and skirts. Worry over Jim certainly helps this along. But motherhood itself can keep you on the go...

Reasonably quickly I regain my figure due to breast feeding and all the activity that is entailed in being a mum and a wife. Six months later you can't tell that I have been pregnant, and my energy is returning.

I also remembered that as a teenager I had accompanied mum to the hospital for her six-week post-natal check-up after the birth of Tina. Whilst we waited, we sat talking to a friend of mum's who was also attending her six-weeks-post-natal appointment too. She was dressed in a slim fitting and peplum waisted suit, looking like she wasn't even married, let alone a mother. I was so impressed by her appearance, and clearly saw that despite motherhood she had kept her figure. Quite unlike all the other women in the neighbourhood that I had seen, who often went to seed, or never really took a pride in their appearance. I had decided there and then that I did not have to 'let-myself-go' like the others, but that one *could* stay slim after birth. I had resolved right then that if I ever got pregnant, I would still take care of my figure. Despite the fact that I had become a Christian, even though one is not supposed to notice how they look, I always had a kind of sense of pride of looking and being the healthiest and best that I could, but without any flaunting or sexy exposure. Tempered as I was by religion, I simply chose not to get fat! I still fitted my wedding dress until I was in my late fifties, many years later... I also develop the habit of taking baby on the bus to visit mum and dad, for they just didn't seem to be able to visit me for a variety of reasons, usually church related.

Naïve Hope

Except for my 'fattening-up' after my stay in the convalescent home, I had always been reasonably slim, so much so that on one visit with baby my mum upbraided me. 'Marni, you are getting too skinny – you look positively gaunt!' she declared. Mum had always had trouble with her weight, being of a different build to myself.

My wrists and ankles were always slim, and I had very good legs and also tapered fingers. My knees had been called 'sexy' by the local boys, at which I had naturally blushed at the time. Though I had narrow shoulders, I had definite hips (and a bit of a JayLo bottom long before they became popular) with a definite waist. Mum also had a definite waist as well as a larger bosom then mine, but she was also heavier boned. A bit embarrassed at the time, I had nevertheless been flattered to have been described as 'curvy' even though I was quite slim. I don't think I really realised my sexual attraction, except on the odd occasion, usually as a result of receiving unwanted attention. Like most girls, I wanted attention, but didn't generally know what to do with it when I got it. My religious conversion made it easier to un-focus on make-up and amplifying any physical attributes and tempered it to my simply looking the best I could - for the Lord... With a definite little tummy swell just below my waist, I would sometimes secretly despair at not having an exact wash-board stomach, little realising that this 'fat' was essential for correct hormonal functioning. After childbirth, when I was slim again, I retained that little bump. Ridiculous really, for looking back I had a very good little figure. Mind you in my teenage years, I only came across a few teenagers who were actually happy with how they looked – movies had certainly begun to have an effect on us, and the Audrey Hepburn and Kate Hepburn looks were just as popular as the curvy Ann-Margret, Marilyn Monroe and Jayne Mansfield types. Today, there is even more ridiculous media focus on shape and weight, though in some pockets of society, a more reasonable attitude is beginning to filter through again.

I am not aware of just how programmed I have become and am becoming. In hindsight, I am ridiculously sincere and genuine, naïve as a child, I am acutely aware of the hurt and pain from broken promises, so I do not break promises or commitments. I keep my word no matter the cost. And in all sincerity, I renew and re-focus and re-apply my promise to follow the Lord and to serve Him.

During childhood, I had often experienced the pain of being let-down. And so because of who I am, not only as the sensitive and too-caring person that I can be, but also because I am now a Christian, I again concentrate on doing to others what I would have them do to me. Whenever and wherever possible. The focus is generally always on giving. Because of my childhood experiences, this is simply building on what I already have learned about life, that in order to live I must please. When I fail, or feel guilty about not doing more for someone, I see myself as the sinner that the Bible condemns us as being.

Even so, sensitive as I am, there are times that I demand from others that which I demand from myself. This is not always a pleasant and welcoming energy to be around. My desire to welcome and help others is also unknowingly compromised and contaminated with my desire to change them – for 'their own good', you understand. In my desire to be of service to the Lord, I accept what the deliverers of the original salvation message (the church) deliver me – initially – and, 'proving' it with scriptures to myself, I then attempt to push it onto others. In my own eyes, I am trying to help to 'save their souls' but in reality, I was as guilty as the church in trying to foist onto others that which I was only just becoming familiar with. The responsibility and mission we are all pressed with during the evangelistic services are that every new Christian is charged to carry the 'good news', the 'gospel', to *everybody*. And to tithe! Yes, every single member is expected to contribute a tenth of their income to the church on a regular basis. Hmmm... Ten members equals one whole salary...

How do you make a church grow whilst ensuring its longevity? You ensure new recruits by getting the 'new'-ies to sign up more newies... Basic marketing. Pyramid selling mentality. And there is no cost for this form of enlistment, for you don't pay for this sort of marketing – you simply quote scripture and guilt them into doing so.

Yes, skeptical I sound, and skeptical I now am, but back then I was naïve, susceptible, too receptive, sincere, and so bloody gullible.

Naïve Hope

The need to believe in something, something I could *count* on, was obviously important to me in my own particular world; one which tended to be of doubt, chaos, and unreliability. With God on my side, I think one subconscious perception ran, my sense of powerlessness and alienation could be alleviated. *'If God be for Us, Who can be against Us'* declares another scripture... and one which many opposing religions assert as their *own* exclusive right to claim.

So cleverly and quietly, misled and conformed, my misdirected missionary zeal overtook my mind, and I have indeed become unable to see my own situation clearly. The 'enemy' *out there* was and is the focus, rather than the enemy within *my own* home and heart. Sure I followed the scriptures to the best of my ability, resisting supposed 'temptations', though truth be told, my own inner guidance system had high moral standards anyway. I didn't drink, didn't smoke, didn't play around, didn't cause mischief, no longer stole, was excruciatingly self-examining, didn't do anything really, that would cause me to be labeled a 'bad girl'. Yet I never *questioned* the apportioning of the title 'sinner' to everyone, myself included. My own issues over unworthiness; well, I must be unworthy if my own parents hadn't seen fit to support me – guilt; even when I attempted right I was accused of wrong – fear; a constant companion was fear of punishment, deserved or not; all conspired to agree. Though the biblical and religious claim that each child is 'born in sin' – and baptized as such - is a smart way to cover all of one's bases.

The idea of the need to be rescued fed into my own need to be freed from the constraints that I had encountered in my life to that point, as well as the well-honed argument by the church that was fully intended to keep one on their toes; For if one doesn't accept the Lord, and because He died for *You*, then his crucifixion rests on *Your* head... The message of sacrifice by the Savior was *capitalized*.

I also add another observation here as I presently realize something else. It is quite possible that in some way, at that time, I am most probably already programmed, and dare I say *addicted*, to putting others first. I am mostly running purely on the survival skills I had to learn earlier in my childhood that predispose me to this.

This, of course, doesn't help one to read a situation correctly or objectively, nor to see alternative ways of dealing with them other than what one has already become kind of wired to; I later learn that the brain works through developed pathways in the brain neurology. This is how we acquire skills and patterns, otherwise we have to make up everything we do everyday afresh every time we go to do something – these repeated actions or reactions can become a pattern that gets embedded, kind of like a ready series of instructions or even as a program, and effectively they save us time. Otherwise we would get up in the morning and have to learn all over again that we need to eat and what is required in order for us to do so; or that we need to work out how to dress ourselves etc.

Emotion is a way of learning, with strong emotion a way of imprinting and embedding certain concepts, perceptions and behaviours. I am explaining this rather roughly but I hope I can get across that when we come to brand new situations, if what we currently know and do isn't working, then we often have to unlearn what we have done in the past, to be able to re-learn how to do something differently.

We can get used to the familiar ways of doing things. And of familiar thinking! Unless we question what we see.

Having said all that about my particular church, I must mention that at least Christianity does not stone its women outright, nor perform nasty anatomical removals on them. I look at the cruelty visited on the women in other religions, other 'faiths' and am amazed that the adherents actually allow certain things to still take place. They seem to prize how things look over the substance of living a truly honorable life – surely honor is about respect, and surely *all* genders and *all* ages deserve respect? The Catholic Church is also now becoming accountable for its misdeeds, thankfully, and the inherent violence in other eastern sects or religions points to twisted and unevolved minds to me. I think the only 'religion' that tends to be the most respectful is Buddhism. Would I ever become one? No, though in later life I more readily accept their philosophical aspects more than I accepted others.

SEAL OF BAPTISM

There is something else here that I have had to work through that may seem insignificant to some, but others may realize a truth contained within. If the following exposé here on Baptism makes you feel uncomfortable for whatever reason, I quite understand if you skip this over to the next chapter. For I want to expose Baptism as a Ritual.

However, I sincerely hope that if Baptism has happened to you and you wish to dare to test if it is or isn't working for you in some way today, then maybe this is an opportunity for you to do something about it. Let me continue; Back to the Seal of Baptism.

The Ritual that is Baptism.

One which subliminally, subconsciously and much more seriously than this, *energetically*, can affect one at an extremely tender and early age. It is this; as a tiny infant, I, like thousands and millions of others, was baptized. I am not connecting this with a discourse on the difference between Methodist, Baptist, Catholic or any section of church organization. What I am considering here is the act and form of the 'ceremony' of Baptism. The one that is done on a very small baby in order to give it a name, and in some cases, a 'god'parent. There is also the Baptism that can occur as an adult such as the one I undertook shortly after my conversion. In effect, I was baptized twice though the second took the form of full emersion in water – similar to the biblical report that John (the Baptist) was said to baptize Jesus.

At a child's baptism, there is usually 'holy water' of some form, together with accompanying incantations or declaration, and possibly ceremonial attire or other accoutrements. It can be performed with a small (or large) gathering, all attendees bearing witness and contributing energetically (and emotionally) to the process. In other words, they, by their very presence, are enforcing and amplifying the procedure. The minister is usually accepted as the representative of God in this ritual. And that is what it is – it is a *Ritual*. The minister holds the baby, performs a prayer, invocation, incantation or some such over the baby, names the baby, and applies 'blessed' or 'holy' (energized in a particular way) water onto the babies forehead between the brow. In the shape of a cross, a plus sign; '+'. Coincidentally, this same shape is also that of a symbol which has the power to close and seal as well as possessing other esoteric meanings and impacts. But I think that the point made regarding the symbol's connection with religion is enough to raise some curiosity as to its application. In short; *He applies pre-pared water in the Sign of the Cross which seals the baby's forehead, the position of the Third Eye Chakra.*

Okay, some of you may feel a bit uncomfortable when I talk about chakras, so I won't talk about it anywhere else in the book, therefore let's simply refer to it as the energy centre at the *front-brain*, the *thinking* area of the brain. A brain that is absolutely wide-open to everything around it as a child, without the ability to filter or reason having yet been developed in any way.

The process of 'Sanctification' is that of dedicating someone or something to the purpose or use of a particular religious cause or of a God. It is the separating of to and for another. It signifies an act of will over another in the case of baptism, over someone that cannot yet *decide for themselves.* Akin to signing up one's child for the army before they can even walk, whether they want it or not. Is this what a Loving Kind God really wants? For it is a traditional way of undermining free will and one's personal religious, and often spiritual, choice. 'Holy' simply means set apart – and there are many groups that set themselves apart, and not for pure reasons either.

Let me put this all together now - Words have power. Prayer is a form of word-power, holding energy. The minister holds power, even if just that ascribed him by his followers. Water holds energy. The cross is a symbol that holds energy. The brain and chakras work with energy. Undergoing a baptism can truly 'seal' one's future thoughts or path. To what? To that *which has been intended in or by the ceremony.* Some may see this as a spell-making, others as a pre-programming of the nervous system and mind, others as a ritualistic method to keep a being or soul or mind conformed to a preferred type, others may see it as a way of taking away the independence, identity and autonomy of an individual. If you liked reading the DaVinci Codes, then you will begin to see the ritualistic aspect here.

And if you are not sure what is being inferred by the reference to energised water, and Holy Water, Dr Masaru Emoto has written some very interesting books on his work and experiments with water, prayer and energy.

In summary, and to explain why I have brought this up here, it is simply this... I continued to have a predisposition to religious authority until I had cleared this symbolic cross and ritual and all it held me to in my own way. If one has been subjugated to authority in a form that is forceful and that has overridden one in some way, it can be a difficult thing to get clear of. This can be any authority, though the religious authority can play on a desire or fear around God. Gurus can be classified as religious authority, and if one has buried or sealed off access to one's *own* inner Guru, one may well be predisposed to looking up to other's ideas rather than one's own.

And as I look back now, I am clearer as to why people get pulled in to religions, especially of the radical or evangelistic variety. For it is the *type* of person that needs religion that keeps it going. It is my own personal opinion and experience that the main reasons are generally these:

- One needs rescuing, as they have some level of helplessness within themself
- They are unable to monitor or control themself effectively and need an outside source to grant them 'forgiveness'
- One has been baptized or sealed to follow an authority or power
- One wants the power and permission that comes with church authority for self-righteousness, hidden superiority and condemnation of others
- One needs a prop, something mysterious that can explain the unexplainable for them, alleviating them from having to work it out for themselves
- If life treats you well, religion and faith is easy to follow when there is no challenge; hard challenges and clear examination can demonstrate loopholes and contradictions
- One needs to belong to something in order to be validated

And I must confess that in various ways, some of these fitted me, I was one of the 'types' that allowed faith and religion to give me my answers to life.

We have all heard at some point of the reality of a death of someone close to us. And of the inevitable question, 'Why did God allow this?'. This is when many have a crisis of faith. But more fool them when they swallow the sugar coated phrases, 'It must be God's will', 'Only the good die young', 'God needed him in heaven'. Sanctimonious tosh, designed to stop one from examining why such as is ascribed to a supposedly loving God with all power. Death is part of Life; and fear of death (or the fear of the consequences of life) is a great way to enslave others to conform.

Despite my apparent rantings, I must also allow to each their own. If a particular faith provides solace, so let it be. My problem is in the act of foisting another's beliefs onto me. Funny, when that is exactly what I did in youth and early marriage. There was no intent to enslave anyone, and my motivations were for the safety of their Soul. So I thought at the time. But I am older and wiser now, and at least I have learned not to do it anymore.

I was forced to confront my religious realities in the face of the events of my own life and all of the unmet promises.

Am I being too harsh, too straight, too honest? There are many more arguments that I still have issue with that I could raise here, but that would take us on another journey. These are my current thoughts on the subject, the result of my own questionings and understandings. Each of us must satisfy our own mind, our own heart, as to the validity of any claims of faith before adopting them. For compliance brings one mindset, and this can prevent us making new decisions and different choices for our own life.

And even then, we are allowed to make mistakes. Mine is haunting me still.

Preacher Jim; Saviour

In due course, Joseph is baptized. By the Pastor. Mary and her husband, Stuart, are named as the godparents. Though there was actually very little, in fact, *no* co- or god-parenting. Ignorant to

Naïve Hope

how it worked, it seemed to me to be just a necessary baptismal component, not an actual role.

At the time I have no reason to doubt anything of the baptism event, having been baptized myself, and at the time, I fully believe with faith that this is the correct thing to do.

The baby's birth is over, things are settling down again, and I am being a good wife. Surely now that I have my figure back and Jim is able to have sex whenever he wants or demands, things will begin to improve? That was what *I* thought, imagined and hoped. But Jim is still not happy, and still getting moody. Naturally, I default to examining myself again.

'What am I doing wrong?', I ask myself... *I* question *myself* over Jim's behavior. It is a habit now, this feeling somehow that it is because of me in some way. I am still far from viewing Jim as his own problem, and still naively blind. But life is about to bring me another **lesson** – though it takes me quite some time to actually realise that that was what it was. A valuable lesson on who Jim really is...

For now something that is so ludicrous, so ridiculous takes place that even now I am still bemused with it all. Did it really happen? Absolutely.

So my friend, there I am, out of habit, trying to turn myself inside out to do the right thing – and there, my friend, was one of the big contributors to this; my thinking it was all me, all my fault, and that I wasn't trying hard enough, doing enough, being enough, giving enough, loving enough:

It is late one night and I have been waiting up for Jim and attending to baby and also taking this opportunity to catch up on the chores - when my husband comes home well past the church closing time with a young woman in tow.

She has short curly light brownish hair, bright red lipstick on, is slim and attractive, young and feisty, wears a very smart fake ocelot fur coat, appears somewhat glamorous and after the initial introductions, she lets *him* do all the talking. So Jim explains.

Her name is Elsa.

She needs a bed for the night!

It turns out he was Witnessing and handing out Tracts – those flyers on Jesus and being 'Saved' - on his way home when he met her. He had been trying to 'save her'.

And she has no place to sleep for the night. So Jim has brought her home in order for us to help her. As good Christians should.

I listen, wondering why this is happening, and somewhat bewildered by such an unusual event.

But wait – there's more!

Oh, and by the way, she is a *prostitute*.

He has brought a prostitute home. Into our house!

And to keep her off the streets, Jim was good enough to Witness to her about his faith in the Lord, and about Jesus's saving grace. 'Jesus Saves' again!

And he gave her a tract about Jesus.

And tried to 'save' her. He really did!

His disjointed story continues as I listen and wait. For I can see that there is more, though I have no idea what.

And he slipped up trying to 'save' her.

For he had actually ended up sleeping with her. He said that he had 'made love' to her. Actually used that term! Hah!

What he meant was that he had fucked her, for crying out loud.

A prostitute.

And he brings her home. *Home!*

And now *I* am being asked to show *Christian Compassion* and give her a bed for the night to *Keep Her Off The Streets!*

Not only that, but it's made clear that it is now *my Duty* as a *Christian* to assist her.

Oh, and by the way, he was so sorry for transgressing. And he has sought the Lord's forgiveness...

Naïve Hope

And so naturally, of course, and, as *instructed*, it was now up to *me* to automatically *forgive* him, just as Jesus forgave Mary Magdalene who was supposedly a harlot (though my later studies showed me that this is actually doubtful). Because, you see, Jim had now *told* me of his transgression, and he had *confessed* that he had strayed, and *couldn't* help himself, sinner that he is, and he was *sorry and asked for forgiveness*, and God has forgiven him, that's why he *needs* Jesus anyway, and he's bought her home to *help her*, and now would *I* be a *Good Wife* and show her some *Christian Kindness* as it was *The Thing To Do*, and would I *say no more* about it...?!

Oh! The bliss when you can do whatever you want, ask God to forgive you, and you are automatically forgiven; and all of this without having to make amends to any injured party – for after all, what argument dare others have if the great Almighty is on your side?

But this is not all. For, get this, the *only* bed available in the house is our fold up couch, and yes you've got it, this was *our own bed*! I kid you not! And poor breastfeeding and hormone befuddled brainwashed me actually tries to *comply*! Duh!

Every argument I can think of fails in the face of the assault of Bible quotes that are aimed at me by him. I am actually beginning to feel uncomfortable. My befuddled brain is swamped. I am now made to feel ashamed. Then guilty. I am actually beginning to feel *sorry* for him. And her.

It is now past midnight and late, we are all tired, and so I prepare the couch bed for the night. I don't like this, not one bit, but I am now made to feel so shamed, guilted and pressured into this. Arguments of a biblical nature continue to force me to comply. I am just too stunned by the unfolding events, and don't have a clear compass on this, so I err on the side of compassion. I want to be a good Christian after all...

And so of course I try to make room in the bed. Knowing and feeling like crazy that there is something wrong with this picture, but I have no voice, cannot find any more words, and now feel like I have no choice. I think that I am still stunned by all of this and I cannot think straight!

And the niggles I have about it, the urge to thump him and kick him, and to smother *her* with the lipstick, perfume, *anything*, in her handbag just doesn't exist in my world, does it?

So I bury my un-cried tears, and call on my missionary zeal and ideal of 'love for all'. Ha!

And I extend Christian kindness.

And I hope to God that in the morning I will be able to think clearer and have an answer to all of this.

Things quieten. The light is turned out and we all lay down, Jim placing himself between Elsa and myself. Things go deadly quiet.

However, when I am eventually lying squashed in bed, next to him lying squashed next to her, holding my breath, and I feel the very thing beginning to happen that I will *not* allow to happen, that *subtle* movement that you know is hands-beginning-to-go-where-they-shouldn't-be-going, and definitely not anywhere on I body but on *my husband's* body (or even worse, on *her* body), then I literally vault up out of there like a jack-in-the-box, and yell at him and her that 'I cannot do this, I can feel something happening in the bed, and I cannot sleep like this. I will *not* put up with this. This has to stop.' I surprise myself at my conviction on this and at my own anger and disgust!

And now of course, I am not being very Christian-Like, not very *forgiving*, and in fact *I* have a dirty mind. And for days later *I* am the one who has done the wrong thing. Go figure!

Baby starts crying. Baby has fully woken up with all this happening and I have to settle him down again. I start boiling milk for a night drink. There is further discussion, proclamations of her or his or their innocence, and condemnations toward me for kicking her out of our bed. But I am now so furious with what he is calling me, for turning her out, and then blaming *me* for asking her to leave the house and so *Causing Her To Further Sin* that I lose it. In all of this, Jim has said something that sparks a red rage in my mind. He accuses *me* of not showing Christian kindness!

For the one and only time in my life, I throw something at Jim as he leaves - I fling the jug of heated milk at him as he escapes through the door to take her somewhere else for the night. The

Naïve Hope

door slams, and I do not remember seeing Jim for the rest of the night. I do not know if he returned. He probably did not, because nothing else registers about that night, I think the shock of what happened caused some kind of 'freeze' to happen in my mind. Though I vaguely remember trying to work it all out as I calm myself whilst I nurse baby. I do remember my surprise at my taking such a step as to physically protest and object in such a violent way; I am somewhat amazed at myself as, after baby is settled, I dazedly clean up the milk mess on the floor. Then I muse that he didn't turn back to hit me over this rebellion against him. I think he too was surprised. But even though there was, I realised, a degree of safety with someone watching – the prostitute girl - one can only push one's luck so far.

The following day, nothing more is said about it. I am too confused, upset and angry to trust my voice, and he probably is too guilty at what he caused to happen. But he acts polite and quiet, and does not provoke any further violence. Chocolates and flowers are proffered without a word, but the association is implied yet his attitude of *me* 'not doing the right thing' taints the giving. I am not allowed to question how this incident – betrayal actually! - happened. Somehow I feel it is my fault in some way...

For sanities sake, the incident is buried. For the sake of the marriage, I have to bury it deep. And I forgive. And I did. And I move on. Enough said.

And life goes on. For *'better or for worse'*, after all.

Though at that time, this incident was another message, a warning, that I *clearly* didn't hear, but I daresay I wouldn't have known how to handle it in any other way.

In the relating of this little engaging story, I burst into laughter at the ridiculousness of the whole situation. How the heck could I have been so duped, so silenced, so compliant as to have put up with this absolute crap? Even to *let* her into the house? That is what programming does to you! And bullying! And using the Bible for your own ends! Stupid me! Stupid cruel crafty devious itchy-pants Jim!

It never occurred to me that this was grounds for divorce. It never entered my mind to consider leaving him. I had submitted to his abuse, I had yielded to his position as 'head of the house', I had resigned myself to obedience to the marriage vows and the church, filling my mind with aspirations to be good and virtuous, 'turn the other cheek', and consequently there was no room in my head or my heart for anything other than the preservation of my family and my home with whatever sacrifice was required of me. The contemplation of a 'broken home' was deemed damning in those days, so could not possibly be part of any equation for safety or survival for me and the children. For what would happen should Jim leave us? How would we cope? How could I cope? What condemnation would I receive from the church for 'not holding the marriage together', for everyone knew (didn't they?) it was the woman's duty to do so.

These questions and their terrifying answers - *if* they had could possibly have flitted through my mind, trailing their devastating repercussions behind them - these thoughts would have left very little mark, whisp or spectre behind that my mind could fasten onto to, for they were contrary to all that I stood for, all that I claimed as a Christian. For hadn't God promised that he would take care of those that follow Him and His ways? The spiritual, domestic and material provision of my children was what mattered, and in order to keep that, I must continue my role, in the Hope, the *naïve Hope*, that God would see it all right in the end.

And recording this, *another* thought occurs, something that was beyond *any* thoughts I could have had at that time – so unspeakable for me even now, but knowing what I know now of others, it is possible – did he want a *threesome*? Shit! Perish the thought! Would he have tried to pull the *'the marriage bed is undefiled'* Biblical quote out for that one?

Yuk. I will stop right there!

He couldn't 'Save her'? Couldn't 'save' himself more like!

Naïve Hope

MORAN. JAMES MORAN

Truth to tell, though, soon enough Jim did try to make it up to me over this. God, that charm of his – it must have covered a multitude of sins. He now turns it on. What is it with this man? Does he have no conscience?

So now out comes the Goody Jim and his little gifts, with his charming attendance and attempts to contribute or to be considerate. This did make it easier to put it behind us and his charisma shines forth again like the sun. I am paid compliments, brought roses and chocolates, and this becomes further establishing of an apology-pattern; together with at-the-moment-heartfelt-apologies-'*cause-I-can't-live-without-you.*

I am plied with flowers to make amends and in a moment of awareness, or maybe just guilt, he talks of taking me to the pictures. His stance now seems to veer toward this *Mistake* of his – as it is now referred to, if at all mentioned or hinted at - being solely the result of all of the stresses of a new child, with the relevant new responsibility, and our lack of time together with the deprivation of no longer having time (or dates) as young marrieds; and other new-agey type of phrases that we were coming across on radio programs or in the odd newspaper that had made its way into the house.

So as you can imagine, I was a bit surprised, but happily so, when he suggested that we go to the movies together. This was new. And very welcome. Yes. Well it had all been a bit intense, and we always seem to be living such a serious life. I think in part his mum may have been involved in this. I have no proof, but that is my thinking trend on this. His mother was a simple woman, and even though she came to the church occasionally, she and Jim's dad still held into in a rough kind of way their own beliefs. Jim's mum was a Catholic and his dad was a Protestant, and they had come over to England from Northern Ireland when Jim was a small child. The difference in their religions simply meant that Jim could follow either. Hard-working and hard drinking, his mum, Ginnie, had a heart of gold – when she was sober – and she may well have told him to take me out occasionally, because I cannot think of anyone else who would have put such a clear thought there. Not unless it was myself and I have forgotten? Had I said it in an argument maybe that we didn't go out anywhere? Possibly so. Anyway, this idea was not a bad thing, and after the austerity and duty and responsibility it was a welcome change for us.

Did I bring up that the church frowned on this sort of thing? No. Possibly because there was now some small recognition filtering through amongst parishioners that couples need to do something other than go to church together to stay together. There was a bit of loosening up on the phrase 'The family that prays together, stays together'. Thank God!

I remember the movie we went to see. It was a brand new movie, and Sheila had spoken about it to us. She was always up on trend about things, was Sheila. Thank God for that too... She had seen it with her husband and thoroughly recommended it to us both.

'Why don't you go and see it for yourself?' she asked. 'It's based on a book by someone who worked for the Intelligence Service'.

'Who is that?' Jim said.

'Ian Fleming. The book he wrote is called *From Russia With Love* and it stars a really good actor, called Sean Connery. It's about spies, and he plays a member of the British MI5. You will really enjoy it.' Then a bit of a rave followed from her, together with the description of a couple of exciting episodes, and Jim was hooked. *We* were hooked. Diversion. Hallelujah!

We went to the movie. Sean Connery was every man's ideal of being a man's man. And most women's ideal of being the sort of hunk she would love to be rescued by. For days, my mind replayed bits from the movie, and even Jim carried a different air about him. He found a copy of the book of the film at a library, and this was the beginning of a new persona for him.

It impacted us both at a time when we needed some diversion, and at a time where in our own ways we were both groping with this whole thing called life, and this thing called marriage in particular. I read the book after him, fully recommended and raved on by him to do so. We start to work our way through all of Ian Flemings' books, and over the ensuing years we have both read and seen

Naïve Hope

every one of his books and the films based on them. This was the start of a new chapter, for now Jim began to try to imitate Bond.

Jim had never had a proper suit, usually preferring his old fashioned check sports jackets, shirt with detachable collars and a pair of complementary trousers. Shirt collars that I often had difficulty starching and ironing in the same way as the Chinese Laundry he used to use. For even though collared and cuffed shirts had been available for *years*, Jim had insisted on using cufflinks and shirt studs for his collars. So old-fashioned! Jim never had much style really, though he did generally wear worsted jackets that were of quality. Or so I thought at the time. They were usually some sort of check, but I realised later that this was how a lot of Irish dressed in those days. And these were the cheapest to buy, because he bought them from second hand shops!

Both Jim and I didn't own jeans, and it was to take us another thirteen years to get some. This happened when we went a little mad at finding a jeans direct outlet and everyone in our little family started to wear jeans and jean jackets, all matching to some degree or another. Even I eventually had a denim skirt. But I am getting ahead of myself. So during the James Bond movies we were exposed to Saville Row suits, smart outfits, classy shirts and ties as well as the then trademark Trilby hat that Bond wore. Jim insisted on having a suit made to measure. With a matching waistcoat. And it had to have a red silk lining like one of the James Bond's suit, he insists, with double splits at the back of the jacket just like the one James Bond wore. We also shop for a similar overcoat, and Jim also gets himself a Trilby hat; *the* Trilby. We saved up for all of this, and as I was glad of a bit of classy tailoring on him for a change I went along with it all. It seemed harmless at the time. I had been used to snazzy dressers before I met Jim, anyway. And I must admit, James Bond made a change to Holy Roller or Demented Nutjob.

He practised James Bond poses. And I tried to style my hair like his leading lady, Tania Romanova. Except that I couldn't afford hairstylists, and still had to observe the unwritten limits as to how much I could fix myself up.

To be fair about this dose of fantasy which was a new thing to me in our limited relationship, I am glad of the change from ultra-serious church-ification, We are even softening up at home and watching the occasional TV program. I had anyway found a bit of a role model myself in Emma Peel of *The Avengers* fame. She never exposed her breasts, always dressed well covered, though I had to alter my dress and skirt lengths to be a longer length. But she was always stylish and classic and slightly more modest than the current trends. With my limited budget and means I could occasionally copy her style, though it was mainly in growing and wearing my hair the same way. Not only that, but she didn't let men push her around. She was smart, savvy, articulate and strong, but still a lady. The show itself was a bit of a fantasy statement on the capability of women, as well as bringing a well-dressed fashion trendsetter with style and humour into my lounge. Plus, despite the odds, she always came out of it in the end! What was there *not* to love about it?

But I knew it was all make believe. Or I think I did. After all, I was still a young woman who had very little in the way of peer examples to style myself on. Most of the women in our church lacked aspiration in the fashion department, and dressed very dowdily or very expensively which pushed things right out of my reach. James Bond movies had woken us both up in this area of style to some degree. This didn't mean that we attended lots of movies. No, we just waited for the next Bond movie to come out.

However, if I had been listening more carefully I would have been aware of the whispers of identity confusion that all of this heralded. They say that imitation is the best form of flattery. I am not so sure. Because later on it became Cliff Richard that Jim tried to emulate... Me? Well much as I admired Marilyn Monroe and Audrey Hepburn and still do, I had too many other things to keep me occupied so I didn't try to emulate them. But whenever possible, I did keep in mind Emma Peel's style. As I would often have to resort to sewing my own clothes I did keep a look out for similar patterns, but did not really manage it. After all, she wore designer styles, and if you know anything about sewing, the style pattern grading would have been 'Difficult' as opposed to 'Easy' or 'Beginners' patterns. However, I did dare to occasionally dream!

Naïve Hope

Meanwhile, life goes on. And I haven't gotten rid of my maternity clothes just yet, though I did manage to gain my figure back very quickly. Probably because I had decided that I didn't need to carry too much flab around with me like lots of other neighbourhood women I had grown up with. Also, whatever I wore had to do double duty for church attendances as well. So it was basic stuff mainly, with keeping one's 'Sunday best' for church. This was still England after all!

By the time I was almost nineteen, despite what I told myself in order to keep going and to keep believing in the best, I was feeling like a woman condemned. I hid this from myself in order to survive, for I was not yet ready to recognise him as the bully he was. I assumed that what others had told me was true and that early on in marriage you are still learning about each other, and trying to sort out how things work together. Buoyed by many of the religious and biblical promises I simply hoped it would all sort itself out. I didn't demand that he support me as I supported him. I wasn't really allowed to even if it had entered my mind. My ministrations towards him of the best of all I possessed as an obedient and devoted wife were gradually and increasingly being repaid by the misguided use of his strength and position toward me. My response was predictable; to try harder. I can now see how in some relationships that the more one partner gives, the more the other takes and eventually the more that person resents them for the giving. How raw at marriage was I still!

Before too long, I discover that I am again pregnant. Fortunately it was not immediately after Joseph's birth. And the enjoyment of this little first one had given me amnesia – like most women, the beautiful essence of a child can certainly help one forget the pain and travail of birthing. One's own child is such a magic presence; delicate skin, with robust muscles and structure, the smell of innocence and freshness when they are not poohing (though I can still remember those Oh-my-god-revolting-oozes that seer the nostrils, you know; the Number-Threes!), the satisfied beatific smile when they are clean, fed, cuddled and asleep. All things infant and new. Yes, I forgot what I was in for. But other women had survived; I had already survived, and could survive again. And now we were to have a brother or sister for Joseph.

Mothers-in-waiting was the term given in those days to pregnant women, mums-to-be. But it wasn't all just sitting around and waiting. Thankfully I have not been attacked like my mother was when she was pregnant, being kicked down the stairs by dad and ending up with a natural pregnancy termination. Though how I or anyone can possibly see this as a positive thing in view of Jim's own bad behaviour, I know not.

Did being pregnant grant me immunity from physical upsets? Does it protect me from Jim's moods and the odd push? No.

For there is another obvious clear physical thumping from him, based again on some perceived disregard on my behalf. Does the 'story' or excuse of why he attacked me matter? Not really, as nothing qualifies a physical attack. This time I go round to the Pastor's house. Mum and dad haven't achieved anything when I asked help from them. Mary and Stuart's intervention has also failed to make a lasting impact. Maybe this time the head of Jim's Church will have more influence? And after having a talk with the Pastor, Jim's behaviour did indeed change for a while.

I thought that this was to be a long-lasting solution. For now the Pastor himself knows, and Jim always honours the Pastor!

So Jim is put on notice to behave himself.

Meanwhile, Sheila gets married and it is a joy to attend her wedding. This may mean a little less time spent together, but our friendship remains strong.

1965

~ Second Chance ~ Second Coming ~ Dumb Promise
~ Instant Karma ~ Dangerous Moves

SECOND CHANCE

It is now April. I, or rather we, have just celebrated (if you can call an acknowledgment with a tiny cake and a Birthday Card a celebration) my twentieth birthday and my second born child is almost ready to join us as a home birth. My belly is now so huge, seeming to carry him much larger than my first. My best friend Sheila is down to keep me company for a while today as I am now well overdue. We are preparing food for dinner together, and we are joking and messing about. Whenever we get together, life always feels lighter. We have such an easy and shared sense of humour.

Anyway, in these last weeks of my second pregnancy, I am now a couple of weeks overdue and so *huge* that Sheila and are joking about my size and due dates. Sheila is also pregnant now, though its early days and she shows very little still. Both Sheila and I are in an 'Eric and Ern' mood, joking and making light of things. So, joking and comparing, it happens that on a whim, I suggest that we measure me, just to be sure that we are right on how humongous I appear to have grown and I go and seek out the tape measure. We start at the top of my torso downwards and discover that my breasts measure an amazing forty inches across – F-O-R-T-Y! We start to laugh. As big as Sabrina, the bustiest lady on film that we knew of. Next to Jayne Mansfield, that is. Okay, now let's see what I measure around my waist, you know, the one that isn't a waist anymore... Fumbling with the tape, we finally get it around my middle, and we both burst out laughing when we see the measurement - F-O-R-T-Y! This is hilarious!

I knew that I was so much bigger than I appeared to look with Joseph, but this is ridiculous! Okay, last one to do now; the hips.

So it was with mounting mirth that we measure my hips. I was gob-smacked – then I showed her where my finger was on the tape.

She looked at me, and I looked at her, my mouth open with amazement, then her mouth opened in amazement – and we both couldn't stop ourselves from hearty guffaws as we hooted with hilarity. Another F-o-r-t-y!

A barrel!

I had actually gone from my usual normal 35-25-37 measurements (in inches of the old days) to an amazing 40-40-40. In metric, that is actually over a hundred centimetres, 102 cm to be exact! This was for breast - waist - hips. We found it so hilarious that we ended up laughing ourselves silly, to the point where I actually have 'an accident' through wetting myself, no matter how hard I held my legs together.

Sheila carries her child so petite-ly, has hidden it so well that she didn't start to show anything till she was over six months pregnant, whereas I would 'show' as soon as 8 weeks. So Sheila just couldn't compete with these measurements! We both literally had uncontrolled hysterics that lasted for ages, and when Jim came home and found us still bursting out into sporadic and contagious laughter, he eventually caved in with us. It was good that he was laughing about it all too. A precious embarrassing memory!

My confinement date was given around the end of March. March has come and it has gone. My birthday has come and it too has gone. The doctor says all is well with me, and that my home confinement is still a safe bet. So I simply have to bide my time. But let me tell you that this child carries very differently from the first. It has a very powerful kick to it, and in this last month, the banging of the head against the pelvic bones is actually quite painful. Around the end of April, slow pains start and the midwife is called. She arrives ready for delivery and after her examination, suggests that I have an enema in preparation. After three enemas, with nothing to show for it, and after two days of continual long slow contractions, this baby is finally getting ready to emerge.

One month overdue, it is a long drawn out and painful labour, again without painkillers and using natural methods. My second son is born at home in Chorlton-cum-Hardy and weighs ten pounds at birth. He is a real bouncer. That is a lot of baby! He was slightly longer than Joseph (I think he was around twenty-two

Naïve Hope

inches long) and I needed several stitches afterwards. I had suffered a long and what was referred to back then as a 'dry' labour that had lasted a couple of days, and was just plain relieved for the birth to be over with.

There had been no painkillers, and when the midwife had finally brought out some gas in the last minutes, they had no effect at all. Plus with all the effort, I was pretty much spent.

I cannot dare contemplate having any more children again after this, especially as the doctor who arrived after it was all over proceeded to mend my tear with several painful stitches that he insists don't need an anaesthetic – despite my yells and painful shouts, he simply stuck to his 'You won't feel a thing down there, it's still numb from the birth.' This idiot would know... how? The attending midwife looks on in horror, her face unbelieving and she gripped hold of my hand for comfort whilst this deliberate torture went on. He chooses not to believe the evidence of his eyes and ears, but to believe some claptrap he thinks he knows or had probably been told by someone else who knows nothing about the realities of birth. It seems that I am obviously stupid and don't know my own body, nor pain from pleasure...

What? Since when do men who have *never* given birth become *experts* on the rigours and pains of labour? But this was not the only time I would come across a trained medical professional that knew absolutely nothing about the very thing he was attempting to fix. So after that, whenever I come across a doctor who actually *knows* more than he has been taught and who tries to keep an open mind, I count them as a great asset.

It was my claim to name this second child. And I still could not come at the full James-Henly thingy. So during the final months of pregnancy I had been casting about for a suitable name. I had been reading a novel called 'Exodus', a modern day account of the Jews in Israel and their fight for freedom. Jesus was a Jew, and a hero in a sense, so I gravitated toward naming the second as a biblical hero, as Jim had done with the first-born. This time it was not the name of a martyred person as Joseph had been named after. With some possible names for a boy and for a girl in mind, I decided that I would wait until baby was born to see what name suited him or her before fully committing to the new 'label'. However, when baby was born, after taking just one look at him I saw that the preferred name did indeed fit him. And so he was named thus. Ben James Henly; Son of James Henly. This then, was also satisfying Jim and his parents, as it was in keeping with the 'James' naming tradition. Though Jim's dad scratched his head at the time, he realised that Ben could always call himself Jim too, and that this family name will still live on. So our second born boy is birthed in April 1965, shortly after my twentieth birthday.

Ben was very well developed at his birth having been born that whole month overdue. Within minutes of his first bath straight after the birth, the nurse picked him up and put his face onto her shoulder as she walked around the other side of the room toward me. We were both surprised when we saw that he was actually lifting his head up, trying to turn it toward me, or possibly the sound of my voice. Or he just might have been curious and wanted to look around. Whatever the reason, his neck was obviously very strong for him to be able to even attempt this. And he has a thick head of black hair, with a line of hair that trails down his back some way.

As you know, Ben had been very active during that final time in the womb, and I had often wondered at the severe pain when his head had banged against my pelvis. Now I knew why. Such a strong head and neck accounted for why I had so often been victim from these inner head-butting. I am so glad to have this over.

Gradually I recover at home, and with a midwife coming round to check on me and with Jim being on his best behaviour, I somehow manage with both children and begin to recover from the ordeal.

Two boys now. So I can use some of Joseph's clothes for this little one, maybe.

For a short period, peace reigns. The long labour is over and the birthing process eventually begins to feel like it is behind me, I am slowly gaining strength again, and home is relatively quiet.

So I am thinking that this is a fresh start. Jim's charming and good side is evident again and maybe we have both learned from the past... I dare to hope again.

Naïve Hope

New home, new baby, new responsibilities.

More maturity for I am now twenty and Jim is at the ripe old age of twenty-four, and he is even more involved with the church; a respected father of two, and expected to be leading a god-fearing and blameless life. And of course, we now live practically next door to the Pastor! Maybe that is my protection?

Little Ben is such a cuddly type of little boy, not that Joseph wasn't, but Joseph seems to be smarter and more sensitive somehow, quick with his words and his imagination. There were moments when it was such a joy for them to both be fed, washed, dressed, happy and settled. A routine begins to establish itself, and breast feeding is a breeze, though I do have to pay attention to tender breasts as Ben loves to linger…

Jim has not threatened me nor frightened me for some time now, and I never dream of bringing up what happened with Elsa, for I had forgiven him. The door has been closed on that episode, and we now have a full family to take care of. Jim has been considerate and helpful, and I am gaining my strength back, and my figure is returning with all of the activity that is demanded of me by the children. So one can understand that I was not expecting or prepared for what happened next. And within such a short period of time.

Even though we are living a quiet life, and Jim is attending church more than I was able to because of the newborn and having two children to care for, a nagging sense of all not being right starts up again. There is a shift in atmosphere. Longer silences between us. Again that sense that I wasn't quite doing something right that I ought to have been doing right, though I had no clue as to what it was or is. Despite the false sense of security I allow myself to be lulled into and grasping onto this inner picture of us being a 'happy family', I now realise that instead of things improving, there actually is a growing darkness that appears to be descending again.

I catch Jim looking at me out of the corner of my eye. I cannot read his face or fathom his thoughts, though he is quick to question me, asking me what I am thinking. He is treating me as though I am holding something back from him. But this wasn't really about me, and I didn't have a clue of this at the time. Being too aware and empathic of another's feelings makes me all-too-ready to make-things-better. Now, however, I began to feel unsettled, and concerned. Why is Jim becoming broody again? Was it a lack of sleep? Am I not spending enough time or energy on Jim? Can I do more after recovering from this second, more damaging and painful birth, is there something I am not doing right? Am I making the wrong meals? Not praying long enough?

I didn't know. I don't know. And he doesn't say. Only now he shows his displeasure, for he starts up again as he gets on to me over little things. Pick-ons. Put-downs. Nothing heavy, just niggles. Then he spits it out. The six week post natal period is taking *far* too long according to Jim.

'What do the doctors know?' he states. 'This is just an excuse to avoid your duties'.

He actually, even after *two* births, *doubts* that six weeks is required to fully recover from childbirth. It is as though he believes that I am deliberately withholding sex from him, deliberately denying him what he thinks is rightfully his! For my part, I couldn't have cared less about sex after what I had been through. Stinging and cruel pain throughout a long labour for such a big baby and also having the birth stitches didn't help, and the recovery time for the stitches to heal without stinging or breaking open again is essential. Exhaustion at having to attend to two young littlies, wash nappies aplenty, recover from such a long labour, these had already fallen off Jim's consideration list.

Was Jim concerned that he now had yet another rival for my undivided attention?

There is a lot of trauma that happens in the genital area through childbirth, though some people seem to think that it is simply a matter of expulsion and everything simply springs back together again like a rubber band. No harm done. Immediate recovery.

Not so. They forget that everything in the abdomen has been totally moved around, even displaced, to make room for the being that grows and feeds on the mother host. Taking nine months to accommodate and requiring at least a *little* time to recuperate to return to normal. In days of close families, it was usually easy to convey to young fathers the processes around childbirth, yet here this man was, without a clue as to self control, consideration as a husband, or what it actually means to be a 'father'.

Eventually, at the six week check-up, I get the go-ahead from the local doctor. Too soon, for my liking. But a Christian wife is not allowed to make decisions over her own body, and after the doctor says it's okay, then I have no further excuse.

Amazing that according to the Bible, a woman's body belongs to her husband! And so bloody chauvinistic, misogynistic and archaic.

However, the husband's rights are restored, and temporarily, things in Jim's world return to normal. Though there is a pattern happening that takes me years to see, years to put together. And it is this; Jim becomes suspicious if he cannot have sex. He becomes testy and vindictive. Then when he has had sex, he becomes guilty at what he has done, it is like sex is a dirty word, a dirty deed, a dirty need. At the time, I think that we just thought of the situation as something that we needed to know more about – was I 'doing' sex wrong, what did I need to know to be able to 'satisfy' Jim better – for it was becoming known (Hah!) that I was the one that was amiss in my sexual service.

We never just simply have sex, leastways, I don't. When I want sex, it is not from the viewpoint of lust and rampant orgasm, a dirty thing to be done in the dark, a shameful thing to hide or to be ashamed of. It is usually from a loving, committed, almost spiritual side of sex, that which is the giving and sharing in a loving union. Yes, I get yearnings and urges, but I generally tend to see them as a need to connect with him in a way that restores intimacy besides fulfilling some biological need. Like a heart urge combined with a sacral urge. I realise that this is hard to define, and some may think me a prude, yet it didn't seem like that to me, though I usually felt discontented afterwards, little realising that I was getting some stimulation, but little actual satisfaction.

Though there was nothing about satisfying the woman in the marriage vows, so get over it, Marni!

I just didn't have the same style of sex as Jim had. And it is possible that my style exposed his approach to himself, that of whatever was going on in his head at the time, the sort of sex that is fucking, rutting, humping, rampant, desperate, rather than a communication of body, heart and mind. It was to be many years later for me to experience the burst of bliss, energy and pure love with a man. But right then I was too young and inexperienced – and ignorant – to know this. And so was Jim. Naively, I expected him to be having the same experience as me, and when I opened my heart as I opened my arms and legs to him, I thought that our exchange would be one of harmony. For the first few years of our marriage, I would lie awake after sex with Jim, resorting to thinking about lists, of what had to be done next, or of things that he had said or done, in an attempt to process whatever it was that had taken place. My attempts at making sense of things, I guess.

In a way, I was only just learning about sex, and of a woman's anatomy. We discovered that there was a book out around this time in the sixties that explained about a woman's anatomy and of her sexual capacity. I cannot remember its title now, but I think it may have been called something like *Discovering the 'G' Spot* or possibly *The Female Eunuch*. A bit like *Lady Chatterley's Lover*, simply because it was about sex, it was considered somewhat risqué, but it was ground-breaking in that it woke a whole generation of women up that had been taught that sex was about the missionary position with the exhortation to 'Close your eyes and think of England'... It was Jim who obtained a copy and gave me instructions to read it. When I shared certain passages with him which I thought were instructive and would bring us closer together, it seemed to titillate him and in the end he read the book himself.

There was indeed some sort of temporary improvement in our relationship after that, and I hoped that Jim having a more educated wife at sex would keep him calmer, whilst the discovery of the orgasm would make the whole experience more satisfying for me.

Naïve Hope

SECOND COMING

One would think that we are now on the home stretch, having now obtained a better sex foundation that would optimistically support a better marital foundation. I was actually getting some enjoyment out of sex, and this was making Jim feel better about the whole deal now himself. Wasn't it?

Not for long. For our differing sex styles had only been part of the issue. There is more to discover.

There is no other way to put this that to say it right out loud:

Jim 'Saves' (and Falls) - Again.

Unbeknownst to me, Jim has other fish frying. Let me tell you the story.

Ben is now about five months old. Jim has been acting a bit weird. But this was somehow different to the moods I had experienced from him so far. I have no way to counter what is happening in his weird world, so just do the best I can to avoid antagonism. Eventually whatever he is wrestling with gets the better of him. It is Sunday after lunch and I am getting the children ready for an afternoon nap. So I continue changing nappies whilst he begins to tell me that he has something he *has* to share with me, and makes me first promise not to be angry with him, but to hear him out. There is some urgency in his voice, and I listen to this preamble of his but I have to finish the nappy changing to give him my attention. He gives me no option but to agree to his request. This sounds serious, and how else will I know what is going on? So with some trepidation, I agree.

Even so, I am totally unprepared for what comes next, and even after he tells me his tale, for a few moments I simply cannot believe what he is proposing and is about to take place as he explains – if one can call this explaining. I have finished attending to the urgent needs of the children by this time, and turn to face Jim directly.

Jim starts off by telling me he has something important to tell me – okay, now he has my full undivided attention. He begins his story. He is in earnest, for now he has me by my both arms as he talks to me. He is now a bit panicky and obviously pressured by time and I can feel this in the urgency of what he is telling me and in his grip. This all has a familiar feeling to it, but I haven't quite gotten there yet... His tale unfolds.

He tells me that *because he has felt neglected by me* that he is supposed to be *meeting someone in the park* around the corner in about *half an hour.*

Neglected? But what about that 'great sex' he has been talking about that we have been sharing? I haven't denied him, have I? My mind whirls to think of a time when I did neglect him... Whilst I am doing this, the next piece of information hits me.

Meeting someone? I stop looking for incidents of neglect and wildly consider this snippet. Who on earth could he mean? 'I didn't know there was an open-air church meeting on' I burst out.

He continues, 'I am supposed to be meeting a young woman in the park'. He still has hold of me. He is not threatening me the same as he has in the past when he has held me like this. His words sink in.

A young woman...

What? I am floored. Gobsmacked.

He is telling me that he has arranged to meet a young woman in the park!

My immediate reactions and thought are confusing... in a millisecond, a multitude of niggles pass through my mind. Struggling with money, doing my best, making do, challenged on small wages to take care of everyone and still tithe to the church, breast-feeding and missing out on sleep, having to be on tap for sex – etc. etc. etc. The usual things for many a young mum, and in fact for a young father. For he was having to make big changes too now, with two small children in our care. But it appears that it was possibly and quite probably harder for him to adjust than for me, and this must have been his answer to it all.

It certainly wasn't the sex, because he made sure that I knew that I could not refuse to do my *duty* as a wife, and that I had to take care of his *needs* – actually looking back at this as I write, I don't remember ever hearing about him really looking out for *my* needs;

it just wasn't in the mindset. Even the sex book adventure was about how he could have better sex for himself.

How far has he gone with her? This was another fleeting question mark inside my head.

... and that he has had sex with her...

Ok, *there* it is. Yup, it's happened again. For right now here he is telling me about *another* woman he is having intercourse with. I am floored. I struggle to keep up.

But that isn't enough.

For he rushes on to tell me he *doesn't* want to continue it, though *she does* want to keep seeing him. What? I replay the thing in my head, in case I hadn't heard right. *He has had an affair, it's now over, yet he is meeting her, but he doesn't want it to carry on...* 'What?' screams loud in my head.

A banner flows past my eyes announcing that Jim has cheated on me yet again. This is Jim's admittance of a second affair and this time with someone he tells me is called Dilys. The names Elsa and Dilys pass behind my eyes.

But apparently that's not all. I am still taking this in, still reeling from his confession with unseeing eyes and an internal disappearance into his betrayal and desertion, when he shakes me back to the present moment and to what he has to say next.

There is more? *Yes,* (God Help Me!) there is more...

For now he drops *another* bomb-shell – No, this time he doesn't ask me to take her in – she has her own place. And no way would I ever consider a repeat of that last fiasco, I will *not* be caught out on Christian duty to even a *hint* of a thought at her staying with us. No, this is different from the last time. This one is just as challenging though.

... you tell her it's over...

What? I didn't even know it had *started*! Before I even get to the 'how long has this been going on for...' he is urging *me* to do this thing, and to do it now. *Now*!

For right now he is urging me out of the house. He turns my shoulders to the door and hands me my coat as he instructs me what must be done immediately. This time he tells *me* to go and see this woman instead of *him* seeing her. Tells me that *he* can't face her to tell her he won't be seeing her again.

And for me to explain to her that he is married and has two children. And take the children with me to prove it. And that it's all off. That he won't be seeing her again.

I ask you. I bloody well ask you!

'*And time is running short*'. He is now due to meet her in about ten minutes. It takes longer than that to get to the park. My body wants to drag as my mind momentarily races then switches to stun. I am still trying to digest this information, lurching mentally from thought to shock to thought again.

Yes, he is actually telling me of his guilty, dirty actions for no other reason that I am aware of other than sheer cowardice, that he has been seeing another woman, and I had *no* idea of it? Yes, he is. He actually *is*. He's done it again. *Again*!

I can hardly believe it. I am in a nightmare. How the *heck* did this happen?

But I am not allowed the luxury of dwelling on this earth shattering news, not allowed to question him about this... For now he continues to press *me* urgently to get out quick and meet her, he is shaking my coat in front of my face. She needs to know. *She* will be wondering and waiting! Again *I* am made to put my considerations aside and to attend to *his* needs – and now *her* needs. I am still struggling with the inertia brought on by this shock.

Finally, he again pulls out the guilty Christian card; for *I* am now made to feel *guilty* that this poor woman is waiting for him to arrive in the park. So it's up to *me* to do this. For as Jim says, 'She will wonder why I haven't turned up'.

Now. Come on Marni, pull yourself together and for the sake of your marriage go do this unsavoury thing.

Naïve Hope

Let me take a moment to clarify the situation again – let me get clear about this -

This *man,* who is *supposed* to be my husband, is asking for me to speak with this woman-who-he-has-fucked (though I still didn't use the 'f' word back then, but the reality is the same!) and probably been fucking, on his behalf to help him to stop it continuing....? I just can't seem to take it in. On top of all that I am dealing with, he seems to be full of excuses and reasons which escape me now, for the next thing I know somehow he is succeeding as *I* am made to feel guilty that it is because *I* am not giving him the same time, energy, sex, consideration, whatever as I used to do. Well, hello, that was before two small children. And boys at that! Busy boisterous demanding boy toddler and baby boy, both of whom I love dearly.

I again make the mistake of thinking in some way that *I* have failed, and so I force myself to try to take this all in, adjust to the situation and do what needs to be done, especially as he swears and promises that he will *never, ever* do such a thing again. Really? And I, fool that I am, am still willing, or rather desperately wanting, to believe that he won't. If I do this for him, then it will be the last time. okay. Deal.

Aren't women ever the practical one's hey?

So I have been given my orders, and put the children in the pram as instructed and sent to keep his *date* and meet this woman, I leave to tell her, my mind in a whirl.

I find this woman, Dilys, in the park waiting where he said she'd be. She is not as flashy as Elsa, and wears glasses. Mousey-brown hair, tweedy clothes, a quiet presence, I establish that she is the woman Jim was going to meet. 'Are you supposed to be meeting Jim here?' I ask her tentatively. She is as surprised to learn of my existence as I was to learn of hers as I explain to her that I am Jim's wife. 'Oh', is all she says. I deliver his messages, and I leave her, and hope that I will *never, ever* see her again.

And as I walk back home pushing the pram, the delayed shock begins to hit me. I feel a whole raft of emotions. I feel ashamed. I feel let-down. I feel dirty. I feel confused. I feel lost. I feel broken.

The emotions tumble around as I try for the sake of the children to hold myself together. Thoughts and feelings fly backwards and forwards, round and round as I search for answers, explanations, understanding. Amongst them I am feeling so embarrassed that this man didn't have the *guts* to do his own Dirty Work! My tears come unbidden. I am ashamed at where I find myself. What happened to my marriage? How could I let this happen?

I don't even wonder how he met her, I don't ask how they managed to have sex and create some sort of connection. I am too busy trying to hold my world together, to hold on to my side of the vows. I do not question him on these things later, and he certainly doesn't offer to tell me.

I am floored that my marriage is having such challenges, while I am trying so hard to meet all his demands and to do everything right. Though I don't yet know it, I *am* doing everything right. I am the *only* one doing everything right! Only there is no-one to tell me that it is *not me* that is wrong, it is *not me* that is messing up this marriage. And this has not been part of my plan, my dream for my marriage. I am still asking the wrong questions, questions that have imprinted themselves on my mind over time, and which I have been too compliant to argue with.

Oh, my... how one mistake can lead to another...

Dumb Promise

My tears dry on the way home as I try to make sense of things and I go into solution solving mode looking how not to have this happen again.

And I slowly walk back home reflecting on how this could possibly have happened. And of how I had absolutely no idea about it until he told me. And on some level I find I hold myself to some of the blame. How naïve I must be not to have been able to see or even feel what was going down. Well, then, *I* must be to blame, for this is the *second* time this has happened.

It *must* be me. My fault. I wasn't attractive enough anymore. I wasn't attentive enough any more.

Naïve Hope

Somewhere in my mind, in order to live with myself, in order to live in this situation and to survive it, in order to get past this to take care of my children, I come to a cross-roads and make a decision – a decision based on an assumption, a very faulty assumption, one that assumes that somehow this was my fault and that this was avoidable.

For this time I *swear* to myself that the marriage *will not end because of me*. I vow this to myself over and over.

I determine that I *will not let myself go* as other wives, that I will *do my best* to take care of everything and everyone, and that I will persevere. That I will give him *no* cause to *ever* do something like that again. The level of intense emotion locks this in to my psyche. If you have seen *Gone with the Wind* and watched Scarlett O'Hara as she swears that she and her family will *never* go hungry again, then you can imagine my similar commitment, for that is the sort of vow that I made.

Unbeknownst to me at the time, though, this now demonstrates a hidden problem, one which we hadn't really gotten to the bottom of, and quite frankly, we didn't have the tools or support or intelligence around us to show us how, or where to go to know. We or rather, *I*, do not yet have the knowledge that will help me to recognise our true situation.

Our Christian teaching, or rather, brain-washing, claims that good is from God and that all evil or sin or temptation is from the Devil. This can actually translate into lack of accountability in many ways, though I realise now that what is 'sin' or wrong to one person, is not necessarily so to another, particularly when the interpretation of sin itself is at question. I am not talking about the basic ethics and morality that are written on the hearts and conscience of all good souls, those who don't need the ten commandments because they are already a part of their being anyway. I am talking about the interpretation of 'sin'. For example, we weren't allowed to listen to popular music, particularly after John Lennon was said to have claimed that he was more popular than Jesus, which inflamed and incensed every Christian of the day. Not listening to gospel or church music and listening to something worldly instead was perceived as sin by some. Jamaican girls weren't allowed to go sleeveless or have short skirts (at least not in Jamaica, according to one Jamaican church friend called Maisie). The same with reading women's magazines, or of having too much make-up on (define 'too much'), or of swearing, or of inappropriate hugging, etc, etc. Or even of differences in religious approaches or tenets.

Living in a world of blaming The Devil (poor sod) for all the 'sins' and slip-ups, blaming temptation for our Straying (yes, you've got it, again through *The Devil*) I am unable as yet to recognise or realise that this *man* has serious problems. And that in my allowing things to continue down the same road, then so have I.

After all, it wasn't really him doing these things, but the devil (wasn't it?)...

And another bi-product of this was repression – for both of us of our own unacknowledged lack of self understanding. But for Jim it was also Denial and Repression of his own guilt and shame. For what follows and haunts us unrecognised throughout the rest of our marriage, demonstrated by these and other later incidents, is that on some level Jim also expected me to do the *same* to him, to have my *own* affairs. Because *he* was capable of this behaviour, I now realise that according to Jim and his own guilt, it followed that so was I.

It could also have been a subconscious attempt to bring me to the same level, to make me of the same guilt and tone as him, to make him feel more comfortable with what he had done, *because I had done it too!*

And I think that over time this imagining of reciprocation by me became part of his thinking and behaviour, even though it never occurred to me. It later occurs to me that his hidden shame and guilt somehow became so linked in to his silent thoughts of love, sex, marriage, fidelity and 'Weakness of the Flesh' that he now takes to accusing me accordingly. His own guilt and shame hounding him and thus he expects others to act like him?

Sure, it was becoming clear that he already was a jealous, suspicious kind of guy, but I feel that somehow these urges of his back then were conveniently projected onto me. What other reason could he have for continually accusing me of things I never entertained of doing, was even too scared to go anywhere *near* that sort of thought? Back then I had so little knowledge of the functioning of the mind, or of the subconscious. Now I dare to ask what it was that caused him to be like this? What did he experience that linked love and sex to betrayal and violence? Or is this really the actual essence of the man simply expressing itself? I still don't know for sure.

My own continued searching for meaning beyond the God of the Bible, the church, faith and religion, and my efforts for further self-understanding after the marriage ended, led me to eventually understand in a much deeper way some of the motivations, impulses and reactions that were involved, and endured.

It is obvious that Jim can be pretty violent when he wants to be. He is prone to moodiness and sulks. And this doesn't change throughout our marriage, only the guise in which it shows itself. For every now and then he would simply erupt. These were not regular occurrences, like as in a foreseeable cycle, so one couldn't predict when it would happen. Leastways I couldn't, for it took until after I had left him to see that our anniversaries were also an issue. In these days, before he returns to his pre-Christian drinking again, there were more occasions when he was charming, loving, considerate and kind than the violent ones. He *tried* to live up to the standards that he professed, or so it seemed. As did I. When he was in a good space, it was *great* to be around him. His smile, his charm, his care, his attraction, his physique, all shared and poured forth like balm. For a moment. But in retrospect, he had many inner conflicts, some of which I don't think he could put words to anyway, and which I was trained not to question. And I guess, living close to the Pastor did help to keep a lid on some of the stuff he was grappling with.

His parents were simple Irish folk, one from Northern Ireland, the other from the South, and as I mentioned, one Catholic, one Protestant. I was told that both were alcoholics though I hadn't as yet been present when they had been drinking so didn't see this side of things till much later. Somehow they seemed to get on as regards religion and their differences. His mum had come from gypsy stock, and it was her husband, James Henly, who taught her to read and write after he married her. My Jim was the eldest of four boys and two sisters. Apart from Jim's Born-Again religious similarities and projected desire to make a real difference in the world I really didn't know much about him when I married him except his strongly professed love of the Lord and his forsaking of worldly things. Maybe because I had met all of his family, who weren't Born-Again's like us, I figured that he would be totally different from them, and I was blinded by the possibility of godly potential as well as the altruistic vision of service for others.

I naively took words at their face value, as *I* had always tried to mean what I said. Years later, long after we were divorced, I came across some of his school photographs that I had never seen before and which he had left with his mother. This threw further light on how he grew up and of his own journey to become school champion boxer, revealing to me his need to take it up in self-defence and possibly because of his short stature. This skill definitely equipped him to put-them-back-in-their-place, whatever *that* was. Through joining the Merchant Navy, he was able to see some of the world, escape home and learn many skills not available to him normally in his Irish sphere that would give him a better chance for employment.

In the navy, he also learned how to drink hard, though I suspect his family background would have already taught him this. I also learned about ten years into our marriage of how he would come home from being out own on shore leave, and drop into bed in a drunken stupor. In the morning when he got up, he would find that his pockets had been emptied of money, and he learned it was by his mother, who would take and spend his cash on drink. So I guess you can add some mistrust of women somewhere into the mix of his inner conflicts. Another fact that didn't sink in till later was that he was also a champion fighter on the ships he sailed, and won many fights. Not forgetting, of course, that he was Irish, and the reputation of their feisty tempers, love of the blarney and oft times irrational thinking had spread abroad - though it had not yet reached me. Add these ingredients together, and you may well have a cocktail of hidden depth waiting to explode. A hidden state requiring a lot of energy to keep concealed. We certainly did. When he is in one of his 'moods' it often felt like I was being punished for something that I had supposedly done, yet had no idea about.

It is not unusual for me to hear about the fights between members of his own family, and of how his mum had no hesitation in hitting 'the old man' as she called him – Jim's dad – over the head with a bottle. Really! Usually when he was too drunk to put up much of a fight. Because I had never witnessed their behaviour, they seemed more like stories, and their reality didn't reach me, now did the idea of Jim being the same way occur to me. I didn't doubt that he, like myself, has suffered in childhood. And this I guess is also part of the equation that has drawn us together. One of the similarities that we had recognised in each other.

So violence was a real part of this man's background, too. This was what he had learned, but instead of changing it during his own marriage, he fell into continuing it. And possibly when he couldn't understand what he was feeling, or maybe not have an answer to something, or he was angry at himself or life, then, as the closest to him, I would take the consequences. It was usually me to blame, for over time and constant repetition, I came to learn that I was and am responsible for his behaviour and feelings with his continuous 'This is *your* fault for *making* me do it'; and neatly and conveniently *I* am made responsible for his deeds.

The violence begins subtly. That first dig in the ribs on the bus, then increasingly heavy and harder hits and slaps, and over time these develop into thumps, bumps, black eyes and broken ribs through *directed* punches, until that final Good-Hiding, that last Beat-up, that he gives me years from now, and for which I have to call the police. But this is nowhere on my horizon yet…

In my search to make sense of all of this at a later date, and long before I realised that I was dealing with a sociopath, and possibly a psychopath, I generously considered whether he had been suffering with undiagnosed Depression. I have also since learned that the illness of Depression can run in families, and can be passed on through heredity. I know that many, many years later, I found myself suffering from Severe Depression, and had to resort to medication to settle things for me whilst I dug away and resolved the reasons and causes behind this illness. There is a cost with simply 'getting on with life' – the body and psyche can absorb shock and trauma (which becomes stored memory) and cushion one from these for a time, but they cannot carry the burden indefinitely. There is a cost! And sooner or later, it must be attended to.

I guess my mother had also had depression to some degree too. And so in retrospect, I can guess that this was also a possible cause in some of Jim's issues. However, as I never treated anyone as he did, then I also consider that how this illness is expressed is also related to what is *inside* the person, the real *essence* of one, the part that *can* make a difference to the outcome of their family experiences, and the impact of family culture, programming, mistakes, and expectations; and *can* make the difference in one living a *better* kind of life and overcoming these behaviours.

For all the hitting and putting-downs though, we showed a united face at church. This was all part of the hidden culture, the very ego, of the church, the unspoken attempt to hide shame from other eyes. No one else saw this side of him, and so he is well respected by others. I really bought into the 'United as a Family' front. You know, the 'You and Me Against the World' mentality that may work in certain situations but not necessarily in everyday peacetime situations. Duh, what a dill! Loyalty really was something I valued, though not being fully aware of exactly *what* one is being loyal too is a BIG mistake. And I was naively and blindly loyal.

Had I married my dad? Did I become my mum in some ways? Quite possibly! Though initially – and remarkably - I only saw all of the *differences* between Jim and my dad. It wasn't until long after the marriage ended that I was able to recognise the many similarities. And to see how I had mirrored some of mum's life and long-suffering in my own marriage.

But the eventual result of it all, years down the track is that I can also see where I *did* manage to break the mould, and refuse to do it the same way as my parents and as the church dictated. I guess I can now honestly say – and with a background tune you will get it:

> *'The record shows*
> *I took the blows*
> *and did it Myyyyyy Waayyyyy'.*   TaDah!

Naïve Hope

INSTANT KARMA

I was very slow to recognise psychopathology in this man whom I had taken to be my husband. And praying for God to fix it obviously wasn't working, no matter the degree of Hope I had.

But I haven't told you yet about Jim's **Instructions on Hugs**, have I? Yes, didn't you know that there is a *Hug Protocol*? Neither did I, not that it was called this back then. Jim's own extrapolation on the church's attitude to acceptable-familiarity-in-the-church. It goes like this.

Well apparently, I am being too friendly with my greetings towards people at church. I am now duly shown by Jim how I was to hug people, depending on whether they were a man or a woman, their age and their relationship with me and with the church.

You can only hug certain men with a handshake and a lean forward so that no part of your body is touching, particular the upper body (though what he really means is 'the breasts'!) Older known godly (and proven 'safe') men, you could possibly allow a shoulder to touch. The same with women, though you could allow two shoulders to touch. If they were large in the upper body (big breasted) and it couldn't be avoided, it was permissible for the accidental chaste grazing of upper body (read breast), but attention must be made to ensure there was no sexual connotation. Close friends were allowed to hug or embrace above the waist with females and around both shoulders with males. Strangers had to be treated with less familiarity, especially men, and great care must be taken in just how much touching was involved. Definitely no touching between both bodies apart from a handshake. Anyone observing must be able to see that there is nothing offensive, suggestive, over familiar or sexual about one's hug. This is in line with the church stance on not giving any cause for another to misread one's actions. Whilst this is intended to give a certain kind of worship and praise to God by *acting* 'blameless', it is also a limiting way of expressing how you feel toward a person. It is also about appearances, a way of avoiding independent thinking and it is a way of *acting*. Acting! Not Being, but acting. Following these instructions, however, whilst squashing spontaneity also lessened the chance of accusations from Jim.

To continue along my storyline, I am now learning to read some of the signs of Jim's impending violent urges. Clever me, hey, though this does help me to avoid some bruises, it doesn't altogether solve the real problem, really.

We are still living practically next door to the Pastor, however I still have to be careful who I could talk to. The upstairs couple on the third floor were professionals, and the husband was foreign. I actually liked them. they were friendly, respectful and seemed very interesting. But I was instructed by Jim to turn down any invitations by Letitia or Balthazar Marquis as they clearly weren't Christians. But I could talk to the brothers of the Pastor, as long as it was in the hallways.

On this particular day, a pleasant day, not too warm not too cool, I am not wearing a heavy cardigan and Jim is in his shirt sleeves. We have had breakfast and been to church without too much hassle and I am attending to the never ending demands of two small children. We are living in the one huge room still at the front of this huge house, though later on we occupy the whole of this ground floor. The kitchen area is closest to the huge bay window, and Jim has been making a cup of tea and looking out of the window, musing. Something shifts in the air. He turns to face me, sipping his tea, the other hand in his pocket. The atmosphere is pregnant. I continue to soothe and minister to the boys.

I don't know *exactly* for sure just what sparks Jim on this occasion, it can be anything, though it is probably that things are overdue for him to blow his valves again. I was always watchful of what I did or said around others, and of course at home for I really think that his thoughts just run away with themselves. Would that they caught a bus and train and kept right on going, with him in tow! Though this thought was furthest from my mind right then. My notion would be more likely 'Uh-oh!'

He mentions old Mr Stanfield. And waits for me to say something. What can I say? He is a nice old man. Is Jim laying some sort of a trap? If he is, I don't yet recognise it.

It soon turns out that on this occasion the excuse he uses to escalate his growing testiness is his steadfast belief that I had been too familiar with this particular church member. It now comes out

Naïve Hope

as an accusation of his (incorrect) interpretation of a hug with this elderly church goer, to which I naturally attempt to defend myself. He is a dear harmless old man, and he had just been through a bit of a bad time. Of *course* there was nothing in it! I don't know how anyone could have misinterpreted it. Except for Jim. He had been irritable before church and through the service he was a bit kind of testy, though I had hoped the service would have rubbed the touchiness out of him.

I heard something in his voice as he talked about how I greeted old Mr Stanfield at church, and I can see the watchfulness in his eyes. The kind that is watching for the best time to pounce, just looking for that opportunity when the mouse is well and truly cornered before the attack. I see the signs, I get the signal. Whilst I have been attending to the children I have been positioned by the table which is near the door to the hallway. Something keeps me by the door as a possible scary scenario begins to appear in my head. Oh, no, not again! Part of me is looking for an escape, an exit point should things come to that, for I have been cornered before. In my mind I can already begin to see and feel a few punches coming as I watch and feel Jim start to clench his jaw, curl his fists and look at me in that 'fixed' way. Jim now instructs me that I come to where he is. 'Come here,' he says as he puts his tea down. 'I'm going to show you what happens when you get too familiar with old men, with any man,' he continues. 'Pushing your breasts up against him,' he now sneers.

What? I never!

In the face of idiocy and stupidity, rational thought by a rational person is totally impossible and totally unacceptable to the irrational, and in fact, becomes a red flag to an inept enraged and stupid bull. Pardon my reference to a bull, I do not intend to insult the animal.

I am about to suffer for something, I can see that, and this talk about an inappropriate hug is the short straw on it. Whatever has been building in his own mind before this is not what he discusses with me. He doesn't show his hand, he *rarely* shows his hand. But I know in my heart that I did nothing wrong with that hug so I cast about for what actually brought this bout on. I cannot for the life of me think of what it is or was. *It is not rational anyway, so I would have to be as stupid as him to follow his thought processes.* Why did I bother? I guess it could have been *anything* I have said or done that he considers contravenes some sort of hidden script or rule of being or behaviour.

I can now see him circling toward me, telling me to come to him, trying to manoeuvre me away from the door, toward which I had been subconsciously progressing even before his accusation. No shouts from him, no yelling, just clever and calculated footwork from him. I turn myself round the table to move closer to the door as I recognise his tactics and feel his desire to punish for now he is heading intently toward me. At this time, I distinctly do *not* want to be hit again. It bloody hurts! I am scared of him, that's for sure. And my thoughts are now totally focused on getting away from him and those damaging fists. Forget about defending yourself with words, girl!

I am still nearer than Jim to the door leading into the hallway, and from here is just a few steps to the front door entrance of the house. The chips are down now, both hands are now evident as we are both committed to our paths and we both know just what the other intends – He to attack me, and me to escape the said attack. In a split second, I calculate my chance of dodging his fists and making it to the door and out of the house and I know if I let him take another step forward I will miss this opportunity. I will have to yank our door open inwards, get into the hall, and yank the front door open inwards to break free from this threat. I can just about do it. Sort things out later, just don't get thumped again.

I see my chance to get through and out of the house first, and as I see his fist tighten again I take a risk. And in a fast fit of independence, I dash for the door, in the hope that I will escape from what is inevitably to come. In a few steps I am in the hall outside the front door. I make a frantic grab for the handle at the front door, and yank it wide open – just as Jim catches up with me and pushes hard against the same door to close it again...

The door slams shut!

I am not in time to escape. But a miracle happens...

Naïve Hope

The sound that follows stops us both in our tracks.

Glass shatters everywhere as we both simultaneously realise that Jim's hand has connected with one of the lovely old fashioned coloured lead glass door panels. And his arm has gone straight through it! Blood is flowing from a deep cut in the top of his arm on his bicep, soaking his shirt in a matter of seconds.

Oh.My.God! Instead of me, *he* has sustained injury. And *he* is bleeding! Not what either of us expected.

The brothers of the Pastor upstairs hear the noise and commotion and they both come running out to help. Our fight, or whatever the heck it was, is set aside to deal with this emergency. Jim needs stitches and I jump into first-aid mode to bundle him up with hasty padding around his upper arm. It is a nasty deep cut on his right bicep, and surely requires stiches. One of the brothers recognises the seriousness of the situation and off he rushes to organise transport in order to drive Jim to emergency hospital, for I don't yet know how to drive.

Meanwhile I attempt to contain the situation whilst we are waiting for the car to come to the front of the house. I tell Jim that I am sorry that he is hurt, and sorry I was. I didn't intend for him to get hurt. And I am secretly further concerned in case this means that I will have *more* to be sorry for when he is recovered and again able to settle the previous score he had in mind.

But when he returns from emergency, he is too busy nursing his arm, being the wounded soldier... I think he got a shock on how it had gone wrong for *him* instead. And he now has a convenient distraction to deal with.

Part of me steps out of the situation, and I am kind of in observer mode as I watch how the dynamics have changed. Interestingly, the original drama causing all of his intended action has actually been eclipsed by the *novelty of Jim getting medical attention*. At this time, I also wonder if his ego does *not* want to dwell on his failing to 'get' me, so his focus now is on him being treated and getting attention. But, more importantly, I am also just plain relieved that I have avoided another belting. For the moment.

This time I have escaped, and not in the way I had envisaged. I am so relieved that I hadn't ended up getting twice as much punishment. Not then anyway. Not that he didn't store it away, and settle it later when dishing out for some other 'wrong'. Who is to know? But at the time, it actually seems forgotten, for he never refers to it again, and I think he got quite a surprise that *he* could be the one getting hurt!

Though I didn't yet know anything about Karma consciously, was this a case of Instant Karma?

Plus his punching arm was out of action for a while. Hurray!

Dangerous Moves

Anger is not always well controlled by those who don't understand *why* they are angry.

And this can mean that logical thought, reason, or even simple commonsense can take a back seat. Which can simply create further complications.

For instance, giving your partner motor vehicle driving lessons is not always the best idea. Add to this scenario someone who is erratically volatile. Alongside this, include the tendency for swift violent action from some idiot who is capable of serious physical damage.

Place all of these ingredients together in an older style car, garnish with children on the back seat, place at a busy inner city roundabout setting, complete with incomplete road signs; shake or stir, and voila!

A few yelled instructions, a grabbing at the steering wheel, and a solid stinging slap across the face and the head *whilst going round the roundabout*, and you have the recipe for serious danger – a serious accident. But fortunately the driver, me, who sustained the slaps, kept her head, and avoided smashing into someone else.

Yes, that is the scenario on one of my 'driving lessons' with Jim. We couldn't afford professional lessons, and this is the only way I can get to learn and to share his driving chores; and anyway, Jim

Naïve Hope

knows how to drive, how to cook, how to do this, how to do that, etc.etc. so he is obviously well equipped to teach me to drive.

Yes?

No! We could have had a serious accident – All of us!

Apologies after? Naah!! It seems to me that he thought that it was his God-given right to do or say *what* he wanted, *when* he wanted to, children present or not. Totally oblivious to possible consequences of his dangerous actions. But then, this man is not that smart when it comes to thinking.

Actually, thinking is too much of a stretch – the brain activity is more a kind of circling. You know, like in the old westerns with covered wagons, going round and round and round... Did I mention that he was Irish? Of course, I did! Sorry to the Irish, for I recognize that there have been some brilliant scholars and minds that have come from that country. However, there is a line of Irish that are less than bog-standard and are just plain stupid (and one of my girl-friends is Irish, and even *she* gets me and agrees with me on this). A compensating factor to hide this ignorance and stupidity may well be the offset of the gift of the Blarney, and this was probably to prevent them from being killed off in early childhood. Or possibly later, before they could pro-create. But in all fairness to the Irish Jim was more than Irish, he was also sociopathic!

For any right-thinking man would surely have recognized the possible consequences, and might have thought differently about those actions.

As I said, this is not a right-thinking man? The more I remember the stupid things that he did, the more I am amazed. Amazed not only that I survived them. But that I didn't recognize that this man *must* have gone over the edge somewhere! For, years after we split up, I could get angry remembering some of his *stupid* and *dangerous* actions. But I still didn't understand them. Now I can look back and recognize certain behaviours and that there *was* a serious problem with him.

Take for example the following scenario a few years later... This happened on several occasions.

We are just driving along, and he has a bee in his bonnet about something. Sometimes after a short day trip, driving back with the kids tired and spent, their heads lolling around in the back seat, Jim would start his badgering. Without the children listening and watching he would progress to accusations no matter my response.

Then his master-stroke of intimidation – he deliberately swings the steering wheel right over, and therefore the car, to the centre of the road, then to the curbside then quickly back again, causing a sudden swerving of the vehicle out of its current pathway. This can be really scary when done unexpectedly and whilst driving over a hundred kilometers an hour along a two-lane highway in the country, with ditches and trees on either side. The maneuver is done in a split second, as would be the damage if he had miscalculated or met with some sort of extra mechanical problem.

Imagine my consternation and fear when he also did the same trick going over the Westgate Bridge – the *tallest* bridge in Victoria - and this brave and gallant action is followed up with 'That's all it takes *– for everything to be over* – for you, for me, for the kids!'

Big *brave* man. Holding me in fear like that! Threatening his kids like that. Sure he may have thought that he had a firm grip on the wheel, (though none on reality) but I am not to know that, nor to trust that – for this man was a *tyrant*! And messing with other people's heads and hearts. *Anything* was fair game if it kept me in fear. If this man *was* all words, then one might view this threat differently, but because he would act out words I didn't dare to doubt what he could possibly do. He certainly delivered a serious message to me with these actions. The message that my life was in his hands, under his control! And that if I didn't behave, the children would also suffer.

Big, brave, clever man! He needs branding with 'Coward' – on his forehead, his chest, his hands and his legs! It's already on his heart - and his Soul! Grrrr!

How can one really *know* when someone is going to snap? He had 'snapped' so often with me over things I had not done and that he had accused me of – who could guarantee that he would never snap on such an occasion, when he was in one of these dark and

Naïve Hope

punishing moods? Hadn't he already tried attempted suicide? Albeit reasonably safely, however, it had still carried a risk...

On some level of my being, I *felt* that this man truly did have the power to cause the death of us all. Charming though he may be when in his 'right mind', the consequences of when he was *not* in his 'right mind' were truly terrifying. I truly did not know what to do to stop all of this, to protect my children and myself better, for any power I may have had I had allowed the church to take away from me in my desire to do or to be good.

'Do unto others...' Well, that is one thing, but this one; *'Forgive them their trespasses...'* And to have to *keep* forgiving...; What a load of crock when you are dealing with someone who should have known better. And who continues to do the same...

Easy to say now, but then I was also doing just the same... accepting things. Stupidly locked into a survival mode of *Getting Through This*, that I had developed a pattern in my own head of managing what was going on that was so deep, ingrained and labyrinthine, that I couldn't yet haul myself up onto any other horizon in my mind that did not include *Obey, Forgive, Service* and my own mother's words from the very first time Jim thumped me echo back to me: *'You've made your bed, now lie in it!'* Thanks, mum!

So in a way, this was all my own fault, anyway. I believed what I was being fed, I accepted it all. Despite the fact that there was no one else on hand, no other mirror present, no other argument available to tell me different – at this time...

1966

~ Twenty-One ~ Pay-Offs ~ Mind Reader

TWENTY-ONE

In many ways I am still an optimist and an idealist, always seeking to see the positive, and ready to hope and believe that things will get better, and comforted by the words of the Bible that declare 'Delight thyself also in the Lord and He shall give thee the desires of thine heart. Commit thy way unto Him, trust also in Him and He shall bring it to pass'. Surely God meant what He said? Surely He will deliver if I just have enough faith, patience and love. Lofty ideals, romantically hopeful dreams, these helped keep me going. But they also kept me in my head, trying to run another reality to fool my heart in order to get me through. I was still idealistically believing that when Jim was in a good mood, then that this was the norm, his real state, and that his odd Bad Mood would pass if I did the right thing. I was running two opposing stories, two different realities. Had to, to get through.

I have to put aside my reality and to hope for and attempt to create another reality. My expectations of others remain distorted as I still hope for them to 'do the right thing', to do what they promise, to meet my own standards of reliability and honour, yet a hidden part of me also expects that they won't, that they will disappoint me. So many disappointments in my past, I do not recognise where my hopes are contaminated with illusion, disenchantment, unreal expectations, defeat and distress, and instead, my 'faith' fills the hole with hope and daydreams to 'expect a miracle every day' from the Lord. I am hooked on God.

For some, indeed, for many, the world is too harsh a place to contemplate directly, without a cushion of fancy or belief.

In some ways having children brings you down to earth. Taking care of them requires practical application of everything you know, and challenges you to learn more. And more.

Naïve Hope

For family I have learned to stifle *my* wants, needs and desires, to ignore them, to disown them. It has now become part of my mental armour that I can't afford to have any. And my own young family requires my undivided attention. Most new mums know some of this for themselves, as they focus on the fresh and promising life they have created. But this is not just a Mother Thing, nor only an overnight thing, for I had been pretty much in training for this from an early age, as eldest, and as Parent to my own parents. Not that I had any real clout or any real authority of course. But in so many other areas I took on the role with its responsibilities. Yes, one could argue that I had little children to think about now, and also little choice, but basically I was entrenched in a certain way of life and of thinking for I didn't know of any other kind – just yet!

Approaching twenty-one was a wake-up call to check in on my life. The universal age of maturity; and as such it can often cause us to review our lives. After all, most people create a huge celebration around turning twenty-one and in those days it was about 'getting the keys to the front door'. Which I already had, of course, and without fanfare or flourish, I had had for quite some time.

During my life I have sometimes dare to make notes of events. Not a lot written during my marriage, though in the latter years I did keep tiny handbag diaries with a kind of shorthand code in it in case Jim saw the entries and questioned them. So nothing that I couldn't defend or justify completely with Jim was dared to be written – for him to find.

Recently, as I gathered dates and perused my old diaries, I came across the following article I had written about this momentous time in life, in anyone's life. It was obvious I had been musing about how things had been, and I had written it as an essay many years after my divorce. Composed in the third person, it had been put in writing as an exercise for one of the courses I did during my initial time of self discovery and self-development. Being still somewhat disconnected from myself at the time, and being driven on several fronts by pure survival, when I came to pen this bit, it came out exactly as I have copied it here. So I will leave this as I originally wrote it, in the third person.

Twenty-One Today

A distinct moment of the meaning of Marni's life had been frozen in a memory, filed in the recesses of her mind, of her 21st birthday. In the search for identity and authenticity, this well preserved memory is excavated and examined.

It was on this day that Marni remembers thinking to herself 'So, this is how it feels to be Twenty-One'. At that precise moment, she was leaning over the porcelain bathtub. In the bath were twelve terry cloth nappies that she was hand washing. A messy job... smelly... but performed with acceptance, persistence and conscientiousness. Hands red and wrinkled somewhat, she had thoroughly cleaned them of the putrid baby-bottom-debris first before the comparable luxury of swirling, hand ringing, washing and squeezing in soapy water had begun. Now a daily occurrence. She had no washing machine, no rubber gloves and this was before the days of disposable nappies. There had long been a sense of further resignation to her fate, and a foolishly commendable attempt to see the beauty in where she was placed, and pride in how clean she was getting the nappies. Back aching, muscles sore, she could only see the pile of waiting nappies that these smelly things were to become.

'Cast your burden upon the Lord' she repeated to herself. If happiness is in an attitude, an acceptance of one's fate, she was reasonably happy. She had no other choice. Jim wasn't angry just at the moment, the children were healthy, there was food in the kitchen, and, of course, 'the Lord will provide'. The children were depending on her, and wasn't it commended by the Bible to take care of and to serve others? Whenever her thoughts strayed about her lot in life, she mentally went straight away to the passages in the Bible about 'the virtuous woman'. This is biblical propaganda for keeping women akin to 'The Stepford Wives' (similar to those in the movie released in 2004 about how women were re-manufactured to suit and serve their husbands).

The Bible states in Proverbs chapter 31 that a virtuous woman rises early to take care of her family. She fears God, she is responsible for the running of the household, she finds bargains to help financially. In short, she is the perfect example of the woman

Naïve Hope

who goes out of her way in order to self sacrifice and serve others. And for this she is called Blessed, and of course, she goes to heaven. So to claim the promise of heaven, this reward, which was certainly a lot better than life on earth, Marni noted to do whatever she could to attain this insurance.

So. No party, no silliness, no celebration. Just getting on with it. Any thoughts of Twenty-First cards, flowers, gifts, cake or celebrations that others reputed to have enjoyed were quickly dismissed in order to keep at bay any associated disappointment and regret. For this was where she found herself, and no amount of dreaming or wishing would change things. If God had willed it otherwise, then it would be so.

Whenever there was talk of Coming of Age and the reaching of the milestone of Twenty-One, Marni would always remember the circumstances around her own. The clear non-emotional thought that had become a life defining moment for her at that age. Age Twenty-One. Coming of age. The decided reiteration and resignation that 'This' was her life.

You will probably be wondering if Marni had any faults at all.

Well, she could be a perfectionist, but didn't realise it. She was overly serious and it took a long time, years in fact, for her to eventually drop her nervous laughter and develop a true body laugh.

She was quite naïve, though thought that she was wise, but this was only true to the extent that she could quote scripture on practically any subject. She was not yet able to really think for herself, and was handicapped in her expectations of life and of how it should be, though in reality she lived with many idiosyncrasies and hypocrisies without recognizing them for what they were because of her religious faith training and unrealistic belief in ultimate goodness.

She was a mite self-righteous though she also didn't recognize this for many years. She was longsuffering (God help us) and went out of her way to put others first, and subsequently had difficulty in realizing that she brought it upon herself that she was always giving and not getting back to anything like the same degree.

In her own mind, as in most people's who have idealistic tendencies, it was hard for her to see her own shortcomings. But if any were pointed out to her, she was like a vengeance upon them to eradicate them. A pity she didn't apply compassion to herself more. It was only to be expected really, that such hard lessons came her way, in order for her to learn and go beyond compassion for others, and through this, to have compassion for herself.

But all is not totally lost, for there is a saving grace in all of this. Later that day, there is a postal delivery. Sheila has sent her a Twenty-First well-wishing congratulatory card.

Sheila never forgets!'

PAY-OFFS

I have to admit to the truths I wrote.

Since that revelation I have learned to drop a lot of this self-sacrificial stuff. After all, I didn't have much left to give away. And I eventually and illuminatingly came to realise that *I am* responsible for *me*, aren't I? The trouble is that it can take quite a while to reverse a way of being, a long-standing pattern, though the first step of course, is to be able to recognise that pattern.

Many of us often operate from so-called 'Pay-offs', where we get to acquire something else under the disguise of *not* getting something. Does this sound confusing? Let me try to explain it this way. We can do something or not do something, by choice, which can often be subconscious. But underneath that we may have another agenda. And if we do, this hidden agenda is the one that gets fulfilled, even though on the surface we complain or make a story about things not being how we want them to be. In other words, we can fool ourselves! We can say we are doing something for one particular reason, when all the time we are doing it for some other reason. Which we may not care to mention, talk about, think about or even be consciously aware of!

Nobody is perfect. Recognising what we do, why we do it and what *Pay-off* we are looking for is part of true integrity and authenticity. If you don't know who you are, and why you do things, how the hell

Naïve Hope

do you expect anyone else to? How are you yourself able to correctly recognise what others are doing?

What do I mean by Pay-offs? What sort of things are these? These pay-offs are where a situation has been created that enables certain things to occur, develop or happen where you are seen to be doing one thing (or the right thing), but in actual fact are achieving another objective. You can complain about being unwell, and in fact you are unwell, and possibly have made yourself that way because you then get something you don't get normally, which is; to be taken care of. Many people work hard because others rely on them, or because they don't know any other way, but for a variety of reasons they don't look after themself, or they get tired of always doing so for others, or they need an excuse to avoid doing something; so they get unwell. The mind is a very powerful thing, and can manufacture un-wellness, or even create accidents that cause a need to be looked after. This is not to say that the only reason for 'an accident' is so that you get to be taken care of. There are many reasons. But in the case of one's own hidden agendas, this is an example of a possible pay-off. And knowing yourself just how involved you are in the outcome of an event can be very empowering. For what you know about yourself, you can either embrace, or change. A pay-off for getting drunk is that you don't have to be responsible for your actions whilst drunk. Or you get to avoid certain feelings that cause deep pain, so you avoid the pain, and you also get to avoid dealing with *fixing* the pain. You may cite the reason for getting drunk as 'having fun' with your friends, of relaxing after a hard week, or of any number of things, but the real reason may be quite different.

In short, a pay-off is something you get that is not apparent or is not the immediate reason behind something.

The usual Pay-offs are when you:

- Don't have to grow up
- Don't have to take risks
- Avoid getting hurt
- Won't have to feel (certain) feelings
- Get to avoid responsibility
- Won't have to remember a painful experience

- Don't have to confront an issue
- Can get taken care of by other people
- Don't have to admit being wrong
- Get to look better than you really are
- Get to fool people for a bit longer
- Get to avoid something in yourself that you don't like
- Get to be a martyr
- Get to blame someone else

To name a few. These are what's called 'Fear-based' Pay-offs.

There *are* more positive ones where the pay-off is getting to feel genuinely better or happier or that have a less selfish agenda. The difference is that we may *think* that we are doing something good for another, even though we are actually doing it for ourself – in order to feel good about it. Get it?

But it is the effect of the Pay-off that is more beneficial for oneself and makes for a better world. These may include when you:

- Save someone's life
- Ease someone's pain
- Put another person first
- Atone for guilt
- Be of service
- Make the world a better place
- Genuinely make someone else happy

To name a few.

Yes, we may have a personal pay-off of doing something that makes us feel good, but the motivation, The agenda, the pay-off can also include pay-offs for others.

Learning what the Pay-off is can be a huge clue to self-motivation and self-understanding, but one has to be honest with oneself to do this. Getting past the pay-offs that prevent us from being all we can be, whether they are positive or negative, and being aware of them can give us greater authenticity and autonomy in our lives. And another benefit is the growing ability to be aware of the pay-offs of others.

Naïve Hope

Had I known about pay-offs earlier, I probably would have searched out and questioned my own pay-offs in staying with Jim. At the least I would have been more aware of what was actually happening behind the scenes, rather than just the dramas on centre stage.

MIND READER

I Know What You Are Thinking.

Jim was very good at reading minds. Or so he thought. It was a game he played throughout our married life.

He would *tell* me what I was thinking. It wasn't a question, it was always a statement.

'I can tell you are thinking ...blah-blah-blah,' (fill in the blank of whatever it was he wanted to *think* that I was thinking at the time) 'by the look on your face,' he would say. I don't know where he got it all from, but he was very rarely right. Though he would claim that he *was* right.

I could be looking blankly out of the window wondering if I was going to do the washing first or the mending, or what meals to have next week, or remembering a recipe, or whatever it was at the time, but you could be sure that *he* would *know* what I was thinking, and no matter what I said, he *insisted* that *he knew*. He would be so insistent that he knew what I was really thinking that I often had to practically prove what I was thinking with a complete explanation and all of the steps of my thinking to arrive at that very expression he thinks he 'caught'.

Duh!

One of the most common things he claimed that I was thinking was that I was planning to *leave* him. Hmmm, wonder where he got *that* idea from? Would I be so stupid as to think such a thing whilst around him, even if it had occurred to me? With such a transparent face, the fear of him finding out would be far too dangerous for my health, now wouldn't it? The next most common thing was that I was thinking about someone that I *fancied* at work, or at the church or the shops. Or of some other some such related subject, depending on what he had been musing over or fuming about during the day. Later on in our married life, I could even guess what the guys at work had been talking about that day, because he came home and projected it all onto me, as if I was planning whatever their wives, girlfriends, mistresses or whomever had gotten up to. Or the men themselves.

It is almost impossible to persuade someone to see or think something different if they have convinced themselves that something is so. Silly bugger. Idiot nut job! I can call him that now because I can see how stupid this all was. Now! At the time, though, it was challenging and confusing.

This telling-me game was sometimes interspersed with another version of the same game.

'What are you thinking?' he would ask. 'Tell me what you are thinking. Now!' I would be hounded until I told him what I was thinking, or until he was satisfied with what I told him I was thinking. Guilty conscience? It was certainly not *my* guilty conscience, for these things almost always came out of the blue for me. Jim wondering how he could please me? Hah! This, of course, is a flippant comment, as I find myself thinking how ridiculous it all is now, yet how serious and scary it was back then.

No, just narcissistic I think, and a bit psychopathic. Did he think that by monitoring my thoughts he could control me? Who knows? I think that actually it was always about him. And his constant thought-friends; Control, Fear and Inadequacy.

Eventually I learned that saying clearly 'How do you know what I am thinking?' also had to be followed up with something more like 'But you are not in my mind. I am. There is no way you can truly know unless I tell you.' And then run!

Anyway, I survived all of that, for here I am telling you this ridiculous habit of his.

Between devoting myself to family, the youngest son was now big enough for me to go back to work – and we sure needed the extra money. There are only so many hours that Jim could work. He had changed jobs and was now working for the Corporation – the Council – and was learning how to drive a large vehicle so he could drive a City Corporation truck which paid even more. He was

Naïve Hope

working as a Sanitary Engineer, with perks. High falootin' title, really. Basically he was now just a *dustbin man*, and would be a dustbin truck driver, and the *perks* were access to first choices when 'stuff' was thrown away. Don't get me wrong – some 'stuff' was brand new, just possibly outdated or back-stock or dribs and drabs not sold in sales. This helped to supplement our income somewhat, especially when good food items (mainly tinned) were cleared out. Even though some nights he would come home quite smelly, after a shower or good bath and a change of clothing, there was no harm done, and everything he brought home was disinfected. My dad was still having trouble with work, and after learning from Jim how it all worked, dad ended up joining the dustbin brigade too, and there was a bit of camaraderie there for a while. Even though the job was dirty it paid well, so we all coped.

It was obvious by now that we would not be missionaries to the Congo or some other so-called needy place, and Jim's focus was on providing for the family as we were no longer assisting with the Youth work. He had stepped-down his duties and I had been replaced in this area when I had fallen pregnant.

But our need to be doing something 'for God' was still strong and our guilt not to be doing so was even stronger and was continually being enforced at church. We had even had an idea of making evangelistic tapes with mum and dad and selling them to assist in converting others to Christianity. The idea had been sparked when Jim was introduced to the new tape recording systems. A super-duper model was available to him through his contacts with his old job and so he had gone ahead and purchased a Brenell Tape Recorder. Initially, he wanted to make tapes of bedtime stories for our sons whilst he was at church, but then other possibilities began to present themselves. Bible readings for the blind, sermons for those who couldn't attend church, songs to encourage the housebound; the list was growing. Mum and dad were impressed with its recording quality and saw the possibility. Being under the spell of the church and its injunction to get the Word out, they were also quite keen to get involved.

We had a brain-storm meeting one night and came up with some ideas which ended up in Jim and I registering a business name for our project. We called ourselves 'Focus Four' because there were four of us. Just as we were about to approach a bank manager for a loan to launch the project, dad had second thoughts and pulled out. I never did really find out what the reason for this was. But you know, I am so glad that he did. It would have been absolutely *disastrous* for us all to have been so bound together in such a venture. Someone would have killed somebody!

In all we produced one bedtime story. Though we did record some messages of other missionaries. And expensive exercise in all.

Meanwhile, our family has grown and we find that we are just too cramped. With missionary ideas now shelved, we can focus on improving our own lot in life, and it is time to recognise that we need a bigger place to bring up the boys, and a separate room for them to sleep in, so the decision to look at what we can afford is made. Even expanding into the other ground floor rooms as they became available proved unsatisfactory.

We discovered that paying for our own property and covering rates etc. was a real financial challenge at that time, as it was for many. Therefore my return to work for wages was essential for us to be able to manage. The search for suitable work for me was now on, only this time, thank god, I did *not* have to work in the same building as Jim! Gaining a position in an office as a Credit Sanction Clerk with one of the large Mail Order Warehouses mushrooming up at the time, I was able to occupy my mind with things other than domestic problems and Bible quotes.

Eventually we saved a little money, enough to put as a deposit on a little terraced house in Rusholme, an area which was a bit closer to the city. 'Two-up-two-down' describes the type of terraced house that was a small solid brick two storey dwelling which included a small kitchen and an outside toilet. The series on British TV called '*Coronation Street*' illustrates the sort of place accurately. A bathroom had been added at some stage upstairs, making the back bedroom somewhat smaller, but also making life in one of these little places more livable. A tiny yard where there was an outside toilet, was just big enough to swing a cat and to hang laundry, though not both at the same time. It was small.

But it was our own!

Naïve Hope

Maybe now life will begin to improve for us all.

Meanwhile, even though we are living in Rusholme in our own house and she is not seeing Johnny anymore, Sheila continues to be a part of my life and on many a Saturday night she would come round and spend time, joining us as we share our favourite take-out meal as a treat from the local shops. This was a combination of Indian curry and rice, with the most amazing fresh crispy chop-suey rolls I have ever had.

Sometimes she would also arrange to come at other times when there was a special meeting on at church, and she continued to 'keep me company'.

1968 THE LAND OF OZ

~ The Ends of The Earth ~ New to Oz ~ Diane Drops Me In
~ Freedom Bid – Mobiltown ~ Merry vs Sloshed ~ The Sixties

THE ENDS OF THE EARTH

One day Sheila arrives at our tiny house a little earlier. Jim is still at home, having for some reason or another decided to go out witnessing later.

So we all sit down to have a cuppa whilst the boys are quiet having their afternoon nap. And we get to talking about Australia and migration.

Sheila has some relative in Australia who keeps sending her positive reports of what it is like over there. She has kept Jim and I informed of some other members of her family who have decided to emigrate. I also have a cousin called Victor who had emigrated to Newcastle in NSW several years earlier, and who had met an Australian woman called Robyn and was planning to marry her.

Interestingly enough, Jim and I have had a conversation on this subject of migration, as he had told me about his time in Canada. His description of Canada had really impressed me, and it had also built on the knowledge I had gained whilst I was at school, for I had been writing to a Canadian pen-pal friend called Ann Hughes, who had been living in Toronto. I really did like the sound of Canada and the idea of living there had intrigued me. Jim and I had occasionally, though not seriously, talked of the possibility of doing such a thing. I had researched it a bit at various times, and loved some of the things I learned about the place.

Things were so tough in England, and we were finding it so hard to keep on top of the expenses, especially with growing interest and council rates, and the struggle to keep a little place like ours was a real test. Sheila and her husband Peter had well paid jobs, so it was easier to own the sort of posh-er house they lived in, though I never begrudged her in this.

Naïve Hope

And then she tells me that mainly due to the feedback of this family member, they have now given it serious consideration and they had decided that both she and her husband Peter are definitely going to move to Australia, though they would have to sell their house first.

What a surprise! This is my closest and bestest friend, and truth be known, my only true friend. And I am fascinated, and also challenged. I don't want to lose my friend, even though I had vague ideas that we might possibly go to Canada at some stage. I am glad for her. But at some stage, we would have to part if or rather when we did go overseas.

Well, anyway, there we are sitting in the kitchen, Jim in one of his charming 'good' moods and quite open to conversation about things. It was one of his good days, I think. And we discuss the merits of migration to Canada, and the merits of migration to Australia.

You realize of course, that we don't have definitive knowledge about all of this, but lots of shared information. Australia had a current migration policy to help new migrants provided they work continuously and pay taxes for the first two years. In exchange they fund the trip over and provide a form of accommodation to rent. Canada costs of migration were beyond our reach. Australia had this, Canada had that. And so it went on. As we talk and as Jim explores living in Canada, and we learn about and compare it with Australia, the Southern Continent sounds so unbelievably great that I hear myself saying out loud 'Well if Australia is so good, what are we doing just sitting here in the kitchen talking about it? We should be over there already.'

With these words, we all look at each other, for this is a moment of destiny. So it is decided – that we make serious enquiries and take it from there. This Monday!

And within three months of my first contacting the Australian Embassy in Manchester, we have put our house on the market, have packed up our packing cases for shipment and we are on our way over to Melbourne on the P & O Line ship, the 'Oriana'.

Wow! Things can move very fast indeed. But this was surely meant to be. And it has been one of the best decisions of my life!

Sheila and her husband Peter and their little girl Yvette eventually follow us over, but it takes them a couple of years more to do so. We settle in Melbourne, they in the Sydney suburb of Camden. And we continue the friendship for many more years.

And that is how we moved to Australia in late 1968, leaving England and family behind and braving a whole new world with and for (we were convinced) our two sons, Joseph and Ben. For a better life! And so it was. For despite later events, I feel and think that it created an opportunity for us all to have a better chance at a brighter future.

New To Oz

It was a whole other experience for us upon our arrival in this new land of Australia, or Oz as some Australians referred to it. I could further expand upon the early trials and tribulations we faced and the essential adjustments, and about what living in an ancient corrugated tin hut is like, as well as the adventure of sampling sometimes eatable migrant hostel food, and the life at the Broadmeadows Migrant Hostel we were allocated to, out in 'the sticks', as outer suburbs were referred to then by a lot of the migrants. But the following record should give you the picture.

Our first night was horrendous. After the luxury of the ship, anything would have been a letdown. But to walk into a tiny converted army Nissan hut and to be greeted with the ancient worn furniture that was meant to be our home was certainly an unexpected shock. There were no cooking facilities, no inside bathroom, just a small lounge/eating area with a small sink that also served as our sleeping quarters. It was furnished with a small square table and four small chairs, but no bed, just a convertible vinyl covered two-seater couch that doubled as our sleeping divan, an old wooden cupboard / wardrobe and another small room fitted out with a chest of drawers and two bunk beds for the boys.

I thought there had been some mistake at first, but realized that there was no mistake and that this was it. Had we jumped out of the frying pan into the proverbial fire? This reality had *not* been included in the flash migration videos shown us at Australia House!

Naïve Hope

It was clear that we just had to make the best of it. I burst into tears. 'What have we done? What are we doing here?' I upbraided myself. We had been told on arrival at the hostel office about the common canteen and that we could get something to eat there, so tired and hungry by this time, we all trotted along there to be faced with congealing unappetizing rations. The lady behind the counter must have felt sorry for me after seeing the stunned-mullet look on my face, for she said, 'Things will look better in the morning, lovey. Just put up a few posters and it will soon look a bit more homely.'

Though it wasn't strictly true, after a sleep, it was a matter of bringing out that British stoicism again, and simply 'getting on with it'!

What a culture shock!

The weather, the mozzies, the food, the clothing, the slang, the drive-ins; a whole new world. The many types of salads available. Trams in Melbourne instead of buses. Taking a train to get to the city. Migrant Italians and Greeks running taxis. The heat in the sun - every day. The sweating. The Ozzie Christmas where weather dictated salads; anything other than our Christmas plum pud after hot stuffed turkey, which was best on a cold chilly day. Business men wearing short trousers and long white socks with sandals. Panty-hose instead of stockings. People calling you by your first name instead of your title.

Most of the Australian working women appeared to be ahead of their English counterparts, for at work all of the women are wearing pantyhose, when one only wore stockings and suspenders in England. Though I accepted that this was progress, I felt more comfortable in suspenders because it was less clammy than full hose. But when I began work I was counseled to wear hose by one woman in particular who had commented that certain stairs at the office allowed for a degree of peeping by some of the men who were lucky enough to be stationed nearby. I took the hint, and even though my skirts were always longer than the other women, felt more assured of modesty in this department.

Not only that, anything to avoid the Inquisition by Lord Jim.

Within days we had sorted the boys' school situation and had met a few other migrants. And found ourselves a Throngs of God church, strongly connected with the Pentecostal Movement.

Getting work in the city and bringing money in again was now crucial to surviving and making this adventure work. We had arrived with only forty-nine English Pounds left in our bank account, as the house was not yet sold. Not that there was expected to be much equity after costs, but at least something to get us started.

I find a job first, and begin work before Christmas. Jim has a harder time but eventually finds work early in the New Year. I quite enjoy my job doing Accounts Payable, and am actually so relieved that my new job takes me out of the horrid atmosphere in the hostel. Travelling daily by train into the city gives me a bit of time to myself, though the time on the train is usually filled with planning the day's work as well as planning meals and making lists of 'to-dos' when I get home again.

We had only ever seen Australian advertising material on the new hostel units, and not anything on the old (and still current) accommodation, so eventually, after getting over some of our culture shock we asked questions to find where the newer accommodation was located. Then we put in a request for a transfer. We found that living in a tiny corrugated tin hut with two children was not much fun. After several harsh months, there is a vacant place for us and so we move down to Altona, nearer the water and nearer to our kind of church. It is still only an old army hut, but there are new hostel units here and so we put our name down for one of these. The old quarters are a bit of an improvement on the Broadmeadows hostel unit so it is a bit more comfortable to live here until one of the new Monier Besser brick hostel units is available for us.

Our story was similar to many others. We make friends with a young couple who also have two small children. Diane and Harry were close to our ages, though not church folk. Nevertheless, there were similar problems in some areas, such as children, schools, good cheap clothing and finding English food etc. - all the general issues of adapting to a new and different culture and environment.

Naïve Hope

They are both from England, Diane is English-born, like me, and Harry is Irish born, like Jim. Diane and I fell into often catching the same train together, as she also worked in the city. She is a very attractive outgoing shapely young woman, blonde and flirtatious. And she has such a happy laugh.

I am enjoying my new job, working in the city for a Japanese import and export company, and I make a new friend there. Julie Murray lives in Warrandyte, and is so very different from myself, but we click, and lunchtimes often finds us both striding up Bourke Street to shop or buy a sandwich together. To keep up with the professional dress standard at work, I have to pay attention to improving my wardrobe to suit. I do *not* have a problem with this, and in fact welcome it. Fortunately I can make many of my own Summer clothes.

I am beginning to adjust to the weather, though it is still so very hot in comparison to England. But I can begin to see a future for us again.

The sense of new life begins to emerge, and I can feel new hope surfacing. Yes, we made the right choice; we did the right thing. And Sheila writes me that she will be coming over here soon anyway. How wonderful that will be!

Diane Drops Me In

Jim and I begin to draw closer together in Australia. We have obviously experienced a lot of stress with this upheaval and move, which has forced us to face difficulties together. This has caused us to be more mutually dependent on each other because of these shared experiences in a new land. So many different culture differences – though not as bad as someone who can't even speak the language. We quickly discover more freedom and lightness here, so despite our challenges, we begin to enjoy some of the things we find here, especially when Jim can finally afford to buy a second-hand car. Then we can get to church more easily instead of having to be picked up by the church bus or a member of the congregation.

I am also gaining more confidence in myself and without really realizing it, I am beginning to grow into a more attractive young woman. My dress sense and standards improve, especially as Julie, my new friend at work, shares her knowledge with me. For she also used to do modeling for Fletcher Jones Ladies Wear. Our boys seem to be doing well at school and our home standards are improving as we can also now afford to buy an electric kettle and fry-pan to have home cooked meals. It is beginning to feel like a home now, and moving into our new accommodation at the hostel, we feel like we are on the home stretch. Our little terraced property in England pays less than we had hoped but enough for us not to feel cheated. This is now safely in our bank account as we watch the pennies grow.

We have been so busy with work, and focused on saving and managing that Jim doesn't seem to have the time or energy to spare on creating drama. Anyway, there is no reason for him to do so and I have forgotten much of the abuse in England as enjoying our new united state of togetherness.

Our fellow migrant next door neighbours, Diane and Harry occasionally catch up with us, but we are all living quite busy lives. I naturally spend a bit more time with Diane because of the shared train travel. Jim keeps more to himself with neighbours than I do, and most catching up with others is now usually in the hostel kitchen or over one of the children's birthdays.

Diane and I occasionally share a couple of recipe ideas, and this is how we learn about the Aussie barbeque – eating outside had been an unfamiliar experience in England, and cooking outside was previously unknown in our limited experience. So we are now introduced and educated to some of the joys of outdoor entertaining. It is at this time that Jim begins to have the odd beer at any BBQ's though he continues this mostly at home alone - it doesn't seem to be a problem. At present.

And we get caught up with another new release of a James Bond movie and before long we have read through *all* of Ian Fleming's books. No, I didn't get the bug the same as Jim and I wasn't an Honor Blackman Pussy Galore, or any of the others that followed. Though I still did wish I could look like Tania Romanova in 'From

Naïve Hope

Russia with Love'. In an attempt to freshen my look, I coloured (or rather, dyed) my hair again for the first time in many, many years – since my attempt at school actually. I was inspired to do so through my new work friend Julie, after she suggested that it would look good on me. And it certainly did. And for some reason, James now takes a bit of appreciation and interest in how I look, as I take a somewhat moderated interest in fashion. Though I still don't dare to wear my skirts as short as the other women at work.

It would seem that life is now being good to us; we have a local church, we are enjoying a limited version of Australian lifestyle, we are both in gainful employment, we are building a fund for our own home and we are all healthy.

Anyway, forward to one day when out of the blue, a spanner is again thrown into this temporary harmony to cause a new problem.

Harry comes knocking in a real panicky fashion on our front door. He needs to speak to me urgently, and is that ok with Jim? Sure. Jim invites him in, and the poor guy is quite frantic.

Harry asks me directly 'Do you know where Diane has gone? Do you know where she is?' and I had absolutely no idea what he was talking about. He seems more than very upset and I can't work out what the problem is. He asks me again, but I cannot answer him any differently. Jim enters into the conversation, and we finally make sense out of what Harry is carrying on about – Diane has left him, for *good*. Gone. Run away with someone she met at work. Left him and the children. She has actually just dropped everything and left them all. I am stunned!

And surely she *must* have told me, us being so pally and everything.

And I didn't have a clue. She had told me *nothing*. Not even said goodbye to me, well, not in any way that I would have recognized as significant. The last time I had seen her was the morning before on the way to work, and there was not a sign, not an inkling, not a clue. Now I am surprised as I thought we had a reasonable friendship together.

Poor Harry is totally distraught. And has no idea how he is going to cope with two little children. I did remember Diane complaining about him to me. About his sometimes being boring and of his lack of romance. But I didn't know she was going to leave him! And she never talked of being unfaithful or of other men.

But none of that really matters as this is not my business, it is not my problem. And yet, it is made to be my problem.

For now, and for quite a while, I am treated as if *I* put her up to it, as if *I* knew all about it, as if *I* encouraged her! Jim is now watching me like a hawk, questioning me over *everything*. Asking me what I am thinking even more now. Totally mistrustful of me. And I didn't have a bloody thing to do with it!!

Eventually I have had enough of all of this. He was driving me crazy, and was now beginning to drink a bit more. Not every night, but at weekend in binges. That other side of Jim is hanging around more often now, the charmer seems to have hidden, and the consequences of this Diane situation are now a real concern for me.

Somehow, *I* am tainted with *her* unfaithfulness.

When he drinks he gets morbid, more suspicious, messy, abusive, disagreeable, and nasty. Now he does odd and unusual things, like pulling my head back by my hair at the slightest perceived provocation, gives me sly elbow digs and flat hand hits even if there is no obvious reason for him to punish me. On a whim. And here there is absolutely no-one else to go to – no family, no friends, not even Diane now.

FREEDOM BID — MOBILTOWN

I can take no more.

Jim the Bible-Basher was showing real promise as Jim the Wife-Basher!

One day after 'the Diane affair', I am stretched, stressed and have totally had enough with his accusations and manhandling. I decide not to go into work that day, being physically bruised and feeling emotionally damaged by him. I am so hurt with his behavior and accusations and treatment that I now get really pissed off about it. I actually dare to feel anger at him. This anger now drives me. I decide that I have simply had enough. What's the point of it all? I ask myself. All along I have been doing the right thing, keeping the faith, honouring my vows, working hard, doing right, but what for? For *this*? I am so upset I can't think straight.

I am being punished as though I deserted the family, as though it was *me* that walked out on everyone. I might as well leave *myself* if I am getting punished for someone else doing so. I cannot take another day, another hour of this, and I determine that I am going to get the next train out of here. Where to? Who cares! I just have to get out of here.

We have no small suitcases suitable to carry, so I pack the shopping trolley with some clothes and a little makeup, and leaving the unit, I walk down to the train station to leave him. Remember I am fed up, and angry as all het up, and I have absolutely *no idea* where I am going to go. All I know is I *have* to get away!

So I begin the walk down to the Mobiltown Train Station down the road about three hundred metres from the Altona hostel. I am struggling as I drag my shopping trolley along the rough stones on the road to the train tracks. There are no pavements. This hostel too is out in the sticks.

It is another hot day in Altona, but that does not deter me. I will do what I have to do to stop this. Resolutely struggling and bumping the trolley over large stones, I am a quarter of the way to the station when a car pulls up, and a *gorgeous* guy winds down his window and asks me if I need a lift.

Probably because I am not thinking clearly and somewhat emotionally mixed up, I am so surprised at the offer. This was totally unexpected as my head was full of anger and arguments with Jim. I was also disarmed at being partly flattered by this attention, and just as relieved to get out of the sun and the dusty dirty walk and before I know it, I have accepted his offer. And I get in the car.

A moment of reality hits when he asks where I need a lift to. So I tell him I am going to catch the train into the city. Usually I think several steps ahead of my actions, because I need to know what I am letting myself in for. This is a habit I am honing in my married life. But not today! For I have not thought this through. The guy now offers to drive me directly to the city as he is going there himself.

Somehow at this point I come to my senses, just in time, and kindly thank him for his offer, but that I already have my ticket and I prefer to get the train. But thank you so much.

My face must have been a picture! He must have known that I was facing something difficult or uncomfortable in my life. And I surely could have made something else happen that day if I had been that kind of person or in that kind of mind, and it probably would have totally changed my life. But I was well warned when it came to strangers, and I guess I was being looked after. For with some hesitation, he graciously drops me off, and goes on his way.

And I sit at the hot deserted station for about half an hour while my temper cools itself down, despite the heat. The flush of anger has worn off, and reason is able to return again. I begin to think about what I am doing. It is at this point that I recognise the enormous risk I had just run by accepting that lift. And of how fortunate I had been in having come across someone who was sympathetic and not pushy. I feel so terribly alone again. But now I also feel even more vulnerable. And I miss my children already.

I now fully realise I have nowhere else to go, no options, and no real stomach to leave my children. But I also have no place to take them to away from this, even if I waited for them to come home from school. And so I have no option other than to walk that rocky road again to go back 'home' – to the hostel.

Once more, a little part of me has died. I have submitted again.

The contradictory behaviour of this man, my *husband*, is confusing. He would be fine for ages, months. Then he would get 'that look' in his eye and you knew, you just *knew*, that in his mind the words playing out are 'It's *your* fault'. And next would follow something, some accusation of what you have done wrong; the shirt got ironed the wrong way, you should have put the spoon here not there, I can't find my ... where did you put it, you're too this, you're too that, you flirted with ..., you should have known that I blah blah blah...

Naïve Hope

Part of you gets to believe it, he is so self convinced that *he* is convincing, and you again wonder what you did to attract it all. And later, when he swears he will *never* hit you again, that he *truly* loves you, that he can't *live* without you, that he *needs* you, and that because he loves you *so* much he can't help losing control, you can fall into the trap of *hoping* and believing that he *is* telling you the truth and that he *means* it when he says he will *not* hurt you again. Which he is. Self convinced. In that moment. And *only* in that moment. And this was a really hard lesson that I had to learn about what he said and what he meant. He may well have meant it in the moment, but that doesn't mean that he means it for life, or that he had the capacity to follow through with it.

I begin to hesitate over whether he really means it, for haven't we been in this place before? Does he guess this? His pleas now become more appealing, more desperate. Because he is now begging '*Please* don't leave me. I will *change*. I will *never* hit you again. I love you and I need you.' Which is also followed with 'We *do* love each other, don't we?' And even 'We *need* each other, don't we?'

When you live in a new country and know hardly anyone else, and you have two young children dependent on you, you always have to think what is in their best interest, too. Part of you is also hoping that this time it's different. This time it will *be* different, and he *will* change.

Only it's never different. You even accept his 'forgive-and-forget-flowers' thinking they will seal the deal. But they don't. Then part of you is *too ashamed* at what has happened, at what you have allowed, at actually *believing* him and at waiting for him to keep his promise. And this is not your shame that you are carrying, but *his*, for somehow he has transferred it along with his irresponsibility to you, yet you don't realise that, you just feel the weight, the energy of it.

You have invested so much in this relationship, so you stupidly continue to hope and to wait for him to keep his promise, just like you waited for your father who promised to take you to that movie, that film, that treat, but who didn't keep his promise, *never* kept his promises, and who never got around to making you feel like *you* were at the centre of his universe. Just once. You stay in someone else's shame and fear instead. Until you finally learn.

And the brain-washing from the church, the continued being preached at, keeps you scared of doing anything that would let Jesus down.

One of the greatest gifts I got from all of this treatment was when I finally faced how *my dad* had let me down, and how I had looked for someone to *not* let me down. But in the doing so, the letting down is *implied* so I attracted men that *would* let me down.

As a much older and wiser version of myself, I one day truly got that my dad *couldn't* give me what I wanted, could indeed *never* give me what I wanted him to give me. He was *incapable* of doing so, and no amount of waiting, hoping or replaying opportunities for him or any other man in my life to do so would change that history. I had to recognise that it couldn't be done. I had to grow past this.

And to *let him off the hook*. Yes, I had to let my dad off the hook that I had him on, the one that wanted something that he could never and would never give me.

The day I did that, my relationship with my dad totally changed, and I could relate to him in an unconditional way that I hadn't been able to do so before.

When he died, I had no regrets, and was able to let him go peacefully, for I had made peace with myself over this, and was able to make peace with him.

Dad loved me as best as he was capable. And his way was definitely *not* my way. I guess in his own way, he had done the best he could, and I had to accept that.

This valuable lesson I hadn't been learned just yet, though, and there are a few more surprises in store until I finally get it. I am not free just yet.

MERRY VS. SLOSHED

During that first year in Australia, I am relishing my work at the Japanese-Australian company on King Street, just round the corner from Bourke Street. These were in the days when that was a clean

Naïve Hope

and classy area of Melbourne, not the crappy night-slum area it is now.

Most of the people working there were Japanese or Australians, and it seems I was the only fresh English person. I look after the accounts and shipping documents and there would be times when all the wool buyers were in from Japan and other parts of Australia, and it would get quite busy. But I enjoy the variety and the mix of staff, and I have a reasonably good rapport with some workers, that is when the mega differences regarding my Faith and beliefs did not get in the way. Which they did from time to time. Religion and beliefs *will* find their way into work situations at some time or another, won't they?

A day arrives when my faith is challenged, and I could *not* for the life of me keep quiet about it. One day one of the guys, Peter, who is actually a really nice guy – normally - is bragging about his previous night's exploits and of how he was still suffering with a hangover. This was in the days when my own husband was having only the odd drink, so I just didn't get it. It wasn't the first time I had heard the guys at work boasting and swaggering about their escapades and competing with each other over what they had drunk, where they had drunk and who had drunk the most etc.

It was actually none of my business, but tell that to a zealous self-righteous Born-Again Christian – if you can. I just got so *incensed* over it all. It somehow pushed my self righteous (or self deprived) buttons and I think I felt offended, but I really shouldn't have been. Anyway…

I was not used to this talk of drinking exploits and ego fights over it, and my overzealous mind went into overdrive about it. After all, I had been taught that work is *not* the place to bring your personal stuff (says Miss High-and-Mighty, straight from the land of appropriate and respectful office workers – the British!) and so I gave this poor man, Peter, a dirty look. He saw it and took me up on it, challenging me; 'What's up your nose?' said Peter. Now Peter and I usually got on quite well. I realized years later, long after I had left Jim, that I had usually found him friendly, pleasant and likeable in some ways, and I may even possibly have found him somewhat attractive – though I think I was too scared to realize it enough to admit this to myself. I do know that the guys there often commented on me and my looks and judging by these, they tended to see me as attractive, especially since I had started making improvements to my appearance. But being so terrified of other men – and naturally so with my fear of and experiences with Jim - I totally denied this to myself. It was only later that I realized that attraction is one thing, flirting is yet another, and taking it someplace else is also an even more very different 'other'. But I did not dare to acknowledge any of this to myself, for if I did, it would also show in my face, and Jim would see it, because I would be in fear, and shame and guilt and then I would surely be punished when I got home.

I didn't know then how to handle people that were simply attractive! I hadn't yet learned how to do that. I was punished for noticing anything like that so by default I had had to learn to live in denial and to wear blinkers to keep myself safe, or at least to prevent supposedly justifiable punishment.

And so, without realizing it, because I had a charge on the situation, I too brought my own personal stuff into the situation. I told him that 'I am disgusted with you talking about a hang-over and getting drunk. It's a bad habit, and disgusting. And you shouldn't be talking about it at work. And anyway, alcohol is poison. How can you poison yourself like that? '

Well, the poor guy was quite taken aback, but also a bit bemused by this. Peter looked at me a bit puzzled, and then he asked me 'Have you ever *been* drunk?'

'No, and I don't intend to either' I retort somewhat self-righteously. But Peter wasn't through with me just yet.

'Well, don't criticize it until you have been drunk yourself. You cannot condemn or comment on what you haven't tried yourself.' He looks straight at me, without the sort of look that Jim would have given me if I had just attacked him the same way I was attacking this man. I am practically spluttering at his comment; 'What?' He then informs me, 'Don't talk about what you don't know about.'

Naïve Hope

I find my words at that. Because Miss self-righteous thought she knew about it and was not finished yet, and now has her final remark to make on the subject.

'I don't need to drink poison to know it is poison,' declare I, triumphantly. 'It's enough to read the label on the bottle. Everyone knows that alcohol is poison.' Turning on my heels, face red, off I go. Bemused looks follow me as I get myself back to work.

But afterwards I think about what Peter has said. And I reflect on his comments. For I have *never* been drunk! I am twenty-four years old and never experienced a hangover. Being fully Tee-total as a Christian I had *no* idea what it felt like to be drunk. Whilst growing up I had only ever had a little nip of the occasional Christmas Sherry, and on my sixteenth birthday dad had first introduced me to alcohol. He had taken me and mum to the local dance at the 'Wagon and Horses' Hotel to celebrate all our birthdays. Dad, mum and myself all had birthdays within three days of each other and as this was my sixteenth, I got some special attention. As well as dad giving me a bit of a dancing lesson - the waltz and a bit of a foxtrot – he also showed me how to respect alcohol by nursing my birthday 'Babycham' alcoholic drink, (referred to in the advertising as a Champagne Perry) most of the night. He was very clear in his instructions, so I took notice.

'Just sip slowly, and enough to keep you *Merry*', he said, and then he had kept an eye on me whilst I did so to see how I was handling things and until the 'Merry' kicked in. After several minutes and a few times of checking on how I was progressing, his repeated question of 'Now how are you feeling?' finally met with a soft and slightly blurry 'Good, thanks' from me, which had indicated to him that I was now getting the relaxing benefits that alcohol could induce when used correctly. His next instruction was also clear: 'That is the feeling you want to keep when you drink. Now slow down even more, and just occasionally sip to keep that nice feeling going. Don't gulp or glug and you will be in control of it. Too much or too quickly and you will not be in charge. You will leave yourself open to being taken advantage of by others.'

With that, he gave me one of the greatest gifts in life with that little lesson. I only needed that one drink to last me the whole night, but that is not surprising as I was only young and not used to it. After that I never could see the attraction of lots of drink when the other teenagers around me were socialising, though not in the quantities that today's youth tend to consume. However, even then it was too much, too fast, and then vomited back up. This never appealed to me. I didn't like it when I was sick for ill-health reasons and so could not see the attraction in being sick deliberately. I hated that feeling of the room reeling when one is feeling ill. Now I had learned the benefit in relaxing with a drink without a hangover.

Hardly drinking afterward was in part due to this valuable lesson, my own disposition and the fact of limited teenage funds. Then becoming a Christian meant that drink was further discouraged and also led to any further experience of alcohol being limited, and so my mindset was naturally against getting drunk.

But I could not stop myself from questioning what Peter had said. Was I being unfair to him? What was it really like to be drunk? Was there a reason to risk feeling sick after all?

That night when I got home from work, this conversation with Peter was still on my mind. This would also have shown on my face in some way. And when Jim resorted to his usual control practice and asked me 'What are you thinking?' I just blurted out to him 'Have you ever been drunk, Jim?' I knew that he had at some stage, but couldn't remember much about what he had said and certainly not any details. Of course he wondered what this was all about, and I daresay he was somewhat alarmed, so there was more than his usual agenda and interest in what had happened when he asked me why. So I briefly told him the story and asked him if he would tell me what it was like because I *knew* I was right, but I was not sure if I was being *fair*. And I had no experience to call my own on the subject.

Well, of course, Jim wouldn't tell me *anything* until I had conveyed every detail of the whole conversation to me. He then told me a little of his exploits in the Merchant Navy, and of what it felt like to be drunk. But this was *his* experience, and still hard for me to know what this dizzy feeling was about. I had been sea-sick on the ship coming over, but still couldn't get my head around it.

Naïve Hope

So Jim suggested that I try it myself to see what it was like. Well, there's a thought. In trepidation, we planned for me to try it that weekend, so I could ensure I would be ok for work on Monday. Come that Saturday night, Jim bought a bottle of Brandy and proceeded to give me measures of it neat with a couple of blocks of ice.

It was a horrible experience. After a short time the room would not stay still, and with my eyes closed I felt I was flying off somewhere in a circular motion. So I kept them open, but my stomach felt weird, and I couldn't walk properly. In retrospect, it could have been softened with a mixer or he could have chosen something other than Brandy, but I only knew of Brandy because it had been called medicinal. Nor did Jim come up with any other suggestion. And I *should* have at least taken some water with it somewhere along the experience. But neat?!

After attempting to work my way down through the bottle, and realizing I couldn't possibly have it all like he had suggested, I got up from the couch and had to get assistance to go to the bathroom to vomit some of it up and then lurch to my bed. Oh what a dreadful feeling... I thought I was going to die. And in the morning – oh boy! I suffered most of that day, not knowing about the need for water and hydration. I felt really sick, old, achy and sorry for myself.

On the Monday I had recovered somewhat. And managed to make it into work ok.

When Peter saw me, he asked 'What's wrong with you? You don't look too good.'

Before I could stop myself I blurted out 'I knew I was right. Alcohol is disgusting.'

The astonished look on his face eventually softened when he realized what had happened. 'You actually went home and got drunk?' he asked, a bit more kindly now.

'Yes, I did. You said I shouldn't talk about what I don't know about. Well I do now. I still think it's disgusting!' says I, getting pinker in the face, which wasn't helping how I still felt.

Well, he burst out laughing at that. I think he was quite surprised and bemused at my self-confessed actions. 'And what did you get drunk on?' he asked, really curious by now.

'My husband bought me a bottle of brandy, and I had some of that.'

'What! Just brandy? What with?' He looked a bit surprised.

'Nothing, just some ice.' I wondered what he was getting at, and why he was asking me this. Later I understood why.

'He didn't give you anything else with it? And this was your first time getting drunk?' he queried, followed by raised eyebrows and then he whistled a long low whistle. I think he was quite surprised that this had been my first real encounter with strong alcohol. Most of the lunches that the buyers attended usually included wine, beer or were mixed drinks. Which is a softer way of going about it, and in retrospect, possibly more fun!

We never talked about it again after that, but in some way, I think that Peter had a new kind of respect for me, and I had kind of gotten off my high horse about things. After all, I could not ever say again that I had never ever been drunk, could I?

But I think it was more than that. I had dared to examine something for myself, hadn't I? I was done with drinking for it was all I thought it would be, even worse!

But Brandy neat?! Woah! Jim, what *were* you thinking?

THE SIXTIES

While we had been working away in England and living the Christian way, we had brought two children into the world in a time of major change. During the sixties we had both individually converted, we had met, gotten married, started a family, bought a tiny house and finally we had moved right across the world. The sixties was a time of incredible change, I have heard it said. People talk to me about me being a baby-boomer and having fun in the sixties. It took me a while to work it all out. But the real truth is that I was *not* a baby-boomer, for I was born *before* the war ended. I think this was later referred to as the Great Generation. Anyway, we had lived on rations for quite a while, and I even remember the ration books that mum had for certain groceries. And as for having fun in the sixties, I really didn't know much of what was happening in the world of music and celebrity. The musical 'Hair' meant nothing to me. The open-air concerts were something I had never tried. Who was Abba? So hearing about Woodstock and other hippie and drug happenings simply didn't register anything until much later; it just wasn't part of my experience.

I knew nothing about pot or hash or any other substance, though I heard the odd hint of Christian disgust at drugs in the world. Talk about leading a sheltered life...

Add to this the fact that I didn't smoke. Couldn't. Had tried it as a teenager, buying the then popular Alpine brand cigarettes because it at least had a menthol taste to it. But on my attempt with a second pack, and whilst sharing the cigarettes with the other girls outside the shops after school, one of them had criticized me.

'You're not dragging, you', she said indignantly. 'You're not inhaling it. You're *wasting* a *whole* ciggie. That's a *waste*, that is,' said she.

'Oh, well that's because I cough too much', I replied, and then I tried to draw in the breath again. But my lungs would have none of it. Each attempt created more coughing and choking. Everyone laughed and laughed, and in the end, red-faced, I gave it up.

'Here, I'll have it if you can't smoke it' said my 'caring' good friend. But she did do me a favour. Embarrassed at first, I took it in good grace and realized that smoking was just not for me. And I didn't need to try and make it look like I smoked. It was ok.

Back to the Sixties.

The one thing I do remember hearing about during the sixties was that John Lennon had made a name in Christian circles because he had claimed that he was more famous than Jesus Christ. Though that wasn't *exactly* what he had said. So it wasn't until much later in life that I came to hear and appreciate his music, actually his later work. And grew to love it. And it was Abba's second time around for me to get to hear and love them when they made a revival appearance in Australia.

So I missed out on a whole hippie hoo-hah. The drugs. The free love. The gypsy clothing. The ban-the-bomb-ing. The music. The communes. The pot-peace-pipes. Not that I am bothered now. And it actually might have done my health a favour.

Was I a mother and a prissy righteous Bible basher? Who is to say?

Meanwhile, life mainly plods on in the hostel and in our little world. With the odd cooking triumph, the odd optimistic creative endeavour, the children are thriving, generally, and we are in a new land enjoying the sun and variety, albeit complete with sly mozzies and stubborn flies. But there is opportunity here if you were prepared to work. And we are hard workers.

I am better learning to choose my times with Jim, and to wait until he is receptive or in a reasonably good mood before I approach him about things that need discussion or attention. And I think and hope that I am adjusting to his moods and bouts and odd binges. He occasionally brings me flowers to make amends and we get to church still, though not as regularly as before, but life goes on. James Bond movies continue to tie us together in some weird way. The Secret Service adventures seem to appeal to him in a way that I cannot understand.

1971

*~ Fitzroy ~ Hungary, Not Mad ~ Jenny ~ Failed Protector
~ New House; Fresh Start ~ Talking of Accidents ~ Geelong
~ Shift in Plans*

FITZROY

We are still determined to own our own home again, and we are fired with the success stories of other fellow migrants, and inspired by the plentiful possibilities that are open to any and every Australian. We are now feeling a bit more like Australians, and have well passed the two year migrant probationary period. We are on our way to becoming Aussies...

After a year or so of living at the Altona hostel with our names on a waiting list for 'real' accommodation, at the first opportunity we move to brand new high-rise flats in Gertrude Street in Fitzroy. Though it is a two-bedroom unit in a tall concrete building, it has manicured gardens, a huge outside playing area, and pathways that the boys could cycle along. Once we had sorted out the problem of being too close to the noise caused by the building's generator, we settle down again to work and save.

Some of the neighbours children would taunt the boys at school and pick fights with them, calling them 'Pommie bastards'. Some projected their parent's issues, prejudices, dislikes and even their tempers, which could be quite simply because our boys were English born. Just like a lot of the Italian, Greek and other nationalities, my children and myself were insulted just the same. Funny thing was that most of the initial migrants were from the United Kingdom anyway, places such as England, Scotland, Ireland and probably some from Wales. But this seemed forgotten by some that had descended from those first early migrants. But its part of starting anew, I guess...

We intended to build our own home, and so the first step was saving for a block of land. The cheapest land that would fit in with our budget is in a new development in Werribee. This is some distance away, but it is also closer to our church, an important consideration for us both, so the resolution is made and carried. We are able to afford one of the new sub-division allotments opening up in the Iramoo section in Werribee, and this is where we purchase for our future. Because of the Westgate Bridge that had just begun construction, this and the new road connections it would create will provide a much better and easier highway access between the city and the south western suburbs for future years. Currently, the only way to access these southern communities is through narrow roads. The bridge would be a huge improvement and make our decision to build in Werribee more feasible and workable.

Living in Fitzroy also meant travel in and to the city for me was easier, and I would be working closer to home. This means less transport costs, less travel time. When the bridge is completed and we are living in Werribee, we will benefit from the easier access.

Meanwhile due to office restructuring I have left the Japanese Company and am now working for Lilla Distributors (Knitwear) in Collingwood, a suburb right next door to Fitzroy, employed as the pay clerk and accounts clerk. Closer to home, easier access, it gives me more time with the boys and for my domestic duties. And it is very close to Smith Street shops, which helps me to shop for items and pay bills during lunch.

Jim's work has come to an end, so he seeks out new work, but he misses out on working with the contractors building the Westgate Bridge at that time. Word had gone around the hostel, and there were queues for any available vacancies. All of the work done on the bridge was extremely well paid - but he also missed out on being amongst those injured or worse when it actually collapsed during the early stages of its construction.

Jim has an interesting though conflicting attitude to my work. We needed the money that I earn, and when I find a position that pays more than him, he is very happy for the money, but there is also more of an edge to him, as though he is resentful that I could earn more than him.

I can understand that this is a man-thing, but you can't have it both ways. His inadequacies certainly showed through from time to time, usually after he has had a 'relaxing' drink. He is still looking

Naïve Hope

for a job that pays more than me, and in honesty, this will certainly give us more money toward our own home, so I can only be glad about it. And I am.

His next money-making opportunity is working with the Natural Gas conversion and the new pipeline connections, which means travelling throughout most of Melbourne.

Jim now sometimes earns more than me, and seems to satisfy him in some way. This also means more in our bank account for the day we start our build.

Hungary, Not Mad

However, my job in Collingwood now begins to become a problem. The boss, a Jewish Hungarian lady called Magda Volkovski, is all sugar and light when I first start working for her. I organise the accounts and learn her system of piece work wages for the staff. I am a very competent worker, but she is highly emotional and erratic and within a short period of time she has become abusive and insulting, and she now begins to put me down and even to shout at me in the middle of the sewing area.

In the office, she also starts to blame me for non payment of the accounts whilst she is on the phone to suppliers, saying it is my fault for not preparing the cheques which she was actually literally *physically* holding in her hands herself so they can't be paid on time. She does this even while I am sitting in the same room! At first I think she has made a mistake, but when I hear her story several times, and how she is blaming me as being lazy or inept, I am appalled. I realise later that she must have had a whole game going on in her head, which keeps the creditors at bay, whilst she using me as the scapegoat. (A very unfamiliar role for me, hey?). I need the job because of our plans, but it begins to really get to me, for it goes against everything I believe. Anyway, I get so stressed, I can't sleep. I actually get a doctors script and start using Valium to settle my nerves.

Eventually I knew I cannot handle it anymore, whether I need the money or not; enough is enough. So I just have to leave. This is a month or so before the Christmas holidays, and I take a few weeks to recover and begin to sleep again. Knowing what I know now, there is no way I would ever put up with that sort of situation again, but back then, with two small children and the need to work hard and get our own place, I didn't consider any other options. Not until it all got too much.

One day, a few weeks later during the Christmas school holidays, I bumped into Suzie, one of the women who worked there at the same time as myself. We were both shopping at the time. And she asked me if I had known when I left. 'Known what?' I asked.

'Did you know that Magda was preparing to leave?' Suzie elaborated.

I had no idea what she was talking about, and so asked her what she meant. It turned out that all the workers had turned up for work after the three-weeks closure over the Christmas holidays to find the place locked up. After making various phone calls, they discovered that Mrs Volkovski had cleared out the bank account, taking the full overdraught, and had *left* the country, absconded, fleeing to Israel apparently. I have no idea of what these workers must have gone through – they were usually migrants and homely people, being paid for 'piece-work' as that they got paid for every piece of hand sewing and hand assembly that they did – this was the basis for their wages. Some did it at home, some at the factory, and most of them depended on these earnings to make ends meet. What a sad and destroying experience for them. They had sometimes called her 'the mad Hungarian' when she wasn't within hearing distance at work.

I had not heard or seen any of this coming of course, for I had left in time not to be party to any of these eventualities. All I know is that she had used me as an excuse not to pay those she owed money to whilst I was there. And she had tried to blame me for not paying on time. But as none of that was true, and she was about to be found out after I left, maybe I was lucky in leaving when I did. Thank goodness I did! As I said, I quickly found another job, and recovered from the Valium after-effects.

The next job I applied for after mad Magda's was again in Fitzroy, and I well remember the interview for the job. The secretary of the company was also the personal assistant, and she screens me

Naïve Hope

before I am interviewed by the boss. It is her job to put forward the most suitable applicants, and her name was Mary Kent. She chuckles when I gave her my answer to why I left my last job so quickly, after only a few months.

Me, being the honest type, tell her that my last boss had been a 'mad Hungarian' who has made off with the company's money (about thirty thousand dollars I think I had been told – quite a lot in those days). After the interview with her, I immediately had another meeting with the boss, Tom Munro. Mary had already recommended me to Tom for the position based on my résumé, and I am thrilled to find out that I have joined their little company. On my first day of work, and whilst we have our morning tea, she watches my face as she calmly tells me that she too, is Hungarian. Oh, My! I was mortified... I fall over myself to apologise, but she just smiles, saying that all Hungarians are *not* mad. We laugh about it and I eventually manage to overcome my embarrassment. Mary turns out to be a treasure, for she is a great sport, an astute asset and especially efficient right-hand secretary to the boss, and a good and understanding friend. I learn much from her professionally and socially, as the company does a lot of work entertaining, and her encouragement inspires me to learn more.

I really enjoy working here. The company is in a huge warehouse in Gore Street, and we do shopfittings, as well as interesting theatre and ballet scenery and special exposés and cut-aways for the motor shows. The work is varied and generally always interesting, and the men by and large are friendly and highly respectful. Tom always treats his staff well. He demands the best, and he certainly gets it from his men. My working hours are always interesting and satisfying, and the pay is good. And it almost feels like family.

This feels like a good phase in my life. Work atones for other areas, and I feel like I am prospering.

Hope is not dead yet.

JENNY

Meanwhile, life in the flats continues. There is a period of unsettlement initially as we adjust to people living above and below us, together with all the noises that can be heard through ceilings. Because most of the building is concrete, items that accidentally get dropped onto the floor above reverberate through the room below, and of course, I become very self-conscious of dropping anything myself or of the children dropping things, because I now know what it sounds like to those on the floor below me.

Work is good, and we are carrying out our plan to build, saving at the top of our agenda. For a change of sorts, we pay visits to the larger more mainstream churches in the city, and become familiar with some of the services there. Scots Presbyterian Church, Collins Street Baptist Church and St Paul's Cathedral gives us a change of pace and are handy alternatives to the hot little Scout Hall in Altona which houses our usual assembly members.

Things appear to be going well as regards external appearances, and I am kept very busy keeping the flat spotless and ensuring that all the necessary things are prepared for school, work and Jim. We develop a routine. I know now how to iron a shirt – as instructed by Jim – as though it has just come out of its flatpack straight from the shop. This means that I actually have to iron, yes, *iron, creases* along the fold lines, which I have also had to master. I simply *cannot* see the sense in this, but Jim absolutely *insists* on it! So needs must that I comply. And, stupidly, I actually become proud that I am able to accomplish that just-out-of-its-box look! Mind you, I just might get a compliment on my handiwork instead of a slap around the ears, hey?

When I said things are going reasonably well, what I really mean is that the domestic schedule is running smoothly, because I am *making* it run, goddam it. Ooops, not allowed to swear. But I can say it now, swear, that is, though I would never have even *thought* it back then. So it is not surprising that beneath this Stepford Wives spicky-specky exterior, I am somewhat currently nervy as Jim seems to now be developing a regular habit of having a drink. As it is still restrained and because Jim isn't doing a lot of drinking, one could be forgiven for not seeing a future problem with alcohol. Which I don't. For it never enters my mind really. However, for some reason it still makes me feel a bit uncomfortable and it is expected of me that I don't upset the applecart by complaining. I am still not interested in having a drink, though I do attempt to try the odd glass of wine with him, and in an effort to find agreeable connections, I occasionally experiment with him by trying a variety of wines over time. This also helps me to develop a better understanding of Australian culture. Like all good beginner imbibers, we start with the initially sweet but tolerant Spatlese Lexia, then the Traminer Reisling and gradually mature our palate to the dry white wines and robust reds. But my limit is a sip or two, and I often find a way of passing it onto Jim or of disposing the rest of it without having to drink it all.

Thinking that we are becoming somewhat more educated and sophisticated, Jim begins to bring home different types of casks of wine. Though I find that I cannot digest them, and even a glass tends to upset my stomach. Not surprising, as these wines are nearly always inferior and tend to have a variety of nasty additives that not everyone can tolerate.

As I mentioned earlier, since we had arrived in Australia, Jim has lost his father, then his brother Johnny and then his next brother Danny through drink. Maybe this was the sobering thought that keeps him on a straighter path.

However, a new development occurs, for Jim has stayed in contact with his family as I have, with letters and the odd phone call. On our last visit back to England, we were flushed with our plans to build and had invited other family members to join us at anytime.

As a result of our encouragement we are now awaiting the arrival of Jim's younger sister Jenny. Through regular letters and the odd phone call, Jenny has expressed her interest in seeing what Australia is like and is open to staying if things work out for her. She takes up our invitation to stay with us for two years. It seems to us both that this is a great idea to expose her to something other than what she was experiencing in England, particularly living in such a limiting Irish family environment. I quite liked her, and I thought that it would be a nice change for her from living with her rough and ready family for a while. Maybe she could be some kind of company for me, too? It will be a great adventure for her, and some good family company for us. Besides, we are living in a three bedroom flat, so it is no problem for the boys who are used to the bunk beds anyway, and are eager to see their Auntie Jenny again.

It is a joyous day indeed when she arrives. She is around seventeen and has never travelled before. Though in some ways, as we had been, she is wide-eyed, she is also a willing learner, and she has some intelligence that can maximize this opportunity. A dark haired young girl, she has a cheeky grin, and infectious laugh and a grateful demeanour. Within a short time, Jenny has a good job at the local supermarket, and begins working her way up with her abilities and through hard work.

We all bundle into our car and drive down to the beach, and we get dressed up for Sundays in the city church. I think Jim is proud to be playing the big brother to her, and to show her what Australia has to offer that we had not been able to enjoy in England. But there was also a dark side that began to emerge with Jim. And it is kept behind closed bedroom doors.

'Don't you dare say anything bad about my sister,' growls Jim the first time I say something that he does not agree with regarding Jenny. He seems to see any comment on her as negative, rather than questioning. I do not know Jenny as Jim knows her, nor do I understand her childhood for I didn't grow up with her, or his, family. To me I am attempting to understand, and also to get some attention from Jim, for his focus is now mostly on her. He is nice as pie with her, playing the Big Brother, the expansive and successful (and surviving) one, and nothing is too much trouble for her. But he does not apply this to me, and am I not his wife?

Naturally, Jim and I begin to have arguments that now include her. It gets so tense that I wasn't allowed to mention her to him now unless it is to complement her. If I didn't understand something about her and I want to discuss it with him, things can turn nasty.

If I had thought or dared hope that Jenny's presence in the house would put Jim on his best behavior and provide me with some sort of protection insurance, I was sorely mistaken. Sore being the operative word. Jim played being the benign older brother to a tee, deserving an Oscar. He is one way to me when Jenny is around, and another way with me when we are on our own. It is confusing, but I eventually get his message. Because one night he hits me so hard that it knocks me sideways off the bed. I bang my head on the concrete floor and have a bruise where he knocked me.

Naïve Hope

Why did he do this? It was because I couldn't understand something that she had done and as she was his sister and knew her family background better than me, I had dared to question him about it. In effect, what I had done was to complain about her to him. I make the mistake of applying the exact same rules Jim applies to me onto *her*, and he doesn't like it. So I have to 'shut-up or else'. There are a couple more times when he attacks me over her, for the second occasion I only had to make a 'look' about her, and this was apparently sufficient cause for him to thump me.

When she is next out with her new boyfriend, it is the opportunity for Jim to 'deal with me' and put me back in my place. I don't hold any of this against her, leastways, I don't think that I do. And what good would it do me, anyway, if I went there? But that is not me. And anyway, she is a nice kid, and we occasionally get out to the shops together, though not as often as I would have liked.

Even though we enjoy showing her around Melbourne and Geelong, despite our inability to always discuss any issues related to her amiably, and even though Jenny loves being here, and also now has a devoted boyfriend, she still misses her family in the UK too much. And this was certainly understandable.

And I wonder, could she possibly have been aware of what went on behind closed doors?

Failed Protector

A short time after Jenny has gone back to the UK, I find I am having difficulty climbing the stairs to the flat, and in walking long distances. So I organize to visit the doctor who has a clinic on the corner of Gertrude Street, just opposite the flats. I am on the pill since Ari's birth and require a new script, anyway, and I also need more sleeping tablets. Because I mention to Jim that I will also be seeing the doctor about my having trouble breathing and I want to ask him about my pain with walking and lying down, Jim, of course, insists on coming with me. I didn't know why at the time, because the black eye I had was almost healed. *Don't ask, for you may well have guessed by now.* Despite my assurances, I have to allow it. The doctor examines me, then he looks over his glasses at Jim as he takes X-rays. But the doctor can already tell that I have two broken ribs! And when he asks me how I came by them, I dare only say that 'I fell down the stairs'. He *knows* this is not consistent with the damage, but fortunately (or unfortunately) doesn't press me further. But I know that he knew. This was in the days before abuse or violence was needed to be reported.

This particular attack was not about Jenny, but about me at work. When I had related a funny incident at work to him, he had decided that I was having an affair with the one who had made us all laugh. Oh, sorry, had made just me laugh! For that is how he replays it back, that Tommy, one of the storekeepers at my work, had been flirting with me, and by the time Jim has finished with what I have said, it is edited to the point that we were not in a group with everyone contributing, and Tommy having the final punch-line. No. It is somehow now just the two of us having a private joke and then having sex. What??

When a lie has been told, and there is an attempt to rectify that lie and to re-present the truth, and that someone who has lied has an investment in keeping that lie going, and who also has a pay-off in the continuation of that lie, it is sometimes true that the wrong-er he is, then the right-er he tries to become, using not only all of his argument ability, but even all of his force and might. As if this will somehow make that lie the Truth. But Truth doesn't work like that. And will eventually 'Out'!

For my pains in attempting to re-establish the truth for what it was, I paid the penalty. No blood was drawn, but bruises were birthed, bones were broken, spirits were silenced. Jim's authority was reasserted, his wrath was therefore, temporarily assuaged; I was subjugated, again, and Jim felt better. However, when someone in authority knows the truth about such slime-bag behavior, and lets that slime-bag know, even in just subtle ways, that he *knows* the truth, it has the remarkable ability to slap a bucket of cold water on him doing the same thing again. Leastways in sight or hearing of the said authority.

Hence, Jim was especially nice to me for a period of time after this visit to the doctors. Of course.

I slowly recover and consequently let a few things slip in the housework area for a period of time. At least until I have healed to

Naïve Hope

a degree and can move forward again, allowing these things to be slowly put into the 'back in the past' basket.

It is not too long before we realize that we have now saved enough to go ahead and start the build on the house in Werribee. Jim hasn't beaten me in the same way since that last bone cruncher. Ever the optimist, I continue to hope that this is a *real* 'Fresh Start'. This will give us our own place, this will be our own little bit of God's Australian turf. Here we could establish ourselves, and make a real home for ourselves and the boys. Then perhaps Jim would finally settle.

At this point, I still haven't recognized something major about marriage and about how to make it the success I had automatically, blindly and naively hoped and assumed it would be. For it is usually and commonly accepted (particularly in the church) that it is the *woman's* role to nurture, value and support her husband and her family and to help prepare their children for adult life feeling loved and supported, and this is done by using all of her talents and skills and sensitivities to the best of her abilities. But less is spoken of the fact that it is the *man's* role to nurture, value and to protect *his wife* and *her role*, sensitivities, feelings and contributions as well as raise his children in a balanced way that helps them fulfill their own lives as adults and progenitors of the line.

Jim's job really, despite what the church says, was supposed to be to *protect me* as the mother and primary female protector and nurturer of his own offspring, and therefore assure his own immortality and perpetuation of his seed and name and family through them. But the male role wasn't ever emphasised as the *Protector* but rather the 'Master' of his wife and children. And subsequently in all of this he failed abysmally. Rather the focus was on the 'not sparing the rod' on the child, and being the chief *over* the woman. Just patriarchal, archaic and controlling approaches. Whilst my failings were through naivety, trust in the wrong things, and blind obedience, his was in bad leadership, perverted or non-existent protective instincts and downright selfish and immature tantrums and destructive behavior.

Men have *no* excuse when it comes to violence toward their women. Absolutely none. Women are generally labeled and designated as being physically the weaker sex in most cases when it comes to fighting or lifting heavy weights. But consider this; consider that women are able to grow and nurture the product of their coming together, to develop the unborn within, for they feed not only with their own nutrition, but with their own *life force*, energy, love and continual care. Women can have children and sustain the rigors of pregnancy, birthing and nursing in ways that men cannot possibly hope to equal, demonstrating their ability and capability as the stronger in a stamina-and-persistence aspect of strength and energy in females.

They are deserving of immense respect at what their bodies can produce and what they endure. They put themselves at great vulnerability, they give over their bodies and beings to be inhabited in a very restrictive way by another being. The female body is designed to look after and deliver at full term as best they can, and then to continue with a further twenty years or so of mothering and caring. But they require protection in doing so. When a man has inseminated, it has cost him little, and takes no more energy from him. His contribution should now involve the protection of his woman before and after birth, and of his offspring as they grow and develop.

Protection of the species begins with protection of the birth-er; the mother. Not only that, even without children, the woman performs certain functions in a partnership that usually cannot be performed by the man, for he is after all the man, and she is after all the woman. Her intuition and sense-ings about things can support and benefit the relationship if these are cared for and respected. His strength and abstraction can be harnessed with these two joint perceptions, benefitting and promoting the success of their joint relationship venture. Derision of her abilities does not mean that the man is after all the bigger, the better and the more logical, for it serves only to inflate his ego, which can be quite mindless and insatiable, and demonstrates his blind spot in choosing to demote a valuable companion and partner in a world built on more than just being brutish.

Regarding the Protection of woman, it is interesting how many men claim to be protecting them when they use non-disclosure and actually deny the truth about themselves or their actions to her.

Naïve Hope

Not telling the truth in order 'to spare' her feelings is not necessarily protecting her as he may claim, but often rather it is protecting *him* from the responsibility and consequence of his *own* actions, and a handy avoidance technique and conscience tranquilizer. If a man fears that his woman can't handle the truth about him, he is denying her the chance to decide for herself, and he is also denying sharing who he truly is. This means that she is relating to a mere image or false presentation of who he is, and not the real being himself. And if he is ashamed of his actions, and not willing to learn not to do things that work against the relationship, he ceases to mature and to evolve, and risks remaining a small man. Do the genes from this type of male contribute to the evolution and improvement of a better civilization? What do you think?

There was once a general desire for a man to be seen as a 'gentleman' and a woman to be seen as a 'lady'. Regardless of status or title. There has been confusion in exactly what is meant by those labels. Both terms actually denote a sense of refinement, of manners and respect, of culture and of civility, despite the left-over snobbish connotations. I understand that society generally now wants to be seen more as being either a 'man' or a 'woman' without supposed airs and pretensions. However, if you have ever been around a real lady or gentleman, a person of true quality and character, there are no pretensions, no airs. There is a genuineness, a generosity of spirit, a mind prepared to meet others as equals, though holding to their own moral code. There is respect, often shown in courtesy or politeness.

Manners often seem to be lacking nowadays, cheerfully showing a lack of pretension, yes, but it can also be just a small step downwards and sideways to reach the slope of disregard and onto the slippery slide of self-absorption or ignorance of another being and their rightful and due place in the world.

Enough of my rumination on this. I have said my piece, my opinion, and am bemused that this is the run-off of my working through how some men (and indeed women) can be and can act when in relationships. Am I being too demanding of consideration? I don't really think so. Am I being too stuck-up and unrealistic over partnerships. Again, upon further examination of myself and my motives, I don't really think so. Just voicing my preferences I guess, in a world full of its own opinions. In a way I am letting my own thoughts and voice speak out. Which is not such a bad thing after all this time of holding back or not even daring to think on such issues.

Out of all this, another recognition emerges. The Finding of the sort of partner that shares, accepts or reflects your own 'style' of relating and communicating. How precious and uplifting this is. Surely this makes a marriage or partnership more workable, more able to last the distance? One would think...

New House; Fresh Start

Meanwhile...

We have bought our land. We have shopped around for examples of homes being built, and have found what was affordable for us. We have checked out and adjusted the plans and the position on our block. We are moving ahead! Life appears to be exciting and full of promise again. I am enthusiastic about life again.

Sure, there is a lot of travel involved at weekends in checking and monitoring the progress, and I am working hard to keep up with all of my other duties, too and we get down as often as we can. We are both working hard, but I do not have the luxury yet of putting up my feet or having a massage...

It is one of those ready designed homes that you can do a bit of individualising with, and we have been through a lot of these exhibition homes to see what we could afford and what would suit us. There was some flexibility in the layout, so I was able to alter the house plans to better suit the family needs, and I have designed a front courtyard, where we plan to grow fruit trees, and we will have more space in the backyard for growing our own vegetables. Jim seems ok with all or at least, most, of my ideas in this area.

It isn't a fancy house, and is mainly comprised of Monier Besser bricks, but it has solid timber beams and will be new! And ours! We appear to be a bit more now united again as our project comes together. Our excitement is building. Our dream is growing!

Naïve Hope

The ultimate day arrives when we move in! Oh joy, oh mud, oh heat! But it is home!

Living in the suburb of Werribee was interesting. As all of the houses were new, some of the homes didn't yet have proper gardens formed and when one drove by one could observe the various building stages in process.

Though the house is solid, maybe I had been too optimistic in thinking that every contribution and suggestion I make would have been considered, or acceptable. Early on in the planning I had proposed that we earmark some money for air-conditioning, and that this is taken into account when laying the concrete slab flooring. Jim, however, had decided to disagree with me on this, and dug his heels in, fighting me all the way. I eventually run out of steam and so I give up. However, in our first summer in the house, he has cause to eat his words. Not long after moving in it gets *so* hot in the house that he is forced to change his mind and we have to source an air conditioner that can be adapted to a home built on a concrete slab. As the house has been built with no provision for this, it means that we don't have the money to pay someone to dig a hole in the slab, we have to do it ourselves! This means that the two of us have to take it in turns to sledge-hammer away into the concrete slab for the hole to take the air-conditioner wiring and pipes.

A difficult job and it is only way we can afford to install the split-system air-conditioning in the lounge room, as this was the central hub of the house. This does make a difference and it becomes more bearable to during the summer as well as allowing for some airflow through to most of the other rooms. Yes, messy to have to do it this way about, but it gets done. I don't dare go down the 'I told you so' road, not then anyway. But after all of the effort and hard work, we proudly fall back into bringing the rest of our ideas and plans together.

Planting trees is a pleasure and a pain, but amongst the mud and dirt, we manage to lay some paving stones, plant some seedlings, dig over the back garden, and design a rock garden at the front. Limited means make us inventive. But it is becoming more and more our home.

And we have something that we can leave to our children when we pass on.

Sure there are times when Jim is spiky, but I think since the challenge of establishing the property, he is taking pleasure in coming home to our little place, which seems to take on something new each week. We have done the hard slog of managing the build; we can see the promise of the finished product. We are both focussed on this endeavour together and I was beginning to feel that we had truly 'arrived' in Australia at last.

And there are times when life felt liveable again. The joy I feel as each room finds order and the pleasure that the boys have in sharing with us has been worth all the work and angst.

I get busy with the sewing machine, and colourful curtains appear at our windows, matching cushions on the couch, and if I must say so myself, all looks great for a do-it-yourself job. We install shelves together, and save for and enjoy buying the extra bookcase and odd items that we need for the new home.

We talk about how the orchard will look when we are old, and we joke about rocking chairs on the paved area, and being able to pick fresh fruit from off the trees. This is my dream and his dream and it becomes our dream. Over the next few months, more detailed plans are drawn up and trees planted that will give us variety, shade and plenty of fruit. Consideration has been given that they all work together to provide us with year round fruit where possible. We look at what plants work best when placed with other plants. We dig. And dig. We nurse and tend the lawn seeds, watering, bird chasing, fertilising, reseeding, and eventually mowing. Jim found and killed a couple of poisonous snakes in this virgin farmland so with greater care we continue with our gardening plans.

The front rockery takes shape, and little dumpy or spindly bits of green foliage quickly develop into bushy celebrations, interspersed with colour and smiley flower faces.

The mail box at the front driveway helps complete our dream and illusion of married bliss.

Naïve Hope

TALKING OF ACCIDENTS

To some degree we are happy. There seems to be some sort of peace settle as we establish a new schedule together. The boys settle into the brand new school just over the fence and within a few metres of our new home.

We continue to work to fund the extra costs that are part of establishing a new home, but there is more pleasure and joy in it now because we can see where our money has been going and what it is bringing us. There is a lot of satisfaction for me in all of this. Our bid to create a better life for our boys is beginning to pay off. Jenny had gone back to the UK just after the concrete slab foundation had been poured, and so it is again the two of us against the world. Correction, it was again the four of us.

However, it is not all love and light. And other factors begin to make themselves known. Because of all the stress and excitement and the pushing to *do*, to *complete*, I am now on anti-biotics. I am fighting off a serious case of flu, probably due to all that is involved in the demands of building, funding, settling building instalments, the actual move and all of the associated minor stresses associated with such a move. The travel to and fro to my job with Mary at Vivien Expositions in Fitzroy also impacts on me. I love my job but the travel has been telling on me as I have so much more distance to travel now.

And now something even more disastrous occurs. I guess it was only a matter of time really. There is a serious car accident shortly after we move to Werribee; and I have caused it!

I have tried to beat a traffic light, and my judgement was so bad, that I was literally sideswiped as I tried to go through the intersection. How on earth did it happen? Well, it took me a while to realise this myself. I was in denial initially that I could actually cause an accident. How *could* I have made a mistake like this? What happened was a bad case of faulty miscalculation. I had actually tried to *beat* the lights, and I realised later that I had become accustomed to doing this, and I had to unlearn this very bad habit. And because I was going uphill, I momentarily misjudged the braking distance and stopping versus my speed. One of the thoughts that had gone through my head was that 'if I brake now I will end up in the middle of the intersection'. I was very badly mistaken, and so the car was written off. I had reacted to the red light far too late – I had made a *bad* decision.

It was my own silly fault. Part of my focus had been my state of mind in worrying about my two sons, and my husband, and the allied duties and requirements. Too much going on – in my head. And I had forgotten that this part of the road was uphill. My little car was just *not* built for this challenge. I learned a major lesson! When emergency services arrived I got them to phone the boys school as well as my husband to explain that I would be late home. I think I gave Jim and the boys a bit of a scare, and I was certainly sore for a long time after.

My license was taken off me for a couple of years because I had run a red light. And I had the embarrassment of having to retake the driving test after the set period. But I was *so* lucky to escape with just bruises and whiplash. Eventually kinesiology, chiropractic and a very helpful technique called Hyperton-X - which resets all of the muscles affected by the whiplash – gave me complete muscle freedom again. But this was not until many years later when I had taken up looking at certain natural therapies.

The loss of the car places a bit of a strain on things at home. We have to sort out alternate transport and rearrange schedules, but we get there.

Even though we are still enjoying our new home, things begin to take a turn for the worst again, and life seems to be getting murkier. Or rather, they were getting clearer as darker frightening patterns began to emerge.

We are attending less and less of the church services. The Altona Pastor we knew when we first arrived in Australia has now moved on and was replaced by another that didn't seem to 'suit' Jim as much. Continuing to travel to the city churches simply meant we were in the city nearly every day of the week, and also means too much travel. Our time is now at a premium, as we also ferry the children around and attend other extra school activities. Squeezing in time for grocery shopping, taking the children to Little Athletics, washing, cleaning, ironing, gardening, car maintenance and work preparations etc cuts into our weekends and leaves little time or energy for church. Still reading the Bible intermittently, and having our own odd moments of 'prayer-time' is about all we seem to manage now. This doesn't give us much time for nursing our 'faith', but for me it is also an interesting experience, as it gives me a different view of life, and begins to show me to a degree just how much the church really means, and just how much support it really gave. And I begin to question the genuineness of it all.

Our house had been re-designed to make four slightly smaller bedrooms instead of three, so now we use one room as a dedicated 'prayer-room'. Here we take time out for 'Quiet-time' and prayer and reading the Bible undisturbed whenever we can. And this seems to be enough. At present.

Life now seems to be more about 'living the life' and practicing one's values and beliefs rather than 'playing' at church... It is much later that I see just how much self-responsibility and accountable is actually practised, and just how much of this gets forfeited when one always has a handy 'Saviour' to forgive one's 'Weaknesses' and 'Sins'.

When we first moved in to Werribee, Jim took to buying and having the odd beer, then when the air-conditioning was installed and we are doing the garden it becomes a regular daily beer. Or two. His drinking now becomes that; drinking. Not just a drink. Curiously enough, he never goes out drinking. He does not want to find a local pub and develop relationships external to work or home. Instead he maintains the image of innocent church goer and Christian whilst gradually claiming further immunity by insisting that a man was entitled to drink in his own home. I have no grounds on which to argue as I don't yet recognise the beginning of the rot that this signals. As yet I have no evidence on how his argument fails, no experience on which to gauge these developing events, nor would I have been heard, much less likely obeyed, if I dared really question or oppose his growing habit. And there was no exposure to external criticism that could have alerted me. Hiding one's drinking behind closed doors, whilst lording it over family and his domain is a recipe for disaster which I have not yet realised, nor fully experienced, though it is in the process of fomentation.   Currently, there is nothing to challenge his conscience on this.

On another front, there is plenty to occupy our main attention and focus. Ever since we arrived in Australia, we have stayed in contact with family, and we still manage to visit family in England every five years or so and have been back twice during our vacations. We had also had discussions on the boys' future, Joseph now almost eleven and Ben nine years old. Our future plans and enquiries have included private schools such as Geelong Grammar or Melbourne Grammar and we have been working our way through a variety of brochures on these and several other good schools for them when they are old enough.

My job is now paying reasonably well after a couple of raises and a generous Christmas bonus so we can dare to plan. Bonuses were paid out every Christmas, but only if there were no sick leave days taken during the year – the bonus was lumped together with the sick pay – and so guys only took sick days off if they absolutely needed to. Deadlines were always met, and this meant that productivity could be pretty much guaranteed, and also that the men could appreciate the extra pay out together with the holiday pay at the expensive silly-season. Christmas costs were covered, as were holidays. Sweet!

However, the winds are primed to take another shift in direction. We are poised on more dramatic happenings, though on the surface we look like we are happy and prospering.

GEELONG

Jim's job with the Natural Gas conversion is completed in Melbourne and now the new pipeline begins to extend out further. This means travelling throughout most of Melbourne's outer eastern surrounds, and down to Geelong and its environs in particular.

I think some of the gas guys he works with made unhealthy kinds of impressions on him, and I daresay that they were quite disrespectful of females, judging by certain snippets and accounts that eventually emerge from Jim. In some ways I think he is disgusted, but also doesn't know how to keep his mind clear of their minds, and he gets influenced, possibly the suspicious part of him replaying their suggestions and applying them inappropriately. He comes home sometimes with dark thoughts, ones that I had nothing to do with causing. On top of the Diane-desertion, this doesn't help my situation in view of his lurking jealousy.

Because the distance in travel sometimes calls for him to stay overnight to complete jobs in a certain area and he would sometimes start work early in the morning till late at night, he needs regular and affordable accommodation for when he is working in Geelong. Jim is away during the week a lot, and doing much more travel.

His pay now includes a well-paid living-away-allowance which together with his car allowance makes all the difference as to how much we can manage for the future. We now have second used car, two growing boys at school and many expenses – and plans. Importantly for Jim, he is now earning more than me.

Rather than have to put up at a hotel in Geelong, which can be quite expensive, Jim finds a Bed and Breakfast situation with a lovely old couple. Mr. and Mrs. Roffey are both retired folk who fuss over him and cook for him and generally take good care of him. They are so kindly and friendly that sometimes at weekends we bundle the boys into the car and we all go along to see them, often going on to the YouYangs for a picnic lunch. But even though he is in a secure, safe and comfortable environment when away from Werribee, this doesn't stop Jim from becoming even more suspicious now that he is not at home every night to check on me for himself. After the initial 'absence makes the heart grow fonder', his mistrust seems to grow with his time away, and it seems his actions and demeanour when he returns are becoming more and more erratic.

When he is home, the questioning over details of everything I do gets worse. I am to account for every day that he has been absent, and sometimes, every hour.

He is becoming more demanding over sex, and now there is often a darker sense to it. It scares me, and I have to refuse some of the things he wants me to do. Not that I am a prude, but this feels degrading and insulting. Somehow I am able to distract him and mostly manage to veer him away from these things. Most of the time.

Shift in Plans

Life goes on, and with life, there is always the constant of change. Whether or not these changes are for the better or for the worse is often an individual perception at the time. An initial perception and observation itself, however, can alter over time. What we originally notice, what we primarily conclude, is based on what we can see and know at any given time. Often, further insights and peripheral information gained over time can give us a different picture or conclusion on the total impact of events. Not understanding why things happen the way they do may cause us to react in a certain way. And understanding is often achieved over time.

We are now a family of four, with our own bit of land, still establishing ourselves in this new land. It seems that the neighbours have tired to some degree, of having a go at the Italians and the Greeks, and now it is the turn of the English. The boys come home with bruises, and tales of defending themselves when insulted as 'Pommies' and even when attacked by other kids. This behaviour from other bullying children is, of course, all to do with what they hear at home. I became aware of the famous Aussie 'chip on the shoulder'. It is our experience at this time that quite a lot of Australian people were making complaints, saying such delightful things whenever possible about 'whingeing Pommies', which was a common joke at this time. Yes, there were a few Pommie Whingers. But it was also kind of funny when I saw so many more British struggling gallantly and valiantly with their typical stoicism who were anything but whingeing. And I listened, amused, as Aussies did most of the whingeing! Some of them were forever complaining, but appeared to be too lazy to do anything about things, and they were very resentful of some of the other 'New Australians' such as the migrant Greeks and Italians who were working all hours for their families and getting established as quickly as they could. The newer migrants had clearly seen the opportunities that were available here, as we had. However, it did present some issues with those who were territorial, resentful, lazy or jealous.

The 'She'll be right, mate' was being somewhat challenged. The laid back attitude and sometimes lazy work ethics of some

Australians, but definitely not all, were probably being threatened by the determined and the hardworking of other nations. We have no alternative but to deal with it and live with it, even though we do not as yet understand it. This also causes our little family to keep a bit more to itself, and some of our immediate neighbours' attitudes discourages any further attempts at neighbourliness. We cope.

We arrive at 1974. An unexpected bombshell is dropped. For I now find that I have become pregnant again. This was so surprising and seems to have happened far too quickly, for we are only just settled. And I am still on the pill!

Another major change is about to occur. I don't even know how it could happen. How could this be, just when we were beginning to build our foundations in Australia and have a home of our own? A home with a back garden. And a future for the children.

I still can't understand it because I have been taking the pill faithfully. What I didn't know then was that even though one is taking the pill, when you also take a course of anti-biotics, these actually can negate the pill's effectiveness. It was also a surprise to read the small print to discover that the pill itself is not one hundred percent infallible for complete birth control. I had been taking the birth control pill for over nine years since Ben was born. And things had been fine. But just one serious course of heavy-duty medication had compromised its efficacy. Of course, thinking back I then realised that I'd had a cold then bronchitis during the upheaval of the move, followed by further strenuous activity. My illness could also possibly have been due to the dust when excavating the concrete for the air-conditioner unit. It later occurred to me that maybe the car accident had added to my stress load and caused the bronchitis? Who knows? This development changed everything. What was I going to do? I worked out that I would be thirty years old when this next child was due to be born. Thirty! That also meant a ten year gap between children. To start all over again from scratch. Was I prepared to do it again? What if this time, I had a little girl? I had always wanted a sister that I could relate to, and mum sometimes borrowed my good clothing from me, saying that when I had a daughter of my own, I would be able to borrow her clothes... What if, hey?

This was major decision time. And it was basically left up to me, considering the warnings issued by the doctor. I was eighteen when I had my first, twenty when I had my second and now I would be thirty. I was offered a termination by the doctor because most women at that particular time in history were having children in their late teens and twenties, and thirty was actually considered as a bit old, and consequently a bit of a risk birth-wise. It is so different today, and indeed not so long ago a relative had three children after she reached the age of forty. And all without any negative effects; all healthy and compus mentus. But back in 1974 it was a very different picture.

So I took a little time for serious consideration, and after further talking with Jim and the doctor, I decide that I will go ahead with the pregnancy. It also seemed to me that in some way, this was (again – when will I ever learn?) a last chance for our relationship. Knowing nothing about how stress works, in those days I just pretty much got on with things. It was basically 'now or never' to have this, our last child. So the new baby-to-be was embraced and I begin the preparations. Of course I have to give reluctant notice in. It is with a sorry heart that I have to leave Mary and Tom and the gang. They were most generous in their leaving gifts, and I was so glad that I had worked with them.

After the decision was made to go ahead with the birth, it surprised me when Jim actually said to me that he thought that I had gotten pregnant deliberately. What? Go through all that again for *fun*? I think he later realised that I was as genuinely surprised as him, and anyway, there was no possible reason at that time for me to *plan* or want to have another child – truth be known, I hadn't considered it one bit, as I was only just coping with everything else that I had on my plate.

In retrospect, it would appear that not one of my sons was planned for. What I mean by 'planned' is that that we had decided beforehand that we would try for a child. We hadn't. Not once. That is the problem with 'Living By Faith', you never knew what was going to be thrown at you, because you had to accept whatever came along anyway as though it was part of some sort of Grand Plan. Believe me when I say that in hindsight for my Christian marriage, as it turned out, not much was part of any Grand Divine plan ...

Being married so young Jim and I have had to learn things as we went along. But in the circles we have both grown up in, families or rather children, were inevitable, so we hadn't even queried this aspect of planning – I hadn't heard of anyone who had actually 'planned' to have their children when they wanted them. Maybe this was to become the luxury of following generations? Or possibly just part of the socio-economic group that I came from. Yet I can honestly say that each and every one of my children *was* wanted. As soon as I knew I was pregnant, I had started planning straight away. Though with John I did consider things first, I still went against doctor's suggestion not to continue. I did not regret having any of my children, and had quite accepted naturally each of their arrivals as, well, natural. I later once heard one of my grown sons say that they thought they weren't wanted. I had no idea where they got this from, certainly not from me and I had to correct him because there is a *huge* difference between being unplanned and being unwanted.

So, a new baby on the way... Now life is ready for another new phase. Plans for college for the boys were now shelved. Nursery preparations now happen in a small way – and we have the space. God will provide. (I hope!)

And Cliff Richard, the converted pop star is arriving to sing in Scots Church in Melbourne! By now, the fear of popular song has given way to the new cry 'Why should the Devil have all the good music' and once tight strings are now loosening. So we go and see Cliff in action, and within a short time, Jim has permed his hair and is wearing the latest rolled-up short sleeved shirts in bright colours aka Cliffie-Baby. It might have been another identity confusion issue for him, but then, I was still sorting out my own identity problems, though not in the same way. As he was happy being this new version, I wasn't about to be anything other than positive about it.

But things still aren't quite right at home.

Jim had lost his father within a couple of years of our departure from England. Sad to say, it is now, in the early months in our new home, that he also loses his mother. I think this affects him more than he cares to talk about. In fact he doesn't have much to say about it at all. But I know it must have affected him. Was this why he was becoming more morose? For he seems to pull into himself more and more. And paradoxically, that other more unpleasant side of him emerges more and more.

Hindsight is such a valuable thing. But nearly always comes a little too late. For with the death of my own parents, I watch how each member of the family individually deals with any unresolved issues, things that have been left unsaid, promises that were left unfulfilled, expectations that were unmet. And I realise that Jim was quite possibly dealing with a whole raft of issues, or rather, that he wasn't dealing with them, yet they were haunting him. I am attempting to be kind here, but I don't actually know the truth of my assumption. And I may never know. Not that it really matters now, anyway.

1975 WERRIBEE

~ And Then There Were Three ~ Heather Westerly ~ Forgiveness
~ 'Home Is Where The Heart Is' ~ Alcohol

AND THEN THERE WERE THREE -

The pregnancy lumbers on. The work in Geelong ends, and Jim is again looking for another job.

He scores a position as a Security Guard at The Page Newspaper on Bourke Street in the city, and seems to have found a nook that suits his suspicious nature. This may work for him as regards his professional duties, but it has an entirely different impact on the home scene. For this role feeds something within him. Shift work is now more involved, a roster of evenings, afternoons and days, though these are offset with extra days off work between shifts, all part of his award package.

During these later months of pregnancy, I still have vivid memories of Jim coming home from working shift work at all hours of the night. I am no longer working by this time, but even so there now seems to be a deliberate attempt by Jim to avoid coming home quietly. Indeed, he makes all the noise he can to disturb me. One would think it was the middle of the day. It also becomes apparent that I am now to keep him company when he has finished his work. Make him a hot chocolate, a cup of tea, a sandwich, pour a beer, listen to his complaints, anything. On some level I can understand this. With loving and close couples there is always some pleasure in being around each other no matter what is happening. But this *didn't* feel that this was just to keep him company, or because of the need to delight in my presence and essence. It feels more like a need to *disturb* me, or for me to have to suffer along with him because he is working abnormal hours.

Now I find relaxing at night when he is not there harder to do. I begin to wait for the sound of his car arriving home when I know his shift is due to end. If I wake in the night to go to the toilet due to the pressure of pregnancy, I also find myself lying awake until he is home. Sleep becomes elusive, disturbed and intermittent. I don't know what sort of a mood he is in, and whether I will have to sympathise with him or feed him. When Jim goes to sleep, no matter the time of day or night, all is expected to be quiet, and to be *kept* quiet. Or there is a huge row. There is no such consideration for my sleep. No matter how sleep deprived I am, I will still be expected to get up at the same time as my husband to help get him ready for work.

The third child is delivered in Werribee Hospital. A normal birth, though the midwife had been on a break from work for ten years, a bit like myself in a way, for I had had a ten year gap, too. Because this is her first birth back at work again, she fails an observation and misses an instruction and I am ripped again as she helps to pull him out. Ouch!

It is a boy! Another boy.

I push my disappointment down deep, and welcome this healthy little bub for who he is. I am truly glad that he is with us, and many regrets are washed away in the charm of his presence.

The boys totally embrace him, despite the fact that their own opportunities have been impacted because of him. Or maybe they just don't realise this yet. All babies bring such joy and freshness and promise, and this infected all of us. We were happily giddy at his safe arrival. Jim is actually pleased, and dare I say it, it appears that Jim is somehow different with this birth. It was almost as though he is more prepared for this child than the previous two births.

I later came to understand and to believe that it is not until a man is in his thirties that he is really ready for all that a family entails. I also later reflect on this and I realised that my own dad wasn't really happy about children till my second sibling came along, and dad was well into his thirties. As I said earlier, when Joan was born, it was like the sunshine shone from her and she could apparently do no wrong. So it is now with this third child of ours. It is as though this child is born to be the next saviour... It feels as though Jim fully embraces him, and actually really loves him, rather than just accepts him as it had felt with the other two boys.

Naïve Hope

He seems to revel in every infant development as though this is his first offspring, and he is far more understanding and lenient and tolerant with him than he was with the other boys.

Or so it seems to me. It may well have been that I too, am less anxious about children and their rearing. But I do notice that there sometimes seems a bit *too* much focus on what this little one wants more than being fair with all three boys. I am glad that Joseph and Ben don't appear to take exception to this, and seem to truly love their little brother so freely and deeply. But I do sometimes wonder how they might be feeling in their own hearts about little Daniel getting more preferential treatment. Yes, we have both agreed on naming our new son Daniel John.

I am now well and truly out-numbered by males. Will I ever be able to watch a girly show on TV again?

I begin to recover from the birth, and it seems that it is no time at before it is our first Christmas.

Jim is hard at work and temporarily absorbed in the newborn. Little Daniel is a definite distraction from deeper issues, and we are all involved in his growth and development. The spare room becomes his nursery, and I feel or rather hope, that things are moving forward. Meanwhile, buying bottles of beer is no longer enough for Jim, and he is now experimenting with home brewing kits. This is in order to save money, you understand. Initially alternating his distillation experiments with regular beer, it soon becomes a regular thing as he finds his inner brewer. He still continues to encourage me to join him in his drinking, but fortunately I am breastfeeding. And I don't like the taste of beer anyway, so I am glad of this plausible excuse.

Over the next few years Jim takes to home brewing by the economic barrelful. This really begins to bother me, but I cannot stop him. In just three years time he will increase his quantity of batches brewed to almost two barrels in a week. Which only he drinks. Not that this is resented, nor anticipated, by me at the time. Yes, it may have been more economical to make it one's self, but not in the amounts he tots up. He only misses a weekly brewing if he still has some still on hand.

Our home now often has that yeasty smell to it. *Yummy*!

Even though I was getting quite concerned and signalled this to him, I could not discourage him, as he insists that he has every right to drink in his 'own home.' And didn't Jesus turn the water into wine? And didn't they have wine in church? There was no way that I could have foreseen this. I didn't know of any other alcoholics, didn't really know how it affected people.

Meanwhile, for a while, we appear to be a reasonably happy group and our first Christmas together was mostly pleasurable.

During the school holidays, the boys play word and giggle games with baby. As he grows and develops, they seem to love encouraging little bub to follow them, playing games to encourage him to catch them and then they would roll around on the floor together. Jim is very active in encouraging his developments, taking a real interest in his activities and when little Daniel was old enough Jim invested in some home tutoring games and lessons that encouraged spelling and learning words. The boys were all encouraged to participate in this. Unfortunately these happy family nights did not hold sway over the unresolved undercurrents, though they did provide a temporary happy interlude.

A ten year gap can be a lot of forgetting. And I had to relearn – again –child rearing. At the risk of being boring, both back then, and again with my youngest grand child I had to review what I knew of this. For it has long been known that early life at home influences a child in many ways, and can set the stage for the patterns they form in relationships. The old schools of thought on childrearing that older generations mainly grew up with were generally centred around teaching the child that they must fit in with what suited the parents. That is that they had to come to learn that feeding was supposed to be only at certain times and not when they were actually hungry, that they had to learn to cry without being attended to if it was inconvenient to the parent or the schedule they were teaching or imposing, and other similar ideas.

This lack of support and attention that is withheld or not given when it is needed, can build a deeper sense of not being supported and cared for, and this can then become the pattern for life on a deep hidden level; the subconscious storing of all those times when they needed help, love or support and it was not given. This can build a sense of lack or abandonment and is often part of how they may well further interact with life itself later. They may often display less real inner self reliance, self-worth, lack of self-belief and a whole raft of other contra-necessary traits that would have enabled them to be able to live a full and unhindered proactive and satisfying life. These are my understandings only, of course. But hopefully you get the idea.

The newer school of thought (which for older ones amongst us was actually similar to the old school of thought) is to respond immediately to every need, to give the child whatever it wants when it wants and if possible at the moment it wants it. That is the short version of this radical theory. Inconvenient it may be, but it can save a whole lot of future problems, for this same thought believes that when a child cries and needs comfort, attention or soothing in any way and that this need is not met, it registers within the child that they cannot and will not get their needs met – and that this can give them a sense of abandonment, low self-worth, and can contribute to a sense or fear that their needs are insatiable or unsatisfiable – though these are actually my words and my interpretation but based on my understanding of the method.

I have since seen this in action, actually my little grandson John was brought up this way, and a happier five year old I have yet to meet. Difficult as it can be for young mums I would now consider this method as worthy of real consideration, but I also acknowledge that we also generally live in a time when we don't usually have lots of family support or close neighbours to assist with this.

I must also mention something else that this marvellous thing called hindsight can give. What is not always as recognised along with this method is the way that children can absorb their mothers emotions when in the womb as well as in early infancy – whether it is joy and happiness or fears and anxiety – which that can affect the hormonal system and possibly can last a lifetime.

Children and the unborn do not have developed filtering systems and are so prone to environment. So when a mother is subjected to abuse of any kind, or unusual or deep stress beyond the normal in life, this will surely register upon the unborn in a way that can lock it in at a deeper level than merely cellular, or intellectual. It can penetrate into the actual nervous system and into the psyche. They may find themselves held back or haunted by something they have no possible hope of identifying, simply because they had no tools of recognition, no way of understanding or filtering or labelling their experience apart from the memory impact it registered upon the place where they 'lived' or were 'housed' – the womb, and therefore the mother.

Certain reflexes are a natural part of life, and these can be compromised or affected in a way that can inhibit future physical or psychological development. The impact can also register within their nervous system, and if severe may possibly cause inappropriate behaviour, responses or even physical problems later.

I myself had trouble with the Moro Reflex until it was worked with through a therapist who employed neurological techniques combined with the memory and emotion release techniques sometimes used with kinesiology. Moro Reflex usually develops to the Startle Reflex, but when arrested as in my case it can cause ultra-sensitivity with noise, sudden movement and over-reaction to these things. Added to this were my experiences of violence and abuse throughout childhood and married life. Even though I had learned to handle most of this reasonably well, when this Reflex was corrected it certainly made a difference in my reactions and how I felt about certain things.

There are a range of therapies to help one uncover frozen issues or hurts and also to release them relatively easily. A bit like a personal-history house-clean. Psychology may assist to some degree but based on my own experiences, I found this was not always sufficient and I combined it with a variety of other therapies such as kinesiology, body work and nutritional support. There are some great books out now about how experiences can get locked into the body as memory or create blockages that may cause pain on a variety of levels.

But enough on this.

Naïve Hope

Heather Westerly

With the birth of little Daniel an extra dimension was added to our lives. For a while I didn't have to work as I recovered from the rigours of childbirth and went about getting myself, my body, the house and our lives in order again.

Neighbours in the street where we lived were not easily engaged. And as most of them were Australian and we still had strong British accents, we weren't easily included in local issues. There was also trouble from time to time when that Australian chip-on-the-shoulder found expression by the kids in the street actively picking on our boys or by non-cooperation with the adults over parking issues. Sometimes it would flare up and I guess because we were these strange 'Born-Agains' the differences became uncomfortably apparent. But we managed. This is our home and we are determined to make it work.

A new friendship sprang up for me with a new neighbour who I met whilst shopping. She didn't live in the same road, but just a few streets away. She was a new arrival to the area too and we just seemed to click. Heather was a nurse, and seemed to be straightforward, a quality I appreciate. I liked her. Her husband had been in the armed forces, and he had been away in Vietnam. Tony was now home recovering and working on rebuilding his health and life. But he had suffered badly during the war, and was prone to unbalanced episodes and violent bouts. There also appeared to be little being done by the government of the day to rehabilitate these war veterans properly, and he apparently had seen some horrendous sights whilst over there fighting. Heather shared this with me after she had been through another irrational outburst from him. I think that he was getting some help, but it didn't appear to be the right help.

Naturally, it is not long before I invite her and her husband home to meet Jim. And so when Jim and I spoke about the church we belonged to – despite what was going on behind closed doors, we would still attend the local Throngs of God church and Witness to others about our Faith –we invited them to come along. Tony graciously declined, but Heather came along. At a later meeting on her own she 'accepted the Lord as Saviour'. This bought a temporary reprieve in the drama of their relationship. But things apparently didn't change enough, nor could they really, for this was not about faith but about damaged health.

Heather and I had both found ourselves pregnant at around the same time. I was first, and just a few months later, Heather announced her pregnancy.

It was after her giving birth that, as they say, the 's..t hit the fan' and she suddenly left her hubby and took up with another guy, who was clearly (or so it appeared) besotted with her. She even brought him round to meet Jim and I, and to explain how hard it had been with Tony, hinting at some small measure of his violence toward her. Eventually, she left and moved interstate, taking the baby, and divorced Tony. And so I lost another friend. Even though I didn't tell her everything about Jim's violence, which had been somewhat temporarily arrested due to my pregnancy, we had had a good shared friendship. She was sorry to go, but I could see her need to do so. And I sincerely wished her well.

Not only did I lose a good friend, though. Yet again, I was made to pay for someone else's 'betrayal' of their marriage in Jim's eyes, and subjected to accusations of intentions to 'run off and leave' whenever I could get a chance. This 'man' was again unreasonably suspicious. Ok, so that's two couples in our immediate circle of acquaintances and friends that had split up.

Was this Jim's fear? That our marriage would split up? Did he expect me to do the same thing? To run away?

Wonder why?

And I can't help asking myself, if *this* was his fear, that couples divorced, how many other couples around us were still happily married? Or at least, married, still? Like his parents, my parents, Mary and Stuart, both just a fraction older than us, like the Pastor's daughter, who had married six months before us. Why should *we* be any different from them? Weren't we Christians, didn't we have a better chance with God on our side? And if he *did* think our marriage was in jeopardy, then, Duh! What was he doing *positively* about it?

Naïve Hope

Just keep pushing, Jim, you just might get your wish! I wish I had had this thought years ago. Instead I just kept putting up with the silly bastard!

Forgiveness

By now there is a clear picture of the difficulties emerging in the marriage. Not that they weren't there all the time, they were simply not as obvious to me. There are bouts of Charm and him doing all he could to make up for his abuse or failing, and these make the sun shine, the birds sing, and God very present, or so it seemed, in our life. All of this, is of course, a matter of perception. What one chooses to believe, is usually how one will interpret the incidents and events that occur around them.

Though his dark and bad moods were damaging, the accord that I thought I felt with him between times, with my focus on doing the best I could in whatever situation I found myself, this accord, this connection, when he was actually wanting to be connected with me, was what I craved.

I hadn't yet learned or realised that I put up with an awful lot of crap to get to those points.

His moods had usually been short-lived, and his endeavours to make up for things nevertheless indicate some sort of remorse or at the least, acknowledgement; to me. I always gave him the benefit of the doubt, and because of his apparent sincerity, I *believed* him when he said he was sorry and he would try to make it up to me. I automatically assumed that he was genuine, capable of sincerity, meant what he said and so he wouldn't do the same thing again. If I had allowed myself to consider and expect changes, I also hadn't known how to create those changes and to instigate manageable consequences. The balance of power was always in his court and so I hoped that he would eventually get it. That saying about thinking that your love can change a guy... I must have believed that at some stage, because it really doesn't work like that. I also now realise that patterns simply keep repeating themselves, and I hadn't as yet allowed myself to recognise that we were living with patterns. I lived in hope. And faith. After all, the Pastor had already been asked about forgiveness. Still a major concern for me, I had sought answers to his early abuse and even been to the Pastor himself. And this, too, had yielded little to help me.

After Jim had sustained the stitches in his arm, there had been a fresh opportunity to speak to the Pastor about Jim's abuse again, as Pastor Parratt had been enquiring after Jim's injury. He had heard from his brothers of the incident and had probably suspected something. Jim was out at work, and the Pastor popped in to see me whilst visiting his brothers. I told him that Jim had been about to beat me and I explained what had happened. He listened sympathetically.

Then I said to him, 'I know we must forgive, but Jim is still hitting me. How long is he allowed to do this? How *many* times must we forgive someone?'

Because of Jim's sporadic but nevertheless persistent abuse, and because I thought that there had to be a limit as to how much this should happen and a limit as to how much someone should be allowed to 'get away' with something, I needed to know just how much a good wife is expected to put up with. I think this continued unreasonable abuse also went against what I thought a Christian should be in that the whole idea was to be a *better* version, a better person – wasn't it? - and to attempt to be like Christ surely? After all, we were Christians – *followers* of Christ - weren't we, and didn't we have a responsibility to be an example of the grace of God in our own lives?

But Pastor Parratt floored me when he replied 'You must forgive as often as you need to. We must always forgive.'

I still wasn't sure this was right, and that I was just supposed to keep putting up with things. I also wondered why it was okay for this to continue and Jim not to be called to accountability.

With this in mind I asked him 'Do we still keep *having* to forgive, even if they keep doing the wrong thing and keep on making the same mistake over and over again?' And his reply was 'The Bible says we must forgive seventy times seven – this means the fullness of numbers. We must keep on forgiving. We must *always* forgive no matter how often or for how long. Just as God forgives us.' This was followed up by the biblical quote; Matthew 18:22. Of course.

Naïve Hope

This is both the pitiless and pathetically pitiful counsel that I got. This was the counsel that later put my life at risk, not to mention how it affected my children. Pitiful in that this was the *sum* of the *best* he could provide in understanding, with its lack of content and lack of support for those being abused; Pitiless in that there was no pity for the abused, no recourse, no mercy for appropriate relief, challenge and change for them.

It also assumed that I had the patience of God. Hah!

One might expect violence in a 'godless' marriage... but when the Church itself sweeps it under the carpet and insists that the wife has no rights apart from that which her husband allows her, then it would appear that the Church itself condones it...

How enlightening it might have been if I had gotten correct and proper relationship counselling at the time. Or if this older and supposedly wiser 'man of God' had taken the time to find out more of what was behind my questions and concerns. Or if Jim had been warned off about his violence by them, by the church authority!

I was still at a loss sometimes as to how to broach subjects. Being so tuned in to other people's reactions, and concerned or sometimes even scared about their responses, I hadn't yet fully learned to find my own voice and question things that were in direct regard to *myself*. It was always easier to defend others, or a greater cause. Except for 'A Talk' with him by Stuart, and the Pastor, Jim had never really been taken to task about it, and all of this 'forgiveness' and lack of understanding, not just about lack of self-control, but also as to what lay underneath this anger and disrespect, all of this ignorance didn't help us one little bit. Jim couldn't help himself, I came to see. And in some way, because it just kept happening, this must mean that I was not helping him correctly. In fact he would often say to me 'You're my wife, you're supposed to know how to fix it.' What?

How ridiculous in hindsight! How primitive! How brutal!

So for someone who doesn't really have to account for bad behaviour, and who is not taken to task about self-control, they are more likely to see that lack of punishment is actually a kind of covert *permission* to continue with the same? From where I currently stand, it looks like that to me.

And this is precisely what happened. I was not aware that I had options, and that I could have devised consequences for his behaviours. But I guess as I had had to accept that he was the 'head' of the wife and family, I didn't really have any say in it, did I?

Oh, how ridiculous it all was. How appalling. How un-supposedly-Christian-like. But then that is a whole other story. You may have guessed by now that when one claims to be a Christian, I no longer automatically give them the benefit of the doubt. Not any more. I simply examine the fruits of their spirit. This is biblical and a good litmus test; 'By their fruits ye shall know them'. *Yes, I will use quotes to make a point, just as quotes have been used against me. If they don't like it, then they can just stop using the Bible at me!* And I no longer condemn other beliefs unless they, too, show the same lousy and rotting fruits of a good many self-righteous and self-deluded people, no matter their faith, ideology, beliefs or claims. Bad is Bad no matter the faith or religious label.

Back then I still paid attention to the descriptor, the tag, the labels, and believed the claims people made. Naively. I guess it came probably because I was pretty honest and upfront myself, and I had been brought up to tell the truth. I always had trouble getting my head around it when people lied or intended hurt or harm to another. Even though I had challenged this myself with my attempt at stealing, my reward at that time of not being prosecuted had flagged such behaviour as not only unworthy of me, but also of only leading to failure in that department anyway. A Major lesson that, in my case, further underscored avoiding any attempt to try to deceive intentionally.

In those days there was really no place to go for victims of domestic violence. It didn't really even have a name then except to be labelled as a 'fight' or 'trouble at home'. We all grew up with it in some form or another, either in our own homes or hearing rows and fights in the immediate neighbourhood. Usually smacks or thrown dinners in most neighbourly cases. In my own case, dad having to rush mum to hospital because of a split lip that required stitches, and in another instance because of him kicking her down the stairs and her consequential spontaneous abortion. Though our family did seem more thorough and dramatic in its delivery of the usual *'king of my own castle'* routine than some of our other neighbours. In a lot of lower class and I guess middle class families it was simply accepted though generally hushed up. You were so very lucky if you had a family where this behaviour was recognised for what it was and avoided – a dysfunctional pattern and a perversion of love. Though with what I know now, I must also include that any class is not free of this particularly insidious practice and that it is the culture of violent men rather than class that must be addressed.

Though Jim was not battering me continually without let-up, and any injury was sometimes more discreet than some I have described, his beatings were generally short-lived and usually driven by temper, and also as I explained, were almost a part of the community culture. Though this was true, I *still* couldn't get why someone would hit or hurt another.

Usually his past attempts at charming me back had worked, though I was now becoming less convinced that he meant these apologies for nothing was changing and these episodes hadn't yet stopped. Given that I had subscribed to this charter of forgiveness in the way that I naively had, there was still little option for me to do other than try to love and forgive it all better. As you can guess, when the charm was full on, painful memories were forgotten – rather like childbirth in that way. But what do you do when the charm begins to lessen? When it is diminished and you are left with only blank or moody-sulky breaks between the outbursts? And what do you do when a new tack is employed, one that is designed to make you feel as though you are nothing? I have become familiar with the hits and smacks, thumps and suspicion, moods and charm. I was not prepared for the next and rather strange practice that now emerges into our little family life.

With the newness of life with little Danny, the positive was that I could feel reasonably safe whilst Jim was employed in basking in the little one's fresh and innocent energy. During the day!

Now Jim was becoming more and more a Jekyll-and-Hyde. The Hyde part was happy with Danny, Jekyll was moody with me; and

Jekyll-and-Hyde were swinging in different ways with the other two boys. After Danny was settled down for the night, Jim would turn his attention to his beer tasting. And to finding fault with me. Beer now lubricated and escalated this practise - it starts to become a pattern. When he is home evenings from his work, his nightly drinking saw to it that I kept myself to myself and avoided antagonising him in any way. But that was no guarantee of safety. For something else now occurs and again, this was after the boys have gone to bed and are supposed to be asleep.

As Jim's work now included shifts and some evenings when he wasn't working, he now began to allow himself to get drunk. Tempers flared, or rather his temper did, though initially I reacted to his erratics, being unfamiliar with how alcohol fuels things until I learn to avoid engagement instead. It would seem like Jim would drink enough and muse enough to reach a certain point. And then he would get up from his armchair, grab me by the arm, which still had an extremely firm grip as witnessed by the many arm bruises I sustained with all of this, and he would manhandle me like a security bouncer escorting someone off the premises to our front door. Whereupon he would yank it open and physically push me through the door.

His slurred mumblings now centred around me having to 'Leave. Don't want you here. Get out. Stay out.' And then it would appear that he would go back to his drinking some more before eventually going to the bedroom, drunk as Larry, happy with his little game and with the fact that I couldn't do anything about it. All pretence at refinement had gone out the window, with loud toilet sounds followed by flushing occurring and not a door closed. Belching, hiccupping, farting, peeing, spilling, dripping, stinking, followed by snoring. Yukks! What could I do? He was bigger and stronger than me, and at that time I didn't know of anywhere else that I could go to. And why would I wish to leave my children and go? So how did I deal with this atrocious yet scary behaviour?

I would usually have to wait until Jim was asleep in bed as attested by his snoring before I would go round the back of the house and knock for entry on the children's bedroom window. I would have to knock just loud enough to wake them, but not wake their father. Then they would let me in through the window, and sometimes they would let me sleep in their bunk bed or we would take it in turns to lie on the floor. Though I suspect the boys gave up their beds for me more times than I slept on the floor. I tried to inconvenience them as little as possible, but I was having quite a bit of back trouble with all of this. It took me many years to realise these aches and pains were directly linked to my life with Jim.

But what on earth were my children learning by being present to all of this? And there was yet nowhere for me to go, or to take them.

It didn't happen every night, nor necessarily every week. But enough for me to say that eventually this certain bad behaviour had come to stay.

What a way to live. I was not comfortable with any of this, but there was always fear in the background. Result: 'play it down, don't make it worse'.

Yes, he may remember and be sorry about it at some stage and try and 'make it up' again. Or he may not. But this was becoming more often a habit of him forgetting, or worse yet as proven by later events, of him ignoring that it *ever* happened.

I was feeling humiliated and embarrassed. But he wasn't actually beating me in front of the children, so I had no grounds to complain of physical abuse, now did I? Honestly, when I look back at the crap I put up with, I could kick myself. But then I remember that I have to have compassion for myself, just as I would if it was someone else who had been in the same place, and who didn't dare to share with someone else as it was seen as betrayal, someone who could take them aside and tell them the facts of life – the facts being that this man who was a misogynist was harmful *as* he was even *without* the beatings, was probably *never* going to change, did not care for or protect or respect them, took total advantage of them, abused them, and excused himself all in the name of a supposed faith or religion. Whilst still declaring himself a 'Christian'! Hah!

And that this man had serious, *serious* hang-ups with himself, women, sex and life.

'HOME IS WHERE THE HEART IS'

Sheila is now living in Sydney and I am still ridiculously either too embarrassed or too scared to tell her of what Jim puts me through.

There is no-one else around to talk to either, and isolated as we are, would I ever go to mum and dad again, whether they are in the UK or not, or phone them for advice about this?

What do you think? You are right if you guess that the answer is 'No!' And unbeknown to me, my tolerance gauge is now set to even worse violence anyway. It seemed to be in so many places around me, and in major relationships in my life. *And let's face it, Christ himself was subjected to major violence and abuse, as were some of his best fans, biblical and otherwise. Christianity is a religion with its origins in violence, despite Jesus's actual fundamental message, which often seems to get lost amongst the spoutings and clap-trap of some of the apostles, and other fans of His.*

Even though I had always desired a harmonious and peaceful and happy home life which on occasion I have momentarily experienced, this hopeful 'model' of mine of how home life *should* be was contaminated. I think I am also kind of pre-programmed by what I had lived through and experienced prior to all of this.

My first and major model of home life and therefore my first experience and model of 'love' was, of course, with mum and dad. Like most parents would, they had the greatest impact through my early and most impressionable years. And this relationship standard was one that was interspersed with such varied pictures of mum and dad waltzing in the lounge and kitchen, kissing and cuddling, dad throwing plates and whole meals around or at mum, doors banging, loud and violent arguments, rows over money and other women, mum sobbing, mum sitting vacantly like a sack of potatoes in a chair, the sound of dad's motorbike starting up angrily, me and my brother in the kitchen peeling potatoes, washing washing and more washing, mum sweating with housework and washing and wringing clothes by hand, my brother and myself repairing worn shoe soles with dad, polishing sundry silver boxing award cups and trophies messily with brasso and silvo, being shouted at by dad, clips across the head and around the ears off dad, getting 'the belt' literally off dad – his army belt –

Naïve Hope

across the backside, handed pieces of chocolate by dad as a rare treat when watching a favourite or special occasion television program, playing Monopoly or Playing Cards, dad dressing up with funny faces or wigs to make us laugh, dad telling the same old jokes yet still getting laughs, comedy shows, snatched moments to read kids comics, reading books, listening to 'The Archers', 'Sherlock Holmes' and 'Dan Dare' on the radio, stinging slaps round the legs, wet mattresses, cold shivery nights when even dad's army coat on the bed didn't bring any warmth, getting up in the freezing cold and preparing the coal fire downstairs, icy toilet seats in the middle of the night that froze the bowels up again, walking to school in the snow and rain, digging in the garden, playing on the tyre hung from the old oak tree in the avenue, being called in to prepare dinner or for dinner, coming home to an empty house from school and having to wait for mum to come home, being hit for something Joan did, Christmas pudding and sherry, etc etc etc. A real mixed bag of chaos, despair, shards of fun, permanent surviving, getting-by.

I now know that what we experience early in life becomes the template or equation on which we build our own major love and life relationship – until we learn to do it different.

It took me some years, but I eventually got the lesson!

As I have previously shared, on the first occasion that Jim had attacked me and given me a black eye, I had run home to mum and dad. Though they seemed a bit sorry for me, when I asked for their support and advice on what to do about Jim's violence mum looked at me with tight lips and said 'Well. You've made your bed. Now you have to lie in it.'

My own mother was resentful of me having married a Christian man. She eventually admitted that she was a bit jealous of me having such a God-fearing man when she had been through what she had been through all her life. Violence was probably what my mum had grown up with from her own family, as well as having lived this out with dad in her marriage; yet despite how much she had suffered, here she was dishing this out to me. I was totally thrown when she flung this at me. Slap! Jealous Slap! Join the (Abused Wives) Club; Slap!

Gee, Thanks mum!

And surprisingly, rather than giving me something more supportive, more practical, more caring, even simply more *Christian* to hold onto, she jealously defaulted to what her mother had probably told her when she had sought help. Good mothering Not!

Thanks mum!

So I couldn't possibly go back to *her* again for help with this. And dad had just hung his head. How could he do otherwise, guilty as the similar perpetrator that he was? And dad was an ex-champion boxer in his regiment. Imagine my surprise after a year or so of marriage to discover that Jim had been a champion boxer, and not only in school, but also in the Merchant Navy!

Oh my God – *I had married my father!*

Short though Jim was, he was stocky and of well-built solid Irish stock. I had not recognised this trait connection, had not see that coming! Great physical stock for the gene pool, yet not even as intelligent as dad. Though that statement is possibly questionable too, wouldn't you agree?

Then the Pastor, peddling his own watered down support to pin me to a life of martyrdom and sacrifice. And this will help God *how*?

So lesson on Not Going To Others For Help was well and truly learned.

Now we have a habit of disturbed sleep before and after Daniel is born.

It is any wonder that both Danny and myself suffered sleep problems for many, many years? Mind you, maybe a skinful of beer would have sorted out that problem for me nicely, hey?

But not only that - further events occurred. I know this sounds like one of those commercials, that goes like '*But wait, there's more, and you get a set of steak knives with that...*' But that is what it feels like as I list these things.

All this forgiveness, but nothing is changing!

Now I am getting more concerned.

Naïve Hope

Previously I had thought 'I will hang on to God and He will see me through, He will fix this'. For sometimes, one's faith can help one to get through. So they say. However, absolving personal responsibility and choosing – whether consciously or not - to live in denial so as not to have to take action can create further problems. Just hoping something will resolve itself is sometimes simply pointless.

There is another saying; 'Keep doing what you have been doing, and you will keep getting what you have been getting.' Same actions yield the same results. If you want something to change, then you have to do something differently. I hadn't yet learned this. But I was about to.

All of this praying for God to help, for the Lord Jesus to help, to guide, to save – but nothing is happening! All of this 'delighting' in the Lord, being meek, keeping centred on only good thoughts, but no rewards are in sight! Reading the Bible, praying. All of this Witnessing when one can, standing up for God, but *who* is standing up for me?

Something was starting to not add up in my mind, the 2 + 2 that had previously been misread as 22 were now showing me a 2 + 2 that = 4! And I was now becoming more observant as to what was and was *not* happening. Though I couldn't put a finger on things, though I didn't as yet have the right *questions*, let alone the right answers, something was working out that this was *not* right. Others were getting a better deal, and they definitely weren't Christians – how come? They weren't sacrificing like I was. What were they doing right that I was not, that *we* were not? Where were the fulfilment of the promises if we kept to God's word?

Before now, I had honoured the saying 'Watch and pray' – now I began just to *WATCH*. And listen. Praying wasn't helping. I was beginning to hear other further rumblings and warning sounds in the distance.

Alcohol

Because it is becoming more and more a part of our life together, let me take a moment to look at our friend, *Alcohol*...

I was not aware on a conscious level of what it means to live with an alcoholic. In my experience, my own parents weren't anything like that, though Uncle Frank had shown me what being drunk looked like. 'Uncle' Frank was a friend of dad's. He lived in Panfield Road, just a short walk away, with his wife Doreen. Frank was a large, rough, burly, friendly Scotsman, and he sure could put away the drink. He wasn't drunk all the time, but he could binge drink at weekends, though we didn't have that word for it back then. Frank and Doreen McHugh had several children, and we had met their children during school holidays one day whilst out on a rare walk with mum and dad in a peaceful period; a time of truce. I was about ten when we first started playing together with his children, and up until I was thirteen we were pretty solid friends. Ian and myself, and sometimes Joan, would play with Frank's children during school holidays, our favourite game being Monopoly with a second fave being playing cards. Carole was the eldest, then Jacqueline was next in birth order, then Eddie. Jacqui and Eddie were around the same age as Ian and I. Frank and Doreen also had a younger daughter called Linda, who had been born after a bit of a gap, similar to the six year gap between Joan and Tina. Like our Joan, Linda was the spoilt one, the favourite, the blameless one. She, like Joan, gave her siblings hell. 'Uncle'

Frank's drinking had now progressed to weekdays, not just weekends. There were times when we would be playing together and 'Uncle' Frank would come home drunk, having lost on the doggies or the horses, and everything would be total confusion, fear and chaos. The same would happen when Linda didn't get her own way. Our game would be interrupted and one of his children would be to blame for whatever was the perceived 'wrong' thing at the time and out would come his belt. We were told in no uncertain manner to go home at this point, to 'Get oot of my hoose'. But later we were allowed to catch up with our friends again and the stories would come back to us. When Frank was in a good mood, he was funny, friendly, jovial, but when he wasn't...

So to my mind, being alcoholic was being drunkenly out of control, like 'Uncle' Frank. Mum and dad had never let me see any open drunkenness, so I didn't consciously recognise it nor connect it to my own family situation. Nor did I know anything about predispositions to it. After all, *I* didn't have a problem with alcohol, as I had very rarely had any, and didn't fancy that funny heady feeling that everyone talked about. It was as though I had a healthy respect for it, and so I hadn't abused it, for I had never yet in my life been drunk myself, not until that one time in Altona Hostel. Somehow, I had never 'been driven to drink' as some others had.

But as a post script to Frank's story it wasn't a happy ending for him; One day, his wife; Doreen, came home from work and quietly packed a suitcase. Coming down the stairs with it as she answered the front door to her boyfriend – which we didn't have a clue about – she put her head around the living room door, saying to Frank 'Well, I am off. I have had enough of your drinking, gambling and abuse. You are welcome to everything here, and if you come after me, he (her boyfriend) will sort you out, you drunken slob. You will beat me no more!' and promptly departed before Frank had any chance to react. I was there. I saw it!

It is not a pleasant story for him and his children after that, and the last I heard, most of them left him as soon as they could, and his beloved Linda was no comfort to him at all. C'est la vie!

I think that drink is the result of old and buried pain, and an attempt to forget it. But drink doesn't solve the problem, it just avoids it. Getting 'Saved' does *not* automatically fix everything. A drinking problem is not solved by choosing a different set of beliefs alone. Running from the symptoms driving one to alcohol, does not deal with its cause.

1977 BEGINNING OF THE END

Abuse Escalates. Courage Wins Through.

~ Alarm Bells Ring ~ The Perfect Wife ~ Back To Work

Alarm Bells Ring

About six months after little Daniel's birth, I fall pregnant again. I am not yet back on the pill.

I kid you not, but I heard the recurring sound of alarm bells ringing at full pelt in my mind and my inner 'ears'. Along with this uncanny and unshakeable sense that, if I have this next child, I and the boys (all three of them) and this new life would not only be totally trapped, but also that we would not survive to tell the tale. It felt like some kind of 'Death Nell' to me and it so impressed itself upon me that I could not ignore it. I thought for a little while about the consequences of proceeding with this pregnancy but I had to listen to these warnings. In my heart of hearts I confess I did secretly want a little girl, but my fears were far too real, and too well based on current fact. And I was responsible for protecting my other children as well. In the end I chose to play it safe and to have an abortion.

Jim is drinking more now and is getting even more moody when little Danny was in bed. The writing was on the wall.

Sure there may have been some financial considerations, but that wasn't my prime concern. It was the bells and forebodings that made the decision for me to go this route. Fortunately when I discussed it at length with Jim I was able to use this argument of money and he quite agreed that we couldn't really financially afford to have another child. When I had fallen pregnant with little Danny, the doctor had warned that I might be pushing it a little age and health wise, and to be prepared for problems or complications with a 'late life' birth. And so this again was an important factor and now my trump card. As I was now over thirty-one there was even more risk to have another child, and the dangers of difficulty and deformity were now quite substantially increased, according to

Naïve Hope

the current medical information at that time. This being the prevailing trend I was now able to fully justify this decision without having to defend it too much, and also to have my local GP's full support and approval.

The average age since 1975 for getting married and having children has increased dramatically owing to medical evolution and societal changes and lifestyles, with couples choosing to work for longer before making conscious parenting choices. And having children later in life has not only become the vogue but also the norm, as more women first establish their 'careers' before creating their children.

The feeling of foreboding that I had experienced had an accompanying and compelling sense of *death at Jim's hands*. (Maybe I was starting to pick up on some vibes, on some signals?) There was nothing concrete that I could quite put my finger on. Just this impending and inescapable sense of death and doom and finality and entrapment. The overwhelming feeling that if I had another child we were all as good as dead. Every time I thought about a fourth child this sense got stronger. Somehow I knew that this would push Jim 'over the edge' and that we would all pay for it. Pictures of mass family murder and suicide kept coming into my consciousness, and I took this as a serious warning. My prime concern is preservation and protection of my family as best I can.

And so I go into hospital for the termination, along with an added procedure at the same time to have my fallopian tubes tied. Jim had absolutely *refused* to have a vasectomy after little Daniel was born, insisting that it was *up to me* to sort this side of things out. In fact, though I am sure you just might possibly find this hard to believe; he actually got *upset* about it! Told you you might not believe me!

A Tubal Ligation, as they called it, was also to safeguard the need for me to take further birth control pills and to avoid further pregnancies. I had been taking birth pills since Ben's birth. It has been almost ten years of suppressing normal hormonal activity. It may have seemed appropriate action back then, but medical updates now filter through on the dangers of continuing this practice. Years later, there arose 'new' understandings and supported research that long term use of these birth control pills could create future problems with health, not to mention the confusion visited upon a woman's normal hormonal cycles. I later understood that many women were actually the experiment for these pills at that time – it hadn't as yet been fully researched. It was also convenient for men, as it did away with the need for them to use the desensitising contraceptive condoms. Or to go the dreaded 'Snip'. (That is, it *was* convenient, until the later outbreak of Aids, which in lots of cases was traced back to the lack of the use of condoms.)

So several problems were 'solved' for myself and Jim by this decision. Though underneath all of this, I think it also fuelled Jim's suspicious nature that I could now have sex any time (and with anyone, I dare say!) I wanted without running the risk of falling pregnant again... Not that *I* considered this at the time.

I would have loved to have a little girl, and the boys would have appreciated one too. But it was not to be. Maybe in another life...

Though the sixties was supposedly a time of sexual revolution, the permissive and experimentation-al aspects still hadn't quite caught up with me. Not surprisingly. There had been some progress past the basic 'missionary position', but we were still, I think, a bit at a loss to some degree. I always sought a deeper meaning to sex, and my approach was more spiritual than for some. To each his own. But hearing about the Kama Sutra and some of the other sex education books going round at the time caused some interest. I knew somehow that there was some connection between sex and spirituality, between the energy of love and the energy and love-making that was much more than we had been experiencing, but it had somehow seemed out of reach. Because there was so much that was amiss in our relationship, in our actual togetherness on an emotional level, I was becoming curious if improvement in our sexual life would improve other areas. Jim seemed to think about it more than I did. This was to be some sort of theme in our lives, this preoccupation with sex. The focus on technique was only part of the solution though.

In his books it was still my job as his wife to keep him happy after all, wasn't it? I wanted to feel more connected on other levels as well as to enjoy this essential part of our marriage more. Maybe if this improved Jim would be somewhat happier?

Over time, we became more educated, learning from books and each other bodies. There did seem to be some improvement in the quality of our relating. And I had taken this as confirmation that we were on the right track. But I also *had* to come to realise that it didn't really *deal* with his issues. For this really wasn't about 'performance'.

Interestingly enough, every anniversary we *ever* had (and where I would usually go out of my way to make it enjoyable) always but *always* ended up in a horrible fight. For one usually makes a romantic effort on an anniversary, and attempts to ignite a renewal of love. Which usually and often ends up with intimacy and sex. And that is what happened. With some couples, there can be fights actually ON the anniversary. Generally not so with us, though this did happen from time to time. If there wasn't a row actually at the time, then it would follow shortly after, usually taking a day or two to filter through, but sure enough there would be some horrific argument or fight and I would be accused of flirting with someone, of infidelity, of cheating and lying, or something else that had absolutely nothing whatsoever to do with what I had done, but with what he insisted that I had done. Or thought. Or was going to do.

Time showed that at each anniversary or at each occasion of true intimacy and sharing there would be a back-lash and an eruption or disruption of anger that had to be dealt with. Instead of the old adage of arguing and then making up with love-making, we seemed to develop the opposite pattern. At the time I thought *I* was too inhibited, and was trying to learn to balance my need to melt into someone else during love-making with being practical and more physical about it. This sentimental flowy part of me that yearned to be a part of someone and allow them to be a part of me did sometimes have difficulties with what was being asked of me. Often, after it was over and the 'after-glow' – or rather, on some occasions, the 'exertion' - settled, sleep would come quickly for Jim, whilst I still lay there thinking of to-do lists. At that time I had no idea, no concept, of what happened energetically during sex, no thought of the interchange of emotions, the dumpings of unresolved issues from one person to another. I just gave my love as best I could, without recognising the consequences of being so open for someone such as myself. Now I know how to accept the love of another, the caring and tenderness, without taking on their problems and emotions. Back then, I didn't have a clue.

In any event, whatever it was that he thought or saw in his own mind seemed to give him the permission he needed to exercise and exorcise his anger and damage on me - for my firm and clear denials to such unreasonable and untrue accusations, and the fact that I *dared* to argue with him all must mean that I *was* hiding something from him. You know, it wasn't till later that I came to understand what he had been doing, as I just couldn't get my head around why there would even *be* an argument. And one needs to see several occurrences to recognise a pattern. I was so involved in the emotion and confusion of the event I couldn't see the wood for the trees. With so many crises, shifts and changes in our life together, this realisation could only come to me a long time after the cessation of such shenanigans.

Any attempts to understand and to bear Jim's burdens did not resolve whatever was happening for him. The Back-lash would follow within a matter of days. Whatever depths we had shared, whatever we had sealed together, there would be disgruntled ripples. In a way it was as though all of his guilt and shame around sex had been dredged up and thrown on me, just like mud, and he just couldn't face either me, or the mud. Stuck as I was in my own approach to things, I sought mundane answers, unaware of how undercurrents related to sexual guilt or repression worked. I defaulted to the usual culprits of reasons such as: problems at work for Jim, me or the boys upsetting him, a meal not cooked to expectation, concern over finances etc. These had been far from the truth, indeed nothing to do with the truth.

No matter what I tried, how I looked at things, it rally was no wonder that I just couldn't seem to sort out how to fix this.

THE PERFECT WIFE

It was natural that after little Danny was born, more subtle changes were occurring in our family dynamics.

Naïve Hope

I sometimes feel that I am seriously outnumbered by males, a lone female in a sea of growing testosterone as the two older boys are entering their teens. I finally began to wake up to the fact that I am a mother, not to three children, but to *four*. It took me years to get that Jim was my very first 'child'.

Though still a strong Christian at this time, I have begun to wonder where 'God' is or was when I prayed for Him to save me from Jim's abuse, arguments, punishments and irrationalities. I was still looking for a miracle. I was yet to learn that the church dealt in false promises. One of the hymns we had often sung was; 'Expect a miracle'...

> 'Expect a miracle every day,
> Expect a miracle when you pray
> If you'll believe it God will find a way
> To provide a miracle for you each day.'

I used to truly believe this. I was still expecting a miracle.

Still stupidly seeking for the 'sin' within myself that had 'deserved' or attracted these punishments, my wounded sense of self-worth was not yet strong enough to reason that I did *not* deserve this treatment. Somewhere inside I knew that I didn't, but all I had was the Bible and my family teachings. But I was learning. A bit like Edison, who, it is said, failed for 1,000 attempts to invent the light bulb. I was still in the 'failing' stream. However, these attempts and searches eventually led me toward the answers to my inner questions.

Meanwhile, I continued to read and re-read the Bible, particularly Psalms and Proverbs 31, the chapter about the 'virtuous woman', whose 'price was far above rubies', and who 'took care of her household'. Thus continued my attempts by being the only one involved in the marriage who is doing the right thing. I still followed the Christian precepts of the model of a virtuous wife; rising early to take care of everyone, being wise with the family money, clothing all the family with the best that I could afford or manage. And let me add, doing so blindly, and without demanding a virtuous husband. I *still* sought to emulate this perfect and godly woman so described in the good book.

My attempts to be this perfect woman were shown time and again, particularly when we had been living in the new Altona hostel accommodation. I had purchased a knitting machine from work (and at cost) from the Japanese import company. Instead of my usual slower hand knitting, I now sped things up, and using every spare waking moment actually turned out over thirty jumpers and cardigans for Jim and the boys and myself for that year *alone*. I would sit up at night, after the evening chores, and again after putting the two boys to bed, knitting row upon row, garment upon garment. What I could not yet afford, I would make. Though it cost a little to purchase the wool, I had cut down on normal costs by not purchasing ready-made garments. My willingness to sacrifice and save for my family did give me some small sense of worth at that time. But what a way to do it!

However, there was one occasion that it backfired... In a major way. I am still wearing egg on my face to this day. We had moved out of the Altona hostel and into the Fitzroy flats – it is the early seventies, when flares and colour are all the rage. And my two older boys, now fully grown men, still remember to this day, and still recall and relate the embarrassment they felt when they were both kitted out in matching purple and white marl knitted jumpers teamed with... yes, you've guessed it ... bright purple flares.

Whoops! Colour co-ordinated - yes. Fashionable colours – yes. Young boys colour, young boys comfort – well, actually, No!

Fortunately, church was where their outfits had the most exposure, and not school or the playground, and church was usually in the city at this stage, with only a handful of other children to laugh and make fun of them. But when these garments were no longer their Sunday-Best clothes and they eventually did have to wear them to school, they came home with unrepairable holes in the knees very shortly afterward. Deliberate? Who can say? Who could blame them?' Not I. Not now. Oh dear! Well, all I can say is that I did my best with what I had...

Eventually they may forgive me. Hopefully. When they have made similar mistakes with their own children. Or they eventually suffer from memory loss. Do I have a red face? Ah well, nobody's perfect... Not all good intentions work out for the best, I learned. Gotta have some funny and embarrassing memories, hey?

On with my story...

BACK TO WORK

Danny is now well over one year old, and we are feeling the pinch financially. Jim's wages is not enough for us to manage, and more money is required in the family coffer so it is time for me to go back to work again. I apply for various positions that are closer to home so that I don't waste a lot of time on travel, especially as the two older boys are all at the new school. I don't like the idea of them being 'latch-key' kids like I used to be, so work close to home is good. I am lucky enough, or just smart and qualified enough to land a job in Altona nearby.

I start work at TOW Chemicals in 1976. I little knew it then, but this was to be the beginning of my independence. I am about to be exposed to many things, some good, some interesting, some enlightening, some bad. From these events would come major change. Things cannot keep going on the same way continually – life is a process of changes and changing, though some things, some ideas, some ways of being that we hold onto may go through a process of evolution and emerge stronger, brighter, wiser, better – mostly. Hopefully.

The days of plenty whilst Jim was working on the gas conversions are over, and things are very lean. I eventually stayed at TOW for about five years, though it felt much longer. It is a large international enterprise with many of the staff having young families, too. Within this first year, through exposure to a variety of types of people, new ways of thinking, new ideas etc I began to see how others live, and over time I do some thinking and growing myself. I see now that this scares Jim, for I was bringing new ideas home with me. This started a chain reaction, though initially neither of us would see this coming.

I am now in my thirties, and naturally have grown more prone to independent thinking and observation. I had begun to watch, examine and challenge things, though mainly quietly and within. I am becoming increasingly aware that our lives have been and still are very insular and protected for I am now coming up against very different mindsets in the workplace, some with quite differing ways of living and beliefs. TOW is a large chemical company and not such a small 'family' company as I had previously been accustomed to. Big organisations work differently to smaller ones and there are more politics, cliques and secrets. Besides learning new systems and advancing on a career level, I am now also exposed to other (and sometimes better) ways of doing things, such as hearing of how other couples and families resolve problems and of how they spent their weekends, and so I began to ask Jim for us to go on trips, visit the nearby YouYangs hills and the seaside, and instead of taking home-made sandwiches, to actually splurge and *buy* cakes and teas or coffees for the boys and ourselves. We begin to enjoy these treats and family outings.

This also helps to make the difficult times of his drinking more bearable.

Jim is still required to work shifts as a security guard. The precision required for both of us being in a certain place at a certain time to ensure that the children were safe and looked after was imperative. There is not much room for lateness or relaxation. Besides this, Jim is well suited to security work, as he was a naturally suspicious guy. Problem is, as you may have guessed by now, that he becomes even more chronically suspicious of me and anyone coming in contact with me. It doesn't get better. In fact, it gets worse.

Jim is now even *more* paranoid about other people and about cars parked at the end of our street, about 'wrong number' phone calls, or those calls where there is silence and no answer. He becomes suspicious about any noises on the line, talking about phone 'tapping'. I am interrogated if the phone rings and no one answers at the other end. I am interrogated if he thinks that he hears 'heavy breathing' on the other end of the phone. I am questioned as to whether someone is checking whether Jim is home or not, and then accused of having a boyfriend who is checking to see whether Jim is in. What?

Naïve Hope

'Who is it? Who are you hiding from me? Who is it waiting for me to leave for work, eh?' he rages. He even goes out and checks out any cars if the dark is enough to hide him. In his mind, it is my 'lover' waiting for Jim to leave, or who hasn't gotten away quickly enough now that Jim was home. Or some other such devious mind-fuck story he had concocted. It was the same when the phone rang and there was no answer at the other end after Jim's initial 'Hello'. An innocent 'wrong number' or misdial does not exist in Jim's vocabulary. The accusation aimed at me claims that the person on the phone is checking to see if Jim has left for work yet before coming round to see me. I ask you! It would be laughable if it hadn't been so deadly serious and scary.

Nuts stuff! But obviously so very real to him.

Throughout the marriage, Jim has continually accused me of infidelity, of having affairs, of being unfaithful, even of doing so in my mind. *Despite* my absolute innocence. Then, after our move to Australia, drink has been added, and together with him working shifts, several factors are now fostering (and festering) his further irrational and mythical suspicions.

No doubt about it, things are increasingly growing worse the longer we are married.

I think I am finally getting the hidden message. Not content with 'You've made your bed...', I now recognise that 'It's a lumpy bed! You are on your own, kiddo.'

The answer to all of this; To forgive him, of course. Do your wifely duty and just keep on *lurving*...

Hah! For this is exactly what I am trying to do. But is it doing any good?

Things now took on a murkier turn. Something else that I don't see coming.

1978

~ Sleepless In Werribee ~ The Inquisition ~ Blackout

SLEEPLESS IN WERRIBEE

Because had been born ten years after the middle child Ben, I had forgotten so much about nursing a small baby and so I had to relearn a few things - again. I had also had to recover from a torn perineum – again - as the nurse who aided the birth in hospital had also been not working for ten years. I was lucky enough to have her at the birth I *don't* think – she forgot to turn the baby's body and consequently I was ripped again unnecessarily. But at least this time I had an injection (ouch) to ease the pain of the stitches required. Again.

But as all women know, after the birth, the pain of it all fades very quickly. And this seemed to be a special time in our lives, as this little boy was so welcomed by Jim that it felt like he had matured in some way. It seemed that he was more fully prepared to be a father than he had been before. And maybe a husband too...? And little Danny was a good child to be around.

Along with the delight of this new little boy, who was indeed welcomed by everyone in the family, came the usual stresses of newborns. Lack of sleep, initial cracked nipples, extra work, nappies etc etc. However, the other two boys enjoyed having a little one around that looked up to them and that they could play with.

And there was much love for a short period of time.

Naturally, over the course of the next three years of Danny's life, I was quite exhausted from lack of sleep. This was because little Danny was in the habit of not sleeping straight through the night. He had developed a pattern of waking up several times during the course of each night. This became so consistent, and affected me to some kind of distraction - Jim had initially helped with a few of the night feeds early on, then after just a couple of months he had simply refused to attend to Danny when he woke up. 'I'm not doing it any more. It's your job, you're the mother!'

Naïve Hope

I guess both Jim and I were a bit worn out by it all, and Jim sometimes suffered broken nights, though he did eventually learn to sleep through most of it. Night care, then, was left entirely to me.

Along with this was the now re-emerging problem of night-time interrogations. I had been given a reprieve from the wild actions from Jim during the newness of this new baby and the natural love injection it brings, but this was not to last. Little Danny could not settle in the night, even after night feeds stopped, and this was to continue for over three years...

I was working during the days and attending to broken nights continually. Alongside this were the dramas of when I would be woken by Jim at his whim, and then also woken by little Daniel who needed attention. Each night presented unbroken sleep through some cause or another. Though I didn't yet know it, I was coming to the end of my tether, coping with family, work, interrogations, expectations, and all the time keeping my cool and not daring to get snappish or angry – *just in case...* I guess the rest of that thought would be; *just in case Jim got worse.* I wasn't allowed to, you see. Get snappish or angry. This could trigger Jim, so I was the one to keep things even, to settle and pacify things. I learned to panic if things weren't going the right way for fear of retribution, and so I guess I was pretty much on guard to be the strong and coping one most of the time.

Danny is now over three years old and still waking up every few hours. We are both working full time and I feel at my wits end.

Medical help didn't solve our sleep problem. I was now desperate for some answers to this dilemma. Doctors couldn't unravel this sleeping issue for Danny, so I made further enquiries and heard that the Tweddle Children's Hospital that might be able to help with this problem. This children's hospital had facilities for mothers sleeping over in the next room to the child which meant that they could be close by whilst the staff attended and observed sleeping behaviours etc and so this seemed like the best solution. We were still with Medibank Private Health Insurance as a precaution with our three children, so our health insurance would cover most of the cost. And so Jim and I took Danny to Tweddle Baby Hospital when he was age three for tests and observation.

I stayed with him for a whole week. Every night he slept there.

And every night he slept right through! For a whole week. Right through each night!

The staff couldn't find *anything* wrong with him. This was not what I had been expecting. Danny seemed to be ok, and as the result was that he slept through the nights without any problem, we had no recourse but to take him home again and see if this new pattern continued.

And of course, as soon as we were home again and he was settled in his own bed, he woke up again during the night! Every night. Again.

At the time I didn't understand it. Only later did I see it.

The problem was not Danny, but the home.

Right then I had no more answers and just put up with what was happening. For we had explored every option available to us at that time. When I phoned Tweddle to tell them what was happening, all the staff could suggest was that 'eventually he will grow out of it'.

It took another six months for Danny to 'grow out of it' and eventually to settle right through the night.

When I noticed that for a whole week he had slept through, I felt like celebrating.

And years later I came to understand that Jim's night shift work and Jim's habits of abusing and interrogating me after his shifts during pregnancy and early childhood had some major part to play in Danny's feeling safe enough to sleep during the night.

And I feel sure that the stresses and fears experienced I had even before Danny was born, together with these early childhood experiences, all affected and continue to affect his nervous system. These are things that negatively impact on a Being, on a heart and mind, even without any memories that can be recalled easily – they simply get kind of programmed into one's body consciousness, or mixed up in the nervous system. These causes to disharmony within the Being of a person need recognition, care, dedication and nutritional and herbal support to reduce or to clear. I hope one day that there are better answers for this type of abuse and buried trauma on the senses and the nervous and energetic systems in the body. Many years later I took to Chinese Herbs and Traditional Chinese Medicine as these gave some help other than prescriptions.

I also learned a little about Reflexes as well as the effect of shock on the nervous system and psyche. Not yet recognising the effect of long buried shock on my own system, nor of the effect of trauma and fear on an unborn child, we all did the best we could to get through it, though there was a cost later in life for me until I had processed and released these effects. One hopes that any child caught this way can address it successfully in later life. Were my children to do this? There was no answer to this at the time, as there wasn't even a question about it.

However, what a relief now that we were getting more sleep. This was a huge help for me as well as for the family, particularly little Danny. As well as for Jim, for I am sure it wouldn't have helped him the odd times that he was disturbed too. I was now looking forward to getting better rest whenever I had the chance to sleep through the nights that Jim was out working, and when I knew that I would be leaving for work not long after he got home.

I began to think again – I think.

The Inquisition

Despite the minor success of finally getting more sleep, it appeared to me that overall things had not simply reverted, they were in fact deteriorating rather quickly. As alcohol consumption increased, erratic and inexcusable behaviour levels rose. And as the rosy love of a new toddler faded, when I looked at what was happening, I realised that increasingly and relentlessly since we had moved to the new house in Werribee, Jim had increased his accusations and tension around imagined affairs and intimacies that I hadn't committed, hadn't dreamed of committing and I was far too terrified to *consider* committing nor had intended ever to do so.

He continued to drink and to increase his drinking. He became more threatening behind closed doors.

For years he had no problem in showing his broodiness and moodiness. If we had been out for a trip and he fell into one of his moods, he would threaten me in the car. Now he took to showing me just how much we were all at risk – we were all at his mercy, and this time it was with *three* children in the car with us. Again, driving over the Westgate Bridge, he wiggled the steering wheel to swerve it from the lane we were in and toward the edges of the flimsy fencing along the top of the bridge. It was quite clear what his message was, even without his clenched teeth and leering voice. It got to be scary going out with him if one wasn't sure exactly what his mood was for the day...

As if this was not bad enough, was not understandable, was confusing, further events that really did my head in were still to follow.

Restrospection indicated that Jim too was under a lot of stress. But taking it out on me was not the answer. Or was it? Was *I* the stress?

It eventually gets so that when he is working on night security shift, I try to anticipate his return and wake ahead of him so I can at least be sitting up in bed should he burst in on me like this. But I don't always manage this. Sometimes, even in these foul tempers, he has actually left for work in a good mood. Now I can no longer match his mood when leaving home to when he arrives home. My heart begins thumping the moment I hear his car in the driveway; I am on alert. The moment I hear his key in the lock, I am praying.

At first it didn't make any sort of sense. I am doing nothing different, just taking care of domestic business and working hard and conscientiously. But I think I was also coming into my peak, my prime period. I am now looking more attractive, I am gaining more confidence at work. I am learning about how others at work did things. I am also getting a bit smarter about life. But being around men at work is causing a problem for Jim; accusations of cheating, teasing and unfaithfulness are increasing... I have to *entreat* Jim to believe me and my fidelity. I am increasingly imploring him to accept my faithfulness. No matter what I say, however, it's like there is something made up in his own mind that I am already guilty of that he cannot, or will not, be persuaded from. Like a terrier, he worries and tugs and worries at his own niggling idea, playing it all out on me.

In order to navigate through our life right now, and to get the things done that need to be done, and in order not to stir the mad-dog I am living with, I have to spend a lot of thought on placating Jim. I try to dance ahead of his moves. Though I think he does a hip-hop step I am not familiar with. Life is now a balancing act as to how much I dare be proud of about work – domestic and professional - and how much I can dare complain about. The fact that we need my money to manage financially helps to keep me working at TOW, and for Jim (graciously-not) to allow it.

When we lived in the flats, part of my domestic duty was to ensure that the place is spotless before I go to bed at night and that due preparations have been made for the following day – *Never put off till tomorrow what you can do today, happy happy hurrah!* or I would be punished for not doing as a wife should. Now we have three children and even though Jim helps on occasion, I still have to manage things more efficiently. Even though his stringent expectations had relaxed to some small degree by now, I still have to ensure that the place was reasonably tidy and clean before I could lay my head down, or engage in marital duties. And now with this emergence of his further irrational suspicions, it became more imperative that I do so. Or he would look for reasons as to why.

So before going to bed I regularly ensure the place is clean and preparations for the following day have been attended to as much as possible in order not to provide any obvious excuse to wake me up for Not Attending To My Duties. When he is at home, I will still try to lie motionless in bed and pretend I am asleep and pretend to ignore any banging about that he does. If I keep quiet and don't Provoke him, I will have a better chance of things being okay. Right? But we have already established that this wasn't always so. One lives in hope, and it is a game of daring to be awake when he comes in and thereby inviting his unwanted attentions, or of attempting, futilely or otherwise, to avoid his interest. It's all a fifty-fifty chance. Damned if I do, damned if I don't, kind of thing.

If his mood was off, for ANY reason, then I would cop it. And with the possibility of an entrance guaranteed to scare me, he continues to menace and threaten me, and to dominate me and interrogate me. And, of course, to refuse to believe anything I say to him in my defence.

I think the nights he leaves me alone, he is just too darned tired to say or do anything. For which I am truly thankful, Amen.

What a bullying bastard, hey? But inside him, what a scared little man he must be! What is it that makes a man mistreat his wife like this, especially when she has done absolutely nothing wrong? Of course, it took me many years to recognise that he was projecting his own guilts, his own inner demons, shames, fears and inadequacies and shortcomings onto me.

He must have been pretty scared of me in some way to have to treat me like this... I had no idea what it was; all I knew was that *I* was scared.

Life feels like I am living in enforced isolation – there seems to be little fun in my life, only the sort that comes with enjoying one's children when possible, or of a job well done. Normal life appears fraught with fear, and I work my way through it on a daily basis.

I was so used to this treatment, so used to having to defend myself, so scared of incurring his wrath, that as I write and admit to this sort of insidious treatment of myself, I am amazed that throughout all of this I had never been introduced to any other way of averting this kind of behaviour. Yes, I realise that it is obvious by now that this man wouldn't necessarily have stood for my rebellion anyway, but it just didn't occur to me that there were other ways of dealing with it. I don't think I am an unintelligent person, but some part of me was certainly duped and stupid.

There is no way it would or could happen to me now. My nerves would not stand for it. I would not stand for it. My conscience would not stand for it. He would be out the door in a flash. 'Here's your hat. What's your hurry? Don't slam the door on your way out.'

Naïve Hope

BLACKOUT

There has to be a price to pay for being on one's toes continually. There has to be a time when the mind just cannot take it any more, and steps out of the room for a 'smoko'.

That time did come for me, just for a short time, but it came. Though I didn't recognise what it really was about at the time. But then, that is nothing new for me, is it?

Working at TOW had introduced me to a whole new world. Maybe any subtle changes in my outlook and the new ways I was beginning to think were because I was in my thirties and naturally moving into my prime, not that I would know that then. It was therefore natural that some aspects of my life, body and thinking were becoming more mature. Maybe the experiences I was subjected to at home had switched something on in my brain, or conversely, switched something off... In any event, I was clearly beginning to question things. Of course, I had to do a lot of this mostly inwardly. And I think some of this thought-processing was happening even at below my conscious awareness level.

I was now spending most of my daytime hours working in a quite large organization, with a variety of personalities, and in a way I was also being exposed to how a lot of other people lived their lives. And some of these were good and kind people - *without* them having to be 'Born-Again's'. I was also seeing how other families spent their leisure time. Out of, and away from, the direct influence of blinkered Christian parents or a controlling church and their ways of doing things, I was able to observe how happy and productive and moral and kind others could be, and who were living their life and doing things in a very different way to us.

And quite possibly I was also subconsciously recognizing in some hidden way that no other woman I knew was getting at home what I was. Despite what was happening privately, I was doing well at work, and being given more responsibility. Working hard and earning recognition because I was reasonably smart with work duties and challenges, there was also a lot to do domestically. On top of these demands, the sort of unjustified and unnecessary stress I was experiencing through Jim was also taking its toll. For I was on the edge of a nervous breakdown and didn't know it. Not then.

Another flag arises, one that in hindsight was a clear indication of the stress that my life had become and part of the cost of all of the upheavals and issues I was attempting to deal with. For my brain now decided to take a holiday. Well, it was actually more like an anaesthetic... I was so rushed off my feet, that one day I have the weirdest experience. I think this was a sign to me, another sign, that I was heading for a nervous breakdown... or worse. Though I certainly didn't know just what it signalled at the time.

One day after our Tweddle Hospital stay with little Danny I am driving down the freeway, somewhere between Werribee and the city. We have only the one working car between us at that time, so our schedule requires careful managing. Oo accomplish using it for both of us to get to work, We have sorted out a system.

Suddenly I seem to 'wake up' in the car. It is as if I have just woken up and take notice of my surroundings. But...

I cannot remember what day it is, where I am, what time of day it is, where I am driving to, and where I have just come from, which way is North, which way is South, what I had for breakfast, anything. Just blank! Clean slate...

The only thing that I remember is that I have just turned off the freeway, though I don't know why I did that, as I am disoriented and no longer sure in what direction I was heading. Which freeway? *Dunno*. It is as though I have just mentally stirred and awakened and found myself sitting behind the steering wheel! Magic. Asleep in bed, then Voila! - in the car!

Where *am* I? Was I now driving along Kororoit Creek Road or Derrimut Road? To the city, back from the city? It looks kind of familiar, but I don't recognise it as such. I still don't quite have a grasp on things to say the least. I simply could *not* remember what I had done to get there, nor of why I found myself driving along this section of road. My mind races searching for what I had been doing and where the heck was I?

'*Where am I? Where am I meant to be going? Is it morning or afternoon? Where have I just been?*' These, and other, thoughts are spinning round in my mind as I mentally scramble to find my bearings. I do not recognize what section of the road I am on, nor

Naïve Hope

which way I am going, and as I can see that there is no parking allowed along most of this section of highway I just have to keep going till I *do* recognize something or I can pull over. All of the internal reference maps in my brain seemed jumbled up, and I cannot pin down where I am. *What am I doing here? Think! Remember!* Even my eyes have difficulty focusing...

Okay, Marni, let's slow down and think about this. Where have you been? I don't know! *Okay... What time is it?* I don't know, my watch has stopped working and I haven't gotten it fixed yet. No clock in the car, so that's no help. *Okay, do you recognise any part of the road you are driving along?* It looks a bit familiar, but Nope! *What day is it?* I don't know! *Which way are you heading, to the city or away from it?* I think I am heading away from the city, but I am not a hundred percent sure. *Okay, let's go with that. Are you going to work or to the crèche with Danny?* I look at my rear vision mirror, and do not see Danny in the back seat in his high riser safety seat... *Where is Danny?* Where is he? *I don't remember dropping him off at crèche, I don't remember him in the car at all...* My mind is a total blank! I feel as if I have been hit in the head with a mallet and I *cannot think*, let alone think *straight*. By now I have found a safe place to pull over by the side of the road, and I check the back seat again, properly. *No, he is* not *in the car.* I now really have to think logically about this. What do I remember doing? Well, actually it is as if I have only just gotten out of bed and put my head on. Yes, that is exactly how it feels.

Okay, let's start from the beginning. Let's assume it's a weekday, for there is no other reason that you would be driving along all by yourself, is there? No. For if it's a weekend, Jim usually drives. *Good! That's good. Alright then, let's go through the possibilities. What do you do when you first get up in the morning?* Get the kids ready for school, and take them to the minders till school time. Then I go with Jim to the city in the car with little Danny, so that I can then use the car to continue to crèche to drop him off and then on to my job. Then I sometimes use the car at lunchtime to pay bills at the Post Office. At the end of the day, I collect Danny from crèche and drive on to the city to pick up Jim so he can drive us home. *It looks like you are nowhere near the Post Office so we'll discount that for the moment. Does it feel like the beginning of the*

331

day, or the end of the day? I don't know. *Probably the beginning of the day, my clothes feel fresher than the end of the day. Okay. Now if little Danny isn't with you in the car, and you are heading away from the city, then you have probably dropped him off. Yes?* Possibly. *Then what can you do to check this out? Are you near the crèche?*

I start the car again and drive on a little further until I come to a road sign, and again park the car. I am on Grieve Parade, just past Dohertys Road, but I am still so confused, for in some way it doesn't look that familiar to me, even though I must have driven down it hundreds of times. So I take out my map book and check out where I am, based on the nearest road sign to me. This settles me to a degree, as I recognise that I am between the crèche and work. I *must* be on my way to work, but I am *still* not convinced, for I don't remember anything that day until a few minutes ago. If it was the end of the day, I would have Danny in the back seat. ...I think...

Come on Marni. Think!

It takes me several minutes to orient myself again to where I was. Gradually I recognize the area and then the road. But I still wasn't sure if it was morning or evening. If it was evening, where was I going to? If it was morning, then *where* was little Daniel?

'What have I done with him? Where is my son?' I still couldn't remember. I am beginning to panic. I am still quite disoriented, and Logic had to somehow be found, brushed off, have its face wiped and be brought into this – so I go through it again;

'Ok. *Then where have I just been? Have I been with Jim to the city centre, to drop him off at his work at The Page Newspaper in the city? Am I now taking Daniel to kindergarten crèche before work?*' But if so, then; '**Where IS he?**' I am now panicking. The struggle with trying to get my brain to work is scaring me, and shaking my head isn't working either. Even though I can now begin to see where I possibly *could* be according to the road map, I can *not* fathom where the crèche now was in relationship to me and my current position. Grrr!

Naïve Hope

I am usually excellent at map reading, yet it takes me a full *five minutes* of struggle with the map book to finally realize that I must have already gone passed it. I am stopped by the side of the road to again question which way I was facing, so now I check through everything again, for I still can't see little Danny in the kiddies back seat of the car when I look in my rear vision window. A mother should *know* where she has put her child, surely? I was beginning to fear that something had happened to him. Quite unreasonable, but reason wasn't in the car with me right then. Let's try again... Had I passed the centre? Must have. Do I have time to go back to the centre to see if Daniel was there? *No, not if its morning, for you'll be late for work. And won't it look silly if he is there?* But it must be; for why would I be driving along here at this time of night? *But you don't know that it's not evening, do you?*

Why don't you head on to work and check for other staff cars in the carpark. If you recognise any of them, you will know that it is a work day and that you are on your way there. If they are there, go into work and get on the phone. You can call the crèche as soon as you get in to see if Danny is ok, and make up some excuse to check that he has everything that he needs. You'll think of something to say. Good idea. This way, if I don't recognise any cars at work, I can head back to the crèche to check if things are different to what we have just sorted. *Good, then off you go!*

I found my way to work. I looked for other staff cars. There were. I went in.

Confusion began to clear after I phoned the child care centre to 'see if little Danny has settled in alright this morning' – he had; all was okay again. Phew! I could gather myself together again, and eventually I settled down to work again. Panic over! But this had given me quite a turn and a part of my mind filed this away. What was all that about? This was a major prod to let me know that all was not right – but I didn't know what to *do* with this. I wondered what the heck was going on with me. This was not like me. This was *not* me! I made a mental note to see a doctor if this happened to me ever again. It didn't! Fortunately!

This episode demonstrated the effect of the pressures one can be under when they don't take time to themselves, and of how close to a nervous breakdown I was. In fact, I guess I was suffering from a kind of nervous debility, all things considered. Along with the other things that were taking place at home, I almost thought I was losing my mind.

It wasn't till many years later that I realized that in all those years after I became a Christian and got married, in all those years of caring and mothering, I *never* took time out for myself, to nurture myself, time just for me... Christian wives (supposedly, or so we were told) didn't go in for self-indulgence, for personal fun, for 'fashion', nor for any other type of Selfish Thing as her main concern was her family – and I had made it my life's mission to be this ridiculously perfect martyring woman of Proverbs 31. Spending time doing Non-Productive Things had always been a No-No for me. And the unrelenting nature of Jim's compulsive suspicion was certainly affecting me detrimentally. Ridiculous as it all may seem to me now, this *was* my reality.

During my lunchtimes at work, I never just sat and read a paper or magazine. No time. I would grab a quick sandwich, often eating on the run, whilst I went to the local shopping centre close to work to go to the bank and post office to pay bills, or picked up groceries that we needed for dinner that night, or get school items for the other boys, or something Jim had asked me to get, or... or... always on the go rush, rush, rushing... though I must confess to occasionally staying at work for the very rare birthday celebration for someone in my office, or to have the odd lunch in the company canteen if I had run out of stuff at home to make my own sandwiches. Over time this eventuated into allowing myself to be pressured to the odd pub lunch for someone's birthday cake celebration or for a group invitation by the boss. All of which were always closely scrutinized by my husband.

How counter-productive this all was.

One thing I later realized about all of this, and I sometimes still need to remind myself today – is that I didn't have much 'fun' in my life – never had, not even as a child. But later in life when I had finally woken up to this anomaly, I allowed myself time to change this and to *begin* to learn how to enjoy myself, however simple and

Naïve Hope

limited it may be. And I can say I have had some measure of success. Though it still needs work!

After experiencing this brain-dead-moment that morning on my way to work, and the scare it gave me, I watched and waited for another such episode. Fortunately I was spared this and things fell pretty much back into the usual pattern again quickly. Years later I understood the pressures I had been under.

After that scary event, whenever I had little Danny in the car with me, I always kept up a bit of a conversation with him. I needed to know that he was safe on the back seat, and with me.

1980 FINAL STRAWS

*~ Violence ~ Lover, Not a Fighter ~ Fix It Yourself
~ Not About The Money, Money, Money ~ Broken Vows
~ The Telling Dream ~ To Lie or Not To Lie?
~ Women's Refuge ~ Resigned ~ Contracts ~ Unstable Jim
~ Go Ahead; Shoot! ~ Counting the Cost ~ Half Hour Tryst Twist
~ Games People Play ~ Critical Mass ~ 'No. No. No.' ~ Blinkers Off!
~ The Tide Turns ~ 'You Will Pay' ~ End Time; Counsellor
~ Three Times Strike ~ Last Christmas ~ Action Time*

VIOLENCE

Could things be any worse?

Funny how some people will stay in a relationship because it's not yet bad enough to force them to leave. I have had people say to me that their relationship was okay simply because they somehow manage to put up with abominable behaviour. This was me at that time, this is what I did, even though I wouldn't have recognised it, let alone willingly admit it. I have since totally shifted on my acceptance of this idea. Had to, really. Now, I would rather manage and strive alone than have things made easier materially by living with a bastard. What's the point? I knew that my marriage was a struggle, but I still somehow had this idea that things *might* change, and that if I did the right thing, then things would come good. Oh fool! Dream on. Right before my eyes, things were getting worse - and harder.

I was having to forgive more. Well, I was now *almost* forgiving; not quite fully, just enough to put it aside and get on with things, but to begin to keep a tally of misdemeanours made by Jim against me. I was also getting more fed up with it all. I hadn't yet reached the point of critical mass, but things are building as humiliation is piled on top of humiliation. The huge question of how to manage on my own is not yet ready to be addressed by me, for I thought I knew the value of having a father for my children rather than *not* having one. That's how much I knew, hey?

Naïve Hope

The fact that I was still so busy and occupied in looking after everyone and everything (or at least most things it seems), also kept me so fully engaged that I had little time for real and full reviews of my life and my options. At this point. But as you can see, things have been heading in a downward curve. And those same things are mounting up at the back of my mind, and piling up in the corner of my heart. My prayers do not seem to be accomplishing anything. No matter how hard I pray, *nothing* is improving.

Again, I ask, 'Could things get any worse?' Yes, of course they can. And they do.

For one of our few occasional 'date' nights, we went to the movies and watched 'Kramer vs Kramer'. Meryl Streep and short Dustin Hoffman were the Kramers, and it was about the wife upping and leaving because she couldn't cope. A great movie, a lousy aftermath. Somehow this was translated by Jim as a forecast of me leaving him. Yet again. Can this man not separate fantasy from reality? Can he not *get* that I have been with him for nearly eighteen years, and if I was leaving I would have left by now?

Meanwhile, Jim's drinking is becoming more and more a time for increasing irresponsibility, angry outbursts and violence. His moods, which have previously included some odd periods of charm, have now progressed from mainly moody and sullen towards me, to the gathering of *permanent* storm clouds, followed by further hail and rains of darkness as he increasingly becomes more critical, derogatory and accusatory, with intermittent showers of extreme downright rage. Even little Dustin Hoffman didn't behave like this to drive Meryl out of the home! These rain-bursts and outbursts are now beginning to show when the children are up and awake, rather than Jim waiting to intimidate and bully me when they are asleep in bed. Sometimes even the furniture now takes some of the battering.

We now progress to the real meat in all this, the unavoidable proof of this man's madness and insanity. Interrogation about phone calls and parked cars is no longer enough. Waking me in the night is not enough. He becomes more deliberate in his interrogation procedures.

He hasn't as yet hit me in front of the children, so in my deluded mind, I figure that what they don't see can't hurt them. I had absolutely *no* idea that kids *do* in fact see. They see with their emotions, they see with their hearts. Though we say to them that nothing is wrong, they *know* on some level when something *is* wrong. And as I learned in my own childhood that when what I felt was happening was denied by my parents, the very ones that I trusted for my life, I had started to doubt what I had felt, to doubt myself, to doubt my own intuition. I allowed their opinion or rather, their false cover up, to become a truth. I stifled a part of my own knowing. And this is precisely a definite element of what had led me down this path with this man. And what had kept me here.

A part of me *must* have known what he was like, but had ignored it, denied it, had let it be overridden, had doubted it, had not believed it. And here I was doing exactly the same thing to my *own* children. And *not knowing* that I am doing it! God forgive me! When will I wake up from this delusion, this illusion?

There are now no longer any apologies after his tirades, and not even any related conversation about it, let alone discussion. Most of his explosions appear to be conveniently forgotten, as if they hadn't happened. I was to learn this is a usual and convenient memory issue for things done whilst under the influence of alcohol.

We are still both working hard, with lots of travel to and from work and crèche, and school extracurricular activities. Any attempts at discussing the improvement of our communication and situation, of my suggestions to create positive change are now simply generally rejected outright, and only those things directly related to the running of the house and immediate domestic problems, or to my accounting of my movements are tolerated. We no longer attend church. Mainly because of his shift work. So his story goes. And I am no longer inclined to push for attendance, either. We still read the Bible, though usually separately. Danny's nursery room has become our Prayer Room, and he sleeps in the bedroom next to the big boys at the other end of the house. The Prayer Room becomes our personal church, both of us taking it in turns to pray on our own whilst the other looks after and monitors the noise level of the children.

Naïve Hope

His current work means that he is required to do rotating shifts for about ten days each shift. These shifts alternated to ensure coverage for eight hours over a twenty-four hour period. Each shift lasted about ten days and he would cover, say, the day shift, then the following next ten days or so it would be the afternoon shift, and after that the evening shift. This latter shift meant that he knocked off from work at about three am in the morning.

As I said earlier, things could and do get worse. Now, when Jim comes home now in the early hours of the morning after finishing his night shift, he it's as if he is determined and set to terrify me. There is still the odd occasion where he was so tired that he almost literally falls into bed, and I thank my lucky stars. But this is more the exception now. Our bedroom is at the opposite end of the house from the boys, to allow for zoning and privacy. However, now it is a little *too* private. His previous interrogation techniques now are deliberately uglier. Is he just totally exhausted and on the edge of a nervous breakdown? Is he somehow drawing strength from my fear or something similar? Is he running from something within him? Who can say?

This erratic and unpredictable behaviour and these very successful attempts at intimidation are now becoming a habit of his. They seem to happen for no apparent reason, but then his conduct had always been somewhat inconsistent anyway.

Just imagine this; It is dark, either late at night or in the early hours of the morning, depending on which shift he has just finished. I am lying in bed.

The scene is set as Jim arrives home from work and comes to the bedroom not long after. Sometimes it is from the moment he has closed and locked the front door. He now bursts into the bedroom as though it is the middle of the day whilst at the same time turning on the bedroom light, and then he proceeds to deliberately lock the door. His next step is to jump directly onto the bed to ensure that I am awake. His launch is designed to land on top of me, with both his knees on my shoulders, pinning me down.

These are terrifying and disorienting experiences. Bleary-eyed, confused and alarmed I am immediately terrified for this is not just an annoying habit, a disregard and demand. This is now a form of torture.

If I have been silly enough to have been asleep before this treatment, I most certainly wake up shaking with frayed nerves at the sleep interruption. Previously, he would shake me awake or throw something on the bed to achieve the same end. But now it is a *deliberate* action, calculated to use as much of the element of surprise as possible. He succeeds!

After making sure that I am indeed now awake (how could I be anything but?) he begins his interrogation.

Jim is sitting astride me and on top of my chest, pinning my shoulders down with his knees. This prevents me from getting up, turning away, or indeed, of making any other avoidance move. Sometimes fists are raised to my face. Sometimes it is just his angry or sneering face that looks down at me. He literally has me at his mercy. Then with me in this very prone position, he begins to question and cross examine me as to whatever imaginary bee he had in his bonnet. Same old same old; who am I having an affair with, what happened at work, who did I flirt with today, where was I between the hours of blank to blank..., whose car was parked at the end of the street, and how long it had been there. And who I had spoken to that day, the names of every single guy in my office etc. And, again, to account for every minute of my time.

I am not only stunned by such a vivid unrealistic imagination, I am totally confused. I have no idea even now where this all comes from. I have *still* never considered having an affair, for I am too bloody cowered and frightened to even dare to let my thoughts go anywhere other than those of the programmed dutiful wife and super-woman.

Initially I protest at this outrageous behaviour, but then I pay for daring to question him, for standing up for him. So the pain teaches me not to. Get it over with, then he will settle. Huh! *Pigs might fly!* And then I also face further accusations that I have something to hide. So I eventually learn to be terrified; and learn it I did, as it gradually became ingrained into my brain and my nervous system, layer upon layer, for what defence did I have from this strong mulish man who I was yoked with?

Naïve Hope

You know the litany by now, yes, that same-old predictable same-old. He accuses me of having an affair, of playing-up with someone and other ridiculous activities. I was generally always scared, and on the defensive. I did not realise at the time that this was abusive and mental torture for it had snuck up so insidiously on me. I was too frightened, no actually I was terrified, and so was fully engaged in this alarm and survival pattern of having to continually defend myself – verbally, physically, emotionally and mentally. Ridiculously, all of this behaviour behind closed doors was kept reasonably quiet (if one dare use that word 'reasonably' in the context of these events) so as not to disturb or waken the children.

God, if he is like this now without me even thinking of having an affair, how would he be if I actually did have one? Well, frankly, I would simply be dead! So we don't even go there, do we? No!

I learned to stay awake until he was asleep. The whole process was deeply disturbing and dark...

Sure I didn't often get black eyes, and certainly had so far had no need for stitches. But as my broken ribs testified, what he did do didn't always have to be obvious – in this way I wasn't challenged to have to continually explain covert injuries to co-workers. Indeed, he bragged that he knew how to beat someone without anything showing externally. I can attest that this is true, though sometimes he did want to give me a visible black-eye for some warped reason as he seemed to like hitting or slapping my face. However, it seems I am now *always* scared of him, and of doing *anything* that might antagonise him. He was a physically powerful man, I knew that I didn't have a chance when he went for me.

Why the heck was I still living in the hope that this man would change and treat me properly? Am *I* nuts?

Did he not get that there are others ways than fear and threats to keep a woman faithful? Is *he* nuts? Easy to ask now, but back then, in the middle of it, it was a different story...

Lover, Not a Fighter

It's not that I am a scaredy cat. As a young girl I avoided fights of any sort, but I never ran from them. Even though soft and sensitive around children and animals, I was often known as a bit of a Tomboy for I loved to climb trees and join in games with the other boys and the mock fights. Especially when it was time to collect bonfire wood which we had nicknamed 'bongy-wood', for Guy Fawkes Bonfire Night each November. I would be picked for these teams often because I was considered a good collector and would try to account for myself by stopping the other friendly rival avenue gangs from taking our wood, but I was never pushing for trouble. For when things got too serious, I sought to solve any fights in other ways.

One day I am faced with a bullying girl in the local park playground. I had been charged with looking after sister Princess Joan, who never did what she was told anyway, and Lord Ian. Consequently one of Joan's actions escalated to the point that this girl now picked on *me* for defending her then challenged me to a physical fight. She had a gang of other girls and a couple of boys around her, and she was obviously their boss, their leader. She had bright red curly hair and her name was Veronica. I refused to fight for there was no reason for it, and anyway I was there to look after my brother and sister on the swings. But her bunch of cronies were now also egging her on and name calling me. Eventually she flew at me, attacking me by pulling my hair at the roots and holding my head in a vicious and painful grip.

It hurt like crazy but *no way* was I going to cry and ask her to stop. Somehow I painfully managed to manoeuvre myself and to grab her hair in a similar fashion, though I could do nothing about the neck hold. But it was enough. In response she applied more pressure on my hair, the pain excruciating. So I applied more on *hers*. Every time she upped the pull on me, I pulled extra hard on her. In the end she realised I was not going to give in, that I was prepared to go to the end with this. Despite my mild mannered appearance, I was not the push-over she had imagined. I was certainly going to give as good as I got! My neck was in a bad position and my face next to the gravel, but I was *not* going to give in.

So after she had tired of getting nothing but the same pain herself she demanded 'Stop pulling my hair,' *'No, you stop pulling my hair,'* 'No, you stop pulling my hair'. There was a no-win in this situation so eventually she made a deal to stop hair pulling if I would. I didn't just give in, I also made her promise, out loud so the others could hear, and she eventually agreed. Slowly, slowly we tested each other with slight releases until we were both free of each other. I was ready to re-engage at any time, only this time I would be ready and not be taken by surprise. When we were totally separate from each other, and my siblings were by my side, she looked at me with respect and admiration then turned to her friends and said out loud for everyone to hear 'This girl's a real good fighter. One of the best I've met.' Then she walked up to me and asked me if we could be friends with each other. I was so surprised. And so I said yes to that, for I felt that she was sincere. Funnily I never did see her again...

Of course, I had scratches and was bruised enough from the assault prior to the hair grabbing and I had a very sore neck and grazes from the park gravel, but I was so pleased with myself that someone else respected me for what I felt was my doing the right thing. But fighting doesn't really solve anything. I chose not to provoke or reciprocate with Jim not just because I was scared of getting hit, but because there was something else about him. I felt on some level that I would never be able to get away with retaliation or reciprocation. That there was some sort of lack in him somewhere, and I did come to believe that he could indeed hunt me down if he didn't 'win'.

I never sought fights. Not consciously. I had grown up with violence; it was such a common and familiar result of another's uncontrolled or misdirected anger. Though interestingly enough I often never even expected it. Despite watching out for it, it nearly always took me by surprise. At home I was often having to defend myself from my younger brother. Ian would pick fights with me and then he would get so mad with rage if I didn't do as he demanded that his face would turn bright red, then he would quite simply 'lose it' and flail at me wildly before he was taught (by dad) how to punch properly. Then I had to learn how to run fast and flee to my bedroom, locking the door by jamming it with dad's big wooden army chest pushed up against it; which I would then promptly sit on to give added weight to, until Ian had calmed down enough or got bored with waiting for me to come out. His punches were hard! Dad had taught him well!

I had accepted Jim's violence because I had had to. And because of the dependence of my children on me and my love and commitment for my family and for Jim. Between times of his violence, when he had appeared to show some sort of remorse and had come home with flowers or been kind and charming again for a while, I had chosen to see only the good things about him and the marriage – how else could I cope, what else was I going to do? I eventually had to learn that we can 'fall in love' (or 'chose to fall in love again') with someone by simply choosing to see *only* the Good Things about them (real or imagined) and to 'fall out of love' by choosing to see *only* the Bad Things (real or imagined) about them. I learned to allow myself to fall in love with what I could see of his good points, and his charm whenever it or they showed their face. After all, I often reminded myself (or fooled myself...), he really *wants* to love God, just like I thought I saw him do in the beginning. I still didn't see him as a Bad Person not for a very long time, and kept excusing him and his actions. That emotional play, that charisma and charm on me had kept me hooked in. But it was fast approaching its use-by-date.

Emotional bonding has been shown to take place with the perpetrators in cases of abduction and imprisonment. The Stockholm Syndrome describes it perfectly. So it is not surprising that our emotions get so mixed up like this, which can go some little way to explain such intricate dynamics of the human heart. And mind.

But now when I add up the sum total of his behaviour and contributions to the family and marriage, I see a very different picture. I now see that he was deliberately setting out to be and do just whatever he wanted, and did not stop to consider the consequences, nor make any real attempt to change himself or his behaviours. That his focus was on belittling or punishing me.

It had begun to crystallise for me after Daniel was born. My comparisons with how other families conducted their lives, even supposedly non-Christian families showed me that Jim's behaviour *was* bad and had also definitely escalated.

Naïve Hope

Actually, I was now able to see that this was indeed *Bad Behaviour*. Whereas I had previously seen it as *Temptation by the Devil* or a weakness that he needed help with – help from me – and that prayer would help. In fact, his 'Christian' behaviour was worse than anyone else that I knew of, as there was no other woman with as many black eyes or bruises as myself that I was aware of or heard any gossip about.

And I had now totally proved that *no amount of prayer* would ever help or change this man. *And it still hasn't to this day as far as I can tell.*

I was also getting a bit tired of waiting for 'God' to intervene – where was He when I needed Him most? Where was Jesus? Did He send someone along to rescue or even simply help me? Did He stop Jim in mid-action of abuse? Arrest Jim's conscience? No.

So where was He? Where is this 'Jesus Saves' when you need Him?

Someone one day commented that 'God doesn't care – He's out playing golf'. And I thought on this. Again I asked fervently for God's help – and of course, didn't get it – no amount of Blind Faith or Naïve Hope or God Belief brought any aid to me. God and Jesus were not in the building!

And then I heard the words – 'God helps those who help themselves.' Hallelujah!

'God helps those who help themselves.'

I saw Hope open one eye...

Now what could I do to help myself? To begin with I had to take my faith-blinders off, and stop this waiting-for-God-to-intervene, waiting for Jim-to-do-the-Right-Thing - I had to be open to see what was *actually* going on – what was *wrong* with the picture – how should things *really* be – what could *I* do to change things – what did I need to *stop* doing to change things – the emphasis now was on *me* watching to look to change things in a different way rather than on *Jim*; placating him or praying to God to avoid beatings!

But this was still a while to fully manifest – rather this was a *dawning* in my mind, heart and consciousness that I needed to take note of what was going on ... of how I wanted things to be ... and not to simply *accept* what *was*...

For the moment though, I am still mindfully occupied with the progress and development of the children and of their care and nurture and of my own work when I am not involved with Jim's mood management and interference. It is a work in progress.

Fix It Yourself

This beginning of awareness, this crack of light in my mind, this miniscule 'other'-disconnection from Jim and blind unquestioning obedience to him and church authority allowed me to become a more observant, though I wasn't fully *aware* of *becoming aware* at the time. It was like I was now totting up in my mind the things that I did to support and help the relationship and the running of the family, whilst at the same time noting just what it was that Jim was, or more importantly was *not*, doing to support and help. I was surprised with the data and results that had been in front of my eyes all along that I had not been able to see before.

Because I had not really looked! But now I was doing some bookkeeping, some balance and check-ing on many different levels of our life together.

I took care of most of the work around the house, the cooking etc was mainly my domain even though I was working full time. He might assist with the household grocery big-buy at the supermarket, but it depended in what else he found to do. Of course tending to his beer brewing and testing (tasting) the loving brew in the barrels took up some of his time, and those weekends when he wasn't working shift and we were around together were the times he 'relaxed' and read the papers, or pottered with the cars. To be fair though, he did spend some time ferrying the boys to their Little Athletics meets, though he made it clear he wasn't that fond of hanging around with other dads. And I suspect that depending on his mood, the boys might occasionally pay for it if they did not perform as well as they could to warrant Jim's efforts in this area.

Naïve Hope

Because of the running around that had to be done and his shift work, things had eventuated to our owning two cheap second-hand cars; we each needed independent transport. Our wages didn't yet run to two late models and we still had his second-hand Ford car. Jim had seen the new little run-about by Diahatsu. It had a two-stroke engine and made a really extraordinary noise, but it moved us around, was cheaper than many smaller models and was extremely economical. It had a laughable put-put sound that harkened close to a motor scooter. But you could get it to move if you knew how to change the gears or do a double-clutch with it.

So we put up with the 'squash' to fit us all in the car, and the 'put-put-put' noises, and got a demonstration vehicle a bit cheaper than a new one. Jim had earlier owned a motorbike, so it was possible he could do some self-maintenance on it, thus saving us some money. It was a handy little car, but it wasn't always reliable. After the novelty wore off it, it soon fell to me to use it, and Jim was usually pretty good at attending to any repairs so I could get to crèche and work. But things were shifting and changing in our relationship, and it began to show in this arena, too.

One Sunday he had spent a lot of time trying to fix it yet again. It was a warm day. I had attending to the weekend household chores and minding the children whilst he had been working. This time he had had enough. The car had stumped him, and he came in mid-afternoon, sweating and fed-up.

'I'm *not* doing any more work on that car anymore. You will have to fix it yourself, or find someone else to do it, or make other arrangements.' And he went off to have a shower and get back to his beer, and to leave me to sort out his statement and this mess. End of story. That was it.

I would get no more help from him.

The car wasn't working. And wasn't going to be fixed. Not by Jim anyway.

Was this a trick statement? Understandable though his frustration may have been, *I* certainly couldn't afford to fix it. I had no money of my own, all of our wages went into a joint account and most of it was always accounted for as we had a strict budget – we had to in order to manage. I didn't have money for extraneous things, so no hope of personal savings. Yes, I 'paid' the bills, but Jim was the 'boss' of the money.

So I had to work out what to do and how I would get to work in the morning. We had kind of made friends, insofar as Jim allowed any 'friends', with one of the older guys at TOW called Bernard, he lived a mile or so down the road, and had helped out once before when I had been in straits for a lift to work. So I found his number and phoned Bernard, and organized for a lift. A nice family man, he was very helpful, but not a push-over as he had his own family to look after. And I suspect that he was having a few problems with that himself. Things were arranged, and I got my promised lift. Jim's response was a 'Harrumph1' then no further comment when he was informed. Ok...!

On the way to work on the Monday morning I spoke to Bernard of my dilemma, because I really had to sort out this unreliable vehicle issue. I hadn't thought about it until he mentioned it, but he suggested that I look at getting a loan and buying a newer car for myself, a 'demonstration model'. We were members of the RACV (the local roadside assistance for motorists) and I could apply to them for a loan using our track record of membership with them and my working at TOW as a credit reference. *What a great idea.* It was worth a try! And I found out that I had just been given a raise at work. How amazing! Here is the answer. But let's check the figures first.

The budget checked out. And it would probably be cheaper than the cost of the repairs we had been forced to keep paying out on. Back home I ran it past Jim, but he was only half listening, whilst fully 'relaxing' in his spare time with his beloved beer. And I don't think he wanted to hear about it anyway. By all appearances he had lost interest in my transport situation, and couldn't seem to care less. So I went ahead with the idea and took action.

Within just a few days I had organized a loan for a second-hand car, and had seen and bought myself a demonstration model Datsun 200B in Sky Blue. I was thrilled! The payments would come directly from my wages, and my raise now made it affordable. I was so relieved that I had a good car. And it was so quiet!

Naïve Hope

The reaction from Jim was really interesting. I had kept him informed of what I was doing – no choice otherwise really – and all along he seemed only part interested. Even though he fully knew everything I was doing, every step I took, I think he didn't believe that I could or would do it. And probably he expected that I would be begging him again to work on the car. Or to be fair, quite possibly he really had had enough of car repairs and it was beyond him to keep trying to sort them out. Maybe he was really hoping I would remove the problem from his shoulders. Whatever. Anyway, by now I am over making excuses for him. The vehicle was not just for my work, but to ferry the children, so he had been just as responsible as I was to sort this out.

However, when I took the Daihatsu in as part-deposit, I think it was *then* that it started to sink in for him as well as for myself what I was actually doing. When I came home with the car, he walked around it slowly (and somewhat begrudgingly, though he tried to hide this) doing his 'tyre-kicking' by picking at it, but he couldn't really fault it. I really do think he had trouble fully realising what I had done. But whatever his real reaction and his distancing on all of this, the car was comfortable, sound, powerful in comparison to what I had been driving, reliable and it looked good.

I was so happy about it. I had gotten myself a real bargain. And more!

This was a first and a very real step for me toward self-autonomy and independence, though I didn't yet know it. Financially we were still attached-at-the-hip but as he had told me *himself* to '*make other arrangements*' he couldn't very well go back on his word, could he? Even though he was relieved from having to work on the car anymore, it was obvious that for some reason he wasn't really as happy for me as he had tried to make out that he was. I think that underneath his bravado and face that he was very surprised. And scared. And jealous. But on some level, I no longer cared; couldn't afford to. I had a job and so the means to pay for it, and it was in my name, and I now had a reliable vehicle, rather than relying on his mood for the upkeep repairs.

After a year of regular payments, I was also later offered a Credit Card by the RACV, which I took them up on. Wow! I now had my own credit card, though I wasn't sure what I would use it for, probably if there was a housekeeping shortfall and we were waiting on wages to come in to cover unexpected emergencies. Whatever the case, it was in my name and my name alone. But at the time Jim didn't really get this.

In a short period of time, major changes had occurred in the balance of power in our house, for me buying my own car really stunned him! Getting my own credit card had affected him even more. In hindsight, he obviously saw this as there being an opportunity to escape for me. Though this was furthest from my thoughts when I got the card.

When I look back now, I can see that there were a whole lot of games going on. I wasn't playing them. Well, yes actually I was. I just didn't know it. He would say 'Jump' and I would say 'How high?' But now the games were changing. I had stopped playing his games the same way.

I think he resented that I had some freedom now, and that I was trying my wings. Though I never consciously dreamt of or intended to leave him then, despite my shelved self promises and contracts, and was not consciously developing a master plan of escape, I simply needed a solution to good transport! Not that it was in his make-up to be sincerely pleased for me or proud of me.

Not About The Money, Money, Money

It is more than clear that Jim does not trust. Me, or others. Can it get any worse than him hitting me if he chose not to believe me during an interrogation? Can things go downhill even more after this physical, mental, emotional and psychological abuse at his hands? The short answer is; Well, yes they can.

It seems that he has planned a new phase of attack, though I have lost count of his phases, and let's just say, like with the steak knives advert; *But wait, there's more...*

This particular day is just another ordinary day in our household. The children are home from school and have been fed. I have finished washing up from the evening meal, and Jim is getting ready to leave for work. He is gradually getting into a bit of a foul mood. Okay, if I am smart, I can get through this okay. He was okay earlier on, but there seems to be a change as he contemplates his night work. Does he not want to go to work? I have no idea. He is tight-lipped, literally.

Collecting his prepared work 'lunch', keys and vacuum flask off the kitchen countertop he heads for the front door. Turning, he stops and looks at me.

'Marni, where's the cheque book?' This is more of a demand than a question.

'I have it in my bag, I was going to take it to work to pay the electric with it tomorrow lunch-time', I explain as I point at my handbag.

'Give it to me' he instructs, holding his hand out.

'What do you need it for?' I misguidedly dare to ask, just in case there is another bill I had forgotten about.

'Just give it to me', he insists. You don't argue with Jim unless you are absolutely sure about it. So I translate this posture in his stance as 'Don't argue', so I don't argue. I hand the cheque book over.

'Is there something I have forgotten to pay?' I venture timidly as I see him go through the cheque stubs.

'No. Now where is your purse?' he asks, his eyes on my handbag. Obviously, I reply 'Why, it's in my bag.'

I watch him as he goes over to the kitchen countertop where my handbag is and he calmly yet determinedly takes my purse – What? - out of my bag and empties it completely of cash; notes and coins. These he puts into his pocket and throws my purse down on the countertop. What? I have to say something, I cannot help myself. 'What are you doing? What's the matter?' I gasp.

'I don't trust you, so I am taking your money with me,' he flatly states. His face might show no emotion, but I swear, he is enjoying this.

I scramble for words. 'But why, what do you think I am going to do?' I am somehow trying to make sense of this needless and humiliating action. I have given him absolutely *no* cause to mistrust me with money in any way. I don't even have a bank account of my own.

'I'm just making sure you don't have any money to skip away with,' is his response. 'I will give it back to you in the morning.'

This is nuts. I feel so utterly helpless, so powerless, so degraded. 'Why would I leave? And what if the children need some emergency medicine or some other emergency?', I appeal.

As usual he has all the answers. Remember that this nutter is always right. He scuttles my ship with 'They are fine at the moment, and there is nothing wrong with them. If there is a problem, phone me at work.' He leaves.

I am left there speechless. And breathless.

It is as if he has punched me straight in the solar plexus. And I do know what that feels like, believe me!

What on earth had happened that day to cause this? Nothing that I can recall. So this beats me! Which is what he is good at after all, isn't it? I peruse my day, I replay the last couple of days. Nope, nothing, didn't see that one coming, did I? So if it wasn't through anything that I could see that I did, there must be something else going on. Try as I might, I cannot think what that is or was. Nor, in truth, could I possibly know what was going on. Not then.

If my continually having to Prove my Fidelity and loyalty in some way, despite my innocence, isn't enough, then what did I think would be enough? *Did* I think on any other plane about this ridiculous behaviour? Not really. This stupidity, this stupor my brain had been put in regarding this abuse kept me in a certain thrall, a certain grip that was hard to break free from. He was the persecutor, and my place was to be the submissive victim. Okay, so put it under the guise of dutiful wife, but it's all the same in the wash.

But this disgusting action of his, this disrespect, this disregard, this humiliation, this new and unnecessary (though, weren't they all unnecessary) type of abuse of his, this financial bullying grip that he now practiced over me, this was to be a major precursor to my further moving away from him. He had taken it to a whole other level. Something in me cracked emotionally. Did another part of me die then? Possibly. But another part of the marriage hypnosis was now being challenged. No other woman I knew had experienced this. This was total humiliation and not part of any love equation. This was worse than a sneaky and cowardly emptying of the bank account, like dad had done. For Jim had done this in front of the children. He had chosen to deliberately humiliate me and demean me without cause in front of our own.

Anyone with any sense would surely now realise that this man is much more than a control freak. If this was him and his continual battling of his inner demons, then his coping method of creating me (or the children or someone else) as The Demon was cruel, evil, hypocritical and unbearable. Is this what I am working for? Is this why I draw wages? Put up with hiding bruises? So my husband can treat me like this? Something in me was now watching even more closely. For a deal-breaker, and a chance to escape...

This was the start. He was to do this inult as a regular practise. Was he picking up resentment vibes from me? Because I certainly started to feel resentful. Though I still behave myself.

For now, this is just the occasional practise. Which didn't make its impact on me any the less. Even if I assume that this was because of his insecurities, and his claim that he Didn't Trust me, then what did all the years of proven and continued faithfulness, forgiveness and support from me mean? *Why* was he doing this?

Many years later I learned of other women who had done big spend-ups and had taken their men to the cleaners. This was unthinkable to me; one didn't do that to someone you loved or cared for. Nor to someone whom you thought was part of your family. Yet he had grouped me in with them because of his own fears. How little he knew me.

When I had acquired my own credit card, Jim now takes to cutting *that* up whilst pocketing all the money. I was gobsmacked the first time he reached into my purse and took out my credit card and attacked it with a pair of scissors, deliberately in front of me and the boys.

'What did you do that for? You have no right to do that' I fumed. 'Now you won't run up a bill on me' he stated. What? 'But this is *my* credit card. It is in *my* name.' 'But I am your husband, and so I am liable for all your debts' he rallied back. 'I won't be held accountable for your spending', he yells. I don't know who was in his ear but this man was a disaster waiting to happen. What spending? I didn't 'spend'! At the first opportunity I re- checked on this possibility to confirm that as it was in my name alone and on my credit rating and with my signature alone then he was *not* liable. I told him this then I had to apply for a new card, claiming it had been lost.

But did this stop this mindless power need of his? No! For it happened again; the next time he did a cash-strip on me and he had *again* cut up my *new* card on me I reminded him *again* that he was not liable for my debts. After this second time, I made some serious enquiries about this at with the bank manager himself.

I then repeated to Jim what was told me; as I had got the credit card in my own right and my own name, and *without* his signature then I was the *only* one responsible for any debts on the card, and that he was not liable for any expenses. (That may have been the old way, but things were now changing and today ordinary women had their own bank accounts and bank cards.) I was also *so* (quietly) pleased to inform him that he could be *prosecuted* for destroying bank property and *my* personal cards! Jim was stopped in his tracks - he had been using the card cutting as an excuse for bullying and control. But no more... 'Go check this out with the banks yourself' I stated.

He didn't like me telling him this, but because I had brought the Bank and therefore *authority* into this, it kept him in his place about it and he stopped cutting up my cards. But where there is a will there is a way... He simply took to taking them out of my purse along with everything else. It never *occurred* to me that I could call the police and claim that the card had been stolen from me!

God, he really must have been terrified that I would leave and take everything. But what he did eventually do was succeed in pushing me so far away, that when I did eventually leave, I was never, never, *ever* going back. And when I did finally go I did not even leave of my own accord. This man was stupid enough to achieve the very thing he feared the most and *he* actually was the one to finally push me away! But that comes a little later.

Broken Vows

Working at such a large company as TOW Chemicals, with its variety of departments, offices and a whole research and development area as well as the actual manufacturing plant allowed me ample opportunity to meet a huge cross-section of people that I hadn't been exposed to before. Little Danny is growing quickly. In a different way I am too, though I hadn't pushed forth the fruit of this particular inner growth just yet. Life, however, had been inevitably forcing me to find and make and possibly take some of my own independent steps.

During my time working at TOW I have obviously accumulated several acquaintances, despite my Christian prickliness. Though I tended to classify them as friends simply because we were friendly and working for the same company, I had still to learn that not everyone has your best interests at heart, as you may have for them. And some of them proved friendly to my face, but not so nice behind my back. Feedback always comes around and I was learning who I could talk to and who I couldn't. My BS-barometer was not yet working fully, whether at home or work. And being as lonely as I was, I was in dire need of a good friend.

One acquaintance who was more straight talking stood out to me, even in my naïve state, as being someone who might be more trustworthy than others. Even though he was male, I felt a bit more comfortable around him. I liked him and we would sometimes bump into each other at the coffee station. I was a bit skittish around other males in case they flirted with me and I would have to answer to Jim. Even though he was around the same age as myself, he didn't flirt, I didn't feel threatened and we never talked about intimate personal things, it was mainly about work, children and domestic stuff in general.

However, this man was a lot more experienced in things of the world, not having had such strong religious inhibitions and protocols as myself, and on occasion he had been helpful with a few hints and tips about local items. So a kind of trust was developing.

This friend, Jan, had recognised that I was at some sort of an impasse in my relationship with my husband. He had also seen that I was actually imprisoned by my beliefs, though I certainly hadn't yet seen this. Jan, to whom I was later most thankful, really challenged me one day. Over the years we had both been working there, he had been subtly and secretly noting that I was getting abused and how I hid it (or more like *tried* to hide it) from others. He became a good platonic friend because he felt safe and seemed to be a very sensitive and gentle type of man. He had obviously recognised some of my symptoms and had waited for an opportunity when I might be a bit more open about things. I was usually quite defensive about my beliefs and very protective of family issues and family privacy at work.

Over time we would occasionally have a little chat that had initially started over the coffee urn. He would ask about my beliefs, which I wasn't shy about sharing; to speak about my faith at every opportunity was after all a prime directive from the Bible. He listened to me and though he would ask the odd question, he didn't belittle my ideas or put me down. In fact he had shared a couple of his own personal experiences, and was very empathic and a good listener. Indeed, he seemed to care. And he did so without compromising me or embarrassing me.

I hadn't realised that he had some of his own thoughts and ideas on what he had himself perceived about my situation, for I had said nothing about any violence at home. Being the type of guy that he was, it was only a matter of time before he saw something that he couldn't keep quiet about. One day I was nursing a bruised chin and bruised arm, and I thought that the makeup had hidden it reasonably successfully, but not from hawk-eye Jan. My explanation to anyone else that had noticed was not as acceptable to him.

'Why are you still with someone who treats you like this?' Jan questions in a semi-casual way, whilst watching me and indicating that he is actually a bit disbelieving that the bruise on my face was really the result of walking into a door as I had been forced to state. I couldn't deny the essence of his question and enough trust had been built up to go there.

'Because I made a promise before God: till death do us part', I reply after a momentary pause to consider. He had seen through my cover-up and he was interested and not derogatory. Even so, I got a little bit nervous that he could see what had happened to me. Or was it that I was actually embarrassed that he might recognise my situation?

'What exactly *did* you actually promise?' he wondered out loud, genuinely appearing to be interested in my next response.

'To love, honour and obey, til death do us part'. I thought this was pretty worldwide as a marriage promise, so I state it quite definitely, almost challenging him in my tone so he can see that I think this is an obvious vow and promise. I wondered why he was asking this in particular, but didn't see the need to hold back.

'And what did your husband promise?' Jan further pursues, with a slight knowing glint in his eye.

I went back to the day we made our vows in church. I saw us both standing there in front of the minister in church. There had been no choice over the words of ceremony, no personal contribution. We had used the time-honoured ones as recommended or rather *instructed* to by the Pastor who married us – good old Pastor Parratt. Trapped me good! *I* had been genuine and serious about my vows, and still am, and I had assumed that Jim was too.

'To love, honour and cherish' I remember out loud. I hear my own voice slowing as I am saying the words and I almost argue with myself over a response that I now feel but don't have words for. Not yet anyway. Jan waits a few moments as I look at him, wondering why he has asked this, and hearing my own words again in my head.

'And has he? Cherished you that is?' he enquires in a gentle tone. Jan just stands there waiting for my reply, giving me time to hear what he is asking, time for this to sink in, time for me to think. Eyebrows raised, he now has a slight but questioning smile that invites an honest answer. So I take the moment to think about this. I am now looking down at the ground – it is as though I am running through the video files in my mind, seeing reruns of Jim's behaviour, looking for the moments that would triumphantly shout back that he *has* cherished me. But I can find none that would came to mind, none that can cancel all of the abuse. All I can see and hear are his accusations, his moods, his false charm and meaningless apologies, his drinking and his threats. My fear of looking at the real truth was now giving way to the truth and the real fear in my situation.

'No', I eventually and slowly reply, as the truth begins to dawn through my inner 'shoulds' and 'shouldn'ts'.

'No, he hasn't. ... And I never realised it before...'

Jan continues to study me and my responses. My mind is working overtime. *How could I have not seen this? How could I have allowed things like this to happen? This was all so bloody obvious, how could I have missed it?* I retraced my thought processes – the ones that made me continue to love, honour and *obey*. But I hadn't missed it – I had been through this a hundred times in the back of my mind but not consciously. How come Jim doesn't have to obey? Well I knew that already, it was biblical; the man has rule over the woman. But then what about this bit, about *cherishing* – Jim clearly hasn't, his behaviour has been atrocious so often. I was beginning to feel quite uncomfortable, I am being really challenged by this. Then also the reason why I had *continued* to put up with it, with this obvious mind-programming; the thought-numbing reason was suddenly clear...

'But I have to *forgive* him, the Bible says so.' I blurt out before I can stop myself. Being so used to defending myself, I launch into what I think are the reasons behind my reality.

'I promised God...', I stumble on, as Jan waits and as my mind reels to take in what is being said, what is being revealed. I had forgiven. Jim didn't forgive – there was nothing to forgive – but even if I had done something wrong, it was now obvious wasn't it; Jim *didn't* forgive. Or CHERISH.

Jan had sized it all up – he already knew the answers to those questions. He also knew something about these things, knew what I didn't yet know.

'You made a *contract* with him, which *he* has *broken*, so you are no longer *held* to that contract. That is what the law says,' my friend

Naïve Hope

continues, gently but firmly seizing the moment. He lets this sink in. I wasn't settling for that though. I *am* been genuine with God.

'But I made my promise to *God*, not the law' I exclaim. 'There is no way I would dishonour my vows to God, no matter how things have gone'.

'Yes' Jan continued, making sure that everything he said was making sense. 'But Jim has also broken his vows to God regarding you, and this means that you are no longer held to be in the same situation. And when you got married, you made not only a religious contract by marrying in a church and making vows before God, but you also made a moral and social contract with Jim before others by pledging to him and consenting to live with him, and you both also made a legal contract that was entered into the Births, Deaths and Marriages records.'

I had to agree with him when I thought about it. Those were the steps we had taken besides our vows in church, though I had mainly remembered only the religious side of it all.

Jan took his time to make sure that I understood what he was getting at. My mind was already whirring with what it had just glimpsed – the very fact that Jim has been derelict in his own vows. It has not yet fully dawned on me that Jim insists on *me* keeping my side of the bargain but doesn't keep *his*. I had been doing the right thing all along. But has Jim? Before I can allow myself to hear the full answer, the *obvious* answer, Jan has more to say.

'He has broken each of those contracts by his treatment of you. He has not cherished you. He has abused, assaulted, mistreated & probably cheated on you. And in law, when one party breaks a contract, the contract is then deemed as broken. The contract between you is already *broken*. *He* has broken the vows, broken the contract, *not* you. And you are therefore no longer held to those contracts. They are *already* broken. *You* are the *only* one upholding them.'

This patient probing friend pauses as I struggle to take in what is being revealed. Enough has been said. My face was grave. The blinkers were falling off. And my inner eyes were beginning to open and to *see*.

'Think about it' he said before indicating that he had to get back to work. But he left with a gentle smile on his face, as if to say 'Sorry I had to tell you that, but someone had to do it.' I also got that he actually *cared* to dare saying something so deep, so personal, so challenging that could possibly have ended the growing trust in this platonic friendship under any other normal circumstances.

The first opportunity that I have, I check the dictionary for the meanings of cherish. I am appalled at what I read. *Jim didn't do that!*

This had quite some impact on me. This was yet another nail in the coffin, another straw to add to the pile. Another reason for me to wake up. And marked the dawning of 'the end' for this particular status quo. Enlightenment can be very painful at times. It causes one to assess where one is, to see with real eyes, to 'real-eyes', to 'realize'. When one becomes aware of where they really are, only then do they have the power to change things.

This 'Enlightenment' eventually came at a price, at a cost, but heralded in freedom for my heart, mind and soul.

I filed this new knowledge in some part of my mind and heart. I cannot not yet challenge Jim on this, for it was only just apparent to *me* what had happened. I never told Jim of this conversation, and because there was no sexual ambiguity from Jan, I felt no guilt in saying nothing. Not only that, I had to hold this deep in my heart. These thoughts could be conceived as traitorous ideas, especially judging by the way Jim treated my previous attempts at proving my fidelity.

But fair to the end, I am still held in misled compassion to give Jim a chance to show that he can be other than he was. Have I missed his attempts to cherish me? I now add this to my 'Watching and Observing' program. Despite this resolution, things just simply seem to escalate at home. This, like other experiences, other realisations, only adds to the growing evidence of what my marriage really was in actuality, and not what I thought or wished that it is.

It had taken me many years to realise that Jim did not cherish or honour me, either, though many would have picked it already. As regards him having 'loved' me, that is also doubtful. But that is enough regarding this lack of being 'cherished'.

I am waking up more and more. What else is there for me to now let myself 'see'?

THE TELLING DREAM

The mind is an amazing instrument; it can think along several lines at once, both conscious and subconscious. And sometimes, those ideas that we have trouble framing in a conscious mind can be served up to one in a dream. A telling dream; a dream which is trying to tell something, though in a language that is not always familiar to the conscious mind.

If I had looked and listened more closely, I just might have read the symbolism in one particular night's dreaming.

It is Ireland in the middle of winter, with much snow on the ground. Well rugged up, I am dressed in sixteenth century winter clothing, a fur cuff cosseting my neck and a fur muff protecting my hands from the crisp air. I am waving goodbye to my family, as my new husband is driving us both away from my lovely big family home. We are both sitting on a sort of sleigh, like an open carriage, and it is drawn by an enormous dappled whitish horse with flowing dark hair around its huge hooves. The horse knows me well, and I feel comfortable with this magnificent creature. There is a sense of promise, an exciting journey and a new life ahead, yet somehow there is also a sense of doom and gloom in this scene. Am I never to return?

The next scene; I am in a small smelly dark room, one that houses myself and my children. Lying on the floor, exhausted and in pain, I strongly feel the neglect of my husband, this same man I drove so hopefully away with. His anger and projected self disgust coat me so strongly that I can smell it. And I know that I am dying and no longer able to protect myself nor my surviving children from him and his cruelty.

At the time I do not recognise the man as Jim. It is to be years later that I have a similar dream, and this time the identity of this abusive and dangerous man is revealed, for it is the man I have chosen as my husband this present lifetime; Jim. The dawning realisation that we have spent several lifetimes together, lifetimes in which he treated me badly, impacts upon me in this dream. In a flash I recognise that this current marriage was in order to give him another opportunity of addressing and correcting his history with me and my children. But in the same burst of awareness, I also sadly realise that it was an opportunity that he cannot recognise, and will not utilise. And so he seals his own fate. Whilst I move on. I let his etheric chains and bonds fall away from me as my face turns towards a different future, one with no further encounters with him ever again. This is now his karma, not mine.

The church says that the Bible does not accept the concept of reincarnation. Yet, as a Bible student with an open mind, I say that it is there for the reading. I still use my Bible Concordance. These dreams were valid evidence to me when I myself later verified and accepted the concept **for myself**.

TO LIE OR NOT TO LIE?

Life continues, but doesn't really improve. My observations serve me with mostly bad news, bad views. My half formulating ideas and suspicions, once never openly admitted to myself, were now growing in vigour and noise, and are beginning to clamour to be bought out and thought out into the open to be looked at properly. Presently they continue to niggle away at the back of my mind...

Before the sh.t really hits the fan, there are to be *two* more *scenes played out, two further significant occasions*, two additional *extreme* events to disclose that lie behind this opening of my heart and life for all the world to see.

These are things that imprinted me and shook me and left a mark on my heart for more than quite some time.

I carried this hurt and pain for many, many years until I was finally able to deal with them. What occurred would not and could not be undone. It forever changed me; and the course and tone of what I still then called our marriage.

Naïve Hope

It is 1980 when I have my first real 'Death and Danger' wake up call – as if I wasn't reading the writing on the wall, these messages were in neon lights and underscored; for things happened that challenged everything I had ever believed and everything I had ignored. If I thought threats to run us all off the road was a scary thing, if I thought a few punches and broken ribs was the worst that could happen, if I thought that taking all my money was as bad as it got, I was about to be convinced otherwise.

It started off as any other normal weekend day. Or so I thought. Birds are twittering, plants are being tended to, grass is getting a haircut. And now it's time to finish and to have a meal, and to ease our muscles and to think of preparing for work the following day. But first, Jim was resharpening and oiling the machete for storage.

We had been doing some work in the garden, weeding and cutting down some really tall grass. I thought nothing of it and the day had gone reasonably well. I cannot even recall there being any problems that day, and so I guess that is why it seems to come right out of the blue.

I don't know whether I was altering in ways I wasn't aware of, because in my own head I was still very present to being a good wife, and going about married and family life as before. I had maybe suggested some new ideas as to possible future outings or family fun ideas that I had gleaned from other family minded people at work. Maybe I had allowed myself to catch up with one of the girls at lunchtime and we had gone to the shops together. Maybe I was taking an interest in what I was wearing. Maybe I was trying a new hairstyle. I have absolutely no idea, but *something* must have triggered this reaction and subsequent unnecessary and crazy behaviour in Jim.

I *always* tell him what happens during the day, any day – because I *have* to. If anything different occurs, he wants to know. though I have buried my conversation with Jan so that I do not have to account for it to Jim – I know that he would misinterpret it all. He has been in the habit of asking (and telling) me what I think throughout our marriage – he is also in the habit of jumping to conclusions about what I think or even what the children are thinking. In basic psychology I learned that this can be referred to as Denial or Projection. This I realised later, but at the time I just had to deal with it. What else could I do? It was still 'Till Death do us part'...

And I now understand that it was probably because of what is in *his* mind, *this* is what is projected. He *sees* his own mind in others. Just like I see honesty in everyone, he sees dishonesty in everyone. He sees all of his dark fears, his self-deceptions, his deviousness and self loathing not in himself, but reflected in others – his ability to recognise is misdirected, and is acknowledge by him thinking that he 'sees' things in others. Usually me.

That would be his usual story wouldn't it – that it was because of something that *I* was doing that did this *to* Jim? Well, I now know that that is *not* true. Jim's mind worked in its own little devious way all by itself, without any input from me. *Any* one deviation could mean anything to him. Whatever it was that he wanted it to mean.

So, on this particular day, he suddenly becomes quiet. I accept it as tiredness after the gardening. I think everything is ok, though things do feel a little tense. I am still not aware that anything is amiss, that I have said or done anything that would niggle him and cause him to ruminate on negatively. So why this tension? *Did* I do something wrong? Though he could just be tired from the day's efforts.

But oh, no, it wasn't that. Uh-oh – what now?

Jim has been thinking. (*Watch out!*)

So what has he been thinking? It is soon revealed. And as I am changing out of my dirtied gardening clothes, he enters the bedroom and closes the door behind him, facing me with one hand behind his back. What unfolds is that which I shared with you in the beginning – for now he reaches round and turns the door lock. As the butterflies and discomfort begins I wonder what he is going to do to me now.

He is placed between me and the bedroom door. And then he brings his arm around to the front of him – in his hand is the machete he had used on the grass earlier. I gulp. This does not look good. I pray he is just going to show me something connected with this knife. *Keep calm, Marni. Don't get too excited just yet.*

The machete is sharp, clean, and in his hands, not a pretty sight.

He lifts it up to near my face. There is a glint in his eye, a dark and dangerous fixed stare...

His face has changed again to 'that face' of his – the one that is not only looking for trouble, but has already found it.

'So what have you got to tell me?' he growls.

I have no idea as to what he is referring. All I know is that now I am getting scared. *Now* I am excited - I begin to tremble inside.

'What about?' I ask, trying to keep my voice steady.

'Don't come that with me' he grunts, inching his body closer toward me. 'You know what about. I can see it in your face'.

'?' I blinked. Again, I repeat, I had absolutely no idea what he was talking about. Nor what he was thinking – which was a danger for me, as I now didn't have a chance to sort this to set his mind at rest.

I check what my face is doing and has been doing. And I do not see what it is that he 'sees'. The scared barometer is rising. I am now in a seriously tricky situation. Before it has only been his fists, and they are powerful enough as it is. This is a whole new ball game.

'What's going on at work? Who is it that you fancy?' he intimates, as he moves the knife forward enough to touch my neck with the tip of the machete.

The feeling of cold powerful steel against a vulnerable point fires my imagination – and this is precisely what he has intended to do. He wants me scared. And I am. *Bloody scared!*

'There's no-one at work' I say. 'Nothing's going on at work'. And there isn't. I have always had to tell him about anything that happened at work. This is fact; I have been totally faithful to him. My face registers my emotions and it is again like living in a glass house – what I feel, you can see. But there is *no-one* at work. Or maybe I don't even know it myself? I begin to doubt myself. I am *not* after anyone at work, I do *not 'fancy'* anyone at work. Labelled *'The Ice Lady'* because I don't share in the smutty office jokes, and because I refuse to flirt, or to join in some things with them. Yes, maybe I am learning to thaw out my self-righteous attitude to others and to be a bit more accepting of other ways of living and being. But as to *carrying on* with anyone, how stupid would I be to even dare let any thoughts of that kind enter my head. Did I have a death wish or something?

It would be more than stupid of me to consider doing anything like that with a husband such as this. And I have my own morals anyway. Even my conversations with Jan do not register to me in any of this; for there has been no cheating, no flirting, no lack of commitment, no betrayal in thought or deed. I know that I am not a Diane, nor a Heather. But does this man? Apparently not!

Jim holds the machete closer down to my throat, getting closer to the jugular vein. He continues to have it in his head that I am carrying on with someone. 'I know there's someone else' he states. 'Who is it?'

This is insane! Nothing is making sense...

As vivid pictures race through my mind, I pray for help; I am now terrified. Oh God, Oh God, Oh God, Jesus (*though why I bother praying, I don't know...*) help me *pleeease...Can He hear me*?

I am visibly shaking so badly that my knees are giving way and I have slowly, carefully sat on the edge of the bed, the knife following my slow movement downward very closely. Tears well up in my eyes at the injustice of these false accusations, at his lies and at my own fears.

I *know* that what he is saying is not true. I don't know where he gets it from. *God* knows it. I keep doubting myself, checking my past thoughts, scouring my mind for any possible forgotten misdemeanour, any ignored slip - while he continues to keep on questioning me, over and over and over. The machete stays close to my neck. He won't believe me when I tell him the truth, and I am beginning to think that at any minute he might crack up and slice me up.

This man has already punched me, broken my ribs, threatened me, insulted me, interrogated me, falsely accused me and kept me on egg shells for such a long time – and now he was resorting to

Naïve Hope

weapons... My worst fears begin to yammer at me. *You never knew what it was that was going to trigger him.* Neither does he, and this was the power he exercised over me. And also what makes this dark side of him so dangerous. Victim to his own feelings or inclinations, apparently without any compassion or impulse control.

My thoughts are dictating that I might not see the night through. Continuing to tell him 'The Truth' was just not working, and now it was a knife that he was threatening me with, not just a hit or a punch.

Stomach churning, fear firing through my body, blood rushes to my head, draining from my limbs. I cannot think straight and I fight to regain control of my own limbs as I feel weakness flow through me.

I search my conscience again doubting myself, he is so sure of himself. No I have *not* been unfaithful to him in any way. I repeat this to him again and with conviction. But still he refuses to hear that.

My thoughts turn to a possible outcome; what will happen to the boys if he kills me? Jim's eyes are so intent, so dark, so full of anger and hate that it seems he is seeing something or someone else. He is not 'seeing' *me*, he does not want to hear me. I don't know how long before he really snaps and does something irreversible. I am defenceless.

He does not want to know the truth. What else can I do? What alternative is there? I wildly cast about in my mind – what else is there but The Truth? I have *always* told him the truth.

Yes, but does he believe you? Does he *want* to hear the truth? No? No! Then *what* does he want to hear?

In a flash I got my answer... *Why, a lie of course!*

In my mind I hear 'reverse psychology' – and so I take a gamble – I do the only thing that I could think of to do in the situation now – I tell him what he *wants* to hear.

If I tell him what he wants to hear, maybe that will be the solution to this insanity. After all, this is totally insane! Don't argue with him, instead *Agree* with him!

But what if he wants details? Then *Make up a story, Marni! Any story!*

Jim is living his own scene, his own version. Okay, then, I will join in with this charade. What else have I got to lose?

'I know that you are fancying someone'. I agree. 'Yes, you're right.'

That was easy – too easy!

'I *know* you work with him', Jim states; I agree. 'Yes, there is someone that I fancy at work.'

'And I know you have even dared to kiss him'; *What! Don't even go there, Marni, just agree.* I agree. 'Yes, I didn't mean to, but it just happened.'

He asks for a name – I give him a name. He asks me when it happened; I make something up. I have surrendered to this man's perverted whims. I may be safe from the knife, I just *may* be, but there is something else that this has cost me.

The realisation that one would say anything to hold onto their own life hits me. What have I done? I scream internally...

Okay, so the kids won't now get up in the morning to find me in pieces all over the house and blood everywhere. So I did what I did to save myself and to save our 'family'... But there is something seriously wrong with my side of this event. There is now a serious internal disconnect within me. Something has been broken within – I am deeply wounded in some way. I feel that he has somehow won, and that I have somehow lost. And I have. My Self-respect.

There forms within me a deep, firm resolve – I *swear* to myself that *if* I survive the night, if I get out of that situation and live to tell the tale, if I make it out of the bedroom alive, *that I would find a way to leave him, to escape!* That I would *never,* **ever** *tell a lie to save myself from him* **ever** *again* – the emotional, moral and spiritual cost is too much to bear. I do not like this person that I have become. Someone who will lower themself to this depth in the face of something, or rather someone, like this. I would rather be dead! And something within me recognises the dark in this man, and that he is beyond any excuses. Part of me now turns its back on him.

I feel so ashamed that I had been forced to this, that something within me has changed toward him *forever*. He had crossed some line in a way that could never be repaired. *I* had crossed some line in a way that changed my relationship with myself and particularly with him forever.

I was too disgusted with myself for lying simply to stay alive. I could not live this way. I did not know how, but somehow this *would not* happen again!

Sure within days I had to consciously put aside any immediate action on this promise to myself, on this decision to leave him because of the needs of the children, but this was *not* totally forgotten; it simmers deep inside and started to grow and solidify to make my backbone strong when I needed it to be. Strange as it may seem, in some way I was getting stronger inside, though I hadn't yet recognised it. The incidents were mounting and accumulating, the scales getting heavier, the balance was shifting, and this huge wedge of bastardly and dastardly misery and disgust had somehow lodged a hold in my consciousness that was beyond forgiveness or acceptance. Though I hadn't as yet got around to challenging myself – or him - how come *he* could be forgiven for an actual sexual infidelity, yet I could be so hounded over just *thinking* about one *even though I had actually not done so*. Such is the power of fear and of living in survival mode.

Things may have appeared or seemed to get back to whatever 'normality' was. But I was still scared, and I now fully realized that I couldn't again lie in order to live, I just couldn't face myself or live with myself and betray myself any more like this again. I decided if there was any way I could escape, I would do so.

It wasn't long before I had an opportunity for such definite action.

WOMENS' REFUGE

It was shortly afterward that something happened to give me my answer, my next step out of this horror I was living. Interestingly, it was through work that I came across the number of a refuge home. And with that came a glimmer of hope, an opportunity for freedom for us all, and I now fully intended to contact the refuge and to take the children there with me.

Meanwhile, something must have shown in my demeanour after this latest episode, and I found it a hard thing to hide from everyone, though I was accustomed to putting on a good face. At home with Jim, it could possibly be interpreted as resignation, as me having been put back in my place. And so I was once again quiet and submissive. But this was actually a quiet determination.

Fortunately the only person at work to notice anything, or rather to *say* anything to me outright, about what I had been going through in my life, was Jan. He was still observing me and didn't always just take my initial responses that I was tired or had been kept awake by the youngest at night. He saw it in my demeanour and challenged me that something had happened. I wouldn't say anything about it, but he knew. Later on that day, I bumped into him again at the coffee bench. He said 'This is for you' and gave me a piece of paper, with the parting words 'Use this if you need it. They can give you and the children a bed till you get sorted' then he was gone.

On the folded piece of paper was the name of a *Women's Refuge* and their phone number. No address, just the phone no. I memorised it and destroyed the paper. I didn't dare let it be found on me.

And so I waited. In taking the time to steel myself for the first opportunity I was also giving Jim yet another chance to change his way of being. Now that I had the means of escape, let's give it one more go, hey? But of course, a change from Jim wasn't to be. And soon we're right back again into his usual attitude of entitlement and bullying.

The knife incident had been the first of the two extreme events that had thrust me face to face with my own mortality, my own boundaries, my own honour.

After Jan had given me the refuge number, it didn't take much time for fate to force me to use it. For it was merely a matter of days later that Jim again humiliates me, and this for no real reason other than his mad imagination and his own projected guilt and shame.

He is about to leave for work with his usual snide remarks and contempt as he does on these occasions. Yes, it's true that when wearing his charming self, I would sometimes get a kiss on the cheek before he left for work. But not today. His dark side was just more and more in evidence, and it so outweighed those moments – any kisses now felt empty, as though there was no longer any substance behind them. My beliefs were crumbling, but were valiantly – and blindly - seeking the best outcome.

However; I could no longer so easily believe what I had wanted to believe about this man, the things that had made me see only the good in him and to believe that there was a chance that he could change was in its final death throes. Not only that. We had now embarked upon a darker road together. That night with the knife has done something to me, it had cut something in me, and I was resolved now somehow to take things into my own hands – it couldn't go on like this, surely? And now I had a contact number!

The moment Jan had given me that phone number I had been ready to leave right then. But I have to bide my time. If Jim got wind of these intentions and possibilities, then we would all be toast. He would be delirious that he had been proven 'right', and he would be justified in venting all the wrath and vengeance he could upon me. So, from the moment I had been given that number, part of my mind had gone into overdrive, weighing up justification for using the phone number and the impact all of this war on myself was having on my children. I had to be so very careful that I gave nothing away – not easy – but I was determined to use this opportunity to escape this cruel man and I had found a place that took in children as well! I had hidden his abuse from others, now it was time to hide things from Jim.

I would have to make contact with them and find the best time to suit. What if they wanted us to come straight away? So with the skeleton of a plan in my head, I had waited for this very moment, I had waited for the next humiliating thing he did before he left for night work. I couldn't afford to have Jim trace my call from the home phone, he had me so paranoid about his boastful capability to track me down by his stories of what security guards were able, allowed and entitled to do, and I had no reason to know or believe anything other than this. Remember, this was in the days pre 'Google' so I wasn't to know anything different at that time.

And here it comes – yup, 'that face' again, reaches for my bag, takes my purse with a self satisfied 'That'll teach ya' look on his face, stuffs my few measly dollars for emergency items into his pocket, together with my credit card. 'Where's the cheque book, eh?' is next, like as if I'm a naughty schoolkid trying to deny I made the cricket ball hole in the window. I had earlier been planning on paying some bills that were due, and so it was out ready on the kitchen bench, behind the due bills. Drats! So it too gets handed over. And with a final flourish, the loose coins (around ten dollars?) also joining the party in his pocket.

And off King Jim goes to his throne at work. He was only a security guard, for crying out loud. Mind you, at 'home' – some home - he was pretty much 'king' of the crumbly castle.

After he has gone off to work I gave him about a quarter of an hour before I lurched into action and I drove out to phone the refuge. In all good conscience, the boys were too small to leave at home anyway, so I take *all* the boys with me even if this did not work out for tonight. This way we are also together if we are able to take off for a place straight away. Gathering a hasty bag that could be filled with a few emergency clothes yet still be explained as 'washing' should he catch us in the act, I woke the children up, and shaking, I bundle them, pyjamas and all, into the back of the car. Well I couldn't take everything with me, but I could take a few overnight things. I didn't know if they could offer me a bed for the night straight away and only hoped that they could, so I am only a little prepared. The important thing is to get away! 'Stuff' can be sorted later.

Getting up the strength and daring to do this much was a huge effort, and I only had a few thrown together clothes for the boys in the car. Nerves taut, my teeth are chattering gently as I organise all of this. But the main thing here is the getting away, and before we see Jim again.

Naïve Hope

So this is my opportunity – I had the hope of a place to stay now. Let's go kids... *Hold on, children, let's go for a drive.* We get in the car, and I furtively check for Jim's car as I drive all the way to the phone box in Werribee central, in case Jim has twigged that something is afoot and has set any traps to follow us. Ridiculous I know, but it's not surprising how my brain must have been with all that had been happening. I was really, *really* scared. This was a huge chance I was taking here. If he found out and got hold of me, I shuddered to think how he would respond. *Stop that, Marni, focus on getting there.* I couldn't afford to think about the consequences or I would do nothing.

So with quaking fingers, I dialled the number. I was still inwardly trembling, just in case something happened. Just in case Jim suspected something even now and came home and found me missing. It was a major consideration and very nerve wracking, but also a potentially freeing attempt. Part of my heart was singing that we had a way out... the other part was quaking at this huge undertaking...

And so I got through to this woman. Yes, it was the correct number. Thank God!

The conversation with the Women's Refuge (I can no longer remember the name of it) went something like this:

Me; Hello, is that the women's shelter?

WS (Women's shelter); yes, how can we help you?

Me; I need to get away from my violent husband and I have my children with me. I believe you have beds and somewhere to stay that is safe?

WS; Yes, that's right

Me; Good. Can we come over tonight? Now, before he comes back home?

WS; Yes, yes, of course you can. And we do not give information out to husbands or partners, we provide a safe place.

Me; Thank God! What is the address?

She gave me the address, and I wrote it down with trembling fingers. Then she gave me some directions and added:

WS; Bring forty dollars cash with you or a cheque, and come over straight away.

Me; But I don't have forty dollars on me.

WS; Well then we can't help you.

Me; But you don't understand. My husband took all of the money out of my purse. He also has the cheque book and my credit card. He took them all to work with him.

WS; We do need the money up front, I am afraid.

Me; But I don't have any right now. Look, I get paid next week, on the 15th. I get a whole months' salary – I work for TOW Chemicals, I will have lots of money then. Please, please help me.

WS; I am sorry – those are the rules. Unless you have forty dollars with you right now we cannot help you. I am sorry, that's the way it is.

Me; Cant you do anything to help us?

WS; Sorry...

And with that she ended the call.

I put the phone down in shock.

What has just happened?

One of the children was crying (Danny), another (Ben) was peering out of the locked car parked next to the phone booth at me, and the eldest son (Joseph) was hugging my legs, shaking and upset, whilst I had been on the phone.

I felt like I had swallowed a boulder. My nerves are still buzzing, and my eyes aren't seeing right but feel fuggy and kind of foggy-misty. I feel like a balloon full of liquid manure had just burst above my head... I feel foul...

What happened?

Now, instead of heading off somewhere safe, I had to stay – again – and face this disaster. Dreams had just been exploded around my

Naïve Hope

head, and I was still dazed by the shock of it all. Supposed solutions and hopes lay smashed to smithereens around me. I couldn't think. Then I realise I am still in the car, holding the paper with the address the woman had given me in my hand.

What happened?

I also realized that saying 'What happened?' to myself wasn't helping. I had to rip the paper up because if Jim found this on me – well – it didn't bear thinking about.

I now unthinkingly bundled and settled the children back into the car. Presently, after I had taken several deep breaths, I dragged together what remaining energy and courage I had left to drive back to the house again. All the time praying that Jim had not come home and discovered anything amiss.

But before I could drive back home, I sat in the car outside the phone box and went over everything again in my mind to see if I had gotten straight these stressful moments.

Just what had *happened?*

I had asked for a place to stay for me and the kids. They had told me the address and told me to bring forty dollars with me. I had explained that I didn't have forty dollars, that Jim had taken all of my money. They said they couldn't help me. Even though I had explained that I was salaried, and that a whole month's payment would be in my bank the next week (in about five days time away), they said they *still* couldn't help me, that I *still* had to bring the forty dollars with me.

Which I didn't have.

Because Jim had got it all!

I was devastated.

How could I ever leave if Jim kept taking my money? How could I accumulate any without him knowing for every dollar was accounted for? And more importantly, how could I ever *dare* to do this again? What was the point?

No-one seemed willing to help me.

Escape Aborted! Hope died, thrashed to a miserable death.

RESIGNED

What The..? Where To Next? Is There A Next?

My shock cannot be described. It was like I had suddenly walked into the twilight zone. I had no recourse. No escape. No way ... I was helpless... could do nothing...

The possibility of escape with some support had died – I was so alone again. And a prisoner. Though at the time I didn't really get how he had imprisoned me. He had been very cunning, and I had been outwitted. And stymied.

Somehow I managed to comfort and quieten the boys down, pretend that really nothing had happened, that this was just a little adventure, and to say nothing to daddy, and to get them home and back into their beds safely. And asleep, just in case he did come home early for whatever reason.

I do *not* know *how* I survived that experience.

It took all I could not to burst out into tears, though they came later, when the kids were back in their beds.

I already knew what it is like to want to die. And here it was again – the feeling to want to just disappear rather than be a slave at someone else's control. And to feel so totally powerless, to be so totally *unable* to help your family, your children, your very blood and yet have no other choice because of these lives that are dependent on you. By taking all my possible resources, Jim had me by the short and curlies but good.

The bastard had ruined my chance of getting those boys out with the least amount of scarring and of myself being free from him. He *must* have known that what he was doing to me was pushing me away and that my attempt to leave him was going to be inevitable; he *must* have realised on some level that what he was doing and how he was treating me would result in some attempt to seek escape. Mustn't he? And he had cunningly made sure that I couldn't *do* any such thing.

This vicious, mean, vindictive, unstable and cruel man was intent on punishing me. And through the children he had another tool. I was still not prepared to walk out on my children, simply because I couldn't take them with me. So we all stayed.

I buried my anger and torment.

And another little part of me died.

I did not entertain this idea again. It had taken a lot for me to get up the courage to do what I had done. And now I had spent all of the emotional energy that was required to achieve such a monumental break-away, and it had simply come crumbling down around me. I did not dare risk another disappointment, my heart was already overwhelmed with the effort and pain of it all.

And I had to emotionally recover, if that was possible... Well, as it turns out, it was not possible. And so I had to bury it, deep away, so that every time something happened, every time I looked at my children and wished that we could all be somewhere else, I would not remember we had had our chance and lost it. I needed to function for them. I needed to stay alive and find another way, though God only knew how. For I didn't.

CONTRACTS

Wedding Vows, Short Memories, Programmed, Brain-Washed – these are the words that come to mind when I think of my confrontation with my husband many, many years later. At the beginning of 2011 to be exact. That's the date I recall as I record this section.

A funny thing about this man who claimed to be a 'husband' was that later on after these events, he claimed he could not remember many of the things he had done. How he had broken his contract to love me or cherish me did not enter into any dialogue at *any* stage. At the *time* of the violent events he might apologise and try to beg and flatter me back. But that was in the early days, before drink got into his blood. Initially on occasion, say when I had a black eye, (and this visual reminder couldn't be avoided for some time till it healed, or if I had become really withdrawn or quiet or scared) he would apologise guiltily, and try and make up for it. He would be (or more accurately *say* that he was) really, really sorry, and say how much he loved me, and what a good wife I was, and how he would never never never do it again. And not to leave him. Because he *needed* me. What would he do *without* me? He *depended* on me. And did I mention, he 'loved' me?

Yeah right... Until the next time it happened...

But further down the track of our marriage and drink, he would simply try to carry on as normal. Or he might be occasionally subdued whilst he recovered from his hangover. He *never* acknowledged he had a problem. When he had broken things or thrown them, he *never* apologised or cleared up the mess.

And I was even subjected to the odd old excuse of *'It's only because I love you that I hit you. If I didn't love you so much, I wouldn't care enough to do it.'* Hah! What absolute *rubbish!* I realise this *now*, but had no choice but to accept it at the time, even though somewhere within me it didn't feel quite right. Oh what falsity is that excuse, a hang-over from cave-man times. What they really meant was 'I hit you because I *can*,' though they equate passion and anger in the same breath as love. Ridiculous! And some of *these* same Neanderthals call *women* emotional!

But I, of course, was *still* programmed to forgive... I had made certain contracts, and I only knew how to honour and keep them. After all, contracts are meant to be binding. Even those one makes with one's self, whether consciously or not...

I had promised in my wedding vows 'to obey'; this was my **second contract** in life... My husband's vow 'to love, honour and cherish' had somehow been forgotten, and was never, *ever* preached on or sermon-ed on as the duty of every husband.

So with my encounter with possible death by hacking, my inner vow about not going through such a thing again became *another* contract I clearly remember making regarding my relationship with Jim. The **third** was as mentioned earlier, when I promised myself that I would *not* be unfaithful, or be the one to cause the marriage to fail.

The very ***first*** **contract** I had made with myself before I met Jim, when I had promised myself that if and when I got married, there would be *no way* that my children would ever have to see the sights and scenes that I had seen, or be forced to witness things like I had as a child.

This *first* contract was still in place, as past assaults had taken place in the bedroom – behind closed doors. I thought I was protecting my children by complicity with Jim to confine this abuse to the bedroom whenever possible. I had fooled myself into thinking that I could draw the line of fire away from the children.

What I had *not* realised at the time, or maybe did not want to consider, was that the energetic dynamics, the emotional innuendoes, the unspoken motivations and intentions that were the dynamics of the relationship, were already being imprinted and burned onto the very psyches of the children. Had I known this consciously, I think I would have again tried to leave him, and in a heartbeat.

But I didn't, and was doing the best I could under very difficult circumstances.

Later, as you will see, these inner promises, these self-contracts, came together in full fruition, and I didn't plan any of it consciously. But I willingly own up to what I eventually did.

So let me just take a moment here to recount what Contracts I have now set up that currently impact on my relationship with Jim – and in what order;

1. There is no way that my children (if and when I have any) will ever get to see what I saw as a child
2. I promise to love, honour and obey my husband
3. There is no way that I will be the cause of the failure of this marriage
4. I will never, ever be in a situation that forces me to tell a lie to save my life again
5. If I live through this I must find a way to leave this man. I never want to live through this again. I would rather be dead

I think that's enough to be going on with. For these were bubbling below the surface of my mind and I had no idea how they would be resolved. It certainly gives a picture of the corner of the room that I had been painting myself into or that I had been painted into. But these also became also my 'get-out-of-jail-cards.

I was yet to discover other things that had also influenced events, and that I was about to challenge. One of them was this: *'What happens in family, stays in family. We do not tell others what goes on within the family or beyond these four walls.'* Great code for supporting family members, especially if others are out to 'get' you or your family - though realistically, there would have to be something pretty damaging to have taken place to be in *fear* of others knowing about it. It is also a great concept for keeping secrets, keeping control, for covering up unhealthy ways of being. Though I guess a lot of families have this similar attitude to a degree. It is self protective of course.

But it can also be used to *blind* those in family who are getting a raw deal, and keep them from usurping the status quo – for how can you have the spotlight of clarity and reasonableness on something if you cannot discuss or compare with other options, opportunities or ideas when you are forced to 'hide' everything? So each family and each individual eventually, in order to mature, has to work out the line between loyalty and allegiance to one's family (and others) versus one's allegiance and loyalty to oneself and one's own well-being. And those with good consciences, hearts and souls usually desire to do so without harm to others wherever possible.

Who knows what goes on behind closed doors? Some ask 'Why does a woman stay with an abusive man like that?' when a better alternate question might be 'Why does *he continue* to do that?' followed by 'What can we do to *stop* that?' Thank god family abuse is now considered a crime and people are exposing it and talking about it more and more – domestic violence is being more readily aired and in some cases being reported and prevented. As in the following case.

Nigella

In the news a short while ago was the story about Nigella Lawson and her famous hubby Mr Saatchi, the past advertising mogul. And that in itself is a possible clue by the way – he was a mogul in the *past* – what claim to current fame does he still hold? Not much at present, except a certain current notoriety. In the newspapers and on the media, we are shown photographic shots of him gripping her throat whilst out at a restaurant. This was apparently his *acceptable* behaviour whilst in a public place. I remember wondering about what went on behind closed doors if this is what he did in front of others. I already knew that my husband wouldn't dare risk letting others know of some of his behaviours and treatment in private. Jim was too much of a coward and a hypocrite to do anything like this in public.

Saatchi's gallant response anyway was to spread it abroad that Nigella has a drugs problem and this was his excuse to do what he did in public. Her side of the incident is totally different, and more believable to me. Having been through what I have been through, I have learned to listen and to more easily recognise a battered or abused wife.

The story that unfolded in court was of her past cocaine-taking in company with her first husband who was dying from cancer. I can understand this and do not condemn her. It was reported that the only other occasion she resorted to it was when she 'felt isolated' in her marriage with this current husband. She talked of *Intimate Terrorism* in their relationship. (I 'get' this too). The court reports stated that when asked about the picture of Saatchi gripping her by the throat, he said he was challenging her about using drugs. Her story was that she had commented on a child in a trolley being pushed past the restaurant and had said what a pleasure it would be to have some grandchildren. At this point he had grabbed her by the throat and said 'I am the only one you should be concerned about. I should be the only one giving you pleasure'. These are the words of a narcissist. That was when she mentioned the term 'Intimate Terrorism'.

And to me it is a big reminder of the type of mentality that ran Jim.

At this point the television journalist on the morning show airing this commented in a sneering manner 'Yeah, and I've heard that one before!' That ignorant comment riled me. I would hazard that this man has no idea or understanding of what she and other women have been subjected to in their relationships. And let's hope that he's fortunate enough not to experience that, hey? But I was very disgusted with this, and got so riled up that I had to change channels immediately. This was too close to home for me, and then I realised the reason I had gotten so angry with him was because of the many times that Jim had done the same thing to me behind closed doors. How come I could forget about such a thing? It's called being 'Stupid' and I mean this in the pure sense of the word.

Oh, one last word. He had previously threatened her with 'exposure' and accusations on her drug taking which had happened ages previously, and that he would destroy her. Such love, such dedications – shows the type of man he really is to threaten such things. And this 'gentleman' (not) has now proceeded to do exactly that by using this opportunity to create this 'exposure' rather than admit what he was really doing at that restaurant. Power hungry jealous manipulator.

Pardon me for sounding less than sympathetic, and lacking supposed Christian-compassion on this. A bit close to home for me.

Far from this incident shaming her, I think that she has gained the sympathy of many who can identify with her. Her program is still popular, and that says a lot.

Unstable Jim

I think I have painted a pretty accurate picture of the atmosphere of life in Werribee whilst I was working at TOW Chemicals.

Parts of the marriage were working still, others were trying to catch up, still others were totally stuck in old patterns and were getting worse. And some parts were now *totally* broken, irreparably damaged, though these were not easy to see.

I had been allowed for some time to wear makeup again, though I was always discreet and only used smidgins. Mainly to keep up with my position at work. My clothing had been updated and I had been sewing more suitable office clothing. And as I now had my figure back again, I enjoyed being a little more fashion conscious, though I was still governed by practicality, as at home there were always three sets of possibly grubby hands to deal with as well as domestic chores.

Naïve Hope

I was coming up with new recipes, new places to take the children for enjoyment, talk of what other people did to keep their relationships alive. I was open to new ideas and even gathering and developing my own opinions, simply because I was being asked and being heard, even if not agreed with at work.

I was thinking of how we could improve things for us both, of how we could get some magic into our relationship, of possible 'romantic date' ideas, shared hobbies, anything that wasn't just work, children and the Bible. I was seeing the positive effect that having some fun could have on a family. The old mantra of 'the family that prays together stays together' had been morphing into 'the family that plays together stays together' in an attempt to save the relationship

But it would appear to me that at each step of my exercising my own mind Jim met this with blocks, abuse, threats and punishment. Excuses not to participate in new ideas, not to try new things, were just so easy for him to manufacture. And giving me the benefit of the doubt seemed to be a real challenge to him.

Some things he had taken on board, when it suited him. He knew that I was good at quite a lot of things, like letting me be responsible for paying the bills for instance. It's what I got paid for, wasn't it? Or actually, and more accurately 'This is what you do at work, so you're supposed to be good at it. *You* do it. You're better than me at this. You keep records of the accounts and take care of the bank statements'. And of course one could make an argument for other reasons for handing this job over to me. Fortunately, I was a good bargain hunter, and not a spender, and very conscientious of all of this – again the biblical Proverbs at work. So there was never much cause for accusation over bills, I was never a 'spendthrift' or shopaholic nor did I pay for expenses that couldn't be fully justified.

When Jim had been charming and in a good mood, it had been a real pleasure. I think this is in part how I managed to put up with the abuse and stay with him through this time. And also the belief that he would eventually change and possibly be like this all of the time.

He would do anything for me at certain times – though guilt may have been involved at some level I never did quite work out the rhythm, rhyme or reason of this, I only recognised them when these times were upon us. If there was some change that I knew that we needed to make life better, improve the home or the functioning of it, or in some way make us happier, I had to save it up for just such times. I had to do this to ensure that the boys got new shoes when they really needed them, when they needed extra money for a school outing that he might say a firm 'No' to otherwise. If he had been like this naturally more often, things could have lasted longer. But I think that there was probably just too much wounding in some way within this man, some sort of warping or corruption for it to be other than it was – this is the excuse I have sometimes used for him. For the only other options are to see this man as socio-pathic, or a man of extreme anti-social behaviour, or a misogynist, or a very sick and mentally unstable man. Or all of these things! And as we have seen, he can be totally and crazily insane on occasion.

Again, I remind myself that this book or journal is to set the record straight, so I am countering all of his absent accusations of me with this record of his acts and perpetrations. What I mean by absent accusations, are those allegations, those blames and shames, those lies, those charges against me that he made after we had split up.

And one day, I would like to give him a copy of this so he can see for himself just what he has been in denial of and to remind him of that which he wants to forget. This is *not* about revenge – for how can one punish someone who has no conscience, no compassion, no ability to make any changes to better themselves? Someone who has demonstrated such thoughtlessness, such cruelty, such twistedness?

No, this is about me finding *my voice*, and at least saying 'You may choose to conveniently deny or forget what you have done, *but I know the truth* and this is it. I am speaking up for myself now, because *I couldn't speak up for myself back then*. This is who you were and probably still are.' This is also about Justice and about Domestic Violence and how the church, amongst others, allows it. Frankly, what he does with all of that, with what I write, I really don't give a damn. Not any more. I am not a vengeful person, that

Naïve Hope

is not the essence of who I am. But I am no longer a mat to be walked upon either.

Regarding his interrogations, I have revealed some of the things that he did that were beyond most 'normal' family situations. What I still find hard to understand is the escalation from inquisition to torture, from charmer to terrorist. For what else is it when a man threatens you with actual harm on your life and also your children's if you don't obey his wishes, if you don't do what he wants you to do or say what he wants to hear? Since I left Jim, no man has ever laid a hand on me again. *For I would not stand for it.* I now know better. I am wiser. I myself would not have dreamed of doing this to someone else. I also know I will never again be imprisoned by a man in a mental, psychological, financial and emotional way. This is something that simply would not be allowed to happen again.

However, during all of this, with my sons as the ransom and death as the threat, when one is emotionally attached to a man whose job is supposed to protect you, whom you are allied with on so many levels, then when they use brute force to back up their threats and cowardly stance, one just might crumble and lose sight of one's Rights. This is because they have been taken away from one. Even though the chains and whip are not visible, they are still in place.

It is only now that I can recognise this element to the games he played. Sure I heard his threats and his words at the time and was appalled by them. But being in the grip of fear and being faced with possible direct action at that very moment to carry out a threat firmly places one in pure survival mode. Survival mode can lock the brain into a kind of cycle, a stupor, a kind of focus that is totally occupied with how one can survive the perceived threat, and in that long moment all of one's resources are brought to bear on this. These long moments can quickly become long hours. Then days. Add to this a familiarity with violence and threats whilst growing up, and you have a brain that in some areas of life and living has become soggy with fear and kind of 'Stupid' and cannot think clearly or cannot think differently about it, though one is capable of clear thinking in many other areas and other issues. But not in this. Stupid! Stupid as in being in a 'Stupor': 'helplessly amazed' or 'dazed'.

If I had known at that time that I might have been able to take all of these 'threats' of his to the police and get direct action to stop it, I would have done so. But even so my mind wasn't looking in that direction – it was too busily engaged in keeping this man pacified, in catering to his moods and needs, in keeping 'the peace'. Learned patterns, lifelong programmed behaviours. And I was in a stupor, a helplessly amazed state still. If I had have been able to be aware enough to look for them, I would done so. But I didn't know what I was looking for, what I needed. I only know I had to avoid danger and violence for me and my children. *I had to keep us alive.*

I had become 'punch-drunk' with it all. In a way, one part of my mind had had to adjust to this as a way of life in order for me to continue to function. And this one part seemed to be activated most of the time in order to preserve not only my life, but also to avoid anything that might be directed at me that would also include direct action against me and the children together. I had seen him hit the boys, but he had never gone at them in the same way that he had gone for me. And a master stroke to keep me in check was this threat of his. It can take some processing after an intense and long hostage situation to deprogram and rehabilitate someone who has been brutalised or dehumanised like this.

As it was for me. But I am not out of the woods just yet.

Go Ahead; Shoot!

Because of circumstance, I had to shelve the decision made during the machete episode. I thought this was as bad as it could be and didn't envisage that there would be anything worse. I was wrong.

And quite naturally (I use the word loosely here), Jim had remorse later. Not that I remember any apology, for it wasn't spoken of later. I think his remorse was not obvious even to him. But I noted that he made attempts to 'make-it-up' to me. The usual; getting my favourite chocolate, taking us out for a drive that weekend, cups of tea, doing a chore or two around the house. But this time I felt so numb to it that it hardly registered.

I had buried the attempt to leave for now, as I didn't have any other answers. The energy it had taken to summon up the courage that

Naïve Hope

had been required to take action and to follow through on such a thing had been *huge*. And I was emotionally exhausted.

Meanwhile, somehow the machete had disappeared on us and he had managed to acquire a cheap lawnmower. Little did he know that I had disposed of it with shaking hands the very day the rubbish bins were emptied, and I had to pretend that I knew nothing about where it had got to. I do *not* regret lying about such a thing and I now openly confess to it. I didn't want to *ever* go through that again. I hoped that something like that wouldn't happen again...

But Jim still isn't through yet...

I should have seen the writing on the wall when he passed his security guard exam and came home boasting about getting his gun license.

Not long afterward he came home proudly parading a hand gun. I had never encouraged him down this path. But for someone who was semi-skilled and not that intelligent he had had few options – though he used to brag about having more 'common-sense' than I did (Huh!?) – well, that's what *he* thinks.

He made a great show of this new gun to me, and he did as he was instructed to by his employers – he secured it someplace it couldn't he easily taken from; he drilled holes in the concrete floor just inside our bedroom wardrobe and screwed on to the concrete a tough metal box with special bolts that had a heavy duty lock. He spent a few minutes showing me with special pride his new acquisition, proof that he was now a fully qualified security guard – and after he deliberated with it for a few minutes, with subtle hints about having a new 'friend' that could back him up, he placed the gun in the box and locked it away. The key went on his key-ring and into his pocket. The bedroom door lock was rechecked and he was satisfied. For the moment.

That gun gave me the shivers from time to time, but he had momentarily reverted to his charming self again, proud of his accomplishment of getting a license and being further qualified in his security work. Proof that he was smarter than me, I guess. See he wasn't such an ignorant Irish man any more, he now had real worth, and others will think twice about messing with him now, wouldn't they? Yes Jim. Whatever you say, Jim.

He developed a new habit of preparing for work now, which included making a show of the gun belt and holster and the gun. I am sure it gave him a feeling of power. And he would come home and replace it in almost a special religious routine kind of way. I was always glad when I could see that he had locked it away.

It is now one evening after the children are in bed – funny how he always did this, isn't it? Waits till the boys are in bed – no witnesses? He has finished work and is again in a suspicious and foul mood. And again he embarks on his nutty interrogations.

But *this* time, it wasn't to be his fists.

On this particular evening we go through the usual things, as he starts doing his usual schizo act; accusing me of having slept with someone, kissed them, done sexual acts with them, blah blah – goodness bloody knows why, because it was all such a predictable and regular litany by now. For god's sake, if you feel like hitting me then just do it. If you need a screw, then just demand your rights, instead of this mindless false crap.

As I closed off part of my mind to the script, automatically responding with my usual denials, I was watching him in a different way. Things had changed between us, not that it showed in any of the domestic rituals and habits, but it was as if I was seeing him in a different kind of way. Yes, there was fear there, there always is when you know you could end up with a black eye, or a sore jaw again. But after the knife incident, I knew that I just couldn't give in to him by fulfilling his imaginary wild fancies again.

Whatever it was that he finally settled on as the reason to try, sentence and condemn me, his actions are fixed in my mind as if it happened yesterday. You know, I cannot honestly remember what issue it was, only what he did, what the result of it all was. I think that shock and this continued chronic abuse can block out some segments of traumatic memory whilst it can also highlight others, and anyway, these interrogations and abuses were now so much a part of my life with Jim, that I had become accustomed to them, almost accepting the ritual unless they were marked by something *different*.

He could probably feel my withdrawal, but I had no control over that. It was a natural consequence of the wounds in my heart and mind.

It is almost impossible to remember everything that happens when placed under such stress. Though the impression stays. My, does it stay. And the key words get burned into your mind. Why I clearly remember this one is because this one was different.

The next step on the road of danger; this time, he brings out his gun to threaten me.

The boys are in bed, presumably asleep. He starts what appears to be a normal conversation in the lounge room, speaking about work and the changes happening there. Maybe he has finally believed what I said about having stayed faithful to him? I don't yet know. Maybe it's good news... One can only hope, for the next thing I know is that Jim goes into the bedroom and calls me in after him. I don't refuse, how can I? and his demeanour doesn't indicate any threat.

Then Jim locks the bedroom door and next he opens the wardrobe door. Initially I wonder what he is up to, thinking he was probably going to tell me something about work, or he might even have a gift for me by way of an apology, like he used to do; because I don't remember seeing that same look in his eye on this occasion, that 'I'm going to make you pay' look. But he has locked the door, so maybe *not* a gift then... I still have no idea of what is to take place, I am not at all prepared for what happens next. Maybe I was going through a 'numb' phase and operating on automatic – I don't honestly know. I was not prepared...

He takes a key out of his pocket, bends down, and as soon as I realise he is going to the gun-box I start to hold my breath. There is a quiet intensity, a purposefulness to his movements, a kind of deliberation as though he is setting the stage and acting a part...

Just like a snake, one that appears to be harmless but is in fact just waiting for you to be unprepared enough for it to strike...

Exactly like with the machete episode, I think he used these shock tactics to really get to me, hijacking me without displaying his usual pre-amble of accusations. Thinking back now, again there really was little to alert me. He appeared to be planning his actions coldly now. The element of *surprise* – that was his new make-me-feel-like-a-man-toy and weapon.

I remember clearly, all too clearly, that he put a bullet in the gun then held it up and pointed it directly at my head. It was an inch or so away. No words yet from him, just his implicit threat of annihilation. He was looking for a reaction. I froze. Ah! So let's try this, he must have thought, as for extra effect he then held it next to my temple. He actually placed it *fully loaded* against the side of my head! I was suddenly wide awake – all of my nerves screaming - what was going on? He is messing with a loaded weapon, and this is no longer part of my survival manual – this is *way* beyond what any one person is allowed to do to another, no matter the deal.

Is he going to kill me?

Is this it? Is this the end? Is this the sum total of my life? Is this all I deserve?

This can't be it? But I can't take any more of this. Something has to change.

Now, too terrified and resigned to see if he is bluffing, too caught up in this incredible situation, one you only read about or see in the movies, I await the click of the trigger, the sound of contact with the firing pin. Does my life pass before my eyes? Kind of. The futility and the end of it just like this does. The grim result of all my efforts. I see a newspaper headline: 'Werribee Man Shoots Wife'. I wonder who will look after the boys. How they will cope. My own mother's shocked reaction when she learns of 'the bed' that I had made and ended up lying in. The Pastor's face at who Jim really is.

I am shaking like a plucked guitar string – no sound, just vibration. My eyes are no longer seeing the room as inner visions race past my mind. And there is nothing I can do about it. I am powerless at this moment. At the mercy of this madman, this unhinged lunatic.

Naïve Hope

Now I was *more* than scared – I am absolutely terrified. Again. I was barely breathing. And he then began his questions.

'Who was it you saw today at work?' This was the insane opener. Then in his next breath: 'Who are you cheating on me with?'

'What? ' I stuttered. 'No one!'

'If I think you are lying I will shoot you *now*. If I thought you were cheating on me, this is what will happen to you. And you will never see the kids ever again. And they will never find your body, because *I know* of places where to put it'.

He scared the shit out of me, and I knew that he could be pushed the wrong way and be tipped over the edge.

What can I say? How can I stop this? I *can't*. I wasn't aware of any rights at that time, there was no internet then, no way I could have Googled solutions beforehand, would that it was available to me back then. I only knew what I knew. And what he told me.

The next questions were about the men at work, and what they had said about woman and the things that they got up to behind their husbands backs. Then it was about what I had worn that day, did I wear my good underwear, and what were the colour knickers and bra that I had had on, and if I had bent over in front of any of them at work etc etc etc...

This man was just a *Sicko*! A bloody sicko! And I was married to IT!

Something shifted, something changed. In me. I suddenly came to a place where I *didn't care* any more if he *did* pull the trigger. I had hit overload. I was done. I was through if this is all my life was about. Why bother any more if you do the right thing and get this as your reward? God had deserted me, that is if He and Jesus had ever actually been on the job. I was over it.

It was like '*Go ahead. You might as well. It's no better or worse than life here with you. And then I won't have to go through all this again.*' In fact I think I said as much to him. In my head, I was now ready to die – I couldn't live like this anymore. '*You might as well kill me, because I haven't done anything wrong and I might as well be dead if you think I did*', I think were the words I said out loud... Long seconds of frozen time with the gun against my head whilst I waited for that final explosion.

I couldn't stop him. God wouldn't (or couldn't) stop him. Nothing could stop him. I was done. I was ready to go. *What are you waiting for?*

The gun was lowered.

And I can't even remember exactly what happened next, of how it ended. I have a vague idea he muttered something about him now believing me that I had been faithful.

I was in such shock that I think I was still shaking for a while after. Again, I can't remember exactly what happened when he left me alone in the bedroom, the door unlocked. I have only vague recollections of that part.

But I do remember that he had terrified me so very profoundly and personally. He had also made some threats about the police finding us all with bullets through our brains. Him included. Life made no sense anymore. This was too much for anyone to take.

If this man didn't really intend to kill me, then this 'man' was totally set on wearing me down to totally disempower me. And he was getting some sort of kick or fix out of it. Otherwise, why do it?

I numbly went through the days that followed. I had reached something, some state, some place that I couldn't describe. It was some time before I could think clearly. Later came the questions. What was the point in living a goodly life and following your conscience when you got threatened and punished like this and by a *supposed Christian* and for *not* even doing any *one* thing that he had accused me of?

Where was this God that was supposed to help those trying to do the right things, trying to be pure? Where was the Saviour who was supposed to be there for me? Nowhere!

Who was going to help me and my children? No-one!

I lost not only a part of myself. I finally lost my blind persistent faith in a God who wasn't there when you truly needed Him to be. Whose own recorded words of being a 'Loving Father' who 'cared for those who love' Him, were empty, flat, powerless, worthless and now totally irrelevant to my life.

Right then, life was *not* worth living.

I was done. There was nothing much else left to lose, hey?

COUNTING THE COST

November 2013 – It is at this point I must divert from my memories, perceptions and interpretations for the moment. Because in the re-membering of these events, in the actually admitting them and committing them onto paper, there naturally comes a certain amount of re-living.

I have put in a lot of time, energy, money and therapy work to be free of the impact of the traumas I have lived through. This has been a long, long process because of the layer-upon-layer that I had experienced in life. This is not necessarily the norm for most people, but may be a similar path for those who have been quite impacted by such traumatic experiences. A few like myself that have felt so deeply can absorb more of this sort of shock energy than others. Being sensitive to start off with, I have had to learn to shut down and bury certain things, things that were simply just too painful to feel because I had felt so acutely.

The reason for this interjection at this point, for this break in the flow of events is because I have been rereading my experiences of being pregnant, and of when Jim began his interrogations in such a frightening way. The lead up to it all that I have laid out before you. I recognise now, in a way that I did not before, just how badly things had progressed. I had made such adjustments that I hadn't seen the degree of darkness that had become a part of my life at this time.

Buoyed with optimism at being in a new home, at this new life joining our family, I had gradually adjusted to his progressively abominable behaviour. One cannot help comparing current life and how things turn out *after* events when one reviews things. And my inability to be able to judge the situation correctly, probably misinterpreted by me at the time as making Judgement on someone, and which was not a supposedly Christian thing to do, had left me at a disadvantage to see exactly what was going on.

I had become accustomed to things. Gradually and over time, I had become *flattened* so to speak, deadened to the possibility of pro-action on my part to stop things. This stupid bloody concept of perpetual forgiveness is just such utter tosh when I view how badly the behaviour of my husband and of my blinded-allowing-of-it-all has impacted on my sons. This really pisses me off. Forgive they say. *Who* says? The do-gooders who don't recognise that a bad lot is really a bad lot! Instead of getting better, this man simply got *worse*. The more I gave, the more he took. The more I forgave, the more he took advantage and slipped deeper, pushing the boundaries of just how much he could get away with.

And I have to interrupt my writing and editing here; I have to be honest and authentic in this journal, as it documents truly the events of my life and marriage. So I must share with you at this point, and possibly in other parts of my writings, that as I sit here and recall and recount parts of my story, fresh aspects of these events appear. As memory fragments arise they then seem to turn a key in a lock that accesses more information, more memory. They then translate themselves into the full memories at the time that these things happened, together with their associated feelings, for these now emerge; things I had totally locked down, *feelings* interlinked with memories that I had buried *so deep* it had just left a blank page over certain incidents and spaces in my life - these now emerge in a surprising and eruptive way bringing with them the sharp recall of those same feelings, emotions and pain of the time anew.... And as a consequence, I cannot but enter again into the time, with the memories so acutely real and stingingly refreshed – and my unbidden response is to simply break down with the sobs emerging from deep within me. As I do now. This takes me a time to recover, and of course, the emotional energy spent causes me some tiredness. Even though I have worked upon many layers, others not yet cleared are triggered through these writings.

I will try to write my experiences of this next, for right now I need to deal with these emotions. Here follows a faithful rendition of what I went through:

Naïve Hope

I have to break from my work, from this writing to recover. Not only can I not write accurately right now, I cannot concentrate on putting experiences into words for a moment, but I also cannot see for my eyes just stream with tears and my body sobs as I hold a hand to my upper chest and near my throat. The pain is so overwhelming, I just have to allow it, to cease all other functions in order to breathe through this. Tears continue to pour forth. I have to get up and pace around, holding my heart and my throat, nursing my Self with my arms as I do so. I walk the room. Sometimes stopping and rocking on my heels. I work my way through some issues, I work my way through tissues. I sob. I swear. I curse. I hurt.

All else stops until it subdues. This takes time...

And eventually I begin to regain my normal breathing, my composure again.

I make a note of what it is, of what I remember, what is hurting me deep within, what I am feeling so strongly about. If I don't clear them now, I will work through them later with the techniques I have learned through my therapy training. But for right now, I have to feel, to acknowledge. For in the feeling and recognising I have already begun a process of healing, some clearing is already taking place, yet replaced by more underneath it. I have recognised the 'emotional charge' I may still have on any issue that has now pushed its way through to my conscious mind and my attention. This charge lets me know that there is still more to be healed, more to release. I breathe again. When there is no more pain left to feel, the work will be ended.

But oh, the pain while the memory emerges. The heartbreak. The torture.

It takes me time to recover, but during these times of recovery, I must confess that chocolate has became a closer friend, though I do have to watch when it becomes practically a live-in lover, for I just want to taste its creaminess and smooth warmth almost all the time. Fortunately I recognised this need to fill my senses with the happiness or comfort that chocolate seems to provide, and to remember that I need to be kind and nurturing to myself, preferably in a way that is not so physically harmful.

I ring my friend when I have gathered myself. She too is a therapist and we have supported each other through some of our painful times. Each phone call bringing improvement each session clearing more of the pain, the stain, the charge on what has emerged and freshly revealed itself.

'I didn't realise that there was still more to work on, there was still stuff locked down there' I cry out to her in tears and desperation and surprise.

'It's because you had layer upon layer. You can only peel back as you are ready and able to do so. These layers have become intertwined with who you are, and to clear them requires energy, a safe space and clarity. Just look at what you are now remembering. And look at all that you have already cleared. You have worked through all the obvious layers, and now you are hitting the deep stuff. You will get there,' she encourages. And I know she is right.

If nothing else then these writings are freeing me up by exposing my memories to the fresh light of day in a way that is at least chronological. As I record the events of my life, instead of my recording only the most significant and gross highlights, I cannot but help to remember *how* I got to where I got – the progression. And the insidiousness of this creeping and deepening abuse. My lack of recognition at the time momentarily makes me feel like a fool for allowing such things. But I am not the fool, for when I use the eye of compassion I see how I have played a straight game, how I have contributed and given; and I stop condemning myself. If a fool does not recognise when he has it good and pisses all over it, then one cannot change that fool. The fact that I had been painted into a corner by my beliefs and lack of support does not make me responsible for the fool's behaviour, for I gave every chance for change. I honoured my vows. I did my best. And I have since so very much changed my views and my beliefs!

At this point, I also want to note that since July 2013 I have finally been in my own place, my own residence for the first time in over two years. In these last few years so much has happened, and for a while I was forced to live in shared spaces and places, some on the other side of the world, as dictated by circumstances. Now a new feeling, a new breath is coming into my life – the sense of a new start, as I am now in a space and environment to finally clean up the remnants of the past and attend to these foundations of my life and health. And with this has come the space to focus on my boys and on their healings too.

Working further with my good friend Angela, I (and often it's been *we*) have been working through and clearing these old emotions, pain, issues and suppressions and repressions, memories and resonances on a deeper level now that I am in this new space – a place where I can relax in a manner, and I can temporarily call home. For here I can just 'be', I can let my guard down to a degree, and let my own energy fill this space and place, without having to watch or concern myself with the problems and impacts of others to the degree I had before. And this allows my process of release, relief, retrieval, recovery, reclamation and eventual realignment.

Sometimes it feels like sheer bliss. And I am grateful. These moments between the work and processing and clearing and the daily concerns of life are keeping my eye and mind and heart on the possible prize – complete healing for me and possibly for my sons and their families. As I heal, I hope that in some way they heal.

And maybe, just maybe, some of my dreams may yet come true...

Back to my story.

Half Hour Tryst Twist

I was now in such a numb emotional state that I daresay that I had shut down, for it would also seem that part of me had distanced myself from him in some new way. Either that or he had killed the loyalty that I thought I had owed him as a husband. Probably both of these are true.

Truth to tell, right then and for some time before he was no longer related to the man I had married. His charm had deserted him. He was no longer making any efforts to hide this side of him. When I consider who he was then I am clear that he was not a husband, just a thug, an emotionally retarded bully, who was trying to destroy the only good thing he had in his life. But at the time I hadn't seen it as that, because I had been too caught up in my situation, too emotionally fearful and fraught, too busy placating and avoiding unnecessary interludes of triggered insanity and consequently I had lost all normal frames of reference.

Now however, this disconnection allows me to become even more observant, though I wasn't fully aware of it at the time.

Why do men cheat? The short answer is *because they can*. And of course, it feels good. Most men that cheat think or feel that they are 'free' or virile, or it makes them more powerful, or they lack self control, or they lack self-worth and need to prove that they are 'worth' something. Does this then make those same men more aware of the ease and possibility of straying and then project it onto others? A kind of 'If I can do it, then you can just as easily do it'? Their own corruption and betrayal is projected onto others, and in this way they can feel justified. But all it is is twisted tosh! Self lies! Delusion!

I knew that I wasn't having any extra-marital sex. It was all getting very wearing. Because of this continual harassment over my supposed 'affairs', I decided to challenge the ridiculousness of these assertions. I remember one day thinking to myself 'What he accuses me of is not even *possible*. Even if I was the sort of person he accuses me of being, there is *no way* that I could possibly, physically or practically, work it into my packed schedule. *'Too much to do. Not interested. Enough with the one I already have, thank you.'* If I could show him that it wasn't *possible* to do what he says that I do, if I could come up with the figures, then maybe, just maybe, faced with the logic of the situation, he will finally give up this persecution of me. The continual accusations and questions over parked cars in the street, and phone calls from I-knew-not-who, probably wrong numbers, was just plain stupid. I knew it, but Jim had to know it. Surely. Faced with enough proof, maybe this will go away. *So I thought.*

With such a scary and busy background and the current demands on my time, I just couldn't for the life of me work out *how* I could possibly miraculously or in any way even physically be able to make *time* to have this 'affair' he was always banging on about. Let alone have the *energy* for one, or the desire or even the *interest* to take on another male... it just never *occurred* to me. I had enough on my plate. But as one knows, eventually if you hear about

Naïve Hope

something for long enough, you have to question *something* about the basis for it.

With this in mind, and to *prove* its impossibility, I did an exercise one day on working out my schedule to see if I even actually had *time* to consider such a thing.

Being a natural organizer and prolific list maker through necessity, my mind naturally chose this logical way of working out things for itself. *Let's make a list and see then shall we? Did I have the* time *to do such a thing as he says?* 'No way', my mind said. 'How do you know for sure' I asked myself. 'Well, lets' see if it's even possible, shall we, for I don't see *how* even if I ever *thought* of doing such a thing'.

So I did a full schedule for a whole month on all the things I had to do and the time it took. 'Is there even *time* for such a thing to occur? Do I even have the time to *spare* to 'have an affair', hah? I don't think so!'

And of course I didn't.

Oh, but maybe I lie – for after all, *there* it was – I had squeezed out a whole *half an hour a month* that wasn't filled in with chores, work, house maintenance, sewing and mending, Bible reading, bill-paying, messages, driving, sleeping and eating. And of course, Jim.

I checked and re-checked. Yes, there it *was*!

Of all the time at my disposal, I could only muster a half hour for myself. A measly half an hour a month!

And why would I even consider doing something with or for someone else with that half hour, when I could possibly dare to sit down and risk reading a woman's magazine? Or even a book? Check out a new dress pattern? Or just go for a walk along the pier near the shops, and just breathe?

A *whole* half an hour. A *month*! Didn't even know that I had that time free... During one of my lunch hours. Thirty minutes a month. What on earth had I done with it before today? Probably had a proper lunch instead of rushing around every day...

So according to Jim, I could only find one reason for that half an hour; according to him, I would rather go through the lengthy process of trying to find a 'lover' (with all the stress and underhandedness and sordidness and sweat and discomfort that it would probably entail) rather than get my hair done, read a book, do my nails, window shop, enjoy an espresso or coffee and relax. *Relax*?! Yup, that would be my choice. I had actually discovered that I could have a whole half an hour a month totally to myself – just for *me*. Where I don't have to be *doing* for someone else. Laughable and pathetic. And I hadn't even been aware of it. Gosh the fun I could have been having with that half hour... Knock myself out looking at the sea at Altona, for instance. I *love* the sea! Mind you, as lunch time was only thirty minutes, it would take me about seven minutes to get there and the same to get back, so I could just about have fifteen minutes to muse at the waves... Which possibly cut down my affair-making-time to fifteen minutes, too, as Altona shops was the nearest civilization to the plant.

I thought Jim's unparalleled belief in my ability to perform the impossible so laughable, so pathetic, that I underscored this finding, and wrote the ironic words 'Half an hour a month in which to find a man, develop a relationship, then find a place to go to 'make-love' and to conduct an affair.' Me, with my transparent face where you could always *read* what my feelings and emotions were, how on earth could I have pulled *that* one off? Even daring to *consider* risking such a thing. What a *ridiculous* idea. To me this proved *conclusively* and beyond doubt that it was *totally* impossible.

And let's take this a step further. Suppose that I *had* the energy, that I was even *interested* in putting my family on the line by doing such a thing, I am *not* the sort of person to just seek casual sex. I need an emotional and an intellectual mind connection with someone to allow feelings to develop that would take me down that road.

This was how it had been before I met Jim, and there had been no reason to change it. I had been so very emotionally connected and devoted to him and to my marriage in this, that there was no room on any level for someone else.

God, you would have to be pretty desperate to think that half an hour a month would be enough to develop a connection with someone and act upon it? Or desperate enough to have to wait a whole month in the hope that you could do something sexually worthwhile with that half hour? Assuming you didn't have to travel for it...

Having completed the time study exercise and demonstrated to myself conclusively the utter *unfairness* and ridiculousness of the situation, and putting it on one side in my purse for the next time Jim accused me of it, I carried on with my duties. And it must have taken me at least half an hour to work it all out, so there goes my chance of an affair *that* month! Okay, so I jest. Weeell, it is pretty silly stuff really isn't it? I mean, the very *idea* that I could actually organize, establish and conduct a clandestine relationship that was satisfying (otherwise why bother?) with *fifteen* minutes a month (remember the travel time *away* from work somewhere!) was so *laughable* to me that this seemed like the final proof; that it was now so *obvious* that it would *totally* quieten all future accusations. Knowing all of this made it easier to deal with life until the next time Jim went into his moody and jealous hissy-fits, where I would be able to now *prove* him wrong, hey!

Or so I thought.

For before I knew it, and I have *no* idea how this happened, Jim had 'found' (or so he said) this little schedule and was waving it in front of my face gleefully proclaiming 'See, this proves it. Now I *know* that you are having an affair. You've even worked it all out. Look!' The man was practically jumping up and down with himself over this. He raced round the room waving it in the air. It was surreal. Like watching a kid who had just won the best prize ever! By now you will have guessed that all the protestations in the world were *not* going to change this guy's mind. He was angry. He was adamant. He had proof! But there was something else...

There was a *jubilance* about it all, a *glee* that he had found something that he interpreted to make him 'right' about it all. Then more hammering questions as to 'who', 'when', 'where' etc. followed. This went on for a couple of weeks, which of course I denied. But that didn't stop him. Oh no. He had found 'incriminating evidence'. He became even more relentless and insisting with his accusations after this. For he totally refused to accept the real reason why I had done the exercise.

He had now *proven* it. End of story.

How stupid of me to write it down? Absolutely, but how else was I going to prove to myself, or, as I had planned, prove it to him? And what sort of a person is it that so desperately wants to prove his worst fears, and cannot see what is in *front* of him, or who chooses *not* to see a truth or a reality that is contrary to how he wishes to see it? A fool, that's who. A fool believes what he chooses to see. But I myself had also played the fool by believing that this man was other than who and what he truly was. *A sick suspicious unintelligent unworthy and inadequate ignoramous of a fool.*

Why had I thought that he would see the truth and use common sense in all this? No matter what argument or proof was brought to Jim about my fidelity and loyalty, he would still choose not to believe or accept it. I once heard a saying that so applies here, and to a lot of other situations. Can't remember exactly where it came from, possibly paraphrased from Romans in the Bible.

It goes like this: '*He who is persuaded against his will, is convinced in his own mind still.*' And Jim didn't want to change his mind about me having affairs. I wonder why?

And I was so *stunned* with his reaction, so amazed, I *totally* overlooked that this man had been through my personal things... For how long I wonder...?

GAMES PEOPLE PLAY

To say that all is not right in our little neck of the woods is possibly the understatement of the year, if not longer. That someone somewhere is not doing the right thing. And that someone was *not* me. Could someone really behave so abominably? Someone who most people view as friendly, charming, helpful, understanding? Absolutely. All that I have shared with you is *true*.

If you think for one moment I would risk writing down what is not true to make any 'points' against someone, and set myself up for a further round of false accusations, then you have another think coming. Or of me to have to tell lies that would make a good husband look so bad that even his mother would turn in her grave? Why bother? I am out of it now, and his mum is dead...

Why get this book written at all, then? Why create problems where there might otherwise seem to be none? Why possibly risk everything I love by setting this all down on paper? Why do any of this if this wasn't *true*? Why would I bother exposing all of this, all of my family pain and humiliations and dysfunctions and despairs to anyone who didn't know all these things already? If I was not 'done to' in the ways that I proclaim, then why bother? Why stir up something or bear false witness to lies if it wasn't so? What could I possibly gain from telling lies about all this?

And why make myself look so stupid for putting up with it for all those years? For being so duped, even calling myself 'Stupid' or in retrospect, let's go for 'Stupefied' hey? Surely one would only do such a possibly damaging thing *if it was true*? It is too much to risk, all these revelations, with the possibility of risking hurting those innocent others that you love – unless it is for a higher reason.

If this 'telling-all' was about making money, or getting recompense, I am sure there are better ways of doing it. Why, in that case I could simply go down to this 'man' in Werribee, and stand over him now (he has had a stroke and mainly uses a wheelchair) and really threaten him, and nobody would be the wiser would they?

Or, why don't I get a ghost writer instead, and get them to tidy up my notes and journals and insert a bit more sex and 'commercial scripting' into it and go flat out for a best seller and at least make some money for this set of whacky ideas? Base it in weird and wonderful settings, include a bit of drug running, prostitution, devil worship? Hmm?

I have no need to tell other than the truth for I am *not* playing games here! These events are what happened to me, and in the telling of them I am *Setting The Record Straight*. As I have said before. This is not a game. I will no longer let bad things be said about me or remain unchallenged by this liar and dictator who tried so hard to destroy me!

Who influenced my very own sons against me, belittling my relationship with them, setting me up as the person at fault in our lives together, and succeeding in brain-washing them with his corrupted and warped ways.

He played games. Mind games. Cruel games. You may have already recognized them or seen some of them in others around you. So if nothing else, maybe someone will learn how to recognize some of these traits, and take notice, and possibly avoid getting caught up in them as I had.

Some of the games he played included *'Humiliation'* and *'Being Right'* whereby one person gets to feel self-righteousness and proud that they are not 'doing what the other person is doing' by calling them on perceived 'wrong' things, or even making things up and calling them as true. Usually the stories are made up anyway and are often a reflection or mirror of the person's own behaviour. They are, after all, only opinions and perceptions. Unless these same accusations or stories are also supported and verified by other people who one sees as honest, fair, reasonable and believable.

This only works if the one being called on is prone to or had a history of being made to feel ashamed or been made responsible for the happiness or well-being of others. Well, that was me for sure, *but no longer*. Other games are *'Taking the Power'* because inside they feel inadequate and powerless, and by getting them to dance to their tune because they think they see that the other person is the stronger of the two, this weaker inadequate one feels more powerful. Or thinks that they are. This game is usually successful if the other player has been made to feel disempowered at some time in their life. Of if they are in a position of dependency.

There are other games I have not mentioned here. One of these was a favourite game he played called *'See What You Made Me Do'* where he got to blame someone else, usually me, for his actions, his feelings, his thoughts, his attacks – you can read more about games in a book by Eric Berne called *'Games People Play'*. I learned a lot from reading that book! There were parts of the games called *'Alcoholic'* and *'Now I've Got You, You Son Of A Bitch'* that often came into our interactions. Oh, and the *'Yes But'* was a great one, I see it so often when people want to look like they are doing something about something and yet they really aren't.

But I won't spoil the surprises for you by telling you of them all. It wasn't until twenty years after our marriage ended that I came across these books. How I wish I had read them earlier.

There are also Dances that people perform in life and relationships. The series of books by Harriet G Lerner were a real eye opener for me, and I have shared them often with my clients over the years. The series included such titles as *'Dance of Anger'* and the *'Dance of Deception'*. Anyway, it is clear by now that this man was playing games, and I didn't have a clue. I was too caught up by my conditioning, and my own morals of conscientiousness and sincerity, seriousness and service to see what was happening. But I eventually learned!

This need to play games that are harmful to others can only come from someone who is not quite right. I think. They must be damaged in some way. Or, as a good friend pointed out, they could well be Narcissistic. Or psychopathic. I only know that I came to understand that this freak was nuts! Don't ask me to be compassionate about this. I have used all of that up and there is none left in the barrel for him.

CRITICAL MASS

By now, you might be forgiven for feeling somewhat frustrated that this state of affairs had continued to the point that it had. Or that I had somehow allowed it to do so. In some ways I was ready to leave and certainly had justification to do so. In other ways, I was still struggling with how this would play out, and how I could take care of my children as well as find them and myself proper accommodation. The earlier foiled attempts at freedom hadn't exactly encouraged me in this area. I certainly wasn't ready to abandon the ship of marriage just yet until I was sure that I had exhausted every possible avenue to save it and find a way out. I wasn't yet sure if that was the case. And I had absolutely no intention of being apart from my children or of causing them any further distress if I could possibly avoid it. I had been through enough as a child and I wished none of this on them.

Not all of this thought processing was fully conscious on my part if I am honest. There is a part of the mind that will take a thought and whilst the front of the mind so to speak is dealing with cooking, cleaning, washing, driving, working etc and quite occupied in everyday tasks, this other and more hidden part of the mind will often be working away quietly. Almost like a computer that has been given a task and is working its way through all of the possibilities before it does a 'Hey Presto!' moment and spits out a particular answer.

I didn't believe that Jim hated me, rather I was still living with the idea that he actually loved me. And this is possibly so. But his version and expression of love was now alien to me, fraught with his moodiness, harm and though I hadn't yet admitted it to myself, betrayal. Quite probably there was something about *himself* that he hated and this was what was projected onto me. And maybe I was living with the idea of love that it came and rescued you from difficult situations? I think that there are a myriad of explanations of how and why this relationship was such an imbalanced one and would therefore never work as a happy partnership.

Interestingly I never really saw myself as a battered wife. Even for all the bruises. Not then, not for a long time, though the evidence was mounting and in my face to such a degree that I was now nursing repressed thoughts that I wasn't yet ready to acknowledge. How could that be? Well, I guess because of those odd moments that had seen Jim when he had been in his saner and more loving times. And initially there *were* those odd moments. However, the dynamics that had been established gave the man certain foundational rights and coupled with the continual blasts from the pulpit about everyone being sinners from the womb, and needing salvation all fed into this twist on marriage to make it a kind of prison. The picture I had of suburban violence was that it happened to others, and the poor wife was scarred or couldn't physically move afterward – though this was actually cases of violence in the extreme. In my mind I figured that the man never really loved the woman involved and had no inner desire to do the right thing by God or his wife. *Others* behaved like this. And anyway, hadn't those in the church and my own family that I had turned to kind of agreed that this was acceptable?

Naïve Hope

I must also acknowledge *my* part in the contribution of all of this in that I myself had brought this tendency to help and *want* to help others first to the relationship. This would never really change until I stopped this and looked at the cost to myself. I was not quite there yet and must have still believed somewhere in my battered and confused hoping heart that things would change, that something – and it would probably by now have to be a miraculous something – something would change and Jim would wake up and be the person that I had somehow thought I knew that he could be – the guy I first saw in that park in Manchester.

One great lesson I also learned was that a person is *not* their *potential*. If they don't exercise and nurture their potential, then it will never manifest. Mothers do this one very well (and some fathers) – we see the potential in our children and quite often already have prime job possibilities lined up in our heads – and we get somewhat surprised when a son could actually be very successful at something simply ends up just doing whatever he feels like. And by rights it is our job to encourage them to do what they feel is right for them. The trick is to encourage them to pursue their excellences without funnelling them away from their heart's desire.

Potential is not necessarily the *possible*, for we often end up with the *probable*. That's life I guess.

Even though things were certainly getting worse, I had clung to every moment when Jim had been normal, and every time he showed any tenderness to any of the children. Was he just canny in sensing when I just couldn't handle any more and that would be when he would throw out some kindness or consideration that would give me a glimpse of hope again? All I know was that I was still going through internal struggle. I had gotten a handle on some of the levels of things that were happening in the marriage, but it was all still very hazy to me.

Was I being fair? Had I left something undone that could help? I just didn't know and even though physically, mentally and emotionally I was quite depleted, I was still to a large degree held fast in this situation. Obviously. For judging from my previous reports in all this I would have surely have escaped after his first life threatening gestures. It seemed to me more and more that I was some sort of catalyst to him, and that I inflamed him somehow, no matter what I did or didn't do. Maybe if I wasn't there, he would calm down, and his love for Danny would take over? I just didn't know. And I did not want to leave my boys. They were my life! They had been entrusted to me and I would do the very best that I could for them.

But something has to give. Things are shifting, things are moving. The terrain itself has taken on new bumps and troughs so to speak, in the foundational shape of our marriage. Things that I thought were true and lasting had given way to shattered illusions. Possibilities of a shared higher goal had now moved to simple survival-mindedness for the least amount of damage and hurt. My love for this man had now been so compromised and challenged that I was simply hanging on because I had promised to, and I was now simply living out my duty to him. All of these and more were where I now lived inside of me, but I didn't even yet fully know it. For my focus was daily on how I could now get myself and the children through the day with the least amount of difficulty, discomfort and displeasure.

We are now fast approaching a critical mass in our family life. A build-up that cannot be ignored. Any pretence at a happy family life was completely disintegrating. We had embarked on our relationship in such a serious manner and had experienced no fun to cement us together. I hadn't seen yet that behind Jim's angst and anger with me was actually huge resentment and blame. If we had have been able to spend more time together before making our vows, I daresay I just might have had second, third and fourth thoughts. Possibly.

Still struggling to find acceptable solutions to the tension in our relationship and to somehow alleviate the issues that seemed to trigger escalations of Jim's suspicions, I had mistakenly thought that we did not have enough 'couple-time' or fun times together.

Jim continued playing the *'Yes, But'* Game when I suggested regular romantic dates, counselling, shared hobbies, joint gym visits etc . It goes like this; there is a problem for Player A and Player B presents a likely solution. Player A – usually the one with

Naïve Hope

the problem – finds something wrong with that or some kind of drawback: '*Yes* that's a good idea, *But* it won't work because ...' (whatever they find wrong with it). Player B then comes up with *another* solution, Player A then finds some reason why that one can't happen too: '*Yes, But...*' and so Player B goes through all the possible ideas and solutions they can come up with, until *all* options are exhausted. Player A is still in the same situation, and appears to be or conveys that they are really willing to solve this dilemma. But nothing is acceptable or workable, so both reach a stalemate and Player B can become convinced that they just haven't yet found the right solution.

Unless they wake up and see that Player A maybe isn't really looking for solutions. Maybe Player A doesn't really want one. It might mean change for them, and this may be too scary for them, as they may not know how to handle it. Or they secretly may really prefer things the way they are and they then don't have to take responsibility for the consequent results. Whatever the reason, and there could be many others more, when you get involved in this game another spin-off is that this Player A gets to enlist sympathy, admiration at their attempts to fix things, albeit failing spectacularly, and they 'take' the energy, attention and life-force of another by their falseness, their engaging and their resistance. If Player B continues to try to solve this problem for Player A, they will end up depleted, frustrated and exhausted from it all. And Player A will still be looking as though they are the victim in all this.

We had been playing this game consistently and thoroughly.

'No. No. No.'

Prior to all this revelation, I had still been in the mindset that my marriage just needed help, not that it was the mess that it truly was. For I circled from 'get out, escape' to 'what about the children' to 'how can we solve this' to 'happy family dreams can still come true'... I still was caught up with that early dream of us growing old together, sitting on our rocking chairs in the front courtyard garden, chuckling about the things we had been through together, surveying our garden and orchard and watching our grandkids playing outside. Together. We had even joked about it when we were building our house and planting our courtyard. However to keep to that dream, to reach that place again I needed to reconcile what was happening in our marriage. But I couldn't do it alone, for in truth, it was the two of us that needed to reconcile the disparity between the dream and the reality. How can we discover the necessary solutions to the peace and harmony I want? And I assume, that Jim wants?

Putting on that united face, the good old 'It's just you and me against the world' had become corrupted to outright repression of what was really going on and hiding it from everyone. That 'Us versus Them' mentality of the church and of families with things to hide had really taken over. But it was now gradually breaking. The revelations I had gained through Jan had given me serious cause to begin thinking – and questioning - consciously.

Something *had* to change. But what. I began to seriously research and consider new untried ideas that would help us to review the relationship and put it on a better footing. I did not want to end it all just like that. I had been seventeen when I married, and we had been married nigh on *eighteen years* – longer married than single – I had a *lot* of history and investment in this relationship. Did I want to throw it away? *No!* Certainly *not*. I had worked too hard and too long at this. Did I want Jim to stop the violence and drinking? Yes! Absolutely yes!

During this last year or so I have dared to ask Jim to go to relationship counselling with me, and he had been very resistant. I have told him that I am very concerned at what was happening between us and of how I want to protect the boys from it, and that it was getting harder for me to continually keep seeing the effect that our disharmony (what else could I call it?) was having on them. But Jim simply expected me to handle it and still didn't see the need for outside help. 'You're my wife. You sort it. You're supposed to help me.' This was still his less than intelligent response evoked by my plea.

I was at a place in life where I could no longer wait for God to intervene. It was past that and I was changing inside. After thinking deeply about where we were at I came up with three possibly workable temporary solutions that would not end the marriage but give us both time to assess and to think. I expected that he would find at least *one* of these ideas agreeable. So I suggested the following three options to him – and all of this was to be of a temporary nature to give us time to cool-down, think, consider and also hopefully undertake counselling;

1. Jim moves out for a while to allow things to settle down while continuing to see the boys as often as he wanted
2. I move out for a little while, maybe up to a few weeks or months, taking Danny with me, as he was still too young to leave him at home without me, whilst I rented a room nearby, to defuse the situation and provide space for us both to think and continue to work through things together
3. I move out for a few weeks or months on my own, (renting a room nearby) to help 'defuse' Jim's angst with me and hopefully improve our situation whilst we undertook counselling and talking together

I didn't classify any of these as a separation, and didn't actually *see* it as that, more as a diffusion and de-escalation. The idea of taking a room nearby, and I went out of my way to explain this to him, was that I would come over at night times after school, actually after my work, and cook for them and spend time with them, but that it was clear that I slept apart whilst we worked on sorting out the tension in the marriage. And get counselling. I would have them at weekends as well if that was okay with him, and we would work out what was best for the boys whilst we sorted things out.

These suggestions were my effort to give us both some space and time to review, as I did not want to simply throw away these *eighteen years* of marriage and emotional investment. It was also to give me space to decide what to do to rescue our marriage. And for Jim to calm down a bit. I guess I also hoped he would then find a way to get help, help that I couldn't give him. Things simply could not continue the way they were. And as events had escalated in their intensity, I knew something had to be done before something more horrific occurred.

He had pulled a gun on me, for crying out loud!

I was still invested in the marriage, and did not want to be the one to cause its demise so wanted less fraught opportunities for us to work on it. My idea was intended to give us both some respite from the tension and cycle or pattern we were falling into, and a chance to sort out where we would go from there. At this stage I had no intention of 'just leaving.' The term 'Separation' didn't even occur to me. To me it was a necessary cool-down.

The first time I came to him with these suggestions, he was most irate. He didn't even take a moment to talk about this. As I gave him each separate possible option he just said a loud and firm to *every one* of them; 'No!' What could I do? Wait until the next huge row or drunken expulsion from the house and ask him again?

I did. After the next outburst, I had taken the three options to Jim again after the gun incident. That's now *two* opportunities for him to seriously think about it, and again he said 'No' to each suggestion ... 'No! No! No!' He doesn't even *consider* them, still dismisses them out of hand. His words are more or less spat in my face, almost triumphantly.

But things had become so bad that I beg him to move out for a while so that I and the children would have some peace. I think my tears must have gotten to him, as I was becoming so fraught with all of this hidden madness. He must have recognised on some level what was happening for he eventually agreed to give it a try and to move out for a couple of weeks. I looked through some local short-term share situations for him and brought these to his attention. However, and totally against my advice, he went to stay at the People's Palace in King St, run by the Salvation Army and near his work. The rooms were horribly miserable. I had done my best to encourage him to stay in a share situation instead, where there would be some company and a more comfortable environment. But Jim chose to stay in this awful atmosphere in just the one windowless room with only a bed, a chair and cupboard, and all he had for company was the Bible and his beer. Consequently and understandably he got more and more morose and insisted on coming back home before the week was out.

When he came back, he was moody for days. But on that first day back his angry statement to me was 'If anyone is going to leave this

Naïve Hope

house, it's going to be *YOU*, because *I'm not!*' It was now getting clearer to me that he *wasn't* willing (and probably not able) to make any change for the better.

Within a short time, of course, he would again feel the need to show that this house we shared together was *his* castle. And things escalated even more once he was home again. After just a few days of harmony and calm when he was gone, living with him was emotional chaos again. The short sweet peace I and the boys enjoyed was again subject to his moods and rampages, his disgruntled return to drinking and his insinuations and accusations and a return to pushing me out of the house.

In much later years, with its hindsight, I wondered if someone had suggested to him that I had planned to get him out of the house and to take over the place for myself, and that he would lose it. I hadn't considered this at all, as didn't realise *any* of my rights at the time, so it wouldn't even have entered my mind.

Suggestions again to get counselling were continually met with cynicism, refusal and self-righteous outrage. Several times he had said to me: 'You're my wife, you should know how to fix this. I don't need a counsellor, as a wife it's your job to sort things, you should know what I need.'

(?) Running out of options there, laddie. Your 'Yes, But' game has dried up my lake of options. The little duckies have all flown away.

In retrospect, I did the best I could, but I didn't know what to do about all of this. Nor should I needed to have. Not having any training in psychology, and having lived the blinkered and 'unworldly' life offered or rather, mandated, by the church and its 'ministers', who themselves were certainly *not* proficient in personal or relationship matters, there wasn't really much more understanding available for me to draw on. Wisdoms called on had often been snippets from the Bible, which were often administered 'ad hoc', and often totally out of context. The only 'relationship' understandings that were available were mainly those in the Bible – basically obey God, who will 'love' you if you are good, and will 'punish' you if you are not.

Simple really. Yes, very simple. Very, very simple. Very bloody minded bloody simple! *Unthink*-ingly simple! No thinking required! Is that angst showing? That's not angst, it's a venting of the obvious.

BLINKERS OFF!

I came to realise many years later that not only was this view so unthinkingly simple, it was also rubbish. Tosh! When I prayed to God and to His Son The Lord Jesus, did they keep any of their promises? The ones where they would look after those that placed their trust in them? Like this one for instance; 'delight thyself in the Lord, He will give thee the desires of thine heart?' Nope!

God hadn't forgotten me. He just wasn't there! Not the sort of God that I had been taught about. The One person that responded to you, that cared for you, that reassured you! Right now was the time when I was at my wits end and I was really looking for some help – but would any come from Him: Hope coming from that quarter looked like it was in a coma.

It was clear that there was very little free time for me, no personal time, no 'down-time', time to do my nails, or even simply read a magazine; except for that fated half an hour a month, hah! Yet it was ok for Jim to kick off his shoes and sit down so he could drink and drink. And drink. And I would be rushed off my feet, and then have to contend with his tantrums and moods on top of everything else. This came to a head for me, when it became so totally obvious – if you looked for it – just what was going on.

One morning I do just that; I make a mental note to see exactly what contributions *he* is putting into the running of the household and family, and to note just how much *I* put in to it. I was now Consciously in Observer Mode at exactly *what* Jim contributed to the family welfare apart from his wages.

For years, and remarkably *despite* the violence and the drinking, we had been in some sort of habit of having a little Bible reading and 'prayer time' in most mornings to try to set the tone for the day. We could no longer do it together now, as I always looked after the children whilst Jim had his prayer time, even if it was only

5 or 10 minutes. And he would occasionally do the same for me. Initially, we had started off with a longer prayer and Bible reading time, but as the children grew things had got busier. We had been trying to keep this practice up for peace of mind and for reasons of our faith. It did seem to help us, I thought, though now I am not so sure. These *'Quiet Times'* had even continued off and on through his drinking bouts and his abusing ways – in the past it might have prompted an apology, but now it was just a way of getting one's head together before work and of finding a Bible verse or phrase to help get one through the day. Interestingly, even reading the Bible would produce the odd religious insight that he might share with me – who was I to knock this back – and of course this helped maintain my blind hope in our current situation improving.

However, now it has becoming increasingly harder for me to get Jim to take his turn to look after the children whilst *I* have a prayer time too, and many mornings I have lost-out because of lack of time.

This particular morning I was so desperate for some time out. I was now feeling like I was being driven to the edge as I the boys had started hammering on the toilet door whilst I am in the toilet, and they are shouting and arguing with each other and demanding my attention. Amidst all this, Jim is now just going about sorting himself out and getting his things ready for work and is not at all bothered about handling the situation for me. I can understand that we all come to this at some stage, well, *some* of us can come to this... But I had spent hours ironing his shirts the way he demanded ('With creases and folds as well, just like they have just been shop bought!'), preparing meals, organising, lunches, cleaning etc. and just needed a few minutes to focus on going to the toilet! In peace! You know what I mean. Just like Jim I have a full day of work ahead of me, too.

So I yell out and ask him to see to the boys whilst I am in the toilet, but he won't. Flat outright refuses. 'No!' *What?* I was desperate that I couldn't think, couldn't focus on doing what I was in there to do, and the din was too much to control from this side of the door. And Jim just refuses to respond to requests. Even when my shout *Please, Please!* for help.

So I took notice of this. Strike 1.

When I came out of the toilet, I ask him for a few minutes in the prayer room.

Jim had had his quiet time and 10 minutes reading the Bible whilst *I* kept the boys quiet, so I thought this was only fair. So it's maybe my turn now? By now I was really desperate for some time out before plunging in to the next lot of chores and preparations for work at the office.

So I am stung when Jim tells me point blank that he won't look after them. *Strike 2.*

I practically beg him to give me just a few minutes quiet in the prayer room. Moodily and doggedly, he refuses.

It was then I realized *just how much* I had been giving and giving, and helping and helping yet getting very little back in return, and I decided that I was *no longer* going to be as giving or as helpful as I had been any more if *my needs* continued to be ignored or denied like this. I would watch what he put in, and *match* it. And *only* match it. No more, no less. I was now consciously becoming aware of just how much I put into the marriage and the family wellbeing. Now I wanted to see what *his* contribution was.

I am being pushed to grow. To grow up. To take note and to be responsible.

Something had switched in my head. Something was coming back to reality. The drip feed of religiosity was drying up? The mounting evidence of contradictions too large to hop over? The weight of all the demands too much to carry any more? All of this and more.

Through my conscious personal internal accounting, I was making notes and discovering to my surprise that *I* was the only one seeming to do most of the house work, his uniform ironing, food preparation, organizing and handling the boys and their homework or chores, and yet still handling a full–time and responsible job, paying the bills, making all of the lunches, attending to Jim's demands and all without much support or help from him.

Hmm, let's see what happens when I *don't* do as much as I do...

Naïve Hope

I now take action, or rather, I took 'inaction' and I dare to stop 'finding the time' to make his sandwiches up for the following day. I start a go-slow that isn't obviously noticeable, that has understandable reasons behind them, but nevertheless it cuts down on what I can achieve in the mornings. It takes me longer to do this, or I am busy doing that, though I have actually just allowed myself to drop down a notch from flat-out 'mad superwoman' stuff to 'efficient' in doing the task I currently have to hand.

I dare to drag my feet!

Being used to things always being done in time, Jim is a bit stunned when I start to say that I haven't had time to do them. I have *always* made the time at the risk of being late. Well, on this occasion I just don't do it, and I decide to only go out of my way for him if he went out of his way for me – I want to see *for myself, eyes wide open*, just how *much* he is prepared to put in. See if he picks up the slack.

He fails. Abysmally! He does no more than he is absolutely *forced* to do by his own necessity. *Strike 3 and he's Out!*

This marks a major change in the relationship dynamics, as I begin to make a few decisions for myself instead of being dictated to all the time.

It would also probably be seen by him that I was being derelict, or that something else was up that was causing this subtle change in things – and I daresay it gave him fuel for his own doubts and fears. I didn't think about that at the time, but he probably really started to worry if I had someone else on the side. I hadn't. And that is not why I was doing it. All I knew was that in some way, blinkers were dropping off and I was beginning to see things I hadn't seen before.

But there was more to come – and the changes that were occurring in me now seemed to take on a life of their own. Oh I admit to being totally responsible for this. But you see, the heart also lives out through our actions. Yes, we can control with our thoughts, our minds, forcing ourselves to be a certain way. But the *heart* has a way of acting up on us if we ignore it for long enough.

And I had.

THE TIDE TURNS

So much was happening concurrently in these recent months and it was to continue for the next few months. Like the last year or so, it is difficult to be absolutely correct on exact their timelines. But the events I have described all happened so very close to each other that it doesn't matter which I write about first.

Things now definitely felt like we were heading toward something, and I have deliberately backed off doing as much as I used to toward Jim's well-being. It has taken on a life of its own. Little details, little helps that I used to attend to were now being dropped as I waited for his positive and supportive input into things. I was really aware of and smarting at the unfairness of his ridiculous accusations, and his downright stubbornness and lack of willingness to address the situation in an active positive or affirming way. I got hit anyway, so why not be less hassled about things. I had continued to encourage some sort of shared hobby between us, in those moments when he was approachable, for I had heard how this helped other couples. But he wasn't really interested, and kept coming up with excuses; his typical *'Yes, But'* reaction.

However, what he did eventually agree to begin having 'dates', which meant that we could spend time having fun instead of just work-work-work.

Permission to read the paper had come about automatically as a result of him working at The Page Newspaper and reading them himself and I wasn't going to go against this, now was I? So in the paper write-ups they gave reviews, and over several months we tried out a couple of the recommended restaurants. One day, possibly in one of his guilty moments, Jim had asked me what I would like to do, and I remembered the enjoyment I got out of dancing. Now Jim points out a restaurant called 'Peanuts' which has a little dance floor and offers commendable plates alongside reasonably priced drinks, together with a good selection of current dance music. This was around the time of the Boogie, 'Saturday Night Fever', The BeeGees and Disco. It was down one of the 'Little' streets in Melbourne.

Naïve Hope

It sounded fun, which we sorely needed, and we went to check it out together. We actually *enjoyed* ourselves. I must say that I felt that Jim was being a good sport at the time. I used to love dancing in my early teens – were hopes of some sort of connection being resurrected again? I think the joint exercise to music did not only me some good but also Jim.

For me, this was a wonderful discovery! We just might have found something that would help to keep us together, a shared interest that might bring us close again, inject some romance back into our relationship, some fun! But I think I was having more fun than Jim and didn't realise it. And I think this turned out to be his next 'Yes, But' issue. I had loved dancing in my early teens, and I know I had been a good dancer then. Jim's form of dancing was very basic, and even though he was able to keep the beat, he didn't know what to do with his hands and arms, and did a kind of march with them raising each alternately above his head like he was yanking on a bell-pull. It looked very mechanical and out of rhythm, but I wasn't about to put him off, was I? I was dancing!

We went another couple of times, but unbeknownst to me, Jim was now looking for criticisms. It wasn't long before we were there one night when a guy came up to us as we were sitting down between dances and asked Jim in a friendly manner if he could sit at our table as the others were all taken up. Jim charmingly – *hypocrite* – said 'Yes, please do so'. And we had a brief polite conversation, as one does when sharing a table. That's it!

Jim's tirade on the way home afterwards was all around it being so obvious that this guy was setting us up for a threesome etc – and seemed totally *beyond* me. What? I would never have guessed that! Apparently, I had encouraged him and I was having a laugh at Jim behind his back. What? Rubbish and balderdash. So, later at home again, I had to reassure him and re-commit my loyalty and attentions toward him again - before we were to venture out the next time.

Ho-hum! This does get boring doesn't it? Even I am bored at this very moment with having to continually tell of this man's need to be this control freak, demanding to be the centre of attention in my life, but that *was* the current state of affairs - And you can guess that there would be quite *another* argument before he felt guilty enough to 'reward' me with our next evening out again.

By this time, we have reached Critical Mass.

The weights have been set, the scales have struggled to stay balanced. Now true gravity comes to town, and, at the risk of mixing more metaphors, the milk is about to be well and truly spilt.

The slippery slide Jim had begun in his own mind was about to come to its natural conclusion.

Not long after this, and getting close to the Christmas season, I am amazed that I have eventually managed to persuade him to lift the mood and go out with me for a 'date' which has been long overdue. Jim had promised off and on for a while to take me out dancing again - I can't remember precisely why he was willing to take me out on this occasion - as I said earlier, it was most likely his way of compensation for his drinking and the subsequent effects. His way of apologising now? We had organised this date time but it had been cancelled several times, as tiredness was his excuse. More like he had been recovering from the drink. His last promise had been firm, and he assured me that he would *definitely* not back out the next date we made, so I was really looking forward to this, deprived as I had been for any entertainment and fun. It had just seemed like work, work, work. Not just for me, but for both of us.

The date-night arrived, but when Jim finally came home from work the night that we were due to go out, he said he was just too tired. Disappointment was written large all over my face. Let down, yet again...

So you can imagine I was *floored* when he suggested that I *go out on my own*; this was unprecedented and previously had been totally unthinkable. My immediate response was not to take this offer up. I would never normally consider going out without him.

But then he insisted, and again he reiterated that because he was too tired, and he had promised me, and he was sorry, yes, do go out without me. I think he was secretly hoping I would stay at home. Again. I hesitated but I had been so disappointed several times with all the postponements, and with my heart had been set on us

Naïve Hope

finally having a dance night, I actually seriously dared to consider it. It seemed like ages since we had been out. Since *I* had been out!

Now we all know that in the old days I would have read what he wanted – and then done it. But this was Now and too much had been happening. Life had been running hot and cold, as had Jim. Arguments that escalated to fights, followed with me then begging Jim to get help or defuse these situations by us finding a way to have our own space for a while. Then his half-hearted attempts to try a suggestion only to come back with the usual *'Yes, But'*. After his hyper-suspicion about this poor bloke who hadn't said boo to a goose really yet was accused of plotting a three-some. And then Jim dragging his heels at our continuing to go dancing. I must have been more disappointed than I had realised. I certainly needed and deserved some sort of fun and pleasure even if simply because of the pressures of having three children and a full-time job, let alone living with this nutter. I didn't smoke, I didn't drink, didn't swear, didn't do drugs, didn't gamble, didn't spend madly, didn't stuff my face, didn't put him down or rebel against him, didn't flirt or cheat with other men. The only addiction was religion and the marriage. I still fitted my size 11 wedding dress, was developing really good dress and fashion sense and knew what suited me. I was in my prime. Firm, fit and attractive, and I knew this through the feedback at work. Jim was becoming an old man. Even his dancing was old-man dancing whereas I was watching the new dance steps and able to copy them quickly. Maybe this was one of his reasons for his inevitable refusal to not go out. For I loved moving to the beat of the music.

Usually I would be too scared to take him up on this offer, or too fearful of what he would do if I said yes. But I was fed up with how things were, and needing to have a break from work and worry all the time, and possibly because Jim was obviously feeling guilty at letting me down again.

And now he offers for me to still go out. On my own! This was indeed heady stuff! When I realised that he was still insisting that I go out and that I could actually escape the house for a couple of hours, it only took me a moment to decide.

I surprised myself at how quickly I took the opportunity to go dancing on my own, as I had never done this since before I got married. It seemed like a taste of freedom, and it was. I can see now that on a sub-conscious level this was a set-up for a showdown for us both.

I continued getting ready, kissed him goodnight, got my car keys and handbag, ensuring I had just enough for my expenses and I went out.

I felt *amazing* driving to 'Peanuts'! Oh, what a great time I had dancing there, there was no lack of willing dance partners, and I felt safe for this was in the days when it was mainly innocent disco, and you could leave your drink still safely unattended at your table. This was well before the days of drugs and violence that is now night-time inner city Melbourne.

And so it was that that night, that a man I danced with paid me such a lot of attention, made me laugh and have fun that I felt carefree again. Compliments, easy conversation, he bought me a couple of drinks. No pressure, no demands. He made me feel so good about myself and even insisted on walking me back to my car. Caught up with gratitude I allowed him to kiss me there and then.

That is when it happened - I ended up being intimate with him. Coarse though it may seem, we had sex in the back of my car. I couldn't call it making love, and I didn't climax, but he was careful and considerate, and it almost felt like simply a matter of course, as though it was ready to happen and inevitable. Consciously, I had had no intention of doing this, I had *never* dreamed that I would do such a thing, I had never *planned* it. It just seemed to happen.

Am I so irresponsible that I can have casual sex with a complete stranger and not feel any guilt about it? Is that who I am? What did this say about me? Is this what I do the moment I am out on my own?

I don't think that was me at all. I think this was something inevitable that simply had to happen. I had been the property of Jim. I had been totally loyal to Jim. I had done all that he asked and more. And his reward and appreciation and love and cherishing had not measured up. In any way!

Naïve Hope

This was *me* telling *me* that I had *left* Jim emotionally – I was now emotionally divorced from him. He no longer held me as his emotional prisoner. I didn't understand this then but came to realise it later, after the initial consequences had worn off.

And I also later realised that this action had also been part programmed in by Jim's constant accusations and intimidations. I had been punched time and again for something that I hadn't done – so here was the equalizer. Something had had to give, and this was the sign that things had changed for all time. I had had no intentions of having an 'Affair' as Jim insisted on calling it, or of seeing this guy ever again. I hadn't gone there with any such ideas in mind, I hadn't set out to do the Wrong Thing, this was purely a wake-up call. My 'love' for Jim, it seems, was totally dead...

You can imagine how bemused I was driving home afterwards. Normally I would be terrified in case Jim guessed, and of what punishment he would mete out to me. But somehow, I just wasn't bothered the same. I had no feelings either one way or the other. I had no feelings period. I was a bit numb. It may not have been a passion made in heaven kind of experience, but I also had no misgivings, no regrets.

When I finally arrive home that night, Jim was lying in bed, pretending to be asleep – or did my arrival actually waken him? Hmm! I *was* extremely quiet.

Anyway, as we already know, it's nothing new for the bedroom to be the place for him to question and frighten me. Jim now stirs and asks me how my night went. I tell him it was good and I enjoyed the dancing. But this is not enough. It's never enough. And, of course, he had had all evening to concoct ideas in his head about me. And Bingo! He comes up with the novel idea that I had been flirting with someone. Someone I had met that night. *And what else had happened, Marni, hmm?*

Whether Jim had realized something was amiss or not, his usual habitual accusations would have served him well this night. Even though initially I say little and avoid, pretending that nothing has happened, he probes and quizzes, grills and interrogates as usual. I wasn't going to blab about this and risk a beating, now was I? But if Jim was always believing that I was going to have an affair - and he has kept on about it long enough - he just might actually get lucky on being right about it sometime, hey?

As you know, even if *nothing* had happened that night, judging from past experience my going out on my own *anyway* was still prime material for him to get his teeth into for questioning and accusations.

And this time he is proved right. For I cannot continue the lie. I tried that once before and could not live with the consequences!

So I confess.

I tell him.

'Yes, I did have sex with someone'.

Stunned silence for a moment...

I.Had.Been.Unfaithful! You could hear this echo round the room in silent screams. The air was alive with the confession of Jezebel!

It wasn't easy over the next few moments after that I can tell you. Waiting to find out if it was the gun, or another knife, or the fists, or...

A stunned moment. A further stunned moment. I didn't know what to expect, but I had been through it all before anyway. There's no escaping whatever the consequences are.

Jim now is sitting up in bed, looking at me as if he doesn't see me. I wonder what he will do next. But I think I am beyond it. I am now removed from it all and again watching the scene from out of my body. I do not know what to expect next. This has not happened to us before. This has not happened to me before. I wait.

My wife has had an Affair... My wife has had an Affair... My wife has had an Affair... I hear him repeating this over and over to himself.

Well, am I *stunned* when Jim's next response is to suddenly catapult out of the bed and instead of reaching for a weapon or my throat he wraps his dressing gown around him and goes into the kitchen-lounge area.

Naïve Hope

I sit up in bed, waiting for him to come back into the room to punish me, but then I hear him talking to someone and realise that he is on the phone.

I am floored with what he does next. There is no more sleep to be had in that house that night; for he spends *all night* on the phone calling people; Alex Kenworthy's Night Line, The Crisis Line, and any other emergency phone line there was. He has the Yellow Pages and the White Phone Book on his lap and is flicking through, dialling the next, then the next, hell bent on telling *everyone* that he knew and *anyone* he could think of that would back him up or tell me how bad I was or how badly he had been done by. He is working his way through the calls, telling them all that his *Wife Has Had An Affair*, that he had been waiting for this to happen, that he *knew it would happen* etc. How devastated he was etc. He just couldn't tell *enough* people about it. Lapping up their condolences, reaping in their sympathy, fuelling his self-righteous hurt at my devastating and awful betrayal. I have no idea who he is speaking with, I just hear his repeated bleating and accusations. Over and over.

Whilst I am forced to listen to it all.

Yet all those years ago when he had done *The Wrong Thing* by me, not once, but several times, *and I had told no-one*, I did not react like *this* – I had had to 'forgive' him, swallow it down and keep schtum about it all.

Jim couldn't see this, he wasn't *able* to see this, see past his own stuff, to question what drove me to do such a thing, to ask himself some serious questions. It was all about what *I* had done wrong and how he had *'been waiting for the other shoe to drop all these years'* (yes, those were his exact words, and the first time I had ever heard them) – the other shoe that had been in his head over his *own* self-guilt after his own unfaithfulness toward me I suppose.

I still didn't quite get this 'one shoe drop' thingy, and he wasn't in the mood for me to ask him about it. It wasn't till much later I ruminated over it. Did he think that my having a so-called affair – let's be honest here and call it what it was, it wasn't a blasted *Affair*, it was only a *one night stand* – did he think this was a 'tit for tat' thing? Why would I wait all these years getting the bejaysis punched out of me when I could have been having it away with Tom, Dick and Hairy (no, that is not a print error) anytime and have reaped the same reward? Why? Because *that's not who I am*. That is not my thinking. But surely, based on this reasoning of tit for tat, then things were *now* finally straight, the debt evened up so to speak?

Look I really don't know. Who can say what is in this twit's mind. All I know is that I didn't set out to cheat on him that night, I didn't *deliberately* plan to have this happen, to jeopardise my marriage. But it sure sent both of us a message each.

And any remaining respect for him was totally lost at his ineptitude, his inadequacy to act as a man in *any* way in this.

That was how the *whole* night went. Neither of us got any sleep. And over the next couple of days Jim brewed and stewed, and I had no idea what was going to happen next. I was on eggshells, for I fully expected him to erupt and to threaten me or to bring out the weapons again. It was like a dark cloud over my head – and yet I *still* couldn't really feel much remorse about it, couldn't feel anything much really. I found it strange that it somehow didn't really reach me, this terrible thing that I had done – I just couldn't feel much regret. I *knew* it was the wrong thing to do, but I couldn't *feel* that I had done wrong somehow. Had Jim been right all along? Is this disloyalty what he had always seen in me and been trying to stop? Well, *No*, it was not. If he had been right all along, I would surely have found a way before now to betray him. But truth was I had never entertained infidelity. Not before this.

How strange was that? I was again living an hour at a time, observing his reactions and wondering where this all might lead. *He should have gone for me by now. Surely?* Well, I knew that something had to give, that his brooding meant no good, and soon I received his considered opinion on the matter.

There was no conversation with me as to *how* this could have happened. No recognition on his part that he just might have pushed me toward this outcome that so rocked our marriage. No attempt to work anything out, to understand my side of it.

Naïve Hope

Instead of fear that our union was being threatened and there being an appropriate response to this wake-up call, Jim took the victim stance. He was indeed *justified* now, he had caught me out, *proven* how wicked and bad I could be. Now the whole *world* should know what I did! He would get the world to punish me. He was just filled with his own thoughts, fears, angers, worrying and pride. For my part, I was still just pretty numb. Part of me wasn't even in this circus. This guy I danced with had meant nothing. I myself was somewhat surprised (if I could even muster up enough energy to feel surprised) that I could have had sex with someone and feel this blasé way about it, but my emotions were pretty messed up by now anyway and were also pretty dead toward Jim and what he was now going through. I didn't even think or remember to bring up how he had been with the prostitute and the teacher (Elsa and Dilys) or anyone else he had possibly been with since then…

I couldn't feel enough to care anymore. I didn't even know if I was really sorry for what I had done. I was not aware of any 'tit-for-tat' or revenge attitude toward Jim, not aware of any need to punish him, for if I had gone that route, my keenly honed survival skills would have talked me out of it anyway. No, it was more likely a combination of things, and let's face it, by now I guess you could say I could legitimately claim that I had finally been brainwashed and pushed into it. Whichever way you looked at it however, what I had done *was* my responsibility for it was *me* that had done it without force or coercion.

'You Will Pay'

But the volcano of Jim's emotions weren't satisfied with getting the world to condemn me. He was working out his own punishment. He was biding his time.

His final determination on the matter soon came. After he had exhausted all outlets for publishing my errant deed and so-called 'Affair' he set about handling things in a more immediate 'Jim-satisfactory' way for himself. Counselling was not now considered sufficient to humiliate me, and the sympathy that came to him that way was not enough, nor the advice by others he had spoken to had been what he really wanted to hear.

Within a couple of days or so, when all was reasonably quiet in the house and the boys had gone to their rooms to sleep, he chose his moment to deliver his judgment. Foolishly, though understandably, I did not really expect what occurred next. How could I, I never really knew how he would react to things, and was still living moment by moment. Externally, I thought that if I agreed to counselling again and allowed his put-downs and insults, this would allay some of his previous modus operandi of reactivity to be alleviated. Or that the fact that this was an entirely new situation for him, one with a reversal of roles, that we might gain some sort of arena to resolve things.

Who am I kidding? I had *no* idea what was going to happen next. I had lived in fear through doing *nothing* wrong, now I was living with fear through doing *something* wrong. Who knew what would happen next? Whichever way things went, I had little opportunity for self-defence anyway. This was a new chapter, a new crisis to deal with.

He came into the bedroom as though nothing was wrong, and closed the door as per usual behind him, though he didn't lock it. Maybe he thought it wasn't necessary as he was between me and the door. I felt his determination and knew something was about to happen. I thought he was going to give me a tongue lashing again, and waited, barely breathing. Now speaking very coldly and distinctly he claimed that he was now going to give me a black eye for what I had done.

'I will mark you for what you have done, so that everyone can see what you are,' he declares. And before I have chance to do anything about it, to plead my case, to beg him not to do so, to flee from the bedroom, he sets about it.

Before I can make a move to defend myself, he throws the first unexpected punch to my face. I felt it connect and immediately pulled my arms and hands up to cover my face. This doesn't stop him though, as his course is clear and set. Determined and grim, Jim just continues to thump me wherever he can. Anywhere and everywhere. This time as the blows reign down on me I am *really* scared. I feel the fear afresh for he is now so methodical and vicious, almost clinical, with each of his punches. After the first

Naïve Hope

couple of thumps he has knocked me to the floor, and I cannot get up - yet he is still pounding into me.

At that very first hit, something in me had said *'Get Help! This is different! This is danger!'* After a couple more of those brutal blows, and because Jim had not stopped, I heard the thought *'He really means to hurt you, he might kill you right now with his bare hands. And the children are in the next room. Get help!'* This felt different to all the other times he had hit me. I had glimpsed death in his eyes before, not often, but it had been there, though somewhat bridled. I now saw it again and I did not like my chances this time – he had just cause now, didn't he?

I just could not keep quiet this time! I refused to 'Shut Up!' anymore and to just take it. I started yelling out *'Help. Help. Stop! Someone call the police. Jo, Ben, Police! Get the police. Help! Police!'*

My screaming didn't stop Jim, didn't have *any* effect on him, he was like an automaton. He was pure determination, pure cold steel. He had planned this, he had cold-heartedly decided that he was going to leave his mark on me. Or more. He just kept punching into me, searching for soft spots, going for the face as much as he could, but if he couldn't get me there, he would go for wherever he could land a punch. It seemed Jim would not stop until he had gotten to my face and pulped it.

And his thumping action was as though he had a piece of dead meat in front of him and he was just intent on pounding it and pounding it to nothing without any breaks between his blows. A few more punches and I was past yelling, I was now *screaming* bloody murder. Bugger hiding this from the children, from the neighbours, this could be the end of me, battered to death by this man. I was getting pulverised, being battered and bruised as never before.

I was twisting and turning, hurting and feeling the pounding and then suddenly I was free. Tears pouring down my face, I was sobbing and crying, and the boys had managed to pull him off me. Joseph and Ben had come running, found that the bedroom door had not been locked and had pulled him off me. My poor boys who I so wanted to protect, had had to protect *me*. From their father.

And one of them actually went and called the police as I had asked and kept on asking in my bloody and bleeding state. Thank you God!! For this was the *only help* from 'God' that I had gotten. So whichever son it was, thank you, thank you, thank you – for you probably saved my life.

I will never forget my sons' expressions when they had seen what was going on. The look of horror on their faces at seeing their father pounding into me like this, and of having to hear my screams. I can still see the panic and fear on Joseph's and Ben's faces as they bravely separated Jim from me, pulling him off me. And little Danny's face behind them, eyes round and terrified, as he put his hands up over his mouth at the sight of it all. These lovely little souls saw such brutality! Even now, as I remember these events, the tears flow.

I think that the children witnessing what Jim was doing put the brakes on his actions continuing. For he stopped. He was not drunk, so was cognisant that they could see what he was doing and what he had done. Their stunned reactions and their shocked faces may well have caused him to reconsider what he had embarked upon. The promise that I had made that no child would see what I had seen as a child was now in my face; here they were, seeing this abuse and disgrace, this violence and brutality, this shame.

The police duly arrived. I dare say the fact that a small child was phoning about their mother being beaten up had a bit more pull than a battered woman herself asking for help. I know it sounds a bit sarcastic but it has often seemed to me that men stand together and back each other up when it comes to a woman trying to stand up for herself. Leastways it may have been the old way of thinking. I hope.

I stayed somewhere else that night after the police came - a hotel I think, I can't even remember where, only that I was allowed to take Daniel with me because he was so young.

In retrospect, I am surprised that the police didn't organise or suggest a hospital checkup. I was traumatised and in pain, but I guess because I could still walk, they didn't bother. Grrr!

Naïve Hope

Before the police moved me out of the house for the night, they took Jim on one side and asked him what had happened. His response was that I had provoked him and I had had an affair etc etc etc. Blah blah poor-badly-done-by-husband-rant blah etc. And he had wanted to teach me a lesson by leaving me with a black eye. They told him he'd gone *too* far and that he should have gone for a walk. 'Keep your hands in your pockets next time, mate'. But they didn't prosecute him. It was a 'domestic affair'. In those days their hands were tied. What? Yup, they told me that it was a domestic affair and that they could *not* interfere!

Slack Bastards! Bloody Boys Club!

I took most of the week off work to recover from this attack. Too much of a mess to show my face, you might say. Something was now more than dead. I now totally lost *any* remaining vestige of respect or compassion for him over this, I had also lost *any* left-over love, caring or patience for this man to grow up and to get it.

I could not avoid comparing the quality of our differing actions and reactions throughout all of this. I had had to stand up and take all the mistakes that he had made and all the stuff he had thrown at me, yet at the first time *I* had done something wrong he had grandly fallen apart and was like a moaning kid in a tantrum, going round like a spoiled brat telling anyone and everyone what I had done. Kicking and spitting. Then this brutality!

Meanwhile, even though raw and battered, something has changed yet again within, I somehow am feeling stronger. I cannot avoid the reality of the real state of our 'marriage' any longer, nor the damage it was doing. I have taken the first step in speaking up. I have broken my silence. I have demanded that he stop!

Now the *authorities* know about his violence.

Oooh, and that is *scary* to coward Jim!

END TIME; COUNSELLOR

The following morning I am forced to come back home, badly bruised and sore.

Now Jim takes up my earlier suggestions and *demands* that we go to counselling. Previously it had been me wanting this. I have *implored* him to go with me to assist us both, but his pride or whatever it was had gotten in the way. And anyway; 'You're my wife, you're supposed to know what's wrong and to fix it!' Duh?

Now things have changed and I am required to attend with him because of my betrayal. We had already had a counselling session before all of this kerfuffle when he had finally given in to my concerns, though he had insisted that it was with a male counsellor for fear that he would be at a disadvantage with a 'conspiring female' on my side, as he put it. After that session, he was too busy, too tired, or whatever excuse he could think of to attend. I had given it away after that, too. By now, I feel that I am done with counselling but to assist with whatever needs to happen next, I go.

The counsellor is again male at Jim's request. It seems that Jim feels that because he is male that he will be on Jim's side and that he has an ally in this man. But as the counsellor asks us both pertinent questions, Jim is not too happy about things. He keeps bringing it back to how I have betrayed him, how I have been such a bad wife. He cannot seem to get past it. And so it now becomes clear that the only purpose of the session is for the counsellor to beat me up on how badly I have behaved, and to put me firmly back in my place.

Jim didn't want to know about sorting things out through the counsellor. Jim has decided that *I* am the one that needs counselling because of that fateful night out on my own.

As we talk, I realise that I am *not* connected to him in the same way anymore, for I am not concerned about trying to make things work anymore. My emotions for him have completely changed and my respect and feelings for him have died. Jim seems to be fighting over a bone that I am not even interested in. I had no desire for affairs, but I have no desire for Jim either. I realized later that he had killed what we had. He had pounded it into the ground until there was nothing left. Not only just with his final beating. This had been coming for a while.

But he gets a bit of an unwanted surprise when the counsellor drops the expected line of reviewing how things came to be the way they were and now takes up the line of 'So you are now getting ready to exit the relationship, Marni. We need some guidelines as to how to do this, how it can be done the easiest and best way for everyone concerned.'

Common sense, really. And pretty obvious. Yet Jim argues about it; he just can't let go of this bone of contention of his over what I have 'done wrong' *to* him. Jim totally misses this whole point. He wants me punished and can't see past that. He cannot see that I am actually really *not* in the relationship anymore – I have already emotionally moved on and am leaving. Still not fully aware of this myself, I think I am just biding time because I don't know quite what happens next. I am feeling my way one day at a time. I only know something momentous has occurred, that I did something so out of character with me and that went against everything I stood for, everything I promised, and that I am still digesting it myself.

I hear the counsellor's words, and I now see what he sees and what he says. He is right. This is not about Jim anymore. *This* is what we need the counselling for, to get us *through* this transition stage, and for us to explore and to learn from it what we can. And to navigate and negotiate and parent for the boys in the best possible way.

But Jim still isn't getting this, *for he isn't getting what he wants.* And I now am given permission to refuse to go to the sessions as the counsellor has insisted that *Jim* continue to see him by himself for a while. Well, you can imagine Jim's response in answer to that. Yes, you guessed it; the counselling stops. Oh, and I am accused of getting 'pally' with the counsellor. And the counsellor is accused of the same, and we are both against him, and the counsellor wants to get into my pants etc etc. Yeah, yeah, yeah, whatever! Simply because the counsellor refuses to lock me in the stocks and pile crap upon crap on top of me, like Jim wants him to do.

Our history on co-operation shows quite clearly Jim's stance.

He had shown that he was simply fundamentally suspicious of everything and everyone. And I was his main target.

If we look at the issue of *'Projection'* – it is this; it is easier to see what lies in oneself when we 'project' in onto the screen of another's life or activities or perceived thoughts. If I am basically honest, I will see everyone as being basically honest. If I am a liar and a thief, I will watch out for others being a liar and a thief. If I have had an affair, I will watch out for my partner having an affair. Because we are a certain way, we can often make the same mistake of seeing everyone (or most) as being the same way. Until we learn differently. For we are each different, with different morals and values as well as intrinsic beliefs. But some people don't wish to 'learn' that others perceive differently from themselves. Generally. Although I also admit that there *are* the sharks of this world that see everyone else as the 'little fish' that they are going to 'reel-in'. But to me these aren't really people or even human, they are merely reptiles in human skin.

As things became even more difficult, and tension is increasing, I am still looking for other answers to this uncomfortable and untenable situation.

THREE TIMES STRIKE

Jim was still raging for 'justice' and he was just as difficult to live with.

Again, I sought to defuse what I sensed to still be a dangerous situation, which felt like it could still possibly escalate further. He seemed to be on an increasingly short fuse, and I was still walking on egg shells all the time. Everything I did and said was watched, questioned, doubted, examined and contradicted. Naturally.

I needed time to think things through and to do it without continual threats hanging over me. I needed a place and space where I could get clear as to the right and appropriate thing to do from here. And to allow an opportunity to see if there was *any* chance that we could fix what had been so badly broken.

Was this possible? I still somehow somewhere held hopes that if this was handled right, things just might improve... before my heart and body had totally checked out of the situation. That was my

Naïve Hope

conscious thinking. Though I more than suspect that without realizing it my heart had already made up its own mind.

I reviewed where we were at, or rather *not* at, and asked him if he would again consider leaving for a break. When he again said 'No', I again presented him with my three previous suggestions.

This was the *third* and *last* time I did so; he had now had *three* opportunities for him to listen, to pay attention, to redress the tide of things, to get the lesson. But there was to be *No* consideration of the options from him still. It was the same as before; 'No. No. No.'; all in one breath. Not even the slightest hesitation to think about *any* of it. A clear message that he had *no* intention of working on improving the situation or the marriage. Rather his attention was on proving how wrong I was and how badly he was done by.

Something had to change. I could not wait or count on God to help, for if anything He had shown that I had to help myself; nor could I expect or hope that Jim would ever get on board. Someone had to do something.

It was up to me now. I was now ready to take action.

For hoping and wishing does not make a thing so.

Last Christmas

We had our last Christmas together as a family in 1980.

One would be forgiven for thinking that nothing was wrong if they observed us as we made the usual family fuss with Christmas presents, traditional Christmas turkey and trimmings, with the mince pies, pudding and cake etc. Though this year I made no attempt to cook my own, and there was a more subdued atmosphere all round.

Plenty of Christmas cheer in alcoholic terms, as our house had a bumper share of barrel-beer. We didn't go to church that I can remember, though we did watch some old Christmas movies. It was a bit like an anti-climax – not the best choice of words, but there you have it...

Looking back it felt like Christmas on a shoestring. I cannot possibly remember what we bought for each of the boys – I think my head was still dealing with the detachment I was feeling. My marriage didn't feel like a marriage any more. It felt like I was simply going through the motions. It wasn't clear what was what just yet. Underneath, I think that I was fed up with having made so many attempts to fix things and having failed so miserably, and realised that this guy was never going to be any different.

I was also still dealing with his reactions to my 'Affair', and my own emotional fall-out on it all and I hadn't yet connected the dots; my behaviour when he had his affairs versus his behaviour right now. Do right and I get punished? Do wrong and I get punished? What the heck?

Having had the police round was no guarantee that he wouldn't do such a thing again, though the fact that the authorities now knew was a kind of dampener on him. But then again, when one is intent on getting rid of whatever irks one, and when you really want to do something, then nothing can stand in your way. Newspapers have reported stories of fathers taking their wives and children 'out' first before disposing of themselves in a grand final act of destruction. In other words, do your worst, then don't hang around to get caught or face the consequences. Brave, hey? Can one afford to take chances? When you have seen the nature of the beast, can you guarantee that a violent and damaged nature will not demonstrate those same traits over again? Only a fool would do so, as the unwise early releases of murderers that murder again as per the reports of late would attest.

So, from Christmas to possible murder, in a few short paragraphs. But these were the facts from the bowl of life that I was currently swimming in.

Action Time

So. Christmas comes and goes and we are still in the long six week break that is the school summer holidays in Australia.

I was now more than ready to take an active role in removing myself from this dangerous man. He would not move out, he would not change, he would not look at himself or at what we could do together to make things work. My children had now been scarred with what they had seen. He would not leave, he would not go; he had made that more than abundantly clear. So it wouldn't stop. Would he beat me again? For sure he would! My own personal promise was now being called to accountability; that my children would not see what I had seen as a child. It was now up to me if I wanted to stop them from seeing worse - I had to remove the danger from them and their eyes. I had to move out.

I was now seriously questioning whether I could be bothered in trying with this man anymore. My patience and compassion had been stretched beyond repair. Yet I still had *eighteen years* of being together to resolve and they were still tugging at me. We had three children together, and you don't just upend all of that in a hurry. Did I want to end the marriage? Did I really want to 'throw it all away'? Whereas before I certainly hadn't considered it, right now it was almost an inevitable event, but I just didn't know which way to go, what to do, what would be best for the children – for they were now the prime consideration.

So if nothing else the idea of some sort of neutral space for me to move into and hopefully allow some de-escalation of the situation will help me to decide if I have anything left to work on the relationship with; to ascertain what we could do with what was left. It wasn't about *us* anymore; that time had come and gone.

But I was still torn. I *also* had to consider that this was also about me, did *I* still want it to work? I needed time to decide, to sort through this. And would Jim now get it, and wake up to it all?

This was our last chance. Particularly in view of the increasing violence and masked hatred, and the fact that Jim would not entertain leaving the family home at all. But Jim also probably didn't like the idea that I wouldn't be where he could get at me, either. There was much to think about. And I needed a place to think, to take some time out of the home horror, and review my marriage by myself. To sort through the catastrophe's, to review my life and my marriage, and what *I* had contributed to its current situation. To see what was salvageable, to see what was not. I didn't want to make any more *reactive* decisions – I had not entered marriage lightly and would not exit it lightly. It was too momentous a decision to be made flippantly and I needed space to consider as well as to allow these horrible happenings to fade from the boys' eyes and the opportunity for us to attempt to conduct a normal civil relationship at a bit of a distance till I had thought things through.

I was now also on my own holidays from TOW, and as it later turned out, the last month of my living in Werribee. Jim knew I was hunting for a share-place, after all he had made it very clear that it was I that had to be the one to leave.

Going through the local community paper I looked for and found a share-accommodation room in nearby Altona close to work. 'With garden'. Perfect. Near work and near the boys; close enough to see the boys three nights a week, come back to Werribee from work and cook dinner for them. Though I would not sleep in Werribee I would see if I could have them come stay with me at the weekends.

I phoned the woman advertising the room. Her name was Suzy and she was happy to meet with me to see if it was suitable for us both. At the appointed time, I knocked at her front door not knowing what I should find. A neat detached three bedroom brick home off the main drag, in a nice semi-circular avenue, she had a tidy garden with fresh plants. She was expecting me and she came to the door with a friendly smile. 'Oh Hi, Marni, I'm Suzy. Pleased to meet you,' she said as she proffered her hand for a handshake. Inviting me inside, she asked me where I was currently living, and I began to tell her of my particular and peculiar situation. Her home was inviting, comfortable with some antiquey type furniture, a little old fashioned with some quirky new accents. Suzy was a slim, tall, dark haired and attractive lady, somewhat younger than myself. She was neat and easily approachable, genuine and not profusive. She had some breeding, or let's call it 'class' and I felt immediately comfortable around her.

When she asked how long I needed the room for, all I could tell her was the truth. She needed to know this, it was only fair, as I would be living under her roof. So I said 'I have no idea to be honest. It may only be for a couple of months, it may be for six months, it may be for longer. At this point I have no way of knowing. I have been married for eighteen years and don't wish to throw all of that away. I just need time to see if things can be worked out.'

Naïve Hope

Her response was comforting. 'You can have the place for as long as you need. There is no lease required, and you will have to pay monthly, but we can sort something out. When do you think you will be needing it?' She made it all so easy and welcoming, but then as it also later turned out, she was a good judge of character.

At that time, I had only given a little thought to the timing, though I did have a vague idea that it should be pretty soon, in view of what was going on at home. We sorted out how I would pay the rent, and I had previously done my sums when I first saw her advert. Because she didn't require any bond, and it was going to be paid monthly which was when my salary was paid, I could manage it all. And so I organised with her to move there around the time of my next salary payment, which was on the fifteenth of the month, within a week or so, and I would be letting my husband know when I got home that I had found a place. If things changed at all then it was agreed that I would call her back.

Suzy explained that she was not set up for children to *live-in*, but because of the backyard there was space for them to play, and she also made it clear that they were welcome to stay over occasionally - so this was fine too. She also had a lovely cat, and in all she provided a very comfortable place. It all seemed to be the solution I needed right now. She was an angel, didn't ask a lot of questions, but obviously had good intuition to take on my situation at face value. I have a lot to thank her for.

And so I went home and as soon as Jim was settled after work that day, I told him that I had now found a place in Altona which would suit both of us as it meant that I was still local and thus able to come over and feed the children weeknights while we sorted out things. Or had further counselling. I told Jim everything I was doing as I would probably have to keep him informed anyway and further reminded him that after what happened we needed to let things settle down.

He listened and nodded to show that he had heard me. After a few minutes silence whilst I attended to domestic stuff he spoke; 'When are you thinking of moving out?' he asked. Wow, he's not putting up any difficulties, I thought - maybe we can get through this and sort things out after all. 'I told Suzy that I would be moving in after the 15th, around the end of next week, say Saturday the 17th or Sunday the 18th. How does that sound?'

'Grmph' or some-such was his response. Until later. He usually takes a day or so to sulk, think, muse, stew or whatever it is that goes on with him. As usual, he silently fomented and fermented. He brewed and he stewed, saying little more. Then within a couple of days, after his day shift, he comes up to me and says with a grim kind of pleasure 'You can't go then. The kids will still be on school holidays. You can't leave while they are on holidays. It's too unsettling. Leave it till they go back to school.'

Well, he didn't tell me that I couldn't leave... Oh. Okay then. Hmmm, I guess it's not entirely fair that I leave *before* school holidays are over. Let them enjoy the hols without this upheaval. Okay. I thought about it and agreed – it was a reasonable suggestion and meant that the boys would have a relatively normal holiday period and the new arrangements would start to coincide with the beginning of the new school year. Daniel was now five years old that year and he would also be starting school. But as I had already made arrangements I needed to check if my delay in taking up the room would be agreeable to Suzy.

'Okay Jim, you are right. I will see if it's okay with Suzy for me to move in to Altona after the school holidays,' and with that he appears to be placated. I just hope that it *is* okay with Suzy and that this doesn't put her off having me because she has to wait for rent money for longer.

So the following day I give her a call, and I tell her that 'I have had to rethink the move-in date because of the school holidays; and 'Is it alright if I move in the first weekend they are back at school, Suzy?'

'That's no problem, Marni. I fully understand. See you then. You will let me know if you change your mind, won't you, though?'

'Absolutely Suzy. But I am *not* changing my mind. I will be moving in as soon as I can, and that is the best date, so if it's alright with you, I'll see you then.'

And that was that.

Naïve Hope

So it was arranged. I think this surprised Jim. And Jim then had no further argument about the dates. He wasn't happy about it, but he couldn't say anything else to stop this from going ahead.

Could he?

I thought that things would settle down somewhat now it was imminent that I would be out of the house soon, and Jim would have the space to himself and not be so het up over me or with me. Looking back, I have *no* idea what could have possibly contributed to make me think that, for I certainly wasn't as good at reading him as I thought I was. Being so habitually responsible for when things went bad, it was hard for me to kick this habit and stop being so self centred and self conscious about problems. I hadn't yet learned to allow him to be responsible for himself, nor indeed,for me to be responsible for myself.

Despite this initial appearance at acceptance, Jim still kept on stewing and brewing. Initially and in his tight-lipped way, Jim had put up little argument. He had been pushing for me to go if *anyone* was to go anyway, for it was clear that *he* certainly wasn't going to. Though in actual fact he really didn't want anything to change. Least of all himself. What a dilemma, hey?

Well, let's face it – it was currently very convenient for him - he could simply shut me up or shut me out anytime he felt like it. When he couldn't bear to look at my face because of his own bad thoughts, shame and guilt, and because he didn't know how to stop it all, he could simply push me out of the way and out of the lounge, in fact, out of the house. This would achieve a couple of things; he could avoid seeing me and drink in peace *and* he could show how much bigger and stronger he was than me. Hide from his own inadequacies, and put me down where I belonged.

Yes, he actually took to physically forcing me out...

If he had been drinking, then first would come the thrown (and now empty) decanted bottles of beer accompanied with abusive language and insults. Next he would grab me by the arms and march me through the house and then physically force me out the front door. No amount of wriggling or struggling to get past him worked, so I learned not to bother. The door would be slammed in my face, and I would quickly go round the back of the house so that the neighbours did not see my humiliation and disgrace.

Even just staying silent was no protection from this act for he would find a way to pick a fight. Woe betide me if I dared to actually push him back, and anyway he was far too strong for me. There was often no time to get a coat or cardigan, before he had pushed and *locked* me out of the house and definitely no handbag was allowed. As with his moods and behaviour this was something that couldn't be hid from the boys with excuses or by sending them to bed for an early night. Not that this helped, for while the kids were in bed there was still the chance he would end up telling me to go.

'Go, leave. Get out! I don't want to see your face!'

Next he would have another drink or three, before going off to bed, leaving me outside, neither worrying nor caring about what the kids thought, or indeed anybody or anything else, and finally he would fall into bed. I would then be forced to wait outside, quietly listening for the snore of his drunken stupor, after which I would go to the kid's bedroom so they could open the window for me to climb in. Poor kids, as they sometimes ended up sleeping together in one of the bunk beds or even on the floor. When this first started, I was forced to sleep in with them, on one of the mattresses or bunk beds, or take the floor when my back could handle it.

We always had to perform all of this quietly, just in case Jim had gotten up to go for a loud and splashy toilet visit and in case he checked on any noises.

Good one, Jim. Smart lad! Let's keep doing this some more, hey?

And why did he not want to see my face? There was nothing wrong with my face. But there was obviously something about me that bothered him... and it certainly wasn't to do with me, but it was to do with him. And with who he really was and what he couldn't face about himself.

1981 THE END

The Final Insult. The Final Shove. The End.

~ Final Curtain ~ Final Push ~ Angel Suzy ~ Life on The Outside ~ Time To Talk ~ Church Prejudice ~ 'Danny First'

FINAL CURTAIN

Not long after we had moved to Werribee, after Danny's birth and the Heather incident, Jim had told me quite clearly that if I ever left him he would find me and destroy me. He clearly told me that if I ever went against him, he would seek me out, wherever I was, and fix me.

He claimed he knew the ways and means of tracking people down, and of disposing of them so they would never be found. He bragged that his work in security and his knowledge and contacts now equipped him with the means to do so. He had been very cold and calculating when he told me this. This wasn't the drink speaking at the time, for he was sober. This was his clear warning to me, his statement that I had nowhere to go that was safe, and that he would do *whatever* it took to teach me a lesson. Initially in our marriage, it had felt like I was dealing with two different men sometimes; the nice charmer, and at other times, the vicious vindictive viper. But now they were running into one another and were now just more and more the muddier and darker one. And nastier.

He was contradictory, hypocritical, cruel and ignorant. To mention a few out of the many... Despite his threats if I dared to leave it was ok for him to make me leave if he felt like it. Jim's humiliating habit of pushing me out of the front door when he had been drinking is pivotal to what happens next.

Even though he never apologised the following morning for any of this sort of behaviour (probably conveniently 'forgotten' by him), and indeed it became almost a 'normal' routine, I was somehow able to convince him that we needed a sofa-bed for those occasions when his 'snoring becomes too loud' for me to sleep.

He argued the idea at first. It was as if he was totally unaware that he was doing this, which of course he was. Until one night when the boys and I simply could not sleep because of the loud sounds that were ripping through the whole house. So we placed a tape recorder outside the bedroom door and actually recorded his horrendous and sonorous sounds.

As I have shared, Jim had his moments of charm, and so at the next approachable moment the kids and I jovially joked about the noises he made at night. He was in total denial and quite jokey about it initially. Then we produced the tape player and played it back to him because he didn't believe us. Not really a good move, but then how is he to know? He got very dark that I had dared to record him. He tried to make it sound a bit jokey for the boys sake, attempting to save face, but I could see that warning glint in his eye. Fortunately for me, the boys stood up for me and this snoring became the focus and argument for the spare bed. It was only a cheapish fold-up foam couch, and we had room in the front lounge room, which was so handy. Plus it gave us extra seating. But it was a godsend.

Now I had the possibility of not being subjected every night to his imprisoning us both in the main bedroom. And I could also use the sofa to sleep on after creeping back in from an eviction. Sure, it was only foam rubber, but it was heaven to be away from right next to his snoring, and the horrible smell of alcohol, or indeed from lying next to this awful man.

I still did not realize at this time that this behaviour was alcoholic behaviour and I did not know about A.A. Obviously we were all scared by now, and just tiptoed around Jim, especially if he was drinking.

But what happened next was also *not* due to alcohol.

Final Push

We arrive at the final countdown. To mix a few metaphors; The die has been cast, the hole dug, the compass set... Chance after chance has been dispensed and also been thrown back into the abyss.

Naïve Hope

I didn't leave of my own choosing after all... Even though I had planned for this space, and an amicable sort of gap to explore for any possible way of us working through this, Jim has decided that we had to do it his way.

It is now the last week of the boys school holidays, and about a week before I have organised the new date to move in to Suzy's. I am mentally preparing myself and the boys for the new schedule, and enjoying the last few days with them. Having told them that I would be home three nights a week on weekdays to cook for them and to see them to bed, and that their father would attend to them on the other nights, and that they would also be coming over to my place on weekends, I thought that this would settle them for the foreseeable future.

Brooding Jim has other plans for me. Probably, I guess, because I have taken affairs into my own hands. And Jim must have felt the need to exercise his 'control' over events yet again.

'Very convenient for you to leave right now, isn't it?' he chirps up. 'Had your fun, destroyed my life, shamed me, and now you think you can just leave us all like that. Hey?'

And here was stupid me, thinking that we had made an agreement about all of this. Obviously not. *Now* what has he got to say?

'Off to your girlfriend's so you can carry on more affairs, hey? Think you can come back at any time to see the kids, hey? Think I'm going to make it easy for you, hey?'

He wasn't making any sort of sense. I knew we didn't have much time left before I leave and this was just not fair. Why oh *why* couldn't *something* be done peaceably and right?

'Well, go on then, go *now*. What are you waiting for? You want to go so badly, then you can go right now!' His eyes are flashing, his jaw set, his stance determined. He is resolved to make even this situation difficult. It has to be drama, drama, drama!

He has picked this fight, and now throws further accusations at me about me 'leaving the children' and how very typical it was of me, and how can I do this, my fancy man would be waiting etc, and the same old stuff was aired. Same-old same-old.

I later think he was doing this because he is so scared that I would do what other women had done; for I later hear that *some* women actually kick the man out, claim the kids, then refuse him access to them whilst taking him to the cleaners. That may be, but that was not me. This man really had no idea *who* I was. And if he couldn't *see* who I was with all of my years of 'service' and loyalty and right and respectful treatment, then *no* argument was going to convince him or make him see otherwise.

Now the big brave *'man'* starts to push me out the door. 'You're leaving right now!' he boasts as he moves me closer to the door.

'Please don't do this Jim'... I ask, attempting to defuse the situation yet try to hold on to my dignity.

'Why not, you're going anyway?' More push, more shove.

'Yes, but not yet. She's not expecting me, she won't be ready, and it's still school holidays with the boys.'

'I don't care. You're leaving. *Now*. Go!'

The children have heard the commotion, his raised voice and my plea and they are watching us both, tension and worry all over their faces. I could see this was a hopeless situation, I could feel the determination in his moves, I could see that 'look' in his eye again, I could hear his decision in his voice.

I continue to try to make him see sense, to argue the case, but he will have none of it. His mind is made up, I was leaving, *Now*, and his firm shoves toward the front door were getting firmer. Much firmer.

So I have to agree to go. Now. That is if one *could* say that I remotely had *any* other option than to 'agree'. But at least I could try to exit with some small dignity.

'Well at least let me take some clothes with me if that's what you really want' I said, playing for time.

'Take what you want. Just pack and get out. Now! I want to make sure you go. I want to see you go. Here, I'll pack for you.' And with that he pulls down the suitcase and goes to where I keep my clothes, pulling drawers open haphazardly.

Naïve Hope

Humiliation again! He wanted to pack my suitcase for me!

I can see his hands are itching to get at me. He is all stirred up and it feels like he is looking for something, anything, that will hurt me or give him an excuse to hurt me in order for him to feel better...

I took the suitcase off him, or rather, I dared to yank it off him. 'If you want me to go, then let me do it!' This is going too far. What does he think I am, a child that he has to pack for me? 'You don't have to do that. I'll pack for myself, thanks.' I am now determined to pack to shut him up. I have had enough. And I start packing by myself. I attempt to close the bedroom door so I have some privacy, but Jim now jams the door open using a stool. Pulling up a chair to sit on whilst he taunts me, he now insists on *watching* me pack to ensure that I *did* pack and leave. His arms are folded across his chest and I think also to keep his hands off me. He has a malicious grin on his face, and appears to be enjoying the scene that has been put on at my expense. The show couldn't have been more obvious. His message: *'You go when I say, not when you choose; you take nothing but what I allow you; I humiliate you in front of the children, they see that I send you away; you don't dictate to me, I dictate to you.'*

He sits there smirking, arms folded, chair placed firmly and squarely where he could watch every move. He is now waiting for the exact moment he can give me one last final triumphant push out of the house. His ego is doing a right old dance.

But he fails to see the serious significance of all of this...

I say to him, and I say it quite clearly and meaningfully, 'If I go through the front door like this it will be for the last time, and I promise you that I will *never* ever sleep under this roof again.' Does he stop and think? Does he listen? Can he hear? No!

Jim refuses to budge, in any way. He is still insisting 'Just keep packing and get out. You're not wanted here. Go on. You've already got a place. Go to it. You want to leave, then go!' and he continues to sit and harass me, watching and goading with further snarky comments and with his arms still folded righteously across his chest. The children are still looking on in awe at these events, frightened and unable to do anything about it.

They did not want me to leave, I could see that. Jim could see that. But did I now have any choice? Jim was just too strong and too scary.

Again I tell Jim 'If you continue to push me out and if I leave right now, then I will never *ever* sleep under this roof again. I really mean this Jim.' Can't this man hear what I am saying? Doesn't he realise that I am again giving him a chance to sort this in a way that doesn't close *all* doors? No. He is too dumb, too *stupid* to see what is in front of his very nose.

He just laughs in a bravado sort of way, urging me back to my packing. He is now almost beside himself with glee, practically jumping up and down on his chair, crossing and uncrossing his arms, folding and unfolding his legs, itching to get up and *do* something.

I am now packing blindly, aware I can't see straight, fully aware that this is a momentous occasion and I really wanted him to see this, to realise, just *what* this could mean. The air is electric. I also didn't know if I would get out of there without another black eye. Or if he would go get the gun. Or *what* he would do.

Just be dignified, Marni. Don't goad or argue with him. Just pack and leave. Take anything that makes sense and get the rest when he is at work. There is now no other option. It is clear he will not back down. Well does he realise that if I go, I will *not* be back? The enormity of what was happening is so very clear to me. Sometimes there is only so much a dog can take before it is prepared to fight back. I was trembling. There is no going back from this. The boys are still watching, confused but unable to do anything, well knowing their father's stubbornness and his volatile nature.

I try again for the last and final time to reason with him. After all, three is supposed to be a magic number, and maybe this time he will reconsider. He can *see* that I am packing, he can see that I will actually have to leave, for he is giving me no alternative, so surely he can see that he is the *only* one that can change this.

Again I warn him - for a *third* time I give him notice against this step, this irreversible insistence, attempting to convey to him that I really mean it. 'Jim, please...' I begin, 'If I leave now I will *never*

Naïve Hope

return to sleep in this house again.' I am poised with my hand on some sort of garment, looking at him, telling him with my mind, with my eyes, with my body, that I fully intend to carry out what I am saying, and that this time I will *not* attempt to come back into the house as though nothing has happened. After all the years of keeping my word, of fulfilling all my promises, does he not see that this will be no exception?

There is no surprise here then, to inform you, that this sincerity of mine was only met with more childish glee. He still doesn't stop to think, he simply cannot control or help himself. He laughs and smirks and continues harassing me to hurry up and pack and to '*Go on. Get out of here*'.

I cannot possibly have been any more specific, any clearer on the consequences of this current action of his. Now I accept that this final appeal was all that I had left to fight this with. There is now nothing else left to say to him. He has made his choice. And in my own heart of hearts, I know that nothing, but *nothing*, would ever induce me to return to sleep under the same roof as him again.

True to form, his rampant ego, his small-minded bully idiocy has him too tied up in this attempt to display control over me. He is too lost in his own perceived little triumph to consider the repercussions, too caught up in what he is doing rather than in listening and hearing.

And for this, he *must* accept the consequences.

In my own heart I am too frightened of his growing combustibility around me, and of how it affects the boys when he we are together to now insist on staying further. I now knew *what* they would continue to see should I stay in that situation exactly as it was. It is not good for any child to know or to see that their mother is pushed out or beaten up in front of them – I know this from first-hand experience. What I thought would be a temporary solution to us sorting out our relationship has become a catalyst for this bizarre and final expulsion.

I give the boys Suzy's home phone number and my work phone number. With a quick hug and a sad wave goodbye to each of the boys, seeing their stunned and scared faces, I am forced to drive away from my home, my family, my life as it had been. For I know in my heart that I will never return to Jim's bed, and only ever visit to see my children.

I hold back my tears; it is too emotional a situation as it was, and I was *not* going to let Jim see me cry! What! Have him score *another* victory over me at my hurt as well as my humiliation?

The tears came later.

And even later still, over thirty years later to be exact, I finally had to deal with what I had failed to recognise at the time. Yes, I later learned that I *could* go legally back to this home at *any* time and continue to live there, as he did *not* have the right to evict me – the house was in both names and we both paid the bills. But would that have worked, anyway? Would that have changed this deplorable situation? I don't think so. As he had said, if anyone is going to go, then it had to be me.

However, something more momentous was also happening, something that I did not and could not possibly recognise at the time, so convinced in the power of truth, right and love was I.

For little did I realise that along with my desire to stop these attacks from Jim that I was also giving up the chance of truly having my children again. I just didn't realise that then. Only now, *in this last year* has this really come home. And I haven't been able to consciously acknowledge this before because the *pain* at this realization was just *too* overwhelming – it was easier for me to stay angry and hurt at his behaviours because it was *easier* than feeling the pain of being *forced* to leave my children. I had locked down this part of my heart. Only recently have I really understood the agony, the torment and despair that I had buried that day – *the day I lost my children.*

I DID NOT REALISE then that leaving without them also meant that I could NOT GO BACK AND GET THEM!

My heart *broke* that day, I realised later. For I had thought that I had done the best I could at that time, this had kept me going. But I hadn't realised the true cost to myself and to the children. *I had lost my boys on that day.* And I was later, much later, to learn, that Jim had totally claimed them psychologically, emotionally, and physically. And branded them in the following years with *his* view of my leaving.

For he was to claim, and to claim it often, that I *'had deserted'* him and the children!

*I had **deserted** the children!* Lying bastard! Twisted Soul!

And right then, I knew NONE of this!

Along with this experience, along with the huge change that this event triggered, other dramas were still yet to unfold. If I thought that one problem had been solved, however badly, I had another think coming. This wasn't solved yet – not by a long shot. Though on some level, part of our unfinished business together *is* over. Part of our destiny together has just been completed.

But what a way to treat a Cinderella! Where *is* my fairy Godmother when I need her?

Angel Suzy

Maybe an angel of mercy will do?

As I had already made forward arrangements with Suzy in Altona, perhaps this option was still viable. I hoped that I still had her place to go to, and so I arrived on her doorstep with my suitcase that very afternoon, much earlier than I had planned. Fortunately she was at home when I arrived, and I so wasn't left on the doorstep worrying longer than was necessary.

Though this was an unexpected turn of events, I had been honest about my current situation. She already knew that I had no idea how long I would need the room, and it was now quite obvious even to her that there were problems with my marriage. Consequently my early arrival was not totally a surprise.

When Suzy opened her front door in answer to my knock, she could see the upset on my face, and the unshed tears brimming in my eyes, and she welcomed me in immediately. No hesitation. There immediately followed a good strong cup of tea to help me gather myself and to give me time to stop shaking.

My world had been turned upside down and I was still traumatized by all of this upset – it also felt like I had been trying to do all the right things, act in ways that didn't hurt others intentionally, and always aware of my responsibilities, yet I had still been hostage to Jim, his moods, his abuse. And his humiliations. Now I had been forced out of my own home in a most undignified way.

After her showing me what was going to be my new bedroom, my first request that night was to ask for a lock on its door. I was so unreasonably scared of Jim finding me and coming after me. I could see that Suzy found this a strange request but at the time it seemed absolutely *essential* to me, I was so frightened. I was so scared still that it took a while for me to settle enough to drop off some of this fear and to stop shaking. And ages to get to sleep that night. I was still too stunned to cry. It's probably because I was still in shock.

As this move had been earlier than expected, and I had nothing with me other than the few things I had been turned out with, I borrowed her spare camp bed for the night. All I needed right then was a bed, some clothes and my toiletries. The following day while Jim was out at work I organised a van for the sofa-bed in the lounge, and also collected my old sewing machine and the rest of my clothes. Somehow I managed to turn up for work the following day as though nothing had happened. Jo was now seventeen, Ben was fifteen and little Danny was just five years old. It fell to Jo to take care of the others until school resumed again.

Directly after work that first Monday night, I went straight home to Werribee to see the boys and to let them know I was ok, and to see how they were. They were so glad to see me and to spend time with me, though they were all a bit subdued and confused with the highly charged and overwhelming events. I gave them as much comfort as I could and lots of hugs, I tidied up the place a bit and cooked them dinner. They reported to me that the night I had left their father had had a few drinks, put them to bed early and there had been no further trouble. I breathed a sigh of relief and was about to leave the house just as Jim was arriving home. Jim was now working just day shifts, so he could be home in time for the boys finishing school. I had already given the eldest son, Joseph, my phone number so they boys could talk to me whenever they wanted. Before driving off, I had a few words with Jim about the boys, giving him the new home phone number for emergency purposes. Jim was civil, but distant and quieter than one would expect. I think he was in shock. Who wasn't?

The die was cast, I was out of there, and I was without my children. But maybe now that perpetual tension, that angst, would give way to rumination and reflection, and a chance for us to sift through the rubble and resurrect a relationship of sorts that would better support the children. I stuffed all my feelings down so that I could put on a brave face, and I am sure that each of the boys did the same thing themselves. I had no idea of the legalities of the situation, nor of my rights and no knowledge of any recourse at this time. It didn't occur to me. I had just wanted the horrors to stop and for us all to be safe and I had thought I was doing all that could be done to achieve this.

I drove back quietly to Altona. It was a strange feeling to realise that I was now living away from my own home and that a new chapter had begun. I simply had to make the most of things, allow Jim time to adjust and hope for the best.

It transpired that a week or two after moving in to Suzy's, a much younger guy arrived at her house to share with us and to take up the third bedroom. He had also responded to her ad, and had organised to arrive around the same time as my original date. Graeme was a young guy in his early twenties, a serious hard worker, but when he joked, he had a great little sense of humour. He had moved back down to Melbourne to be closer to work, and had just finished with his girlfriend. So he, too, was licking his wounds. He would occasionally get a bit of good natured ribbing off us, but he wasn't a sop, he was just a genuinely nice kid. Suzy was in her early thirties, and was an intelligent professional who worked in a major insurance company in the city, She was secure in her work and relaxed in her skin. We spent a little time filling each other in on our backgrounds, though she was never pushy or needy, and she had a lot of depth and understanding. Suzy also explained to me that she was recovering from a nasty divorce, and needed to let the spare bedrooms to help pay her mortgage. This allowed us to commiserate with each other to some degree, and we all got on really well together. We would sometimes have meals together, but this wasn't a regular thing. Somehow we made it all work. A peaceful pleasure after all of the dramas and fights I had been experiencing.

I was now aged thirty-six yet still so much at sea with life.

LIFE ON THE OUTSIDE

Ben was soon back at school and I missed out on seeing him start his first day in a new class, and I missed seeing Danny start his very first school. However, I could not afford to dwell on these thoughts as it was far too painful. I swallow it down, for I have enough to deal with right now. It was important for me to maintain contact with the boys, but if could avoid Jim as much as possible, whilst keeping my word, then we just might be able to navigate through this until the dust had settled, and reason prevailed.

However, life now felt like I was living in a daze, like someone else was living this life. Part of me was relieved that I was out from under his clutches, but another part of me wondered what the heck would happen next, despite my idealistic hopes.

When I had picked up the sofa-bed, I had also taken with me the bank mortgage pay-in book at the same time. I knew that Jim couldn't cope on his own, and I intended to pay for the house by myself as a kind of maintenance for the children even though I was out of the home. This was not about later laying any claim to the payments or the property, as I didn't even know about any part of equity claims at that time. This was about me doing the right thing and doing what I could for the boys well-being in a practical way. This way the children would still have a home to live in, and it was my way of paying child maintenance. No one had to tell me to do that, it seemed to be the natural thing to do. I am sure any conscientious father would do the same thing should he have left the marital home. And because I didn't know how they worked out these things, I thought that I could budget for it somehow and it was simpler than trying to work out what to do about groceries for the boys or electricity bills etc. This was an essential bill towards the boys upkeep and accommodation, and something that Jim could count on as a contribution to assist him. And it was enough of an extra burden financially for me anyway.

Naïve Hope

Altona was just a few miles away so that I could have easy access to my boys. But as it turned out this wasn't to last as long as I had expected.

My initial suggestion to Jim had been that if I took thinking time away from home, that I would also come home straight from work for two to three nights a week to cook for the boys and provide them with some sense of normality and continuity. And that I would have them at weekends, and they could stay with me. This seemed like a good plan to me and *was* a good plan, but only if *both* parents make it work.

At the first opportunity as promised, I had turned up to make dinner for the boys, and put together whatever I could that was available in the house. The next time I came, I brought some food with me so I could plan and cook something solid. For a short while, I would turn up, cook dinner, then leave them all and go to Suzy's to sleep. But after a few weeks, I found things were getting increasingly harder for me. After my initial home cooking visits I had noticed that Jim was also leaving all the dirty dishes out in the sink for me to do, and there was grease and spatter everywhere. By the time I had cleaned up then cooked something for the boys I was absolutely beat, and spent, and it was late. This was exhausting me mentally, physically and emotionally. Jim wasn't making this one bit easier for me, he was working against me. I gradually saw that he was doing nothing to assist, and that he was leaving all the kitchen cleaning for me to do.

Then the next problem to present itself was that I couldn't find anything to cook in the house and I didn't always have the money to go out and buy food, plus it meant really late meals for the boys. Even driving round looking for a local shop open took time, energy and funds. And my credit card debt was growing bigger.

Whilst living with Jim, there had always been a set plan of forthcoming meals so we could budget and shop in advance. This now all went by the board, and Jim didn't shop for much it appeared, and I was lucky to find any canned food or even vegetables in the pantry. I had my own rental and living expenses now, as well as still paying off my car and the family mortgage. I was really trying to be fair about everything and somehow cope financially myself.

'You don't need me here to heat up beans on toast, Jim,' I said to him. But he didn't offer anything in response to this. Did he make the effort to get anything else in? No. He told me that I could go out and buy something as he has been too busy... So, not willing to apologise then, for no food being in for the boys? Not willing to make any mends, not willing to work at this with me, then. No possible c-h-a-n-g-e in his attitude...

What was the point of me only heating up baked beans and toast if this was all Jim said that he had in? He wasn't that hard up, for I was paying off his largest expense, the mortgage, wasn't I?

This was getting more and more painful for me. I wanted to take care of the children, but found myself being a household skivvy again and being taken advantage of by Jim. I couldn't do this on top of recover emotionally from the situation. I was struggling financially myself and looking at working extra jobs to fund things, and I just didn't have the energy to take care of Jim's responsibilities and games as well. If it was simply that he couldn't manage, then this was not the impression that he gave, for it rather felt like an absolving himself of any household duties and an expectation that I was to come home and act as cook and cleaner still as well as struggle with the extra travel and picking the children up for the weekends. This all felt like just another one of his games.

I twigged to this and told him that I could only cook if he had something in, and if I also had a helping hand with the dishes.

But nothing changed. No matter my willingness to visit and to cook for the boys, giving them some sense of normality, it became obvious that Jim was not going to assist me with this and I realise now that he had other plans. He demanded the keys to the house and I had no option but to hand them over. Even though I was still paying off the mortgage.

I was still trying to be mother, but he wasn't interested in co-parenting. And so sadly I eventually stopped going back there to cook at week nights anymore and I had to let him know that I

Naïve Hope

couldn't do this. He didn't tell me about it for quite some time, in fact he *never* told me about it, but it transpired that Jim's answer was to get a live-in 'housekeeper' complete with her own son: I will not comment on this except to say that she apparently proposed to him some months later but he turned her down, and then he kicked her out; so I will let the reader draw their own conclusions. The result of all this was that the children 'didn't require' my cooking services and could manage very well without me, thank you very much. And I was only to see them at weekends from now on.

Even though this reduced in part the physical running around for me, I still felt that I had become superfluous, lost, hurt, unwanted – I could now not maintain regular weekday contact with my boys, and the wedge was being driven in ever wider. I thrashed around inwardly in my pain, wondering how I could fill this gap in my heart and life. As a mother who has been deprived of her children I felt as though I had lost my arms and legs... and part of my identity. This was really hurting!

The next step in Jim's sabotage of my relationship with the boys occurred over the course of several months; the children were no longer around when I called over at weekends or on any pre-arranged night. This eventuated to it becoming harder for me to catch them at home especially if I was even a minute or two late. Within 9 months I had moved from Altona and was now living in Brighton having been forced by Jim's actions to leave my job at TOW. This was not of my own choosing, and nothing to do with Suzy, but rather other events. But more of this later.

Sure I understand how difficult it is for parents that split to co-parent together. I can also appreciate that Jim had a lot to deal with and that now that I was no longer there to take the brunt of the domestic organisation he would be quite challenged. But this is what *he* had forced, not me. If there was any acknowledgement to himself that he had stuffed up grandly by forcing me to leave, then he did not show it. Nor was there any attempt to woo me back, nor to acknowledge the events that had forced things to this state. I offered plenty of opportunity to discuss the situation, especially in the early months, and I would be friendly and available to talk about things whenever I phoned regarding the boys. However, Jim saw this as an opportunity to *appear* to be friendly, then to hit me with some verbal, emotional or psychological hammer. It took me many years to recognise that he was a snake. Some snakes may be fascinating or appear to be charming creatures, but their bite is full of venom. Particularly in Australia! I eventually had to stop leaving even this door open to him in order to stop this further verbal abuse, blame and shame on me.

Meanwhile my visits to the boys were now mainly at the weekends. I continued to pay the mortgage, as my contribution to the family maintenance, and when this was finished, continued to pay regularly to the family upkeep. I now had a part-time job every third weekend working for a research company, and sometimes they would throw me an extra weekend. Inadvisable to refuse, as I sorely needed this extra income, I had to try and re-negotiate the weekend with the boys. This must have played into his hands, as I later realised that he was still looking to blame me at any opportunity. And sure enough, instead of what was best for the boys, Jim included this as another hurdle for me - he admitted that if I was even just one minute late past the due time, he would make sure that they would not be there for me. And so it was. If I got held up in traffic, he would send them off someplace else, and he wouldn't tell me where they were.

It became clear during those following months which grew into years, that Jim was still bent on punishing me, and it seemed that he did all he could to prevent me having easy and peaceful contact with the children. Access became a lottery as to whether the boys would be home when I got there, with Jim trotting all sorts of excuses out about them not coming back from friends' houses, being suddenly invited to parties, having already eaten, and so on.

Jim just wasn't getting over it, but there was no way I was ever going back. It couldn't just go on like this forever. So I invited Jim to divorce me as he appeared to feel so bitter about my leaving, but he refused to do so. I figured that this way he could say that he divorced me, and keep some pride. But to him it wasn't an option, he couldn't let go. Things did not improve between us, even though I kept offering him to talk at any time. He remained difficult to deal with and I remained scared of being controlled by him again.

Naïve Hope

I had no idea of my rights about any of this. I didn't know many divorced people. Apart from Suzy who didn't yet have any children, I didn't know of anyone else who came close to my situation. I didn't have any real friends. I only had workmates. And I didn't like to tell them of the catastrophic happenings at home. It was all I could do to manage to carry on at work.

It was a stressful time all by itself, but spending emotional energy, time and petrol travelling to see my boys only to be turned away time and again, was frustrating, hurtful and cruel. I began to realise that I had to fill the aching void in my heart with something besides work. The pain was so deep, the hurt at the injustice of it all was so acute that I had to find something to totally take my mind off not being able to have them with me or to see them. I searched for hobbies and interests, then eventually hunted to find extra work besides the research work to support the cost of it all. Meanwhile my new credit card was taking a real battering and I was riding the roller-coaster that came with needing one.

TIME TO TALK

All of my attempts to employ this time amicably and all of my offers to talk about what had happened - about the separation, about the children and what to do, about how we handle things, about how Jim manages now I am not in the house etc., all of these or indeed *any* of these things - were met with hostility, self-righteousness, or plain nastiness. You would think that *he* had been kicked out of the house with only the clothes on his back! I had been faced with my own identity crisis since being evicted and was trying to find me and my roots again – and where I belonged. But one thing I knew, there was no way that I could or would go back to him, no matter how tough things are.

Despite all of the things in my life, I still tried to offer a friendly ear or shoulder to Jim. But every time I offered to be there to talk about things, On *each* and *every* occasion he stayed true to form. Even when it was not done obviously and openly, it was still there; Nasty, vindictive, secretive, brooding... Look, I knew that it was hard for me and therefore naturally must have been hard for him and I also knew that he no longer had me there to confide in, to sort things out, to 'fix' things, and he now had the boys (which he had insisted on keeping with him) to look after, mainly by himself, so I gave him a little slack. But...! There is a limit.

Even this huge shift of geo-location in our relationship did nothing to make him 'wake up' and look at what part he had contributed to this. Every time I rang the boys between visits, I also ensured that I speak to Jim at the same time to see how he was. Would he take any of my suggestions? Of course not.

Except for the odd occasion that he appeared to show some sort of concern where he kept me talking and asked me questions. He pretended to be interested in what I had to say. At this stage I was still naïve and still seeking to see the best in people and so I would open up to talk about things. I didn't realise that he was pumping me for information that he intended to use later. For I discovered over time that he would store things up and just when I thought we had some sort of common communication going, he would turn what I had shared against me. This happened often enough that eventually I vowed not to let him in again, not to open up and share. And this took a few hurt heart moments before I was able to cut off totally emotionally from him. Which was not helpful when it came to jointly dealing with what was in the best interest for the boys.

Jim still insisted on playing games, only they were now new ones and so I didn't recognise them straight away. And this was where he really proved himself as the destructive person he was because now he was including the boys in his little power games.

It would appear from the disjointed moments of conversation we had that he was still determined to destroy me, for he said as much.

'You'll get nothing! You deserve nothing!' he had said when I asked him about some sort of settlement approximately six months after moving out. Several times I had tried to engage him in serious or peaceful conversation to discuss our situation and to see how we handled our new set of circumstances. Between the pretend times and the *You're-Late*-games he had trouble even being near me. Phone calls became hotbeds of angst, questions by me were not only fielded way out of the park, but they were received like angry spears and returned like fire rockets with follow-up sleeper bombs attached. It was incredibly difficult to get any cooperation from him. His words were flung at me like spiked and loaded barbs, and any phone calls by him later were hidden attempts to get into my confidence again and then to try to use whatever I said to him against me. He was a master at sniffing out opportunities designed to bring things down and undone, rather than to seek solutions and the best for the children.

Church Prejudice

Where was my Lord and Saviour in all of this? Where was the God that I loved and that I thought loved me back? The promises that I had read over and over in the Bible *hadn't* been fulfilled. I had obeyed all the rules, I had followed the precepts and requirements as best I could. Yes, I had betrayed my marriage, but then, the marriage had actually betrayed me. I truly believed that I had tried every which way to save my marriage, and I had explored all of the options available through what I knew of God and the church and faith; and still God was silent, Jesus stood by doing nothing. I alone had had to be the one to act… Little realizing that this was part of my spiritual development, and the shift needed for me to no longer perceive God as separate from myself, or the Divine Source as being an authority outside of myself, I was yet to realize that I was actually taking the right steps and moving in the right direction for the safety of my own Soul. The outer trappings of my beliefs were yet to be dealt with, the breaking of the web of beliefs and the one-way commands and promises were being addressed, albeit on a still yet hidden level to my conscious mind.

Now, consciously, it was time that I broke free from the commitment that I made to Jesus and that way of life that night, and from its insidious influence. And this was to take me some time, but the process had already begun. It had begun long ago during my marriage, but now it was a more conscious process, as I gradually examined the codes I had been living by.

Meanwhile, I am a woman out of her marriage, a woman who still knows little of life outside of marriage, indeed, of living a single life. For the first time in my life, I am not living in a family situation. And I sorely needed assistance and encouragement.

Now I found myself without even the pitifully poor support of the church that we had belonged to. They now demonstrated quite clearly to me that they were 'funny' about newly (or even long-time) separated or divorced women. It was as though they were, and therefore *I was*, some sort of threat of having their *own* husbands taken from them by the newly independent female, no doubt. All of my so-called church friends, or to be more generous, my 'Christian acquaintances' were now just too busy to entertain, visit, talk, phone, anything, once they knew I had left Jim. But surprising and unexpected as this cold-shoulder treatment was to me, it also clearly showed prejudice and a lack of kindness that alleged Christians were supposed to be recognised by. Instead, they were just a group of fearful and suspicious people who couldn't handle something different from the safety of their own familiar structures and were probably *terrified* of their own vulnerability to temptation of any kind. I didn't *care* about anyone else's husband, I simply needed to get through. And they were *no* help, just showing me cold shoulders and lack of availability.

Whether Jim had said anything I don't know, though another thought strikes me, and it is possible that the night of my dastardly 'affair' Jim had included the church lot in his blabbing and broadcasting, too. How very kind and considerate and Christian of him, hey? Goodness knows what Jim *had* said to them – it doesn't bear thinking in light of his mindset, his lying, denying and his own multiplistic behaviours.

What *did* people think I wanted from them?

I have come to realise that there are huge numbers of people that cannot think independently by themselves or for them self. What I mean by that is that there is of course a certain amount of reasoning that everyone is capable of. This is usually according to certain basic assumptions, statements and beliefs that one operates one's life by. The ability to question these basic tenets is a real skill and of inestimable value. With one's given stance and thoughts in life there may sometimes be a blind spot if you like, the need for another inner question to be asked that would progress one onto a different outcome or possibly to further information that might change the outcome of one's original thoughts and decisions. This is often through not being taught how to follow through on a line of thought to its conclusions. Or it may be that any other possible outcome may be undesirable for them on one level or another, or for one reason or another, consciously or subconsciously.

The thing about most people who belong to a group and who are invested in that group, and in particular a faith or religion, is the *preservation of* that same group. The *Cause* itself becomes the thing to preserve *above* other things. Because of their need to belong to the group and so to validate themselves with and through that group, one may carry a torch of grievance for anyone who thinks or acts differently, or they may be unable to discriminate between a real or an imagined threat, with the result they often see *all* as a threat. Some may not always be quick in utilising positive opportunities for their own self advancement, they envy those who do, or create perceptions of being badly done by, when they just can't be bothered to do anything about things themselves. Or they may become co-dependent, or parasitic in their personalities or behaviours, living off others and giving little or even nothing in return.

Not that this type of person is confined to church people, nor to any particular group of people. They can be everywhere, even in families that are well educated and privileged.

In fact, when I look back at my way of thinking at that time, the thinking that went along the particular lines of thought that were familiar to me and that I had maintained in order to stay married, I really had *not* learned to think correctly for myself. I did not question sufficiently what I was being told, I did not argue when I saw fluffy spots in logic or promise. I had few wordly life comparisons, and had been taught to put complete trust in the Bible and in the church's accepted interpretations of it. But when one subscribes to pure *blind faith*, then the key is in the word 'blind'. I was *blinded* to any other way of conducting my life.

No more. Enough!

For what had the church given me, what could it offer to me? I already had my own Moral Codes and had been acting on them before and during my conversion. Written on my heart were the sentiments of Jesus anyway, and the Ten Commandments were part of how I generally lived. My humanity had caused me to err on several occasions, yes, but I didn't need to be told what was right or wrong, I already knew; I knew not to kill, I knew not to cheat, I knew not to lie, I knew not to commit adultery (in my own heart I was no longer married to this man and had 'fallen' under extreme circumstances), I knew not to bear false witness etc etc. All the church could do for me was to pour guilt, fear, shame, unworthiness and obedience onto me. And claim my money, time, energy and allegiance. Applying Bible rules, quotes and philosophies may work for some, but they hadn't worked for me. Nor for Jim, by all accounts!

What else can I say? Well I can say that I have since learned to think for myself. I have learned not to accept what someone says unless I have challenged and been satisfied with the supposed or actual authority behind what they say. This now *cannot* be taken away from me. I observe each person I meet and befriend to see if what they *say* matches what they *do* or who they present themselves to be. I no longer need them to approve of me as before, for I owe no man anything, or woman. I no longer need for them to trust me. *I* trust me, and so I do not need to prove anything. And I am human enough to understand when I mess up, for none of us is infallible. For *I know* my heart's intentions are usually innocent, though certainly not all-knowing. I am basically a good human being, and still have moments of being more 'human' than 'good'.

There is such a thing as maturity, and this in itself should assist in bringing a better thinking process, surely? But usually maturity often requires time, and a willingness to develop...

'DANNY FIRST'

I am not exaggerating here when I tell you that this man now showed that he had no scruples, indeed no respect and no backbone.

You would think that he may have gotten some message from the fact that I didn't go back home as he later confessed (thirty years later in fact) that he had expected me to.

Naïve Hope

Did he think about getting real help? I doubt it. If he was crying out for help, he wasn't crying out the right way. He had been and still was hitting out!

I had now been living at Suzy's about six or seven months. Jim had the home number, and he called me there one night. Initially I thought it was to have a shot at me about my next 'scheduled' visit, but I was stunned by what he has to say to me. And certainly not expecting what followed next.

'Hello, Marni,' was his opening line, as was usual .

'Hello, Jim,' I respond cautiously and I wait to hear what he has to say.

'I am just phoning to let you know that I am going to end it all. I am going to kill myself,' were his next few words.

What? *That* was unexpected! Was he kidding, or what? Keep calm, Marni, and anyway, why is he telling you this? What does he want *you* to do about it? Whilst part of my mind is in overdrive, pursuing this information and its terrible consequences, Jim drops his next dramatic statement into the void.

'This is my last Goodbye.'

He still had his gun for as far as I knew he was still with the security firm. Habitually reacting emotionally and mostly sympathetically to his calls for help in the past, this time I thought I would call his bluff. Things were no longer as they had been and I had heard not to overreact when someone threatens suicide, but to be calm about it. So I now try to engage him and talk him out of it, but he seems dead set – pardon the pun.

'Is there nothing I can say to make you change your mind?' I ask him as encouragingly as I could.

'No. Nothing' he replies quite dispassionately. I wonder how he can be so calm and yet sound so determined about it all. But I keep hold of my original thought and also consider that maybe he just wants attention and he is seeing how far he can go with this new mini-drama with this sensational 'confession'.

Meanwhile, my mind is still working things through as best it can under such circumstances, and whilst our conversation is taking place, somewhere at the back of my mind I am wondering what is going on with the other children, and a cold dread passes through me. If I remember correctly the two older boys were at a school camp, so I knew they were not at home with him. But what about little Danny?

His next words cause my heart to flip and cold fear to course through my veins. Not again. This man is doing it again – fear and threats and nastiness and badness!

'I have little Danny here with me, and he is going to go first.' He delivers this with deliberate coolness and sounds quite detached. *What*?!

'What do you mean?' I dare to ask as calmly as I can manage, just to clarify I have heard him right.

'I will shoot him first, before I shoot myself.' He is still using the same dispassionate voice. But his words pack terror and horror. Jim is threatening to *kill* poor innocent little Danny. His own son! The monster!

I felt my stomach flip and flop and slap around inside my body. I felt sick. The old fears came back again. *Hold it together, Marni. Don't make waves... Don't be the one to push him over the edge.* It is all I can do to keep the tremor out of my throat and tongue. Initially, I respond as calmly as I could, asking him why he thought that this was necessary, but he just wasn't making sense. I also remembered someone saying that if a person is going to commit suicide, they usually don't tell you about it, they usually just go ahead and do it. But was Jim your 'usual' kind of guy? Did he do 'usual' things? When my calm, accepting reasoning didn't gain a different response from him - for there was no way that I was going to gratify him with begging for mercy with a 'please not to do such a terrible thing', or any other dramatic carryings on that had been our life together – I tried a different tack. Somehow I manage to keep my voice under control as I attempted to bluff him that I didn't care for I could do nothing about it and so it was entirely up to him. But I was panicking. *Boy, was I panicking!*

For some reason, some ridiculous and naïve reason, I had *never* thought that my leaving the marital home would cause Jim to redirect his anger and nastiness toward the boys. It *never occurred* to me that this would or could happen. I had believed that his problem was *with me,* and that if this was addressed then the situation would be alleviated. And I guess this was me being guilty of Projection myself. Because *I* wouldn't dream of doing something like that, I had assumed that *others* wouldn't do it. Because I followed the adage 'Do unto others as you would have them do unto you' then I naturally gave others the benefit of the doubt. I was too riddled with Christian ideals and homilies and hopes still to be able to see when others weren't. And I was to fall for this ignorant mindset error again before things were to be sorted between us.

Would I ever threaten any of my children like this? *No,* I certainly wouldn't! Not in a pink fit! So if it's not in my mental makeup to do such a thing, how could I possibly imagine that someone else would do such a thing? Especially someone professing to love his children? And whose anger previously appeared to be directed at me, and not the children?

It blew my mind. This was not appropriate or acceptable behaviour! Of course, Jim could have been bluffing... But was I prepared to take a chance on that? No way!

He continued to talk to me for just a short time in an effort to draw out his farewell, and I said 'Goodbye' as he requested. But my mind was now already racing and planning.

The moment he ended the call I was onto the Werribee police straight away. I gave them the address and the exact words he had said, and I added that 'He may be bluffing, but I cannot afford to take a chance. No one should threaten my son or any child in this way. Please, *please* get someone over there to make sure that Danny is alright.'

They were on to it immediately, and said they would phone me back as soon as they had checked out the situation. I was itching to get in the car and drive around there straight away, but I followed their instruction. So I waited by the phone. Besides, it would have taken me a while to get round there, and not only that, if he had his gun and *had* gone off the deep end, my arriving there without the police just might escalate things even more. Please remember that this was in the days before mobile phones so if I wanted to know what was going on, I really had little option other than to stay where I was until they got back to me on the home phone as they had instructed me. Would they make it in time? What would they find when they got there? I sweated and paced whilst I waited for the call. Within the longest three quarters of an hour of my life, the police phoned me back. 'You can come round and collect your little boy, Mrs Moran. He is safe, and your husband is safe too.'

With that, I grabbed my keys and raced round. I was allowed to take Danny home with me for that night, but when I begged them to let me keep him, they said that there was no custody order for me to do so, and he had to remain with Jim. But that they would be keeping an eye on him for any future threats like this. They also told me that they had 'had a serious talk with him'.

And that is all? Yep! *And that fixes it all I suppose*, I thought to myself.

Jim didn't speak to me for three weeks after I had called the police on him. My phone calls checking on little Danny were left unanswered.

I did *not* want to go through this again. I did not want to keep any of my sons in danger with this man. I did not now trust Jim with the boys, and I wanted to know if I could keep Danny with me.

I again sought legal support and advice. Citizens Bureau. Legal Aid. Anybody? After I had been evicted from Werribee, I had sought legal advice. When I had asked about having my children living with me out of the home, I had been told that, I could *not* take the children from the *family home*, as it would be perceived and prosecuted as 'kidnapping and abduction'. I found another solicitor and put my situation to him about getting the boys away from Jim. This same information was just repeated to me again, and hadn't changed in any way even under these new circumstances. It was quite clear that even despite this occurrence with Jim that it still stood as before. My hands were again tied, and much as I wanted them with me where I *knew* that they would all be safe, there was *nothing* I could do to get my children away from him. And as *Jim* occupied and owned the family home, it would be seen that he was in a better situation to house them and therefore the he was better provider! Tommyrot! Total Tosh!

Naïve Hope

I could not even go for full custody of Danny because of how Jim had positioned me, as I could not afford any other rental just then other than my current accommodation. Even worse, Jim now threatened to go for full custody himself. There was nothing more I could do to protect my children, only try and see them whenever I was allowed to.

When the police had had their 'word' with Jim they reported that he had told them that he didn't really mean any of it, that he didn't intend any harm. But he had no answer to the question of 'Well, sir, if you hadn't really meant it then *why* did you do such a thing? Surely you realise this could be viewed as a serious threat. Best not make any threats at all, hey? We don't want to come out to see you again.'

In Jim's desire to hit back at me, to hurt me, to attempt to destroy me, he was using the very ones he was duty, morally and love bound to protect – his own flesh and blood; his children. They were just pawns in this man's blind games and mad thrashings for attention and control. He did *not* deserve to keep them with him!

And yet I, who *was* more fitted to have them and look after them, had *no* recourse to claim them back and *no* financial backing to fight any of this. Without family or close friends nearby, who was there to stand behind me and support me in any of this. This was crazy, and yet just another thing that I had to swallow down and suppress so I could get through the daily round of 'living'.

If I had had the money, if I had the means, I would have taken him to court over this. But I didn't at that time, I was only just making ends meet. And I couldn't afford to 'hate' this man, because I had to stay present to my children when I saw them, and I had to be up to working, and living in hope that something would resolve all of this in a much better way. And let's face it, I was still pretty scared of him.

How can one possibly *consider* entering or staying in a marriage with any *other* hope or dream that is not with the best outcome or intention in mind? How can one bring children into the world if they thought that any of this kind of thing could happen? Why bother at all? This was definitely not what I had signed up for when embarking on this supposedly 'blessed state' of marriage. This was bullshit.

And another nail in the coffin of blind faith and naïve hope. For we were all still living a nightmare.

Leaving behind my 'Christian' understanding of life-and-the-world, I needed some other way to make some sort of sense of this world, as I had very little real tools of life other than Bible 'rules'. I only as yet had the memory of confusion and dysfunction experienced both at home with my family of origin, and in my own marital dynamics.

SINGLE LIFE
Life After Marriage. The Fall-Out. Lessons.

~Four Jobs And A Holiday ~ Distraction ~ Not Happy, Jan!
~ Help? Anyone? ~ Tall Dark and Handsome ~ Who Am I?
~ Sinking Ship ~ Kerry ~ Denis ~ Out Again
~ Spiritual Path ~ Divorce ~ No Longer Mum

Four Jobs & A Holiday

Within a couple of months of me moving out I began to recognize that I was 'free' of his violence and the prison he had created for me. For the first time in over thirty-six years, I had a *holiday*. Because I still learning how to juggle my extra expenses, I used my brand new credit card. This was not the best way to go, but my repressed and bruised personality and psyche needed some sun and sea. And some freedom. I had been suppressed enough. I needed to forget about the horrors and the pain and to think about myself a bit, especially since all of my plans had been so successfully sabotaged, in cooking for the children, in seeing them regularly, in having them live with me. Even Suzy suggested it to me when she saw the state I was in about things.

I took my first holiday by *myself* ever. I count this as only the third *actual* holiday I had in my life, if I don't count the Convalescence from severe anaemia in Wales at twelve. The *first* holiday I had been on was with mum and my brother Ian when we were children. We spent one rainy week in a caravan on a cold and wet deserted beach. The *second* was a week at Butlin's Holiday Camp at Skegness, with Jim and the two boys before we decided to come to Australia. Our 'honeymoon' had actually been a busy conference at a Christian Youth Camp where we were involved with other Christian youth all the time, attending prayer meetings, Bible study and other similar events. So I don't count that as a real holiday either. After we moved to Australia, every few years we would travel to the UK to see family, for his father had died not long after our migration and his alcoholic mother lived on her own, and so our time was often spent racing round from family member to family member. I can't really count these trips back home to see family as real holidays. It was always exhausting and expensive and we had to do all the travelling to catch up and connect with people. No fun, relaxation, sight-seeing and partying involved.

No one from my family had ever visited us here in Australia, I was always the one to visit and stay in touch. So; very little rest or recuperation, then.

Here I was, tired, exhausted, stressed and emotionally bruised. And ready for a *real* holiday! My rebellion kicked in and I decided that for once I would have what *I* wanted.

I spent a week at the Broadbeach Hotel in Queensland. A whole glorious irresponsible week. Sheer extravagance, sheer bliss. I had a view of the beach from my bed! *Actually* from my bed... it was glorious. I had seen the advertising picture in the tourist booklet, and wanted 'that exact view' – and I got it. Yahoo! Sure there was some measure of discomfort being totally by myself; not used to it you see. But inevitably the break was extremely good for me and I managed to get a bit of a tan. Yes, I had to put the cost of all this on my new credit card, but I was past worrying about money at that moment – the need to get away was overwhelming. I don't think I could have carried on without this break.

Then it was back to work, back to the grindstone, and as I had voluntarily taken the Werribee house mortgage bank pay-in book with me, I continued with this as my contribution toward 'maintenance' for the boys; I now needed to focus on work and get more money in.

I could not have my children suffer because I had been forced out of the marital home, and if it was at all possible, I would do whatever I could, practically and financially.

As you know, before being evicted, I had tried to come to an agreement about living arrangements to defuse the situation – the result had been three very clear refusals of No No No. This stance had taken its toll in more ways than one. I was a mother that had been forced away from her children. I had a *huge* hole in my heart, that only being with my children and knowing they were safe could fill. I wasn't able to be *with* them as I wanted, I wasn't able to *care* for them as I wanted, I wasn't even consulted on any issues regarding them. This hole was getting bigger, and every time I thought of them I had to push the pain down further and further. Eventually something had to give, and I had to find a way of living with this pain.

DISTRACTION

Living with Jim had been so oppressive.

During our life together, we had occasionally had discussions (or rather Jim had issued his own fixed statements) that had left me feeling uncomfortable about the world we lived in. When famous or successful women came up in the news or in a success story, he had been fond of sneeringly stating that they made it to fame only because of 'the casting couch routine'. His insinuation was always that women got what they wanted by using sex for their ends. In short, the only way to get ahead was to sleep with someone influential. He had always been adamant in this attitude. I didn't believe him. This was not how I lived, not what I had yet seen around me, so I naturally totally disagreed with him about this. Even though I no longer dared to contradict him openly for fear of the consequences, I secretly held that this was *not* true, could not possibly be totally true for all women, and that women *could* make it by talent and abilities alone.

Maybe it was a kneejerk reaction, maybe I wanted to prove something to him, maybe to myself. I was about to prove him wrong. Sure one could consider this as me being reactive. But I was also being *pro-active*, and pulling out those horrid weeds of negativity that he had planted in me about women time and time again. Whatever the reason, and there were many reasons to do what I was considering, I sought further education and involvement to, in-part, replace the time I would normally have devoted to my children. Something was needed to fill the space in my heart and in my life.

Distraction! That's what I need – distraction!

Maybe I could find some hobbies that I can enjoy, involve myself in something, learn a bit more about myself I thought to myself. For I was done with church and wasn't sure what I was looking for at this stage. I wasn't yet ready to do any art, nor hairdressing, just not really that interested in them at that time. I looked around to see what fun things I could do, remembering the play I had been in as a child. So I circled the acting, dancing, shorthand and book reading courses for the moment. I thought that these would help occupy my mind and my spare time, and to cover up some of the pain and distress of the difficulties involved in seeing my boys. Any classes I took up would require funds, too, but I had my credit card at the moment. I was still trying to run from the hurt and destruction in my life, from things that I felt I had no control over. As yet I was still so unused to being able to look after and nurture myself because I was so 'other' oriented. And quite probably was not yet aware that I was still in shock from all that had happened. I daresay my mind was struggling to cope with all that had transpired, and to adjust to a difficult situation as best it could.

This was all an entirely new and interesting experience – part of me free and ready to spread my wings in a way I had never done, or never been allowed to do before, with another part of me very wary after what I had been through with Jim, yet another part wanting the stability of home and family life, another part yearning and grieving for my children, and another part still believing in fairness, equality, romance and the basic goodness of others, whilst yet another part was not knowing who I was or what to do about it all. Initially it was all a bit confusing, complicated and distracting. But I am willing to learn new things as I go.

This was in actuality the beginning of a whole new side of my life – learning and experimenting and discovering. In a way, this set a pattern for the rest of my life, as I was later to become interested in many things, and in other ways. But I had to start somewhere. And I started with a short course on acting first, the teacher being Barry Michael. Then I put my name down for a modeling course – both a good way to go considering there was so much I subconsciously had to prove to myself. And getting rid of some of the labels placed on women by Jim seemed to be a positive idea. In any event, these courses appealed to me before anything else.

They proved to be a lot of fun for me besides being challenging to my mind and psyche.

Naïve Hope

After this short taster on acting with the Council of Adult Education, I followed through on the modeling course with Elly Lukas of Collins Street in Melbourne. Elly was pleased to have me on her books and I was her oldest model, most others being quite young and some a bit scatty. I enjoyed doing deportment and practicing catwalk and disco-catwalk sessions as well as modeling assignments for Schwarzkopf and others. I had so missed dancing since being married and this played into my sense of rhythm. Besides awakening my aesthetic side again, for I really enjoyed the artistic side of the make-up classes. Along with this, I was also enjoying female acquaintances and I made a couple of new friends. Following this I did a radio course and played around with accents. A lot of fun. And a sense of self discovery.

After I did a second adult acting course, I was informed that Barry Michael also ran an agency for acting, called **BMA** – Barry Michael Artists – and he did casting for Television work for extras and actors. I was invited to sign up, and I did my first 'walk-on' extras part in the very last episode of 'The Sullivans'. Freezing cold, and tired because I could not sleep the night before from sheer excitement at fulfilling yet another dream; I was exhilarated by it all. The pay was good, so this became one of my part-time jobs, and over the following years I got to work on 'Prisoner', 'Cop Shop', a couple of commercials and a variety of movies being filmed in or close by to Melbourne. I got my Actors Equity card after that first part, and I still have that card!

The acting later turned into regular paid work, which I enjoyed doing. Besides, I had needed extra money to pay for the added load of renting and separate groceries since moving out of home, as well as to pay for my car and my holiday.

This progressed to my doing amateur theatre and was another fascinating way of expressing myself creatively, and I was so pleased when I scored parts that were based on auditions, presentation and skill and not on any 'casting couch routine'.

I fairly thumped the air whenever I scored a part, and inside I laughed at Jim's idea. I had proved him *so* wrong. Later, of course, I had to acknowledge that some stars or models did indeed follow this route, but I also found that others refused to do so yet still made it big. This whole thing was not necessarily about me getting to be famous or about me being 'big' – I had no such ambitions - but about the conviction and integrity of my beliefs being proven right. It was also about my doing some of the things that had been denied to me through devotion to parents, siblings and then later to this tyrant. I was doing work that I wanted to do, and work that was also fun. And I felt like I was reclaiming something.

I enrolled in other courses and saw new sides of myself developing.

I undertook training with Morgan Research to help fill some of the lonely weekend hours doing public surveys every third weekend. All of this kept me occupied, and able to avoid the ache in my heart to some degree. And helped pay my expenses. Even with paying for an accountant to do my tax return, I was ahead.

The income from my TV bit-parts was a real help, and with a couple of nights a week waitressing or bar-work, there was a bit more money. I also worked occasionally for the big football and cricket ground caterers. *Add that to the pot, Marni.* So in the end I was doing three part time jobs besides my full time job, essential to cover and manage my living expenses since leaving home. But I was coping. By myself! And I was fulfilling my responsibilities towards my children. And still learning about myself as I went along.

I watch for Jim to either make a change for the better or divorce me.

Neither of these, of course, were ever to happen.

NOT HAPPY, JAN!

I was still struggling with this huge hole and void in my heart and life that the separation from my children and the breakdown of my marriage had caused. Distraction was helping to a degree, but the ache was still there, underneath it all, like an undercurrent.

Whoever said that 'Whatever doesn't kill you, makes you stronger', or words to that effect, needs their head examined. The truth is more likely this; the strong are the ones that mostly manage to survive, dragging up their inner strength in order to do so, whilst the less-than-strong may not be able to fully recover and can even

Naïve Hope

become broken. And even the strong can be weakened by continual onslaughts! It is sadistic to believe otherwise. The strong get tested (as we all do) but unrelenting fatigue can cause depression, which has nothing to do with 'strength'. Whoever it was that coined that phrase if I ever meet him or her, I will give him or her a piece of my mind!

The torment I had suffered during my marriage and the steps I had taken to sidetrack this had cost us all. Not just myself, but the children too. Over the following years I pieced together how others conducted their divorces, and compared it with how ours was being played out, and I was amazed that there were actually civilized divorces. Every step along the way with this man, he *had* to make it difficult – he *had* to fight. I dare to say now that he was mad, nuts, a mad stupid Irishman, because that is how he was with me. Nuts!

Shortly after this huge shift in my life, the final push of the eviction, the beating, the attempts to see the children, it became clear to my workmate Jan that something immense had happened. He had been away on an assignment, then on his holidays and now he was back. I hadn't seen much of him for a while prior to this as he had been doing an intensive training course. Within a couple of weeks he had asked me what was going on at home. He knew that something had happened, and could he help in any way? No, nothing you can do really. Then he prised it out of me. So I told him the refuge idea had failed, and of my much changed current situation.

'I suggest you get some advice on the children, you don't want to leave them with him. And it looks like he may have *planned* to get you out of the house so he can claim it from under you.' He said. I didn't want to believe this, and I found it hard to think that Jim could have cold bloodedly planned on throwing me out. But I was concerned about the legal side of things, and so very ignorant. I had a counscling session coming up, so I asked the counselor, and he agreed that I should find out my legal position, as it is often very hard for a spouse to take children from the family home without a court order.

I was recommended a female lawyer, who was supposedly renowned in fighting for women's rights in the divorce courts. Let me tell you, she charged fees like a wounded bull, and apart from one possible protection option, one I couldn't really agree to, she was very remiss in her advice. Even further consultations with a male lawyer on her staff left me vulnerable to Jim's games. I was obviously small fry in their eyes, with only a small settlement for a little house out somewhere in the suburbs. But that is no excuse. Anyway, again, no matter how I looked at it, the legal position was as I had started to fear – I could not just go in and get my kids, I could not 'remove them from the family home'. Not possible. Even using a proper solicitor would leave me open to legal action and I would be facing a court hearing and possible jail.

Well, Thank YOU! Bloody Thank you! So *still* I can't go and get my kids no matter *how* badly this man has behaved towards me? And what about *them*?

Talk about injustice!

Not long after this, I went on a social outing to the group for single parents called PWP: Parents Without Partners. I only went a couple of times. Without exception, *all* of the men groaned and moaned and winged and whined about what they had lost. Carrying on about how *all* the women had it good. Did they ask me about why I was separated? How I was coping? Not *one* of them. *All* stupid, boring and selfish men. I couldn't believe how they moaned about their wives leaving them as if it was some totally unexpected surprise; even when questioned most of them *admitted* that when their wives had told they would leave if blah-blah-blank didn't happen, they still couldn't believe that she actually would. These silly men totally ignoring messages and then blaming the woman. Options to engage, to change, to grow, were *all* ignored. I could not stand it. It was a moaning-misery club for verbal wife-bashing and hammering the wives legal representatives. Here was I, having suffered what I had been through, and these lazy, self-centred men grumbled without knowing the half of what others went through to try to save their marriages. Not that I really connected with many women there, but judging from my own situation, they might have had a similarly tough time connecting with *any* male there.

Back to my own legal situation. Their only suggestion, possibly the only decent legal protection advice I was given, was to force the sale of the home if my husband defaulted in paying me out on settlement. But if for some reason Jim defaulted, that would mean my kids would not have a roof over their heads. I had a picture of them being out on the streets and just *couldn't* do that to them, the thought was impossible to consider. I told them I couldn't possibly do that, as it might mean that my kids have nowhere to live, and I couldn't have them put out on the street. I have no idea why I would think that he would default, but I must have known somewhere that he could and possibly would... Did they come up with any other protection clause instead? No. They didn't even consider a proviso which occurred to me years later, that if he didn't pay me within a certain amount of time then he would incur ongoing interest until he did pay me out. And these legal guys were supposed to be *professionals*! Spend a small ridiculous fortune and all they really did was legalise things; cross 't's' and dot 'i's'.

All they had to do was to have inserted a clause that interest on what he owed me would accrue until he had finally paid out what he owed me. But then, it wasn't a big settlement, my property wasn't in the millions, or even the hundreds of thousands. I was small fish. So why should they bother? I would *never* go to this firm of solicitors, this big fancy supposedly standing-up-for-and-helping-women agency ever ever again. And if you want to know who they are I will happily tell you. But for reasons of law, I cannot name them here. 'A Tiger for Women' they had been labeled – what utter crap!

I had paid for a *proper* sworn valuation on the property. The (male) judge, however, cut down my share to a paltry sum, sticking instead with Jim's minimum guess-timation assessment of property value. And I was instructed to pay maintenance. Which I had already been doing via the mortgage and which I did continue to do. Talk about men banding together!

Property settlement went through the courts based on a lower sum than the property was actually worth, alongside an application for joint custody. My solicitor's didn't even contest the settlement sum. I was consequently to wait for over three years before Jim actually started paying *anything* off the property settlement he owed me, whilst I had still continued to pay for the house mortgage! I had been badly caught, though Jim didn't tell me that he was the one holding back... He said the delays were all due to the solicitors. I was raw on many levels for many, many years over how this was all conducted.

Jim had *said* that he would destroy me – and he certainly succeeded in destroying many plans and opportunities for me. I *never* really recovered financially from this, even though I continued to work hard and long all my life .

In fact, after eighteen years of 'Hard labour' as they call it in prison terms - which I felt that I had been doing whilst married to this man - I got to walk away with *nothing*. I had to wait nearly four years to get a repayment plan off Jim in writing, then I had to wait for this lying Jim to get the message that he actually had to legally *pay* me whether he wanted to or not. I was the one who was in fact paying from the moment I left home. By the time enough money for a deposit had trickled through from him it was 1985 and he had achieved his objective; to stall my chance of starting over again.

In case you picked a slight tone of anger in any of this, you just could be a teensy-weensy bit right. Underneath my hurt and pain and fear of this man there lay a healthy (or unhealthy if you like) slab of anger. Never being allowed to show anger as a child, never daring as a Christian or married woman, being the target of the anger of others, compromising without gaining benefit, abused and afraid, I had *trusted* this man to come good in some way, *any* way, and in the process I had been in the direct path of his hidden anger and violent wrath. I had absorbed some of his anger as well as holding down my own. I had trusted *God* and this is what I got. In writing about this, I can recognise and release his anger, for it never belonged to me. But also I am being made aware that with all of the pain that I had suppressed, underneath there was such anger at how he had disgustingly treated me, and also my children.

As I write this I also feel my own anger at this weak and miserable man, this pathetic and limited soul, this person who was so emotionally and psychologically inadequate; and I get pissed off at how he got to punish me and his children for his own jealousies, fears and hidden shame.

Naïve Hope

For Jim was indeed a weak man. *And he still is!*

Help? Anyone?

You may ask the question, wasn't there someone that you could go to about all this? Good question. The answer is simple really.

There wasn't anyone. Any 'friends' or acquaintances that I had thought I had were mainly from the church group. And the church together with its members, especially the women, were suspicious of a newly 'separated' woman, particularly given the publicity Jim had given; so not much help there. They also kept their husbands away, quite naturally of course, so basically I was on my own. And prayer hadn't and didn't fix anything up either – I was still learning that I had to do things myself, for there was no one else to count on.

Neighbours? Many of the close neighbours had ended up building their first home here because it was an outer suburb therefore less expensive. Like us. Families setting up their own families. Like us. Families bringing new hopes with them to a new area. Like us. But in reality one couldn't expect much help from them. As long as they had their parking space and you didn't overly complain when they had noisy barbeques, or interfere in obtuse ways that they could find offensive, then you were left in peace.

Church; The pastor for help? That's a laugh. Hadn't I already been told quite plainly that I had to keep on forgiving? That was the prescribed remedy. Hah! A supposed cure-all.

Friends? Sheila was living her own life with her own family in Sydney, and now that there was such distance involved, and Jim generally discouraged personal friends now that we were here, it wasn't the sort of thing that I could simply put into a letter or have a phone chat about. Heather? She had moved away. Mary and Stuart? They had accomplished sending us a few chatty letters and calls, and then zilch. And their letters were always so boasting. Would they understand, would they help, and what would Jim do if I wrote to them about things? Nope, not worth considering.

Family? Well I guess the answer is also simple. 'You've made your bed, now lie in it'. And; Refer to previous notes on church.

Work? Now who could I dare involve at work that could actually help me and make a difference to things? Apart from my one platonic friend, who had his own problems and was making plausible headway with a new relationship, there was no way I could conceive of him intervening that might accomplish anything.

God? Ah, there's a thought... Oh, but hasn't He been too busy these last eighteen years to do anything yet? Sent Him letters, prayers, begging – done duties, suffered, followed rules, paid tithes – been kind, forgiving, patient – mmmmmm, wonder why I haven't had any help from Him yet? Maybe He's out of town?

Myself? Now, let's see – have tried to improve. Have tried to be good wife, good mother, good woman, yet still in a pickle. What am I missing here? Yes, what *am* I missing here? If *only* I knew!

I was still to learn that I had to be *my own* best friend and my own strongest resource for myself. And this was to take me many years.

TALL DARK AND HANDSOME

Several months after moving into Suzy's, I received an invitation from a brand new night club that was opening up. This came about quite accidentally – I was given it impromptu when I went out one free night with a girlfriend from work. We were sitting at a bar, enjoying a drink and a chat together. By this time I did drink the occasional alcoholic drink, but no more than one because I couldn't really afford it, financially or head-wise; the Brandy episode had not encouraged me otherwise.

Then this guy comes up and starts chatting to us both in a friendly way. We weren't staying long because we had work in the morning, but he spent a couple of minutes asking us what we thought of the place where we were, and what we liked about it, and how often we went out. He must have liked us because before leaving he handed out these cards which were formal invitations to the Opening of a brand new club called 'Silver's Night Club' at a posh hotel. It stressed black tie and tails, and dress-up evening or cocktail dress for ladies and was dated for a couple of weeks time hence.

Dinner and drink was included, and the current Miss Australia was going to be part of the Grand Opening. We both had double passes,

Naïve Hope

so we could invite who we wanted along with us. My friend had something happening already that night, and seeing as she couldn't make it she gave me her ticket.

I didn't know any guys at this time, and no one else to ask really. But over the next day or so, I showed my tickets to Suzy asking if she wanted to come along to the opening. She was a bit interested, and when I asked if she had someone, a guy, she could invite along she said she did know someone who would be interested. Great! Now all *I* need is a partner. When Suzy asked me who I was taking, I confessed I didn't know anyone. 'Oh, that's a pity' she said. 'If my friend knows someone suitable would you be happy to go along with him? It would be a bit of a blind date, but a foursome, and at least you would have a bit of company beside me' Suzy suggested.

'Mmm, I guess that would be ok', I answered. Why not?

'What sort of a guy would you prefer, that is, if he knows someone like that,' she then asks me.

I thought for a minute. I gave my imagination full reign. Well, why not, I asked myself. It can't hurt to ask. 'Someone tall, dark and handsome,' I smilingly replied, wondering if there was such a person outside of the movies.

Suzy laughed. 'Well why not. I'll ask and we'll see what we can come up with.' And so I waited to see what could come forth out of my request. If anything. Meanwhile I madly set about planning what on earth I could wear, or what I could sew in time.

Suzy tells me a few days before the evening that her date for the night had invited a friend of his, whom, he thought, fitted the bill. Oh, how exciting! But as I didn't really hold much in the way of expectation, as long as he wasn't a disgrace, then I was sure I could manage for the evening. And anyway, Suzy was going along too, so we were sure to have some fun!

The evening of the Grand Opening, Suzy and I get called for by our two escorts. My God! Tall, dark *and* handsome! On the button! And he was very appreciative of me too. His name was David, and we had a great time that night. No funny buggers, just a great time. An *extremely* attractive man, he was quite interested in me and was much more than just looks. There was quite a bit of depth.

Amazing what you can manifest when you are clear and when you are ready! Even if only for a few hours, I felt like I was in another world, and starring in my own movie...

David and I saw each other quite a bit for a several months after that Grand Opening. I learned that he had been involved with a famous celebrity, actually a national and world famous model, for quite a few years just prior to meeting me. Recently splitting up with her, he too, was sorting himself out. We were very good for each other, and went cycling and on dinner dates together, but even though we shared a bed, neither of us was yet ready to go into anything deeper at that time.

I also realized that Jim's previous jokes about 'Its not how big it is but what you do with it', was a short-sell (pardon the pun), and of how much enjoyment and satisfaction I had missed for all those years, and without complaint! Was his degree of inadequacy commensurate with his degree of suspicion? He wasn't only small in stature, that was for sure!

In a short time David and I were having deep and meaningful conversations. He was making a change in his own career path and was rethinking many things, as was I. One subject we discussed was what happened sexually when you came out of a long term relationship. Even though sex with Jim was not always the romantic or spiritual expression I would have wished it to be, it was a reasonably *regular* experience, and one which the lack of took some adjusting to. Having left home and Jim, I no longer felt held to my commitments of fidelity to him. I wasn't going back to him again, and saw no reason not to have sex with someone else. I had paid physically and emotionally for it over and over anyway, though this was not my reason to do so. Talking with David about just this issue, and even though we were sleeping together and enjoying each other's company, he shared with me how he had previously resolved this problem of lack of sex with an appropriate person prior to meeting me. He, like me, preferred quality and connection rather than just humping. When he had split up, he decided that he would solve the problem by being voluntarily celibate. He promised himself that he wouldn't have sex for the next six months, and instead, he would devote that energy toward his studies, creativity, meditation and the furtherance of his career. He would channel his sexuality in a way that served him.

And it had worked, for he was in the middle of a complete change of career direction; he had completed training and qualifications and was even starting up his own college on his new vocational subject. By being celibate, *he* would be in control of his sexuality, and *not* sex being in control of *him*. Being a Scorpio, there was no lack of sexuality about him, but I really admired him for this ability to work with sexual energy this way! When we stopped seeing each other, I too decided to be consciously celibate.

I found that so liberating, and no longer felt that I needed to find a partner or to be so desperate in finding 'The One' – who I hoped existed after the disaster called Jim! And when David and I kind of drifted apart, and if there was no one else on the horizon, I just extended my celibacy vow and explored more of who I was.

But I cannot tell you just how much good dating David did for my self-esteem and confidence. His calmness and depth gave me much comfort and he was a great sounding board. Over the years since then we have remained friends though nothing more. On paper most things could have worked out long term, but there just wasn't the full chemistry there.

But what a *great* time we had! Amongst the debris that was my life, this was an uplifting and positive experience.

Maybe there is some hope for me after all?

WHO AM I?

Meanwhile, I still have my family life to deal with. Actually, I still have my husband to deal with.

I persist in seeing my sons whenever possible and permissible, for my initial ideas of cooking for them a couple of times a week and seeing them on weekends had now being adjusted to whatever opportunities I could get when things were made relatively easy to see them. Though usually organized, I think it often stressed me out to the point I was sometimes getting there late. But even when I was late by only *one* minute, I would somehow miss out on them being home. Travel in Melbourne wasn't always easy at the best of times, and I would sometimes be a little late because of new road works, or some other new obstruction. As I mentioned, Jim could make it very difficult and would still punish me for being even a couple of minutes late and I would often arrive to find that the boys were out-somewhere-at-a-friend's-house even though we had arranged the visit. This continued to be a heartbreaking and painful affair.

Sometimes it felt like it was almost not worth the bother of driving all the way there from the other side of the city only to find that the boys had been sent round to a 'friends' house. Jim was not very co-operative for the good of the children with any of this, and I think this contributed to my eventual shut-down in some ways – my family was no more, I was denied having my children, and continually somehow at war with Jim – still.

Six or so months after moving out, I was still living at Suzy's place, and still working at TOW, and in fact I had been promoted from accounts to wages for the whole plant. Much more responsibility, and consequently I sometimes had to work back a bit to complete anything that hadn't been completed for the day.

Despite all of the upheaval and concerns, being away from Jim's continual interrogations was reviving me to some degree. I had lost the stress of being woken up and interrogated in the night and his continual accusations and even though I had exchanged it for another kind of stress, it still felt better for me than when I had been living with him. I was expanding my horizons and doing some real searching for answers to my life.

I was searching for who I was now, trying to discover the 'me' that had got lost somewhere along the way. I was straddling two different ways of being – still a part-time mum, still working, and holding down another part-time job at this stage, and then there was this other side that I was having to learn about and understand. I knew who I was as 'Marni as wife', 'Marni as mum', 'Marni as sister', 'Marni as daughter', 'Marni as Christian' and 'Marni as worker' – but I didn't know who 'Marni as a person' really was.

Even at this time, I wasn't yet fully cognizant of just how much I had missed out on by getting married so early. For most of my life

Naïve Hope

I considered that my motives had been pretty unselfish, and unfortunately my thoughts had just habitually been so 'other-centred' that working out who *I* was and what *my* thoughts and even opinions were exactly, I was now in the process of uncovering. I guess my thoughts had often been very idealistic and so often overshadowed by 'a Higher Cause' that thinking of *self* had always been seen as purely 'selfish'. I now know that people have different thinking parameters and central motivations. To me *now*, there *are* times when it is important and appropriate to think of one's self first. And there are times when it is appropriate to think of another first. Being selfish and being selfless are part of the interplay of life, both necessary and part of a healthy image of Self providing one knows when to be on either side of this central theme of managing the self. But I hadn't gotten there just yet.

Even though my parents had never really been there for me, we still had a reasonable relationship. And I was still the respectful daughter. They weren't deliberately obstructive, they weren't deliberately ignorant, they were just mainly unaware and still pretty involved with their own stuff. Running a lot of their own early conditioning and programs, religion had tempered it to *some* degree, but they were not really as self-aware as they thought they were. Neither was I at that stage when it comes to it! I loved them after all. They were my parents, and they were Christians. I could see no conscious reason not to love them. Without realizing it, I was in quite some denial. All of my hurts and pains and angers at their betrayals and behaviours had been locked down or buried away or excused, and I wasn't as yet equipped in any way to deal with or to change the conditioning and programming that I had received in my childhood. So mostly we had good relationships, and I was always respectful. Leaving Jim, or rather being forced out of my home, was a huge event, and as they hadn't been that helpful earlier ('You've made your bed now lie in it') I not only wasn't quite ready to let them know, I also didn't quite know *how* to let them know.

Over the years my parents and I had kept in touch by letter and also had phoned each other and talked occasionally. Dad would only ever write to me in verse, though he called it poetry. This was supposedly because an early ancestor of his had had a reputation for it, and though dad did have a way with words, after I moved to Australia and he started to mature and grow, he took to writing to me as a bard. Bless him. I wish he had been like that when I lived with him and mum. In his last years he was to confide that being a father was the hardest thing he ever had to do – not surprising really as he had really sucked at it. And this coming from an ex-Commando and Commando trainer! Though he never went as far as to actually apologise...

Jim and I and the boys had visited England at roughly five-yearly intervals. We didn't really have holidays; we saved our holiday time and scrimped our money and revisited the UK to keep in touch with everyone. And so it was natural that Mum had phoned me from England a few times in that first six months as she hadn't heard from me for a while. I could not yet face her on it. So Jim had taken yet another message from her for me to call her. And at my next visit to the boys, he now states to me quite bluntly that he will not take any more calls from her. What? I think that what he means is that he felt uncomfortable about it and he didn't want to be the one to say anything, which I can understand, so it was up to me to phone and to tell mum. So there it was. I now had to face them and to let mum and dad know that we were separated.

It actually took me six months after moving out to screw up enough courage to call her back. So *why* had I avoided it? Well, mainly because they were Christians. And despite the platitudes and declarations otherwise, there was and is so much condemnation in the churches about 'failed marriages' and divorce. Well, in truth, that was part of it. And I had already experienced the prejudice from other church members. I also didn't want to be preached at. Especially in view of what had happened. I felt ashamed that I had been through what I had been through. Yes, I know that it wasn't my fault. But mud does stick. And this man had been throwing it round by the bucketful.

Another reason, and the more important reason I later realized, was that I hadn't told her because I thought she would stop 'loving' me. Yup. The religious codes were so strong that I thought it would impact on her love for me. How strange is that? Yet this was a very real fear. And all part of being a daughter I imagine. And so I had put it off until it was unavoidable and until I had

Naïve Hope

gotten a handle on what all of this huge drama had meant in a spiritual way to me and my 'lost' faith. For I no longer knew at this point *what* I really believed anymore and I wouldn't be able to answer her on this topic when it came up. And her earlier words still kept haunting me.

Eventually, I haltingly phoned her; taking some deep breaths and after the initial familiarities, I told her that I was no longer living at home. There was silence on the other end.

'I have had to move out.' A sigh from mum on the other end.

'About six months ago, mum.'

'Oh, Marni, I am sorry to hear that.' A pause.

'Is there any chance of you getting back together again?' she tentatively asked.

'No mum. No way.' I am so definite that I let it hang in the air.

Another longer pause. Then her question 'Why didn't you tell me sooner?' Yes, why didn't I? As I asked myself this that's when it hit me, and I hadn't seen it till just that moment – and so I blurted it out 'Because I thought you might not approve. That you would stop loving me, mum'.

Now that impromptu revelation was a surprise to me and yet was the truth of it. I had finally found the words for my fears...

And I heard her voice saying 'Oh, Marni, I will always love you. That won't stop me. I'm your mother.' And as she spoke those words, I burst into tears. And I knew that no matter the wrong counsel I had been given, the constant preaching, the judgments, the lousy childhood, the mistakes, etc, that in her own way she truly did try to love me.

Then mum was curious. 'Why did you think that I wouldn't love you, Marni?' So I had to answer her honestly and explained it was because of the church beliefs on marriage and divorce. But she assured me that that wouldn't make any difference. Though she did ask again if there was *any* possible chance that I would get back together with him. 'No way mum. Not after what has happened. I don't love him anymore and couldn't ever love him again.'

So I told her some of the basic stuff, how things hadn't been working out, how I couldn't have the boys and kept it upbeat. I was too ashamed to go in depth or to tell her everything. I explained that I had tried everything I knew before I had eventually split from Jim, and mum understood. And I dare say that she might have guessed to what extent I must have been pushed to no longer be living at home with him.

We re-established contact again after that, and I continued my visits back home, always receiving a warm welcome from her and dad. There was certainly love between us, even though so many of my needs had gone unmet in childhood, and I came to realize that she had done the best she could. And when she died in 2011, there were no regrets in my heart, for I had made my peace with her, and had eventually come to that place within where I could let her 'off the hook' as it were – the hook of past unmet needs, the holding on for something that it was far too late to get from her, the hook from my little inner child within who didn't get the understanding from her that it had needed; for I was now old enough to do that for myself.

For some reason, fear Jim as I may, I had not got to the point of hating Jim. Not then and not for a while. I think that underneath I was angry with him, but I was also just too busy dealing with the hang-over of my fears, still living in my own survival mode. My main concern had been to keep us all alive, so to speak. Then to escape being the cause of triggering his anger and to prevent consciously pushing him to this edge that he continually seemed to be courting. As I said, love is an action, not just a feeling, and I had created deep habit tracks in working through marital love in a Christian setting – I was not yet really capable of gathering myself to full out rebellion-regardless-of-the-cost. My family was just too important. As was my own health and life.

Sinking Ship

Dealing with my wounds and navigating the waves on which I now found myself was all consuming for me at this point. No older voice of wisdom to guide me, I was simply learning as I went. Well, more like being forced to learn, really. At sea with life and my own

Naïve Hope

direction, attempting to locate my Polar North with a battered compass, I was both elated that I was no longer under Jim's thumb, but also terrified because he still held onto the seed of my body and what had been my real meaning to life and marriage – my sons.

Things took yet another turn over time – just as I had been pushed out of the family home, Jim now advanced to doing the same thing to the eldest born son, Joseph. This time, a drunken hissy-fit and Joseph is ejected. Or rather, escapes. This was the first of the boys to experience what I had. Not surprisingly, and over time, Jim actually gained the proud distinction of ejecting each and every one of the boys out of his castle. What a clever dad! And a clear declaration of his supposed love for them! Unsurprisingly, each occasion was when he was in a drunken state.

Jo cleared out of the marital home about six months after his dad had ejected me. He was kicked out the night that Jim couldn't 'bear to see his face again'.

I still don't know the full story to this, all I remember is that Jo turned up on my door and I was just so glad that he had come to me. Yes, his dad was drunk again and had flung him out, and he was glad to leave. I was cramped in a one bedroom flat, but fortunately, within a short period of time, Joseph had shared accommodation with one of his work-mates. We got to see each other in a more relaxed state than before, though we have never really spoken about what scars may have been sustained with all that had happened. More recently, over these last few years, we have been able to talk about some of the things. I had recognised that Jim had sometimes displayed a real problem with Joseph, a real sense of rivalry and a clearly demonstrated desire to put him down and belittle him. Whatever this was about wasn't clear at the time, and I have only guessed it over the years.

But this eviction fact was a relief for me on Jo's behalf. Not that I would have wished it to happen that way, but because he was now *out of there*, complete with life and limb so-to-speak. He was so hurt, so demoralised, so emotionally exhausted that he could only say over and over how much he *hated* his dad and that he never wanted to see him ever again. I didn't force him to at that time, and gave him space to sort it for himself.

However, the toxic poison of having lived with this man was not resolved overnight for him, nor indeed for any of us. Many things have been hidden from me and even today I am still not party to it all. There again, my own journey with my abusive and violent dad is mostly unknown to my siblings, and was quickly forgotten by my mum when Christianity came to stay. I did not know at this time how to help my sons except to be available for them as best I could.

I was still dealing with my own scars. It was up to me to sort through the abuse I had experienced and to find a way through. Part of this was to match what my mind knows about not deserving this kind of treatment with how my heart felt about what had happened to me; and to also realise and recognise the body memories that got imprinted at a nervous system level. But that was to take time. As a mother, I felt for my children and did so for many years. They hurt; I hurt. As I mother I wanted to protect them. And if I hadn't been able to protect them, then I wanted to deal with the perpetrator and give him what he deserved! But right now what price would there be – it would only stir up everything again. Until such time as they want redress, and it is safe to do so, we get on with life.

Kerry

I had now been working at TOW for over four years, and during that time, employees swapped positions with each other, taking up similar or more advanced posts in another branch or in another country.

For the last two years one of the guys doing research and development in the Altona plant had been working for the company in the United States. Kerry was a chemist. In the early days of my employment at TOW, Kerry had shown some interest in me by making enquiries about me to some of my co-workers. A couple of the girls at work had tried to get me to join them at the pub lunches, as it turned out that he had asked them to get me there since he was quite taken with me. But I didn't know he even existed at the time. I had very little to do with him, and he just wasn't on my radar. I was too busy being the faithful wife and dutiful mother. So when they eventually shared with me that

Naïve Hope

'Kerry wants to get to know you' I was even more determined not to attend. Somewhat embarrassed by any unwanted attention by 'another man' I was not only scared of Jim getting sniff of this, I also didn't really know how to handle it myself at that stage. The overriding thought though, had been that I did not want to provide any opportunities for Jim's jubilations at my being or feeling compromised. Besides which, I had a reputation at work as the 'Ice Lady' to maintain. Then Kerry had been sent overseas and there was no further threat to my peace of mind. I had also started to create better working relationships. During the time Kerry was overseas I had been softening up on the previously imposed deprivations of avoiding social situations at work, and had joined in with others a bit more.

Now I was in a totally different situation. I was no longer just taking time out from Jim to work on the relationship for there really was nothing I could work with. The dynamics had changed totally since I first thought of creating this breather space between us. We were now well past the idea of a trial separation as Jim had made it quite clear that he didn't want to resolve anything or work anything out. He was just plain hell-bent on punishing me. I had no option but to consider myself as separated. And separated from Jim I now truly was. The relief for me personally was welcome and unexpected, but the ongoing pain regarding my children was still to be endured. Meanwhile, I feel quite different about men right now, fully convinced that my romantic ideal was quite possibly and quite likely out there still. With this in mind, I was set to not only explore myself but also to explore the world.

Within months of my moving out of 'home', Kerry had arrived back to the Altona division. Having shown active interest in me prior to his departure, this time around I allow myself to be intrigued by him. I heard that there was a birthday party being set up for him and though I still wasn't interested in him per se and I went along.

My real reason for attending was because of another new guy at TOW who would also be present at the party, actually the new boss of his department, newly arrived from the States. This darkly attractive man had somehow persuaded or rather challenged me to the odd game of lunch-time squash with him – a rewarding way to spend my half hour a month, hey? Though now my spare time had increased from half an hour a month as I was no longer running round at Jim's beck and call. And when this enticing guy had shown interest in me, I had responded in kind. He told me that Kerry's party was basically the department sharing lunch together at one of the local eating holes. I cheekily invited myself along so I could sit near the new man - why shouldn't I expand my horizons?

And when I had two men paying me attention, and paying me compliments and showing interest in me, I lapped it up. I had been starved of this most of my married life; fun, compliments and appreciation without any insults and interrogations. Besides which I apparently was ready for some flattery. That part of me that had been subdued was shining forth because I was no longer being continually put-down and repressed personally by Jim. I was running from this huge hole within that needed filling, but I also wanted to explore more.

When Kerry had first arrived back from the States, I had only done a couple of my part-time courses and wasn't fully involved with acting yet. But my self discoveries and new found confidence were radiating from me in all directions. I had a new glow about me, and it certainly wasn't the fanatical zeal from attending Church!

This was all running parallel with my part-time paid job in market research and my attending modeling assignments, and when the Denis-situation came up, which I will share with you shortly, it was reasonably early days with Kerry. With Kerry's return to Australia, his romantic interest was reignited and this man wooed me from the moment he set eyes on me again. And this time, I was vivacious, I was bright, I was free of beatings and continual repression, I was in good shape in my mid thirties and I felt attractive. I was beginning to have confidence with a capital C.

Within a couple of months, Kerry had no competition and we had seriously started seeing each other. He had started off by writing me notes in work, then jokes, then poems. He would send me flowers. I would find surprises at my desk. I took to visiting the Research and Technical Dept as often as I could and we would find any excuse to talk, linger, and flirt. Then he took me to the theatre, out to dinner, and parties without making any moves on me. Keeping it quiet from co-workers made it that bit more tantalizing.

Naïve Hope

One night after a party at his place, I was tuckered out after having fun and dancing and I was the last to leave. Or rather, I kind of fell asleep on one of the couches.

He had a huge company house. The party had been held in the huge lounge room which had plenty of big fluffy inviting couches. I had closed my eyes for a while as he saw the last guest out. Instead of him taking advantage of me, he came over to cover me with a blanket and let me sleep there whilst he took himself off the bed. But not before he had kissed me gently on the forehead. I remember I was still part awake, though tired, and very curious about what he would do next and so was pretending to be sleep at this stage – he passed my test with flying colours. No work in the morning and so he woke me up with a glass of fresh squeezed orange juice, fresh good coffee and some lovely breakfast eggs. Oh. My. God. Heaven! Then he got out his guitar and sang and played to me. I was enthralled.

We spent a weekend away in the snow where he showed me how to ski. He was very caring and made no approaches but just spent time getting to know me. He wasn't the handsome type I usually was interested in, but he was attractive and his quirky and quixotic side began to appeal to me. He had a sense of humour, and importantly to me at that time, he was very romantic.

When we did finally make love together, he was caring, gentle, romantic, absolutely gorgeous – and it was also funny – he made me laugh so much and we had such a good time that we ended up falling out of bed together and laughing uproariously! Yes, definitely hooked! This man was the perfect mixture!

We had to fight hard to keep this all quiet at work. We didn't want nosy people making fun as he was not supposed to mix work and pleasure. When he had a Sydney conference to attend, he insisted on me coming with him and staying at his hotel with him whilst using a false name to quieten work gossip. In the evenings we went to the theatre, saw 'Evita' and then dined out at a top restaurant. Back in Melbourne he met my boys and we all spent time at the beach together.

My heart was again captivated. Life was exciting! I was being wooed, courted, romanced, involved, loved... Hope for a better future began to raise its head and heart again...

Within a couple of months of our connecting, Kerry took me to New Zealand to meet his family and we had an amazing holiday together skiing on the South Island. On the plane back to Melbourne, he told me how important this trip had been to him, and that he needed a commitment of some sort from me. At the thought of committing something, anything, especially my heart, to another person, I felt my physical heart beating faster, almost in a panic. He was pressing me for an answer, and I had to give it some consideration.

Considering what I had been through in my marriage, I knew that I had the ability to commit, but was I really *ready*? I still felt scared around relationships, and his courting had been not only exciting but also easing and calming for me. My heart was still recovering, but his romance and generosity, sense of humour, intelligence and all the things I knew about him meant a totally different deal from my marriage. Even so, I still had to seriously think about this before I could answer him on it. After a couple of hours on the plane, I decided that this *was* worth committing to, and I gave him my answer. Our heartfelt kiss and embrace now assured me that I had turned a corner somehow. In New Zealand I had met his children and family, albeit under the guise of being a work colleague, but we had all hung out together, and it felt that we had somehow created a foundation that we could further build on.

Kerry had opened up a whole new world, new horizons. He was attentive, romantic, thoughtful, sexy, fun, intelligent, attractive, kind... I was in heaven. I had a place to go, I had a man who cared for me, and I no longer needed to be where Jim could get hold of me ever again. It felt like he had my back and would protect me.

I had not had this experience before. And this was unfamiliar territory...

Naïve Hope

Denis

The tide of energy behind the events that catapulted me from the family home in Werribee late January 1981 were not done with yet, for they are about to take yet another turn.

During that first day of singledom I get called into my boss's office one day. Denis, the current head of my department, is over from the United States, and he had been assigned to TOW Altona for the last couple of years. He was a bit older than me, and a well presented man, with an American accent. Denis was a solidly built man and fair hair and he wore fine-rimmed glasses. A smart and fair guy, he had given my skills and work performance good feedback and had encouraged me to take on the new promotion.

I kind of liked him as I respected him, though I had been in no way attracted to him, and saw him only as an interesting new boss. And he had been the perfect boss, despite what was about to be revealed in this meeting. At first I had no idea what he wanted to see me about. He was a bit tight-lipped, so I got a little concerned. I couldn't think of anywhere that I had fallen down on the job, though I must admit I had felt a bit challenged with some of my new duties.

I had thought I was managing the stringent schedules and extra study required, but...

I was absolutely shocked when he asked me what I had told my husband about him. Actually, I was speechless. Ijust gawked at Denis. I couldn't think why he was asking me this. I had to think about what I had said to Jim, but there was nothing apart from reporting who I worked with and answering all of Jim's questions about work. There was not much to tell him about Denis anyway. When I managed to find my words I asked 'Why, what's happened? I have told him you're my boss, naturally? What's going on?'

His response was 'Well, that's what I want to know – what's going on? Your husband has phoned me a couple of times about you working here, and today he phoned accusing me of having an affair with you!'

I went bright red with the blush of horror that my husband was now making false accusations against my boss. And me. He was interfering in my *working* life. He was causing as much trouble and nastiness as he could to get at me. Again. I felt invaded. It felt yucky and revolting. I felt like the wind had been knocked out of my sails. I felt eyes in the workplace, Jim's sneering and hate, and it felt awful. Is there any getting away from this guy and his horribleness?

But even worse, I now had to explain my personal situation to my boss. I had to tell him that I had moved out of home and to try to explain that this was the sort of behavior I had had from Jim for a while without giving him too many details. I felt ashamed enough as it was. Humiliated, and embarrassed, Jim's mind-filth was sticking like mud to everything he could access that was connected with me.

Denis seemed to understand, but he warned me that if Jim did it again he would have to take it further, and that might mean that Jim would be reported to the authorities and would lose the use of the home phone. Not a good idea for someone with children. He said he was sorry I was going through all of this and if there was anything he could do to assist, please let him know. I was a valued worker, and this was not the sort of behavior he was used to. Nor should I be. Call in to talk to him in his office anytime.

Thank you, Denis! He had genuinely taken it really well when you consider the audacity and rudeness of this bloody idiot man I was involved with – still! Jim could have been legally prosecuted. That evening I phoned Jim and told him what Denis would be forced to do if he did it again. But he had been drinking, and so was difficult to get through to. He didn't ring Denis again that I am aware of whilst I was still there. However...I couldn't take a chance on that.

Not long after this, I left TOW. Even though I didn't have another job to go to, I felt too uncomfortable to continue there, knowing that Jim could call at any time creating mayhem or further trouble for me. He had taken any joy and security out of it, just as he had planned it to. And who knew how and when he would strike again?

I needed a place to live and a new job. But finding work elsewhere right then seemed to be an elusive mission. My part-time work was not enough to manage on and I was running out of money; I had to reconsider my living arrangements. But when Kerry heard of what was going on with Jim phoning work, and that I was leaving TOW, he insisted that I come and live with him. I could *stay* with him. Actually *live* with him! He genuinely seemed to be head over heels with me. Soon afterwards I moved out of Suzy's house. I thought this was the solution to my problems, and that I was finding my path, and a genuine love to clear away all of the pain I had been through. Could things be as simple as that for me?

Despite all that was going on around me and the courses that I was doing, the extra part-time work and this new relationship, I remained in denial of the continuing effect of Jim on my life.

Interestingly enough I can see now that I was angry with Jim, but not yet willing to face it or face him with it. Just like in childhood where fear kept me in my place, my fear of the consequences kept me in check. He could still beat my brains in. Even more importantly, he still had my children, and I couldn't afford to rile him. Somehow, they were ransom to stop me from retaliating in some way. But being the basically honest person that I was, this honesty tricked me. For in order to manage my situation, I had to bury my anger along with his anger toward me. So that I could not honestly see it.

Instead I only acknowledged the other side of the coin – the side of pain and hurt. Alice Miller wrote an interesting book which I read many years later. It was called *'The Drama of The Gifted Child'*, and is basically about *all* children and how they live in glass houses when it comes to emotions. What they feel is what you see – a child cannot suppress its emotions or hide the expression on its face, it doesn't yet know how to. Eventually over time they learn something different about their emotions, though. They learn this through the reactions and actions of their parents. If a parent sees emotions that the parent him or herself cannot handle or they find scary, unacceptable or unmanageable, that parent may remove their love, approval or protection from that child. A child may even bury their own emotions out of sight and out of grasp so that even the child itself doesn't know where they are rather than be abandoned like this. In this way, the child can avoid expressing these unacceptable feelings and emotions, and so learn to adapt his behaviour.

A parent's disapproval can have devastating effects on the sensitivities of a child, and that child wants more than *anything* to have the love and approval of that parent. Naturally so. They are thoroughly helpless without it, for this is the basis of their food, shelter, nurturing and care until they are grown and developed enough to do these things for themselves. This is all simply part of their survival mechanism. So disowned and buried emotions and fears and angers do not just disappear, they do not just go away. For they still exist in some form, and they *must* come up at some stage and at some time from where they have been buried or from where they are rattling around in order to be addressed. If they are not dealt with they can lead to illness, if not just dysfunction of some kind. The body and the mind and emotions are all linked. Emotions are simply energy in motion, and when unexpressed correctly they can become blocked or locked emotions.

Mine were still being held in check.

OUT AGAIN

Life in Brighton was like the sunshine after living in the dark. I had the run of a large comfortable and well-furnished company house, a garden and outdoor entertainment area; food was provided, things looked good. Lots of romance. Poetry, roses, shared interests. Great as this seemed though, it wasn't *all* roses. I was beginning to get restless - the thrust for me to find another good job was on me again. I had to get work. I had expenses, didn't I? Kerry wasn't responsible for these, *I* was. It was up to me to keep up my end of the boys upkeep with the mortgage, and to do so I needed a job.

The modeling course had been significant to me in that it assured me that women could be attractive on both the inside and the outside. I must also now agree, though, with the advent of Supermodels, that it is obvious this is not necessarily so for all models, nor for all women. So when I took up the modeling it was with one of the top agencies in Melbourne and I had started to get small assignments. One day Elly herself had a proposition for me, seeing as I was one of her more mature models, and gave me a contact to follow up. She didn't know enough about it and wanted someone she could trust and who was smart enough to check it out before she passed it on to any other of her younger student models. It all seemed above board at the time. However close inspection revealed that there was a side that I hadn't seen, a darker side that could eventuate and I discovered this before any harm was done

However, Kerry being a man of the world had already recognized the possible dangers with this particular opportunity and tried to warn me not to pursue it. In fact, he *told* me not to follow through on it. I went ahead in pursuing it to check out its validity despite this. And there were many reasons why. Not least of all there being hidden in the recesses of my mind the thought that I was done with being dictated to by men. But there were other far more obvious and weighty reasons. The project paid extremely well, and if viable, could provide me with the means to solve my financial dilemma and clear my debts more quickly.

I also had never really had a man take care of me properly before, and except time of work for pregnancies, financially I had always been accountable. So I didn't know how to *allow* Kerry to take care of me, I was so programmed to be otherwise, to be the one that others depended upon. Another part of this was that I also did not want to be seen as a 'kept woman', to appear as someone living with a man for support – which to me still amounted to services for money. I simply was not used to *not* having to pull my own weight all the time, and found it difficult to adjust. Anyway, what if this man got fed up with 'looking after me'? But underneath all of this, which took me many years to work out, was an old buried belief that *I didn't deserve it*. Even Jim had labeled me as this. This was detrimental to me accepting love from a man, particularly so soon after all of the abuse that Jim had handed out. Even though I believed that I was safe with this man, the wounds from my marriage had gone deep.

Things had been going really well between us before this. It only took me a couple of days to see the danger in the project. And as soon as I did, I told Kerry he was right. And that I wasn't pursuing it anymore and I conveyed my findings to Elly. But by the time I realized that I had made a faulty decision in going against Kerry's advice and in checking this opportunity out, it was too late. In less than a week, Kerry was telling me that I had to move out from his place. I was stunned. Why? Hadn't he been talking about a long term relationship just a few short weeks ago? I realized things had seriously changed, and I hadn't even seen it coming. I began to think that I had done something dreadful, simply by going against what he had said – well, that was pretty much the story of my life to this point, wasn't it?

But then the things he *hadn't* told me started to unfold; there was something he hadn't told me...

Whilst Kerry had been in the United States it now turns out that he had encouraged a female co-worker over from the states, and she was due over in the next couple of weeks to join him. Apparently they had continued corresponding after he left the U.S., though he had never mentioned her name to me. Now he is telling me that she is coming over and that he cannot (read that as will not) discourage her! What is later eventually revealed is his relationship with Sherry whilst over there. But at this time he only tells me that he felt responsible for encouraging her to take him up on his suggestion and offer of accommodation. Oh, sorry, SHE was taking him up on his offer. But he had *said* 'they'. Mmm! She was only young – read that as ten years younger than him, and me - and he said that he had promised to help her if she ever came over to Australia. And I couldn't do it (help and assist her) *with* him, he had to do it all by himself, you see, because it was his, not *our*, responsibility. You do see that, don't you? Grrr!

No! Of course, this I *didn't* get. We had been a couple, and had been living together for several months, had an understanding and now he was saying that he *alone* had to sort out this friend. These, then were my marching orders.

I had become addicted to the romance he promised. The separation from him tore at me. He had wooed me when I was at my most vulnerable, he had opened doors that I had thought were shut to me forever, he had forced me to make a serious decision about our relationship early on which meant a real commitment by me, and I had done so. And now this...

I was raw from my marriage, hurting at my loss of employment, confused and in pain at Kerry's revelations, in deep grief with my children, and now in survival mode for money to keep a roof over my own head.

Naïve Hope

Of course, when one feels betrayed, rejected and unwanted, one cannot necessarily see clearly. Besides there was so much confusion going on in my life that it took me a while to see he had had this 'get-out-of-jail' card in his back pocket all along. He hadn't told me about it, about her, and as long as I was who he wanted me to be, then everything was okay. He had two previous divorces, and I now think that he had been grooming her (like he had been grooming me) but then his two years in the States were up. Obviously they had remained in contact, and she had probably somehow gotten whiff of me, and had decided to 'follow her man' so as not to lose him. Smart advice. He chose the younger more malleable model with less mileage, and he had kept his choices instead of keeping his commitment!

To encapsulate what happened next it was this. A mad dash to find an affordable place. She was due over within a few days. I moved out. She moved in. Within a couple of months they had both moved over to New Zealand with his work at TOW, and shortly after that they got married. Fresh blood works wonders for some men.

Would I have made different choices if I had known about her sooner? Would I have lived with him if I had known about her? Would I have been able to adjust to a man paying all the bills? Knowing what I know now, that is an interesting question to muse. And I am not too sure of what my answers would be... But lets face it, I had fallen for a 'flake' without realizing it... This ''love' business stinks, hey?

I had to find accommodation quick and so I moved into a share situation with a woman who had advertised for a flat mate to help cover the rent. It was an apparently nice property at Rowena Parade in Richmond, within walking distance of the parks and River Yarra. At least I would be a bit closer to the city, so less travel to see the boys in Werribee. But talk about the bad-luck fairy following me around; things are still not settled. Within a week of me moving in, another bomb is dropped; this share-mate was moving out, in just two weeks time, and I could *'keep the place on and continue to pay the rent by yourself, or you can sublet'*. What? Did I hear right? I just got here and you're leaving? I hadn't had a chance to find work yet and you think I can pay *double* rent?

I could *not* afford this place on my own. Broke, and broken. Again. Aaaaagh!

I managed to bluff my way into some bar work which I had never done before (the acting classes paid off) and then quickly learned how to do cocktail waitressing part-time whilst I found a proper job - this satisfied a small part of my situation. And kept part of my mind off my immediate personal problems.

I also somehow managed to find a cheap one bedroom flat where Abbotsford met Richmond, now known as 'Little Vietnam'. Within a short space of time I was fortunate enough to land a good job at a small boutique advertising agency in Richmond, handling production accounts and media reconciliations. In fact this position with DPB turned out to be one of my favourite jobs. It was different to anything I had done before and I had a bit of a learning curve as I worked alongside the other accounts girl.

Whilst I was working at DPB, my boss, Alan, was very happy with the day work I did. The time came when Barry Michael had another TV part for me and the pay was too good to turn down. Could I do this as well as my normal job? I spoke to Alan about my acting assignment as I knew that I would need the odd afternoon off to do so. We came to an arrangement easily. As it was a salaried role, Alan was both flexible and very understanding and our agreement was that as long as I got my job done and *on time*, then I could mix my hours. It was not unheard of for me to work back late till nine or ten o'clock or to turn up to work on some Sundays to ensure that Production and Media charges were correct and completed. What else was I going to do with my spare time when Jim had the children, and I had no partner to occupy me? I gained a good friend for quite a while in the person of Debra Henty until we lost track of each other. Debbie had a great sense of humour, was easy to get on with, and I felt like things might not be at rock bottom after all. She taught me a lot initially about how Production and Media differed from normal bookkeeping and accounting principles, and through her I learned to enhance my previous accounts reconciliations experience to the more difficult

Naïve Hope

and fraught detailed television and radio media accounts reconciliations.

I continued with my TV and acting and scored a part in an amateur theatre company that was happily entertaining Footscray and the inner North of Melbourne as Osa Johnston in *Chamber Music*. Loved it and got rave acclaims. Later I auditioned with another Theatre Group and played Toby Landau in Neil Simon's *The Gingerbread Lady*. Fantastic! Again, rave reviews, fun and pleasure! I did a tad more amateur theatre. I was now using both sides of my brain and gaining in confidence and satisfaction to some degree.

It was interesting that I could become, almost, another person and put aside my own personal life for a public endeavour. A bit like how it was being a Christian; when you are not entirely thrilled by 'suffering' as a Christian, so you believe and 'trust in God', push aside and don't let others see your doubt, just hold onto the image, promise and idea of God being the solution to all your problems. You are after all doing this for the Cause! Hah! Yet, when at home, my emotions, mostly trepidation or fear, were just too transparent. If I unconsciously reacted and felt angry, it would show, and incur the 'master's' displeasure and disapproval, so I had learned to push it down, cover it up. Was this what had triggered Jim's insistences that I was 'hiding something' from him? Possibly. For I had had absolutely no idea who I was back then, and was always so involved in the process of emotions or defending myself or some other form of distraction or drama. Now that a lot of the continual crisis was over with at home, it was easier to be more of an observer. Not that I had come anywhere near perfecting it, I was just a beginner, but this all somehow gave me some kind of inner space to relax my *re-actions* and to pay better attention.

The acting was both a challenge and a pleasure, and I was also enjoying the structured accounting side of agency life along with seeing the results of the creative and expressive functions of branding, launching and advertising. It was a small but highly creative agency, winning awards in a short time.

But there was another aspect of me that was co-existing with this apparently satisfying part of my life. I could fool myself some of the time, but I couldn't fool myself all of the time. The cracks in my protective persona showed itself when I was on my own. This process of life, of healing, of restoring would take some time to full recovery. Career-wise, I was busy and occupied. This new position with this fascinating creative company helped to occupy and support me while I licked my wounds over my life and the TOW man. I had made a genuine heart commitment to him, and when I do, I do. If I had been smart enough to recognize where I was at, emotionally and psychologically, maybe I wouldn't have made such a commitment, and my heart would still belong to me and in my own hands. Emotionally, I was devastated.

The River Yarra became my haunt and refuge; it was the hider of my tears. Walks along the banks of this major river in Melbourne, right next to the huge Botanic Gardens helped me in some small part. On Sunday mornings, before others filled the picnic and barbeque areas, I would wander and think. And cry. As I walked I fought with demons to stay alive for my kids. Sunglasses veiled most of my tears, and I was always equipped with tissues. Birds, trees, swans, flowers – and when I could handle the sunlight, that too, helped to get me through this phase of my life. I felt isolated, totally alone and misunderstood, emotionally distraught, betrayed, heartbroken, abandoned and powerless. It took five years before I could walk by that river without bursting into tears. So with the changes in my belief systems, and this fresh wound on top of the raw pain of my marriage and children, I had good reason to seek the solace of this area. I watched seasons change, and gradually came to terms with where I thought I was at. Of course, when one has never been in a certain situation before, one simply does the best one can. It is sometimes not until later that we can see more clearly the greater picture and landscape of the journey.

With hind sight, I later realized that there was a strong possibility that because of the long eighteen year marriage I had just exited, I was just not emotionally really ready for such a deep commitment to Kerry, in fact for *any* commitment.

And yet I had done so. Duh!

On the other hand, this just may have been why I chose this mercurial and flippant man. I had given as much as I could in my marriage, and I was so fragile still, and still working out who I was and in truth I really wasn't ready to handle such another serious commitment so soon. I had been living such a very blinkered life for so long, living the life of a Christian wife whose limited horizons included church, family and self-sacrifice that I was probably really quite overwhelmed with what I had to learn about relating to the rest of the world. And to myself.

Maybe I had known that this was too good to be true?

Maybe the illusion of romance was an experience I needed to have? Maybe this was just some sort of recovery phase and a distraction on the way?

Maybe I was a magnet for charmers…?

Or just maybe I was still tainted by nasty energy of that arsehole of a husband and just couldn't reach the good men yet…

I had another yet another emotional experience whilst I was licking my wounds in **Richmond**. I took the self protective step of having a HIV test, as the possibility of Aids had suddenly become a huge scare. Not that I was promiscuous, but I had had a couple of boyfriends, since Jim and I was no longer in a 'safe' married and therefore monogamous relationship. I also wanted to be sure that not only was I 'clear' but also that I was not a 'carrier' of any sort. And as I later came to believe that Jim had not been as faithful to me as he had demanded I was to him, this was a smart move. At the same time I also had a pap smear. Anyway, the HIV test came back as clear. Sweet relief!

But the pap smear test had picked up an abnormality in the cervix area. A Dysplasia. They wanted me to go in for a biopsy test in case it was cancer. Cancer! The 'C' word!

My world suddenly fell apart – again - I felt like the earth had opened beneath my feet. I didn't feel like I had anyone I could tell about this, I didn't feel that there was anyone to support or comfort me, and it felt absolutely horrible. I was again faced with the possibility of death, and my life was pulled back into some other sort of alignment. Facing the operating room for damage removal and further biopsy tests on my own, it was a tense week or so until I got the results. But I lived and died several deaths during that time. The overwhelming sense of relief was like a breath of fresh air to me. I now turned my attention back to resolving my situation.

Was it resolvable? Hmm...

SPIRITUAL PATH

My Blind Faith had been cracked, my Naïve Hope exposed. Though the process of re-examination and re-building was to continue for many, many years.

The trials of my life forced me to face issues not everyone has to face. I got to be challenged in my most sincerest of beliefs. And with all that had happened, I realized that I could not continue on in the same way anymore. And I am therefore now impelled to examine even more my ways, my thoughts, my values; in fact *all* my beliefs. And in examining one aspect of life, I came up with questions on other areas of my life. One cannot rip up one area of flooring without it affecting another part. To do a good job, you have to do it all...

So did I live a lie when I was a Christian? I knew that I hadn't, but it just didn't fit in the same way anymore. I needed new answers.

For this is now a time in my life whereby all of my previous spiritual experiences had been insufficiently explained. For the mould that once fitted has been thrown away. Just what did these experiences mean *now*, what did they stand for? What sort of a Christian was I now? Was I still a Christian? What *is* a Christian?

As a Born-Again, a Pentecostal, I had had some interesting experiences, one would call them spiritual. One of the main differences of belief of the church or 'faith' I was converted 'under' was the reference to the day of Pentecost. That's why they called themselves Pentecostal Christians. Similar attitude really as the Charismatics and Revivalists in that though they each claim a slight difference, by focusing on one aspect or another of Bible 'doctrine' – which basically means that *they* alone (that is each individual sect) have the *right* doctrine – they get to claim that all the others have simply missed the point, missed the mark, are *wrong*. Ridiculous really. But at the time, it seemed like we had the 'truth' whilst others just didn't quite get it. A kind of spiritual superiority really. I call it spiritual snobbery. Separatism, Being Special, Snobs. Though of course, they would claim the opposite in order to be seen as humble. Humbug!

Anyhow, when I got converted, as a Pentecostal it was required that you had full body immersion in a baptism to prove your faith and commitment – to Jesus. Along with this was the 'laying on of hands' and the 'receiving of the Holy Ghost'. I am not going to go into doctrines here – I have studied the Bible and my concordance a lot over the years, as well as other faiths and religions, other philosophies and theosophies, ancient scriptures and old scrolls. I now know hood-winking when I hear it. I now recognize tradition and enslavement when I hear it. And whatever one chose to believe is just that – what they *choose* to believe. From a smorgasbord of different labels and interpretations. I will not take to people door-knocking to 'save my soul' in order to earn a ticket to heaven – I do not go to their house and insist they believe in what I believe in – and I tell these people that the Bible in fact instructs that *they* 'are saved by grace, and that not of yourselves, it is the gift of God, not or works, lest any man should boast' and also to *go home* and 'work out your *own* salvation with fear and trembling', all Biblical quotes – and they leave me alone.

But I digress; for this is the real crux of the matter. I was taught to have *faith*. Actually I was taught to have *blind* faith, along with a lot of patience, and that if God thought it right He would help me like he promised. So I followed all of the rules. Obeyed all of the commands. Was obedient to the end. And God had also promised that he would take care of His flock. That if we called unto Him He would answer. Blind faith is workable and not a con, if what you were promised eventuates. I have faith that when I sit in this chair, that it will support my weight. The manufacturer has promised it. My eyes can see that it is reasonably sound. Then my body acts upon this faith and sits upon it, and it holds my weight. So my faith has been rewarded. I had total faith in God, that He would honour His promise. I had full and blind faith in Him even though I had never seen Him rescue me, I thought I knew that He would come and do so if I really needed it. And I had needed it, but so far I was still waiting for Faith to be honoured...

I had been *told* to have faith in Him and His Word, according to the Bible. How had *I known* this was true? Because I had been *told* it was. How could I test this for *myself*? No, you *can't* do that, you *must trust* that it is all true. What if I *don't* trust that this is so? Well, then there is *no hope* for you, you are *hell-bound* and *you* have crucified the Son of God yourself. To trust you must accept the Bible as God's Word. No proof. Just blind trust, blind faith. Or you are really *really* bad!

Apply this to anything else in life and you would be accused of being deluded, stupid, irresponsible, mad or possibly even possessed. Talk about snake-oil purveyors clothed in the garments of righteousness and authority. For faith is supposed to be eventually rewarded with the fruition of whatever one has put their faith and trust in. Right? Otherwise faith is simply stupidity!

Well, I needed to prove *right now* that the Bible is not just empty words. I have trusted as I was instructed, as I was supposed to do. Now is the time for my faith to be rewarded. Surely? I have suffered enough, we all have. And I am really hanging out in faith for His help.

Yet it all seems to be a one-way street.

For *now* when *I* needed God, or the Lord Jesus, He did *not* help me. Not in any way I needed help nor could recognize as help. And I *finally* got that I *wasn't going* to get an answer to my dilemma, I was going to get any help – so in a way, I got it, I got my answer. Some say that God only helps those who help themselves. Well I finally got that I had to help myself, and that is eventually what I did. I needed to do something as God wasn't going to. His promises didn't seem to hold for me. All my faith in Him had gone unanswered. And I will spend no more time on this side of things. Or on individual beliefs and interpretations, as these require too many explanations and would require terms that may well cover varying meanings, depending on how they are used – such as what the reader associated with those terms, words or phrases and what they actually eventually mean to each person.

What I am getting at here is that I could not deny that I *actually did* experience the baptism in the Holy Spirit, and actually had experienced an amazing spiritual event. I had demonstrated this often enough during the church services. I had also belonged to a church that believed in Divine Healing, and saw some genuine healings, and some not so genuine, and some non-healings too. But I could also not deny what had happened to me, and what was still happening. And because of that I had to rethink *all* my spiritual experiences, and all that I had known and been taught up to that point in my life and experience.

I hadn't wanted this marriage to end, I had meant every word of my vows and promises. But end it already had.

Because it had, I had to examine all that I had known, all that I had believed, all that I had been taught, all that I had experienced. I had to make a new sense, a new understanding of my existence.

And so when I had to leave my 'Blessed by God' marriage, I no longer had the heart or the belief in the same God that I had once had. In fact I had a hard time with the kind of God who could allow this sort of thing to happen at the hands of a supposed 'son' or 'man' of God. The Bible claims that our 'Heavenly Father' is a loving and merciful God. And that He is our Father. Father! Imagine... So I imagined how my father treated me, and made it bigger and more powerful – nope doesn't fit for me. So let's see if I get a better picture if I let God stand on His *own* merits as a Father.

Mmmm...Let me see now. He is supposed to be a Loving Father... Well, my God had not been very loving with allowing my husband and dad to do what they did... Nor had he been merciful in helping me... So Him being a supposed Loving Father now meant nothing to me.

My father had not been the loving and kind father that our Heavenly Father was said to be. And my husband had *not* been a caring and kind man. And when I needed spiritual outside help from this same God who I once thought was so close, He had totally ignored me. And had endangered not only me but my children too. So it was hard in view of this original model of my father and in how God had fulfilled his word, or actually how He hadn't, to see this as being the good thing it was claimed to be. So scrap that picture.

This was now too much of a stretch for an intelligent woman like myself. I had given it everything I had and this was the pay-back. Not such a great deal, was it? I think I had been short-changed somewhere... And I allowed myself to feel snarky and done-by over it all. I had hidden it for long enough, I had put up with it for long enough, I had good reason to be fed up with it all, to feel a bit cheated and let-down.

I realize that I am not the Christian I once thought I was. And with that came real fears that had been installed and instilled in me. I had dealt with standing up for myself by not going back to live with that tyrant of an ex-husband. I had thought things through and realized that the God I had counted on and trusted had not helped or stood by me.

Besides nursing a broken-heart from the end of my old-age dreams of a long and successful marriage I had suppressed grieving for my children so that I could cope. This had been quickly followed by my experience with Kerry, creating yet another raw wound.

Now we move onto other bits of the old religious equation... Here comes a further fear to deal with, the turning over of another stone that had kept me stuck and in a tomb called marriage...

It was to be almost another five years after eviction from Werribee before I came to terms with the following really deep piece of church dogma. For almost daily I would actually look out my window to see if people were still walking around in the street; I would check upwards to the sky; I would watch for signs of the biblical prophecy of the 'Coming of the Lord', just in case I had gotten left behind. It took me a while to realize that I had been trained, programmed, brainwashed if you will, into following the church, or the Bible, or that particular way of belief though this fear - fearing for my Soul not making it to 'Heaven'. Fear that I would not be worthy enough to be taken up in 'The Rapture'; the promised reward to all who follow The Lord. Oh, the threats of the End Time that is written about in the *Book of Revelations* in the Bible. I had been told that 'God was Love', yet had been fed a God of fear and intimidation, an angry God; and I had *experienced* a God that was not a God of love and compassion or one who fulfilled

Naïve Hope

His promises to help those who put their trust in Him. Oh boy, had I trusted. For over eighteen years I had trusted.

You see, one of the difficulties was that I could no longer believe in the same way. Just couldn't do it now – my eyes had been opened... But then how did I account for the feelings I had had when praying to this same God, to this same Lord Jesus? The same one who said 'Come unto me all ye who are weary and I shall give you rest'? 'Lay your burden upon the Lord', 'Cast your cares upon Him' 'Trust also in him and he shall bring it to pass'? I thought that I had truly felt that He would help, that He was there somewhere, I had even sometimes prayed and felt myself kind of float like I was meeting Him in Heaven – yet despite that all of this Christian Marriage crap had actually happened? And where was He now? What was going on? But I still couldn't deny those experiences. It finally came to me that the experiences were true, and that I was really a spiritual being inside. I had connected with my Spiritual Source. But that the beliefs were simply superfluous trimmings and not even part of my true experience.

My experience is just that: *my* experience – and all I can say here is where I am currently at this point in my journey.

I realized that I can no longer call myself a Christian in the sense that other Christians define that word, for I couldn't believe it all blindly anymore. I do not believe *anything* blindly anymore.

With that came an openness to discover my true spiritual essence, and not to be taken in by cults, churches, 'faiths', religions, groups, traditions, spiritual leaders, gurus, Masters or anyone claiming to have the answers to God. Even this God, this Yahweh God is not who we think He is. The Bible does not give the whole story here, and believe me I have spent many hours with my Bible Concordance studying the original words and meanings. Consequently I have withdrawn all commitment to this God, to this projection, to this definition of a God of love. And I continue to follow the laws of love, conscience, decency, consideration, self responsibility, accountability, true Divinity and spiritual evolution whenever and wherever possible.

Part of my spiritual development was further enhanced by studying astronomy and astrology, both western and the Indian Vedic systems. I discovered that they are a science indeed. But that is not all there is, and sometimes other laws supersede these and void them. 'Curiouser and Curiouser', as Alice said when she was down the Rabbit-hole in *Alice in Wonderland*. And still I search and seek. To this day. And grow and evolve.

One thing I will say here, and hold strongly too; when someone says that you must totally accept something by 'faith' then I counsel you to be very careful. Putting *blind faith* in something is like getting married to a total stranger. One can hope and believe and have faith that they are a good person... but how do you really know? What is the PROOF? Because someone else tells you? Examine their agenda, their pay-off for it. Their investment in it all. And if you don't, then you deserve everything you get.

'Faith' doesn't work for everyone. I have heard so many supposedly 'good' and highly recommended men of different faiths and religions, and yet so many of them have egos or agendas that are not aligned with purity and goodness and kindness, but rather with power, influence, pride, passive-aggressive anger, self-righteousness and control. And how many of them are huge 'sinners' themselves; and their excuse for failure in following their Christian laws and instructions are that they are sinners so they need God and Christ? Rubbish. The whole idea is to *change* for the better. '*Therefore go ye and* **sin no more**.' They need to stop handing over lack of self control and be real about what they commit to do. I have met few really good genuine men of what I call high spiritual calibre, but plenty of pseudo 'masters' – who claim to be of the 'Light' but they are really of the 'Twilight'. The Bible is real when it says 'By their fruit ye shall know them' and also advises what fruits to look for: goodness, kindness, etc. Cruelty, control, compliance is not from the real Godness, nor the Light. Nor is 'Better Than Thou'.

Being innocent is one thing. Even being naïve. Being hopeful is also another thing. But you had better be sure of what you put your hope in, and if it doesn't deliver, then it is hope wasted. Having naïve hope is both dangerous and irresponsible. In my books. And I should know; I got an 'A' plus in it!

Naïve Hope

What I eventually came to understand is not that I don't believe in God, for there is a God, but not the God of the Bible; the kind of Holy Father Christmas God floating in the Heavens that rewarded those that did the right thing and punished those that didn't. The 'God' I see now is neither male nor female but may include both, is bigger than all of us, *is* all of us and is also *individual* within us. Too hard to define here, it would be another book-full of words for me to fully convey, and there are books aplenty on this. And even then, I might not get it right for everyone. Just for now I know that my understanding on this is bigger than it was. This doesn't mean that what I think or believe is for everyone, but it does mean that it is not as restricted as it once was.

Please, whoever you are, *your* life is *your* path, your journey, and therefore *your* discovery on life and the true essence of the highest divine answers that you can find if you so choose to look. And I wish you well on your journey whatever your label or aspiration or calling.

Divorce

The questions 'What happens next?', and 'Have you heard from your solicitor yet?', were posed to Jim at various times after settlement. These were always met with vague responses and continued antagonism toward me.

There was *no* way in this world that I was going to *stay* 'married' to this man in any way!

I invited Jim to divorce me so that he could possibly feel a bit better over the situation, a kind of revenge by divorce thing. I had told him this 'You can divorce me, I will let you. Rather than me divorcing you.' I figured this opportunity would give him some sort of say or control over the situation, that he could *say* that he divorced me rather than me divorce him, that the injustice he felt might sit better with him if he took some action, and that he might feel that it had not been 'done' to him. It didn't bother me just who divorced who, as long as we were divorced! But he refused point blank. I later heard that it was because he didn't want to pay the hundred dollars for the divorce paper. He was loath to spend the money on me. Financially struggling as I was, I was *not* going to let that stand in my way. He had had chance enough and had changed nothing.

I was somewhat concerned about his managing the children for I truly cared about them. But Jim was playing the martyr, or more accurately, the victim. It was as though I had done everything to him, *I* had been the one to do the wrong thing. No thought to his own contributions yet. Within several months, he had lost a lot of weight, and it felt like he was blaming me for his state. The first year he lost so much weight his clothes were swimming on him. Gone was the swaggering guy with the swollen features of a once semi-attractive face, and the developing beer gut. He now looked gaunt, so much smaller, and I was wearing high heels, no longer pandering to his height issue and I was coming into my prime and towering over him instead. Despite his appearance and pallor, he was no less diminished in his vindictiveness. He was now more and more the little boy lost. I took no joy in this, but I was past caring any more for him or about him.

Eventually I learned that Jim, meanwhile, had stopped work, and was now a Stay-At-Home-Dad, claiming that he was no longer fit enough to work and blaming ill-health and stress through the breakup — more like through not addressing anything and being so full of anger and vindictiveness! As he never talked to me about this or told me anything that was going on in his life, I cannot say any more than what I was later told. Him *admit* to pining for me…? I think not. He complained that his health had suffered because *I had left* him, and deserted the children. Yet, even when he was reminded that *he* had kicked *me* out, he still didn't get it. Still no willingness to talk about how things came to be the way they did, still no seeking for solutions, just Cold War fuming and spiky intimations. Meanwhile and unbeknown to me, he was totally *turning the boys against me.*

The divorce however had to be done for there was no going back. He would have held on for as long as he could. But I couldn't. Not to this sorry marriage. And after waiting for about eight months, I realised that I had to go ahead and divorce him anyway for I felt that he would hold onto expectations of me coming back to him. So I went ahead with the divorce. It was inevitable now anyway.

Naïve Hope

I had been evicted from our Werribee home late January 1981. I applied for Divorce 18th August 1981, our wedding anniversary. I had survived over eighteen years of marriage and if we had stayed together, I would have been married that day for nineteen years. Decree Nisi came through on October 15th 1982, twenty years after the wedding.

On my next visit after I had received my Decree Nisi, Jim showed his 'mean' face again and now insisted that I give him back my engagement ring and my wedding ring. I was surprised by this, but he was adamant that because I had ended the marriage that he was entitled to them. I didn't quite get this, but I thought about it, particularly when it now seemed to be a big thing to him and he continued to ask me each time I came over to visit the children. Well, actually he now *demanded* it as his right.

Just before we had built in Werribee and when Jim had been in a good phase of mind, he had finally made good his promise to replace my second-hand pawn shop ring. It had only taken thirteen years to do so. We had bought another engagement ring for me, a little solitaire. It wasn't huge, but at least it was brand new and had not belonged to anyone else. I had been thrilled, and that had helped to keep me hanging in.

But now he wanted *all* the rings back. I didn't deserve them, he said. I had ended the marriage and so they belonged to him, he said. Yet this is the man who had *broken* our marriage, and was now trying to make *me* feel humiliated again, like I had done it all and created the whole thing by myself. He was so angry about these rings, and I can only guess at what they represented to him. For I had no idea on what logic he was operating. Maybe it was to try and punish me; humiliate me by taking back his rings...? Hah! Like that hurts... not!

But as I thought about whether to keep them or not, I realised that they no longer meant *anything* to me anymore anyway, and that I was more than happy to give him back the original rings, especially as it now seemed that in Jim's eyes, taking them back had somehow become some sort of retribution and punishment on me after my supposed bad behaviours in his eyes. So I gave him back his original second-hand engagement ring and the wedding ring.

He had killed their meaning for me. I no longer cared if he had them or not. I no longer cared what he did with them. I was no longer interested in keeping them. He could do whatever he wanted with them now, especially after this harassment. He could stick them somewhere dark and nasty if he liked, far away from me. They meant nothing to me now.

But I kept the newer one because. And after all, I deserved this ring, I had bloody earned this one. I had worked bloody hard in this relationship. No way could he have them all. This one was *mine*. He was not getting to me on this.

The fact that he had also traded up his car for a Datsun Bluebird, the next bigger Datsun up in the range, did not go unnoticed. If he was trying to say that his dick was bigger than mine, then, small as his already was, he was probably right. But did I care? Nope! I wasn't married to him anymore! I was just amused and bemused by it. Meanwhile, I am still paying maintenance yet it is still taking a while for a settlement to be sorted. Quite a while...

The boy's attitudes were also changing somewhat towards me, and hidden aggressions occasionally showed from them. Not surprising under normal separation situations as questions of loyalties to both parents causes confusion. This had certainly not been a mutually respectful separation. They were caught up in Jim's war against me. He was using my children as pawns to hurt me.

No Longer Mum

And hurt me it did. Many years later I was to hear that from the moment I had left, Jim had accused me to all and sundry of my deserting the family and of abandoning the boys. What? Holy What!

Meanwhile, I was still trying to cope with all the hurt I was holding. That's how I came to make a huge mistake with my boys. In order to cover or bury the hurt I experienced every time my children called me 'mum'. I felt that I couldn't be that for them anymore, for I was being prevented from being proper mum, what with having been pushed out of the home and denied proper access. After a few years of the circus we were living through I asked them to call me by my first name instead from now on. Yes, I admit, that is what I actually did, more's the pity. It just hurt me so much when they called me mum. They couldn't live with me. Jim had the family home and my living space was inadequate for them as I couldn't afford more at this time. Jim always made things difficult for me, and I just felt so inadequate to meet their needs as well as I could before. I didn't realise how emotionally bruised and damaged I was after all I had been through. Yes, I was still discovering who the heck Marni was, but I didn't recognise then that this was no way to go.

I paid a long time for that mistake. It had been a cry for help, but to the wrong people. My own children. It was *my* job to continue to be the parent, and I continued to try to do the best I could in very difficult circumstances, but I wish I could have taken this back. And I wished that I could have done better. What did I know about how things worked? All I knew was that it hurt, it hurt like crazy, it hurt so much that I had to stop the hurt no matter what. I didn't realise the impact it would have on my children by asking them to do this. I had buried this torment and hurt deep inside myself, and writing this journal, this record of events, has helped me work through it. But I still beat myself up - I was stupid to take such a stand – and I think *Stupid* is the correct word here!

I know now more clearly why I took such a step. I was still in this huge process of re-defining my life and myself. Never being on my own until I left Jim, I knew myself as a mother, as a daughter, as a sister, as a wife, as a partner, as a Christian, as a friend. But I didn't know who *Marni* really was – What did *I* like? Who was *I* without all of these other roles? What did *I* want in life? I was being challenged to *find out*!

Another big reason, and one I wasn't even consciously aware of until during the last few years and over thirty years after these events, was that *the very day* Jim pushed me out of my home, the very day I was forced to leave, was actually *the day I lost my children*. And that everything else after that was *directly related to the pain of that*.

I pray, oh how I pray, that one day my children will come to understand that dropping the 'mum' word wasn't because I didn't love them, but because it was the only way I could cope at the time. I made no recourse to booze, to drugs, to prostitution, to gambling or any other such thing – though a part of me continued to seek the healing and the love that my heart and soul needed.

Other changes were also changing; I was changing. I *never ever* swore when I was married. Couldn't do it. Went against everything that I believed and what the Bible taught. But later when I dared to use the word 'Damn' – kind of biblical because it was used in the Bible, so in a way allowable, kinda – it just didn't scratch the itchy places that needed to be scratched. Not after what I had been through, not with the residue of emotions I had experienced. When I dared to use a double-barrel swear word – 'Damn-Damn' – that too failed abysmally to express what I was feeling. No real 'Ooomph' to it! That is how I discovered the power of expression and honesty in a simple swear. The feeling I experienced after Jim's further nasty and vindictive actions and my responses being alleviated by saying 'Fuck You' – though not yet to his face – were immense and surprising! To this day I have not yet sworn at him directly. But that is simply lack of right opportunity. If one presents itself, I am more than ready – or should I say more than *Bloody* ready!

1984

~ Eighteen and Sheila ~ Thirty-Nine ~ No, Mr. Policemen!
~ Two Seconds Away ~ Buckets Of Love ~ Home Sweet Home
~ I Hate Dad

Eighteen and Sheila

An interesting observation on my attitude at the time is how I coped when others talked about 'failed' marriages. I actually had come to believe that my marriage was 'successful' because it had lasted for eighteen years. That's a long time. Particularly when one realises that I was eighteen when my first child was born. Why I viewed this as a success instead of a failure, I do not know... But it served to get me through.

At the time and for many years, I actually felt proud that I had made it work for so long. But there again, that was then. Did I want a medal for having lasted so long? I am jesting, of course. But I don't think that was so. I think that had we parted on more positive terms, I could more reasonably claim it as a success. Now I see it as quite a different story, and I no longer need to justify to myself or anyone else that which I had endured in order to ensure that I didn't aggravate a situation that would threaten my life and my children's lives further – I am just so thankful that they all made it out of there alive. Yes, I may have been remiss in not going in and 'kidnapping' them, but I have already laid out the main reasons for not being able to do so.

Here are some facts on what I now see as a 'fated' marriage – that is a marriage that seemed and 'felt' to be 'fated'... Eighteen seems to have been a common theme in our relationship...

My birthday is on the eighteenth of the month. So is Jim's.

We were married on the eighteenth of the month.

I was seventeen when I got married, but eighteen when Joseph was born.

It was after eighteen years of marriage when Jim threw me out.

I applied for divorce on the eighteenth.

The only further comment I will make on this right now is that I understand that this number eighteen can be reduced to number nine, and may be connected with difficulties and completions. If this really is the case, then I could say 'Been there, done that, got the tee-shirt'. For those of you who are into numerology, I will leave you to work it all out. I don't want to bore those of you who aren't.

I caught up with my good friend Sheila occasionally. She was still living in Camden, and I visited her and her husband Peter and their daughter Yvette for a few days. We went to the local best Chinese restaurant, and in general had a lovely time. In moments of sharing, when Yvette was in bed and Peter busy with his books, I told her many things I had not told her when I was married. But before I told her, I had to explain the reason behind the ridiculous plethora of makeup I had brought with me. I had a whole case of makeup – creams and lotions and hairspray and blush and eyeshadow etc etc etc. Of course she thought I was nuts, and I probably was. I had been repressed for years and I was now applying all I had learned to feel better about myself and compensate. Makeup was certainly one of my 'props' to get me through at this time, though I hadn't yet recognised it. Initially I was addicted to it. Fortunately I grew out of it. But right then, she saw me at my 'maddest'. And still loved me!

So when she asked me how the breakup had happened, I told her. I told her of the years of abuse, of his cruelties, of the things I had pretended hadn't happened at the time.

When I initially told her that he used to beat me, she looked at me wisely and kindly and said 'Yes, I knew he was like that'. I was so surprised. And almost hurt. She *knew* and hadn't said anything? How *could* she?

'How could you know he was like that and not *tell* me? Why didn't you *warn* me?' I asked her in amazement.

She looked at me knowingly before answering.

'Would you have believed me?' she enquired gently.

What? Of course I w ..., well, actually ... but surely...

Naïve Hope

Ruminating within myself, I thought about this for a few moments, imagining what I would have said and done at the time. And I realised the truth. 'No. I probably wouldn't', I sadly responded. I knew the truth then. I would have been in denial and stuck up for him. This was my degree of conditioning and honour around family, commitment and loyalty. Now, I know better. But not back then. She didn't judge me about any of this, and was amazingly supportive. She seemed to understand what was happening for me. And commented on me probably feeling like a Jack-in-the-box, now exploring all the things I could not whilst living with Jim.

'You'll work it out of your system soon' she encouraged. 'I went out with his brother remember! They were all mad Irish in that family. But it was too late to warn you about marrying him because you already were when we met.'

Good old Sheila. Spot on of course. Bless her.

Thirty-Nine

On my own, now, I am endeavouring to meet new people, to work out how they tick, learning how to navigate through a difficult situation. Suddenly it dawns on me that I had missed out on having a celebratory birthday on my eighteenth birthday. The same was also true when I had reached twenty-one years of age. It had always been the same-old same-old; responsibility and good behaviour.

I am now nearing my fortieth year and was getting somewhat concerned about that. When I thought about having a fortieth birthday party in another year or so, I cringed inwardly. Hence I decided against it. So what could a girl do to feel like life was worth living again? Before it's too late, she's too old and it's all over? Well, I didn't have an eighteenth, I didn't in fact have a twenty-first either – how about I add them together and have a thirty-ninth instead? Brilliant idea! Get two for the price of one!

This thought inspired me. I was going to make up for what I had missed out on!

Out came the invitation cards, then out *went* the invitation cards. In came the replies. Everyone thought it was a great idea, and they promised me that they would help me celebrate and we would all make up for me not having parties the first time around. Yahoo!

I had a great celebration party! With the two older boys Joseph and Ben and all my good friends, including David, Suzy and Graham (who I had shared with) as well as others I had been accumulating along the way. We danced and danced. Drink flowed, and though I didn't get drunk, it got close. The boys had a few drinks too, but they were old enough by now, and there was no raging drunkenness. In fact, apart from having great fun we were just high on good music and good company. I had a fantastic time.

There wasn't much sleeping room at my little place, but when I got up in the morning, most of the crew had found enough bedding, blankets, towels, cushions, couches, chairs or coats to create a make-shift sleep-spot each. I stepped over their bodies when I got up in the morning. Fortunately I had plenty of brekkie supplies and we had a cook up when they surfaced. Never had another party like that since. Will never forget that one! Nor will they, they assured me. Everyone had a ball!

My old mate Jan was unable to attend as he had just gotten remarried, but he sincerely wished me well. Eventually some years later we lost touch as he himself left TOW and set up his own fishing shop near the water. We both just got busy with separate lives, but those early days had been invaluable in my growth.

Meanwhile I was daring to explore and discover and search wider.

NO, MR. POLICEMAN!

Mr Tall, Dark and Handsome (David) and I stayed friendly catching up socially from time to time. Inviting me out for dinner one night to complete a platonic foursome, he introduced me to another of his friends. This man was a senior officer in the police force, and seemed to be a nice individual. Ray was not as tall or as handsome as David, but he was a reasonably attractive and personable man. And David gave him a good recommendation. I was open to making more friends, and was happy to spend a bit of time socialising occasionally. We had a lovely evening together with lots of fun and frivolity, a good meal and good company. Ray

Naïve Hope

invited me out again separately at the end of that evening and I felt comfortable enough to accept. Considering the fun we had had, I thought it would be worth spending a little more time to see who he was. I wasn't in a hurry for a guy or a relationship, and was still learning about people and social situations like this.

A few evenings later, he picked me up for dinner in his Jag with its leather upholstery and all mod do-dahs (very impressive!) and we go to a lovely restaurant. This fine dining was still new to me, and I was really enjoying the experience of quality eating out, trying new restaurants and well cooked and tasty meals with a drop of good wine. Ray, however, enjoyed his wine more than I did. What I mean is that he had much more than I did, but he kept reassuring me that he would be fine for driving. (This was in the years before drink driving was so stringent.) Throughout the evening he was attentive, well-mannered, affable and charming. Getting into his car to go home I paid particular attention to his handling of the car, but he seemed to be very careful with his driving, and there were no problems. Everything was going along well, and mentally I was considering another date if he asked me.

That was until he came into my place after driving me home.

I had offered him in for a cup of coffee, which I had often heard others talking about after a date. I had some lovely coffee at home, so I did the hospitable thing and extended the invitation to him. To me back then, 'coffee' meant Coffee, the drink! Still does! Being the honest type, what you say is generally what you mean; 'Do have a cup of coffee'. We go into the kitchen, and I put the kettle on. As I am pottering round at the sink, I feel him come up behind me very closely. This is unexpected, a little uncomfortable and I am not quite ready for this just yet. I am still learning about him and not ready for any rush. But I was prepared to give him the benefit of the doubt and I need to slow this down if this is going to go the way it seems it just may go. I have basically only just met him, and need a bit more time. I turn round to see exactly what he is doing and why, and note that both his hands are now placed on the sink edges, hemming me in. He moves in closer, now pressing against me. I begin to wonder what he is doing. I hadn't been aware of putting out any invitations to get this personal or intimate, and at this point I am initially more curious than anything else, though now starting to get a little concerned as he continues to move in closer. Let's see where he goes with this...

'What are you doing?' I ask him in a half-joking manner, giving him opportunity to be the gentleman and to back off.

'Do you realise that I could do anything I want with you, and no-one would know?' he utters in a low deep voice. I am surprised with his words, and register not only surprise, but also alarm. My eyes must have opened wider at this. Where was the gentleman I was with a few minutes ago?

He is moving in even closer now.

'What do you mean?' I asked, this time not as jokingly and I could hear a hint of alarm in my own voice now as I am moving my arms in front of me to protect me.

By now he is leaning right into me, and has me pinned against the sink. He has manoeuvred himself so that I have little space to move without hurting myself. My back is arched to keep away from him, but I am aware of being careful I don't push my body inappropriately into his, in a way that might be taken as an invitation for more than just a cuddle. His next words seal it for me. Shades of Jim!

'I can do anything I want right now, I can take you right here and have my way with you, and there is no way you could stop me. I'm stronger than you. And whose word do you think they would believe? Yours or mine? I am the Police!' He was looking into my eyes now, challenging me to be scared. He is practically leering, but his eyes are hungry. He wanted me, and he was letting me know. But he was also pulling the control card, the scare card, the 'I am Authority and I have the backing of my lads and the whole force behind me' card.

I am more than beyond scared; I am now *bloody angry*!

Fuck this! No way is this bugger going to pull a Jimmy on me! I tense and feel my own fingers curl ready to scratch, my head comes down to level my eyes at him straight on. From somewhere deep in my belly, rising to my throat and emerging out of my mouth is a low threatening response. 'Get your hands off me! Who do you think you are! No way will you touch me.' My eyes are now

Naïve Hope

narrowing as I give full force to my intent. 'You don't scare me!' I continue. 'I've had worse things happen than you. No way will I go down without a fight!'

No more submissions. If I was going down, then I was fully ready to go down fighting. To do whatever it took to stop this guy from just taking what was not his to take. And I would leave my mark in the process to show it. My jaw was clenched tight, my face set, my hands fisted then flexed, my whole body was tense, my feet felt they were gripping the floor and my knees were just the slightest bit bent ready to launch. I would use anything and *everything* at my command and I would *not* stop fighting him until I was either unconscious or dead. I would give as good as I got until I couldn't give any more!

I have had enough of fucking guys thinking they can push me around and use me and scare me. Try it Bud!

Just.Bloody.Try.It!

He actually looked surprised! I think this slapped him into reality. He released his lean against me and looked a mite uncomfortable. I don't think he had seen this coming. Neither had I for that matter!

I carried through to advantage. 'Get away from me, Ray. What do you think you are up to? I would like you to leave. Right now!' Sensing his hesitation, I pushed him away from me. At the same time, I moved away from my position at the sink as soon as he released his pressure, and I had already noted where my nearest knife was. I was ready! Now I had space to move, to hit, to protect myself, to damage him if necessary.

By this time, he had stepped backwards. He had realised that it wasn't quite going as he had expected it. He hadn't made the Hero impression on me at all... He saw his gaff. He had picked on the wrong gal. *Oops, what do I do now?* Well, bud, you're leaving. Forget coffee. This was his goodnight kiss, or as close as he was going to get to it. He was now looking a bit confused as I escorted him to the front door, and he was trying to mumble apologies all the way.

At the door he stopped and held onto the door frame as I said 'Goodnight Ray. Thanks for dinner, but I don't expect to see you again.' And without giving him any more time to try to wriggle out of what had happened, I pushed him out and firmly closed the door, forcing him to let go his fingers and I heaved a sigh of relief. Turning off the hall light, I was now standing there, shaking. I know that he stood outside the front door for a few minutes before I heard his steps going down the path to his car. As soon as I could, and still almost holding my breath, I moved down the hallway quietly, turning off lights as quickly as I could so he had no further invitations to come back. Even though the place had been locked up before I had gone out for the evening, I still checked all the locks and windows to ensure that they were all secure, for this guy was a policeman, and who knows what would or could happen next?

After a minute or three, I heard a car drive away.

When things stayed quiet, I gathered a bit more confidence, and peeped through the window for confirmation of a clear street before I prepared for bed. I had a little trouble getting to sleep that night, but there was no more trouble from him.

This was on a Thursday night. I closed the book on this guy. I had already seen what he was capable of. I was scared of him, and disgusted by him. All memory of the sensitivity, charm, romantic possibilities, pseudo-gentlemanly behaviour was now gone – poof! Up in a cloud of smoke. Two nights later, the Saturday night, I am due to work at a cocktail bar for a few hours, and am almost ready to leave for work. There is a knock on the front door. I answer. There is Ray again. This time he is stone cold sober. As he should be! And he is carrying a *huge* bunch of flowers.

'I came to apologise. I don't know what came over me. I am so, so sorry. I don't usually act like that. Please, please forgive me and give me another chance'- he is begging me. His demeanour matches his words, as he holds the flowers out to me. There are actual tears in his eyes! I look at him. He seems genuinely sorry, and I realise he is. But can I trust this man ever again? Do I have to forgive and forget and let him do it again? I think not. BT, DT: Been There, Done That!

'I am sorry too, Ray. But I can't allow that to happen to me again.' He sees I am on my way out and I can see he is dying to come in and talk about things. Thrusting the flowers practically into my face, he insists 'Please take these. I feel so bad about what happened. I am truly sorry'. I don't need to insult him further; I have said my piece, so I accept the flowers as graciously as I can under the circumstances.

'I have to go somewhere, Ray' I clarify, 'and I have to go in a moment. Thanks for the apology, but I don't think I can do this again.'

He looks crestfallen, and I can see he is really hurting. The message I seem to be getting from him as I look at him and hear him is that he had a great chance with someone who he really, really likes, and now he has gone and done something stupid and he regrets it and he doesn't know how to get it sorted. 'I've never met anyone like you', 'You deserve better than that', 'I'd like to make it up to you', 'Never treat you like that again', 'Another chance, won't let you down again...' He is shuffling, mumbling, beseeching. I think he got some sort of lesson from it, leastways I hope so.

But I have to go.

'Ray, I 'm sorry but I have been in an abusive situation and don't intend to be in another one again. Thanks, but you have to go now. All the best.' And I close the door on him.

Madly running round grabbing handbag, keys, checking doors and windows, these actions give me a couple of minutes to let him go away and for me to steel myself in case he is outside the house waiting. I throw the flowers into some water in the sink to vase up later. Or not. And then it's time to go.

Checking all the cars I could see in the street outside, I can see that he has gone and that there is no-one hanging around outside. That is the last I see or hear from him.

Nice of him to apologise. But what abominable behaviour. And he thinks a bunch of flowers is going to fix it. *Unfixable*! A man that comes on like that has already shown what he is capable of. And what was it all for? To show off? To impress me as to his power and status? To take what he could? Or just some stupid alcohol talking? I didn't know and I didn't care. I wasn't going to risk it.

I had certainly learned *my* lesson. Even though I was a bit disappointed that someone who one would think had so much going for him would act this way, I felt stronger, for I had not allowed him to control me.

And no man has ever repeated *anything* like this again with me.

Two Seconds Away

My great job at the advertising agency was forced to close down due to unforeseen circumstances'.

After a year of me joining the operation, it was discovered that someone in management had taken a bribe of some sort. Sadly around ninety percent of the original staff was finished up and had to seek other employment. I had really loved my time there. I was offered short term extension of employment with the company that took over the advertising accounts, Clemenger Harvie. The existing bookwork required preparation and completion for hand-over to them. Financially, this got me out of a sticky situation. Building on my advertising experience, I was then able to secure another job at JWT, a very large advertising agency in Melbourne, and was now working with television media reconciliations full-time. And meeting some famous people whilst working there was not enough to keep me wanting to stay on. The vibe was different, and the women I worked for were a very different breed from those at DPB. It was no longer the same and I gladly moved on. And talking about moving, I was again moving house to a larger rental place.

This was a solid-brick semi-detached house in Ripponlea and a much bigger and better place with more rooms so I could let the boys sleep over when they came to stay. It had a garden and was much closer to the sea. I still felt really isolated though, and very vulnerable as the fall-out from the huge shifts, changes and stresses took their toll. When one has a different space and is secure on certain survival levels, then the buried things can begin to surface.

And they did. I hadn't yet realize was that I was suffering from repressed emotional deprivation in regards to not having my boys

Naïve Hope

with me. Sure on some levels I knew this, but not the ultimate repressed emotional aspects for I was too busy with managing things to explore the deep hurts. How much hurt and pain can you experience at a time, anyway? This thing could be endless, so you just got on with life. I was used to doing that. But I was still a mother without her children to care for. I was kept busy putting on a good face as well as managing life, loss and past mistreatments.

Even working at several jobs and being involved in a play does not necessarily heal the type of wounds that my experiences had caused. And it was to be many years before I understood this. All I knew was this restlessness and emptiness. I did not recognize my denied pain and wounds. I still did not acknowledge my own buried anger, and Jim's transferred anger and shame – I could not afford to feel these, let alone acknowledge them. All I could feel was the effect from being on the treadmill of repression, distraction, denial and covert worry. Though a holiday had got me through some of my trauma temporarily, I was still emotionally spent, and didn't know it.

A photograph had been taken for a play I was auditioning for around this time. A friend commented that my eyes looked 'haunted'. I got what they meant a couple of years later when I came across it again. But I didn't see it at the time. Maybe because of what I was struggling with. My Soul was so down, so low, so aching at that time and I was in sore need of relief from this.

I have a vivid memory of something that happened one day whilst waiting for the train to get to work. I felt that I had nothing left to live for. I took stock of my life.

'There is no reason to live anymore. Life is too painful. My children are not with me, my ex-husband is vindictively working against me, my parents and siblings are far away, and not on the same page, and I just cannot see any good in store for me anymore. There is nothing left to live for. Life is empty.'

These were my undercurrent thoughts and I had been quietly and surreptitiously thinking these for some time. But now I heard them loud and clear in my mind. Very clear.

I was staring at the train lines. And an express train shot past.

I wanted to die. I *really* wanted to die. I felt a new realization dawning; *Here is a place that I can do that.* The train lines looked so inviting. A mite messy, but *quick*. Once you have made that move into the tracks, there is no stopping the train. It just keeps on going. And then I just keep on going – away from here – for good.

Death is just two seconds away...

I so wanted to throw myself onto the train lines and end it all right then and there. Looking back now, the impulse was so strong, I am surprised that I took a moment before hurling myself forward right then. Somehow I must have realized that I really was actually ready to do this. I felt no fear at all at the idea of moving forward onto the train track. I was numb.

That moment of hesitation made the difference – the next thought that I had was that I had to plan it. I had failed the last time I had tried to end it all – I have *got* to get it right this time. This seems to be a good way to go, a sure way. But is this the best time? Don't want to hurt anyone else if I can help it. All these city workers around me. Might try to stop me. Need to find a time I can do this unhindered. And the best spot.

I began working out the best way of accomplishing it, where I had to position myself for clear access and launch, and all of the details so that it would be complete. And quick. I now fully and consciously realized that I was getting ready to die. I wanted to.

With this deep realization there came a gift.

I had a way out. *Finally!*

Oh, my – a chance to end the hurt for good... A way out of this treadmill of pain, aggravation, unhappiness, struggle, unlovedness...

It is amazing how it can free up one's mind when one knows that there is a way out after all. It seemed like my mind had now started thinking differently, as though I could now see that there was a chink in the dark curtain around me – there was something I *could* do about this after all! This dead-end place, this lonely locked and blocked space, this pit I had fallen into. I began to feel more at peace, because I already knew that I could go no lower, and I now had a solution to *all* of my problems. Just like when I was sixteen

Naïve Hope

and attempted suicide, *this* time I could *ensure* that it was final. I did not want to wake up maimed, or incapacitated, I wanted it to be o-v-e-r.

This was a very real and present option to make the pain stop. As I was standing there, taking this in, I became more consciously aware of the momentous decision I was taking. Then I seemed to hear other thoughts in my head that hadn't been there before. They were mixing with my previously hidden and repressed thoughts. Maybe I had had to consciously recognize and think certain initial thoughts to progress to others? All I knew was that this was an inner conversation I was having. Pros and cons to life? Pros and cons to dying by this method? I was kind of thinking in circles, but the circles seemed to be coming up with some other sort of different thinking as well.

These thoughts were saying to me that now that I had a way out at last, what will happen to my family (boys etc). I was now looking at the full consequences of such an action, a weighing up of the possible effects not just for me, but for those I leave behind. I could not give them any more than I had. There was nothing left to give that did not give me more pain or sorrow. I was empty. I was now leaving this world still feeling *unloved*.

My thoughts became more serious now, another side of me was voicing itself – or was it my higher self? I did not know or care at the time, I was only listening to my thoughts. So, the thoughts went, if you can now get out of this at any time, if you now have a *'Guaranteed Exit Plan'* and you are still wanting to be *loved*, how about you make a promise with yourself? How about giving yourself a little more time to find this love that you want and need, and then if you still haven't found it, you can go right ahead and end it all? Why don't you give it one more chance; just give it *one more chance*.

I was in a totally disassociated space and quite divorced from my feelings by this stage. I obviously listened to these thoughts, thoughts that said to give it another chance. The thoughts continued; *'Why don't you give yourself five years to find what it is you're looking for, to find this love that you think is to be had?'* I thought, 'Well, it can't get much worse than I have been through or that I am going through right now. I am at rock bottom. Is there a possibility I have not yet seen that could make a difference?'

Somehow, I came to a new decision; I would give myself five years, and five years *only*, and that if I had not found the love I wanted and needed, then I most certainly *would* end it all. For now I knew that I could. Five years. To find that love; Five years to find love… That was fair, wasn't it? Then I could honestly say to myself that I had tried, that I had honestly tried my best and done *everything* that I possibly could do before ending it.

Though I didn't recognize it at the time, this began a whole new era in my life. Things didn't just automatically vanish and disappear and get easier overnight, there was still a lot of pain to be endured, but events did start to move me in another direction. I decided that I would not think again seriously about killing myself for the next five years. I wouldn't forget it, I would just shelve it and revisit it in five years time.

And I was also comforted that I had saved some poor soul of a train driver from living with something that would not be his fault yet might affect him for the rest of his life. How glad I am that I listened to that small voice inside.

And why wait five years? I have no idea why this was the number that jumped into my head, though I have found it to be a favourite of mine. Interestingly five is right in the middle of 1 to 10, make out of that little thought what you will.

In fact, the five years came and went, as you will see.

Yes, I had further challenges to meet along life's way, and I seriously considered it again another twenty years later after another really challenging time. After the five years, I remembered and reviewed this promise; I realized that I hadn't found someone to love me, like I had promised myself. *But* by then I had done a lot of grieving and healing and what I had found was more important, more necessary. Because of this deal I had made with myself, I had eventually stopped running around looking for something or someone out there to do all my self-loving for me, and was learning to *love myself*. That actually was the love that I needed.

Naïve Hope

I hadn't realized that in order to experience love, I had been doing a deal. The deal had been; I will love and take care of *you*, and I will hope and expect that you will love and take care of *me*. For I can't do it for myself (and also for I am not *allowed* to do it for myself!).

My self love was so very low. I had grown up feeling so unloved and unworthy of love that in order to get what I needed in love, I had hoped someone else would to do it for me. And I later realized that I had also been stupidly taught that to love yourself, that is myself, is selfish and unworthy as you are supposed to love others more than yourself – that is 'what God tells us through the Bible'. What rot, I later found. And what a misquote, for we are told to love others *as* we love ourselves, not *more* than we love our self. If you don't know how to love yourself, how on earth would you really know how to love someone else? I am talking about real love here. Not the neediness associated with co-dependent types of love, nor the lust of sexual addiction.

During that five years I came to realize that I had huge difficulty in understanding how and why people could treat each other so badly. So inhumanely. Yes, some of this difficulty was due to my own experiences during my marriage, as well as my somewhat love-neglected childhood. But now I was a single person so to speak, and needed to work out who *I* was in relation to the world around me without using the blinkered and narrow lenses of the Born-Again Christian way. I was happy to let the irresponsible side of believing that God's forgiveness was your get-out-of-jail-free-card. I had never used it anyway. But I was meeting other people now who didn't use that card. I was meeting both honest and kind people that were not Christians, as well as sneaky and mean types (who may or may not be Christian). But I had no understanding of how things worked, and of why I would be feeling the way I did when certain things happened, and others seemed to be experiencing a totally different reality. I was still needing to make sense of the world. My own romanticism and idealism and unrealistic desperate belief in the goodness of people was holding me back from navigating through the different personalities and lifestyles and cultures of those I was meeting. They didn't do what I expected, or hadn't gone out of their way for others, as I had. But, so my thinking had run, I had tried to do what they expected.

Therefore they had let me down... What a silly conclusion, a stupid way to live, yet it had been my learned way, my survival way. And my reactions could be quite intense, particularly when it had been a perceived offense over my religious beliefs. Now I was learning about reactivity and personalities. And more.

Over time I got that some things happen simply *because* of who we are, and we have to work through them. I also got that some things happen *regardless* of who we are, and not to take them personally. To a conscientious soul, geared to not wanting to deliberately hurt others as their general modus operandi, coming up against others that wished one harm from the get-go was a challenge. As had been the challenge to recognize when someone you love wishes you harm. Still learning...

I had studied the words of the Bible – 'Love suffereth long and is kind etc' and had no wish to go through that hell again. So when I discovered and read the Gospel of Thomas and came across the words (paraphrased here) 'Whoever knows everything but knows not himself knows nothing' it was a call to understand my own feelings, emotions, thoughts, actions and motivations etc in order to be able to have a hope of being able to understand the thoughts, feelings and actions of others. This then was my next challenge, to know myself, along with discovering how to truly love myself. I had already been exploring myself, but now I was digging deeper.

Events shaped themselves in an unusual way after this. I met someone who told me about this self exploration course which also helped one to open oneself to understanding life, the self and others more. I did the course, which was run by People Knowhow in Melbourne in those days. In fact I did it a couple of times and got more out of it every time I did it... It was based on self development principles together with some metaphysics and spiritual practices. *This changed my life.* It didn't yet solve all of my problems, but it gave me hope and some tools to life.

As well as some self knowledge, it gave me a glimpse of metaphysics and spirituality in a *different* context. This was a major leap forward for me. Further events formed to guide me to further studies, which in some ways saved my life, my mind and my

Naïve Hope

heart. But these events took place over many years, as I sought to bring peace and healing to my heart and soul.

I had yet to realize that my whole life was a journey, a journey to overcome the obstacles to being who I was, and to living and loving authentically.

Buckets of Love

But I still haven't enlightened you about *How* I began to learn to love myself...

And it took me many years to learn this piece of the puzzle.

Because I was having difficulty knowing what loving myself felt like, a self development counselor I saw gave me principle to work with. My job was to practice this regularly until I didn't need to practice it any more. At first I didn't know how apply it. But I had recognized that somewhere within I did deserve love. Even though I was quick to be critical of myself, I began to see I had some really good qualities. It was as if I was ready to see who and what I really was without the labels, judgments, voices and opinions of others. And after all, I wasn't a bad person, I didn't intentionally hurt others. In fact I would often do whatever I could to alleviate any possible hurt toward others. Yet others were totally loved, even though they did horrible things. So why couldn't I be loved? *Why wasn't I loved?*

I will try and explain it in this way.

There were times in my life when I felt better about myself and about life one day more than the day before, or indeed for a period of time before. By feeling better, I include not feeling down, but feeling ready to be with people, not feeling like a truck had hit me, not feeling grotty or crappy about life, but feeling that today is an 'Ok' day. If I felt like the day wasn't so bad after all, that it was a 'better day' than the one before, I would invariably and immediately want to share these happier feelings with someone. Someone like (and usually) a girlfriend or a friend or neighbor or a relative. I would get this impulse to see if she wanted to go to the pictures, and I would shout her the entry. Or feel like going round to see her and cheer her up with some flowers or chocolates. Or to phone or call on someone to see how they were going and to give them words of encouragement. Or see if I could do something for them. Or help them in some way. Or some other similar thing. I wanted to share the good or positive feeling, no matter how fleeting, with someone straight away.

This feeling is energy. Love is an energy.

It was pointed out to me how I just kept giving away my love and therefore my energy to others as soon as I had any. And now I had to *learn to give it to myself.*

Those words were full of mystery at first – how did I do that? How could I 'give love' to myself? So I was told that the very next time I felt like doing something for someone else, I had to stop and do it for myself instead. What? How can I give myself a trip to the cinema? Oh yes, well I know that I could go on my own. But what if there's nothing on that I want to see? Oh, yes of course, I can shout myself something else that will please and 'lift' me. Get myself some flowers and enjoy putting them into a vase at home. Or take myself out for a cup of coffee. Oh, I see, I think I understand. But then I won't be sharing anything with anyone else, will I? I will be cut off. No, that's only part of it. This is about *how much* I give away. And that I don't realize that I am giving. This is also about giving only from my *excess*. And dealing with feeling comfortable with my own love for myself.

I had been so used to running on empty that as soon as I felt it, felt love, felt energy, felt better about life, I had given it away. I hadn't nursed and nurtured it. Now I can choose instead to give some of it to myself, I can begin to build up a store of love-energy for myself, by putting my 'love' energy back into me'. Then *every other time* I feel the same way, *then* I can share this with someone. And this is very important... Share with someone else, yes, but give yourself a turn at giving back to yourself... Take turns with yourself; at giving to others and at keeping for yourself.

I soon had an opportunity to put this into practice. For I found myself driving along after work one day, actually feeling a bit better about life. And I then found myself thinking of phoning a girlfriend when I got home and buying flowers for her on the way home to

Naïve Hope

cheer her up. Then I remembered my commitment to this exercise. Oh, that's right, this is the *alternate time*, isn't it?

Imagine this; here I am in my car, having to give myself the love I wanted to dish out to another. No I am not gay, nor would it matter if I was. I am talking about simple love and caring. But I really had to struggle to 'put it back' into my heart, into my own love battery so to speak. I now found myself parked at a set of traffic lights having difficulty putting this same love I wanted to share back into my own heart. I wanted to give it away, for this was easier for me, this was my habit. But I cannot. *I have to keep it.* I literally swallowed the feelings back down *into my heart*; Yes, Swallowed! – This was how I learned to give myself love – to keep the love I was always so ready to give away. Anyone parked alongside of me might have wondered what I was doing when I was struggling so with it, but they also might possibly have seen the look on my face when I had 'swallowed' this love back down, and then felt so good about it. Eureka! I had done it...!

I didn't need to give it *all* away – I could keep some for myself! And I really felt it. It felt good...

So every other time after that, I kept this energy for myself. I still got to share, but I also got to feel loved, and *without* needing someone else to do it for me.

What I didn't realize was that my 'energy bucket' (or 'love bucket') which had been empty had now got some 'juice' in it. If you look at how a battery works, you will get the idea. An empty battery is pretty flat, and not much happens. When the battery gets charged a little, if that store of energy (or love) gets used up straight away, the battery is just as flat as before. But when you keep adding to it, and adding to it, and don't drain it all out straight away, then it builds up to a full battery. How much easier and more pleasant it is to give from a full store of energy and love than from a struggling and replete store!

I was learning that I had to fill by own 'bucket' of love, and not to keep giving it out to everyone else all the time, in the hope that *they* would put some 'love' into my bucket. Yes, it took me some time to learn, but at least I know knew that I might be able to do something to help myself.

I cannot emphasize how important it was for me to understand this. Some of us are lucky enough to get enough love as a child so that we can call on this anytime we need it. And along with that, some are lucky to have self-worth instilled into them, and to be acknowledged and supported in their choices. And this we can call on too. Those of us who *don't* get those gifts, who didn't get that support, have to work that much harder in life to grow these things ourselves, sometimes with few tools. But the effort can turn lives and hearts around. And possibly bring some wisdom and some compassion along the way.

And so it was, that in my quest I came to understand and give myself permission to *begin* to love myself. And in so doing, I would be able to attract a different kind of love from others. It was quite simple really. When you knew how.

Meanwhile, other areas of my life are also requiring management.

HOME SWEET HOME

In those early weeks and months after I left the family home, I had tried to maintain reasonable and civil contact with Jim. On most occasions, as one can imagine, though I almost invariable was ill prepared for and didn't expect it, he would turn on me. Not once did he attempt to resolve, to recognise or to accept any blame in the break-up, not once did he seek to acknowledge what happened, nor his part in it, not once did he admit to losing control or being unreasonable, not once did he apologise for anything.

Jim was also having his own struggles. Eventually it occurred to me that he had not expected me to actually *leave*. Despite him continually pushed me out and regardless of his statement that if anyone was to leave then it was going to be me. I don't know *what* he had really expected from his behaviour – maybe he thought I would come back to him (again) but I wasn't about to put myself in his untrustworthy hands ever again. And as I was still concerned with maintaining a good relationship with my boys, initially I had to put up with the constraints and endeavour to visit as often as I was allowed.

Naïve Hope

Having a housekeeper for the boys made it even more difficult to organise mutual times for me to see them. And if I was required to work back late or weekends, I would try to make other arrangements with him, though mostly these were not easily accepted by him. And they would be taken as a deliberate slight for which I would suffer the next few times I wanted to see my sons.

The boys didn't like to talk about things at home in Werribee and I believe that it was because they had been asked to tell me nothing. Shamefully I also took to sometimes asking the boys not to say what was going on in my life. This was because when they had accidentally or in natural conversation (I prefer to refrain from thinking in terms of any interrogations on them) told Jim quite innocently of what was happening with me, next time I saw Jim or called by phone I would get snide remarks off Jim. And things would be uneasy again. And so the boys didn't want to get into trouble either way. Quite naturally. But this must have been very difficult for them and was oh so wrong for them to be expected to understand and mediate like this. What a complicated situation. Still nothing was said about property settlements or legal developments even though the Divorce Absolute had come through.

I was waiting and waiting for news of the slow movement of settlement legal machinery to inform me as to progress so I could organise myself financially and buy my own place instead of paying rent. I needed to settle somewhere that I could call mine. But it was a long time coming and when I asked Jim about progress on this score, nothing would be said to me in a clear manner. Whenever I assessed that he was approachable, and asked how things were going in that department, his response was that he simply didn't know, he hadn't heard, he was waiting for them to get back to him – and so on. I hesitated to question further for a while; after all, each phone call to a solicitor is expensive and I had enough on my plate.

When I got concerned enough at this lack of action and Jim's continued pleading of ignorance about it all, I made a phone call to my solicitor. It then came back to me that Jim was hoping to string out the time spent on this case and therefore increase the legal costs to me so that I would walk away *with nothing* from the marriage. Not strictly professional for a solicitor to report on conversations with the other parties solicitor – confidentiality issues and all that – but I think both solicitors were so *appalled* at Jim's plan that they simply had to put me in the picture. I had moved out at the beginning of 1981, yet still by March 1984 *nothing* had been done to finalise the court settlement and Jim's payout for my small share in the family property. He *himself* was actually behind the delay. He knew and *deliberately* sabotaged it.

His solicitor had a word with him about how The Law viewed this deliberate inaction, and also what his delay could cost *him*. This stopped his game playing and his debt to me was slowly acknowledged again. Now I was faced with the job of seeing *what* he could pay and *when* he could pay it. Talk about me being a softie and getting walked over again. But there was no excuse this time for the delays except his bloody-mindedness, and I was realising just how dastardly and bastardly this man could be.

Finally Jim was forced to do something about it, or more precisely, Jim had been *pushed* till he could no longer postpone things, and he had to face sorting out what he owed me from the settlement. After his previous delaying tactics of pretending that none of this was his fault, he then had the cheek to draw out the process of *actually* repaying me.

Now he appealed to me to give him *more* time to pay – he didn't have any money! *Hah! Welcome to the club!* But surely he could get a mortgage draw down, but he kept coming up with problems; more 'Yes, But!' ducks in a row... And he was no longer working, claiming that the boys needed him at home. Yeah, right! I was finding it hard to believe *anything* that came out of his mouth at this point. Anyway, in the end he was forced to take some sort of action and it became clear that the only way I would get any money from him was in dribs and drabs – a thousand dollars here, a thousand dollars there. I allowed this, as I wasn't a mean or selfish person and I was still mindful of possible erratic consequences and I certainly didn't want the children to suffer. Again.

It had taken another full six months after chasing up with the solicitors for me to start getting any money.

Naïve Hope

Through all of this Jim had shown his true colours, deliberately slowing things down, yet continually pretending that it was in no way on account of him, using these delays in his attempt to carry out his threats and beliefs that I 'deserved nothing' and that he 'would destroy' me. Again, he received another serious word from his – and my – solicitor. Eventually he was notified quite clearly that he could go to *jail* if he carried on dishonouring the property settlement agreement, and that this would also cost him in money.

By this time and through such appalling hindering, interest rates were now at an all time high, reaching a record 17 ½ %. Meanwhile house prices had risen drastically between 1980 and 1986. We had split in January 1981, were divorced in October 1982 and it wasn't until around March 1984 that he agreed to look at paying me what was due me, still at 1982 prices, yet he claimed he could only pay me in small instalments. By the time he started paying me and I had received most of the few paltry payments at one thousand dollars a time I could barely afford to buy a decent sort of property.

Finally and after more delays in payments I was paid out by 1986, after five years of my continued paying maintenance. Prices had continued to rise, liveable and reasonably priced residences having been bought up quickly due to the rising interest rates, and consequently what was available was now almost 'bottom of the barrel' for the dollars that I could manage to borrow. People began to hold onto their properties, only selling if they had to. It was all I could do to look for a little timber semi-detached as brick was now out of my affordability range. The house in Werribee had been fully paid up for several years, and I had kept my end up by continuing to send Jim money without needing to be told to, whether working or not. I had paid maintenance, even working extra jobs to do so. Yet this 'man' could not honour *his* financial responsibilities. Talk about being screwed!

It took a lot of travel and I almost gave up. Eventually, fortunately, I managed to get enough for a deposit on a little place in Clifton Hill, which was like the early Fitzroy – old, drab, still cheap, needed work, but a small possibility of rising in the estate market as the as-yet-not-desirable area had future possibilities.

This narrow timber property was professionally noted to need re-stumping at some stage soon, hence its affordability for me just then. This was factored optimistically into my future budget. Even though finances were tight, I now had a place of my own that I could have the children for weekends and visits. But even as this was appearing to be a step in the right direction, things between Jim and myself were still fraught with tension and undercurrents.

I Hate Dad

Within a few years, Jim had had enough of Ben, and as was now proving to be his way, in a drunken state he threw Ben out to the wolves. That is now *two* sons out of there. Both kicked out by a lout living in a beer bottle. Yet another son that hates his father and doesn't want to see him ever again.

I gladly took Ben in, thankful that he too had escaped alive. And that I had the room to do so. Ben was so angry telling me how much he *hates* him. He *never* wants to see him again. And I could totally understand why. Or so I thought. But I was still being the 'fair parent' and possibly gave them the wrong advice; for as each of my sons had left, I had encouraged them to stay in contact with their dad as he was *still* their father. Eventually, the boys *did* maintain contact with him, though it took a while for them to do so. At the time, I think that I was afraid that based on his past behaviour and erratic thinking that he would do something bad to the boys if they tried to disappear from his life totally. Misguided as I was, I perceived that it was important for the boys to stay in contact with Jim. And after all in my eyes, this was the Right Thing To Do... *Little did I know of how he had been treating them.* They didn't like this at first. And in retrospect, I can't help but wonder if I did the right thing. (I was to later regret this stance as for some years afterwards I realised that this had harmed them all further.) I *still* didn't truly appreciate how noxious and 'sick' this man was.

Another son safe. But what of poor Danny? What could I do about that? Well as it turned out, still nothing. For I had no proof of anything untoward. My sons were helpless to do anything either, not that any of this was up to them. All they could do was to try and alleviate any fears I had, saying things like 'It will be all right.

Naïve Hope

Danny will be ok'. I think it was the only way they could cope too. And still nothing was mentioned of any abuse from Jim by them.

So best for me to attend to what I could, eh? But in our communications, Jim still held onto resentment and blame.

None of my children were happy. As their mother, this affected me, and I couldn't be really happy. Of course, all of the continued struggles and tension would impact *anyone* with an ounce of empathy or caring in their body. Or heart. I was helpless to do anything more for my children than I was already doing, and they were going through their own crisis's and dramas, dealing with the personal issues that this too-long marriage and destructively conducted breakup had dished out to them. They weren't happy; I wasn't happy. But I also was to learn more later about the dynamics, the actual energetics of the situation. For not only does a parent, particularly a mother, get affected by her children's happiness or lack thereof, conversely the chidren can become impacted and affected by lack of happiness in a parent. Examining this statement in the light of my own childhood also verified the truth of this to me.

Initially, my relationship with Ben was more strained, and we would have rows about keeping the place tidy. I was too busy to continue to 'mumsy' him, and did not appreciate, let alone know, what had been happening at home with his dad. But in all truth, I wasn't told anything, so had *no* idea of the things that Jim had been doing, nor yet of what he had been saying about me *behind* my back, or of what the children had been subjected to. I had no basis to think otherwise.

Not long after Ben moved in, there was a fire in the roof due to old and faulty wiring. Thank goodness that he was there to help me to identify this in time. The place had tall ceilings, and though I could smell the burning, I could see nothing, whereas Ben was able to somehow climb up into the roof by swinging up into and through the roof access hole in the ceiling and to see the flames. The Fire Brigade was called, and a nastier fire was prevented. The cost of electrical rewiring pushed me well over my budget and meant that I could no longer afford the restumping nor other repairs that needed doing.

I had been stretched to the limit financially, and I still having to keep my other jobs up. House repair costs were now a major financial problem. Even though I had insisted on and paid for a good and proper approved sworn inspection, the wiring had obviously not been properly looked at. And I was told I had no recourse against those that had performed that inspection! I couldn't work any more hours than I already was. I needed to be more available to put in time with the boys when they were with me. So the only thing I could do was sell and downsize.

Consequently staying here in my new home didn't last long.

It was heartbreaking and humiliating. But eventually I found a downstairs unit in Hughesdale, Oakleigh which was simply the better of a bad bunch at the time. Prices had still been climbing as now interest rates were again beginning to drop but also sales were increasing at record pace, and I now seemed to have missed the opportunity to get a comfortable little place with my funds and repayment prospects.

And I know for a fact that Jim couldn't have cared less. In fact I think it rather pleased him. In all of this, there was absolutely no respect to me – the mother of his children. It seemed that I was dirt. Nor for his children either, it would seem. No matter what I did, how I tried to work things through with him, he still was so mad with me, so overtly angry then passive-aggressive. He obviously could not see that I should have been respected, no matter how badly I had dared to behave to him (that is if I had done so) simply for the fact that I had brought his three sons into the world, and had cared for them. Being the mother of these boys *alone* deserves so much respect.

When will this man ever stop trying to destroy me?

And when will I ever discover the truth of what really went on in that house after I had left?

Meanwhile, two children out now, only one more to go and we will *all* have escaped him! And survived him! Joseph had already moved on and was rent sharing with a friend and in time Ben did the same.

Naïve Hope

1988

~ Sole Custody! ~ Lousy Father ~ Danny Out!

SOLE CUSTODY

I have it on record that I was contesting for Full Custody of our son Daniel on 31st July 1988. From memory, though I no longer have the paperwork on the rest of it, this was in response to action taken by Jim. For some reason, and right out of the blue, Jim was again going for full custody of Daniel, and he also wanted an increase of maintenance from me. (I also saw this as an opportunity to try for sole custody myself.) I realised that this was his attempt to get at me by making out that my 'rejection' of him was a direct rejection of the boys. That I was unfit. This from the man who had his own *numerous* affairs, had abused me and kicked me and two of his sons out, and had refused to let me take the children with me!

This hounding for custody was during a tough period in Australian history – the recession of the late '80s.

Due to the downturn in the economic climate at this time, our company had been badly hit and we all found ourselves out of work. This meant that I had lost my job, and so I couldn't afford financially to follow a case for sole custody through to completion. The building sector was among the first to be hit. I had loved working for this company, which was well-paid and in the property and building industry. My bosses had been good to work with and I had grown on the job, increasing my skills and experience.

I had had a very good job, good pay and even had shares as a reward for my contributions and length of employment. But within a short period of time these were totally worthless and I lost thousands of good dollars that could have helped me through. I was again unemployed, and broke through no fault of my own. Like other thousands who were also looking for new employment.

Fortunately for me however, Jim *lost* his sole custody case, and forever to his discredit on the court document and subsequently now in filed in court records, he tried to paint a dishonourable and untrue picture of me to swing the case his way, which was both nasty and futile. If you think you have the measure of this particular man by now, let me tell you that, like me, you just may be surprised by what he tried to pull on me next; Jim *actually* put in to the custody affidavit that I had had my youngest child by *another man;* one of the guys that I had worked with daily, and whom I had only ever first met after starting at TOW when Daniel *was already 18 months old.* Well you probably have worked it out by now. Yes, it was the name of the guy I had given when I was threatened by Jim with the knife and I had lied to him! Go figure! Danny was a year or so old when I first met and worked with this man – a retro conception? Obviously, if you also include sex by remote looks! This was better than the Virgin Birth!

He *knew* the truth of it, yet he couldn't help himself – he just *had* to get the boot in. What a nasty little mind! This was calculated to hurt both me and my sense of truth and justice. He was so blind, so vindictive, sly and stupid that he tried to belittle and humiliate me as best he could. But he had also submitted *false information* on a legal document, all in the hope he would 'win' the full custody of Daniel and keep Danny away from me for good. How sick is that! This was *not* about what was *best* for Danny! This was another game he played, and played to win! Fortunately, I shared this with the solicitor just before she went into court. I wasn't even called in to give testimony. She told me that when the judge read his custody application and heard the facts, he laughed at Jim!

And I retained joint custody.

And this silly man didn't realise that implausible as it was what he had written, this is *still on court record,* and if anyone checks out dates etc they will see how *willing* to lie and deceive and punish blindly that this man was. By his own words he would stand as a *fraud.*

But apart from the rage I felt at his lying words and slur on my character, what really stayed with me was that a *father* would try to take joint custody and access to my son *away* from me, when I had supported him in his contact with his sons. And that he would actually *lie* in court about paternity and *use* his son like that. Condemn Daniel to a life of *no* mother just to get back at me and to hurt me. Bugger about what really is in the best interest of Danny;

just do anything to get time and attention from me and try to hurt me with lies and humiliations and insults.

But as I said, someone somewhere must have been looking out for me as I did retain joint custody despite not having a regular job right then.

Though I would rather have won the *sole* custody from him so that I would be sure that Danny was safe. After this was all over the job market shifted somewhat and I found employment again. Not the best, but something to manage with.

Lousy Father

There *had* been times when Jim had been somewhat gentler and more loving with his boys. But then there were those other times when he was somewhat insane. He seemed to forget they were children and it was as though they were an enemy, out to ridicule or destroy him, out to make him look stupid, or trying to prove that they knew more than him. Of course, in hindsight I can see how this all played out on me, but back then it was hard to see clearly through the confusion, smoke and mirrors. Jim and I were both still learning about parenting. And we basically had only our own dysfunctional childhood experiences as well as the books we were reading, or comments from workmates. Or what the church said on the subject. Which really wasn't that helpful.

Though I could be somewhat tough when required as I felt that boys needed to be taught toward self reliance, I was always free with my hugs and often with treats. There were times when Jim and I would take it in turns to read to the boys, and other times when he would plunge into his moods again and just disappear. I never really got to have 'moods' myself, couldn't afford to, wasn't allowed. At the time I just saw and accepted these times as simply him having had a bad day. I had seen this often enough at home with my own father and learned to walk egg-shells there. This behaviour was already familiar in my own family and therefore too easily accepted. We had little choice to do otherwise. The signal of moodiness was Jim's excuse for brooding and withdrawal, and over time became both a signal and a trained response for the boys and myself to avoid upsetting him in some way. Years later, long after I had left home and the boys were well grown up, the bad behaviour continued; I heard of stories of him phoning them when he had been drinking, verbally abusing and threatening them, time and time again. Whenever any of these stories filtered through to me I found it very hard to simply accept Jim's continued poor and immature relating, and his power and manipulation over my sons. For they were often genuinely upset about his words and actions. In fact, I would become incensed with him, and feel ready to go round there right then and punch his lights out... though I would obviously have come off the worse for it. But it didn't stop me from feeling such rage, anger, hurt and frustration at his stupid and cruel doings. And wishing I could do something about it, because forgiveness sure didn't bloody work!

You would think that when a man loses his wife, then his sons, *One By One*, that at some stage that he would ask himself the question 'What have I *done* to contribute to all of this?' Wouldn't you? And possibly, just possibly, one might even get the inkling of an answer...

But things didn't go that way. Not at all. Jim still maintained the stance of victim, yet continued to treat others so badly.

Though I didn't know the half, I did learn a few things about the way he tried to poison my boys' minds against me, so that even my youngest son had fears of who I was. But more of this shortly. However, I do not know *all* of the things that Jim said about me, though I am aware of some of the effects his manipulations might have on young and impressionable minds. A father is a very important person in a boy's life. I really do understand and accept that the relationship a son has with his father is different to the one he has with his mother. And in my own way I did try to support this.

But this particular family history had created such dysfunctional attitudes. Instead of being acknowledged and respected as a mother I was portrayed as a wicked wife and a bad mother.

I know that my children have been damaged by events during the marriage and by the way the divorce was handled. Jim's subsequent brain washing and continued unrelenting and vindictive assault on my reputation and character hasn't helped. I

Naïve Hope

know that at times, when I had heard some of the things he had said (that the boys had let slip when they were with me), and in response to the way in which he treated my attempts at having time with the boys, that I have been quite angry. Hard not to be with all the game-playing and the toxic fall-out from the issues that caused the marriage break-down. Over the years when I have heard of his carryings on, I have gotten angry with Jim, and said so in front of the boys – I know this, and I am sorry. So sorry. This would have placed them in a difficult position with torn loyalties, but in all honesty, I am also surprised at my restraint considering all that I had suffered, and all that they had suffered by him.

But I also want to believe that one day, they will have totally overcome all of this, and that they will learn to do it differently. Hopefully they will know that I had done my best for them. And that they will somehow know that they were loved and cared for by their mother, despite the mottled history. Maybe this knowledge will help them when they finally come to deal with their relationship with their father (which is inevitable, one way or the other), and help them to get past and overcome the dynamics that clipped their wings, so that they may learn to fly, and to fly free.

And I want to be clear here; just because they had a father like that does not automatically mean that they will *be* like him. For I have watched them over the years, and even though there are some shared genes, they have not resorted in quite the same way to imitating their father's sick manipulations. In this I am so proud of them. Like me, they too have helped to 'change the pattern' for I know that any grandchildren will experience a different childhood to the one I had, and to the one that my sons had.

My sons may not think that they were as successful in life as some because they did not own huge mansions, nor run a big company, nor do all of that flashy stuff. But in this I can be pleased, that I have not seen them passing on all of their father's behaviours; they seem to appreciate love and family; I think and hope that they would no sooner dream of beating up a woman as fly to Pluto... And this is not thanks to me, but this is on their own qualities, on their own account and due to what lays and lives within them, within their heart, not just their genes.

> *One of the greatest lessons in life that I have learned is this: 'You don't really know a man (or woman) until their back is against the wall – then who they truly are emerges'.*

DANNY OUT!

So far, Jim has thrown the two older boys out one by one in drunken fits. I have very few memories of the times spent with them after this, except that our relating was now a bit disjointed. Things had shifted and we were all a bit different by now, so naturally other issues came to the fore. Our relationships were running on several levels; the original connection of love and trust we had when I lived at home as mother, the effects of Jim's actions and brain-washing on this and the subsequent inner loyalty conflicts, unresolved issues around abusive men and being men, and their maturing and personal need to become independent young men. They both handled things in their own way, and our shared space had a different dynamic. Being teenagers they had wanted and needed their own space and were exploring, finding their own footings in life.

Ben moved in with a close mate who lived at home still with his mother. Ben took to calling his best friend's mother 'mum' and did so openly and deliberately with me. This badly hurt, more than I expected. But what could I do about this? I took it, and tried to understand. After all, I had made my own mistakes on motherhood. And wasn't I the one who had told them to stop calling me mum?

It took many years for this to be redressed. I apologised to them some time later when I realised the impact of my request on them and our relationship. Eventually they all fell to calling me mum again. Thank God.

Two children out. Two children and their mother have escaped the wrath of Jim. I cannot tell you what fears now plagued me. If Jim could throw out each of us without apology or redress, and he was still drinking, then what the heck was going on with young Danny?

Naïve Hope

Jim has shown that he has no conscience in using Danny as a pawn in his mind games. How was he now treating him behind closed doors with no buffer, no one else to safeguard or protect him? I was really concerned about Danny, but totally powerless to do anything to get him out of there, to protect him from his father. It was becoming a major issue for me. Even Joseph himself was concerned, though he would always try and set my mind at rest in the best way that he could. I had many conversations with Joseph about this as we spent more time catching up together than did Ben and I. Not that I saw a lot of the boys, as I wasn't the sort of mum to be continually 'in' their lives trying to govern and live it for and through them, phoning and hassling them continually. I guess I always saw it as a two-way street, and was very aware of not being an interfering parent. Maybe I was trying not to overly influence them, and I was also conscious of trying not to be a nuisance or being seen as a needy mom.

Anyway, one night Joseph and I are sitting together in my kitchen in Daly Street, Clifton Hill having a cuppa. We are discussing the situation of Danny, again, and I am, again, airing my concerns. The legality of going in to the house and taking Danny out was, yet *again*, up for discussion, but we were still in the same stalemate position on this. We are both concerned, but we are legally unable to do anything about it. I had failed to get sole custody and Danny is now the tender age of thirteen, seven years after my being thrown out.

There is a phone call and I go to answer it. I am surprised with what I hear – I am distressed with what I hear – I am overjoyed with what I hear! Danny is phoning me from Werribee Railway station. He is distressed, he sounds frightened. He too has been kicked out by his drunken dad, disposed of in a beer haze and destructive self-hate rage.

He does not know what to do, he does not know where to go; he is calling to ask what to do! Oh My God! He is only thirteen! So much younger than the others when Jim threw them out! I have no idea how he has made it to the station, I cannot remember, for all else is overshadowed by the fact that Danny is now OUT! And needing me to come and pick him up! Joseph and I are amazed and so, *so* grateful! But we are also a bit scared for he is not yet fully out of the woods – right now he is on his own with an erratic drunkard at home, and at a station all by himself. We have to get there as quickly as possible.

If it wasn't for the dire circumstances, the fact that this is still the youngest and still at school, we would have been jumping up and down. But this is still a young boy who his father has thrust out without any protection. How cruel! Yet it is also answer to our concerns. And fortunately Joseph is still with me at this precise moment, this moment of freedom for Danny. So we can *both* go down and pick him up together!

We tell Danny to stay where he is, to wait, don't talk to anyone, we are on our way. I let Joseph talk to him on the phone whilst I grab my bag and keys. Then we are on our way – immediately – and we drive down to pick him up. More likely race down with great anticipation. I am so excited. But scared as to what might have happened to him. I conjure up pictures of black eyes, bruising, torn clothing, but I have to settle myself if I am to be of help and support to him in this dramatic and overwhelming situation. None of my children has been what's called 'bad boys', they all have kind hearts, and great compassion. And each has been treated so unjustly and cruelly. Yet I have to contain myself at what I might find.

He is still at the station waiting. Thank Goodness!

I will never forget seeing him when we arrive there. He is so confused, so lost; even now I feel tears welling up at this thought. Each time my children were thrown out by this maniac, I was powerless to take Jim to task. Too scared of what this mad man might do, of the repercussions, of his revenge. Yes I do call him *mad* for I am convinced that he is! Not in the clinical sense, but in the human sense! Though there may be grounds in the clinical sense, too!

There Danny stands, wringing his hands, looking so lost. My little boy has experienced at the tender age of thirteen what I had experienced as a mature woman and was still dealing with. Feelings rush and tumble one after another, anger at this stupid man, pain at what Danny must be feeling, relief that I have found him safe, concern at what damage may lie beneath the surface,

Naïve Hope

happy that all my sons are now out of the hell-house, humble that I can take him under my wings again.

Joseph and I look at each other. It appears that in each other's eyes we can read the thoughts that are just so full of gratitude that he is in one piece, that he is not bruised or bashed, he has not been attacked by any Werribee hooligans, and that he has called for me to come for him. But Joseph warns me not to run out to him, and that he will approach him first. This has to be handled carefully.

At the time, I questioned this. I am his mother. *I* should be the first to hold him, to comfort him, to 'rescue' him. But the reality of it all is that in some ways, over the years of him living with his father, we had settled into a somewhat tentative relationship. In some ways, we felt like strangers. With the degree of mind-messing he had gone through with Jim, and in view of my own experiences, the possible interrogations and questioning about his visits with me, it is not surprising if he had created some form of mistrust or disconnection with me. The question of divided loyalties should never be thrust upon a child, yet I believe in my heart that this is exactly what Jim did or attempted to do with each of our children. I was not aware of practising this myself, as I thought that I had included Jim as part of their family circle and I had been certain to encourage them to maintain contact with him without demanding *complete* loyalty to myself. Yet what Jo is saying feels right. This is about Danny, not me.

I take Joseph's words on board, because I know he has Daniel's best interests at heart, and he also knows what Danny may well be going through. After all, he too had been through something similar. 'Let me talk to him first, mum' he says. So I do. Joseph gets out of the parked car and walks over to Danny at the station as he stands there waiting and looking so lost and vulnerable. There is a school bag on the floor next to Danny that probably holds a few clothes, and Danny is standing guard over it as though it is all he possesses in the world. And in some way this is probably true for him right now.

No physical harm has come to him. Thank god. I still didn't trust such public hang-out places even though in those days it was probably still a reasonably safe place to be of an early evening, and not the sort of place it is today. Joseph gently hugs him as brothers do, and talks to him for a few minutes. Shortly, he waves me over, and I get out of the parked car and go over to speak with Danny and to give him the hug my arms have been waiting and aching to give. But I must take care not to overwhelm him with my own feelings and needs. This is about him, what he needs right now. He needs to feel safe, to know that he has a place, a space, a mother and a big brother.

I gently and tenderly tell him that he is now safe with me, that I have a place for him, and that it *will* be all right. And we all make our way almost carefully back to the car. It feels like I am gently shepherding a fragile invalid as I feel the energetic cotton-wool that both Joseph and I are surrounding Danny with to help him through this tough and difficult time.

I drive us all back to my place. While I make up a bed for him and sort out a supper of sorts, and sort through the little bit of clothing he brought with him, Danny spends a bit of time talking with Joseph, who helps to settle him down. Joseph is great at this, he has a way with children. After the bed is made up with such tender loving care, relief and gratitude, I organise food and ensure that both Danny and Joseph are fed after such an event. As I quietly fuss and potter, doing my best to maintain an air or normality and calm, Danny's story is related to us both. He paints a clear picture of yet another moment of madness from this man who again has allowed himself to become drunk enough and cruel enough to kick out his own son. What this must mean to Danny! 'Abandoned' and 'deserted' by his mother (according to Jim) at the tender age of five and living with such a cruel man experiencing things under that roof that I had no possible idea of, nor could not have rescued him from. And being told that his mum is a … well, let's continue with the story…

Eventually it's time for bed. I take him to his bedroom and settle him down. I am still handling him with kid gloves, for I know he is still in shock and needs gentle treatment right now, *very* gentle treatment.

I tuck him in for the first time in many years, such a healing thing for my own Soul to be able to do again. The bedside light is left on low so he can find his way around. He has been fed, 'debriefed' so to speak, had a bath and is clothed in clean clothes between clean sheets and made to feel comfortable. Something I later hear is that this had not always been the case. So I kiss him goodnight and give him a great big hug, and I tiptoe out, leaving the door slightly ajar so he can hear the hum of our voices in the kitchen not far away. Joseph and I talk in semi-hushed tones about our next steps and what we need to do for Danny and the situation for a while. Joseph is a rock, and so very in tune with what is needed and I am grateful for his input and his suggestions. We are already adjusting to the new situation, and I am so grateful that now all of my boys are out of Jim's clutches. For he himself has thrown them out, I didn't go in and take them. So he cannot claim Danny back now.

They are *all* now free!

And I am so glad that I have been patient in this because they have all seen what he is like. Though truth to tell, I wish I could have spared them all of it, and I am so sorry that they have had to wait for this man to let them go before being able to get away from him alive. Yes, alive; all the way through this I have been gravely concerned that each one of us escapes and gets out from his clutches alive. So Joseph and I continue to talk in the kitchen, making or suggesting possible plans and options for Danny's future. But when I peep in to check on Danny after about twenty minutes, he is still wide awake. I enter the room and ask him if he is okay.

What follows is an eye-opening exchange:

'Are you okay, son? Having trouble sleeping?' I gently prompt.

'Yes, mum.' He rolls over onto his back and pulls the blanket up to his chin.

'What is it? Is there anything on your mind?' I slide onto the edge of the bed the better to speak with him, gently putting my hand on the arm closest to me. He takes a moment or two to respond.

'Well, yes'. I wait for him to elaborate, but he appears to have some difficulty in saying whatever it is.

After a while I say to him: 'It doesn't matter what it is you are concerned about, you can tell me. You can ask me anything. I won't get angry or upset with you. I promise you.'

He looks at me, still unsure and says 'You promise?' His voice says it all. He really needs reassurance. I steel myself for whatever it is he has to say.

'I *promise* I won't get upset or angry *whatever* it is you have to say,' I confirm with a faint smile to him, thinking that he is going to take me to task about leaving his dad or something along similar lines. But I don't yet know and it's no use guessing. All I can do is to listen and be truthful to the best of my knowledge and ability. I put my hands in my lap waiting for him to tell me, a small smile on my face.

So then he sits up in bed, looking down at his fingers and with hunched shoulders he shares his thoughts and fears: 'Is it true what dad says about you?' His head is still down, now he cocks it on one side and looks up at me.

'Is what true, Danny?'

With trepidation and some fear in his eyes Danny speaks - 'He says you are a prostitute.'

He watches my response, waiting for a reaction, probably scared that he has crossed some line, unsure of what to do if his father was right. I cannot believe what I am hearing. Is he expecting punishment for voicing such a thing? He looks so worried and scared almost as if I am going to hit him. But I am prepared for anything, *anything*, and have already steeled myself to handle whatever emerges with Danny and to be truthful about whatever he asks or says. He watches my face and my eyes in an attempt to pre-empt or forecast my responses.

Calmly I say 'No, it's *not* true Danny. Never has been. I can tell you honestly that I have *never* been that or done that.' I smile at him. And wait, for my response is true and congruent. I have nothing to hide. He is still watching me.

'Oh' he says, and lets that sink in. The reaction I read on his face is relief. He lets out his breath. 'I didn't think so,' he says. But he is still on edge...

Naïve Hope

I see him now asking inner questions. There is more. He shares;

'Dad also says you are on drugs and that you are an addict. Is that true?'

This is getting past a joke now. Telling my son I was a prostitute – what sort of man does that? What a foul lie! And now *this*? I am feeling just the tiniest bit angry with this 'man' now, saying such things, and so very appalled that he would put such revolting and despicable ideas about me into my son's head. But I reign in my temper and my surprise that Jim has gone this far to corrupt his young son's mind with all this shit. For we are still not yet fully through this. This is not about how I feel right now, but about how Danny feels.

'No, Danny, I have *never* tried drugs, and don't intend to. That is *not* true. I don't even smoke!' My voice is a tad firmer now. But Danny can see it's not because of him, but rather what he is sharing. However, this is difficult for him and possibly scary if he risks upsetting me as well as his dad. He's just been kicked out of one home after all. I realise that we are still not yet done.

There is still a question in the air, still something more to be said, some bubble still to be pricked. I realise he is not yet through thinking his thoughts.

'Is there anything else that's on your mind, Danny? It's ok to tell me or ask me. I won't get angry with you, I promise', and I touch his arm again to let him know I am sincere. I need to know everything to be able to move on with Danny. If he can let me know we can clear the air and start off with a new slate so to speak. 'It's ok, you can tell me anything, darling' I encourage him with a gentle pat on his arm, sending him love and acceptance whilst at the same time hoping my voice sounds gentler than I am feeling toward Jim right now.

'There is something else' Danny says, looking at me with that lob-sided head gaze again. He needs encouraging further I can see.

'Danny, the things you just said, I can assure you that they are *not* true. I haven't done any of those things. It's ok to tell me if there is anything else that is bothering you. I understand.'

'Then it's also not true that you are a Witch as well?' he blurts out.

God damn this man! What rot, what tripe, what nastiness he has invented. What things to call someone, what soul rotting and revolting ideas to plant in a young and trusting mind and so untruthfully! And this is not about witches, for they, like Christians and non-Christians can be good or bad, but this is about the Christian attitude and indictment on them as Devil Worshippers; this is one of the worst insults and labels they can place on anyone, and this was the level this man had sunk to. The only place he could have got any of those disgusting ideas was from his own filthy mind. But I refrain from saying any of this to Danny, I have to for Danny's sake. I have now seen into Jim's mind. And this poor child has been *living* with him!

Firmly and clearly yet gently I say 'No, that's *not* true either. I have never been that, nor intend to be one.'

With a sigh of relief, Danny's shoulders began to relax.

'I thought they weren't true, but I wasn't sure, because dad kept saying that it was all true.' A moments silence and reflection. Then 'Thanks mum. Thanks for picking me up.' He looks at me, and I feel we are over the worst now. Somehow, despite this man's attempts at poison, Danny believes me and is now allowing himself to feel safer with me. We smile at each other and embrace each other properly now, a real heartfelt hug of love and comfort.

It seems to me now that keeping hold of the family house and depriving me of this as well as warping the boys, was more important to Jim that what was actually best for the boys – for they would have thrived with me as parent instead of Jim, who has *betrayed every single one of them.*

Danny settles down now and he slept well after that. And he settles into the house (and later a new school). Meanwhile, I go back to join Joseph in the kitchen and share these revelations with him. Despite our shared disgust and anger at Jim, Daniel is out of that place, out of his direct influence, away from this man who has overshadowed his life so negatively for the last seven years. We set positive plans in place, and I give thanks for the events of this night. The long wait is over.

Naïve Hope

I breathe a sigh of relief that all three boys, all of my sons had escaped his hands, and are still alive. Our relationships weren't perfect and certainly had been damaged, but they were still here, I was still here. I was ready and I was open to telling them the truth about anything and everything; Jim wasn't, he had hidden the truth from them, and he had also thrown them all out himself. So there was no need for him to stalk and try to get them back. They were finally *free*! *All* my children were *alive* and they were *free*!

I can breathe again!

I loved the fact that Danny was part of my life again, and that I could take him to his new school and do all the things I had been unable to do with him before. It was now in a very different setting that we could be together, without the threats and moods that had been so much a part of our lives previously. In some ways I was a different person from the one who had previously mothered him in Werribee. Things had certainly changed.

Now I had to review my life and my priorities again to see where to next. I no longer needed to pay maintenance, but I also now had further added expense. I was also being challenged to design a different future, a different budget, a different lifestyle.

My TV acting had become regular and I was now getting specific roles as well as speaking parts in commercials; roles were getting more interesting and paying better. Was I prepared to give this all up to make a more stable life for us both? Well, that is easy, compared with having my son back safe with me, it is No Contest.

Besides, when I left DPB my new position no longer afforded the same flexibility. But I was content with what I had gained from out of it all; I had done TV work, some modelling, had some fun and performed in live theatre with some acclaim, and still hadn't resorted to that good ole casting-couch! Live theatre had given me a buzz, for through the experiences with different theatre groups, I got to learn, share and develop. The interaction had sustained me with human intimacy when family couldn't. Part-time acting had had its day and even though I had truly loved it, it was no longer necessary and I was now back to being a mum again. I knew which was more important to me! It was no sacrifice! Acting had been a victory of personal expression for me. But my *greater* victory was in having my son *safe*, and back with me again.

I said goodbye to this part of my life to work on creating a stable life for my son and myself. Dare I revive hope for a more positive future? It is beginning to look like it...

1989

~ Come Into My Parlour ~ Brutal Lesson ~ On Your Knees

COME INTO MY PARLOUR

'Come Into My Parlour' said the Spider to the Fly...

Danny had been kicked out at age thirteen, in 1989.

It is now a year or so further on, and Daniel is happily living with me, and attending his new school. We have established a routine, and I drop him off by car, usually *without* a kiss because he is far too old for that now! Of course. Yucky stuff at that age... So if I really, really want a goodbye kiss off him I have to drop him off round the corner from school.

It took some time for Daniel to forget some of his stress and trauma, though I never forgot his words that first night. Do I question him further about any abuse he may have suffered? Or do I allow it to emerge naturally, and avoid any further unnecessary stress on him that might seem like interrogation? It may have been remiss of me, but I left it to him to tell me and share with me when he felt comfortable about it. I did not reckon on the possibility of him having repressed any dark memories. Indeed, I had not been fully aware of my own. Time was to reveal these shadows when they began to emerge in his thirties. Would he have told me things anyway, now, at this time? Even if I had asked him, or insisted on knowing? Maybe not. Grown up as he is today, he is still loathe to discuss the past, loathe to talk about emotion or feelings, and generally has an aversion to dissecting personal issues, despite his ability to delve deeply into books.

As it turned out, Danny had other more immediate issues to consider when he first arrived. Over the last few years, he had put on a lot of weight. Difficult for me to control as he had been with his father most of the time. But now, he was clearly embarrassed about this and this issue caused further problems for him, affecting his socialisation to a degree. For he would only go to the school baths wearing a tee-shirt over his trunks to cover his tubbiness.

Even when I took him out on the odd occasion with the children of one of my girlfriends for rides and fun by a river or lake, he would feel terribly embarrassed. His father's meals of carbs, carbs and more carbs (read that as beans, toast, coke, chips etc) had done nothing for his health and stamina. He clearly needed more protein, not excess carbohydrates. On a personal level, I was also becoming more aware of health myself and so it was enjoyable to find new ways to provide healthier nutrition and meals. In the end, the best tool I found for him at that time was a product called Herbalife, which was high in protein and herbs. Though he complained on occasion, we stuck with it and he trimmed up quite quickly. I also think the lack of stress from his idiot dad also helped with this. I didn't drink, so he had no fear of me going off my head at him for no reason.

Danny hated his father for what he had been through. I was still aware that this man could do all manner of things if he so chose and I didn't know the half of what he had experienced at his dad's hands then. Accordingly, like I thought a good and fair mother would act, I encouraged him to see his dad again, just like I had encouraged his brothers. In hindsight, I wish I had played the nasty 'witch' role and damned him for kicking the boys out like he had. But compassion had won the day.

It is now almost nine years since I had moved out from Jim. Even though I had plenty to keep my busy I had been seeing this new man for a year or so, and before Danny was kicked out of Werribee, and we had become engaged.

My fiancé Rick and I share a lot of similar interests. Being with Rick has been a major learning curve for me, and it looked like this relationship might offer me the stability, romance, understanding and connection that I had missed in my marriage. We hadn't yet moved in together though we spent a lot of time together and both felt a huge attraction on many levels. Both of us were attempting to work through our separate relationship issues and we were preparing to make really sure before we progressed to a deeper commitment. He, too, was divorced. Rick and I had both been on a self-development adventure, separately and together, and we had attended courses to come to grips with our own personal demons, pains, patterns and histories.

Naïve Hope

Our biggest hurdle was the age difference between us. Though I looked a lot younger and had been open to dating much younger guys prior to him, there was a nine year gap between us which he found challenging. Despite my history, I was vibrant, attractive, intelligent, adventurous, understanding, mature and also spontaneous and we got on really well together as he had similar traits. His problem was that he had been conditioned to be with a woman who was younger than himself, preferably with a five years age gap. Which it seems is what most men believe is the perfect gap – though it still beats me why. The age difference just kept popping up again and again for him, though he was doing his best to work through this. There was nothing I could do about it but be myself and give it a little while. Daniel was also being challenged to adjust to him as he was so different from his father, but it was good to have a man about the place a bit.

For me life was looking reasonably good. I am coming to grips with certain events in my life, discovering more of who I am, learning new tools to move me beyond my past, my son is living with me, I have a job, have a partner, my eldest son visits me, and I am reasonably settled. Yes, I dare say that Hope was resurrected again in my life.

Then one night after work and totally out of the blue, I receive a phone call from Jim.

As luck would have it Rick was round for dinner that night, and my eldest son, Joseph, had also called in to visit me. I was very surprised by Jim's phone call, as we were still mainly at an impasse and any communication was always strained. Time had taught me not to trust him and I was bemused by his phone request. After months of silence, Jim was actually inviting me and my fiancé down to see him and to have dinner with him! *Quelle Surprise!* This was unheard of. He said he had a surprise for us both and made it sound really enticing. Even so, it still seemed really strange and out of character, and sure enough, it was.

He hinted that his surprise had a flavour of a gift of some sort, and when thoughts of him being fairer about the abysmal divorce settlement and making amends entered my head, or even an engagement gift of some sort, I knew that something just wasn't quite right. Though I began to hope that even just an apology along these lines might possibly be at the end of the drive down to visit him. *Just what was it that made me kind of expect him to suddenly do 'the right thing'? Didn't I realise that this man was never going to change?* I think that on some level some part of me *knew* that he was supposed to and was waiting for that...

Meanwhile, because Joseph was there he heard *all* that went on. He quickly voiced his opinion that something was definitely *not* right about all this. He also knew his father well. After some discussion about it, Joseph and Rick came to a decision and decided that they would go down together to Werribee to see Jim *without* me, leaving me behind. Joseph had smelled a rat (or should I say Snake – and unsurprisingly this man was born in the year of the Snake!) in more ways than one! We wouldn't tell Jim that Joseph was going in my stead for Jo insisted that he felt something was seriously amiss, being a mite sensitive and intuitive himself. So off they both go and I await their return, eaten up with curiosity. It felt strange waiting for them both to come back from there, what with all that had happened in the past. But there was nothing I could do but to wait it out as I realised that it was the only way to handle things given the situation. Quite some time later they both turn up at my place again with an even stranger tale.

Apparently Joseph had been absolutely right – something had definitely been wrong. When they arrived there they it became clear that Jim had been drinking. But as he hadn't been expecting Joseph this put him on a back foot. During the evening his own son had sussed him out; Jo realised by careful questioning and observation that Jim had intended to drug both Rick and myself and then to murder us both with a hammer he had semi-hidden nearby at the ready. Jim was now forced to abandon his plan to kill as Joseph would be a witness if he still tried it on Rick.

Joseph and Rick had both spent some time in talking him sober and back into reason and out of his intentions.

That evening back at my place, Rick shared that Jim had become enthralled by what Rick had to say, as Rick was quoting some of the self-development stuff we had been learning at him. In some ways, Rick was quite an aware guy, and could also be very charming,

Naïve Hope

though with a lot more depth and integrity than Jim. Jim had more than met his match, and during the course of that evening dropped all of his original intentions, being overly impressed by Rick to the point that as they shook hands goodbye he pressed a one hundred dollar bill into Rick's hand. Rick thought this whole scenario was really funny. Of course, he would... I thought it was scary and weird and I was reminded again of Jim's desire *to do me harm* in any way he could.

For no matter how you look at it, Jim had planned revenge on me, and on my new possible future. Revenge is about deliberately trying to hurt someone, and here he was again, playing with ways to hurt me again. And to silence me for good... This further confirmed my resolve to have nothing more to do with him unless it was absolutely necessary for the boys. Joseph had been so right over this, and I was so glad that he had been there to help sort this all out.

You know, when I confronted Jim about this event thirty years later, he *denied* having met Rick and claimed that he couldn't even remember that I had been engaged. He denied everything about this incident until I reminded him that his own son Joseph had been there and that *he* remembered.

Ah, the sleep of ignorance and blamelessness caused by alcohol!

Brutal Lesson

Joseph was smart in not trusting his father. He had been badly treated by him on several occasions. Jim would use any leverage he could to hurt us both, though none of us were immune to his manipulations, plottings or machinations. If he couldn't get at me directly, there were other things he could do...

But some background first: in that last year before I had left home, Joseph as eldest had not done as well as was expected in his final school year – in hindsight this should not have been surprising as he is and was somewhat sensitive, like myself, and family is and was very important to him. However what was surprising was that he was usually a very intelligent student, very quick witted, and also smart regarding ideas and creativity; and because he always did well, he usually coasted through most of his work and tests. However, when he got this much-poorer-than-expected final year results, he realised that he had not concentrated as much as he should, him being a very smart lad and all. With that school report he saw that by not seriously applying himself he was now reaping the results and it gave him a major wake-up call; he couldn't just count on breezing through with his smarts as in the past, he now had to apply himself.

As I said though, family life *had* not been easy for any of us then, and this should also have been recognised at the time. By his father. Who *demanded* and ordered that instead of being given another chance, he now go out to find a job and go to work. Like him.

I was horrified, and *knew* that Joseph could do better and could see that he *wanted* to, and he only needed a chance to. Joseph now *pleaded* for another opportunity and one more repeat year at school; in which I *knew* he could easily make good and remedy everything. I could see Joseph's genuineness in this and wanted to support him. So I was all for him doing one more year. But not so his dad.

I was so *very* upset that Jim again refused to listen to what Joseph wanted, and that Jim had to prove his authority by depriving Joseph, his *own son* of this opportunity to change things. Joseph had woken up and was now searching for something, *anything* to apply himself to. But I could see that he found this response of his dad hard to bear at the time. His father and I should have been there to *help* him get it together. It really hurt having to stand by and not be able to do anything. But that was the way it was. My hands were tied. And I think it was also another catalyst for my emotional separation from this man who didn't really care about his children or who was in some way jealous of them and instead of affording them better opportunities as a *real* parent than the one he had had, he had chosen to *punish* Joseph, and sabotaged and stymied his progress.

There had continued to be tension between Jim and Jo for quite some time, and naturally so I believe, as there is some natural boundary testing that takes place with many young males. Add to

Naïve Hope

this, I think, that maybe Jo was recognising unfairness, hypocrisy and seeing more clearly who Jim really was, and was possibly trying to work out why his father was not supporting him in the way a father should.

Anyway, things come to a head. And the next thing I know is that there is an outright challenge from Jo on Jim's authority, or rather, on Jim's right use of this authority. Jim is challenging Joseph to a fight! Yes! He actually *challenges* this lovely lad to a fisticuffs to 'prove' who is the bigger man. Even if this was to prove whether he is a 'man' or not, is this really the way to go? Jim with all his boxing training, and Joseph who loves drawing, reading, ideas. Joseph willowy and taller than his father, Jim stocky and well seasoned.

Jo stands six feet tall, towering over his dad, and he is also much smarter and quicker with his words, and capable of reading back to his father verbatim the things that Jim has said in the past. Jo also tries to stand up for me and defend me, as his father should have been doing. Jim hasn't liked that, and so decides that he is going to teach him a lesson. Jo is also a gentle child, and clever as opposed to physically overpowering. He may have looked like he is on the way to being a strong young man, but he is not there yet. His strength is increasing, and he is often practical in carrying shopping, helping out with gardening and other physical chores. But directed force through the fists is a skill his father still has over him, despite Jo's inner conviction that right will win out over this stupid man. After all, he can see how ridiculous he is being, how absurd. Maybe he thinks, like me, that Truth is Might?

Anyway, he rises to his father's challenge and thinks that he can beat him. I wasn't so sure, but I did not want violence between father and son. It was unthinkable, and not well thought out for either party.

But the challenge has been issued, Jim's authority has been challenged, Jo's pride has been insulted, and something has to give.

And a mother's nightmare takes place.

This bloody bully-brute of a man takes our son, *my* son, out into the back garden, despite all my protestations, simply because

Joseph dared to question him, dared to stand up to him. There is only one natural conclusion, though I had so wished that it was otherwise, for I am in despair and powerless to prevent this slaughter. And slaughter is what it became.

For Jim literally *beats* him up! Not content with simply putting him down, Jim ensures that he is thoroughly defeated and made to look like a loser. (And this has not been for the first time.) Even though Jo puts up a valiant effort, he is too gangly and inexperienced to make good his mark, and Jim *spares him nothing*. My disgust at how my husband behaved with his son is palpable. But this smirking jubilant *pig* of a man walks away from Joseph, leaving him lying on the garden grass, and comes back into the house to enjoy a celebratory drink, or three.

I was beside myself, and couldn't believe how this man could run things like this. I had seen similar with my own dad, and here it was again. *Barbaric!*

It's my opinion that Jim resented Joseph being given another opportunity to do well at school, for if he succeeded, then it would *really* put Jim's own intelligence or abilities to shame, wouldn't it? For after all, just how smart, really, was Jim? Hmmm? In truth, not very and in more ways than one! Didn't finish School Leaving. Couldn't let Jo show him up at that, now, could he? This to me seems more than likely a major driving force in the humiliation he attempted on his own son, his own flesh and blood. This was then followed up by cruel taunting from Jim. 'Get a job, make yourself useful. See what real hard work is about. I have to work, your mother has to work. Why should we give you another year off to mess around?' These were the intelligent and worth enhancing considerations poured onto Joseph to encourage him in life... Sick, idiot, irresponsible arsehole of a man... *Shame on you, Jim!*

Joseph had to take it. He was quite a mess for a while, but he had gotten the message, though not one I was happy with, not at all. But Joseph was not really a lazy boy. Now he applied himself to finding work. It was heartbreaking to see the effort he put into seeking employment, and the harsh setbacks he experienced as he competed with better qualified teens. Lots of teens were looking for work at this time, and *with* qualifications. But he kept at it.

Naïve Hope

After quite some time was spent despairingly searching the papers and answering ads, and being subjected to his father's taunts on being a lazy layabout, he finally found himself a job as an apprentice at a hairdressers.

Thank goodness he had found something. And it suited his creative side. And he had a bit of money coming in. Not that he was at home for long after this...

On Your Knees

With this as part of our family history, and Jim's determination to force me to compliance or punishment, I am somewhat taken aback with his enlistment of others to rebuke and discipline me. Too far away for him to go to the Pastor over my 'desertion', he resorted to other ways in an attempt to shame me. But the shame was on him in the end...

My bridesmaid Mary Strawthorne and her husband had long been associated with the Throngs of God. They were the ones who originally witnessed to Jim before we met, and who were so instrumental in his conversion. Somewhat upper class, definitely of a different class, they were well spoken, well dressed, drove a modern car, always appeared to be caring and beyond reproach. And a little bit superior, though they tried hard to be amenable and to mix with everyone. Generally good people. And I thought they were our friends. When they later started going to another church, we had still sometimes caught up with them when we visited England, and had exchanged letters when we moved to Australia.

In our last few years together, Jim had confided in a drunken moment that he had always fancied Mary, and this was why he originally joined the church, so that he could get involved with her and get into her pants. Those were his actual words...! Surprised as I was, what could I have said – for he hadn't acted on it. But it was also a red flag as to his ulterior motives, for this was a married woman. It also raised alarms at to his motives in becoming a Christian too. Just what had he converted? His heart? His head? His genitals? His behaviour?

Interesting background to my next little story.

About a year or so after my eviction, Mary wrote me a personal letter. It was a while since I had heard from her, not surprisingly. Usually she addressed her occasional correspondence to both Jim and myself, but this was addressed to me alone and had my current address. I realised that Mary must have gotten it from Jim, and they must have been in contact about things after I had moved out. I was therefore a little surprised when I received a letter directly from her. But also curious and open as to what she had written. Until I actually read her missive.

I presumed in view of Jim's relationship with them, or possibly his secret penchant for her, he had written to her and told her that I had left him. Yes, that *I* was the one to leave him. And you can guess that he would have capitalised on his victim-ship and renaming his eviction as my *desertion*... This was the first that I knew about Jim spreading false stories to others overseas about me. And Joseph!

I was *amazed* at what she wrote. After her initial greetings in the usual Christian way: 'Greetings in the Lord, dearly Beloved' (yes, straight out of the Bible) I was promptly and thoroughly treated to a proper dressing down by her regarding *my* 'desertion' of Jim and the children. And of my corrupting the boys... especially Joseph. And further, *How* could I dare encourage my son to be a homosexual (his hairdressing boss was one – and what an assumption; that Jo was now one!!!)? How could I put him in the way of temptation? Not Godly. This is all of the Devil. Homo this, homo that; Rant, rant, rave, rant.

Then she really started chastising and dictating to me; *How* could I have treated Jim so badly? How could I have *deserted* Jim and the children and gone out into the world knowing the Lord as I did. How could I have these affairs with other men? *I should be down on my knees begging for God's help and forgiveness* and for *Jim's* forgiveness for what I had done. Such a lovely and precious and innocent one as Jim deserved much better treatment etc etc etc. And so I got quite an ear full, or should I say, an eye full of judgments, condemnations, accusations and criticisms. All of this unjustified condemnation from a supposed non-judgmental *Christian*. I was flabbergasted!

Naïve Hope

And insulted. And hurt. I had to reread it several times to come to grips with it.

What sort of a person, a friend, a *Christian* does that?

One who hadn't checked on the truth of any of it, who hadn't even asked me **one** thing as to *why* on earth I would do such a thing, what had happened, *what* was it that had caused the breakup... *No such thing.* Hadn't even considered there were two sides. She had made out she was my friend, but here she was condemning me so unfairly and without knowing the full facts, indeed any facts, and believing only what Jim had chosen to tell her.

I did not reply to her letter straight away. I had to think about it, and decided that the next time I visited England, I would meet up with her and put her straight. Because Joseph worked for a gay then that made him gay? Because Jim had thrown me out I had deserted him? What was up with this woman? Well, this is what happens when someone is so bloody prissy self-righteous and quick to attack others. Put-downs are the hall-mark of those who want power over another or want to think that they are better than them. Jim had done it often enough most of our life together, and now he had gone crying to someone who knew *nothing* of what he had *really* been up to and he had sneakily enlisted her in slamming me. But her letter did not shame me, nor make me want to go back to him. Quite the opposite. It proved that hypocrisy is alive and kicking in unaware Christians.

What was the outcome? Well, the next time I was in England, I phoned her to arrange to see if I could meet up with her. We made a time that suited us both and she actually sounded glad that I would be calling in. I had a hire car, and drove to see her at her home which was still in Chorlton-cum-Hardy.

As usual Mary acted elegantly and graciously, as did I. She was a bit taller than I was, but with everyone I ever saw her talk to she had a habit of smiling at you while she lifted her chin, almost like she was looking at you down her nose. Oozing charm, she usually appeared to be a kind and interested person to be around. But this time around, we had the words in her letter between us. And that same letter was in my pocket!

Greeting me at the door, she invited me in and offered me tea and cakes. But I couldn't stomach anything like that though I did accept her offer of a cup of tea.

Without much preamble I told her straight out 'I'm here because of that last letter you wrote to me, Mary. I have something I want to say to you.' She gave me an uncertain look, but asked me to continue.

'Thank you for your last letter. But I was more than disappointed with what you wrote.'

'Oh, what was that dear?' she said smiling benevolently down her nose at me to placate me. She could see that I was being very civil, but not as friendly as I used to be. She could probably feel that barrier I had set up in order to speak my piece clearly.

I pulled out the letter, and laid it out open on the table between us. I spoke to her just as calmly, quietly and piously as she had spoken to me.

With a small smile on my face, I offered her these words. 'Mary, thank you for writing me. However, I think you were operating under a misconception. You never once checked on the truth of things. You never once in your letter ask me *why* I had left Jim; what had caused me to do such a drastic thing. You just made all of these assumptions. You say you are a friend but you immediately took Jim's side of things without checking in on the facts. You just condemned me straight out. That is not what I call friendship.' Yes, this was a bit blunt, but I didn't see the point in all of the niceties and skirting around which would only make speaking the truth harder and more difficult. I wasn't setting out to hurt her deliberately, but I had to tell her to her face what I thought. I waited for her to respond.

She was quiet for a bit, digesting what I had said.

'Oh, I see' she said, eyes down. You could practically see things registering and reordering themselves in front of her eyes.

'Why do you think I would *do* such a thing? Why would I simply throw eighteen years of marriage away just like that? Do you think I am so shallow that I would just walk away because it suited me?'

Naïve Hope

She then started to realise just what had happened. She looked at me and said 'Jim told me you had left him'.

'Yes, he probably did. But did you know what he had been up to before all of that happened? Did he tell you about the things he did to me? Did you bother to ask me?' I let my words hang in the air between us. I wasn't about to tell her all of the details, but I did want to know if she had even thought about my side.

'Oh Marni, I didn't realise.' She seemed to be re-thinking about things with this revelation. And putting it together with her memories of my loyalty and devotion before we left for Australia.

Then she lifts her head again to ask me, 'But we can still be friends can't we?'

I don't think so! My thoughts flew round my head. I hadn't taken our conversation much past letting her know that there was a reason as to why things were the way they were, and it wasn't because of my 'desertion'. Truth was, if I had found the words right then, if I had thought quicker about it then, I would have launched out the following verbal missive: *'You may think you're a Christian, and you may wish to call on my forgiveness-ability in all of this, but you know what, I am 'forgived-out', I have Forgiveness Fatigue, I am empty of it in relationship to this issue. Anything more to do with Jim, there is zilch forgiveness left in the bucket. Anything to do with unfair judgments on myself, I am done with. I am having none of this. No more!'*

Mary's words hadn't been about how wrong she may have been or how hurt I had been, but were rather a smoothing over of any ruffles, an attempt to get back to how things were, of avoiding unpleasantness. In fact, she *still* hadn't really apologised for misjudging me so badly nor did she ask *now* as to *why* I had left.

Mary hadn't known that her big hero Jimmy-boy had kicked me out, and not for the first time. Nor did she know of his own unfaithful past, though for sure he would have told her about my 'affair' as he called that one time stand. Of course he would only tell her what he wanted her to know. That's part of what's called the 'Charm' in charming – C(clever) Harm! And I really didn't care anymore. I didn't need friends like that. I am done. I am ready to go. I stand up to leave and am making my way toward the door, allowing her to match my movements.

'We *can* put this behind us, can't we?' she proffered hopefully and expectantly. There is now pleading in her eyes, and regret. But still no 'I am so sorry, Marni'. Is she capable of apology, or does she just want it to be all sugary-sweet, and 'not to upset the apple cart'?

So again I reiterated 'No thanks, Mary. I don't think you and I will be seeing each other again. And I won't be in further contact. I just came to tell you directly face to face. I wish you all the best in your life. But this is Goodbye.'

She is dumb struck. She stands at the door watching after me. But I cannot give her any hope. I got to my car and took a moment to heave a huge sigh. I was a little sad. But I was also stronger because of what I had done; I had stuck up for myself and said my truth.

I can only guess that she, too, was sad. If I thought she *was* truly sad at losing me as a friend, if she had apologised even, I just might have possibly been swayed. Maybe because of what was said in that letter, I think that her over stern words, interference and *order*-ing in my affairs without knowing what was really going on, and without attempting to find out, had probably sealed it for me. It had cut the cord of friendship. And I was laying it to rest.

A true friend is different things to different people. And we can have a variety of depths of relationships with a variety of people. I know about loyalty, and I am a very loyal friend. After what I have been through with my ex-husband I do not need to hold onto people that put me down or attack me.

A misunderstanding is one thing, but condemnation is another. I have a big heart, and welcome good friendships, but not abusive ones. If someone doesn't even bother to ask me about something and then makes an attack on me, then they are no longer my friend.

Consequently, I have many acquaintances, and few real friends, but the ones I have are true.

2003 and Beyond
~ Counting The Cost ~ PTSD ~ Bloody Angry! ~ Taking a Stand ~ Healing Art

Counting The Cost

Over twenty years have passed, and Danny is living with his girlfriend, Ben is married with three children and Jo is recovering from Emphysema and PTSD. Everyone has gone their own separate way. Attempts to stay in touch always feel stilted, and I often still feel guilty for something though I don't know what it is. Feeding into my own perceptions of my inadequacy to fully protect my children from Jim, and indeed for marrying such as this person who became their father, I am carrying far more guilt and shame than is mine, far too much than is necessary.

Indeed, even though I know that this is not a truth, somehow I am still made to feel that I am to blame for most of the disintegration of the marriage and the unhappiness of my children.

The things that someone will put up with in the hope of being given love in return for the love that they offer. When one keeps giving and without reciprocation, they can eventually run-out. My love and energy battery (or energy bucket if you will) was now being trained and managed better. I was more aware of motivation. But things still weren't right.

Love is such a bandied about word.

'I love this', 'I love that', be it a TV program, a food or pleasure, or a person. Or even simply sex with that person! We have many meanings for the one word – Love – with totally different meanings and implications and results. There are other languages that are more specific in the *types* of love. Rather than digress into the many varieties that exist, I want to focus on the love I referred to earlier – the love that I so needed when I was ready to end it all at almost twenty years ago.

Yes, sure I learned about how to begin to love myself. I was learning about who I was, about how people tick, about how our family can affect us, and about how we can change things. I was learning about how to transform how we view the past, how to release old or stuck or unresolved emotions, and even how to help others.

For the last fifteen years or so I have been following my own spiritual journey through self development, reading, workshops and meditation, making sense of the world and of my own idea of God, life and of what that means to me. My desire to understand the events of my life had led me to some interesting answers. I was now qualified in certain branches of therapy, counselling and in nutritional support. I had undertaken training in the health arts and was slowly building a small part-time client base alongside part-time work at a doctor's clinic and counselling centre.

Gaining valuable insight and understanding, I was beginning to join the dots psychologically speaking, as to how I could have allowed such things to happen as had happened in my life. One therapy session gave me intimate information when I did my training in rebirthing.

I remember my birth! *I actually relived it!* That moment of struggle and pressure as I emerged from the relative safety of my mother and into a world of harsh loud sound and cold fierce air against my unprepared and sensitive skin. No welcome of tender acknowledgment for this quivering body, instead a humiliating dangling upside down followed by a detached yet vicious slap to my behind to ensure full lung capacity. A brutal introduction to life before I was plonked aside whilst the doctor attended to my mother. Face red, shaking and quaking, my choking squawks and pathetic cries of appeal for comfort and dignity went unmet whilst other matters were dealt with. Weary medicos, still snowed under with the aftermath of the returning wounded, mounting casualties from a long and bloody war, I registered low on their list of priorities. My little arms flailing and uncontrollable, freshly released from the warm confines of the womb, still wetly smeared and naked, shivering and writhing, I was thus introduced and initiated into pain and indignity. Like many war babies. The impact this had on my heart and psyche was now being dealt with.

But there were more answers for me to discover for myself.

Naïve Hope

For one would have thought that the dust had totally settled and I could put the past behind me and just get on with things. Well, actually, I was. Getting on with things. *But things aren't settled unless they are settled right,* as Agatha Christie once wrote. There was another important part of the puzzle I was still yet to deal with. And this manifested in 2003 when I could no longer hold things together and the floodgates of buried pain burst their banks. I had reached my own personal crisis, my own Critical Mass experience. There is a cost with simply 'Getting on with Life'; the body, the psyche, the heart, can store memory and cushion one for a time, but they cannot carry the burden forever. Inevitably and invariably, the physical cost must be counted and paid.

In 2000 I had ended a business project and relationship partnership at great cost to myself financially, emotionally and personally. The project had not been honestly portrayed and I had limped back to Melbourne from interstate to rebuild my life. Again. Restarting my therapy practise I thought I was on top of things. But the stress it had caused me and the lack of safe space to process and heal meant that I had buried what I couldn't yet deal with. The body and endocrine system, the nervous system, heart and emotions demanded that I now pay attention; for they were on strike...

This was when I was diagnosed with Severe Depression.

This particular day I had received yet another letter from a professional therapists association. Because I had felt so exhausted and I could hardly get out of bed, I had made a doctor's appointment, so I took it unopened along with me to read whilst I waited.

At the time I was attempting to get a Training Workshop approved by one of my professional boards and we were now over eight years down the track since my original submission. It had been easily approved (and with commendation) within weeks by a similar professional association in another State I was connected with some years earlier. I had also been teaching it for years, yet with this organization I kept meeting with opposition and delays time and time again, and even downright personal disrespect from a certain person on the board, though we had never even met.

But maybe they had finally approved the training and I would have something to celebrate about? One can only *hope*...

I was outside at the time, as the doctor was running late, so I sat in the little public garden nearby, filling in the time. I opened and read the letter.

I collapsed. It was the final straw for me that day... and that year!

I simply burst into tears. And sobbed and sobbed. And found that I couldn't stop sobbing. Previously typewritten, this supposedly professional hand written response was filled with more criticism, manufactured problems and stinging nasty comments. I felt totally defeated. My life felt like shit, I had no energy, hardly any relationship worth mentioning with my children, felt alone, and in such despair that life was beginning again to seem like not worth living. What was the point of it all?

Trying to manage after the devastation wrought by the loss of my property (through the business breakup), attempts to make ends meet and my past marital stress, my adrenals had now totally gone on strike. Kinesiology framed it as hydration and adrenal problems, with compromised kidney energy and function; kidneys are related to fears in Chinese Medicine. It was later confirmed as 'Adrenal Exhaustion'. Unsurprisingly.

I hadn't been doing anything wrong personally regarding my health; I was still tee-total, still eating reasonably healthily, not smoking, not doing drugs, still using natural supplements, not living or working in environmentally toxic surroundings, not raging or overdoing anything. But I was gaining little ground and still seemed to be in such a hard place physically, mentally and emotionally. It was going to be a while before I registered that I was actually *'burnt-out'*!

My sad and stressful history was catching up with me. The 'Turning your burdens over to the Lord' avoidance advice from going to church hadn't helped. Even dedicated sessions to unravelling old emotional issues through Kinesiology, energy healing, correct nutrition, *none* of this had managed to fix things.

Yet, how would I have coped if I hadn't done *any* of this?

My own inner spirit and desire not to deliberately intend anyone harm had also helped to keep me going, faced with all I had had to deal with? But there were so many layers still. And the buried heartbreak and pain from losing my sons that day those many years ago was still not even on my Radar Screen yet…

Here I was suffering from Severe Depression; I had trouble accepting it could not understand it. Regardless, I was prescribed anti-depressants.

Even though I knew so much more than I had ever known before, learning of this condition was a huge shock to me. It certainly explained how I was feeling. I was no longer willing to live, I could not stop crying, and had hardly any energy to get up and 'do'.

I felt that I had engaged with life and hope again, but had been somehow been beaten back. Again. I was emotionally, physically and mentally exhausted. As part of my healing, I had still yet to learn more about the adrenals and the physiological cost of chronic trauma and long-held stress. But I was limited in my understanding of this at the time. The clear solution presented was medication. I felt like an absolute failure.

How had this happened? Even though I had all these facts, I still couldn't work it out. But first I had to get help, get well. Then sort out the mess that was my life. In order that I might function again I quite literally had to *force* myself to accept the anti-depressants. Such was my natural inclination to avoid such things as chemical medications and to not rely on drugs, I had an actual sensitivity reaction to them, for which I had to be re-balanced using kinesiology; so I could take the medicine prescribed without further adverse physical or emotional reaction.

The tablets were intended to balance my huge darkness a little, and give me some sort of emotional equilibrium in order to dig into the real underlying causes of my depression. Medication deals with symptoms *only*, it does *not* necessarily deal with the causes.

Oh, and get this, the doctor told me that I would get well by 'thinking positive'.

I actually saw the case notes he was taking, when he left the room momentarily; he had actually referred to this advice on the onscreen form he filled in at the appointments as 'Gave Counselling' - *for three minutes* of ridiculous and (at the time) *impossible* advice. And he figured that telling me this was *counselling* me! I almost burst out with the cheek and incredulity of this. Then I was appalled! Well, actually I didn't have the energy to be appalled, nor to argue the facts with him. He was too ignorant - and I mean this in the sense that he really didn't have any idea of what I was going through at all, nor was he likely to - and *this* was *all* he knew. God help us!

I took the tablets, and worked ceaselessly on the issues underneath to clear as much as I could. I got through. In fact, the doctor wanted to keep me on them for quite some time, but I started to cut down on these pills by myself. Actually I started stockpiling them. Every time I visited him and he gave me a new prescription, I would get it filled, and I found that I wasn't taking them as often, but he kept prescribing them, so I kept getting them, cutting down on taking them and saving them, eventually taking myself totally off using them. I didn't dispose of them 'Just in case'. In case of what? Well, obviously, in case it came back again. And then again, it might be a cleaner way of sorting out the problem for this life instead of using a messy train line finish?

(However, when I went back to the UK in 2011 to bury mum and dad, I had to flush them all down the toilet. Ah well! No, actually, 'Just as well'!)

During the visits with the doctor he continued to tell me that to get better I had to 'think positive'. And far too soon he wanted me to *seek work* again, when the very idea of work gave me physical pain in my insides and genuinely made me want to howl and hide. Now I love working at something productive, and I am certainly not a lazy person. I like being involved. What he failed to realise that when one is in the grip of Depression, 'thinking positive' is not all that possible. Thinking properly and even the ability to think correctly is affected by this debilitating affliction. Hormonal balance needs to be fixed first, and he apparently had no idea about any of this, but at least his dispensing of the anti-depressants did bring some measure of relief. Years of taking the birth pill had certainly interfered with my endocrine system. I later learned and understood from my own experience how the brain gets somewhat 'soggy' or soaked with the wrong hormones, and forgets how to produce the good hormones, the ones that make one feel 'up' or 'good'. Anti-depressants are only good for a short time. Better solutions are needed for long term solutions. Otherwise you are somewhat of a substance user, relying on drugs to manage the symptoms without improving the real problem.

He had also failed to consider what his advice would mean in practical terms. When I had arrived back in Melbourne to restart again, I had also been racing round for several months looking for professional and corporate employment in order to create some stability to start off again. Only to be met with 'You are over qualified', 'You would be wasted in this position', 'We have been inundated with too many applicants', or even the ignorant response of no reply whatsoever. Taking one look at me and comparing a fifty-something woman with one half my age, who could have come straight from college and so require less salary or wage was the easy way out for a lot of employers who failed to recognise the wealth that experience and mature commitment can bring. Each time I got that I was in the 'too old' age group, it seemed to reinforce to my sensitive mind at the time that I was 'spent', and that the company perception was that I was approaching, indeed, was already there, at my work use-by-date. When this is actually so totally untrue as is being more quickly and readily recognised again today.

Each time I had a job knock-back, it started to feel like a physical blow. For it cost me emotionally every time I put myself out there, and it cost physically and monetarily every time I did a resume, prepared and travelled for an appointment, and was forced to follow up on those that left me dangling regarding the position. And the mental frustration at feeling that one was being cast aside was repeated each time I applied and failed to get a job.

And here this doctor was telling me within a short period of medication and as part of my recovery to start *looking* for work again. If it was just looking, that could be hard enough, but *not getting* for me at that time and in that condition was simply devastating. Not the best advice if you're serious about me getting well again, Doc!

Here *he* is, in a well paid and secure job, not really knowing or understanding about this disability. However, the hard fact was, and upset as I was about it, I had to get over my annoyance at his ignorance and just focus on getting better. So what did I already know, however small, about all this, and what could I learn?

PTSD

In the years following working in the advertising and building sectors, I had explored health solutions. During my therapy trainings and studies I had been taught about how emotion can affect the body, about how experiences and events can cause trauma that can impact on us emotionally, mentally, physically and even spiritually. I had been working on some of what I had come to recognise as 'my issues', but I had not yet understood about the damage caused by long-term stress or Post Traumatic Stress Disorder (PTSD) on the body; on *my* body.

What had happened many years ago in my marriage and my childhood had been dealt with *in part* by my mind and emotions. But not my body. The cost on my Nervous System was now up for payment. Going through Menopause had exacerbated the situation and shifted the balance, and what had only *just* been working could now no longer cope; and now showed signs that it was indeed broken. Sweats, whether it was hot or cold, could be triggered at the slightest perceived threat and was one of the long term results of the traumas I had endured. I had not realised how affected my adrenals were by the stress-response reactions that I had experienced time after time after time.

I could not share anything of this with my sons, knowing that they had their own battles to fight. And boys are usually less open to discussing these things than women are, so I felt quite cut off regarding family, too. Even soldiers in battle got time off and had 'leave'. During the First World War, it was recognised just how battle could affect soldiers, whether or not they were physically wounded. After the war, many wounded or damaged soldiers were sent away to recuperate. The opportunity for those who wished to share and unburden themselves was often provided, but and as well as, (and more importantly) they were given peace, space, time, sun, good food, nurturing or nursing, and a good dose of understanding. I remember a neighbour in Benchill who had lost an arm and also had burn scars on his face. He was pensioned-off but had received intensive healing care, and also nurturing to recover from the shock, loss and trauma suffered. Then he was more able to partake in 'normal' life and activities. In his case, most of his scars were visible. Not all scars are.

Gradually over the following years I eventually put together what had happened to bring this debilitating illness about for me personally. Depression can grip anyone through a variety of causes and issues, often peculiar to the individual and their circumstances. Recognition had taken this long a time because not one person actually had been able to give me the whole picture in my case. Not one person had *known* or recognised the whole picture until it had become so obvious. Along the way to finding solutions, I had been made aware of (and dealt with) other issues such as a problem called Candida overgrowth, which gave rise to some sensitivities. Another issue had been IBS – Irritable Bowel Syndrome – sometimes called Leaky Gut. These issues, though manageable, often caused a drop in energy due to the fact that the body couldn't fully absorb all the nutrition it was being given. Waste of money, waste of energy.

With the Depression diagnosis I had a different angle to work with. These symptoms *compelled* me to pay attention; I was in real trouble and knew that I needed help. I had been addressing my symptoms via the various separate ailments that had individually manifested, but the body was still holding a lot of emotional stress and memory and had not had the wherewithal to resolve these – in short I had sustained a lot of hurt and harm. And I hadn't really known about it, just struggled to get on with life. Now I did.

Knowing about something is one thing, fixing it is another.

It also seemed that my whole life as it had been now came to an abrupt halt, and everything had to be not only rescued and repaired but re-organised, re-viewed, refurbished, redefined, re-valued. Physically, emotionally, mentally, spiritually. But life is about change anyway. Nothing is more constant than the fact of change, for nothing, nothing ever stays the same. Does this fact help? Only in that there is the possibility of change *from* this situation.

Taking the medications I continued to appraise my life and recognise issues, issues that had driven me to be in such a bad way. I realised that the anti-depressant tablets would help settle my emotional roller coaster and curb my fraught tears, but they were only tackling the *symptoms*, they were not dealing with the *causes*. As part of my recovery, I was working on several levels. Costly in some ways yes, but I was investing in my health, my well-being, my future. Using a variety of techniques based on natural methods and techniques and seeing a counsellor, each of these had a positive impact and assisted toward my recovery: we were working on several levels; the mental, the physical and the emotional for each was interlinked with the other. Indeed if I hadn't been pursuing these things, I dread to think how I would have coped, because it had helped keep some of the darker aspects of depression at bay.

Through my professional counsellor, Winsome, who did so much more than simply listen, I was able to grasp the role I had been assigned and undertaken from my family of origin – my parents and siblings. Thoughts and roles that had been collected as a child now had to be addressed, as these were no longer supporting me. Growing up too quickly in order to act as the mother in the family and also be the buffer for the other children was recognised. The peace-maker who recognised unfairness, but who wasn't recognised for herself was acknowledged.

Working through this and more with Winsome I could also see the dynamics in my marriage that had mirrored some of this transference if you like. This included the brutality that I had suffered, though she never actually used that term. It also became clear that I had been afforded little autonomy, and little support, and again, the lesson that I already knew about; that I had not obtained the love that I had needed and wanted. I had to learn more about self-love.

I was also learning more about hormonal imbalance in the Endocrine System. I was now post-Menopausal and life on that level was still a kind of hell. A vital part of my recovery was to discover that the adrenals play a huge part during and after Menopause.

If the adrenals have been compromised and exhausted, then they are not able to take over as effectively as they might have been expected to. Women with healthy adrenals may well experience some effects of menopause, such as sweats, flushes etc. But when the adrenals have been seriously compromised because of severe shock or trauma, or because of chronic or long-term sustained stress without reprieve, then they simply just don't cope. And this will affect *everything* in the body. The body will be attempting to deal with huge amounts of cortisol still held in the body and tissues, the adrenals and hypothalamus will have problems in switching 'on' or 'off' and may be totally confused, which affects energy, sleep, hormones, metabolism, and a whole raft of other things. Even fluid retention and surprisingly the ability to think!

Long-term use of the birth pill without proper studies led to no real understanding that it compromises the hormonal gland's abilities to supply the correct hormones; and I had been taking these for almost ten years after Ben! My hormones were really messed up. I think that gives you an idea as to what it was like waking up in my mid-fifties to discover such an affliction. My body could barely just keep it together, but going through menopause had created a further stress on the body. When this was accompanied by other stresses without a real rest and recovery phase, then the adrenals had just simply 'given up'. Now the only way that I could fix this was to begin to work with my adrenals. Clearing the adrenals of stress and trauma by using complementary or natural therapies was assisting in releasing the memories held in the cells, but even this was also causing further stress on the adrenals through this forced change processes. For change requires energy to complete. So back to the nutritional side of things again to support this part of the process. Along the way it became clear that according to Chinese Medicine, I had very low Yin and very low Yang in Kidneys and Adrenals; negligible functionality. The adrenals can be likened to the starting motor in a car. If that is stuffed up, then nothing starts.

Did it ever end? This cataloguing of problems? Yes. Eventually. It took a long time for me to get into this state, and it took a long time to reverse the harm and the damage.

And part of this was impacted on with what happened even *before* I was born; mother smoking, faulty and ignorant nutrition and lack of peace, support and nurturing. (We're not even talking about the impact from the bombings.) This lack of proper nutrition had continued after birth with restricted food supplies (rations), lack of proper care, anti-biotic course after anti-biotic course to combat tonsillitis and bronchitis when maybe some heating, warm blankets and nourishing soups and good protein would have assisted.

The impact on my health had resulted in early loss of teeth, anaemia, bouts of tonsillitis and bronchitis, and had contributed to some of my eventual Adrenal Exhaustion. However in truth regarding my teeth, periodontal diseases and gum bacteria was not really recognised back then, and so no dentist bothered looking further than merely filling in or ripping out for many years.

But... I also remember that dad was *not* averse to a horsey and greyhound betting habit.

Indeed, my English cousins shared their own memories on one of my UK Trip; mum and dad were very fond of impressing others by buying drinks at the local pub and living a bit above themselves when out socialising. Yet holes in the soles of our shoes was common, and wearing wet socks practically normal. I ask myself; how can one justify not getting proper dental care or providing appropriate warmth for your children and instead put a regular night out singing, dancing, dining and drinking above them? I just didn't get it, but I certainly saw it! Though as a child it was naturally beyond me to understand the mechanics of domestic finances and budgets, I had no other choice but to accept what was meted out. Or not!

It had become my nature to accept so I did.

Part of my recovery journey was to unearth this, to *re*-member what had been *dis*-membered from me, what had been buried away by me in the hope that forgetting made it other than it had actually been. But my psyche bore the neglect, my mind and subconscious had been scarred with the de-valuation that had taken place, my heart affected by the emotional and nutritional abandoning, my body reaped the harvest of poor nutrition, my Being imprinted with small-minded and self-centred people who I looked up to as being smart heroes and heroines. This surely explained some of the later aspects of my life, and my own journey and reclamation of self-recognition, self-recovery, self-worth. At least until I reclaimed them. For clear and claim them I must if I was not to remain a victim for the rest of my days!

Bloody Angry!!

One of the most significant discoveries that I learned in these journeying was that Depression can be a result from Suppressed or Repressed Anger – an *Anger which has been turned against one's own self...*

But I wasn't the angry one!

Was I?

Living in fear of someone can create a form of repressed anger. Not only that, when someone vents their own heavily charged emotions at someone else who is sensitive (like myself) they can very well end up absorbing those same emotions. They may become a dumping ground for the projected energy of anger. On top of the many childhood injustices that I had suffered, and the angers from others that I had absorbed, Jim had also been piling his wrath and outrage into me. That is a *lot* of anger to manage, and because I was so fearful of him, this effectively kept the lid down on it. But there comes a time when this old, buried, repressed anger must be dealt with to remain healthy, or at the least, sane.

And *Depression can be anger turned in on the self.* Woah! Not me. This wasn't me, surely? What am *I* angry about?

Then I got it; anger at the injustice of how I had been hurt and betrayed, anger that I and others had been so cruelly treated, anger that I hadn't gotten out of it sooner, anger that people got away with what they got away with, anger that I hadn't done it different, anger that I had put up with it for so long yet things still hadn't changed, and anger that God had let me down. Yep, there it was! Anger at Him. Interesting discovery.

Now I had to learn to deal with all of this and with these angers for they had also blocked the flow of energy in my body, bringing inflammation and pain. But anger was such a scary thing. It had frightened me since the first time I saw and felt it from others. I tried not to get angry myself, hiding it away and doing the forgiving and Christian bit. But I hadn't actually dealt with such a vital emotion, nor learned how to handle it correctly! That was before I read Alice Miller's *'The Drama of the Gifted Child'* or the books by Harriet G Lerner such as *'Dance of Anger'*.

I also came to understand that anger can actually be a positive emotion, but only when one uses and channels it into a positive outlet; such as a little old lady getting angry with some young pup who tries to mug her, only to come off the worse as grannies handbag is smashed over his ears... or the mother daring to attack a burly man who is beating or threatening her small child... The anger has, in this instance, been converted into positive action... The energy of anger can say; *'Something about this needs to change. Here I am, now use me to change this situation...'*

I recalled my self-development exercises and courses in the late 1980's and realised that I had still more work to do. One of the things they taught was to dare to allow oneself to feel the anger that you held toward someone or something, and then to channel it into something harmless, like beating the hiding out of a mattress or pillow. I always felt rejuvenated after the initial exertion with this one, ending up releasing this anger and feeling lighter in myself. It also seemed to energise me after the initial effort. And I hadn't hurt anyone! Another exercise was to do some Bodywork, which allowed the blocked energy in the body, particularly the thighs, to be released. Kick-boxing is a great one, as is Tai Chi, which can help to bring flow back into a more aware body.

Expressing anger can help to release it, as long as one doesn't dwell on it for too long, as anger energy sometimes seems to *beget* anger; the anger never seems to stop... We have all met that person who just cannot seem to stop being angry. It's important to learn how much anger one needs to release to carry on with one's own life in a more positive way. And to learn to channel the energy positively. I found several safe ways of releasing the charge around anger issues, and just as well, for the stress of carrying that old anger around without harming someone (do unto others etc...) can take a heavy toll on one's health and well-being. Not to mention their capacity for peace.

Fortunately for Jim, I never did erupt and pour all of his anger right back at him... Who knows what I would have done?

I still use one of the exercises I learned about if I feel really angry about something. Now armed with my knowledge of the adrenals, my history, my therapies, anger exercises, counselling support, and my persistence to reclaim who I was, I continued my journey of self-healing and self-restoration. And that was about it. Now I embark on Chinese herbs to alleviate the symptoms and rebuild these organs and glands again. But this does take time. I learned not to do this by myself, as taking the wrong herbs can be harmful, and taking singular herbs does not work effectively as each of the organs and systems in the body works in concert with others, and not as an isolated unit.

And within weeks I started to feel the difference.

And I continue to work on my personal worth and issues, releasing as I discover or rather, *un*-cover the old memories.

After nine months or so of starting on the anti-depressants, I was already reducing my medication and weaning myself off. I could face the idea of work again and had started being productive again as things had begun to shift and change again in my life. Soon I was able to actually and actively 'Think Positive' and to dare to see a future again. I was able to return to my therapy work, taking further studies in natural therapies and counselling whilst also adding this experience to my growing and hard-earned knowledge.

Life felt like it was accelerating, and things appeared to be happening quicker and quicker.

Taking a Stand

At Ben's Officer Graduation Ceremony in 2004, I came to realize that I could not stand to be near Jim or to be in his presence. Too much had happened, too much had been left unresolved and yet here he was, as though absolutely *nothing* was wrong or ever had been wrong. He was all charm and politeness and it felt he was expecting me to comply again. In fact on first seeing me, he acted like an overeager puppy, almost as though I had wronged him yet he was all too willing to prove a point to be nice about it all. He pretended that everything was just fine, that nothing had ever happened on his part, and that we had parted on an amicable note. Like heck! His whole attitude I read as an act to make me look wrong, I could feel his insincerity, I knew it well – the spider to the fly. I was not going to be held in the place he wanted me to be by social dictates. He had used that emotional blackmailing often enough in the past, bugger if I will pretend he is anything other than he is. Forget that, bud!

As a 'family' we got through the ceremony without any embarrassment – I wasn't uncivil, deliberately rude or provocative, I just simply pretended that he wasn't there and acted that way. I refused to speak to him unless absolutely essential, and in fact at one point totally ignored his attempt to engage in conversation. The boys couldn't understand it, I daresay, but I couldn't help myself. Too much had been pushed down, too much hurt and harm absorbed from him. Simply saying forgive and forget just didn't cut it.

Though this didn't help or move us forward to any resolution of any sort, it was also clear that he certainly wasn't going to make any moves to sort out anything with me and most likely he still worked on the premise 'Pretend it isn't there or it hasn't happened – and it will be all right.' It took another four years for me to realize I simply had to face him with this, with the past, for he certainly wasn't going to address any of it. But right then, I had to deal with how I felt and realize that I was not yet over his treatment and abuse of me or his children.

Momentum on this was building again.

HEALING ART

By 2005, in other ways, I had turned yet another corner.

Naïve Hope

As I began to reclaim my life, I began to reclaim my own self worth. By now I had set up my own clinic again, and had placed a couple of decorative pictures up on the walls, but it still didn't really feel right. I felt that I needed to put my own mark, my own signature, on the walls, and that I needed real colour in my space. When I priced the paintings and pictures I liked, the cost was way beyond my reach.

It was also occurring to me that I had to redress having been denied certain opportunities regarding artwork. I decided that I needed something that I had painted myself on my wall. For some reason I fancied that I could do as well as some of the pictures I had come across and I began to wonder if I really could. I had always been interested in art, as you are already aware, having done well at it at school. But as I had been discouraged in pursuing it, I felt in some way a bit conflicted about it all; did I still possess any ability? I hadn't done anything arty since school, except to sew curtains and knit. Would any real art work I did be good enough? Was it too late to try it, to enjoy it?

As part of my ongoing self discovery, I did a short term course of a few weeks at a watercolour night class. I felt unsure of the sorts of paints that I could make work for me, as school days were a distant memory. So I thought watercolour was a good way to start. The teacher was very educative, and had many little tips to share.

I found myself itching to do some artwork for my lounge or clinic practise room, something that inspired or lifted me, or indeed that simply 'felt' like me. So I decided to take the plunge and buy some paints and a canvas in order to put some colour into my life. It needed to be paints and not watercolours, as I still wasn't sure about this mysterious medium. Though that changed years later. At the time. It was hit and miss at first, but when I got the canvas, after more time and some experimenting I came up with what I wanted on it.

And that was the start. Sure, it took me a while to work out how the paint actually worked. At first it was too thin as I had added some water. Then I found that for some things you needed to apply the acrylic paint neat from the tube. I chose acrylic over oils because I had read of the toxic side effects of painting with oil paints. Having had some sensitive reactions to certain substances, I took this into consideration. Just in case. I then did a framing course, and framed the painting. I was so pleased with my efforts that I could feel more self confidence growing. And I realised that I actually enjoyed painting. Ok, so not all of my creative endeavours were as successful as this one, and indeed this first painting took a few goes to get right. But I learned heaps. And got braver.

This was a revelation to me. Why not do another artwork piece?

It was just a matter of time for ideas to begin flowing through my brain. So many that I went a little drunk with it all I think. For a period of time, over a year, I found myself painting every spare minute. Not being in a relationship at the time, I could stay up till 2am 'just to finish this bit' and not have anyone but myself complain about it. And so it was that I amassed quite a few paintings, and then a series of paintings. I hung some on the clinic and my lounge room walls, put some in the hall, and even had one in the toilet. I was exploring me! And having fun!

My walls were becoming alive and my rented residence really felt like 'my space' now.

Clients in my clinic started commenting, even asking if they were for sale and then actually buying some. And so I decided to hold an exhibition. In 2006 I held my first art exhibition. By this time I had painted around a hundred paintings. I sold quite a few but that is another story. I had reclaimed something. I had made peace with that part of myself.

Though I did not make my fortune, this was a huge success and a personal victory. I knew more about me and more importantly I had reclaimed something that had been denied me.

I was satisfied!

2008

~ *Fall-Out*

FALL-OUT

Time moves on. It is now 2008

Over the years, my relationships with my sons continued to be somewhat stilted. Unfortunately, yet understandably, I sometimes took what I felt as a lack of ease with communication and availability as a personal slight toward myself. Though they may not wish to look at it, it is my conviction that they still believe on some level of their being that I walked out on them. Eventually I learned, or in some cases came to realise, that they were boys. That is, that men do not communicate in the same way as women, nor as daughters and mothers do. Ok, so I accept that. But I also felt that there was more to it than that. I had said very clearly to each of them that if they ever wanted to know anything from me about family history, about past events, about *anything* that happened during or after the marriage, that I would *always* be there and be available to talk to them about it. They could ask me anything and I would answer.

This of course never happened. Their lack to question what had happened could simply or possibly be because they are guys and don't want to chew over the past but just get on with it. And also the failure to recognise when something truly is broken. Daughters may well be quite different with regard to this. Also my boys still may well be unresolved about certain things or have loyalty issues. Whatever. Simply because they haven't gone into things yet doesn't mean that they won't. Leastways, that is what I hope. But there is no guarantee about that.

I know that they were all influenced by their father and by the events that happened during and after the marriage. If something happens to me, how will they know what the truth is? If I die before they are ready to look at how the past influenced them in any way and without my telling them, how can they possibly know or access other than what their father would insist on that had happened? Or more importantly, how can they ask what their father has drunkenly and conveniently forgotten? Sure some men don't always want to know the nitty-gritty of things, especially if they have no way of fixing them. And they may well see women as making more of something than it is. But knowing what I know now, and of how repressed and denied events, feelings, buried emotions, trauma and experiences can all get locked into the body and affect a person, and that dealing with these things allows the body to get healthier again, then I am remiss if I do not at least make available to them as a parent those things that I do know and can remember.

This then became a major reason for me to write down my story.

There is so much illness and disease (or should I say dis-ease) in the world today that is often caused by locked and blocked emotion. Emotion after all is only energy. It is the signalling from and through the body on certain situations, events, experiences, warnings and pleasures. It lets us know if something is good or beneficial or if it is otherwise. This is a very simplistic way of explaining it, but you will get the idea. People have recovered from serious illness when they have addressed not just the body, but also the mind and the emotions. We are very complicated beings. The body works so well for us, performs so many amazing processes, and many of them simultaneously. We can often forget what the body is doing in order to get on with something that occupies our mind, our hearts or our feelings. We can force it to do things for us and it will do it. But we can't do this indefinitely. We cannot separate the body entirely from other parts of the being.

There were many causes for my Severe Depression and Acute Adrenal Exhaustion. It could have been worse for me... If I had not been addressing my health I could have been seriously ill. The fact that I didn't smoke, drink or take substances certainly has helped too. My main addiction had been (dare I say it?)... religion? Well, that is if you don't count chocolate! However by this time I have had some rumblings of ill-health, and there have been times when I have been under intense stress. As it was, in 2008, stress in my life had escalated through family issues back in the UK. The tale of my 'minister' sister, who I now publicly divorce as being no sister of mine, is one of theft and fraud. She actually robbed our parents of

Naïve Hope

all their money; raiding their bank accounts and stealing cash from their house, taking everything she could from them the moment they were both incapacitated in hospital together. And even doing so on Christmas Day! I spent many night (and day) hours with other overseas family members by phone and email trying to bring transparency to the situation, as well as doing online research and phoning and shooting emails off to the relevant legal and health authorities to follow-up and resolve these nasty dirty deeds done by this parasite. The sense of helplessness I had felt at protecting mum and dad had seen me devote many sleepless nights to addressing this. I even flew over to visit my parents (and other siblings in the UK) for their birthdays and to support and protect them under these stressful circumstances.

But my year was not yet done.

Arriving back, within a month Danny phoned me unexpectedly. I lived a matter of six minutes away from Danny and his partner's place. He had rung me out of the blue and asked how I was. I was fine, and said that I had been planning to do my shopping. I didn't get to spend as much time with him and the grandchildren as I know was possible, but that was him choice, not mine. I often had to wait for Danny to return calls or to phone me. I was a bit fed up with waiting disappointedly, and so I was ready to be a bit flippant with him and to make him call back when I had more time to speak with him. But then I thought *he doesn't often phone me, in fact he rarely phones me, is everything all right?*

'Is everything okay Daniel?' I asked.

He responded 'Actually, no, mum. Not feeling too well at the moment.'

Now Danny *never* ever complains about how he feels. He usually just goes quiet and into his 'cave'. This was new. I felt a distress flag waving and pressed him further. 'Why, what's happening? What's going on?'

'I was wondering if you could take me to the hospital or the doctors, mum.' He didn't sound well now, even though I could hear he was trying to maintain control with his voice, almost as though his jaw was quite tight or his teeth were being gritted together.

Now this was sounding serious. 'But if you're going out, I will sort something else out' he continues.

'What, no of course you won't. I will be over right away, give me a couple of minutes to grab my things, I will be there in five minutes,' and I was already gathering purse, bag and keys and checking how to make my quickest exit. When I got there, he was grey, perspiring heavily and doubled up. I found it hard to believe he looked so unwell. Usually appearing reasonably unflappable or generally acting as though things were together, even when they may not be, I could easily see something was seriously wrong. Soaked and sweating such a cold sweat, I was getting really concerned. I had already nursed him through a serious New Year's Eve King-Hit attack which had required a further transfusion of five pints of blood, and I again felt this was just as serious if not more so. I don't know how long he had put up with the pain and the discomforts, but I got him to emergency hospital immediately and waited along with him, continually checking until Triage was available and staying until they told me to leave. He was immediately admitted into intensive care and I stayed around til Melinda, his partner, arrived. As only one relative was allowed, I naturally let her take over.

Danny was in the intensive unit for two long weeks, with tubes inserted into various body parts, heavily monitored whilst he did some repairing and detoxification from alcohol. During the time he was there, he had a code blue, which means that his heart stopped and he technically died. Fortunately, he was brought back and was in hospital for over five weeks further, being moved out only because of lack of beds.

In summation of my discovery of the some of the events that had led up to all this, various things now emerged. He had taken to binge drinking at weekends, and I feel this was in order to lock down feeling painful things he had experienced. Things that had happened to him at home after I had left also slipped out during his hallucinations and treatment. I was stunned, then shocked, then angry, and I was ready to visit his father and tear his hair out right

Naïve Hope

there and then. I eventually learned that Jim, despite his professed love of his son, had really psychologically messed with him. The only incident I was clearly told about was the time that his father placed a knife in Danny's hand, and Jim had pressed the sharp point against his own body begging Danny to kill him, to end it all for him, even pushing Danny's hand in against his body. What father would do that? Who could seriously do that and claim sanity?

And more importantly; What on earth could that do to a person?

Then another time came to mind. Danny had insisted on travelling to Adelaide together with his friends in a car, and both Jim and myself had expressed concern. I could not override my son's decision to go as he was eighteen and now old enough to make his own mind up; and this was his desire. Jim disagreed with me, but I could not help that, as I didn't go against him simply to go against him, but because I had no power to stop my son who was well old enough to decide; and I had to trust that he could take care of himself. Most young men have similar adventures, and after you give them the warnings etc, then you have to support their choices, don't you? Well, that's how I thought it should be. I only asked that Danny keep in touch with both us, his parents.

Imagine how I felt when two days later I got a call from Jim, telling me that Dan had been injured and was in hospital. Giving me some sketchy details of him falling out of a moving car whilst en route to Perth from Adelaide, Jim wouldn't tell me which hospital he was in, nor how injured he was. *He point blank refused.* Whilst I was trying to work out why he would do this, he then tells me that he has a message for me from Danny. So I ask him what the message was. I still had no idea what state Danny was in, or how badly he was hurt, and feared the worst, as mothers can be apt to do sometimes.

Once he had my undivided attention, his response was *'I'm not telling you'*, and with that he put the phone down!

I don't know if you can get the way I felt with this. I did not know *how* my son was, *where* he was, *what* he had wanted to say to me, or *why* Jim should be like this still. He could have been at death's door for all I knew. And here was Jim playing games again. This is the sort of man I had married and had borne three children to, and he treated me like that. Still.

And I still don't know to this day the actual facts around all of this, only that Danny was injured. Nor what messages Jim may have communicated to Danny regarding my interest in his accident. Danny is never communicative at the best of times and doesn't say much about things that affect him deeply. So I still don't know what went down then.

This silence on the past, this avoidance to deal with issues and to move on wasn't discouraged by Jim. Rather the past, or his version of it, had been and continued to be used by him as a punishment, as an excuse, or as a kind of proof of his stance or his suspicions. Truth and reality had little to do with it. But my boys were following down the same path. And he was doing nothing to correct this.

I understand that the male of the species likes to go into his 'cave' and muse or mull over things until they find solutions, and until they *do* find solutions they may not take action. I get that. But this disrespect, this lack of giving *both* sides a fair hearing, the posture of blame without looking at their own failings with life and those close to them, is just so bloody cheeky and stupid that one just has to give voice in some way to initiate change in this deadlock status quo. I guess in retrospect this is also just another example of the poison in this man's mind.

I know parents are not always blameless and mess up. But this game with Danny and the knife was above and beyond in my eyes. For my own part, I once told my oldest son that I had had enough, and that I was contemplating suicide. Yes, I actually did that. I cannot believe that I did such a mindless or cruel thing, but I must also be honest and face up to my own acts and sins here. All I can say in my own defence, if indeed I can defend myself in this, is that I was not thinking straight at the time. The fact that I had no-one else to turn to does not excuse me. One could say that at least I didn't ask any of my sons to do the job for me! But it still must have had a huge impact!

However, the mother in me rose to the surface on top of all the outrage and sense of injustice I had experienced during my

Naïve Hope

marriage and subsequent divorce. When I learned of what Jim had done to Danny, of how his past actions when I was not there to protect him had impacted on him, I so hated that man right then and there. For *here* was real proof of what his damaging behaviour had done to his own children. This wasn't about just me, though it reignited some of those buried emotions of inhumanity, disrespect, brutalisation and abuse, and I just wanted to make him suffer like his son had. And I had. Danny would carry the scars from his dance with Death for a while but at least he could no longer live in denial of what he had been doing to himself with his binge drinking as a consequence of the past, and he could now begin a healthier way of life. His pancreas had not only shut down, but was damaged beyond repair. But he came out of it, he survived. As I visited daily and even twice a day, my life was pretty much focused on all of this. The social worker could see my incense and intervened, advising me not to tackle my ex-husband on these things, as he recognised part of what had been happening. But he didn't really know all that had gone before, nor was I going to tell him. I was just so glad to help get Danny back to his home again. We grew a bit closer through this and he would soon be returning the favour.

For my year was still not yet over.

That same year within months, I was admitted for an emergency operation to have my gall bladder removed. The bitterness in the lives of those around me and my sense of gall at the injustices I had seen had taken their toll. I was taken ill interstate whilst attending a work related seminar, and was lucky to make it back by plane from Sydney to Melbourne safely, as flying could exacerbate my condition. And of course, Danny visited me during my all too brief stay in the ward, bless him. Even though he was making major adjustments health-wise in his own life, he collected me from hospital and took me home afterwards.

This was a major year for me. I had really seen some of the dynamics and results of my own dysfunctional family of origin back in the UK, as well as the physical and psychological result of abuse suffered in my own family by my youngest son.

2011 - THIRTY YEARS LATER

*~ Facing the Snake in His Den ~ Cover Letter ~ The Letter To Jim
~ 'Things I Want To Say To Jim' ~ The Response
~ Message to My Boys ~ Ben: An Apology ~ Ben's Response
~ Let Me Say*

FACING THE SNAKE IN HIS DEN

Several times over the years I had felt compelled to speak directly with Jim – to beard this particular spineless lion – or Snake - in his own home. As different hints and bits of stories escaped from my boys, I had impulses to challenge him about his past and even his recent acts and behaviours, but had always thought it better not to 'stir-up stuff'. I had felt such rage toward him that I realized had I responded right then and there, that I might possibly act in anger toward him. My anger was not yet fully resolved, and maybe I had to take actual action to rectify my past feelings of helplessness and pain...

I felt quite fired up particularly in view of reports about him still getting drunk and then phoning and abusing my sons and their partners even until relatively recent times. It was quite obvious that not only had *I* suffered, but also that his bad, inappropriate and troublesome behavior was still being visited on the boys long after I had left the family home. No one would really tell me straight about things, but I was also hearing what was not being said – and putting things together... Were they protecting him, or themselves? Or was it all just too much, too hard for them to know where to begin or even what to do?

Still I was torn with how to approach this; I didn't want to let things just slide, but I also didn't want to make any more waves that would be redirected to the boys and cause them any further concerns or upsets. I knew by now that Jim was a coward and that he wouldn't or couldn't face or communicate with me directly, and I realised that it was a next 'natural' step for him to take his upsets out on the boys.

Naïve Hope

After being bitten enough times, I had finally learned and had consequently chosen to have *no* contact whatsoever with him, and to avoid anything connected with him. Hard when you have children that may be troubled by loyalty issues and who just don't understand *how* unscrupulous and devious their own father could be.

But after Ben's Graduation ceremony experience, then Danny's serious illness, I found that the angers were reignited again and yet still I had to keep pushing it down to maintain peace in consideration of the fragility of everyone around. But I couldn't keep this up. The situation with my sons, in particular with Danny's serious hospitalization, had forced me to really *look* at what was still happening – and that it had been and was still affecting my health in a toxic way.

This time my anger won. It would not go away. It now felt like it was time to speak with him, to face and confront him, to demand explanations or acknowledgement from him.

I worked through this anger to a place of choosing to take the very next opportunity that presented itself to challenge him, not punish or attack him, but ask for *reasons why* his past behaviors in an attempt to understand *why* and *how* someone can treat another so badly and so unjustly.

In retrospect, I don't know if what I did was a wise thing or not. I may never know. It had to be done, though. All I do know now, based on his continuing behavior, (even after my visit to him that I share with you next) is that it is doubtful if this man will *ever* be able to change.

I had learned through personal experience over the years since our separation and divorce that every time, *every single time*, I had extended a hand of friendship or co-operation, he had drawn me in with charm and a pretence at cooperation only to strike with venom where it could hurt the most. As the basically straightforward type of person that I am, somehow it was still not conceivable to me that someone would continue to act this way. Would there always be hidden traps laid to await an ambush-opportune moment on me? Nor could I understand why such lack of consideration was given as to whether or not it would hurt anyone else besides myself, either.

But if I could speak to him, what would I say? What was it I really wanted from him? I needed answers; I simply could not understand how and why someone would treat someone else so abominably, particularly without provocation or retaliation. I had to at least know the answers to this, even if there was no apology forthcoming.

How fortuitous that an opportunity presented itself quite unexpectedly. A close girlfriend who had been interstate was visiting my home city on that coming Friday and we were planning to catch up over the few days she would be here. When she arrived in Melbourne, she phoned to say her plans for our Sunday afternoon get-together had changed. On the last minute her plans now included a detour to Werribee where her grandson lived; she was also now able to visit him and he was living within a couple of kilometers of my ex-husband's home. She asked if I wanted to come along to Werribee with her.

Things suddenly fell into place. This was the *perfect* opportunity. When I ran my idea past her of visiting my ex at the same time as she visited her grandson, she readily agreed it was a really good idea in light of what she had seen me dealing with over the years. She was willing to drive me down there, drop herself off at her grandchildren's, let me take the car to see my ex, then I would pick her up again after. She knew what I had suffered and some of the torment I had felt, and she was more than capable of supporting me through any consequential emotional fall-out.

Working with clients on the Saturday, I quickly wrote out my letter to my ex on that Sunday morning with my questions. Things that I had pushed down in order to survive and that had continued to plague me for over thirty years. I had been attempting to patch my life up bit by bit all along, and now just maybe I could fill in some of those blank areas... As an afterthought, I quickly typed a covering letter, just in case he could no longer read or he wasn't at home.

This all happened so very quickly over that weekend, and so perfectly - I had been wondering for some time how I could resolve these issues and here was a way. When it's the right time and place, then things flow, don't they?

Naïve Hope

My friend and I both travelled down to the suburb that afternoon.

When I arrived in the area, it was a bit like going down memory lane. Driving through the once familiar streets yet feeling so strange and dis-connected from them somehow. For memories of loving my boys and taking care of them were mixed and contaminated with memories of what this man had put me through. Instead of it making me uncomfortable, though, I felt even more resolve. It felt like the right time. The house itself looked a bit knocked about and uncared for. But that was to be expected as he was now a man who was often in a wheelchair for he was recovering from a stroke a year or so earlier. The street was quiet and calm. I gathered myself, but I was ready to see him face to face again. It was time. It felt inevitable.

I knocked on his door and he opened it.

'Hello Marni' he slowly lisped. He was a tired old man in a dressing gown in the middle of the day, and appeared to have difficulty in talking or moving fast. His movements and speech were measured.

'Hello' I responded. I felt no fear and felt calm and in control of my situation. Not because he was in any way debilitated, but because I had worked through so much of my fear, and was now seeking to resolve what remained; my anger and my confusion as to why. I told him I had come to see him because I had something to ask him. I took note of the changes over the years, and of his current obvious lack of threat and bluster. But he always was a master of charm.

Standing outside the front door I am holding my letter to him in my hand. Explaining my presence, I tell him I had written him a letter but thought it better to give it to him direct. Somewhat chubbier than he used to be, as indeed I myself was no longer as slim as I used to be anymore, we had both aged to some degree. I wasn't sure of his vision capabilities, so I indicated that I was happy to read the letter to him, or simply to give it to him. He then invited me in, and as I still felt calm with the situation I accepted. Also it felt a mite better than delivering the letter out loud to him at the door if he couldn't read, for I didn't really know how the stroke had affected him.

He let me in reasonably graciously under the circumstances, though more likely he may just have simply been quiet and subdued, unsure as to what I was going to say or do. I must confess that I was a bit surprised to see a bed in the lounge room together with a motorised wheelchair and a table full of tablets and medications placed near a couch. Jim asked if I would like to sit down, so I chose a chair that didn't look or feel too uncomfortable – this was his home now – and he offered me a cup of tea, which I declined.

I felt no anger, no angst, no anxiety – I was together and I was ready. I did not berate him, I did not raise my voice, I did not threaten him, I did not stand over him. I was polite, calm, reasonable, sensible and honest. Pulling out the letter from its envelope, I read out my letter to him... at his request.

Through it I asked him why, why, why had he treated me so badly... I simply wanted answers, I needed to know – Why?

Along with this I had typed a covering letter in case he wasn't at home, which I also gave to him, and these are the exact words I gave him (pasted and copied here):

COVER LETTER

Jim Moran.

16.1.2011

Jim, I write this letter to you in case I do not catch you in.

When Daniel nearly died in hospital, I was so angry with you I nearly came round to see you and deal with you personally. The fact that I am no longer afraid of you would have been unsettling for you, and the fact that you are in a wheelchair would have been downright scary for you for a change, because I would have the upper hand physically. What you might call, a 'reverse situation' eh?

I did not visit you because I did not want to cause any more trouble for the boys. But in view of reports I have had over the years, and continue to have of your atrocious behaviour and interference, I am speaking my mind.

Naïve Hope

There are a lot of things I could say to you, and most of them would be perceived as insults... the truth, yes... but insults nevertheless. I do not want to sink to that level. I have never sunk to your level.

But it is time I said what I had to say, and lay this all to rest.

I cannot stop your noxious influence on the boys, nor help with your drunken phone calls, nor prevent your attempts to guilt them and control them with your promises and your sporadic charm. I have no influence over them at all, you have contributed to that. But the lack of respect they display toward me as their mother, I lay firmly at your door for most of it. I did not bring them up to be the way they are. [In fact in some ways I did not bring them up at all, because, oh let's see now... that's right... you wouldn't let me have them! But that is another story, and both of us contributed to that.]

The fact that you nursed a grudge and planned to get rid of me and my then fiancé (Rick) 10 years after the marriage, I find more than amazing and creepy, but I have gotten over that. There are many more things I could say. But as I said this letter is in case you are not in when I call.

This has been bottling up for some time, and I have always kept the peace. But I am guided to speak (or write) my mind and so it is. I will not call round again. Whatever is in the highest good will happen. I only decided that I would do this on Friday 14th Jan as an opportunity presented itself.

If I catch you in, I will read this to you, if you let me. And I will give you the opportunity to answer if you so wish. If you are not in, I will leave this for you to read at your leisure. If you do not let me read this to you, you can read it yourself.

I suggest you do not get someone else to read this out to you as you will be embarrassed at the truths I will remind you of.

Don't bother to write or contact me, as I realize now that I may never get an apology from you for the cruel ways you have treated me. My concern is how you treat the boys now.

I suggest you let the boys sort out their own issues between them. Good guidance would have encouraged them to do so.

The attached will say what I want to say to you. I am aware that there are always two sides to any story, but it is about time you had my side, instead of only presenting your side to the world.

I leave you with this, in the knowledge that this act will ease some of the pain you have caused me.

Marni

The Letter To Jim

And here is my letter to him that was enclosed with the cover letter above, exactly as I wrote it;

'Things I Want To Say To Jim'

1. We were married for 18 years; why were you so brutal, and violent and suspicious of me when I gave you no cause to doubt my faithfulness & loyalty to you, the children and the marriage?

2. Why did you accuse me throughout our marriage of having an affair/s when you were the one who had two affairs early on?

3. Why did you disrespect me so badly that you willingly tried to leave me with nothing, even saying as much to your solicitor, and lying and procrastinating in paying me out?

4. Why did you think that I did not deserve anything when I had borne three sons, been faithful, put all my money into the family coffers, put up with your drinking, abuse, affairs and mistreatments?

5. Why did you treat your sons with the brutality, fear, threats, violence, attacks, lies, guilt and harassments that you did? How could a loving father treat his sons so? Shame on you.

6. How come you have never ever once tried to make good, or apologise to me? When you call yourself a Christian, yet it is ok for you to have treated me like you did? Not biblical!

7. Or even to support me as a mother? Instead telling and brainwashing my sons with your absolute & damaging lies that I was a prostitute, a drug addict and a witch?

Naïve Hope

8. Even now, you do not encourage them to contact me, yet I encouraged them to stay in contact with you when you kicked each of them out one–by–one in your drunken rages, and they came to live with me again, and when they said that they never wanted to see you again, and that they **hated** you, I told them that you were still their father. What sort of person are you?

Things you have done that have been hard to deal with, and caused me pain, and affected what was our family, and for which you will be accountable...

9. You had two affairs early on, and were even so dishonouring as to bring one of them (a prostitute named Elsa) home to sleep in the same bed (under the guise of 'Christianity')? And you didn't have the guts to break it off with Dilys, but instead sent me to the meeting place in the park to speak with her & say that it was over? (Gutless wonder!) Don't you realise that it was your guilt and not mine that ate you up with thoughts of my unfaithfulness?

10. You kicked me out time and again when you were drunk, and I had to crawl in through the kid's bedroom window to sleep with them or on the floor. What do your sons think of that, o man, o bully, o coward?

11. What do they think of women after the abysmal way you have treated me? What sort of a role model did you give them?

12. I never, ever, slept with another man, nor thought about it, until I had been so brainwashed and punished after 18 years of your accusations, brutality and interrogations, that I eventually did what you always feared I would do. I had already been punished many times for something I had not committed. The one time I agreed with you that I had had an affair, I had to lie because of your machete to my throat. I feared you would kill me. [You were always on a knife edge, yet refused help.] This changed my love for you for good. Yet you will not accept your part in creating any of this!

13. Your threats about driving off the Westgate with us all on board and in front of the kids!

14. Your threats and menacing with fists, belts, a gun and machete, as well as cutting up MY credit cards, and taking every penny from my purse when you left for work! Bully!

15. *I was a good wife and mother! Devoted, hard-working, loving, caring, smart with money, generous, effective, handy, clever, capable, a good home-maker and honourable. I did not deserve the way you treated me, nor your attempts to destroy me, nor your lies to the boys!!!*

16. *You had a great chance to grow and evolve this lifetime, and I truly loved you, but you killed all that long ago, and I only have feeling of cold anger at the way you have brutally and cowardly treated & continue to treat & manipulate your sons.*

17. *This is the last time I want to be involved with you in any way in these games of karma. You are on your own now.*

I quietly folded the letter and placed it on a surface close to him.

Then I waited.

THE RESPONSE

There was some silence at the end of all this.

We sit quietly whilst the words settle in the air and onto the carpet. I have not yet raised my voice, nor do I intend to. I just want answers.

He did not speak. After some minutes I eventually ask him 'Do you have anything to say?'

After some time, he seems to take a breath before answering. And after all that, *all* of those individual items, all he could say at the end of all that I had read out to him were the following comments – for he apparently had no real answers himself to any of this:

'You are very brave to come here like this.' Then Silence.

I already knew that! I was still waiting for some form of answer to my list. Eventually he spoke again.

'I am sorry for what happened'. And he just sat and looked at me. Lord knows what he was thinking...What does he mean? There was no sincerity behind them, no meaning, no energy; they were just handy words. And I had no response for this.

What was he sorry for? I waited for him to say what he was sorry for. I felt blank for that was not what I had asked him, that was not what I was waiting to hear. My mind could not register his sorry, it

Naïve Hope

was listening for his reasons for his actions. And what I think was happening was that I may well have been having trouble computing in my brain; was he sorry for me leaving, sorry for what he did to me, sorry he didn't actually kill me? Just exactly *what* was he sorry for? I had to let his meagre 'sorry' wait while my mind was still looking for some answers to my 'whys'. He speaks again.

'From the moment you left, I only ever wanted the best for you'.

Jim actually *said* that! Wow, *What*? Hold on a moment... What was that? Rewind.

'From the moment you left, I only ever wanted the best for you'.

Now you *must* be joking... I have *got* to set this record straight!

Just what has he been reading? Just what alternate reality is he living in? This flies in the face of nearly *everything* I have experienced at his hand and that I have just got through reading to him.

He sits there calmly in his old familiar way, and I can plainly see how he conned people with it all, with his air of innocence and concern. And pretence. But that was then, and this is now. And as for charm... well, you can no longer con me. *I was there*, remember, Jim!

I look at him and challenge; 'I think you've dry-cleaned your brain not to remember that you set out to destroy me, and you had even told me as much,' I confront him. I wait. No answer... He sits quietly still, to all appearances he is kindly considering my words. Maybe I will get lucky, and he will begin to remember just some of what he put me through? Surely my words have jogged something in his conscience, if not in his heart? He delivers the next sentence with all the calm and appearance of genuine goodness in the world...

'I thought you were a Princess, you were always so lovely and good'.

What?

What?

Where the hell did *that* come from?

To which I iterate the so-bloody-obvious that I am surprised it is not hitting him in the face; 'Then *why* did you treat me so badly? *Why* didn't you treat me like one?' Again I wait. Again no answer... Is he brain-dead, or just so busy looking for ways to get out of his predicament that he looks so harmless? Time was, when he was a healthy man, he would have leapt out of his chair and decked me immediately. But he is older now, and not so capable?

You stupid little man. You can't just make airy-fairy statements and expect me to swallow them! I repeat, Jim... I.Was.There!

Still no answer to my 'why'...

Ok, Jim, you may be having trouble remembering, so what about *this*?

'You *deliberately* set out to destroy me, Jim. You even planned to kill me and my fiancé Rick ten years after I had gone.' So what have you to say to that? I hear myself think to myself.

There is some animation from him now. He shifts in his chair. His face changes from a kindly blank look to one of offended rebuff. Then...He *actually* denies it. Yes, that is what I said, he actually *denies* it...

'I don't remember these things' he says, clearly affronted, as though I am trying to pin some bank robbery job onto him. To further convince me that he is innocent, and that his memory proves it, he now asks 'Who is this Rick anyway, I don't know *anything* about this.' Again, I am gobsmacked. Rick and I had been together for over three years and were even engaged, and don't you even *dare* to tell me that you nosy, interfering, busy-body-who-pulled-the-boys-strings-as-to-my-whereabouts along the way, that you did *not* have a clue about it!

He doesn't rise to offer anything else, even though I have reminded him of my engagement.

So, ok, not an outright denial of intent to murder, then. Yet another very clever misdirection. But I had proof, I had witnesses, and now I didn't hesitate to use this. Pull out the irrefutable card...

'Ask your son Joseph. He was there, he will remember'. I wait. And wait. Still no answer...

Naïve Hope

This pathetic man now tells me (and expects me to believe it) that he doesn't remember... Slowly shaking his head, his attitude is one of 'take pity on me'. Not so affronted with this answer, then, Jim?... But still un-valiantly wriggling out of any fall-out from your own actions. It's just the same old game – another attempt to try and charm his way out of responsibility, acknowledgement or restitution of things contained in my letter.

I cannot clearly remember all of the rest of our 'talk' that day, as I was still seeking answers to my original questions in the words that followed but not finding any... I was still trying to make some sense of it all, and not getting any; and I was also expecting him in some way to accept responsibility or at least to own up to it. But that really didn't happen. Not one actual admittance of anything that I had claimed, not one answer to my series of 'why's'. I clearly remember the above comments because I was so surprised by them. But still ever the charmer, he actually smiles at one point and said that it was good to see me again. Oh yes, I thought? Really?

He then, most surprisingly, said that he had *prayed* for years that I would come and visit him! Mmm, what does he mean by that? That I have answered his prayers? Probably. That he is a goody-goody and see how much he has changed? Yeah, likely story...

And the alternative thing to admit would have been...? What it really was of course; his own inaction. I then realised something else. True to form he had prayed for something that he wasn't prepared to do himself. This man was still not able to take appropriate steps to resolve things. Was still expecting me (or God) to do the work. *Sit back, hope and pray, let someone else make the moves...*

I asked him 'Why did you throw me out, time after time? Why did you say I had *deserted* when you had evicted me yourself, forcing and then watching me pack?

His stunning response, for which I had absolutely NO answer was to state 'I was only bluffing!' *Bluffing?* Are you as stunned as I am on this? My jaw dropped open. Talk about a different universe, a weird parallel reality...

This man truly is a bog-standard *ijeet! (That is an Irish Idiot!)* I couldn't think where to go after that one for a while...

In all, most of this was not the outcome I had expected, nor wished for. I had hoped for some kind of resolution, some *real* answers. I had expected some resolve to my questions, some truth, some honesty, some admittance... *Why* I had thought this was possible is only testimony to my belief that man can improve himself, can become more than he is. Ridiculous in Jim's case, and this was a reminder. I did not expect Jim to look as though he was calmly appearing to listen and not argue. Or deny. I did not expect, and was surprised, at his too quick, too easy, vague and unclear apology, as I had not seen that coming. Nor throughout did he really say what he was apologising for. I did a review...

'Sorry for what happened...' What? *What* particular thing that happened? That I left? That I wouldn't put up with it anymore? That you accused me wrongly? I could go on, so tell me, sorry what for? These words were lost on me at the time, for his supposed apology really meant nothing, and so had not really registered. For in all honesty it did not ring with true sincerity, more like just a worm trying to avoid the sharp pointy end of the fork... This was somewhat confusing, as it can be in confrontational situations; we later chew over things in our mind, seeing different options of response or direction of communication.

I was still in my seeking-'Why?'-answers-mode and looking for something to mentally grip onto and come to terms with, and his words weren't actually dealing with *any* of them. It was all I could do to remain sitting facing him holding this space in which I was challenging him. I am still looking for answers rather than just being there to make trouble. (So far the outcome was certainly not as I would have liked, not satisfactory or even honest.) If I had had the presence of mind to clarify what he meant by saying he was sorry and gotten clear what he was apologising for, I would have gained further understanding.

If I had had the time to go over possible conversations we might have had in my mind, the possible ways the course of our 'meeting' might have gone, then I just might have been prepared for these results. For none of this was really what I had expected. But who

Naïve Hope

really knows how things could have gone? Had I really been that deluded to actually expect that he would tell me why he had done these things? But he couldn't. Maybe he didn't know himself? Who knows?

In retrospect, his pathetic response had been mainly smokescreens, with no real response or addressing of the issues I had raised. Not one real answer. I was not impressed upon with what he had to say, as it later seemed that he himself had no answers, and probably couldn't really offer any. He didn't even attempt to address or go through any *one* of the point issues I had listed, he hadn't been able to pick out *one* and talk about that.

It had taken me thirty years to get to this point. This had been a *huge* effort for me to see him, especially in that house again, where all of my dreams had been dashed and destroyed so totally. And where he had become such a brute. It was now clear that he had conveniently 'forgotten' or denied so many, many things. Ah, the expedient dream of pathetic alcoholism.

I was still looking for some mental clarity, but I am still not getting much real satisfaction from this exercise, other than the fact that I am actually daring to face him and challenge him openly about things. I feel we are drawing to the end of this meeting.

Oh, wait... Now he speaks!

He suddenly addresses how we got engaged – he says, 'What was that all about? Getting engaged before we'd even kissed?' He is asking *me* why *he* said what he said? Surely he would know more about that than I? All I could offer was that the church had influenced us. That was all I could see at this particular time, though with later thought on the subject, it became clearer to me just how influenced I had been. But what about him? Did he see that? In retrospect, *Jim* was the one that suggested we get married and had made the first move to kiss me, *he* was the one who went to the Pastor for his advice, *he* was the one that precipitated it ... Duh! And I had just followed, like a sheeple...

This really wasn't the time or space for me to go through all of the events that had occurred around that. We were still straying from the reason for my being in this same room as him. My main mission had been to get answers to my long standing questions on Jim's abusive behaviour, and that was why I had put these things in a letter; so I could and would be reminded about them... yet even *I* hardly referred to the list after I read it out. I guess I had mostly needed to say something and just trust to see what his responses were.

And as I write this another thought occurs to me on his last remark? Had Jim thought that *I* was trying to get him to marry me? Did Jim blame *me* that we had to get married so quickly? Is that one of the reasons he was such an arse to me? I don't know and I may never know. But if he did, then he was wrong. Dead wrong.

Suffice it to say, I left there glad that I had been able to say many of the questions that had been in my heart for so long, but I was also sad that this man was in total denial of so many things and did not (and maybe *could not*) give me *any* answers to my questions. One of the final things he said before I left was that he asked me if there was anything he could do. Again, was this just lip-service? I think so, and in view of what happened the following day it was. I would have liked to say – 'Yes, pay me back *all* that you owe me and took from me and return my children back to me' – but could he do that? I think not! So all I could answer was to say that he should look into his heart and soul and he would know what he should do. Did he ask me to be more specific, or say 'Let me think about it, about what I can do about it?' Of course not. That would require action and reparation on his part, and I feel that in retrospect he was simply avoiding my possible anger or retaliation for the years of abuse. Or he didn't want to commit himself to anything real... Or maybe he was simply a man on drugs who could not think clearly and really didn't want to know or deal with any of this stuff. Or really, whatever...

I found myself saying to him that I was never, ever going to go through anything like this with him ever again. In this life, the next or in any other life. That it was over, it was done. It was now up to his Soul what he had done.

I am now at the front door. Just as I am leaving, he tells me that he would probably be a bit sad for a few days about this but that he

Naïve Hope

would probably get over it. An interesting thing or a weird thing for him to say? Probably feel a bit sorry for himself; at being reminded or found out, or seen as the total arse he had been. Who knows?.

I can say that I certainly wouldn't be feeling sorry for his supposed sadness... At this point I couldn't have cared less!

I left it at this and reiterated that I would not be back, I now have to integrate the fact that I had finally achieved what had been on and off in my mind for so long – actually facing him and challenging him. And I was emotionally spent for the rest of the day and the next, my head busily rewinding and rehashing what had occurred. Quite naturally so.

This had actually been a huge deal, a *momentous* occasion in my life, even though I had not gotten clear results. What had I achieved? - *I had let my voice be heard.* I had let Jim know, and in writing, some of the abuse and some of the pain that he had caused. In this regard, it was an absolutely huge deal.

On our long drive back home to my place in Murrumbeena, me and my friend stopped off and had a meal so that we could both debrief from our various visits. By now I was shaking, and exhausted with the effort of it all. So this was a good opportunity to take a little time to rest up before she continued to drive us home. In all, it had been a very successful visit. I thought. But any hope that this could be the start of a healing for the family was short-lived, however.

The following day I had a phone call from the partner of son Danny, Linda. She asked me what on earth had happened, what had I done, as Jim had been on the phone threatening to 'cut him off'. I didn't understand what she meant by 'cut Danny off'; cut him off from what... cut him out of what... His life? His will? I didn't know, as it was all a bit confusing until she eventually explained that Jim had accused him and her of disloyalty and of telling me family stuff that they had no right to tell. Namely that another son was suffering or had been suffering with depression. What? *Who?*

I ask you! One of my own sons has major depression and as a mother I am *not* supposed to know? And I *didn't* know, because no-one had told me!

Jim had drawn his own conclusions and assumptions from a comment during our conversation. During my 'visit' I had mentioned to him that I wanted him to know that if he had intended to hurt me then he had succeeded, and that I had suffered Depression in part because of the things that had happened to me at his hands. From this he had concluded (such a clever man is this Jim) that I *knew* that one of my sons had depression. And he further concluded that the youngest son (see, very clever) must have told me. And he further concluded that this was a betrayal and that his son Danny and also Linda couldn't be 'trusted'. Oh, and he also had obviously concluded that I *had no right to know this at all!!* What...?

Typical Jim, his mind running on very well worn tracks of suspicion, seeking avoidance at looking what my visit was about... And seeking to involve and attack someone else in his discomfort. What further confirmation did I need of a damaged and warped individual? And thinking that *as a mother I had no right* to know anything about what was going on in my son's lives! Bastard!

Danny was most upset that his father was threatening him like this, and even refused to speak to me for a while. Still emotionally unresolved and connected to his father through the abuses he suffered after I left, just like I had been with my dad; only ever wanting his love and admiration and putting up with so much to get it. Fortunately I had clearer lines of communication with Linda. She was working as a counsellor with a variety of dysfunctional family and well being issues, so she was more capable of being in tune with what was happening. By this time, Danny had been building himself a home and family together with Linda, and they had a young girl and a small boy. Linda had taken the initiative and had phoned me to find out what was going on as Danny was so very upset. He must have been for Linda to phone me to see what had transpired.

So after explaining to her about the letter, and even reading them both out to her so she could judge for herself, she realised that Jim was 'just being Jim again', and she then knew how to sort things out with Danny. In retrospect, I was glad that I had confined my confrontation with Jim to what he did to me, and stayed vague with the treatment of the boys. If I had shared the *knife with Danny* incident with him goodness only knows what he would have blown this up into. And would he really get it anyway?

I think I had also somehow thought that this confrontation might help change him – challenge him to look at what had happened. Would that were so! If I thought that by broaching what I did to him that he would get-it, and try to make amends, to make peace, to heal, to explain, to acknowledge – without rebounding back and causing more angst by involving the children – then I was mistaken. For even thirty years later, this man has not taken the time to work out *anything* from the marriage and his own behaviour and to take this opportunity to be or do something different.

What did I learn? That the middle son, Ben, had depression after his stint in Afghanistan with the army. Sometime after this episode, Ben and I had a conversation in which he opened up and shared this with me. Another thing I learned was that this whole exercise had in some way made me somewhat wiser.

Would Jim ever redeem himself from this situation? Would he ever truly acknowledge and apologise for what he did to me? To the boys? Not to me. I think it is far too late now. What reparation he could have made, he has let slip by. He could have stepped up when I approached him, but he chose not to. His actions, or rather, non-action, again spoke for him.

MESSAGE TO MY BOYS

As my remaining years now whittle down before my eyes, and I realise that time is indeed starting to run out, I have to own up and sort things out.

This thought prompted me to reach out to my sons and apologise to them by letter sometime the following year. Putting it in writing gave me the opportunity to get clear on what I needed to say. And it would also give them time to consider its contents. One son, Jo, the eldest, got it straight away and when we next spoke by phone, he said that I had no need to apologise. It hadn't been my fault. But the second son had a quite different response. He was so very angry with me, and he stormed at me that I had *deserted the family* in order to 'have fun' and 'kick up my heels'. Jim's words had surely taken root! This was so hurtful. I didn't know where to begin to explain to him, and he didn't want to know at that time. He was so angry that I hadn't been a 'real mum' to him that I couldn't even get a word in to defend myself or to explain.

Anyway. I think he has had some realisations since.

Over the years, without me having considered it, these issues of my old hurts and harm had also possibly affected my relationship with my sons. Confronting Jim had brought no resolutions or change in these dynamics really. But what it had done was get out of my head all of those 'Why's' and given me some space to see past them and that possibly I myself may have inflicted hurt on the children during the marriage and also when I had left. It was time to look at any harmful or negative impact I had made on them in the way Jim had made on me.

Now I had moved into this headspace, I was also remembering other instances. Of things done that were surely not by someone in a right mind...?

I remembered one time that Jim had taken the belt to Ben. One of the boys had done something wrong, yet establishing who had done what was proving a bit of a problem. Ben was younger than Jo, and more action oriented, and being younger he was slower with his words and not as quick as Jo to deny doing whatever it was that had gotten Jim riled up. Jo had a good grasp of language even at such a young age, and he quickly and verbosely denied doing whatever it was (I forget) so it defaulted to Ben to be the guilty party; though he was not the one to blame, Jo was. But being terrified of his dad's temper, Jo had naturally sought to avoid it. He was only a child, so I can understand his fear. I don't think he realised the consequences, and just wanted to avoid his father's wrath. But Ben was the one that copped it. He just was not quick enough to find the words to convince his father that he was not the guilty one! And for this he was being badly thrashed. I could not talk sense into Jim, his mind was made up. I fought to drag Ben off Jim when I saw the look on his face, and heard his threat of using his leather belt.

Naïve Hope

I tried to stop him taking Ben into the bedroom, but Jim was too strong for me and savagely pushed me to the floor. Jo and I were both screaming for him to stop, and I was banging and banging on the bedroom door, but nothing was going to deter Jim from exacting his revenge. All I and Jo could do was helplessly stand by as we heard the screams and pain and heart-rending sobs emerging from behind that locked door, whilst we held onto each other. This man brutalised this little innocent child without a thought. Fucking ogre. Jo was terrified still, but didn't dare own up to it now. He told me it was his fault, and that he didn't know Ben would get into trouble for it, but it was too late, and the damage was done. After it was over, Jim left the house for a 'drive', leaving all three of us in tears, with poor little Ben sobbing and heaving and with such marks on him. I think it broke a part of him that day, this unjustified punishment by his hero. And I couldn't fix it! In effect, as far as Ben may have perceived, I had done nothing to stop his father from doing what he did. As a child, he would not be able just yet to process and comprehend as an adult could, he would not be able to see that Jim's very actions had prevented me. From his point of view, if he was calling out for help, and mum was outside the door, yet no help came, what did that then make me?

What was it that blinded me to what Jim could do to each and every one of us? What mind-numbing hypnosis prevented me from taking a knife to this man? From poisoning him? What kept me always looking for the best instead of seeing the horrid reality in our supposedly 'Christian' family? God alone knows...!

We - Jo, Ben and I - were all upset, powerless, affected, scared. A man who relies on and insists on using his physical might to force his will cannot be reached by the finer consciousnesses or with any real consideration of the feelings of others.

Even though I was powerless to prevent any of this, reviewing how not only I myself, but also my children have been affected by the events in our family, this too has to be taken into consideration.

But as mum, I could not prevent what happened. I could not stop it. And I had continued to *stay* with this man, in a way condoning what he did. That was the effect of it, even though I seemed to have no other option. Even though the refuge had turned us away, a child's heart is not to know this, nor understand it.

I might have been blameless in all of this, nevertheless, I had married this guy, I had given them this man as their father. And simply by staying with him, stuff had happened, hurt had happened. Sure, if I had somehow left Jim before all of the end-time eviction stuff, things would still have affected them. Whichever way you looked at it, they would have been affected. That's the way it works. We impact on others. Life impacts on us and on others. Now I had to ensure that my sons knew my heart, knew they had been loved, knew that I was now aware that I had been involved in whatever had gone down in their childhood. I had been involved. And guilty by association in some way.

Is there something that needs to be redressed with them? Ever since I had left Jim I had let them know that I was available to talk with, to discuss, to understand any or part of the events that occurred. Not one of them had shown any real interest to this point. No one wanted to look at it. And of course, I can now understand why. If I had had so much trouble dealing with the hurt and harm I had felt, how must it have been for them, how would they have managed with it? How hard must it be for them? Were my boys going to stay caught in the pattern begun in their childhood?

So besides sorting out with Jim where he went wrong, let's find out where *I* went wrong – from the eyes and perceptions of my sons. Give them a chance, another chance, a last chance to sort anything between us. If I have done anything against them... please let's sort it out. It seems that the major focus of my life right now is in resolving family issues, sorting out all of my relationships...

During 2012, whilst recovering from the drama around my family in the UK following the funeral of my parents, and in line with my desire to heal any wounds that I myself may have caused, I sent two of my sons the following letter. One to Jo and one to Ben. After speaking with Linda, we both agreed that Danny was still too fragile to be faced with this just yet. This action was taken in case something happened to me and I did not survive to complete a proper documented record of events.

Naïve Hope

Here is a copy of Ben's letter, with Jo's being almost identical except for a couple of individualised personal references.

To Ben — An Apology

This letter is to my son, Ben Henly Moran. With the intention to let him know how much I love him & appreciate him.

20.5.2012

Dearest Ben,

Sometimes it is easier to say things by writing them down. Things I might wish to say can be overlooked when speaking face to face, and I want to make sure that I say to you the things that must be said.

AN APOLOGY

So I write this letter to say and to let you know that I ask for your forgiveness for all the pain caused by my not staying in the family home when you were children, and for all the subsequent pain caused by my not being there to protect you.

I have long nursed the pain of parting from my three sons, and have seen the impact that the divorce and everything surrounding it and following it has had on each of you, and have felt powerless to change it. I have had to hide it down deep in order to carry on with my life. This has not helped me, and probably not helped you either.

More importantly, I want to say to you that I am really, really sorry that I wasn't there for you, to protect you, to nurture you. I wanted to be and at the time I had no idea things would turn out the way they did – [circumstances prevailed and worsened] - and I know that it may be perceived as me 'abandoning' you [though this is not true] and this may well be how it felt. And for that pain, that confusion, that sense of grief and loss, I truly apologise.

I love you, and as your mother I have always loved you. And I always will! I may not always have understood you, or agreed with you, but that is part of life. If the pain I have felt over you is anything like the pain you have experienced through life events early on (or since) then I understand that it has indeed been a torment for you.

Dear Ben, I remember your birth quite clearly, the days of labour waiting for you to make your 'entrance', the little details of the birth, how you were trying to check out things even within minutes of being born, your friendly smiling face and your loving hugs growing up, your dislike of beans, your delight when in cahoots with your big brother, the tears when Joseph went to school and you couldn't go with him, your love of sugar butties etc, so many, many memories of you growing up, and the pride and pleasure I felt over you. [I can at this point also ask for forgiveness for forcing you into those purple flares! And also for cooking the brown rice, though I don't think it did you any real harm...lol] I remember the importance to me of choosing the 'right' name for you, and when I first saw you, the name did indeed fit you. Still does, I think. [And I hope I don't have to ask forgiveness for this too.]

I am so proud that you could share with me that you were suffering from depression – not proud of the actual problem, but proud that you could let me know even though you were in the vulnerability that depression can bring. Having experienced severe depression myself allows me some understanding. Having to survive it and put my life back together has given me insights, some of which showed me how much my early life and subsequent events had impacted on me, and just how much pain I had pushed down. Dealing with these things eventually helped me leave the medications behind.

As part of my 'healing' I was finally able to speak to your father early last year with my questions and concerns, as previously I had avoided talking to him or taking any further action that may be perceived as 'causing any trouble' for you or your brothers. But doing this helped to give me the space to revisit the possible hurts and pains caused to you by events. I am acutely aware how my inability to be present may have impacted on you. This was not done deliberately, and was a naïve mistake that I could not correct legally or otherwise (though I tried). However, the bottom line is that I know that it has caused you pain. There will probably be a list of things I have done or said that has also been painful to you, and for all these things I wish to say how sorry I am for that/them.

Naïve Hope

Ben, I don't know if or how I can make any of this up to you, or if it could be made up to you, just like my parents couldn't make amends to me. It took many years for me to get that they actually did (in their own way) love me, and so before anything further happens to me, I want to let you know, that I really did and still do love you. I hope that one day you may eventually also see that I did the best I could and did not deliberately set out to hurt you – how could I and why would I intentionally hurt the fruit of my womb?

As you know, last year I was in England dealing with final family matters there and burying both grandma and granddad. Again, I was reminded that we never know when it is our time to go. And so for me to leave things unsaid that could be said is a regret that I do not want to have.

If anything were to happen to myself or you, and I hadn't told you how sorry I am / was, and that I always loved you and always will, it would be another mistake on my part that couldn't be rectified.

Life is such a tentative and unguaranteed affair. I wish to let you know that you are and were truly loved whilst there is time.

I am so grateful that we have re-established some form of contact, and hope that this will continue.

You are welcome to take up this above conversation with me, or to ignore it and continue as we are now, or to ask me anything you care to as I have nothing to hide.

Having said that, I will not refer to this letter again unless you wish to do so. It is my intention to seek self forgiveness and to hopefully receive your forgiveness, but more importantly for each of us to eventually gain peace with the past.

With all my love and blessings, no matter what you do in response to this letter, my dearest son,

Mum / Marni

[My Address & Phone No.]

p.s. I am so proud and pleased that you have such a lovely family, and so happy that you have such a treasure in your capable, understanding and supportive wife and partner. Well done, Ben.

p.p.s There is a favourite picture of me with both you & Joseph at Alexander Park that has been on my facebook page for a while: [facebook page link placed here] (you are not identified so your privacy is secured)

Ben's Response

The responses were not exactly what I expected.

Happily, Jo had told me that there was nothing to apologise for when I phoned to see if he had received my letter. But this opened a door and we started talking like we hadn't talked for years. And he shared some of the ways in which his father had let him down and still continued to do so. Joseph and I had done some sort of resolving through this. Good. Great! A result.

Now what does the next son say?

Ben phoned me to let me know he had got the letter, but that he really wasn't inclined to talk about it. When I asked if he had 'anything at all to say about it then please to do so or I won't bring it up ever again', he did say something.

What followed was an emotive blast. A blast at me for not being the sort of mother he wanted, for me being selfish, for me 'leaving home' to 'kick up my heels', for only apologising in order for me to feel better about myself and not to be sincere about him, that the letter was purely about me, and how selfish I was. I was floored with his angry rant for I hadn't expected anything like this. Our relationship had been mostly sporadic, though I had gotten on well with his wife Jodi most of the time, and had even dubbed her TDIAW – The Daughter I Always Wanted – and had even given her a keychain with that inscribed on it. He had taken the letter so differently to how I had intended it. All of these accusations hit me in the heart. He made it sound like I had in fact deserted them, and for purely selfish reasons, and he would not allow me in any way to defend myself, continuing to hit at me with his words and flattening me. I was so very upset. I could hardly get a word in to

Naïve Hope

explain or respond, I wasn't allowed to defend myself, and found myself quite overpowered by his rage. This was getting more and more painful for me.

His final insult floored me.

'You are only writing to me now to get in with me and my family because you are getting old and need someone to look after you!' he spat out. I took a moment to digest what he had just said.

What? *What*!

I burst out laughing at this for it was so ludicrous, so ridiculously far off centre that I had no other words for it. All I could manage was 'What?' His father was the one with the stroke always phoning to complain about his medications.

'You're getting old and you need our help'. He really seemed to think this.

'No I don't. That's not true. And I wouldn't come to you for help anyway', I managed, ending the call quickly after this. 'I can see that we won't achieve anything so I will say Goodbye and wish you all the best'. And that was that.

After I got over my initial shock at his venting, I came to realise that the letter had opened the door to a whole lot of his repressed and suppressed anger. He was so mad with me! I truly don't believe that I deserved all of this anger, and that some of it was meant for his dad but was unable to be expressed. Leastways that is what I believe, but as you can see, I could be wrong. But he or we had somehow lanced the top of the boil, decapitated the monster and the crap came a-flying-out. I was in tears for days after this of course, but I eventually recovered. I didn't dare phone him for quite some time, for I was not ready to be so hurt again. Thinking that I would let him deal with whatever had emerged for him without me prodding, I got on with life.

However, a tentative phone call some couple of months short of a year later, we started some kind of easier communication between us. Maybe he had processed some of this buried stuff? And maybe his older brother had had a few words with him about what had *really* gone down and had maybe helped him see another side to things. For I think that Ben and his father were more similar to each other than either of them realise and they had been somewhat closer to each other and he had been more led by Jim's mindset than Joseph had been.

For a period of time we talked every few weeks. Not for long, but at least we would say 'Hi'. Within a couple of years, I was able to visit both him and his brother Joseph for by now they were living closer to each other. It was a positive outcome, though there was still no deep and meaningful communication.

So the letter did achieve something.

Should I now send one to the youngest, Danny? Well. No I don't think so, and I decided not to. We were already in regular contact, and I think he already knows the heart of my letter anyway, as I moved to be nearer to him and his children after my stint in Tasmania. Not only that, but I was also with him when he was in Intensive Care and was there if he needed me. For I see love as more than just words; Love is also an action. There is therefore currently less need to thrust my letter upon him and to challenge him with any need to address or action its contents. The next but more important reason is more compelling. Since his hospital stay his health has been greatly compromised. Jim still continues to be a major part of his life, and there is such an emotional knotting between them and some fragility on Danny's part that I will not yet put him through the emotional trawling that this may produce. If I die, he has this book as record. But until then, I will wait and see how he navigates things before considering it again.

You see, when I left to go to England, according to his partner, Linda, it triggered my leaving the marital home all over again for him. I was to discover this on my return. It had brought up for him a sense of abandonment, and this could be felt when we communicated. There are other considerations, all of which simply confirm that right then all he needed to know was that I was around and here for him as best I can be. He has two small children, and the youngest is a little boy. I watch as Danny relives his life, albeit unknowingly, through his little boy. Seeing how having a stable home life for him changes Danny's own history somehow, heals something that went amiss there. As his partner mothers, loves and manages things, and makes family life workable and ordered and stable for the children, so for Danny this part of him is relived and hopefully more satisfactorily fulfilled through this and through his own son's experiences. I hope, anyway. I never had loving or kind grandparents, and my own children grew up in Australia without this. Jim's parents died within a few years of our emigration, and both my parents kept pushing God to each and every one of us whenever we visited. In a way, not having that kind of grandparent was a mixed blessing when viewing this religious hammering albeit meant with good intent. I may not have much to give materially, but I did consider myself to be an easy and loving grandmother, and I love being around the grandchildren. So as regards Danny, I will bide my time, or say nothing and just allow things to be.

As I have said before, the energy of the written word, the magic of seeing that all will work out eventually, and writing about it, I hope will support this intent.

LET ME SAY

If any of my sons ever come across this book and recognise the characters in this, then let me take this opportunity to send them the following message. Or if they were to talk to me about the things that happened during our family history or about any of the events that I have journalled here, then I must also take some responsibility for not being there to protect them when they needed it.

This would be (and is) my heartfelt message;

To each of my sons, if I have offended you in any way, and wherever I have offended you, please forgive me. I did not intentionally mean to hurt you, but I acknowledge that I may well have. Please forgive me and be kind in your assessments. Please also know that I did and do truly love you. I loved and love each of you in different ways, because you are all different. And I loved and love each of you in the same way, because you are all my sons, born of my own body. I only ever wanted the best for you. I would have liked to have given you what I never had, loved you in a way that I wasn't, wished for you to fully experience your true potential.

You may have memories, and probably do, of things that I did or said that may well have hurt or confused you. I may not remember or even be aware of all of these unless you tell me and you are most certainly invited to. I offer no excuses here, I am only human. But I do know what it feels like to feel hurt yet this hurt to go unaddressed and unacknowledged. I don't know all of the legacies I left you with, or of how I have let you down apart from the stories I have included and set down for you here. If I could kiss these offences better, or be given the opportunity to explain them more fully, or apologise most sincerely or simply to hold you close till you get that I did and do truly love you – then I would and I will. You only have to tell me and I will listen - I will be there.

One more thing I would like to add here is this; I had a tough dad, an abusive dad. But I was not like him. Whether you agree with me about your dad or not, you are who you are. You are not your father. You are yourself, and you have your own choices and life to live. Maybe it is about time that you tackle any wounds you may hold within and reappraise the reality of the past and how it has impacted on the current situation?

This book, journal, document, whatever it eventually becomes, is basically all that I can leave to you. I have no immense wealth to bless you with, no amazing faith to pass on to you, no major legacy to hand down to you except to commend that you be authentic in who you are and what you do. All I can offer you is life; the life I birthed you with, the life you escaped your father with, and a better life I wish and hope for you still. This is my record, my attempt to set things straight, my way of contributing to the healing process for you all. I started off life with Naïve Hope and I trust to end it with Wisdom and Understanding, and More.

2016

~ Abusive Men and Domestic Terrorism ~ Reflections ~ Remnants
~ Ultimate Healing ~ Last Words ~ Making Sense Of It All

ABUSIVE MEN AND DOMESTIC TERRORISM

Marital Abuse as it is called in some quarters, is targeted at the partners or wives. Domestic Violence also encompasses the children. This is now being challenged as never before, and adverts to notify the authorities about it are becoming an accepted message. But will this actually stop it? I doubt it. Reporting it will temporarily stop the symptoms of this insidious and destructive disease, but it will not fix it. There is a reason that this happens. Many reasons in fact. And jail may punish but not necessarily address the real problem.

The costs to society associated with the judicial system, Prison and supporting the abused family members is huge. Understanding the real causes has not really begun. A child angry at the injustice in life may continue the same pattern of abuse that they experienced, passing it on from generation to generation. Counseling may help support them and to understand the why and how, as well as the where-to-next, but only if the counselor has a real understanding of what is at the heart of the matter and can offer support together with alternate perceptions, choices and options.

Much (though not all) abuse is basically trapped anger; at life, at birth, at dad, at mum, at missing out, at being singled out, at being hurt, at being helpless, at being abandoned, and so on – so many legitimate ways to be angry. But even though the reasons to be angry may vary, the solutions are similar. I am not talking about those men that deep down inside are real bad eggs, but those men who are lost in some way. And those women, for there are some cases of abuse by a female. But the majority of domestic abuse is male perpetrated, and the numbers of murders by male partners is far higher than that of deaths by war or accidents, or of many other life-shortening events!

Women in relationships are fair game, still. Indeed, it wasn't until the 90's that marital rape became illegal! Though not many women know or prosecute on this point.

I know what it is like to be an abused woman, and therefore I have some understanding of the sorts of things that can help a woman to overcome her deep wounds and to fully engage effectively in life again. But what about the men who dish out this sort of abuse? What of them? Yes, I have been angry with my ex-husband. But not all men are like this man, and I believe that some men actually want to stop the hitting, but simply don't know how to control what is driving them. What if we could give these men back their self-respect, their self-control and self-love instead of self-hate and fear... The usual ways are not working. But there are other ways... Just as I have desired to help other women overcome their abuse history, I have also imagined workshops for men to understand and explore, and maybe one day these will come to pass...

Is this simply a Naïve Hope? I hope not!

Support towards exploring, expressing and understanding old held-in hurt or anger *safely* in order to clear and resolve it, whilst under proper guidance, I believe, can help to reduce the epidemic we as a society find ourselves in. And to arrest its perpetuation. Permission to be good men instead of the current childish tendency toward immature competitiveness to be the worst of men and a raising of the bar on manhood would certainly create a better climate for healthier esteem of females; and possibly provide young women better choices of partners and therefore higher expectations of more respectful treatment.

Strong balanced male role models, tools for self-understanding, lessons for self-development, brain integration, neurological detoxification and support, creative outlets – these could be good investments for treating and preventing abuse continuation and contamination, and besides being cost effective in the long run, would give a more cohesive society in which to grow our future generations. Proper care for the children caught in these situations can prevent their repetition to the next generation. But these are only my thoughts and ideas, and my humble opinions.

I considered what sort of a legacy I would leave my children early on in my marriage. It wasn't quite the one I would have liked to leave them considering events. But it is one of caring and honesty, strength, openness and holding to my values. Their birth was safe, they were loved. What is the legacy left by a brutal man? It is toxicity, manipulation, interference, despair, festering resentment and off-target judgment.

Jim's legacy is something I shudder at.

Reflections

As I review my story, I can't help but ask myself again a really big question: What happened? What did all this amount to?

There have been many lessons learned, some of which I have been able to put into some sort of cohesive form, others I am still finding the words for. Some experiences I would have preferred to have avoided, and with the hindsight that I now possess, to have made better choices.

One thing I have learned, that no matter what has been thrown at me, I have not been put under, I have not let them keep me down. My firm belief in 'What goes around comes around' still remains, despite the fact that I may not necessarily see this in my lifetime.

It is 1st December today.

I reflect for a moment as I update and continue to edit these notes and chapters. I have only been up for less than an hour. It is a Sunday morning, and whilst lying in bed earlier I suddenly remembered the occasion when Jim had hit me badly and then he had felt so guilty about it that he eventually gave in to my begging for a positive change in our communication. This had resulted in him agreeing to us both going away on a Couples Weekend put on by a local marriage guidance counselling service. I need to remember to include it in my writings, and so I make a note of it here. I remembered how they spoke to us about certain ways and styles of communicating and gave us a variety of questions to explore individually and also to work with together. The 'Trust' exercise was also a part of the schedule. This is where you get to fall backward into your partner's arms, in the hope that they will be there to catch you when you fall. They said it takes trust to do this. We worked through that exercise easily, and we both caught each other beautifully that weekend. In that setting. *A controlled setting.* But it's one thing to be amongst others who are mostly strangers and quite another thing to trust, and to know, that your fall will be arrested by your partner when *unmonitored* behind closed doors. I knew I had Jim's back, but hadn't yet grasped that he didn't really have mine. I am sure that there were some things that we picked up from that experience that helped us. But it wasn't enough. And we were obviously both good at creating an image that nothing was wrong – we had after all had plenty of practice at this for years with the church and friends. As for continued counselling. No. That didn't happen. Not until Jim was ready and it suited his purposes which by that time was far too late.

And so I get up for a break again and make another cup of tea. And I am feeling so, so sad. I also realise that another layer of pain is ready to be released. As I reflect on just what it is that I am about to release, hopefully forever; I think of the story of my life, the totality of that which I am writing. And I again review the waste of it all. The sheer and utter un-necessity (if that's a word I can use here, for that's what it feels like) of this outpouring of pain caused needlessly by this man and his behaviour. If I was expected to 'heal' him in some way, from his own pain or from something broken within him, then I have failed miserably. And I have wasted years and years and years on him, and been influenced by his poison for many more years after that. The experience has occupied far too much of my life and my energy. And the truth is that it has. Occupied me. Occupied and distracted me from living an easier and more productive life. In so many more ways. The cause and effect of it all. The collateral damage. Not just in the living together with him, and the watching the boys after I left, but in the facts of how much he *did* manage to disempower me, how he managed to mess up my financial state so I would experience huge difficulties in owning my own property or becoming financially secure, and his bullying tactics so that my health would always be compromised by the huge deficit in my adrenal system due to the stress and abuse I had endured at his hands long term.

Naïve Hope

And the tears flow. Again. How much more different would my life have been if I had never met this man? I feel like I had been hijacked, and set on a path that wasn't really meant for me on some level. That somehow I got caught up in something intended to distract me. Yet more grief is acknowledged and released.

So I look for the cause on all of this. And I realise and confirm yet again that apart from some other possible explanations, (possibly far too weird for this book and this time) that the church itself, supposed 'Faith' encouragers, supposed leaders of the 'Love of God', were the main instigators in me being with this person. It was my 'duty' to 'do the right thing' which was whatever was indicated or governed by the church or its leaders. Though they would deny that. But the threats of serious consequences if you did not follow their instructions gives answer to that erroneous and false response; doctrines and programmings served under sugary coatings or with a hefty dose of threatening Hell Fire.

With what I know now, I can see that behind these religions, pseudo-religions, faiths and cults (whatever they may attempt to call themselves, for basically they are all the same, all about control) is the same message served under sugary coatings and appealing heroic platitudes – Do not trust yourself! Comply! Serve! You are not good enough! You are nothing! We know better! God is power, and this power will be on *your* side! And of course, many more messages that can keep one locked down and not trusting one's own knowing. It's a great way to prevent one from finding and following one's own individual path and destiny. Ever since I left the church I have known this. But seeing it woven through my life from this end-days vantage point, and how it has continued to affect my family on both sides of the world makes me want to shudder.

I allow myself to reflect on these last vestiges of sadness. The sadness at the frustration and futility of events past that cannot be changed. Maybe the sadness is for those regrets, maybe it's at how people get to do the horrid things they do to one another, maybe it's for lost opportunities, or maybe it's my Soul; knowing that though it rose to deal with all placed in its way with honour and integrity as best it could, it has been hurt that this mindlessness had to be. For whatever reason. The things I want to accomplish from this point forward are not quite as easy to do now as they would have been years ago. So maybe it's also the frustration felt by someone watching the sands of time running out.

Yes, I have and am again questioning myself with thoughts of 'what have I accomplished during my life' and though it has been to let my Soul shine through and not to resort to the same as has been done to me, that can seem little comfort in the face of what I know and that I could have possibly offered. I feel the loss of potential and accomplishments unexplored. As I get older and acquire more peace in my life as I work on myself, I am aware that I have gained some handy knowledge (and knowing) which is now available to me and such experienced skills that I could share if given the opportunity – yet I now often seem to lack the 'push' to get it done. My father used to joke 'My get up and go has got up and gone' – I think I now know what he meant!

Is the sum total of my life simply fodder for a book? What did it all achieve? Is this the best I have to offer to the world? I had and have so many hopes and dreams and ideas I have wanted to accomplish. And I am now getting old... Is it all too late for me?

Tears continue to flow as I view what feels right now in this moment of time as the 'ruins' of my life. I only ever wanted a happy home. No big plans as a child, just to love and be loved. To live comfortably, to be at peace, to be productive, to find answers, to share with others. It would seem the writing on my soul was misread instead and deciphered as 'to suffer' what I didn't deserve. Certain limited spiritual thinking could say it must have been my karma from other times, but I now know that is not the complete truth. I have long since learned that braver souls can also make the mistake of taking on the karma (accountability or simple 'cause and effect') of others simply because more advanced souls are more capable, and that lesser souls (yes, I do know what I am saying here) sometimes just do not learn or grow, instead they tend to lean on those who *can* get the job done.

Maybe I am being too hard on myself. Maybe I am still completing the end of the processing of this chapter of my life, and I am getting ready to embark on a new one... Maybe, when I have completed this book, all will appear different, though I do not as yet see how, for these are just a record of events of my life and they have already happened and been lived through and therefore are in the past. It's possible that in the writing of this book that something else 'clicks' into place, that allows a new chapter to begin... what a comforting thought!

Just to be clear about all that has been written here - this story *is* a true story. These are all actual experiences. Some of the names have been changed to protect the innocent. Some of the names have not been changed to inform the innocent.

I would like to think that making sense of difficult, unexpected or somewhat debilitating and disconcerting events is much more than 'half the battle'... and turning an apparent disaster into an amazing opportunity is a real gift from the divine, and attests to the indomitable optimism of the human spirit.

This is my opportunity to set the record straight and to lay the ghosts of my past marriage to its final resting place.

Remnants

I am nearing the end of my story. And today, moving into I have reread the last few chapters. To be more precise, I have just been re-reading about my visit to Jim and of what I wanted to know from him. Memories that had hidden behind my questions, behind my words, spring to mind, bringing with them the painful feelings that I did not go into at that visit. If I had done that, all would be lost for I would not have been able to keep my peace and continue to face him. I was dealing with cold anger that day, steely cold restraint to combat my fears and to fortify my resolve. But underneath anger there is always the pain of hurt. And underneath pain there is always the anger at hurt.

It is the pain that is at the core. And now I feel it. The torment, the hurt, the harm. I fight with it, for I don't want to feel this way. Now the final vestiges of pain and anger battle within me. Suddenly an emotional response erupts from deep inside. Forcefully it breaks through and out of me – such anger surges up, such sense of hurt at all of this. At how I feel I have tried to do the right thing, the 'honourable' thing, and yet still been met with such stupidity, such unsatisfactory responses from Jim; images and realisations that our lives together could possibly have become this waste of love, time, energy, hope. *We could have grown old together.* And there it is! The pain at the destruction of my familial dream. Underneath this there also resided the pain at the destruction of my 'family'. Another buried thorn. I have to deal with this before I move on, for there is more to come. I know it and sense it! So deal with it, I do.

And so I break from my writing and editing to process these last feelings at my thoughts. The final vestiges of what has gone before. Clearing out for the last time, that which had limited me. I hope.

Before I continue:

Sitting here to write about the torment I had buried for so long within. I had been used to the inner fear that had become the norm for so much of my life. Now it is fully exposed.

Having held it down for so long just so I could function, and get on with my life – not recognising how wounded I had felt. It has been easier to see it with my children, rather than to dig and expose it in myself – this man was a brute – he brutalised all of his family – it seems to be that whatever good he brought to his children and to me as his wife has been killed by his actions and tortures.

On so many levels, this man's fathering was and still is toxic.

I had continually lived with the very real fear that this man could snap beyond repair – though I now recognise that in a way he is already well beyond repair.

It has taken me a long time to be able to get to a place where I could face in such an exposed way this man – this tyrant. I think I understand what rape victims feel like when they have to face their aggressor. And in many ways, this man raped *my life.*

In marriage, 'taking' your wife was not referred to as rape – but it is **still** *the very same thing – and I have experienced that – so I know what it feels like to be raped. And if being beaten qualifies it more as a rape, then I have experienced that too. And you can also add into that blend the element of torture – of having a gun to the head, and a knife to the throat – and then spread this over many years of having to cook and clean for this man and carry on as though nothing is wrong, and to avoid triggering this man into* *a rampage in case your children are harmed – all hidden, all disguised, all allowed by the church and you can begin to see the damage that can be done and has been done by this one man – JAMES FUCKING HENLY FUCKING MORAN!!!!!!!*

MORON!!!

Yup, that was my anger finding words.

It is with some embarrassment that I have to confess there have recently been times when I wished Jim was dead. This book has brought up all of the vestiges of unsorted emotion and hurt, giving me opportunity for a final working through and out.

Whilst coming face to face with the net results of the this life lived in such an unnecessary shadow, living with what transpired that should really not have been, in the reliving of these past horrors and in the midst of my processing all of the associated emotions, there were times I wished him harm. Now, and in a more lucid frame of mind, rather than condemn myself for these bad thoughts I acknowledge these as a natural consequence of all the fear, brutality and terror I had been put through. And for the despicable way he had continued to treat his sons, my sons. Whilst exploring these dark emotions, I also became aware of the blame, hate, anger and death wishes I had actually absorbed *from* him; HIS dark energy that was aimed at me during our life together and was emphasised with his assaults and attacks. As a sensitive I would naturally absorb these feelings very quickly without realising the-what-and-the-why of it, nor even realise that Iwas soaking them up in such a way. But this projection of his own sick stuff was his intention anyway.

His thoughts, I think, were on the lines of 'Bugger you. I am angry at you. *You* are the problem, you are the cause of my pain – So take this! And this!'

And I had.

And now I say, 'Bugger You, Jim. You Assoholic! You can have it all back. It's not mine!' I am done!

For right now, rereading these past events again has given me a fresh memory of the day, a revisited pictorial reminder of the obsessive and narcissistic nature of this stupidly ignorant arrogant cruel deficient and weak man.

I let this register for the moment – as I sense another awareness surface. And again, just for this moment in time, it feels like I have always had to protect myself from men – I want to trust them, dare to trust them, then they betray, hurt and abandon me... these are the honest feelings that are now right now being uncovered, that need to be exorcised from me.

So many times I have felt this, and now I feel it again, recognising the primal origin in my vulnerable childhood. Feeling so bereft and alone, so helpless, so abandoned, as this resonance echoes through me at this precise moment; I burst into tears at such a simple yet loaded dilemma... an echo of my life – *where is the man who will protect and support me?* That is the question... And there is no answer back!! For there cannot be. I have had to teach myself self protection, self respect, self recognition and self-responsibility. It has taken many years and much self searching.

I inevitably – and understandably - blamed Jim for what went wrong. I blamed him for the unhappy state of each of my sons. I blamed myself for staying with him. All this blame – all of that anger...Me blaming him for him blaming me... Laughable really. When you consider that one of the main issues was about being self responsible. *If* I had been responsible for standing up for myself... *If* he had been responsible for his actions and inner fears... And the 'what-ifs' gets one nowhere...

Wow, all these old emotions still to come up for acknowledgement and release! Keep breathing through this Marni!

I breathe. I release. Things settle, and I feel freer from that burden. Life, hey? Just when you think you have gotten sorted about men and relationships and life and love, another little pocket of hidden stuff erupts for you to look at and get honest about and sort through...

That's because there is still stuff there to process, Marni... All part of my own Soul's learning.

And as I consciously and in an aware way breathe my way through these occurrences, there goes through my conscious mind the

Naïve Hope

picture of an issue about *being nothing without a man*, something else I was brought up with. That was the reality for most women at the time, but it's different now, and so I remind myself of how capable I am and that being on my own is only temporary, for everything changes. And I breathe that through, too. Calm is finally being reclaimed. Peace is making its presence felt again.

That's because you have processed what was sitting there, waiting for your attention, and for the right time and space to release it.

This last paragraph I am writing a week after that last release – I am now so much calmer, and so much clearer of the toxic energy of that particular residual anger. At least those emotions are cleared out. I can read the pieces that triggered me previously without the same reaction, the same emotional charge. But it did surprise me when those buried feelings had shown themselves.

Gosh, how much more?

As many as it takes to be completely clear, Marni. For when they are gone, there is no more upset, no more emotional charge, no more past hurts to trip you up again.

When I look back at how Jim and I got together, the potential that was there, that I saw in this man, and the mess that it all became, and the part that I played in staying with him even though I couldn't see any other option in view of the influence and pressure of the minister, I now see more clearly that futile games were being played. This man feared that I would leave him, punished me for that fear and in the end leave him I did... I wonder how he feels about it all... Does he get that he could have had it good? That I was one of the best things that had happened to him? That he had some amazing opportunities to work together with me? Does he get that I had somehow been made his enemy, for that is surely how I was treated.

No matter the hidden agendas on a Soul level, it is now my firm conviction that I definitely chose the wrong man to marry, the wrong father for my children. I believed, hoped and trusted too much. Trusted and hoped naively! I was gullible and certainly youthfully innocent of certain things. When a person is innocent, this doesn't mean that they are stupid, it simply means that they are guilt free, that they are free of guile. Or that they are childlike and not yet contaminated.

Does one have to be deceitful to be 'wise'? Not necessarily.

A good man, hey? Someone who knows how to cherish, respect, admire, support and protect his woman; *that* is a good man. Who knows how to love her. For that is part of his job as a man.

Are there such mythical creatures?

Yes, there definitely are.

And so where are they? Well, most of them are happily married being good and loving husbands to their lucky wives. Other wives, just like me, have less-than partners and difficult experiences and then have to learn to decide that they actually deserve better than what they have. It all boils down to me having faith in myself, belief in me. My parents didn't believe in me, my partner didn't, and I had poured my belief into others, into people and things outside of myself.

Until I stopped.

Ultimate Healing

As the repressed and confused plethora of emotions finally sort and settle, I realise that I needed to acknowledge for the last time the confusion of pain, terror, fear and loss that had been locked down for so many years and that were tiered underneath my realisations. I feel that this is finally the last visitation of all of the pain, humiliation and terrorism that I have experienced. I can now let it go. There has been layer after layer to contend with, but there is now a sense of hitting bedrock on the subject.

In order to heal, people of old understood that you needed a safe place to do so. My safe place had been long in coming. But it did eventually arrive, and with it I had the tools that I needed to dare to face these long-held demons. Demons that had been poured into me by someone projecting their energy with such force that it had broken down my own gentler boundaries and created such fracturing of my own self and psyche. As I have worked through this story, through this journal of events, I have had to deal with my self arguments as well as the emotional drain that the process of facing things that had been locked down for so long had cost me. In speaking, reviewing, re-reading, writing and consciously going through events I have in part re-lived them.

In the reliving, I have no longer been able to hide things behind the simple word 'divorced' or 'abused'. I have had to acknowledge what truly went down and I have had to come to terms with things in a different way. It has also been made clear to me through the process of this record-correcting-exercise that it takes energy and emotional resources to not only deal with the emotional lock-downs but also to be able to move forward beyond it again. Separate things. Yet closely tied in together. I couldn't really move on, even though I thought I had in so many ways.

Not until I had truly acknowledged the past, and let my voice out. I had been silenced most of my married life, indeed for most of my life; bullied and silenced. And I had buried the hurt and harm of all this. It takes energy to bury stuff deep where even you yourself cannot feel it, in order to carry on, to function. And it takes energy to bring it up, to face it, to rid the demons, to 'tell the truth and shame the devil'.

I could function very well, but not completely. For at a heart level, there was always a tender spot, an emotional charge when it came to my sons and their futures. And also my own future. To really leave it all behind, I had to remove those stubborn bits that had gotten so entangled with who I thought I was, those bits of toxic bubble-gum sticking to the sole of my Soul and that kept some level of fear of some kind of retribution ever present. For I could no longer ignore those demons.

Even the whole deal of the writing of this story and getting it published, whilst giving me a voice, also raised fears that should my ex-husband know about it then what would he do and say to sway the children that I was persecuting him through this book. Or some-such other manufactured Jim-reasoning or avoidance of facing up to his own demons. 'Thirty years ago, so it's long past' he could well say. Well, that might be his story as he conveniently forgets and leaves it all behind. And this could be so for him because he didn't have to live what I did, he is not the one who was beaten, who was bullied. I have been bruised way beyond the physical, I had been bruised right through my emotional centre and my heart and to my very core and psyche. So deep and so bruised that I didn't even know it was there. If I had no emotional charge of residual pain on anything that I have written, then this book would have just been a mental and language exercise. But the very fact that I have been at pains to complete it, that I have had to resort to my good friend and therapist to help to put me back together at the revival of each incompletely resolved memory, each relived torment, each powerless event, each unjustified and cruel condemnation and punishment, demonstrates just how much more there was still for me to work through in order to exorcise completely the demons and shadows of demons that had plagued me for so long.

Despite my own previous continued persistent healing efforts of these past hurts.

This is not just simply a story of *physical* abuse. This is something that I had no cause to deserve. When someone is taught as I was through the impact of Christianity, or, where it suits the transgressor, that you forgive and then move on by conveniently forgetting, it is usually small stuff that needs forgiveness, or a method of convenient avoidance. I believe still in the concept of forgiveness. But I do *not* believe in the concept of accepting another's lack of responsibility nor stupid-ness as an excuse for bad, dangerous or vile behaviour. Behaviour that is also allowed to be repeated.

When I was doing a self development course, we were instructed to explore our childhood to see what lessons we had learned that didn't serve us anymore, for they were viewed through the eyes of a child and could not be passed through a mature adult-logic filter in order to bring understanding to the perception. In order to do this, I needed to know more about my childhood from my parents, in particular, my mother. I asked her about the past and my growing up on several occasions, and just kept getting the comfortable and convenient church-ified response of 'Oh, That is all in the past now. God forgives.' 'Don't dwell on the past, dear. It won't do any good. If God forgives, then it's all behind us.' 'What's past is past. Bringing it all up again won't help.'

Naïve Hope

Well, God wasn't necessarily the one that those bad things happened to. I understood what is meant by 'His Forgiveness'. But shouldn't one make it right first with the *person* that has been hurt too? Even the Bible tells us to do so. But this gets lost in the feel-good and cast-your-burdens-on-Him and all-is-forgiven flowery stances. If you have chopped someone's hand off, you simply can't say to them 'God has forgiven me (and I will now forget it)' and that should make it all right again, and then just move on. That is rubbish. On the other hand, neither do you have to go round continually apologising for every breath you take for having done harm to someone – though one *should* do what one can to make reparation for it, if at all possible. The self-loathing taught by the church and religion is not helpful either. There has to be some balance between both of these opposite end viewpoints.

To continue on with the story of my request to my mum for information about events in my childhood. After enough times of asking her for this information had passed and after again explaining that it was for an exercise that I was doing, she finally gave me something to work with. It was after I asked her 'Well if you can't tell me about what happened as I was growing up, then tell me what sort of a little girl was I?'

She thought about this, then came up with 'Well, Marni, you were a very complicated little girl'. And that was it. She would say nothing more. What? Was I? I was bemused. I pondered this. I had no reply at that time, because this was such a loaded response and kept me quite busy trying to work out what this actually meant.

What's complicated about a little child? You give them the love they need, surely? What is complicated about a little girl who simply needs love? Doesn't every child need to be cuddled, caressed, given affection without strings? And not have to continuously be on their guard in case they get hurt or let-down? What on earth could I have done that required figuring out?

Just love and keep to your promises and there is no complication. Surely?

With these words I understood in part that the war had taken its toll in so many ways, and mum was ill equipped to deal with a child in such circumstances. And a sensitive soul at that. In short, she didn't have a clue about me. This wasn't about me, it was about her. And whatever had happened in childhood was too painful for mum to revisit. And I had to let this be so. Having written this book I now understand the cost in time and energy of sorting through painful repressed memories, especially when you have no power or tools to change any of the outcomes.

But that is life. We do the best we can. We *be* the best we can be. Most of us, anyway. We do it better for those coming after. If we can. In my opinion. Though now I see this cost as actually being a positive investment. As long as we don't become doormats.

What did I eventually say to mum as my reply? Well, there was nothing to say really. If this was how she saw it, and that was all she would say on it, it really wasn't up for discussion or understanding, and her adage of burying the past was still true for her. But not for me. If a continual sore has a buried splint of wood or detritus at its heart, isn't it better to get the piece of irritation that is causing the hurt and toxic harm out to allow for its healing, and to deal with the resulting irritation pus or matter caused by exposure to it, and through keeping it clean allow for complete healing? Who knows, maybe even the scar will eventually disappear.

I once saw a movie that showed the energetic power of words. I also came across this concept through one of the Terry Pratchett's books. The picture given was of the power that came directly off the printed page, perhaps perceived as a glow or vibration, or even the actual sound or whisper of the words themselves. Spell books giving off and emanating a different power, a different discharge or force than books about comedy do. Each diverse energy giving a different 'feeling' and message. Is this why books were burned in the past, books of knowledge and wisdom? Because of energetic power and emanations and not just information? I understand the fascination in all of this, for I have known people that could walk into a library or book room looking for something and find the exact book simply by 'feeling' where it was.

Anyway, using this idea, this concept, the fact that I have written what I have written in itself begins to set the record straight. The current story, the one told by Jim, the accepted tale, the corrupted

Naïve Hope

version, the deliberate and manufactured lies, will be rewritten on several levels. And I choose to hope that by this act alone, by my writing my story as clearly as I can, the dynamics in the lives of my children will take on a new dimension. The beginning of a different past and the possibility for a different and happier future will emerge. In the very least, they will have a happier mother, one who no longer carries the unspoken and un-exorcised burdens of hidden abuse and fear.

This is the beginning of a brand new year. I feel it is the start of a new era for me. As peace seems to settle over me, I know I can end this part of the journey to begin another.

Where do I find myself today? Good question.

Lately I feel as though I have woken from a bad dream. More and more I find myself waking up feeling easier, happier, more content with my situation. Life still presents the normal run of little challenges that face everyone, but my Soul feels cleaner, less dented, more whole. I realise I have exorcised the demons of trauma, torment and terror. My Soul is breathing again. I feel I have finally come through and not only have I survived, I have succeeded and not been found wanting.

I know I am human and therefore probably have still more errors to make, but I no longer need to repeat those I have learned from. For I am now better equipped. Over the years I have involved myself with natural and associated therapies, gaining professional qualifications. These life experiences have enriched my practice as they become translated into helping others who were also passing through similar rites of passage.

I have had several relationships since my marriage ended, one of which led to an engagement. For many years now I have been on my own and this has allowed me to further examine the various impacts of my conversion and of my marriage.

I also have hardly any contact with my boys. And boys they remain. Not because of how I view or treat them but as my estimate on their maturity. They have still not worked through their own manhood to the point of being beyond this tyrant's power and influence. I still feel this man's poison and toxic presence at each encounter with them. So by choice and for self protection, I avoid contact until such time as they are ready to heal and lose the smell of their father's toxic presence.

Since this previous paragraph, this last year or so has been spent in revisions and edits. When I thought I was close to completion and publishing, I found myself recovering from an accident that saw me hospitalised and quite incapacitated. This mishap led me to realise that *none* of my sons are ever going to be of any help or assistance to me in my life. Consequently I no longer have anything more to give them. It is obvious that the damage done runs too deep. However, the time allowed me to reconsider and review before handing everything over for final editing and processing to Siri.

You may be curious as to whether I have met a man to share my life with? Not yet, though I am dating again. Old as I am, I still believe that there is still a kind of hope – a possibility? - in this, though that anticipation is no longer blind, nor naïve. And whilst I am waiting, there is much to amuse and occupy myself with. My skin is good, my health is surprisingly good, and nutritional support is ongoing. I believe in *possibilities* now, in wisdom and sometimes in 'miracles'.

If you have experienced a similar path, I would like you to know or at least consider, that holding firm to your inner values will bring you self respect and a kind of peace, and possibly its own partnership reward.

I am no longer naïve in the things that I once was.

My hope is tempered. But I am optimistic!

Last Words

I was only a child when I got married, though I didn't think so at the time. I have had to remind myself of this fact many times in order to get through life. Because many circumstances had served to form a kind of 'road' of what life was about for me, I have had to break through these patterns, expectations and programs to discover a different road.

As many others have had to. Gaining insights regarding people's relationships with some of the information that is currently available today may mean that we are less likely to put up with things now than we were in the past. But one thing that may not come through at the time is our own contribution to events and attitudes, and subsequently, to the survival, success or failure of the relationship or marriage. Everyone has a responsibility for their own mistakes, and that includes myself. Through accepting self-responsibility, one can grow and learn. And improve. I know the mistakes I have made. Mostly. And I am willing to explore those that I have still to learn from or that have been observed by others and through others.

Though I would rather not have experienced some of the things that life brought my way, I have mostly learned from them. Not that I always saw them as 'challenges', but rather as things to be endured and got-through. I am older, yes. But I am also wiser. And I can look at myself in the mirror knowing that I have done the best I could for the family and under terrible and tormenting circumstances. Through my life I have attempted to rise to the challenges that came my way and to do things better. I have demonstrated courage in the face of adversity. And have shown that I am not a coward. Nor a bully. Nor a schemer and manipulator.

Lots of women have the same strength. Opportunity can appear to be somewhat disguised in the circumstances I have described, though that were part of my life. But each time it gave me the opportunity to choose to be who I was or to be something other than what was before me or to grow even though I didn't always recognise it. I had to find the strength to carry on from somewhere, and sometimes I had to look deep. But remember that wanting to make things work, to include another person in your life requires risk, and courage, and when things get tough, the strength to go to the next step.

My ex-husband, however, cannot claim that. He has shown himself to be not only a bully but also a coward. So very weak and inadequate. He is in a wheel-chair now, and claims not to remember much of what I have challenged him with. As far as I am aware, he is still on regular medication and lives a very restricted life. Very little 'quality of life' as I know it. He no longer has a car because he can no longer drive. He is dependent on his children and others for variety and sympathy and validation. He didn't fully recover from the stroke he had several years ago, causing a bit of a speech impediment still and slowness of movement. This means that he cannot move quickly as before, and he cannot enjoy drinking his barrels of beer as before.

I have no idea what he sees when he looks in his mirror. Nor do I want to know, nor care, because I have seen his inside persona. And in these last thirty-odd years I have not seen any positive or worthy attempts from him whatsoever to reconcile any of the past events. Whether to simply engage to talk about things and how they came about, or to come anywhere near to accepting any blame or even to *genuinely* apologise for any of the dreadful things that he did.

Through the tendency I had of putting other's needs first along life's way, I had somehow also further embedded a fear that my own needs wouldn't be met. This can be difficult to deal with, and it sometimes felt like a weight at the back of my heart. It even affected me physically in that the muscles in my back behind the heart would 'freeze up' or get stiff, which created referred pain in my shoulders, ribs or usually my neck muscles, giving me a stiff neck. Initially it was considered connected to sitting and working, but over time I proved this mostly untrue. I alleviated a lot of this with work on the physical, emotional and energetic aspects using counselling, natural therapies and chiropractic or Bowen as well as massage. Talking with friends and therapists helped me get to the bottom of the underlying issues, and my own personally therapy training also gave me further insights and helped get me through. This is not necessarily for everybody, but this is the path I took that worked for me. And I have seen similar first-hand positive effects in others.

At this point I could muse about taking other paths, about what could have happened if I had seen and therefore made other choices. What if I had left him after the first affair that he had? But I didn't even consider it because one didn't do that in those days – 'for better or for worse'. Even now I find it hard to think of what would or could have happened in such an eventuality. Though the thought occurs to me that I don't think I would have had the support of my parents then. I would have been totally on

Naïve Hope

my own with a child and nowhere to live. So what other option did I have?

And I consider further; if I had not met Jim or become involved so weirdly with him, what would I have done – would I have continued on to be a missionary? Would I indeed or instead have continued on with my then boyfriend Bob? Or would I have still followed through on the fear I felt when Bob had mentioned marriage and children?

And this leads me to further thoughts and so another question emerges – What would I have done if I had never been challenged spiritually and religiously as I was? What other possible directions would I have moved in? How long would I have been prepared to stay on at home putting everybody else first in the family? Could I have continued to put up with losing most of my wages? Would I have mixed with other more worldly types of people who would have put me wise to what I was doing? Or who could have put me wise to what was being done by family? Would I have gotten into some other sort of trouble?

And so inevitably, thoughts that cannot be answered, that are just an exercise in the imagination or in the musings of 'what-if' can only lead one to an empty space that has no resolution. Imagination can make it possibly a better outcome or a worse one. But it changes nothing of the past and the present. The best application of my mind and my imagination is in dealing with the past (as and when it impacts upon me or my life), handling the present and defining a better future and one that I would aspire to. Though I guess I have to confess that this is only my opinion at this point. And there are many more other worthy opinions besides my own.

Despite what Jim would have liked to think about himself and his supposed Christianity, he really demonstrated that he was not capable of real forgiveness, or love. His focus was on punishment and revenge and destruction. Like a spoilt child he just wanted to make me pay and hurt.

Even though Jim showed such animosity to me and punished me physically, emotionally, financially, and mentally, he has not been able to destroy my spirit. My Soul was wounded but has recovered.

My truth was twisted, but surviving through all of my trials at his hand I have found more of myself than I ever imagined. I have become not only wiser, but stronger, smarter and more whole as a human being. My self-respect has grown, my self-worth has been mostly recovered, and where there was little, I now have self-love. I have learned that even though things may be at their worse, and one may momentarily stumble and possibly consider ending it all, you still cannot crush someone who has strong moral fibre, who truly seeks truth and healing and does not dwell on punishment or revenge. You can try to crush them, you can have a go, but it will wilt when someone finds their own self through surviving a darkness that another has created.

I no longer need to hold on to the harm and hurt that has held me back – it is time for it to go - time for me to recognise my spirit, this brave caring finely-tuned spirit. Time for me to soar.

I believe that what goes around, comes around. And in this world or the next that both Jim and myself will reap our just rewards. And that they will both be quite different.

As they indeed already are now.

Making Sense Of It All

This story would be incomplete without some final rumination and last thoughts on my tale. And a bit of metaphysical insight.

Following all the 'Rules' had not yielded the promised rewards. Breaking free from the illusions and conditioning of religious ideology and their shaming restrictions had helped me to make sense of my life. Being evicted from the family home forced me to look seriously and to question *all* of the various aspects of my life. Losing my children caused me the deepest pain which I struggled with for many, many years. All of this had led me to examine who I really was. What I truly believed, what I would accept as true. I came face to face with the fact that the world was not as I wished it. Was not as I would have it be. It could be a cruel mixture of breathless fragility as well as mindless violence, gentle whispers as well as smashing vindictiveness, loving tenderness as well as the desire to kill and destroy. I knew which I would choose.

Naïve Hope

But I had also had to learn to recognise that others might choose different to me. And the empowering thought that I do *not* have to follow *their* way, *nor* become like them, nor to do what they do, nor have to fix it for them. The crucibles of hardship, trials and deprivation have created a fresh appreciation of those values I still hold dear. I have more than survived. Discovering more of who I really was, I have also evolved. Evolved in experience, and hopefully in wisdom and knowledge. Certainly in depth and understanding. I think and feel that I am no longer the martyr, sacrificing myself to others who do not appreciate it, nor unreservedly offering the disrespectful or lazy to stand on the shoulders of my sacrifice in order to rise to a higher level. I now live my life for me. And for those who understand and value me and my assistance. I love my family and would have done whatever I could for them – however, my new proviso is that it does not cause me harm or damage. I no longer live for them; for I *cannot* live for them.

There are certain spiritual quarters which are somewhat more advanced that those caught in a specific religion, creed or faith. One course of discovery I did centred around the Law of Attraction, and was with one of those involved in the making of the film '*The Secret*' which was in part based on this Law. But those that are limited in their experience can fall into the trap of perceiving only one level of universal truth, which is that 'We all create our own reality'. One concept of this states that; *I am the only one that exists and that I create this world to learn about myself. In that case, I am the only one that exists and I am the God in my world.* I can see how some adopt this perception cart blanche.

The progression beyond this is to drop the arrogance that it is 'all about me', for there are other powerful Souls inhabiting the same space and time. And each of these can impact on another. Now we come to the interesting bit; the tone of one Soul may not have the same morals or ethics as the Soul of another.

I have come to the stage where I refuse to accept being responsible for the bad behaviours of other Souls. It may be that we inevitably incarnate to deal with one's own bad behaviour, our own bad karma – cause and effect; the result of our actions. However, consider this: Some Souls do *not* owe in a given lifetime, but instead are *owed*. But by the very nature of this energetic dynamic, as they are involved in another's debt, they needs must be present to give the other party opportunity to repay and to clear this karmic debt. If the debtor refuses to do so, or defaults back into playing out again the same old habitual selfish role, or unable or are unwilling to learn their lesson, *it is not the fault* (or the creation) of the owed party!

I get that what has been owed to me has NOT been repaid. I accept this and I release it. I don't want good repayment from this Soul. *AND*; I refuse to be party any more to this particular karmic lesson for this Soul. I do not want to and I chose not to ever incarnate or reunite with this Soul ever again. And this recognition of the magnetic dynamic that drew us together now gives me freedom to climb out of the morass created by this other. May they learn their lesson elsewhere, and with another. No more repeats on this lesson for me, for *I have got the learning*.

Making sense on the spiritual aspect of this was so important to me.

At this point, I can choose to create another future reality – one free from these characters. I can move on to freeing myself from other magnetic or energetic bad debts. And I do.

I now brace myself for the new as I truly release the old, and balance the Books of Truth on this story for all time.

ABOUT THE AUTHOR

Siri Eschel ventures into the fiction genre with her timely tale on Domestic Abuse. She was challenged to do so after continually hearing the question 'If he is so violent, then *why* does she stay?' As this was a subject close to her own heart, Siri examines one woman's personal story and the reasons that held her captive in this common domestic jail. Based on fact, the unfolding tale explores one answer to this question and how one woman got caught in a web of hidden misogyny, religious gender bias, closet alcoholism and loyalty conflict.

Siri currently lives on the NSW Coast, enjoying the nearby sea and lake surroundings. She has future plans to write further fiction, though probably in the form of a short novel.

Contents Summary

PROLOGUE To Lie or To Die? ... **Error! Bookmark not defined.**

INTRODUCTION .... **Error! Bookmark not defined.**

IN THE BEGINNING 19
   Humble Benchill 19
   No Voice 23
   School 30
   Celebration 32
   Scary Sounds 33
   Mixed Bag 34
   Grammar School 36
   Bobby Dazzler 38
   Anaemic 44
   Working Class 48
   Don't Break Her Spirit 50
   Ways and Means 53
   Latch-Key Kids 57
   What About Me 60
   Home Dead End 64
   Nightmares 67
   NightLights and Chrissie 69
   To Be or Not To Be 71
   Seeking Freedom 75
   Greek God 84
   Anniversary Crossroad 87
   Faith and Hope 93
   Fate Butts In 99
   The Church 109

1962 THE SCENE IS SET 113
   Strange Romance 113
   Two Day Countdown 126
   The Big Day! 131
   Why Jim? 134
   Married Life 143
   Don't Look 151
   Shoulder Shoves 157
   Christian Wife 158
   Sheila 163
1963 166
   Firstborn 166
   Pride leads to Hell 170
   The Birth 175
   Sin and Saviours 181

Seal of Baptism 187
Preacher Jim; Saviour 190
Moran. James Moran 197
1965 203
Second Chance 203
Second Coming 211
Dumb Promise 216
Instant Karma 223
Dangerous Moves 228
1966 232
Twenty-One 232
Pay-Offs 236
Mind Reader 239

1968 THE LAND OF OZ 244
The Ends of The Earth 244
New To Oz 246
Diane Drops Me In 249
Freedom Bid – Mobiltown 252
Merry vs. Sloshed 256
The Sixties 262
1971 265
Fitzroy 265
Hungary, Not Mad 267
Jenny 269
Failed Protector 273
New House; Fresh Start 278
Talking of Accidents 281
Geelong 284
Shift in Plans 286
1975 WERRIBEE 291
And Then There Were Three - 291
Heather Westerly 297
Forgiveness 299
'Home Is Where The Heart Is' 306
Alcohol 309

1977 BEGINNING OF THE END 312
Alarm Bells Ring 312
The Perfect Wife 316
Back To Work 319
1978 322
Sleepless in Werribee 322
The Inquisition 325
Blackout 329

1980 FINAL STRAWS 336
- Violence 336
- Lover, Not a Fighter 341
- Fix It Yourself 346
- Not About The Money, Money, Money 350
- Broken Vows 355
- The Telling Dream 361
- To Lie or Not To Lie? 362
- Womens' Refuge 369
- Resigned 376
- Contracts 377
- Unstable Jim 382
- Go Ahead; Shoot! 386
- Counting the Cost 393
- Half Hour Tryst Twist 397
- Games People Play 402
- Critical Mass 405
- 'No. No. No.' 409
- Blinkers Off! 414
- The Tide Turns 418
- 'You Will Pay' 427
- End Time; Counsellor 431
- Three Times Strike 434
- Last Christmas 435
- Action Time 436

1981 THE END 443
- Final Curtain 443
- Final Push 444
- Angel Suzy 451
- Life On The Outside 454
- Time To Talk 459
- Church Prejudice 461
- 'Danny First' 464

SINGLE LIFE 471
- Four Jobs & A Holiday 471
- Distraction 473
- Not Happy, Jan! 476
- Help? Anyone? 481
- Tall Dark and Handsome 482
- Who Am I? 485
- Sinking Ship 490
- Kerry 492
- Denis 497
- Out Again 500
- Spiritual Path 508

Divorce...515
　　No Longer Mum 518
1984 521
　　Eighteen and Sheila..521
　　Thirty-Nine 523
　　No, Mr. Policeman!...524
　　Two Seconds Away 530
　　Buckets of Love..537
　　Home Sweet Home 540
　　I Hate Dad.. 544
1988 547
　　Sole Custody 547
　　Lousy Father 549
　　Danny Out! 552
1989 563
　　Come Into My Parlour... 563
　　Brutal Lesson...567
　　On Your Knees 571

2003 and Beyond 577
　　Counting The Cost 577
　　PTSD 584
　　Bloody Angry!! 589
　　Taking a Stand 591
　　Healing Art 592
2008 595
　　Fall-Out... 595

2011 - THIRTY YEARS Later 602
　　Facing the Snake in His Den 602
　　Message To My Boys 619
　　Ben's Response 626
　　Let Me Say 629
2016 631
　　Abusive Men and Domestic Terrorism 631
　　Reflections 633
　　Remnants.. 637
　　Ultimate Healing 642
　　Last Words.. 648
　　Making Sense Of It All.. 652

About the Author... 655
　　Contents 656
　　Signs and Types of abuse.. 660

SIGNS AND TYPES OF ABUSE

Taken from the Australian Domestic Hotline and Marni's own experiences. If you are subjected to any of these, please get help, as it usually escalates.

TYPES OF ABUSE:

- Physical
- Mental
- Sexual
- Emotional
- Verbal
- Financial
- Social
- Fear
- Intimidation
- Spiritual

BEHAVIOURS THAT ARE NOT NORMAL, THAT ARE NOT YOUR FAULT;

1. WONT GIVE YOU PERSONAL SPACE OR PRIVACY
2. PLAYS MIND GAMES
3. REFUSES TO ACCEPT RESPONSIBILITY
4. CRITICIZES YOU IN FRONT OF OTHERS
5. MAKES YOU FEEL TRAPPED
6. IS JEALOUS OF YOU SPENDING TIME WITH OTHERS'
7. MAKES YOU FEEL ANXIOUS
8. ISOLATES YOU FROM YOUR FAMILY & FRIENDS
9. THREATENS SELF-HARM, SUICIDE OR HARM TO OTHERS IF YOU LEAVE
10. HURTS OR THREATENS TO HARM YOUR PET
11. SHOUTS OFTEN & HAS ANGER ISSUES
12. LEAVES YOU WITHOUT ACCESS TO MONEY
13. BLAMES YOU FOR THEIR MISTAKES
14. HAS CONTROLLING BEHAVIOURS
15. MAKES YOU FEEL AFRAID
16. CHECKS YOUR TEXT MESSAGES, PHONE CALLS ETC
17. READS YOUR DIARY
18. WANTS TO KNOW WHERE YOU ARE AT ALL TIMES
19. SCRUTINIZES EVERY CENT YOU SPEND
20. TEACHES YOUR CHILDREN TO DISRESPECT YOU
21. CALLS YOU NAMES & PUTS YOU DOWN
22. CONSTANTLY CHECKS YOUR WHEREABOUTS
23. IS MEAN, RUDE OR INAPPROPRIATE
24. SABOTAGES YOUR ABILITY TO WORK OR STUDY
25. THREATENS YOU
26. HITS, SLAPS, SPITS ON OR RAPES YOU
27. CONSTANTLY ACCUSES YOU OF FLIRTING OR CHEATING
28. DRAWS ATTENTION TO YOUR FLAWS OR MISTAKES
29. ABUSES YOU IN FRONT OF YOUR CHILDREN
30. DOES NOT MAKE YOU FEEL RESPECTED
31. IS HYPOCRITICAL IN THEIR DEMANDS
32. DESTROYS YOUR REPUTATION

www.ingramcontent.com/pod-product-compliance
Lightning Source LLC
Chambersburg PA
CBHW052132010526
44113CB00035B/1922